THE SCM PRESS A–Z OF
CHRISTIAN THEOLOGY

The SCM Press A–Z of Patristic Theology

JOHN ANTHONY McGUCKIN

scm press

All rights reserved. No part of this publication may be reproduced, stored in a retrieval system, or transmitted, in any form or by any means, electronic, mechanical, photocopying or otherwise, without the prior permission of the publisher, SCM Press.

Second Edition © **John Anthony McGuckin** 2005

First Edition published in 2004 by
Westminster John Knox

British Library Cataloguing in Publication data

A catalogue record for this book is available
from the British Library

0 334 04010 8

This Second Edition published in 2005 by SCM Press
9-17 St Albans Place, London N1 0NX

www.scm-canterburypress.co.uk

SCM Press is a division of
SCM-Canterbury Press Ltd

Printed and bound in Great Britain by
William Clowes Ltd, Beccles, Suffolk

For Maria and Lizzy—
two bright souls

Please note the copy on the back cover of the book contains an error. *The Bibliographic Guide Essay* has been replaced by a *Thematic Guide to Reading the Handbook* at the beginning of the book, and the *General Bibliography* is replaced by thematic bibliographies at the close of every entry.

Contents

Series Introduction

The SCM Press A–Z of Christian Theology series provides a set of resources for the study of historic and contemporary theological movements and Christian theologians. These books are intended to assist scholars and students find concise and accurate treatments of important theological terms. The entries for the handbooks are arranged in alphabetical format to provide easy access to each term. The works are written by scholars with special expertise in these fields.

We hope this series will be of great help as readers explore the riches of Christian theology as it has been expressed in the past and as it will be formulated in the future.

The Publisher

Preface

Hope is always a good place to make a beginning. I hope that this book will provide some help in the often bewildering first encounter that students have with the world of early Christianity. Some hope. That world was perhaps even more bewildering than our own, which is complex enough; and even two millennia of hindsight still often make it difficult for us to make sense of the turmoils, passions, and inspirations that gave shape and significance to the affairs of the early Christians. In any case, this book is meant as an attempt to help in that process of sorting, sifting, synopsizing; meant to give enough detail without losing the clarity of the overview. Its focus has been on intellectual matters throughout, and it was my intention to attempt to give a series of brief but sharp portrayals of the major theological issues that formed the early church, as well as of those people who were its major thinkers in the first eight centuries. The book's range is dominated by the two great intellectual traditions of the Greeks and the Latins, but it also attempts to take notice of some of the other voices too—not least the ancient churches of Syria, Ethiopia, and Armenia, not to mention the social currents that were the important macrocontexts for how early Christian men and women developed their religious destinies, their institutional organizations, and their civil and intellectual identities. The book has been arranged in the form of an A–Z dictionary, part of a larger series of new reference works covering the development of Christianity from antiquity to modernity, which Westminster John Knox Press is in the process of issuing. These various volumes will soon accumulate to an extensive and major resource for students of church history and theology, and so I am more than delighted that Westminster John Knox invited me to present the early church within that series. The present volume relates to that formative period known as "patristics," a term signifying the early bishops from the second century through (usually) to the eighth century. Bishops were not the only shapers of the church, by any means, and the range of the entries offered here covers men and women, clerical and lay, in the earliest ages. Nevertheless it seemed right to preserve the designation "patristic" since it connotes the manner in which this episcopal theology of the postapostolic period assumed a position of authority that was, in a real sense, an extension of the biblical era of revelation, at least for the Orthodox and Catholic churches. Patristic theology, for both traditions, represented a good part of formative Christian tradition; and whether or not one has any investment in such issues of theological authority in the churches today, it cannot be denied that the "fathers of the church" in most cases fashioned an architecture for an abundance of Christian attitudes and structures that (for good or ill) often survive to the present. The contents of the volume came together from the confluence of four streams: major personalities and writers, international controversies, key technical terms, and cultural themes and movements. It seemed simplest, and therefore best, to combine these all together alphabetically rather than listing them in separate sections. The result is an A–Z handbook. The strength of that form is that it provides the readiest way to look up something. The weakness is the paradox that one has to know what one wants to learn about before one can learn about it. To help make the individual entries less insular, therefore, a system of interconnected references has been used (words in bold type and italics) so that from one key theme the connections can be traced with other related ideas, and the persons who advanced that topic most notably. This dictionary is unlike many others in that it has been written by one person with (presumably) a coherent view of history and theology formed over many years, while others are (quite sensibly) written by a variety of experts in their own specialist fields. Three widely available reference works in that form of multiauthored volumes are each strong in different ways. The best and largest of them all is the admirable *Encyclopedia of the Early Church*, edited by Angelo Di Berardino. It was the work of Italian scholars, mainly, and in 1992 was issued in a fine English translation (Adrian Walford's) by James Clarke & Co. of Cambridge, United Kingdom. That large two-volume, hard-cover set is a place where readers of this work can go to gain more information, more bibliography, and more details than are possible in the present volume. The final sections of the second volume of Di Berardino are a very important resource for the iconography and archaeology of the early church, and offer invaluable site plans, and timelines for the student. This pres-

ent work stands to that in the relation of a more concise and more introductory volume, as well as being indisputably more portable and considerably less expensive. I highly recommend Di Berardino's *Encyclopedia* as the next step for fuller reference information for those who need it. *The Oxford Dictionary of the Christian Church* (3d ed.; ed. E. A. Livingstone; Oxford, U.K., 1977) is also a good source of further bibliographies, and biographies covering a greater range of (generally less monumental) church writers than have been abstracted here. That single-volume work covers the whole history of Christianity, not simply the early church, but weighing in at 1,786 closely printed pages, it is not easily transportable, though perhaps more affordable for a student library than the Di Berardino. The *Encyclopedia of Early Christianity*, edited by Everett Ferguson, Michael McHugh, and Frederick Norris, is a fine example of modern American patristic scholarship. It was first issued in New York and London in 1990, and has since been revised and amplified. The articles there show a conscious attempt to move out from mere texts into wider contexts of history of culture, archaeology, and iconography, and this character, together with its generous patristic text-referencing system (most articles give a whole list where each issue is treated in a variety of patristic sources), make this a very valuable work as well. I have learned much from all three of these dictionaries over a number of years. There are other, yet more monumental, reference works in German and French, but the majority of undergraduate and master's students might find them forbidding. My own task in this new dictionary has been to retell many stories with a view to what, in my opinion, were the salient issues; refining the people and controversies down to clear lineaments, yet without sacrificing the fundamental importance (and point) of such a dictionary—which is either to send readers away with sufficient data to satisfy them, or to initiate them into the next step of where to go for more information. For this reason every entry in the present volume has a short study bibliography attached to it. These titles have been chosen from works available in English, except in a few cases where the only significant texts were in other European languages. The bibliographies do not attempt to present the very latest works of specialist scholarship on any given topic as much as suggest what would be the best and most comprehensive studies, produced in recent years, that would give a fuller picture for someone wanting to do deeper research for a term essay or something similar. They should be able to lead the enquirer easily enough into a greater range of scholarly materials. Patristic scholarship in the last century has flourished so much that there is a veritable ocean of literature lapping at the shores of almost every single entry in this book. Students with access to a good library ought to ask the reference librarian about the American Theological Library Association (ATLA) and its database of bibliographies, which can perform powerful computer searches of theological articles written over the last decade, on the basis of thematic as well as personal-name keyword entries.

This dictionary may have a destiny to sit on the shelf until required to illustrate a problem. Well and good: and don't forget to dust it occasionally. I hope it serves its function when called to perform. But if one wanted more, even to squeeze the book like a lemon, to extract all the juice, it could then serve a dual function as a historically slanted introduction to patristic theology. In this case I would suggest that one could approach the book in a way less dependent on the random tyranny of alphabet roulette, and use the following strategy. In the first place distinguish the persons from the themes or keywords. The list of names is extensive, but the theologians can collectively be set apart easily enough, and can then be followed up in terms of who were the major thinkers of the various centuries. Following the great writers and controversialists across the various century-epochs (roughly speaking) would give a vivid picture of what issues were occupying the leading intellectuals of the church across significant periods of its development. To assist this, I have made a ready guide at the end of this essay, listing key writers century by century. Just a cursory glance shows how the "pace" of patristic theology speeds up to a climacteric in the fourth and fifth centuries. In the second place, the thematic articles could themselves be subgrouped theologically and culturally. By progressing through a series of related articles, as if they were partial essays on a broader theme (as indeed they mainly are), a good survey of the main stages of the development of early Christian theology could soon be made. I have also provided a thematic guide to the book, at the end of this introduction. But however you use this dictionary, I hope that the list of characters and controversies contained here, a veritable gallery of saints and sinners (much like the present church), will prove to be not only instructive, but even a source of great fun. It has been for me in the writing of it.

John Anthony McGuckin
Feast of the Nativity of John the Baptist
New York, June 2003

Thematic Guide to Reading the Handbook

Selected Major Christian Theologians and Theological Schools in Chronological Sequence

Late First Century

Docetism; Gnosticism; Apostolic Fathers; Didache; Clement of Rome; Polycarp

Second Century

Apologists; Aristides; Athenagoras; Bardesanes; Ebionites; Epistle of Barnabas; Basilides; Ignatius of Antioch; Hegesippus; Heracleon; Irenaeus; Justin Martyr; Marcion; Papias; Polycarp; Shepherd of Hermas; Tatian; Tertullian; Theophilus of Antioch; Valentinus; Victor of Rome

Third Century

Antony the Great; Callistus; Clement of Alexandria; Cyprian; Dionysius of Rome; Dionysius of Alexandria; Hippolytus; Minucius Felix; Monarchianism; Novatian; Origen; Paul of Samosata; Perpetua

Fourth Century

Aetius; Ambrose; Aphrahat; Apollinaris; Athanasius; Basil of Caesarea; Constantine; Council of Nicaea I (325); Council of Constantinople I (381); Cyril of Jerusalem; Diodore of Tarsus; Ephrem the Syrian; Epiphanius; Eunomius; Eusebius of Caesarea; Eusebius of Nicomedia; Evagrius; Gregory of Nazianzus; Gregory of Nyssa; Hilary of Poitiers; Jerome; John Chrysostom; Lactantius; Macarius the Great (2); Methodius of Olympus; Pachomius; Priscillian; Prudentius; Theodore of Mopsuestia; Theodosius the Great

Fifth Century

Augustine; Boethius; Celestine I; Council of Ephesus (431); Council of Chalcedon (451); Cyril of Alexandria; Diadochus; Dioscorus; Flavian of Constantinople; Gelasius; Ibas of Edessa; John Cassian; Leo the Great; Monophysitism; Nestorius; Palladius; Patrick; Pelagius; Peter the Fuller; Philostorgius; Prosper of Aquitaine; Severus of Antioch; Shenoudi of Atripe; Socrates Scholasticus; Sozomen; Theodoret; Timothy Aelurus; Tyconius

Sixth Century

Benedict; Council of Constantinople II (553); Cyril of Scythopolis; Evagrius Scholasticus; Facundus; Fulgentius; Gregory the Great; Gregory of Tours; Jacob Baradeus; Jacob of Serugh; John Climacus; Justinian; Leontius of Byzantium; Philoxenus of Mabbug; Romanos the Melodist; Venantius Fortunatus

A Thematic Arrangement of Theological Ideas

Christology

Christology; Incarnation; Logos Theology; Resurrection; Communion of Properties; Enhypostasia; Hypostasis; Hypostatic Union; Homoousion; Homoiousianism

Ignatius of Antioch; Irenaeus of Lyons; Origen; Paul of Samosata; Athanasius; Apollinaris; Gregory of Nazianzus; Diodore of Tarsus; Nestorius; Cyril of Alexandria; Severus of Antioch; Three Chapters Controversy

Adoptionism; Arianism; Docetism; Monophysitism; Monothelitism; Nestorianism; Photinianism; Subordinationism

Trinity

Holy Spirit; Logos Theology; Trinity; Economic Trinity; Ousia; Perichoresis; Person

Justin Martyr; Theophilus of Antioch; Tertullian; Novatian; Origen; Dionysius of Alexandria; Athanasius of Alexandria; Gregory of Nazianzus; Basil of Caesarea; Augustine of Hippo

Council of Constantinople 1; Monarchianism; Pneumatomachianism

Salvation Theory

Soteriology; Atonement; Deification; Eschatology; Heaven; Hell; Judgment; Penance; Recapitulation

Origen; Athanasius; Augustine of Hippo

Scripture

Canon of Scripture; Exegesis; Revelation; Tradition; Allegory; Anagogy; Apocalyptic

Irenaeus; Origen; Diodore of Tarsus; Theodore of Mopsuestia; Jerome; Augustine; Gregory the Great

Ecclesiology

Church; Apostolicity; Episcopate; Canons; Catholic; Clergy; Communion of the Saints; Creeds; Deacons; Excommunication; Kerygma; Orthodoxy; Papacy; Priesthood; Schism

Cyprian of Carthage; Augustine of Hippo; Donatism; Novatianism; Pope Gelasius

Asceticism

Asceticism; Celibacy; Desert; Marriage; Virgins; Widows; Wealth

Antony the Great; Pachomius; Messalianism; Eustathius of Antioch; Basil of Caesarea; Evagrius of Pontus; Macrina; Palladius; Macarius the Great (2); John Cassian; Melania the Elder; Benedict; Barsanuphius; John Climacus; Symeon Stylites; Tall Brothers

Spirituality

Almsgiving; Apophaticism; Asceticism; Confession; Deification; Ecstasy; Exorcism; Hagiography; Healing; Liturgy; Lord's Prayer; Penance; Pilgrimage; Prayer; Relics; Saints; Soul; Synaxarion; Theotokos; Visions

Aphrahat; Origen; Evagrius; Macarius the Great (2); Gregory of Nyssa; Diadochus of Photike; Philocalia; Barsanuphius; John Climacus

Sacraments

Baptism; Eucharist; Chrism; Burial; Confession; Episcopate; Priesthood; Deacons; Marriage; Anaphora; Epiclesis; Mystery; Ordination; Sacrament; Synaxis

Anthropology

Anthropology; Burial; Death; Dreams; Fall; Family; Healing; Magic; Nature; Reincarnation; Slavery; Soul; War

Eschatology

Eschatology; Heaven; Hell; Judgment; Parousia; Purgatory; Recapitulation; Reincarnation; Resurrection

Papias; Irenaeus; Lactantius

Chiliasm; Montanism

Philosophy

Philosophy; Aristotelianism, Platonism; Plotinus; Proclus; Pythagoreanism; Stoicism

Social Ethics

Almsgiving; Marriage; Sexual Ethics; Sin; Slavery; Virtue; War; Will; Wealth; Widows

Heretical or Dissident Movements

Adoptionism; Docetism; Ebionites; Chiliasm; Gnosticism; Marcion; Monarchianism; Subordinationism; Montanism; Manicheism; Novatianism; Arianism; Apollinaris of Laodicea; Melitian Schism; Donatism; Pneumatomachianism; Neo-Arianism; Nestorianism; Pelagianism; Monophysitism; Monoenergism; Monothelitism; Iconoclasm

Abbreviations

AB	Analecta Bollandiana	DACL	*Dictionnaire d'archéologie*
ACW	Ancient Christian Writers		*chrétienne et de liturgie*
	(1946–)		(Paris, 1907–1953)
Adv. Haer.	Irenaeus of Lyons, *Adversus*	DCB	Dictionary of Christian
	haereses (Against Heresies)		Biography (London,
AHC	Annuarium Historiae Con-		1877–1887)
	ciliorum	DOP	*Dumbarton Oaks Papers*
ANCL	The Ante Nicene Christian	DR	*Downside Review*
	Library	DSP	Dictionnaire de Spiritualité
ANF	*Ante-Nicene Fathers*		Chrétienne
ANRW	*Aufstieg und Niedergang der*	DTC	*Dictionnaire de théologie*
	römischen Welt (Berlin,		*catholique* (Paris,
	1972–)		1903–1950)
ATR	*Anglican Theological Review*	ET	English translation
AUSS	*Andrews University Semi-*	fl.	*Floruit* (the author
	nary Studies		flourished/was active in
b.	Date of birth		this time period)
BJRUL	*Bulletin of the John Rylands*	GRBS	*Greek, Roman, and Byzantine*
	University Library of Man-		*Studies*
	chester	Haer	Hippolytus, *Refutation of*
BJS	Brown Judaic Studies		*All Heresies*
c.	Circa (approximate date)	HDG	Handbuch der Dog-
CCSG	Corpus Christianorum:		mengeschichte (Freiburg,
	Series graeca (1977–)		Germany, 1956–)
CHR	*Catholic Historical Review*	H.E.	Eusebius of Caesarea, *His-*
CQ	*Church Quarterly*		*toria ecclesiastica*
CS	Cistercian Studies	HTR	*Harvard Theological Review*
CSCO	Corpus scriptorum chris-	ITQ	*Irish Theological Quarterly*
	tianorum orientalium	JAAR	*Journal of the American*
	(Paris, 1903–)		*Academy of Religion*
CWS	Classics of Western Spiritu-	JBL	*Journal of Biblical Literature*
	ality (New York, 1978–)	JEH	*Journal of Ecclesiastical*
d.	Date of death		*History*

JHS	Journal of the History of Sexuality	PRIA	Proceedings of the Royal Irish Academy
JLW	Jahrbuch für Liturgiewissenschaft	REA	Revue des études augustiniennes
JMH	Journal of Medieval History	RecAug	Recherches augustiniennes
JQR	Jewish Quarterly Review	RHE	Revue d'histoire ecclésiastique
JRE	Journal of Religious Ethics	RIL	Religion in Life
JRH	Journal of Religious History	ROC	Revue de l'Orient Chrétien
JRS	Journal of Roman Studies	RQ	Römische Quartalschrift für die christliche Altertumskunde und für Kirchengeschichte
JTS	Journal of Theological Studies		
LXX	The Septuagintal Greek translation of the Hebrew Scriptures	RSPT	Revue des sciences philosophiques et théologiques
MSR	Mélanges de science religieuse	RSR	Recherches de science religieuse
NPNF	Nicene and Post-Nicene Fathers	SBL	Society of Biblical Literature
NTS	New Testament Studies	SP	Studia patristica
OCA	Orientalia christiana analecta	ST	Studia theologica
OCP	Orientalia christiana periodica	SVTQ	St. Vladimir's Theological Quarterly
PBR	Patristic and Byzantine Review	TS	Theological Studies
PG	Patrologia graeca (J.-P. Migne, ed., Patrologiae cursus completus: Series graeca; Paris, 1857–1886)	TSC	Second Century
		TU	Texte und Untersuchungen zur Geschichte der altchristlichen Literatur
PL	Patrologia latina (J.-P. Migne, ed., Patrologiae cursus completus: Series latina; Paris, 1844–1864)	VC	Vigiliae christianae
		VSp	Vie spirituelle
		ZNTW	Zeitschrift für die neutestamentliche Wissenschaft und die Kunde der älten Kirche
PO	Patrologia orientalis		

A–Z Entries

---

* Seven Ecumenical Councils.

Abortion   *see* **Family, Sexual Ethics, Soul**

Acts of the Martyrs   In the second century the church became more conscious of the need to preserve a formal record of the martyrdoms of the Christians who had been executed on account of their faith. This was the beginning of the genre of texts known as martyrial acts. From the earliest times the sufferings of the *saints* had been seen as specially blessed by God, with effective power of atonement and intercession for the church on earth, especially the local church from which the martyrs came. The martyr was regarded as one who had imaged the sufferings of Jesus, and had thus "entered into glory" with the power to intercede for Christians on earth (Rev. 7:13–17). The account of the passion of the Lord was one of the first elements of the New Testament, and the synoptic passion narratives demonstrate a coherence and continuity that suggests they were written independently at a very early date: something like the "Acts of the Passion of Jesus." Other great Christian heroes, such as Paul and Peter, were also seen, as martyrs of the faith, to have undergone a mimesis of Jesus in their sufferings (cf. Mark 13:9–10; John 21:18–19). The increase in government-sponsored *persecutions* of local churches, in **Rome**, Asia Minor, Egypt, and **North Africa**, throughout the second century, but above all in the time of Decius and Diocletian (mid-third and early fourth centuries) accounts for the rise of specific *Acts of the Martyrs*. Although all of them are apologias for the martyr, several of the texts were based on the actual court case, recording details of the trial of the martyr and the answers given. The first examples of this kind were the *Acts of Justin*, the *Acts of Saints Carpus, Papylus, and Agathonice*, and the North African text the *Acts of the Scillitan Martyrs*. Some texts such as the *Passion of Perpetua and Felicity*, also from North Africa, have an immense drama, and the latter preserves accounts of *Per-*

petua's prison diary. It was so popular that *Augustine* later complained of it being read in the churches and overshadowing the reading of the Gospel. Christians regarded the martyr's task in the time of their trial to be above all one of witness (*martyria*) or public confession of the faith. The martyrs' fearless confessions before their judges, therefore, were seen to be particularly inspired by the *Holy Spirit* (Mark 13:11), and accounts of their confession were avidly read by the churches (usually after the persecution had abated). The oldest of the major martyrial texts was the *Martyrdom of Polycarp* (c. 155–156), where the theology of martyrdom is elaborated (later to be given a systematic treatment in the second- and third-century writers *Tertullian* [*To the Martyrs*], *Origen* [*Exhortation to Martyrdom*], and *Cyprian* [*To Fortunatus*]). The large numbers of Acts of the Martyrs were analyzed and collected in most useful editions by Delehaye and Musurillo.

H. Delehaye, *Les passions des martyrs et les genres littéraires* (Brussels, 1921); idem, *Les origines du culte des martyrs* (Brussels, 1933); W. H. C. Frend, *Martyrdom and Persecution in the Early Church* (Oxford, 1965); J. A. McGuckin, "Martyr Devotion in the Alexandrian School: Origen to Athanasius," in *Martyrs and Martyrologies* (Studies in Church History 30; Oxford, 1993), 35–45; H. Musurillo, *The Acts of the Christian Martyrs* (Oxford, 1972).

Adoptionism   A theological approach (also called dynamic monarchianism) that tried to defend the monarchy of God (*monarchianism*) by explaining the Christian sense of the divinity of Jesus in terms of his radical possession by the *Holy Spirit*. Adoptionist thinkers are thus distinguished from those who simply thought Jesus was a prophet of God, or a holy man, by the extent of his possession. The term frequently used was "indwelling": that is, the Spirit chose Jesus at some point in his earthly life (some suggested the birth, but the majority thought the baptism) and inhabited his body as in a temple. His possession of the Spirit, and therefore his authority in teaching and acting, was thus incomparably higher than any prophet who had come before, who only enjoyed a temporary or occasional visitation from the Spirit of God. It was a theory that never commanded great enthusiasm from Christian congregations, and seems to have been more elaborated as a theology of individual intellectuals, and then used by later patristic thinkers as a shield against which they could tilt their lances (accusing their contemporaries, especially in the Arian period, of holding similar views that thus reduced Jesus to state of a "mere man" (psilanthropism). One of its weaknesses is that it accounts for Jesus' authentic doctrine, but less for his dramatic acts of salvation in his cross and resurrection. In the adoptionist scheme the *resurrection* appears simply as a reward to Jesus for fidelity, rather than the New Testament manner of seeing it as the dawning of the covenant of the new age. Adoptionism was most famously represented in the patristic era by *Paul of Samosata* (Eusebius, *Ecclesiastical History* 7.30) and *Theodotus* of Byzantium (Hippolytus, *Refutation of All Heresies* 7.35). The *Ebionites* are also generally placed in this category, though next to nothing is known of their precise doctrine. The term has also been applied to a (relatively obscure) eighth-century Spanish controversy over the nature of the sonship of Christ, as true or adoptive. The latter was addressed in Alcuin's seven books *Against Felix*.

J. N. D. Kelly, *Early Christian Doctrines* (London, 1958), 115–19, 158–60.

Aelurus   *see* Timothy Aelurus

Aetius (c. 300–370)   Aetius was one of the most radical of the late Arian theologians (*see Arianism*). He was a metal-

worker trading at Antioch who through native ability rose to the position of renowned sophist and logician at *Alexandria*. He pressed the implications of Christian doctrinal statements to their semantic limits. He was leader of the school which asserted ingeneracy as divinity's fundamental definition and argued that while the *Nicene* party who asserted the essential identity of the Father and the Son-Logos (*Homoousians*) were mistaken, so too were the anti-Nicene majority, which had fallen into two camps, one affirming the essential likeness of the Father and Logos (*Homoiousians*) and the larger school, which banned essentialist language and argued for the vaguer idea of the likeness of the two hypostases (Homoians). Aetius, pressing the point that words (especially scriptural ones) revealed essences, claimed that the relation of the Son to the Father was one of complete dissimilarity (*anhomoios*). If the Father was quintessentially the Ingenerate, then the Son, being Generate, was radically unlike the supreme Godhead. His party, accordingly, called down the fury of all sides against them and were classed by opponents as the Anomoians (the Unlikers: also Anhomoians, Anomoeans). His work later stimulated *Gregory of Nazianzus* to argue that biblical words did not reveal essences as much as relations, and this was an important influence in the *Cappadocian* development of *Trinitarian* doctrine. Aetius was ordained deacon by 345 but was implicated in the downfall of Gallus and exiled in 354. Councils at Ancyra (358) and Constantinople (360) condemned his teachings but through the patronage of Caesar Julian (Gallus's brother) he was rewarded with episcopal rank as a "roving bishop." His devoted secretary, *Eunomius*, became the most energetic spokesman of the school, and looked after Aetius in his old age at *Constantinople*. His chief and only surviving work is the *Syntagmation*.

G. Bardy, "L'héritage littéraire d'Aétius," RHE 24 (1928): 809–27; R. P. C. Hanson, *The Search for the Christian Doctrine of God* (Edinburgh, 1988), 598–636; L. Wickham, "The *Syntagmation* of Aetius the Anomoean," JTS 19 (1968): 532–69; Idem, "Aetius and the doctrine of divine ingeneracy," SP 11 (1972): 259–63.

Africa   *see* **Alexandria, Augustine, Cyprian of Carthage, Donatism, Ethiopia, Lactantius, North Africa, Nubia, Origen of Alexandria, Tertullian, Tyconius**

Agape   The LXX translation of the Hebrew Scriptures, which was the version extensively used in the early Eastern church, uses the word agape to connote love in all its forms: divine, affective, philanthropic, and sexual. This usage ousted the more normal preference of Hellenistic Greek for the term eros. It was a trend continued strongly in the New Testament, where agape became the primary term evoking love and loving-kindness, and was predominantly conceived in terms of divine philanthropy, which called out to humans to mirror the goodness of God in mutual fellowship and charity (cf. John 15:13; Rom. 8:35; 2 Cor. 5:14; 1 John 4:7; and many other instances). As exemplified in John 3:16, the word agape was advanced by the New Testament writers to be one of the key paradigms of a Christian theology of salvation: "God so loved the world that he gave his only Son." The connection between the love of God toward a world in need and the love that was supposed to characterize the disciples as a new community of agape was closely drawn in the early church. Love, in this sense, was understood not so much as an affective feeling, but as a philanthropic regard for the other. God's philanthropy of salvation (*see* **soteriology**) was taken as a model for mimesis, a code of conduct that the church should reflect to others (particularly among its own) since it had received philanthropy in abundance from God. The ethic of agape can be seen especially in Jesus' doctrine of the mutuality of mercy, exemplified in the Lord's Prayer, which asks for the forgiveness of God: "as we also have forgiven our debtors" (Matt. 6:12). The earliest patristic literature, such as *First Clement* 49–50, from the end of the first century, articulates this theology of mutuality as a common bond that unites God and the church, and unites the church among itself as a kind of "new society." The term agape was also used in antiquity to connote the ritual of the love feast. The evidence is obscure, but some of the earliest Christian communities seem to have celebrated a ritual meal of fellowship, within which the eucharistic ritual took place. Paul is one of the first to make complaints about some of the abuses that could characterize this close association of "club" festivity (for the common meal was a regular element of many ancient religious societies) and the solemn commemoration of the Last Supper (1 Cor. 11:17–22). *Ignatius of Antioch*, and parts of the *Didache*, show that the agape as a distinct ritual from the *Eucharist* is still a feature of *Syrian* Christianity at the beginning of the second century (*To the Smyrnaeans* 8.2; *Didache* 9, 10, 14). By the third century the agape and Eucharist parted company across most of the church. The agape continued in *North Africa* and Byzantium until after the fifth century, as a common meal designed to relieve the poor. To this day, in the Byzantine rite of the Eucharist, and the Litya ritual of festal vespers, the custom of sharing blessed bread together in church is an echo of the agape ceremonies.

J. Keating, *The Agape and the Eucharist in the Early Church: Studies in the History of the Christian Love-Feasts* (London, 1901); A. Nygren, *Agape and Eros* (Philadelphia, 1953); G. H. Outka, *Agape: An Ethical Analysis* (New Haven, Conn., 1972).

Alexandria   Alexandria was founded at the Nile delta, to be the great center of Hellenistic culture in honor of Alexander the Great, who laid out its street design and selected its chief temples (Strabo, *Geography* 17.791–795). His remains were brought there from the East to a great hero's tomb in the center that was one of the city's ancient tourist attractions. His successor, Ptolemy, founded a dynasty there and melded the indigenous religious traditions of Egypt with a universalized cultural vision of Hellenism that had a potent effect on the intellectual and religious mentality of the Mediterranean world. From that point on, Alexandria expanded quickly into the second greatest city of the Roman Empire. After the defeat of Antony and Cleopatra direct Roman rule was instituted, and the governor of Egypt was one of the great powers in the Roman world. Alexandria's functional effectiveness as really the only great city for the whole of Egypt made it command the massive resources of the Nile (its agriculture provided the bread for Rome) as well as the international trade routes by sea from *India*, and land routes through Arabia. All traffic from *Nubia* and *Ethiopia* also passed down the Nile to the international port, strategically sited at the heart of the Mediterranean sea lanes. As a great center of trade and military forces, and also as the massive heart of the mystical-Egyptian religious systems, Alexandria was a vibrant capital. In Christian terms it was a city that affected Christian development in major ways, as one of the chief intellectual cradles of Christianity (along with *Rome* and *Antioch*). Almost all Greek *patristic* thought bears the stamp of Alexandria in it somewhere, and many of the city's Christian intellectuals shaped the very foundations of *christological* and Trinitarian (*see Trinity*) thought for the international Christian world. The city might have been the world center of Hellenism (surpassing even Rome in this regard), and from the time of the very birth of the Christian movement, it had also long been the veritable world center of *Judaism*. There was a vast Jewish quarter in Alexandria, and the intellectual life of the Jewish community was deep rooted and flourishing. The city saw the production of what is now known as the Wisdom literature of the Old Testament. In the time of Jesus, *Philo*, one of the world's leading Jewish intellectuals, had already developed a school that carefully tried to lead biblical *exegesis* along a Hellenistic path of allegorical interpretation (long practiced in the Great Library of Alexandria in reference to the classical canon of authors) and had forged a dynamic link between Hellenistic philosophy and biblical religion, in his fertile use of *Logos theology*. This strong rooting in Wisdom literature (aphoristic philosophical religion) and mystical speculations of the Logos movement became constitutive of the Christian communities in Alexandria also. One of the first Alexandrian Christian theologians known to us is Apollos, the Jewish Christian convert who seems to have made even someone as confident as Paul feel the need to improve his rhetoric (see the Western Text of Acts 18:25; cf. 1 Cor. 1:12). By the second century the Alexandrian church was a center for learned private teachers offering *paideia*. Among them were several Christian *gnostic* thinkers, not least *Basilides*, who claimed to have been the disciple of Glaukios who had been a companion of St. Peter. The first attempts at systematizing Christian doctrine in a less mythopoetical way than the gnostics were undertaken by *Clement of Alexandria*. Later traditions list him as a presbyter of the church, but his work is not so much evidence of the formal catechetical school of the Christians (this really only applies after the third century), but more an example of what a skilled Christian philosopher had to say in his own lecture rooms about the function of Christianity as a religion of enlightenment. Clement's emphasis on Logos theology set the terms for much of what would later be taken to a pitch in

Origenes. *Origen of Alexandria* was without doubt the greatest Greek Christian philosopher of antiquity, and with the possible exception of **Augustine** in the Latin West, he was the single most influential of all the early theologians. His systematic work was complex and subtle, envisaging the descent of the eternal Word and Wisdom of God to earth in the figure of Jesus, in order to initiate a great cosmic ascent back to God. Origen lived in an environment where gnostic thought was still active in Alexandria, but set out to rescue the best and most inclusivist insights of the gnostics for the tradition of *orthodoxy*. In this he largely succeeded, but at the cost of alienating his local bishop, Demetrius of Alexandria. Demetrius is an important figure historically for demonstrating the rise of the Christian monarchical *episcopate* to a position of unprecedented power. By international letters of communion with the other chief churches, Demetrius was able to police orthodoxy and prosecute dissidents, of whom he regarded Origen as a chief example. In his administration, in the early decades of the third century, Alexandria was more clearly organized as a church with its own theological school (for the preparation of *baptismal* candidates) and with a firm hand over its subordinate bishops. The peculiar geography of Egypt (with only one metropolitan city in such a vast terrain) made the bishops of Alexandria occupy a unique position in the Christian world, and they took advantage of that to the full, ensuring that they were the single metropolitan of their nation, with a vast array of suffragan bishops under them, all depending on their personal patronage, and needing their agreement for ordination. Because of this the Alexandrian church was immensely centralized, and the power of the Christian bishops grew as the church itself grew and was stabilized, until in the fourth century the archbishop of the city could defy an emperor, and in the fifth century rivaled the power of the imperial governor of

Egypt. The third-century *persecutions* were especially bitter in Alexandria, where the governors prosecuted them with notorious savagery. Christianity had made its headway first in the city, and then more slowly in the country regions of upper Egypt, where the old religion was still powerful. By the fourth century the church had emerged from the fires of hostility with a high reputation for fidelity and a large array of *martyrs*, coloring its later self-image with a pugnacity that the rest of the Christian world often found alarming. In the fourth century the spread of Christianity through the regions of Upper Egypt was rapid and fostered by the burgeoning communities of monks who had adopted the semidesert lands around the Nile as their center of operations, and from that seclusion actually had a strong base from which to communicate with Egyptian culture, and the city of Alexandria, by the perennial highway of the river Nile. Monastic communities following the varied eremitical or community rules (*see* **Antony, asceticism, Pachomius**) were widely spread in the environs of Alexandria (*see* **Nitria, Scete**), and Egyptian monasticism caught the attention of the world and spread widely. Many of the greatest intellects of the patristic age in the fourth and fifth centuries were monks in the Origenian tradition, not least *Evagrius of Pontus*, the teacher from the desert near Alexandria. The fourth-century *Arian* crisis began as a local Alexandrian theological argument, and *Athanasius* the bishop of Alexandria was one of the leading theological voices of the era. The controversy stimulated him to write a powerful body of work, which became the substrate for the whole movement of Nicene orthodoxy. In *Christology* and pneumatology (*see* **Holy Spirit**), Athanasius proved to be one of the greatest of all patristic thinkers. His successors *Theophilus* and the latter's nephew *Cyril of Alexandria* took the see to new heights of influence in Christian politics and theology. Cyril, presiding at the *Council of Ephesus* in

431, formed the substructure of classic patristic Christology in his writings refuting *Nestorius of Constantinople*. After his death the church of Egypt fell into a decline as its archbishop *Dioscorus* attempted to force international opinion to his own increasingly narrow view of Cyril's intellectual legacy. His downfall at the *Council of Chalcedon* (451) led to a progressive alienation of Alexandria and the diocese of Egypt from the currents of Byzantine Christianity. The episcopal incumbents of the city oscillated between Chalcedonian and anti-Chalcedonian allegiance for years afterwards, and the so-called *Monophysite* schism was never healed in any significant way before the Arab and Islamic invasions of the seventh century permanently detached Egypt from the Christian world. The churches rapidly fell into a deep and lasting shadow. The archbishops remained in contact with the neighboring Christian churches of Africa, but after the loss of *Nubian* Christianity in the Middle Ages, its primary link was with the *Ethiopian* highlands, resulting in a close intertwining of the ecclesiastical cultures of these once so disparate parts of Africa. It has often been thought that the Great Library, the massive collection of Hellenistic literature at Alexandria, was burned in the time of Theophilus, although it was only the "branch collection" sited at the Serapeum that was damaged; or that the collection was destroyed by the Islamic invaders. In fact the collection was allowed to be dispersed by sea over a twelve-month interregnum before the invading forces took possession of Alexandria as their new capital in 642. As a result, Christian Alexandria exported its vast resources of Hellenistic and Christian literature, as well as the relics of its greatest *saints*, to the churches of *Rome* and *Constantinople*, to the very end preserving its role as one of the great disseminators of international culture and religious mysticism for the antique world.

[Mélanges:Mondésert]   *Alexandrina: Hellénisme, Judaïsme et Christianisme à Alexandrie: Mélanges offerts au Père Claude Mondésert* (Paris, 1987); R. S. Bagnall, *Egypt in Late Antiquity* (Princeton, N.J., 1993); E. R. Hardy, *Christian Egypt* (New York, 1952); B. A. Pearson and J. E. Goehring, eds., *The Roots of Egyptian Christianity* (Philadelphia, 1986).

Allegory   Allegory was a widely used Hellenistic literary method of interpreting sacred literature (the Homeric corpus or the classics of philosophy) by means of universal symbolic modalities. The need to exegete Homer symbolically, for example, was increasingly noted by late antique religious philosophers who demanded that Hellenistic myth should be reworked to give it a more metaphysically advanced religious base. The Stoic writer Pseudo-Heraclitus, in the first century of the Christian era, argued that unless Homer is interpreted allegorically, all he contains is impieties (*Allegoriae Homericae* 1.1). *Philo* (first century) and the Middle *Platonist* Numenius (second century) also did much to introduce the allegorical method as a way of disconnecting the Old Testament from its immediate historical origins and reinterpreting it as a metaphysically universalist literature. Details in the sacred texts that were unworthy, archaic, or obsolete could thus be taken as symbolic allusions to another level of meaning. The allegorical method was not unknown to the earliest Christian writers, although the consistent allegorical retelling of some of Jesus' parables (such as the second telling of the parable of the Sower in Mark 4) are usually taken to be exercises of the evangelists rather than Jesus himself. Paul, for example, makes an explicit reference to allegorical symbolic readings of texts in Galatians 4:24. He uses a set of other allegorical symbols in 1 Corinthians 5:6–8 (leaven as a symbol); 1 Corinthians 9:8–14 (the ox as a symbol of apostolic rights); and 1 Corinthians 10:1–5 (exodus events as symbols of Christian sacraments). It is *Origen of Alexandria*, however, who brings allegorical interpretation of sacred texts onto the Christian agenda most definitively in the third century. For Origen, allegory means a deeper, symbolic, "spiritually acute" reading of the biblical narrative, and he devotes considerable time in his treatise *De principiis* to explaining his system of biblical interpretation, one that is clearly modeled on elements of literary analysis that had been established at the Great Library of Alexandria. He does not markedly distinguish between allegory, typology, and *anagogy*, though later *exegesis* progressively did. Allegory was then fitted into a narrower definition that saw it as an extended narrative that took elements from an earlier story and used them symbolically in a parallel narrative so as to speak about something else, or in order to erect a digressive commentary alongside the first narrative. The second telling of the parable of the Sower in Mark 4 represents this narrow sense of allegory (the grain really means the word, the rocks mean temptations, the birds mean evil spirits, and so on). Typology, on the other hand, was the use of symbolic narratives or figures from the Scripture, to make an extended correlation of New Testament episodes in the light of older narratives—a system of reading one narrative within the enclosing ambit of another narrative (for example, the manner in which the story of Abraham's taking of Isaac up the mountain to sacrifice him was read as a "type" of the crucifixion story). Type in this sense was like the die that stamped a coin. One narrative "typed itself" onto the other. Christian exegetes understood the antitype (always the New Testament narrative) to be the result of type hitting the object—thus the antitype was legible, printed the correct way round as it were, while the type itself was a reversal, a shadow, or an anticipation. In typological theory the type, although prior to the antitype, needed the later story or event to be itself elucidated. Origen expressed it graphically in his theory that only with the advent of the New Testament did the Old Testament become comprehensible. *Gregory of Nyssa* in his highly allegorized reading of the Song of Songs expressed his opinion that, as with the transmutation of wheat husks into bread, just so the church needed to transfigure raw Scripture into meaningful discourse by means of allegorical interpretation (prologue of the *Homilies on the Song of Songs*). The earliest Christian commentators, however, did not usually distinguish as clearly as we might have wanted them to between allegory and typology. For Origen and his many subsequent disciples, allegory simply meant the finding of a higher message in all parts of the Scripture, even those parts that seemed odd and objectionable when read on a purely historical (literal) level. In early medieval times the random use of earlier technical terms of exegesis was clarified and tightened up to represent "four senses of scripture": the literal (or historical), the tropological (or moral), the allegorical (the spiritual commentary), and the anagogical (the eschatological significance). After the condemnation of Origenism in the sixth century, many Greek and Latin exegetes ostensibly rejected his allegorical approach. In practice, however, it continued unabated, now described as the reading of *theoria* (the higher sense of Scripture). Origen's laws were replaced (for the West) by *Augustine's* extended treatment of the rules of allegorical exegesis in his treatise *Christian Instruction* (*see also* **Tyconius**), and thus allegorization became the dominant way of a universalized reading of narrative until late modernity, when a profound reaction set in against it, and the historical-critical method began to be dominant. Postmodern literary theory in the late twentieth century once more challenged the supremacy of historicist readings of texts, and great interest is again being shown in the early Christian patterns of allegorical exegesis.

R. M. Grant, *The Letter and the Spirit* (New York, 1957); J. M. Daniélou, *From Shadows to Reality: Studies in the Biblical Typology of the Fathers* (Philadelphia, 1961); K. Froehlich, ed., *Biblical Interpretation in the Early Church* (Philadelphia, 1974); J. A. McGuckin, "Origen as Literary Critic in the Alexandrian Tradition," in L. Perrone, ed., *Origenianum Octavum* (Leuven, Belgium, 2003).

Almsgiving   A collective term for the gift of food, money, or help in general to those in distress, for the sake of the glory of the God of mercy (hence the Greek term *eleemosyne*: mercifulness). It was advocated throughout the Scriptures as a sign of fidelity to the covenant (Isa. 58:6–12; Matt. 6; 25:34–45; Jas. 2:14–17). And from ancient times the practice of charitable donations was made part of the fabric of regular church life (Acts 11:19–30; 2 Cor. 8:1–15). From the mid–second century the bishops assumed the direction of the church's relief work (one of the reasons that office grew to preeminence), and the orders of *deacons* and *widows* were entrusted with the task of distribution. In some larger churches this amounted to a considerable social effort. Orphans, prisoners, the sick, *slaves*, and travelers were among the main recipients. *Prayer*, fasting, and almsgiving were commonly regarded as practices that would call down God's mercy on those who observed them, and they were the standard forms of penitential practice of early Christianity, advocated in the *Didache* (15.4). The Shepherd of *Hermas* regards the interdependence of the poor and the rich in terms of their salvation as comparable to the way in which the vine needs the elm tree to support it (Shepherd of Hermas, *Similitude* 2). (*See Wealth.*) *Cyprian* dedicated an entire treatise to almsgiving in the third century (*De opere et eleemosynis*) and after the

fourth century, with the increased opportunities for public relief work of the Constantinian era, many patristic sermons began to advocate a more systematic effort of charitable donations from the church. *Gregory of Nazianzus* presented a famous "Oration on the Poor" (*Or. Orat.* 14), which was one of the first homilies to elaborate why alms should be donated as a matter of justice to the poor, since even the most wretched on earth (he envisaged lepers, and was pleading for funds to establish a leprosarium at Caesarea) were the icon of God on earth, and had equal status with any other human being (not a commonly accepted idea in antiquity, pagan or Christian, where many notions still lingered about the sick and suffering being "cursed by God"). In the classical patristic era, with stirring rhetorical appeals for almsgiving becoming more common an element of episcopal preaching, the organization of institutional church relief work grew accordingly, and into the Byzantine era, and beyond, church establishments for the sick, for lepers, for orphans and the destitute were a common part of life in the larger city churches. The *Cappadocian Fathers*, along with *Ambrose*, *Chrysostom*, and *Augustine*, are among the most eloquent of the church fathers advocating almsgiving as both a doxology of God and an act of merciful justice.

D. Constantelos, *Byzantine Philanthropy and Social Welfare* (New Brunswick, N.J., 1968); I. Giordani, *The Social Message of the Early Church Fathers* (Paterson, N.J., 1944); A. Guillaume, *Riches et Pauvres dans l'Église ancienne* (Paris, 1962); J. A. McGuckin, "The Vine and the Elm Tree: The Patristic Interpretation of Jesus' Teachings on Wealth," in *The Church and Wealth* (Studies in Church History 24; Oxford, 1987), 1–14; P. Phan, *Social Thought* (Message of the Fathers of the Church 20; Wilmington, Del., 1984); B. Ramsey, "Almsgiving in the Latin Church: The Late Fourth and Early Fifth Centuries," TS 43 (1982): 226–59.

Ambrose (c. 339–397)   Ambrose rose to fame as a powerful and learned bishop of Milan (374–397). He was an aristocrat, son of the Praetorian prefect of Gaul. Educated in rhetoric and *philosophy* at *Rome*, he took up a career in law and by 370 had risen politically to be the consularis (governor) of Aemilia and Liguria in northern Italy, based in Milan. In 374 he acted to bring order to street disturbances that had broken out between the *Catholics* and *Arians* fighting over the legitimate successor to the (Arian) bishop Auxentius. His decisive intervention impressed the city enough to ensure his own acclamation to the see, and so he was hurriedly *baptized* and consecrated *bishop*. He proved to be a forceful leader of his city, and a strong advocate of the *Nicene* faith. His pastoral civic care became a model for many generations of bishops after him, and stories about his successful standoffs with emperors gave symbolic grounds for the later Western church's theory of the preeminence of the priestly office, an important element in the rise of the monarchical *papacy*. Ambrose as a neophyte bishop set himself the task of learning theology and biblical *exegesis* from the foundations, in order to fulfill his preaching obligations. He was fluent in Greek (rare for that time in the West), and his work shows an intelligent dependence on *Origen* and the Eastern patristic tradition for *Christology* and *Trinitarian* thought. His sermons include many strong moral appeals for social justice. Ambrose embraced the *ascetical* life and gave much prominence to the idea of consecrated *virginity* in his works, and to the cult of the *martyrs*. His treatise on the sacraments gives an important insight into fourth-century liturgical practice. He is also credited with the popularization of communal *hymn* singing in the Western church, and his own four authentic hymns mark the first flowering of a great tradition of Latin hymnody. Ambrose pressured the emperor Valentinian not to accede to pagan appeals for pluralistic religious toleration, and he stood for the ejection of the ancient altar of victory from the senate house. He also refused to allow Arians rights of free worship in his city and his occupation of church buildings forced the imperial policy of toleration to be reversed. He enunciated the principle for the first time: "The emperor indeed is within the church, not above the church," thereby setting a new standard of ecclesiastical polity. He continued in the same tenor with Valentinian's successor Theodosius I, excommunicating the emperor for his assault on the city of Thessalonica as a punishment for mutinous riots. The emperor accepted public penance and soon afterwards initiated a series of laws licensing the complete outlawing of paganism in the empire.

F. H. Dudden, *The Life and Times of St. Ambrose* (2 vols.; Oxford, 1935); N. B. McLynn, *Ambrose of Milan: Church and Court in a Christian Capital* (Berkeley and London, 1994); A. Paredi, *St. Ambrose* (trans. M. J. Costelloe; Notre Dame, Ind., 1964); D. H. Williams, *Ambrose and the End of the Arian-Nicene Conflicts* (Oxford Early Christian Studies; Oxford, 1995).

Ambrosiaster (late fourth century) This anonymous writer was called Ambrosiaster because his work had been attributed to *Ambrose* in the medieval textual tradition. He was a theologian of the Roman church in the time of Pope *Damasus* (366–384), who wrote a commentary on the writings of Paul that had considerable influence on later *exegesis* (avoiding allegory in favor of a straightforward literal and historical analysis). He is also the author of the *Questions on the Old and New Testaments*, which was formerly attributed to *Augustine*. Augustine used his *Commentary on Romans* and named its author as one "Saint Hilary." He influenced Augustine in his conception of the human being as at once sinner and redeemed. His work shows close knowledge of *Judaism*, and reflects on the relation of the Jewish people to the plan of *salvation* offered in the church of Christ.

A. Souter, *A Study of Ambrosiaster* (Texts and Studies 7.4; Cambridge, U.K., 1905); idem, *The Earliest Latin Commentaries on the Epistles of St. Paul* (Oxford, 1927).

Anagogy   *Origen* was one of the first Christians to refer to the process of a higher symbolic reading of the Old Testament scriptures as anagogical reading (*ComJn* 1.26 [24]; 32.12). (*See Allegory*.) The word *anagoge* literally means "lifting up," and Origen applied it to the manner in which a reading of the text could be "deepened" if interpreters "lifted up" the spiritual eyes of their intelligence, so as to recognize the Christian verities that lay hidden within it symbolically. Origen did not much distinguish anagogy from allegory, which was his more common term and process. *Gregory of Nazianzus* uses the concept of anagogy in the same sense at the end of the fourth century (*Oration* 45.12) to argue for a "balanced" exegetical understanding that is neither "lowly and Jewish" (by which he meant historically contextualized and primarily focused on the literal meaning), nor elevated into "mystical dreaminess" (an attack on excessive allegorization). Gregory thus begins a technical sense of anagogy, which would develop apace at the end of the *patristic* era and on into the medieval church. In this later period there developed a doctrine of the "four senses" of Scripture. The sacred text should, it was thought, be systematically examined for its literal meaning, its tropological (moral) sense, its allegorical (symbolic doctrinal and spiritual) significance, and its anagogical meaning. In the latter case the anagogical sense was how a given scriptural passage clarified or related to the *eschatological* imperative, the end times, or consummation (*see apokatastasis, recapitulation*).

D. Dawson, *Allegorical Readers and Cultural Revision in Ancient Alexandria*

(Berkeley, Calif., 1992); idem, *Christian Figural Reading and the Fashioning of Identity* (Berkeley, Calif., 2002); H. De Lubac, *Medieval Exegesis: The Four Senses of Scripture* (trans. M. Sebanc and E. M. Macierowski; Grand Rapids, vol. 1, 1998; vol. 2, 2000).

Anakephalaiosis   *see* **Recapitulation**

Anaphora   The Greek term means "announcing news" or "offering up." For the Christians it soon predominantly assumed the sense of "lifting up" in the sense of making a cultic offering, especially a spiritual sacrifice. The biblical instances of Hebrews 13:15 and 1 Peter 2:5 were particularly instrumental in shaping the word's exclusively liturgical application. The *anaphora* mainly denoted the act of offering up *prayer*. It particularly meant the central act of Christian worship, the Eucharistic assembly. And soon it came to be a specific term for the central act of the eucharistic rite itself, that is, the main prayer of offering the bishop (later also the presbyters [*see priesthood*]) would offer (at first *extempore*), during which the offering of bread and wine would be consecrated on the altar. In this sense the *anaphora* was what the Western church came to call the "canon" of the Mass. In the early eucharistic rituals of the Eastern church the *anaphora* began with the invitation to the people to "lift up your hearts," and after the singing of the Sanctus and a short preface of thanksgiving prayers for the benefits of God, it moved to the words of institution over the bread and wine, then going on to include the elevation of the gifts and the prayer of offering, the prayer of *epiclesis* (invocation) for the *Holy Spirit's* consecration of the offering, and finally summative prayers of intercession and thanksgiving, before culminating in the communal recitation of the Our Father. (Some writers use it to refer to everything in the liturgy from the Great Entrance to Communion.) The *anaphora* is thus the central prayer of the eucharistic liturgy. In some early liturgical texts *anaphora* also had an even more specific reference. It could signify the bread and wine (those things that were being offered). Soon this use was replaced by the term *prosphora* to connote the eucharistic gifts. *Anaphora* could also signify the veil that was placed over the chalice and paten on the altar. But again soon the term *kalymna* replaced it for this connotation, and *anaphora* remained to designate primarily the process of making sacred spiritual offering to God in the Eucharist. In modern theological writings it is commonly used to refer to the various eucharistic traditions or liturgical "families" of rites. In this sense there are generally seen to be three major branches of *anaphorae*: the Syro-Oriental (Chaldaean), the Antiochene or Syro-Occidental (Byzantine), and the Alexandrian (Coptic). The oldest known *anaphorae* of the church are the *Eucharistic Prayer* of Serapion of Thmuis, the *anaphora* given in the *Apostolic Tradition* of **Hippolytus**, the *Liturgy of Addai and Mari*, and the Egyptian form of the *Liturgy of St. Basil*.

G. Dix, *The Shape of the Liturgy* (London, 1945); J. P. Oesterley, *The Jewish Background of the Christian Liturgy* (Oxford, 1965).

Anathema The Greek word means "suspended" or "hung up overhead" and, through the LXX Greek translation of the Bible, came into Christian usage as a version of the Hebrew *herem*, which meant to "cut off" or "put under a sacred ban" (Deut. 7:26). From an early age it connoted the process of rendering something "sacred to the Lord," such as a votive offering (cf. Lev. 21:6). Cultically, such a gift was "dedicated" and thus out of bounds for the common people. Penalties were severe for illegitimately crossing the boundaries set between the sacred and the profane, and so the concept of anathema soon began to be loaded with punitive and exclusionary significance. In the Old Testament pre-exilic period, the "setting under a ban" sometimes meant the destruction of the cities or people so anathematized (Deut. 7:1f.; Josh. 6; 1 Sam. 15), a notion that later devolved into a form of excommunication involving the "separation" of a person from the community, and the accompanying confiscation of goods and property this entailed. It is this sense of anathematizing that runs on into the New Testament (Matt. 18:17; Mark 6:11; John 9:22), although the actual word is not used until Paul referred it to fundamental offenses that merited exclusion from the Christian community (1 Cor. 16:22; Gal. 1:8–9). The patristic era saw the word first used in a technical sense of denouncing and excommunicating serious (sexual) offenders at the Council of Elvira (306). Experience gained from the second-century struggles with the gnostics had thus been combined with Old Testament and Pauline archetypes to provide the beginnings of a synodical code of canon law. **Cyril of Alexandria**, in the early fifth century, attacked the theology of **Nestorius** by attaching a list of "Twelve Anathemata" to his third synodical letter. While this was undoubtedly a synodical threat of excommunication, it is probable that Cyril used the older Greek sense of anathemata as sacred public proclamations (propositions), to which he demanded Nestorius give his assent. After that time, synodical anathematization became a standard form of the condemnation of heretics. Their crimes and names were read out and bishops collectively shouted out the anathemas. Liturgically this practice is still observed in the Byzantine rite on the Sunday of Orthodoxy, where the classical heretics are symbolically anathematized in church by the congregation. In the West the ritual of excommunication involved anathematizing the person and doctrine of the individual, and at the moment of cursing, twelve **priests** who had been carrying lighted candles dramatically cast them down upon the church floor, so extinguishing them. This ritual was abolished in the revised Latin code of *canon* law in 1983. Anathe-matizing a person was viewed as announcing publicly their complete sep-aration from the body of the church because of the severity of their own deeds or doctrines. Excommunication was distinct from this, and was the dis-ciplinary exclusion of a believer from the sacraments until such time as a penance had been performed.

L. Brun, *Segen und Fluch im Urchristentum* (Oslo, 1931); A. Vacant, "Anathema," in DTC (vol. 1; Paris, 1903), cols. 1168–71.

Andrew of Crete (c. 660–740) Andrew of Crete was a native of Damas-cus who became a monk at *Jerusalem*. Ordained *deacon* at *Constantinople*, he was then appointed in 692 as archbishop of Gortyna in Crete. His homilies were collected and had much influence in the Eastern church as examples of rhetorical brilliance. He is most remembered for his defense of the icons (*see iconoclasm*), his devotion to the *theotokos*, and his poetry. His greatest work, *The Great Canon* (he is said to have invented the poetic genre of the Byzantine canon), is still used as a major penitential hymn in Eastern Orthodoxy during Lent.

B. Daley, *On the Dormition of Mary: Early Patristic Homilies* (New York, 1998), 103–52; D. Chitty, *St. Andrew of Crete: The Great Canon* (London, 1957); Sister Katherine and Sister Thekla, trans., *St. Andrew of Crete: The Great Canon* (Newport Pagnell, 1974).

Angels The word derives from the Greek term for "messenger" (*angelos*) and in most of the many scriptural refer-ences to God's angels (for example, Gen. 16:7; 32:1; Judg. 6:11; Dan. 7:10), they appear as the intermediaries who serve God's will by mediating with humankind. They are especially the deliverers of *revelation* and, as such, play a large role in the New Testament accounts of the annunciation, the birth of the Messiah, and the *resurrection* (Matt. 28:2–7; John 20:12). Late biblical religion, especially the *apocalyptic* texts, saw them especially as the court of God, and in the early Christian literature (espe-cially the book of Revelation and the Letter to the Hebrews) this aspect devel-oped into a vision of the angelic host as the preeminent singers of God's glory: the liturgical choir of divine praise. Jesus referred to angels on several occasions, teaching that they always enjoyed the presence and vision of the Father (Matt. 18:10), and that they would form the accompanying army of God which would return with the Son of Man at the *Parousia* (Matt. 16:27). Some Jewish Christian sects developed an angelology that saw Christ as a high archangel who had come to earth to deliver a salvific gospel. The trend was already advanced in Hellenistic *Judaism* (it can be seen in *Philo*) to imagine the angelic mediators as "manifestations" of the divine on earth (so the law was seen to be given through angels, not directly by an epiphany of God to Moses), and it can be partially witnessed in the anxiety of parts of the New Testament Pastoral Let-ters and the Epistle to the Hebrews to insist that Christ is "far superior" to the angels (Col. 2:18; Heb. 1:4). *Irenaeus* insisted that the angels were distinct creatures of God, not a system of divine emanations as *Gnosticism* imagined and, like humanity, had a destiny to serve and worship the deity (*Adversus haereses* 2.30.6–9). Origen greatly ex-tended the patristic understanding of the angelic orders, with his doctrine of the preexistence of *souls*. The angels, in Origen's scheme, were the original souls created by God, who retained their heavenly dignity and ethereal status. Humanity had once been angelic, but had fallen into corporeality because of premundane *sins*; although one day the faithful soul could ascend back to become transfigured once more into angelic glory. It was Origen who brought the widespread belief in guardian angels into church life, with his teaching that God had appointed angels to watch over the destiny of nations, but also others to care for the safe journey of each soul on earth, until it returned back to its original heavenly family. The Origenian scheme of preexistence was highly attractive to the Christian mystics, such as *Evagrius,* but was never accepted by the larger church. In the fourth century *Gregory of Nazianzus* rescued the doctrine of angels from the implications of Origenian preexistence doctrine, and laid out a system that would become authoritative for the wider *tradition.* God, Gregory argued, had made three creations. The first was the angelic order. The second was the material and animal creation, and the third was humanity. The two first creations were simple and coherent in their ontology, spiritual and fleshly respectively. Mankind alone was a "mixed creation" (flesh and spirit). By faithful obedience, and a constant "ascent" of soul, human beings could attain to the glory of angelic status in the afterlife (Gregory of Nazianzus, *Carmina* 1.1.7). Two scriptural passages caught the imagination of the early Church, where the "ranks" of the angels were described with some differences (Eph. 1:21; Col. 1:16). The early patristic writers, putting them together, came up with an enumeration of five different ranks. *Dionysius the Areopagite* added to that list of five the separate ranks of angel, archangel, seraph, and cherubim, and thus set out the definitive list of the "nine orders" of the angels that would form the basic understanding of both the Latin and Greek churches ever after (angels, archangels, principalities, powers, virtues, dominions, thrones, cherubim, and seraphim). The seraphim occupied the seventh heaven alongside God, and their proximity to the divine presence resulted in their eruption into pure fire (in such a way are they always depicted in iconography). The angels were seen to be endowed with almost infinite mobility and vast powers. In patristic understanding they also

attended the liturgy whenever it was celebrated on earth. In the Byzantine liturgy the deacons often assumed a role of symbolizing the angelic orders, and the imperial eunuchs (sexless, as Jesus had said the angels were in heaven: Mark 12:25) had the special task of singing the cherubic hymn at the time of the Great Entrance: "We who in a mystery represent the Cherubim, and sing the thrice holy hymn to the life-creating trinity, now lay aside all earthly cares, that we may receive the King of all who comes escorted by the ranks of unseen angels" (The Cherubic Hymn of the Liturgy of St. John Chrysostom).

J. Daniélou, "Les anges et leurs mission d'après les Pères de l'Église," *Irenikon* 5 (1952); K. S. Frank, *Angelikos Bios* (Münster, Germany, 1964).

Anhomoians (Anomoeans)   *see* Aetius, Eunomius, Neo-Arianism

Anthropology
Anthropology is the study of the human person, especially understood (in theological terms) as the manner in which the constitution of humanity and its present condition relate to the divine plan of salvation. Christian anthropology was thus mainly occupied with the twin ideas of how the human being was constituted (that is, the nature of body, *soul*, and spirit), and how the human being had fallen from grace (the *fall*) and could return to God's glory. The concept of *soteriology,* or the doctrine of salvation, was thus never far from the patristic consideration of anthropology. The main architecture of anthropology, in both its aspects, was established by the Scriptures. Paul regularly talked about the tripartite division of humans into soul (*psyche*), spirit (*pneuma*), and body (*sarx, soma*). There is hardly a writer of the patristic era, whether in dogmatic, spiritual, or ascetic contexts, who does not speculate on what that might mean: how the various "capacities" (spiritual, intellectual,

psychic, material) of human beings can be correlated and described. Patristic writers were generally dominated by the Genesis accounts of the fall of humans from innocence, and from such exegetical "types" as the detail of Adam walking hand in hand with God in the peace of the garden, they deduced that the first ancestors were constituted as immortal beings who were given the gift of communion with God as part of their *nature*. The contemplation of the face of God conveyed immortality to Adam, and even after he had fallen from that communion, the lives of the early ancestors were immensely long, a sign that the immortality they had lost was only progressively alienated from them. *Gregory of Nyssa*, one of many writers who commented on Genesis, notes that the need for Adam and Eve to "cover themselves with skins" is a record of how humanity's original destiny as a transcendent psyche that enjoyed the divine *vision* had now fallen into the debilitating morass of fleshly concerns (the covering of animal skins). The radical division of humanity into mind/reason (*nous*) on the one hand and flesh/body (*sarx*) on the other was a basic element of much Hellenistic anthropology. In the patristic writings this polarism was combined with, and balanced by, more biblical elements that reduced the Hellenistic desire to identify humanity's finest and essential element only with the rational aspect of life. In line with this Hellenistic "anthropology of reason," women, children, and slaves (those who were regarded as not capable of "free and reasonable enquiry") were generally regarded as subhuman and subpersonal. The Christian theologians shifted this emphasis on rationality (although they simultaneously affirmed it as a central aspect of what the divine image in mankind meant) to define the quintessence of the human person as rather the capacity for communion with God. This set Christian anthropology on a new track of theoretical equitableness. From *Irenaeus*, in the second century, the biblical notion of the *image of God* became central to patristic anthropology. Irenaeus made a distinction not hitherto visible in biblical reflection on the divine image and likeness (Gen. 1:26), noting that any human was the divine image simply by being a creature (because of the race's natural makeup), but could become the "likeness of God" only in terms of a *mystical* conformity to Christ; in other words, through the spiritual life of regeneration. Irenaeus described a whole vision of the accommodation of anthropology to soteriology when he said: "God will be glorified in his creature (*plasma*) as it is rendered conformable and made similar to his own Son" (*Adversus haereses* 5.6.1). In the third century *Origen of Alexandria* drew up the basis in his *De principiis* for a whole systematic treatment of anthropology, envisaging the nature of humans as an inevitable labor to ascend once more to the lost communion with God. In the fourth century *Athanasius* of Alexandria (*De incarnatione*) underscored the link present in the Scriptures, in Irenaeus and Origen, between anthropology and *Christology*, and afterwards this nexus of ideas became inextricable. The *incarnation* of the divine *Logos*, the personal architect of all humanity, now present as an individual human being, was regarded as nothing less than the re-creation of humanity. This new humanity, the "Christ-nature," was different from the old Adamic humanity: as different as mortality was from immortality. The idea of christological regeneration dominated patristic thought after that point, and was taken to a pitch in the writings of *Cyril of Alexandria*, who also connected humanity's ongoing regeneration (transformation into the new Adam) to the regular reception of the *Eucharist*—the dynamic of new life communicated to the church on earth. In *Augustine*, christological anthropology became a focus of all his theology, a lens by which to illuminate every other problem of Christian thought. Through him the anthropological imperative was interiorized; reflection on the inner life of a person (the scrutiny of the soul) became the primary manner of reading the book of God written in the human conscience. Augustine had a dominant effect on the rise of personal subjectivity as a major aspect of Christian philosophy in the later Western church. In Eastern Christian thinking the christological and soteriological emphases of the older tradition remained more dominant.

H. Bianchi, *Arche e Telos: L'Antropologia di Origene e di Grigorio di Nissa* (Milan, Italy, 1981); D. Cairns, *The Image of God in Man* (London, 1953); G. Mathon, *L'anthropologie chrétienne en occident de S. Augustin à Jean Scot Erigène* (Ph.D. diss., University of Lille, France, 1964); J. Pepin, *Idées grecques sur l'homme et sur Dieu* (Paris, 1971).

Antioch   After *Rome* and *Alexandria*, Antioch was the third most important city of the late antique Roman Empire, and its importance is correspondingly reflected in the history of the early church. It was founded on the Orontes River in 300 B.C. by Seleukis I, one of the successors of Alexander the Great. A Christian community existed here from the early first century, and it was here that the Jesus-disciples first started to be called "Christians" (Acts 11:26). The city's church was in ancient times associated with the work of the apostle Peter, and it has generally been taken that the Gospel of Matthew, reflecting generically Petrine theology in its earliest levels, is a gospel tradition that grew out of the Antiochene environment. It shows an original concern for maintaining close relationships between law and gospel, much more so that that represented in the more Gentile-inclined communities of Asia Minor and Rome, where Paul's influence was predominant. Paul began his first missionary tour from the church at Antioch, which funded it (Acts 13:1–2), and his Letter to the Galatians also suggests that Jewish and Gentile Christians in that church were among the first to struggle with the question whether Gentile converts to the faith were required to keep the law's observances or not (cf. Gal. 2:11–21), a matter over which Paul admits that he had face-to-face arguments with Peter at Antioch. Again at Antioch the first signs of the growth of monarchical episcopate (the pattern that would soon predominate in the international Christian movement) were manifested, in the person of *Ignatius* the famous martyr bishop, who left behind a series of letters to the churches as he made his way in chains to his trial in Rome at the very beginning of the second century. Ignatius complains that his church is riddled with heretics who seem to have denied Jesus was a fleshly being. This first suggestion of Antiochene theology in the patristic age appears to indicate a *Docetic* tendency. It drew from Ignatius a robust attack, and thus the beginning of a long strand in later patristic thought to emphasize the sacramentality and reality of Jesus' human embodiment. The Docetic strand of thought, however, is very easily merged with proto-*Gnosticism*, and it is probable that the gnostics had a hold in Antioch as elsewhere in the major Christian cities at this period, though not as much is known of city affairs here compared with Rome and Alexandria. One of the dissident teachers who are recorded was Saturninos, who presented a Christology arguing that Jesus was only apparently human, and in reality was a spiritual epiphany of the divine Savior. The Egyptian gnostic *Basilides* may also have spent some time teaching at Antioch. One of the earliest and most significant episcopal theologians from Antioch was the apologist *Theophilus*, who wrote his treatise *To Autolycus* c. 180. It is clear from his work that the church in Antioch was still deeply influenced by Jewish intellectual currents. Theophilus is one of the first to try to present a *Trinitarian* theology and an exegetical system at the heart of a public apologia for the Christian movement. At the same period the *Encratite* thinker *Tatian* had come in to the city to teach and argue the cause of his religion. He began the collation of Gospel texts and evidences for his work that resulted in the *Diatessaron*, which was conceived as a synthetic totalist view of the Christian tradition (the four Gospels harmonized into a single account). Tatian probably spoke directly and passionately to many sections of the Syrian-speaking Antiochene church (it was throughout the patristic period a bilingual city: Greek and Syriac) with his vision of the Christian movement as a radical sect of ascetical detachment from the world. In the time of the Decian persecution its famed bishop Babylas was martyred there, and after the restoration of the peace, his shrine became a significant pilgrimage place for Christians. In 350 his *relics* were moved to the suburb of Daphne, near the Castalian spring, sacred to Apollo. It was widely thought (among Christians) that Julian's failure in the Persian campaign was a direct result of his insult to the memory of Babylas when later in the fourth century he ordered his relics to be removed from the vicinity of the temple of Apollo, since the god had "ceased speaking" (Christians said Babylas had silenced the demon Apollo; local pagans said Apollo was offended by the remains of a dead mortal near his temple). After Julian's death the relics were brought back in triumph, and the Christian population of the city entered a period of clear ascendancy. The factions were volatile (Apollo's temple "accidentally" burned down when Julian ordered the destruction of the Babylas shrine), perhaps not so volatile as at Alexandria, but it was always a lively set of communities, as many of *John Chrysostom's* homilies demonstrate. A great octagonal church was built as the central cathedral, and was one of the largest then active in the Christian world. In the mid–third century the church witnessed a curious incident when *Paul of Samosata* combined

his role as senior government procurator with the duties of episcopal teaching (260–268). His doctrine (christological *Adoptionism*) attracted much criticism, and eventually resulted in his deposition by a larger synod. Antioch attracted to itself a very large hinterland of bishops who looked to it as the metropolitan center. Most of the Christian bishops in Persia also regarded it as their center of reference. One of the problems was, however, that the territory was very underpopulated and generally mountainous. To gather the clergy in from all quarters was a formidable undertaking, as most had to take the very difficult land routes. The weakness that this introduced into Antiochene church politics would be dramatically exploited in the fifth century when *Cyril of Alexandria* (with his centralized ecclesiastical system) gathered all his forces easily for the *Council of Ephesus I* (431) while *John of Antioch* was struggling to bring order into his disparate and bedraggled contingent. The first great patristic theologian of Antioch was *Lucian the Martyr* (d. 312), who edited the Septuagintal text for use in the church. *Eustathius of Antioch* was another vigorous theologian at the time of the *Council of Nicaea I*. He started out his career in the *Arian* camp, claiming the (now dead) Lucian as his teacher; but when he was installed as bishop of the city, he dramatically changed his mind and announced that Arius was fundamentally mistaken. From that time on he was an ardent defender of the doctrine of the consubstantiality (*homoousion*) of the Son of God. *Athanasius of Alexandria* never trusted him, but Eustathius commanded immense respect among the eastern Nicenes, and lived long enough to see the final vindication of Nicene orthodoxy at the *Council of Constantinople (381)*. With Eustathius the affairs of the church of Antioch were bitterly confused with a rival hierarchy having been instituted with Western backing, which split the Nicene factions into two while the Arians were united against them both (see **Meletian Schism**). In 350 the neo-Arian logician *Aetius* was ordained a deacon at Antioch, though he was soon banished when even the Arians found his doctrine too radical for their tastes. One of Eustathius's disciples, *Diodore* the bishop of Tarsus, began a movement of scriptural interpretation that ostensibly tried to avoid the excessive allegorization of texts, in preference for a simpler historical and moral *exegesis*. Diodore also introduced a christological scheme that spoke of "Two Sons" working in the Christ: the divine Son of God, and the human Son of Man. He was roundly assailed for his "dichotomous" views by *Gregory of Nazianzus*, another of the protégés of Eustathius, but his biblical and christological ideas had a marked influence on late–fourth and early–fifth-century Antiochene theology. In the persons of *Theodore of Mopsuestia* and *Nestorius* (two Syrian teachers who worked in Antioch for several periods), the so-called "Antiochene School" assumed its character. The dramatic clash of the Antiochene and Alexandrian traditions during the conflict between Cyril of Alexandria and Nestorius (Council of Ephesus [431]) resulted in the rapid decline of Antioch as a respected theological center. Antiochene Christology was thus overshadowed as a distinct school. It survived in the original diocesan hinterland, but as this was progressively detaching more and more from the ambit of the Roman world, and thereby passing out of the Greek language into Syriac, its departure was not widely noticed. In the end the Syrian tradition disappeared into Persia, where it endured for centuries, but in obscure and oppressed conditions. One of the most famous preachers of Antioch was John Chrysostom, who was a learned *ascetic* of this church until his virtual kidnapping to serve as *bishop* of the newly ascendant *Constantinople*. With the rising fortunes of Constantinople came a corresponding decline in the vitality and significance of Antioch. Its prestige took a severe battering in the time of Cyril of Alexandria, and it had few theologians of international stature to help repair it. *Theodoret of Cyrrhus* was one of them, but his censure at the *Council of Ephesus II* (449), and again (less officially) at *Chalcedon* (451) and *Constantinople II* (553), sidelined him as an international influence. The major Syrian writers really only survived because of their Syriac editions, though all of them had once worked as Greek rhetoricians in a thoroughly Greek international oecumene. After the fruitless defense of the Antiochene theologian Nestorius, who had been deposed by Cyril at the Council of Ephesus (431), the affairs of Antioch entered into a bewildering phase when (like post-Chalcedonian Alexandria) its bishops oscillated between pro- and anti-Chalcedonian theologians. Syria, once a heartland of the "Two Sons" school of Diodore, soon became a center for *Monophysite* theology. Its last significant theologian of the patristic age was *Severus of Antioch* (bishop there in 512), one of the most powerful intellectual defenders of the radical Cyrilline (anti-Chalcedonian) Christology of the "One Nature." Antioch was a metropolitan see that greatly encouraged its ascetics, who were famed as being the most "severe" in the world. The Antiochene diocese boasted no less than two *Simeon Stylites*, one in the fifth and the other in the sixth century. They attracted pilgrims and disciples from all over the Christian world, and were soon being emulated at Constantinople itself, though the West always professed some disdain for a "too showy" asceticism such as this. Theodoret's *History of the Monks of Syria* gives a fascinating insight into Syrian ascetical life. In its time it was a veritable rival for Egyptian and Palestinian Monasticism. The city fell dramatically and fast. The Persians harried it through the latter part of the sixth century and sacked it in 540. They returned to burn the suburbs in 573, and once more took the city from the Romans in 611. The Arab armies took it in 637–638, and after that point the city ceased to operate as a center of international Christian culture. The Christian communities continued a long and uninterrupted existence there, but increasingly out of touch with the rest of the Greek and Latin Romanity of the other churches, and thus progressively isolated, not least because of their refusal to admit the ecumenicity of the Chalcedonian Christology. The rediscovery in the twentieth century of the works of several of the major fourth-century Antiochene writers has led to a revival of appreciation of their theology in contemporary times.

R. Devreesse, *Le Patriarcat d'Antioche* (Paris, 1945); G. Downey, *A History of Antioch in Syria: From Seleucus to the Arab Conquest* (Princeton, N.J., 1961); G. Elderkin, L. Lassus, R. Stillwell, D. Waagé, and F. Waagé, *Antioch on the Orontes* (5 vols.; Princeton, N.J., 1934–1972); R. Brown and J. P. Meier, *Antioch and Rome: New Testament Cradles of Catholic Christianity* (New York, 1983); W. A. Meeks and R. L. Wilken, *Jews and Christians in Antioch in the First Four Centuries of the Common Era* (Missoula, Mont., 1978).

Antony the Great (c. 251–356) Antony is symbolically the "first monk" of Christian tradition, and an important Desert Father. There were, of course, *ascetics* and hermits before him, but the *Life of Antony* written by **Athanasius of Alexandria**, soon after Antony's death, became one of the most popular Christian texts of antiquity and was responsible for making him paradigmatic for much of subsequent monastic theory. By the age of twenty Antony inherited his father's wealth and became head of his household. He experienced a dramatic conversion while hearing the Gospel read in church: "Sell all and follow me," and taking it to heart, he dispossessed himself for the benefit of the poor, broke his familial ties, and left *Alexandria* for a life of ascetical seclusion in the *desert*

around the Nile, near Fayyum. He began his ascetical life near settlements (and from this period come the stories of his famous "wrestling with demons"), but by 285 he moved deeper into the Egyptian desert seeking a more solitary (or "eremitical") lifestyle, at a place called Outer Mountain (Pispir). Here he organized a colony of disciples under a loose form of early communal "rule" (called "cenobitic" monasticism from the Greek term for shared lifestyle). In 305 he moved even farther into the wilderness to a place called Inner Mountain (Deir Mar Antonios) by the Red Sea. Here he presided over an association of monks living as hermits. So it is that he traditionally came to be associated with the foundation of the three basic types of Christian monastic structure: communes (*koinobia*) under the direction of a senior monk (*Abba*); *lavras*, where scattered groups of individual hermits would inhabit neighboring valleys and meet for occasional worship, under the spiritual authority of an elder (*Geron*); and the eremitical life proper, where a monk would live in more or less complete seclusion. His writings focused on the need to acquire freedom in the inner life, so that the vision of God could be sought with a focused heart. His reputation as a holy man, counselor, exorcist, and thaumaturg, even in his own lifetime, was such that the bishop of Alexandria, Athanasius, called on his assistance and used the power of his reputation to combat the *Arian* movement.

R. C. Gregg, *Athanasius: The Life of Antony* (Classics of Western Spirituality; New York, 1980); S. Rubenson, *The Letters of Saint Antony: Origenist Theology, Monastic Tradition, and the Making of a Saint* (Bibliotheca Historico-Ecclesiastica Lundensis 24; Lund, Sweden, 1990).

Apatheia From the Greek (*Stoic*) term for insensibility, *apatheia* was first used by **Clement of Alexandria** and adopted by the Christian *ascetics* of the fourth century and after, mainly the east-erners of Evagrian tradition, to connote that state of dispassion where the ascetic could sense that he or she had achieved such a degree of control over the unruly heart and body that the spiritual intelligence (*nous*) was now in command of the whole synthetic composite of the psychic existence (*see* **anthropology, Plotinus**). From that time onward the faithful disciple was not so much subject to the regular temptations and lapses that described normal, tentative Christian existence, but rather had been spiritually prepared to receive the higher initiations of the *Holy Spirit*. Many of the Latin thinkers (cf. *Jerome*, *Epistulae* 133.3) regarded the notion of achieving a state of dispassion-ateness as incompatible with their own stress on the complete and far-reaching *fall* of humankind (Jerome misread the word as advocating a state of complete insensibility—*anaesthesia*). After the theology of **Augustine** had popularized the view of the corrupting and endemic state of the fall, the word never commanded much attention in the West (*see* **grace, Pelagius**), although **John Cassian** had introduced the idea into Western monasticism through his reading of **Evagrius**, and so it remained a feature of ascetical reading for both Eastern and Western monks. In Cassian's Latin, however, he rendered the idea as "purity of heart." In the later Greek-speaking church *apatheia* progressively lost its original technical meaning as a state of advanced monastic self-control and discipline that readied the heart to receive mystical knowledge, and came to describe simply the state of the experienced monk who had learned to control the passions (*pathemata*) with some stability.

G. Bardy, "Apathée," in DSP 1 (Paris, 1937), cols. 727–46.

Aphrahat (Afrahat, Aphraates)

(early fourth century)   Known as the Persian sage, Aphrahat is one of the most important of the early Syrian church writers. He was an *ascetic* and probably a bishop (he wrote a synodical letter to the *clergy* of the whole region). His most important work is his *Twenty-Three Demonstrations*. The first ten were composed in 337 as a set of dialogues for the guidance of ascetics, the next twelve in 344 mainly concerned with Christian-Jewish dialogue (*see* **Judaism**), and the last in 345, which is an essay on biblical history and the end of times based on the idea of the "berry" (Isa. 65:8 LXX). The *Demonstrations* show a church in regular dialogue with the synagogue, and are interesting exchanges of different perspectives without the hostility that later characterized much of the dialogue between the synagogue and the church. Aphrahat also has deep insights on *prayer* (especially *Demonstration* 4) and the mystical life, which he characterizes as the priesthood of the inner heart, offering the incense of prayer to the divinity. The ideas of peace and loving forgiveness are central to his thought. Later his writings became very influential in developing the East-Christian school of the "Prayer of the Heart."

J. Gwynn, *Selections Translated into English from the Hymns and Homilies of Ephraim the Syrian and From the Demonstrations of Aphrahat the Persian Sage* (NPNF, 2d series, vol. 13.2; New York, 1898); J. A. McGuckin, "The Prayer of the Heart in Patristic and Early Byzantine Tradition," in P. Allen, W. Mayer, and L. Cross, eds., *Prayer and Spirituality in the Early Church* (vol. 2; Everton Park, Australia, 1999), 69–108; J. Neusner, *Aphrahat and Judaism* (Leiden, Netherlands, 1971).

Apocalyptic

The Greek term means "lifting away the veil." It was translated in Latin as "revelation." Apocalyptic originally represented a theological movement that flourished two and a half centuries before the time of Christ, and though it dwindled away in *Judaism* after the disastrous collapse of the Simon Bar Kochba revolt in second-century

Palestine (an apocalyptic messianic movement), it remained as a potent force in Christianity long afterwards. The apocalyptic imperative was, in fact, one of the founding dynamics of the Christian movement, and has remained part of the inner pulse of Christianity, in varied forms, even to the present day. Apocalyptic writings abounded in the period in question, both before and after the appearance of Christianity. Most of them are now located in the so-called Apocrypha, since they failed to command a position in the *canon of Scripture* as it was being elaborated. Some of the more important were the *Psalms of Solomon*, the *Testaments of the Twelve Patriarchs*, the book of *Jubilees*, the books of *Enoch*, and numerous apocalypses of Old Testament and New Testament figures such as Esdras, Isaiah, Moses, John the Baptist, Mary, and so on.

In the Old Testament the book of Daniel is the only complete apocalypse, though parts of Ezekiel would also qualify as apocalyptic. In the New Testament, while there are many apocalyptic elements in the Gospels and Letters, the only complete apocalypse that entered the *canon* (and then only with reluctance as far as the East was concerned) was the book of Revelation. The use of the word "apocalypse" to describe the genre comes from the fact that in most narratives of this type a prophetic visionary is caught up in rapture to the heavenly court, and there he sees mysteries revealed to him. The veil is lifted away. The prophet sees the cosmic and theological explication of times past, and is then shown the unveiling of the future. The prophet returns to earth to announce a message of *judgment*, explaining the mysteries of the ages past, present, and to come, in order to call the people to repentance. Many of the key apocalyptic themes and terms, such as *metanoia*, the kingdom of God, *resurrection*, the Last Judgment, the Son of Man, and so on, are found as cardinal elements in the preaching of Jesus and the first apostles. The Christian fathers developed the apocalyptic element of the New Testament in new directions and into a more extended concept of *eschatology* (the last things).

The apocalyptic impulse in Hebraic theology had been focused on the notion of justice, where the Lord of creation ended time in order to intervene with righteous judgement on the wickedness of the earth, so as to vindicate his faithful and suffering Israel. Christian theologians, on the other hand, generally drew the line of their thinking on eschatology through the medium of *Christology*. Christians saw the return of the Lord of Glory as the *parousial* epiphany of Christ. His judgment was the establishment of the kingdom in heaven, which he had inaugurated on earth, and to which he now summoned his church as the risen Lord of history. Many scholars think that this christological imperative somewhat "flattened out" the apocalyptic impetus of primitive Christianity, and have described it as apocalypticism's evolution into proto-Catholicism. This may be true in part, but it frequently underestimates the eschatological depth of patristic thought. The apocalyptic spirit flourished strongly in the age of the *persecutions*, and can be witnessed explicitly in the early Christian cult of the *martyrs*. It is also believed to have inspired the rise of monastic *asceticism*, in the era when Christianity was officially tolerated and fostered by imperial power.

P. J. Alexander, *The Byzantine Apocalyptic Tradition* (Berkeley, 1985); W. Schneemelcher, *New Testament Apocrypha* (Cambridge, 1991); J. Daniélou, *The Theology of Jewish Christianity* (trans. J. A. Baker; London, 1964); B. Daley, *The Hope of the Early Church: A Handbook of Patristic Eschatology* (Cambridge, 1991).

Apokatastasis   The term means the reinstatement or reconstitution of a thing (originally the full revolution of a planet in orbit), and has a specific connotation in Christian theology as the doctrine (mainly represented by *Origen of Alexandria* in the third century and *Gregory of Nyssa* in the late fourth) whereby God would restore all things to the condition of primeval bliss, which he had designed for the creation in the beginning. Origen's views were based on the idea that all rational psychic life on earth was the result of a precosmic fall of superangelic spirits. As the spirits were first created (by the *Logos*) they surrounded the divine Word in perfectly blissful contemplation of the divine glory, and were thus stabilized in their being. Some spirits, however, "cooled off" from this first glory (he etymologically derives the word for *souls, psychai,* from the Greek term *psychesthai,* or cooling off), and he envisaged them as lapsing from the state of being a pure spirit and being coarsened in their essence, mutating into souls, whence they lapsed from the vision of the glory and so declined from their ontological stability. In the end, Origen argued, some fallen souls were so further corrupted and coarsened that God had to create a material world for them; and thus they entered into corporeality as a form of penitential reparation for their sins. Origen asserted most emphatically that since God's purposes could not be frustrated ultimately, and since his mercy was infinite, all punishment for sin and error had to be pedagogical. In other words it would be "unworthy" to attribute to God the plan of an everlasting *hell* that had no function except to inflict torture on the wicked (*Contra Celsum* 6.25; *Commentary on Romans* 6.5). Thus, all suffering and pain inflicted by God for the correction and healing of his creation had to be envisaged as pedagogically therapeutic. Origen argued that in the end, therefore, it would be logical to surmise that all spirits (perhaps even the devil himself) would be restored to union with God (*Peri Archon* 3.5.7, interpreting 1 Cor. 15:24–28; also *PArch* 3.6.5; *Commentary on Romans* 8.9). When this happened, the whole original

creation would have been reinstated as a pure band of superangelic spirits once again in communion with each other and in perfect contemplative harmony with the Logos. This is the first and classical Christian concept of *apokatastasis* as the perfect revolution of the wheel, so that "God would be all in all." Because it was so heavily dependent on the doctrine of the preexistence of souls, Origen was posthumously condemned several centuries after his death for holding such a theory. Even in his lifetime he stirred a storm of resistance for suggesting Satan could be saved and that hell was not necessarily everlasting, and he seems to have backed away from the idea as he grew older (*Commentary on John* 28.8.61–66). Gregory of Nyssa moderated the idea of *apokatastasis,* and taught it without censure in his lifetime (or after). Gregory envisaged all creation as making an eternal progress (*prokope*) to God, an ascent that began in this life and continued through endless ages afterwards, which thus enabled a finite creature to participate in the infinite reality of God in a moderated but authentic manner. After Gregory the idea was sidelined and never commanded a wide acceptance in the church even before it was formally condemned in the sixth-century Origenist controversy.

H. Crouzel, "L'apocatastase chez Origène," in L. Lies, ed., *Origeniana Quarta* (Innsbruck, Austria, 1987), 282–90; J. Daniélou, "L'apocatastase chez saint Grégoire de Nysse," RSR 30 (1940): 328–40; C. E. Rabinowitz, "Personal and Cosmic Salvation in Origen," VC 38 (1984): 319–32.

Apollinarism (Apollinarianism)
see **Apollinaris of Laodicea**

Apollinaris of Laodicea (c. 315–392)
Apollinaris was an important intellectual and political bishop defending the *Nicene* cause in the fourth century. He became a liability to the party

because of his views on *Christology*, and was heavily attacked by the *Arians* and eventually abandoned by most of the Nicenes. His works only survive in fragments now, but his ideas proved such a challenge to the later Nicene party, as they were forced to articulate a (different) theory of Christ's single subjectivity in the condition of incarnate *Logos*, that Apollinaris can rightly be regarded as a major stimulus to the construction of the *neo-Nicene* orthodoxy that hereticized him. He was the son of a famed rhetorician and *littérateur* at Beirut (Apollinaris the Elder), who had become a priest in the town of Laodicea. He enrolled his son among the lectors of the church, and both were engaged in a lifelong endeavor to correlate Christianity with the best of classical culture, and to make of their literary labors an apologetic for the ascendancy of Christian culture in the Hellenistic world. In 346 they welcomed *Athanasius of Alexandria* into their house on his return from exile in the West, and soon became his zealous supporters, and outspoken defenders of the Nicene *homoousion*. This brought down on them the excommunication of George their bishop, who was a leading Arian, and so they assumed the local leadership of the Nicene party in an underground church of protest. They encouraged their followers to contest vacant episcopal sees in the East and organized extensive agitation for their version of the Nicene cause. Apollinaris became bishop of Laodicea in 360. After Emperor Julian's death the Nicene leaders presented statements of faith to Jovian his successor (363–364), and here Apollinaris sketched out his theory of the single subjectivity of Christ as his answer to Arian hostile deconstructions of the *homoousion*. They had argued that if the Logos entered directly into a human life (became a man), then he would be limited (passible and mortal). And would not this limitation mean both the introduction of alteration into the Godhead and the proof positive that the Logos was not unchangeable, and therefore not God? To resolve this prob-

lem Apollinaris argued that the Christ was indeed the direct *incarnation* of the Logos, but that the Word remained unchanged and immortal even in the incarnate life, because he adopted a human body, not a human *person*. The body of Jesus was mortal; the person of Jesus was synonymous with the Logos, simply the divinity in human form. The key to this was a theory of "icon." The Logos, according to Apollinaris, constituted humans as the *image of God*. The image was particularly located in the *nous*, the spiritual intellect. This was also the seat of personhood (mind and *soul*). In the case of Jesus the Logos did not need to assume a human mind (logos or rationality), as he was himself the archetype of all intellect. In this one case the image was not *anthropologically* needed as the original was present, replacing it. Apollinaris's hostile opponents regarded this as a theory that reduced the incarnation to a mythological epiphany—a divinity inhabiting a mindless and soulless flesh. Those who were more sympathetic saw that his intention was to make the strongest bond possible between the Logos and the incarnate Christ, to reject *adoptionist* and Arian Christologies, and to elaborate a *soteriological* theory of the incarnation that gave to the human deeds of Christ a fully divine significance. His work was condemned as heterodox by the synods of Rome (377) and Antioch (379) and also at the *Council of Constantinople (381). Gregory of Nazianzus* lampooned it (*Epistulae* 101–103) as a "mindless Christology," but Apollinaris's chief catch-phrase, "One nature made flesh of God the Logos" (*mia physis*), went on to make a large impact on *Cyril of Alexandria* and, through him, on the anti-Chalcedonian churches (*see Monophysitism, Severus of Antioch*).

G. L. Prestige, *Fathers and Heretics* (The Bampton Lectures for 1940; Oxford, 1940), 193–246; E. Raven, *Apollinarianism: An Essay on the Christology of the Early Church* (Cambridge, U.K., 1923).

Apologists (second to early third century)   The collective title of the theologians of the postapostolic period (*Apostolic Fathers*), active before the ascendancy of the late–third-century Alexandrian theologians (*Clement, Origen*) and the classical fourth-century patristic period. Their concern is largely with making a reasoned (philosophically and legally justified) defense (or apologia) of the Christian faith before outsiders. The chief opposition forces addressed are Roman social and political hostility, and Jewish theological attacks. Many of them wrote in times of *persecution* and stress, and several addressed their works (even if only nominally) to the emperor. The main theologians among them are *Aristides, Athenagoras, Justin Martyr, Lactantius, Minucius Felix, Tatian, Tertullian*, and *Theophilus*. Apart from their specific apologetic work, trying to present Christianity as worthy of being regarded as a "licit religion" in Roman terms, they also give interesting sidelights on the early form of pre-Nicene Christianity. Many of them elaborate Christianity's first reflections on metaphysics, cultural theology, and cosmology. Justin Martyr offers rare insights on the earliest form of liturgy. Writers such as Tertullian and Lactantius begin to sketch out the basis of Christian systematic and political theology. Theophilus is one of the first to elaborate a terminology for the doctrine of the *Trinity*. The enthusiasm of the Apologists, generally speaking, for *Logos theology* led to the predominance of that scheme of thought in later Christianity.

R. M. Grant, *The Greek Apologists of the Second Century* (Philadelphia, 1988); F. L. Battles, *The Apologists* (Allison Park, Pa., 1991).

Apophaticism   The Greek term signifies a "turning away from speech." In Christian theology it was first used, and popularized, by Pseudo-*Dionysius the Areopagite*, a *Syrian* monastic theologian from the early sixth century. Dionysius, in his book *The Divine Names*, speaks of the progressive purification of earthly concepts of God. The ascent of the mind through affirmative declarative statements about God (kataphatic theology) leads on the percipient theologian to realize that ultimately the God who is above all essence (hyperousial) is far above "all names that can be named," and that the perfect knowledge of God consists in a radical transcendence of all speech and thought about him (apophatic theology). He developed this aspect most particularly in his short but very influential book, *Mystical Theology*. Dionysius stood in a long line of earlier Christian theologians who emphasized the profoundly limited capacity of human language or thought to capture the deity, even as he stood within an *orthodox* tradition that affirmed the necessity of making precise dogmatic statements about God, in opposition to heretics of various kinds. *Clement* and *Origen of Alexandria* were two of the first patristic writers to develop this proto-apophatic tradition, and their successors *Gregory of Nazianzus* and *Gregory of Nyssa* moved the ideas centrally into Christian consciousness in the bitter struggle with *Arian* disputants such as *Eunomius* and *Aetius*. Gregory Nazianzen's *Orations* 37–38 specifically consider the manner in which knowledge of God leaves all human knowledge exhausted but, even so, rendered speechless in an "ignorance" that is far higher than the "wordiness" of those who think they have fully comprehended God. The Hellenistic Platonic tradition also had a long tradition that preferred to use "negative" terms (ideas negating common attributions) about the divinity. In the later Christian apophatic tradition, when it had been more scholastically appropriated in the West, it was thus thought that taking a negative path (*via negativa*) in theologizing was more accurate. Thus God was, properly speaking, in-visible, in-effable, in-comprehensible, and so on, even though conformity to the faith required many positive assertions of God—such that he was righteous, powerful, loving, merciful, and the like. The Western tradition thus appropriated the apophatic tradition as part of its theological method known as the path of analogy (*via analogiae*). In the East theologians kept the apophatic tradition closely bonded to the notion that the only valid knowledge of God was a *mystical* and ineffable one, and accordingly that the highest confession of faith was hesychastic, the silent worship of illumined gnosis.

P. Evdokimov, *La Connaissance de Dieu selon la tradition orientale* (Lyons, France, 1967); V. Lossky, *The Mystical Theology of the Eastern Church* (Cambridge, 1991); A. Louth, *Denys the Areopagite* (London, 1989); D. Turner, *The Darkness of God: Negativity in Christian Mysticism* (Cambridge, 1995).

Apostolic Church Order

Apostolic Church Order is an Egyptian discipline book of the very early fourth century, also known as *The Ecclesiastical Canons of the Holy Apostles*. The book imaginatively ascribes sets of rules to individual apostles, supposedly during a meeting they had with Mary and Martha present. Sections 4–14 reflect the sermon on the "Two Ways" that begins the *Didache* and presents moral exhortations much in line with other second- and third-century church orders (*see* **Apostolic Tradition, Didache, Didascalia**). The second part of the book (sec. 15–30) legislates on ministerial affairs. It specifies a monarchical **bishop**, with **presbyters**, a church reader, **deacons**, and **widows**. It explicitly argues that women should not participate in the sacrifice of the body and blood of Christ: indicating, perhaps, a rejection in Egypt at this period of the **eucharistic** aspects of the office of female deacons. Originally written in Greek, it was also translated into Latin, Syriac, Coptic, Arabic, and Ethiopic. It enjoyed a high authority since its ascription to the apostles was long taken as authentic. (*See* **Apostolic Constitutions**.)

J. P. Arendzen, "An Entire Syriac Text of the Apostolic Church Order," JTS 3 (1901): 59–80 (with ET); J. V. Bartlet, *Church Life and Church-Order During the First Four Centuries With Special Reference to the Early Eastern Church-Orders* (Oxford, 1943); A. Harnack, *Sources of the Apostolic Canons* (London, 1895).

Apostolic Constitutions

A late–fourth-century book of church order compiled, probably, by an *Arian* theologian, *Apostolic Constitutions* is a collection based on many older materials, especially three previous church order books, which it heavily reuses (the *Didache*, the *Didascalia*, and the *Diataxeis of the Holy Apostles*—the last being a version of the **Apostolic Tradition** of **Hippolytus**). The book gives many instructions on liturgical matters, notably the *ordination* rituals, proper *eucharistic* forms, and the ritual of *baptism* (three versions). Although its liturgical materials are of very high interest (it contains an extensive excerpt from the early Antiochene liturgy), it is generally regarded as not being a sure guide to real practice in the fourth-century church. It offers much pastoral advice on the church's assistance for *widows* and orphans, and advocates *prayer* and *almsgiving*. The reconciliation and forgiveness of penitents is encouraged. In its final list of *canons* (these are eighty-five in number and have been known separately as the *Apostolic Canons*), at Canon 85, it gives the list of the received biblical books, which is almost exactly the one (*canon of Scripture*) currently received, except that the book of Revelation is not admitted, and the *Apostolic Constitutions* is itself included. The Troullan Synod of 692 first recognized clear Arian elements in the book, but believed in its self-proclaimed apostolic origin, and concluded that an Arian interpolator must have interfered with the text. The synod censured the text, but affirmed its ancient canons as apostolic, and thus they survived as authoritative in the juridical tradition. The whole work is now generally seen to be entirely a product of a pseudepigrapher (some say Julian, the *Anhomoian* bishop of Cilicia) using ancient materials interpolated with his own instructions.

J. Donaldson, trans., *The Apostolic Constitutions,* ANCL vol. 17, part 2 (1870); also in ANF vol. 7 (1886): 385–505; D. A. Fiensy, *Prayers Alleged to be Jewish: An Examination of the Constitutiones Apostolicae* (BJS 65; Decatur, 1985); C. H. Turner, "Notes on the Apostolic Constitutions," JTS 16 (1915): 54–61, 523–538.

Apostolic Fathers (early second century)

"Apostolic Fathers" is the collective title for the earliest writers of the Christian church, immediately after the New Testament period (and in some cases coterminous with the later books of what came to be the complete New Testament canon). They are immensely important for the understanding of the formation of the earliest Christian communities, but were relatively neglected by the post-Nicene church as being very different in form and style from current interests in theology, and also not possessing the authoritative status of the scriptural writings. They belong to the world of the house church or the incipient rise of the monarchical bishops, and are frequently concerned with moral encouragement in a markedly eschatological context or outlook. The main writers of the group are *Clement of Rome, Hermas, Ignatius of Antioch, Papias,* Polycarp, and the authors of the letter of *Barnabas,* the *Letter to Diognetus,* and *2 Clement.* The *Didache* is also traditionally included in this group. The two books known as the *Apostolic Church Order* (Egypt c. 300) and the *Apostolic Constitutions* (*Constantinople* late fourth century) already show that in antiquity Christian writers were deliberately archaizing so to be included in this group, partly for theological reasons,

and mainly concerning matters of church organization and ritual.

L. W. Barnard, *Studies in the Apostolic Fathers* (Oxford, 1961); J. Lawson, *A Theological and Historical Introduction to the Apostolic Fathers and Their Background* (London, 1966); S. Tugwell, *The Apostolic Fathers* (Oxford, 1989).

Apostolicity

As clashes between the second-century *bishops* and freelance *gnostic* teacher-theologians (Didaskaloi) became more and more common, it was increasingly realized that some system of recognizing "authenticity" of doctrine was a pressing need for the church. Until the gnostic crisis it had been more or less assumed, unreflectively, that the Christian community would be given coherence and identity by its fidelity to the words of Jesus, and by adherence to scriptural laws. After the second century the whole problematic nature of scriptural coherence became critical. Not only was there not a commonly agreed *canon of Scripture* at this time but, more to the point, before the pioneering work of *Origen* in the third century, there were no commonly agreed methods of biblical interpretation. In the gnostic crisis numerous new texts were being composed and offered to the church as "scriptures" (later classed as Apocrypha) and most of them advocated a particular way of reading the historical and theological evidence (thus many gnostic writings described the God of the Old Testament as a false deity, thereby committing most of the Hebrew Bible to redundancy). Several gnostic teachers claimed that their doctrines were only apparently innovative, since they had actually been committed in secret by Jesus to his apostles, and were now being revealed by the Didaskaloi who had inherited them (Irenaeus, *Adversus haereses* 3.2.1; Epiphanius, *Refutation of All Heresies* 33.7.9). Irenaeus, in the second century, was one of the first major patristic writers to offer the beginnings of a systematic answer to the gnostic problem. He began to draw up several criteria of authenticity for Christian traditions, not least defining the limits of a concept of "canonical Scripture" (there are only four gospels as there are only four corners of the world, he says), insisting on the church's acceptance of a core "Rule of Faith" (an early form of the creedal listing of basic and fundamental doctrines that were accepted by the faithful). In the course of setting out his apologia (*Adversus haereses*), Irenaeus focused great attention on the principle that Christ taught a single, coherent, and simple truth to simple fishermen. The gnostics had complicated and corrupted this doctrine, he argued, and had made it fantastically elaborated. Nevertheless, the truth Christ had taught was given as a heritage to the apostles, who in their own turn taught it to their disciples. This "apostolic heritage" was now represented by the bishops of the early communities, whose own doctrine was simple and apostolic in contrast to the clever complexity of the intellectualist Didaskaloi. It was a set of teachings that were coherent, uniformly witnessed in the major communities of the Christian world, and demonstrable in the bond of intercommunion that existed in the relations of bishops of various cities. The apostolic doctrine was above all represented in the New Testament writings. So, as Irenaeus argued, by fidelity to the Scriptures, as these were regulated and expounded by the legitimate bishop in the church assembly (one who was recognized and accepted by the communion of bishops, and who would thus teach in harmony with *tradition*, and rule out the reading of gnostic apocrypha), all the faithful could hear the authentic teaching of Christ as preserved by the *Apostolic Tradition. Justin Martyr* argued that the chief characteristic of apostolic doctrine was its international uniformity (*First Apology* 42): a concept that was advanced by Tertullian in his *De praescriptione haereticorum* (20–21, 32), and which eventually matured into the

necessary inclusion of apostolicity as one of the four cardinal identifiers of the church (one, holy, catholic, and apostolic). The idea of the bishops as the valid successors of the apostles as teachers gained great momentum from the late first century onward, advocated greatly by *Ignatius of Antioch, Polycarp, Clement of Rome (First Clement)*, and Irenaeus, and emerged as the doctrine of the apostolic succession. It was finally referred retrospectively to become the chief element of what constituted an authentic "scriptural" writing. The Gospels of Mark and Luke made it because of widely accepted theories that they were "apostolic," since they were written by disciples of apostles. The other letters and treatises were all ascribed to apostles. Important texts such as the *Shepherd of Hermas* or the Clementine literature were eventually ruled out of the canon simply because they were not "apostolic" in that primary sense. Most later patristic considerations of apostolicity continued to turn around these twin axes of scriptural evidence and episcopal communion.

J. N. Bakhuizen, "Tradition and Authority in the Early Church," *Studia Patristica* 7 (TU 92, Berlin) (1966): 3–22; H. von Campenhausen, "Le concept d'Apotre dans le Christianisme primitif," ST 1 (1947–1948): 96–130; J. A. McGuckin, "Eschaton and Kerygma: The Future of the Past in the Present Kairos: The Concept of Living Tradition in Orthodox Theology," *St. Vladimir's Theological Quarterly* 42, nos. 3–4 (winter 1998): 225–71.

Apostolic Succession   *see* **Apostolicity**

Apostolic Tradition   The *Apostolic Tradition* is one of the important early books of church discipline. It was formerly known as the "Egyptian Church Order," but is now generally recognized to have been the composition of *Hippolytus of Rome*, an important early–third-century theologian. It has been reconstructed from its appearance in several other church order books. The text includes rituals for *baptism, ordination*, and *Eucharist*, as well as instructions about morning prayers, burial, fasting, and the services for the evening lamplighting attached to a love feast (*agape*). The work has many duplicated passages, which has been taken as a sign it was a compilation of two very similar previously existing treatises, with a later scribe combining both and duplicating only those passages that had variants. Hippolytus broke communion with the Roman pope (probably in the reign of *Callistus* in the early third century) and led a separatist community. The *Apostolic Tradition* was probably his attempt to show how Callistus's policies (such as the reconciliation of public sinners) were not "traditional" while those of his community were. His example of the Great Eucharistic Prayer (*anaphora*), as well as his other liturgical information, cannot necessarily be taken as a sure guide to traditional Roman church practice in that period. It has been suggested, for example, that the written-down *anaphora* he gives is just as likely to be a free composition of his own, illustrating (in an era when the prayer was still commonly made up spontaneously) how eucharistic prayer "ought to be made" by a presiding bishop (*see* *episcopate*). The book was heavily used in the Roman Catholic Church's liturgical reforms of the late twentieth century and was the basis for the contemporary Roman "Second Eucharistic Prayer."

B. Botte, *La Tradition Apostolique de Saint Hippolyte: Essai de Reconstitution* (Münster, Germany, 1963); P. F. Bradshaw, *The Search for the Origins of Christian Worship* (Oxford, 2002), 73–97; R. H. Connolly, *The So-called Egyptian Church Order and Derived Documents* (Cambridge, 1916).

Architecture   It is almost impossible now to determine anything about the architecture of the very earliest Christian communities. Our picture of the condi-

tion of church architecture in the first two centuries is generally provided by the missionary situation of the New Testament communities. The first believers shared table fellowship "from house to house" (Acts 2:46; 5:42). Paul mentions whole households being converted at once (as the master converted so did the household) and sends greetings to the "church in the house" of various people (Rom. 16:5; 1 Cor. 16:19; Col. 4:15; Phlm. 2). New Testament and other early literature mentions Christian assemblies in "upper rooms" (probably hired) (Acts 20:8); lecture rooms (Acts 19:9), and warehouses (*Passion of Paul* 1). It is generally thought that from the end of the first century, villas of the wealthier members of the church increasingly were adapted and used for the purposes of the liturgical assembly, but no solid evidence is available, and much relies on deduction from a very small number of cases. It seems a reasonable supposition that the fluid arrangements of the earliest Christian generations increasingly gave way to specifically ordered church buildings. A rare example of a so-called "house church" from this later period of consolidation exists in Dura Europos, a Roman border town in Syria, discovered in 1920. Excavations in 1939 revealed a small mid–second-century Christian building that had been remodeled from a normal house. The exterior remained the same as other houses in the street, but the interior walls had been extensively redesigned to make a large rectangular assembly hall. Another small room was made into a baptistery, with a canopied font set into the floor and wall frescoes illustrating Gospel scenes. From the third century onwards, some of the houses of famous *martyrs* also became places of worship, such as the house of John and Paul on the Caelian Hill in Rome, which in its elaboration into a church assimilated an adjacent apartment block. Other private villas were given to the church by wealthy patrons for the purposes of worship. In the time of the Diocletianic *persecution* of the early fourth century, *Lactantius* notes in his *Divine Institutes* that the Christian church at Nicomedia was a notable public building, and was deliberately burned by imperial troops. Several prestigious churches at **Constantinople** took their origin from the donation of senatorial villas to church use in the fourth century, a practice that had begun with grants of imperial property and civic basilicas in the time of **Constantine** (who had commenced this practice to afford some form of reparation of property to the Christians who had suffered confiscation of buildings and goods in the persecutions of the preceding centuries). The Lateran Basilica is one example of such a gift. Other churches were custombuilt by Constantine, including the Anastasis (Holy Sepulchre) in **Jerusalem**, and the Shrine of Peter on the Vatican Hill at **Rome**. Both were basilica-style buildings with adjoining martyria. After emerging from the era of persecutions, Christians increasingly built their own churches, as well as adapting basilicas gifted to them by the emperor. After the fifth century many pagan temples were also taken over for use as Christian churches. Some of the most dramatic examples are the Pantheon in Rome, the Parthenon in Athens, and the Serapeum in **Alexandria**. The donation of basilicas had a strong impact on later Christian architecture. The basilica was substantially a rectangular hall, with an apsidal benched end (for magistrates), and was to become one of the most common formats of Christian building, in which case the apse was oriented to the east (an aspect not usually observed in pre-Christian basilicas that were adapted). Churches built over special sites or holy places were often marked by a distinctive architectural shape. *Martyria* (the tomb-shrines of martyrs that developed into churches) were often octagonal or rotunda in shape. Octagonal church building in the East also usually designated a particular commemoration of a site: biblical holy places or the like being enclosed in a clear geometric design, with surrounding colonnades to allow

pilgrims access to the holy place. The great Church of the Anastasis built by Constantine at Jerusalem combined a rotunda over the site of Christ's death, with a large basilica attached to the holy place by colonnaded porticoes. The design of the buildings in Jerusalem had a powerful effect on the determination of liturgical rites (such as processions or circumambulations) in many other churches of Christendom. In the Greek East after the fifth century a new form of Christian architecture came into favor, and was patronized by powerful emperors. Justinian's churches of saints Sergius and Bacchus, later to be followed by his monumental Hagia Sophia at Constantinople (replacing a basilica-type predecessor church on the site) used the idea of a squared cross set under a dome. This "Byzantine" style soon superseded the basilica in the Greek-speaking and Slavic East, but the **Armenian** churches combined elements of both the squared Byzantine cross and the Western basilica, and formed their own distinctive synthesis. One of the common determinants in all matters relating to church architecture was the relative wealth of the local church. *Ethiopia* and the Coptic churches retained a simplicity of architectural forms in marked contrast to the burgeoning of building that was characteristic of the Latin and Byzantine churches in their imperial expansions. After the third century almost all Christian churches were fashioned to reflect a biblical typology of the Jerusalem temple as fulfilled in the Christian mysteries. The altar area (sanctuary) was occupied by the priestly ministers, and was increasingly marked off from the main body of the church (the nave) occupied by the faithful, and from the portico (narthex), which was given over to the catechumens and those undergoing penitential discipline. The eastern liturgies witnessed a regular movement back and forth between the two areas by the *deacons*, who had charge of public prayers. The development of the Byzantine iconographic tradition, especially after the eighth-century iconoclastic crisis, also stimulated reflection on the shape of church buildings as an earthly mirror of the heavenly cosmos. The pattern of depicting prophets and saints, with Christ in judgment typically occupying the central dome, and the Virgin with liturgical saints in the sanctuary area, attempted to mark a linearly progressive movement (from the narthex frescoes of Old Testament saints one entered deeper into the church with New Testament scenes until one arrived at Christ in glory), and also a vertically progressive movement (from the lower walls where *ascetics* and other *saints* gave way in an upward sweep to great martyrs, angels, and the Mother of God). Declining economic conditions after the eighth century made the typical village church in Orthodox lands usually a small and intimate affair (in marked contrast to Hagia Sophia, which still served as a style model). In the West the basilical form proved to be a fertile matrix for a number of stylistic developments and variations, such as Romanesque and, in the medieval period, Gothic and Perpendicular.

F. V. Filson, "The Significance of Early Christian House-Churches," JBL 58 (1939): 105–12; C. H. Kraeling, *The Christian Building* (New Haven, Conn., 1967); R. Krautheimer, *Early Christian and Byzantine Architecture* (3d ed.; London, 1979); C. Mango, *Byzantine Architecture* (New York, 1985); L. Rodley, *Byzantine Art and Architecture: An Introduction* (Cambridge, 1999).

Arianism   Arianism, one of the most extensive ecclesiastical controversies, spread through most of the fourth century and shaped Christian thought decisively. It has been regarded as the archetypal heresy. It began with the theories of *Arius* of Alexandria, opposed by *Alexander* the bishop of Alexandria, which concerned a dispute over the status of the *Logos*. Was the Logos the pre-

eternal Son of God, divine of the divine, as Alexander taught? Or, as Arius believed, was the Logos the Son and Servant of God, but in no way God in the same sense as the Father was God? He might have been a supremely elevated spiritual power of God (as Arius seems to have thought), but was he, in essence, still a creature? Arius elevated Proverbs 8:22 as his supreme proof text. Later radical disciples such as *Aetius* and *Eunomius* (the *Neo-Arians*) would make this a key to their form of Arian teaching: that the Logos was heterousial, of a wholly different essence from God (in other words, "not God"). Many Eastern bishops after the *Council of Nicaea I*, where the party of Alexander had a victory over Arius, later withdrew their support for the imperial policy of the *homoousion* (the Logos as the same nature as God the Father). They were led by *Eusebius of Nicomedia*, one of the chief agitators for the Arian cause (by this stage Arius himself faded into the background as the issue became a matter for international debate across many synods). Eusebius took special interest in trying to prosecute the chief defender of the anti-Arian Nicene party, *Athanasius of Alexandria*. It was Athanasius's ability to command the support of the Western bishops, as well as his readiness to dialogue with a wider range of theologians after 362 (the Synod of Alexandria), that finally led to a growing consensus in the East to the effect that Arianism had to be eradicated by a confession of the full and coequal deity of the Logos. This final stage of the crisis was resolved by the *neo-Nicene* movement, when the *Cappadocian Fathers* (*Gregory of Nazianzus, Basil of Caesarea,* and *Gregory of Nyssa*) theologically prepared the ground for the *Council of Constantinople (381)*, where Arian thought was formally condemned for both sections of the empire. Arianism would later have a revival of fortunes when the Gothic tribes occupied the western empire, but it then only flourished among the invaders and was absorbed into the strong Nicenism of the western Catholics within a century. Arianism was thus a complex and "shifting" set of ideas, against which the Nicene party themselves evolved and changed across the fourth century. It is, in brief, the attribution of inferior status (however elevated its *Logos theology* might be) to the Son of God. The notion that deity could possibly tolerate degrees of difference within its absolute perfection was not accepted by the Nicene party, and eventually the rejection of Arianism led to the formulation of the doctrine of the *Trinity* of coequal *hypostases* in the single deity.

R. C. Gregg and D. Groh, *Early Arianism: A View of Salvation* (Philadelphia, 1981); R. P. C. Hanson, *The Search for the Christian Doctrine of God: The Arian Controversy 318–381* (Edinburgh, 1988); R. Williams, *Arius: Heresy and Tradition* (London, 1987).

Aristides A second-century *Apologist*, Aristides was a citizen of Athens who practiced *philosophy*, and is thought to be the earliest Christian writer who composed a considered defense of the Christian faith (*Apology on Behalf of the Christians*). Eusebius believed he presented his book to the emperor Hadrian in 125 (Eusebius, *Ecclesiastical History* 4.3.3). He makes a fourfold division of humanity and of the race's quest for enlightenment: enumerating barbarians, Greeks, Jews, and Christians, and presenting the four stages as a progressive ascent to the perfection of wisdom manifested in the Christian faith, whose moral code and universal monotheistic doctrine prove both its authenticity and its superiority over all preceding forms of religion or philosophy.

H. B. Harris, *The Newly Recovered Apology of Aristides: Its Doctrine and Ethics* (London, 1891); R. L. Wolff, "The Apology of Aristides: A Re-Examination," HTR 30 (1937): 233–47.

Aristotelianism Aristotle (384–322 B.C.) and *Plato* (428–346 B.C.) dominated the Greek and Hellenistic philosophic traditions and had a marked impact also on the development of Christian philosophical and theological traditions, since in the first century (beginning with Albinus) Hellenistic philosophy eclectically combined elements from the Aristotelian system within a broad matrix of Platonic thought, a synthetic context into which Christianity was born. Aristotelianism had always emphasized empirical method. Its major methodological procedure was classification: the taxonomic identification of the variety of species and their respective inherent *teloi* (or ontological goals) based upon close observation of the natural order and its related phenomena. The idea of natures containing the principles of their destinies, which subsequently unfolded in the pattern and the dynamic of their life-courses, was important to the system. So too was ethical reflection (beginning with Aristotle's own *Nichomachean Ethics* in the fourth century B.C.). The system was also identified with structures of syllogistic reasoning, and gave a prime place of importance to correct deductive method. By the church fathers Plato was generally regarded as more conducive to reflection on the divine mystery, and Aristotle as more of an empiricist concerned with the material order, but this belied the massive amount of Aristotelianism that was quietly adopted by the early *Apologists* in their meditations on the order of the created world, and how it manifested the hand of God within it. Chief among the Aristotelian ideas assimilated by the church were the concepts of form and matter, the metaphysical preeminence of the Good, the idea of First Cause, and the notion of balanced ethics as the median and reasonable position. *Origen of Alexandria* was one of the first to make a dramatic synthesis between Aristotelianism and Platonism in his own systematic theology. He began the rigorous classification of various types of literature, and literary method, thus giving birth to the first (more or less) "scientific" Christian *exegesis*. Origen's system had profoundly Platonic features, of course, but its substructure was provided by biblical exegesis, and that in turn sat on Aristotelian interpretative principles. Origen's disciple *Gregory of Nazianzus*, in the fourth century, was even more explicitly indebted to Aristotle. He and the other *Cappadocians* prepared a wholesale assault on the *neo-Arian* teachers *Eunomius* and *Aetius*, who had elevated Aristotelian syllogism to center stage in their theological method (thus arguing the Son's nondivinity since the category of Son is inherently different from that of Father). Gregory painstakingly used Aristotelian method in his *Five Theological Orations* (27–31) to demonstrate the strengths and limits of the various syllogistic forms of reasoning, and to argue for the Nicene doctrine of the full deity of the Son (based upon the premise that titles such as Father and Son were accidental, or relational, not substantive categories). After Gregory the use of explicit Aristotelian method was "blessed" by patristic authority. After the fifth century many of Aristotle's works were translated into Syriac and had a strong influence on *Syrian* Christian philosophy. In Byzantium, Aristotle's idea of mankind's *telos*, the inherent natural drive that unfolded in an *anthropologically* defining manner, was refined into a Christian spiritual philosophy that saw assimilation to the divine image (communion with God) as the fundamental human *telos*, and in this sense Aristotelian ideas became constitutive of the Byzantine mystical and theological writers, especially *Maximus the Confessor*, Leontius of Byzantium, and *John of Damascus*. Through the latter, especially his theological "handbook" (*On the Orthodox Faith*), Aristotle's influence came back (though mainly in the medieval period) into the Western church.

J. de Ghellinck, "Quelques appréciations de la dialectique d'Aristote durant les conflits trinitaires du IV-ième siècle," RHE 25 (1930): 5–42; F. W. Norris, *Faith Gives Fullness to Reason: The Five Theological Orations of Gregory of Nazianzus* (Leiden, Netherlands, 1991), 17–39; D. T. Runia, "Festugière revisited: Aristotle in the Church Fathers," VC 43 (1989): 1–34; F. Ricken, *Philosophy of the Ancients* (London, 1991), 123–81; B. Tatakis, *La Philosophie Byzantine* (Paris, 1949).

Arius *see* **Arianism**

Armenia Armenia was the first of all Christian kingdoms, predating the Christianization of the Roman Empire, at least in terms of that understood as the adoption of Christianity by *Constantine the Great*. The first patristic theologian, known as the Apostle of Armenia, was Gregory the Illuminator (c. 240–332), whose preaching campaign converted the Armenian king Tiridates in 301. The Armenian scholars Mashtots and Sahak subsequently invented an alphabet for the Armenians and the translation of biblical and patristic writings began in earnest. The seclusion of Armenia (a rugged mountainous land) and its relative linguistic isolation have resulted in this library of translated patristic works surviving intact in the Armenian. Some works by Irenaeus and *Ephrem the Syrian*, for example, only exist today because of the Armenian versions that were made of them in the patristic era. The Armenians were at first ecclesiastically dependent on the church of Caesarea in Palestine, but after the death in 374 of St. Nerses, the catholicos (or patriarch), that relation was repudiated. The Armenian church was not engaged in the controversies leading up to the *Council of Chalcedon (451)*, and was not represented there. While it accepted the first three Ecumenical *Councils*, therefore, it never agreed to the theology of the fourth, which it found to be offensive in its language of "two natures." In 555 the Armenians officially anathematized Chalcedon, and thus began their ecclesiastical separation from the Byzantine and Latin traditions of theology, though both these Christian cultures deeply affected the Armenian church throughout its history in terms of liturgical, political, and cultural developments. The later history of the Armenian Christians has been one of intense oppression and suffering. Its Christian character has been sustained with great heroism to the present day. The liturgical forms follow the rite of St. Basil, and apart from christological theology the doctrines of the church are very close to Eastern Orthodoxy in most respects, although there are several ritual differences.

K. Sarkissian, *The Council of Chalcedon and the Armenian Church* (London, 1965); idem, *A Brief Introduction to Armenian Christian Literature* (2d ed.; Bergenfield, 1974); R. W. Thomson, ed., *Moses Khorenats'i: History of the Armenians* (Cambridge, Mass., 1978).

Art Christianity in the earliest period seems to have shared the aversion common in *Judaism* (though not an absolute aversion as is demonstrated by the highly decorated second-century synagogue at Dura Europos) to painted representations in religious contexts. The Hellenistic world was so thoroughly immersed in art as a religious medium that both the synagogue and the church turned from it as part of their apologia against false cult, and Christian thinkers argued instead for the intellectual, spiritual, and moral mimesis of God as the only valid depictions of the divine on earth. *Origen of Alexandria* in the third century remains immensely hostile to the idea of figurative art, and writers such as *Eusebius of Caesarea* (himself an ardent Origenist) or *Epiphanius* of Salamis in the fourth century were also explicitly hostile to the idea of art depicting Christ in any way at all in the

church's cultic life. Even so, from early times one knows that the "real world" of Christian practice was departing from its rhetorical absolutes, for the later New Testament writings were already describing Christ as the exact picture of the deity, the icon (*eikon; see* **iconoclasm**) of the unseen God (Col. 1:15). The *catacombs* of *Rome* (those of Callistus, Priscilla, and Praetextatus) also show a popular desire to depict Christian signs, and crude representations on the graves and memorials of the faithful, certainly from the mid–second century onward (the Christian baptistery at Dura Europos has several New Testament scenes drawn in fresco around the walls), and growing with great speed through the third and fourth centuries, when the figurative depiction of Christ and the apostles (dressed as imperial senators) marks the beginning of Christian art forms as such. In the Constantinian era there are some signs of the Christians adapting pagan iconography in terms of the good shepherd motif (Christ as a young man with a lamb on his shoulder), or the remarkable mosaic of Christ as Phoebus-Apollo driving the chariot of the sun across the sky (though this time haloed with a cross nimbus) in the early–fourth-century Christian tomb in the Vatican necropolis. But mainly the biblical episodes provided the church with enough subject matter to develop a distinctive art-tradition of its own. Christians for a long time had taken up cryptic symbols to serve as identifying marks of the faith. Notable ones were the fish (whose letters, IXTHUS, made up the confessional statement: "Jesus Christ Son of God and Savior"), the anchor (a cipher of the *cross*), the ship (a symbol of the church), and the praying woman (a pagan symbol of piety and a Christian image of the church at prayer). *Clement of Alexandria* in the second century comments on which ciphers were suitable for a believer to have engraved on rings or other jewelry (*Paedagogus* 3.57.1–3.60.1). It was only in the fifth century that Christian art emerged from the shadowy world of ciphers and cemeteries to become established as a regular part of Christian life. This was the beginning of the Byzantine style of iconic painting, which endures to the present day in Eastern Christianity (though with many developments of style and matter). The so-called Fayyum portraits seem to have had an impact on Christian art style in Egypt. Roman naturalistic painting was the first wave to affect the church, and several of the earliest surviving examples of icons (from the seventh century) show a crude representationalism suggesting a combination of several traditions, not least the Roman manner of portraits of the emperor, the Hellenistic custom of paintings of the household gods and ancestors, and the funerary custom of having a likeness of oneself painted (which would be later inserted onto the shroud wrappings over the face of the deceased instead of an entire sarcophagus mummification process). *Martyrs* were among the first to be iconically depicted, perhaps because of the close relation between the Christian cult of the martyr and the Hellenistic custom of the veneration of the dead. By the eighth century the high popularity of religious iconic art had ensured its progress from private oratories into the churches themselves, and a reaction was soon evident. The *iconoclastic* period marked a split in Byzantium between, on the one side, monastics and popular religious feeling, which was profoundly for icon veneration, and on the other, the army and the imperial palace of the Syrian (Isaurian) dynasty, who were deeply opposed to it and set about stripping the churches of figurative representations. The controversy with its concomitant *persecutions* lasted more than a century, and resulted, from the ninth century onward, in the complete victory of the icon-venerators (iconodules). After this time a whole theology of iconic art was elaborated. Theologians such as *John of Damascus*, Germanos of Constantinople, and Theodore Studite composed treatises in

defense of the icons, drawing a connection between the incarnation of the invisible God in flesh and the permissibility of an icon depicting Christ, the Virgin, or the saints. They also clarified how a Christian could venerate an icon, so that the act of honor (bowing or offering incense) would transmit to the person depicted, not to the icon itself. Worship (*latreia*) was due to God alone, but veneration (*proskynesis*) could be made through the medium of holy icons, to be directed to God, the *Virgin Mary*, or the *saints* therein depicted. Despite a bad Latin translation of the acts of the Seventh Ecumenical *Council of Nicaea II* (787), which consolidated this doctrine of images (the version circulating in the Carolingian empire confused the central terms "worship" and "veneration," thus making a nonsense of the Greek teaching, and making it sound as if the Byzantines were advocating idolatry), the Western church generally wholeheartedly supported the Byzantine iconodules. There even developed in the Latin church a preference for statuary art (which the canon law of the East continued to forbid under the strictest terms as redolent of idols). The East developed its art forms in wonderful manuscript illumination and portable artistic works such as intricate reliquaries, sarcophagi, and church and household goods. Even the Byzantine coinage after the ninth century was stamped with images of Christ and the Virgin. The Latins consistently regarded religious art as justified primarily in pedagogical terms. Such representations could instruct the unlearned, or move the heart to higher things. For the Byzantines the pedagogic motive of art was legitimate, but there was also a deeper sense that the depiction of the holy intrinsically invoked the holy, and much of Byzantine icon theory and practice came much closer to sacramentalism than anything in the West. The Seventh Ecumenical Council (that is, the Council of Nicaea II [787]) anathematized those who opposed iconic art as *christological* heretics (denying the validity of the sacred medium of the flesh for the true revelation of God) and the centrality of icons in the Eastern liturgies was permanently affirmed by the establishment of the "Sunday of Orthodoxy" (first Sunday of Lent) where the decrees of Nicaea II were read out annually and the Iconoclasts were vocally denounced along with all the other heretics from time immemorial.

M. Barasch, *Icon: Studies in the History of an Idea* (New York, 1995); A. Grabar, *The Beginnings of Christian Art: 200–395* (London, 1967); E. Kitzinger, *Byzantine Art in the Making* (Cambridge, Mass., 1977); W. F. Volbach and M. Hirmer, *Early Christian Art* (New York, 1962).

Asceticism   *Ascesis* was the Greek term for athletic training, and was used by the Christian writers, especially the monastic spiritual writers of the fourth to sixth centuries, to take up the athletic imagery first used by Paul (cf. 2 Tim. 4:7) to signify the need of Christians to train themselves by rigorous observances (sexual renunciation, fasting, and deprivations) to observe the commandments with exceptional zeal. The ascetical movement in Christianity is already prevalent in the New Testament literature, which develops apocalyptic themes by contrasting the life lived in accordance with the kingdom with the ease of a worldly existence. The ascetical message resonated well with Hellenistic ideas about the "sober life" of the wise man or woman (*sophrosyne*) and much of late first- and second-century Christian literature, such as the *Didache*, the Clementine Letters (*see* **Clement of Rome**), and the *Shepherd of Hermas*, began to stress the need for sobriety as a fundamental character of Christian discipleship. It is a powerful impetus in the writings of *Tertullian*, who already reports large numbers of male and female lay ascetics in the Carthaginian church of his day (*The Apparel of Women* 2.9; *To His Wife* 1.6; *The Resur-rection of the Flesh* 61). It is in the mid-third to fourth centuries, however, that the ascetical movement really became a powerful and distinctively organized movement in Christianity. Ascetical associations had already existed in Christian life, especially in *Syria*, where orders of *virgins* (male and female) who lived near the church building and congregated for regular *prayer* were a normal feature of local church life. *Baptism* in the earliest Syrian tradition was reserved for those "sons and daughters of the covenant" who were ready to adopt the single celibate life as solitaries (*Ihidaya*—a Syriac word play on single one/only begotten: comparable to the Greek for single person, *monos*, which would give rise to the word *monasticism*). Those who were not ready for this step were considered not ready for baptism. As a result of this practice (later known as **Encratism**) ascetic celibates soon assumed prominent positions of leadership in the church. In Egypt, from the fourth century onward, the movement of ascetics to the *desert* regions attracted wide international attention. Athanasius's *Life of Antony* and other ascetical hagiographies greatly popularized the practice of retreating into seclusion in order to follow a Christian life, alone, in small groups (as exemplified by *Antony*), or in communities (as in *Pachomian* monasticism). The ascetical life in the early desert period was characterized by celibacy aimed at evoking the condition of singleness and singlemindedness, by poverty and seclusion, by hard subsistence labor, and by long sustained prayers and vigils. The movement spread to the Sinai and Gaza regions, and from there to Palestine, and soon to the West. It thus gave birth to varied forms of monasticism, which in a few generations became so far removed from the "flight from civic responsibilities" that had first characterized it that monks (after the early fifth century) more or less commandeered the episcopal offices in both East and West.

P. Brown, *The Body and Society: Men, Women, and Sexual Renunciation in Early Christianity* (New York, 1988); R. Kirschner, "The Vocation of Holiness in Late Antiquity," VC 38 (1984): 105–24; A. Voobus, *A History of Asceticism in the Syrian Orient* (2 vols.; CSCO 184, 197; Louvain, Belgium, 1958, 1960); V. Wimbush, ed., *Ascetic Behaviour in Greco-Roman Antiquity* (Minneapolis, 1990).

Athanasian Creed *see* **Creeds, Trinity**

Athanasius of Alexandria (c.

296–373) As bishop of the powerful see of Alexandria in Egypt, Athanasius was one of the main architects of the Nicene faith—the theological confession of the divinity of the Word of God personally incarnated in Christ. He used allegiance to the creedal statement promulgated at *Council of Nicaea I* (325) to serve as a rallying point against the various *Arian* movements. As *deacon* and secretary to Bishop Alexander, he attended the council in 325. In 328 Athanasius succeeded Alexander in a period when *Constantine* and his dynasty were increasingly abandoning the anti-Arian policy which the Nicene doctrine of the *homoousion* of the *Logos* was meant to represent. He soon became a prominent symbol of opposition to imperially sponsored consensus theology, and was deposed by ecclesiastical enemies at the Council of Tyre in 335. He returned from exile on the death of Constantine in 337, but was soon forced to flee again and took refuge in *Rome*, where he was received as a champion of *orthodoxy*. From this time onward he gained the constant support of the Western churches, who encouraged his resistance. In 346 the Western emperor Constans demanded his rehabilitation, but though Athanasius came back to *Alexandria*, he was exiled again in the same year by the Eastern emperor Constantius. This time he fled into the Egyptian *desert*, where he fostered his relations with the growing monastic movement, whose hero he publicized in the widely influential *Life of Antony* (*see* **Antony**). On the death of Constantius in 362 he returned to the city, but was exiled soon afterwards by Julian. After that emperor's unexpected death in 363, he was able to return to his followers in Alexandria in the following year and, with the exception of another short exile in 365–366, this time he stabilized his ecclesiastical administration and worked in his later years to assemble a coherent international group of Eastern "Nicene" theologians. In a synod in Alexandria in 362 Athanasius made a striking move to harmonize the different parties of the anti-Arian alliance (especially the *homoiousians*) by agreeing that precise vocabulary was not as important as the reality of consensus in a *Christology* organized around the idea of the full deity of the Logos as the personal subject of Jesus. Even so, he managed to secure his own vocabulary of *homoousion* in the process of bringing others on board. Athanasius also clarified fundamentals of Christian *soteriology*—in which the incarnation was articulated through its effect on humankind. His principle was: "As God became man, so did mankind become *deified*" (*De incarnatione* 54). His *Letters to Serapion* were also of major importance in the developing doctrine of the *Trinity*. His work in creating a more widely based "Nicene party" was taken to its pitch by the generation of Cappadocian theologians that came after him, especially *Gregory of Nazianzus, Basil of Caesarea,* and *Gregory of Nyssa*. The policy came to fruition with the accession as emperor in the East of *Theodosius*, who summoned *Council of Constantinople I* in 381 and established Nicene orthodoxy as the subsequent standard for the churches. Athanasius had spent his life in this cause, but did not live to see the final result of his labors. He died in Alexandria on May 3, 373.

T. D. Barnes, *Athanasius and Constantius* (Cambridge, Mass., 1993); F. Young, *From*

Nicaea to Chalcedon (London, 1983), 65–83; bibliog. 339–41, 362–67.

Athenagoras   A mid– to late–second-century *Apologist*, Athenagoras wrote a treatise, *On the Resurrection from the Dead* (though some dispute his authorship), and also an apology entitled *Plea on Behalf of the Christians* (also known as the *Legatio* or *Supplicatio*) advocating toleration and an end to unjust *persecution*. His *Plea* was addressed to the Emperors Marcus Aurelius and Commodus, and was concerned with rejecting the popular charges against the Christians of cannibalism, atheism, and incest. Athenagoras shows a wide awareness of Greek *philosophy* and culture in his work. He takes the moral integrity of the Christian gospel, and its sense of an impending divine *judgment*, as chief supports for his argument that the church is no threat to moral order as its enemies have claimed, but is instead superior to all other forms of religion and philosophy. In his discussion of the prophets he extends Christian reflection about the process of divine *revelation*, and also witnesses an early form of *Trinitarian* theology, as he reflects on the unity of God expressed within the distinctions of *person*.

L. W. Barnard, *Athenagoras: A Study in Second Century Christian Apologetic* (Paris 1972); A. J. Malherbe, "The Holy Spirit in Athenagoras," JTS 20 (1969): 538–42; idem, "The Structure of Athenagoras' Supplicatio Pro Christianis," VC 23 (1969): 1–20.

Atonement   Atonement is a modern term for a wide variety of *patristic* images and theories about the efficacy of the *salvation* brought to the world by Christ. The word literally means rendering the alienated "at one" or bringing about a reconciliation. Patristic writers prefer the more generic idea of salvation (*soteria*), and describe the process collec-tively as the "economy of salvation" (*oikonomia tes soterias*), where the word *economy* connotes the active dynamic of God's work to rescue the world and achieve humanity's restoration to God's favor and the concomitant graces of immortality and divine communion. After the medieval period the concept of atonement became the subject of many theological discussions, particularly in the Western church, and was subse-quently classified as a major aspect of theological thought. In the patristic era the concept of God as Savior is expressed more organically, through a variety of poetic and biblical images, without many specific controversies to give it shape, except the second-century *gnos-tic* crisis, when the whole involvement of a merciful God with the created order was called into question. Then it was that the mainstream Christian writers decisively insisted on the authenticity of the biblical vision of a personal God who was intimately involved with his peo-ple's history, making and restoring covenant with them throughout the ages, and most decisively in the person and work of Christ. Simplistic solutions to the problem of theodicy proposed by *Marcion* and some gnostics, to the effect that the God of the Old Testament was a corrupt daemon hostile to the true spiri-tual God (the Father of Jesus), and thus the entire Old Testament needed to be jettisoned, were set aside, and the greater problem of how the supremely transcendent deity could be reconciled with the suffering and fallibility of the cosmic order was attacked primarily through the biblical medium. The early Christian writers were mesmerized by the story of the *fall* in Genesis, and explained human suffering, ignorance, and sin as a result of the lapse of human-ity's capacities that progressively dam-aged the basic constitution of the person (*see anthropology*). The work of salva-tion was seen as a threefold dynamic of pedagogy (God sent the prophets and saints throughout the Old Testament era to correct and instruct the people); cultic illumination (God demanded of his covenant people true and singular worship, which made them stand out among all nations); and ontological rescue. In this third movement the *incarnation* of Christ was seen as the decisive event of the salvation of the human race, prepared for through long ages beforehand (the biblical record was thus seamlessly integrated with the Christian story in a decisive movement of *exegetical* theory). If humanity had ontologically lapsed from its original immortal condition, once it turned away from the face of God (its destiny of contemplation) and embraced material life (its animal destiny), the potential for divine communion remained in the damaged creature, and Christ was to restore it in and through the divine Word's personal adoption (and transfiguration) of flesh in the incarnation. The first major analogies of atonement in patristic writers followed the richly diverse Pauline language of sacrificial substitution. Christ's blood was a cleansing of sins (Eph. 1:7; Heb. 9:1–28) and a humble atonement for the whole world (Heb. 2:9–10). In his victory over death Christ became the leader of many kindred (Heb. 2:14–18) and brought them out into freedom from their bitter slavery to death and corruption. It was a transactional exchange, whereby those who were assimilated to his death became enfolded in the gift of his *resurrection* and glory (2 Tim. 2:11–13). Christ's work of atonement was a *priestly* activity, an offering up of *prayers* and tears for the sanctification and illumination of the faithful (Heb. 5:1–10). It was also a cosmic victory over all the forces hostile to God (by the *cross* he cast down the demonic forces), and a triumph that definitively changed the manner in which God related to the world, opening the gates of mercy for a new covenant through the mediation of Christ the Victor (Phil. 2:6–11; Col. 1:15–20; 2:14–15; 1 Tim. 3:16). Christ's work was also seen as a pedagogical instruction that gave supreme example of godliness to the world, and established a pattern of behavior for all disciples to scrutinize and follow (Heb. 12:1–4). All of these diverse images are strongly represented in the patristic writers of the first four centuries. The cultic and liturgical images of sacrificial substitution were progressively subsumed into the theology of the Eucharist. Origen in the third century had already explained notions of the divine anger in terms of a pedagogical "strategy" on God's part to induce intellectual and spiritual reform (God was not really angry any more than a wise parent or teacher was when trying to teach a child), but later writers such as *John Chrysostom* preached extensively about the *death* of Christ as a sacrifice that literally appeased the anger of God. It was a notion that was not only common to Israelites during the time of the temple, but of course an idea that seemed natural and self-explanatory to Chrysostom's Greek and *Syrian* Christian audience who lived immersed in the world of Hellenistic sacrificial cults, and whose presumptions about the anger of God registered nothing unusual in this imagery. *Ignatius of Antioch* writes of his impending martyr's death in Rome as his destiny to be ground down as wheat by the teeth of lions, and so to share his master's sufferings (*Letter to the Romans* 4.1). His aim was "to imitate the passion of my God" (*Letter to the Romans* 6.3). The theme of assimilation to Christ's sufferings, however, was never so prevalent in the Eastern writers as it came to be in the Latin theologians (especially in the medieval period). Writers such as *Irenaeus* focused more on the glory of the victory of Christ spread over the world in a cosmically significant mystery of triumph (after the manner of Colossians). Christ the Victor was the one whose struggle had broken the power of the demons (John 12:31). *Athanasius* in the *De incarnatione* (longer recension) explains the choice of crucifixion as the method of Jesus' death as a strategy whereby the Logos entrapped the aerial demons (those which hindered the ascent of the soul to God both in prayer and after death). The conquered forces of the enemy were also described as death, ignorance, corruption, and idolatry. All of these things (along with the demons) are personally and graphically envisaged by the ancient patristic writers. It is often a problem for modern interpreters who might wish to demythologize the ideas, but the concept of the world as literally under the sway of malign powers was one that underpinned the Gospel accounts and was entirely shared by the ancient writers, who see and experience in this aspect of psychic liberation a definite energy of atonement. This explains why so many of the patristic theologians stress the dynamic power of the "sign of the cross," for exorcising and blessing. Undoubtedly this popular piety was a major element in the catechetical spread of Christianity in the villages and towns. Writers such as Irenaeus, Athanasius, and *Gregory of Nyssa* developed the concept of Christ the Victor in terms of his winning back the world from bondage to Satan. As sin had enslaved the race (following Paul in Rom. 6:15–23), Christ came to redeem the slave and buy it back to freedom. The price was Christ's own blood. Sometime the patristic preachers developed the theme imaginatively: Satan is duped into crushing Jesus as an ordinary "sinful man," not realizing that this mistake will void his power over the race. Gregory of Nyssa describes the divinity of Christ as the fishhook hidden within the flesh that captures the Leviathan and brings its reign to an end (*Catechetical Oration* 17–23). Irenaeus saw Satan as a wicked usurper, the prince of the world whose power Jesus legitimately broke as a conqueror. But others such as *Tertullian, Origen,* and Gregory of Nyssa suggested that God had given Satan rights over the fallen race, and Christ's work was a philanthropic "buying back" from a harsh slave owner. The Alexandrian theologians such as Origen and Clement used several of the range of the above ideas, but stressed the atonement as first and foremost a work of education. The Logos descended to earth in order to teach the paths for souls to ascend once more on high. His death was an exemplary one. In patristic writing this does not mean "merely" or only exemplarist, for Origen certainly combines his pedagogical theory with sacrificial views and notions of transactional redemption. After the fourth century the Alexandrian theory witnessed in Athanasius, and later brought to a pitch by *Cyril of Alexandria* and the Byzantine theologians, begins to dominate Eastern patristic thought. This has been called the "physical theory" of atonement, whereby the entrance of the divine Word into the fabric and condition of the flesh so radically reconstitutes the humanity of the race that the mortal is rendered immortal. The image of Christ's fleshly body (his finger or spittle, for example) becoming a divine medium of *grace* and power (healing the blind man or calling Lazarus back to life) is taken as a paradigm for what has happened to the humanity of all people after the transfiguration of Jesus' own humanity. Irenaeus described it in terms of: "Out of his great love, he became what we are, so that we might become what he is" (*Adversus haereses* 5 praef.). And Athanasius repeated it more succinctly: "He [the Logos] became human that humans might become God" (*De incarnatione* 54). After the fourth century the theory of *deification* (*theopoiesis*) dominated the Byzantine religious imagination. In the West the idea of substitutionary sacrifice, to appease the anger of God, remained the dominant and most vivid idea of the atonement. The idea was prevalent in the *North African* writers Tertullian and *Cyprian,* and when it was restated by *Augustine* (in more balanced and philosophical terms) it was set to enter the Western church as the primary motif of atonement theology for centuries to come. It is conveyed in Augustine's statement: "Since death was our punishment for sin, Christ's death was that of a sacrificial victim offered up for sins" (*De Trinitate* 4.12.15). Many modern patristic theorists have attempted to bring some order into the sprawling images of atonement we find in this literature, describing various "schools" or theories (physical theory, Christ the Victor, and so on). The simple fact is that the patristic writing is organically diffuse on the central mystery of Christ's economy, and its context is generally that of encomiastic preaching. The writers used many images, often a combination of them, all of them devolving in some sense or another from the rich poetic tapestry of scriptural texts about the work of Christ. To impose systematic order on this wildly vivid *kerygmatic* witness is often anachronistic and inappropriately scholastic.

G. Aulén, *Christus Victor* (London, 1931); F. W. Dillistone, *The Christian Understanding of Atonement* (London, 1968); J. Rivière, *The Doctrine of Atonement* (2 vols.; St. Louis, 1909); H. E. W. Turner, *The Patristic Doctrine of Redemption* (London, 1952).

Augustine of Hippo (354–430)

Perhaps the single most important writer of the Christian West, Augustine was from Thagaste, near Madauros, in Roman *North Africa*. His father Patricius was a pagan (until his deathbed), and his mother, Monica, a *catholic* Christian who enrolled her infant son as a *catechumen*. Augustine's talent was noticed early, and a wealthy patron, Romanianus, sponsored his education. He studied rhetoric at Carthage, where at the age of nineteen he was powerfully attracted to the vocation of rhetor-philosopher by reading Cicero's (lost) treatise *Hortensius*. His mother pressured him to enroll for *baptism* but Augustine had already set up house with a concubine (whom he never names), to whom he was deeply attached, and he was not willing to threaten that relationship, or to submit himself to the doctrines of the catholics, which he had come to regard as simplistic. He attached himself to the *Manichean* movement (as a "hearer") and belonged to them for the next ten years until 387. Augustine's career took him from Carthage to *Rome* and eventually to Milan, where he occupied the position of rhetoric professor, won for him by Manichean patrons. In Milan he became increasingly disillusioned with the Manicheans, and a series of crises shook his security, beginning with increasing asthmatic troubles (fatal for an ancient orator) and his agreement with his mother's plan to dismiss his partner of fifteen years' standing (the mother of his son Adeodatus) so that he could make a rich marriage to advance his career. His heartless agreement to her dismissal was soon followed by heartbreak at her loss, and his rapid employment of a sexual surrogate caused him to regard his philosophical aspirations with a depressed skepticism; but his increasing contact with one of the leading rhetorical and philosophical circles in the city (the group of theologians associated with the priest Simplicianus and bishop *Ambrose*) opened up new vistas for him. He was greatly impressed by Ambrose, and began to consider the possibility of a similar career as *ascetic* philosopher. He describes his psychosexual and spiritual struggle in a famous autobiography (*Confessions*), which he wrote many years later, and here he depicts the turning point of his life as occurring dramatically in a quiet Milanese garden when he abandoned his destiny to Christ and subsequently petitioned for admission to the church. For a while he stayed with Christian friends who formed a scholarly college around him. Soon, however, he returned to Rome, where Monica died, and then in 388 he made his way back to Africa, where he intended to live with his companions (more cheaply) at Thagaste. One day in 391, while making a visit to the seaport of Hippo Regius, he was seized by local Christians and forcibly ordained *priest* by Bishop Valerius, so that he could help the old bishop in the church administration. He and his companions accepted the forced initiation into church administration, and by 395 Augustine was consecrated as Valerius's episcopal assistant and soon afterwards, his successor. Local bishops in Africa regarded his promotion as canonically dubious, and even his baptism as somewhat irregular—for the news of his early life (both his sexual liaisons and his membership in the heretical Manichees) was common gossip in a church much troubled by the rigorist dissidents, the *Donatists*. To defend himself Augustine composed treatises against the Manichees after his priestly *ordination*, and after his consecration as *bishop* wrote the *Confessions*, an exercise in how self-scrutiny can be a salvific reading of the story of God's providence in creation and in a human life. It was a brilliant answer to his episcopal colleagues who had criticized him for slipping through the rigorous baptismal "scrutinies" of the African church. As bishop, Augustine made profound moves to resolve the schism of the Donatists, which led to his enunciation of important principles that would form the basic substructure of Western catholic ideas of sacramentality and ecclesial legitimacy. His works greatly developed the Latin *church's* understanding of itself as both a heavenly and earthly body (like Christ himself—whose body it was—a complete and perfect synthesis of flesh and divine spirit). Opposed at first to applying secular pressure on dissidents, he reluctantly came to a position by 411 that allowed for the partial legitimacy of such a policy. His immediate context was the lively Donatist threat of violence against him, but his authority seemed to have been placed behind the idea of religious compulsion when necessary, and it was an authority much evoked to justify forms of ecclesiastical oppression in later centuries. The publication of his *Confessions* had caused some outrage in Rome, where a moralist preacher, *Pelagius*, was appalled by Augustine's apparently fatalist resignation of his salvation to God's grace. Pelagius called for a more robust personal commitment and moral effort, and so began a controversy that was to mark all of Augustine's later life, and cause him to elaborate a profound and careful doctrine of *grace* that would become determinative for Western Catholicism. Augustine regarded humanity as having nothing on which it could base its *salvation*: all was a free gift of God. Humanity left to itself could only slip into the slavery of sin and corruption. His ideas were set out as a theology of praise for God's merciful providence, but in some more negative readings of his legacy, the pessimistic tone predominated in an unbalanced way, and Augustine in a real sense has to be seen as the author of a tendency in Latin theology to focus on the notions of *original sin*, and the corruption of the material world along with an ever-present tendency of the whole race to depravity. Most Greek writers never laid such stress on this pessimism, and never adopted as elements of the faith (unlike subsequent Western Catholicism) what they regarded as peculiarities of Augustine's local church (*theologoumena*). After the sack of Rome in 410 Augustine began a work of large-scale apologetic to answer those who laid the blame for the decadence of the Western empire at the door of the Christians. Between 412 and 427 he produced a monumental work called *The City of God*, where he elaborated the first extensively considered ethical and political view of what Christianity conceived of as a civilized order, in distinction to pre-Christian ideas. He stresses the earthly city's (human society's) radical dissociation from the true city of God (the *eschatological* realization of the kingdom) but makes a case for how the earthly city is informed and guided by heavenly ideals. Slavery is a prime symptom of the inherent corruption of the world's affairs. In the midst of endemic violence and disorder the church has the destiny to represent mercy and reconciliation, guiding society to a perfection it might never attain, but to which it is inexorably summoned. To stand with the *Confessions* and *City of God* in his triad of "world classics," we should add Augustine's monumental work of theology, *The Trinity*, composed between 399 and 419. In this he constructs a major anti-Arian apologetic around the Nicene faith in **Christology** and pneumatology. He demonstrates from a wide variety of triadic cosmic patterns the reasonableness of the **Trinitarian** doctrine of three divine persons subsisting in one single divine nature. Much use is made of triadic patterns of human psychology (the **soul** as the **image of God**), and he emphasized once again his deeply sensed connection between self-scrutiny and theological method (something common to Augustine and the **Platonic** tradition). His vast corpus of writings became, of course, his own form of ascetical exercise. The great extent of his work made him function as an encyclopaedic theological authority for the next millennium in the West. His spiritual writings gave a great impetus to monasticism as the organizing structure of the Latin church (something that **Gregory the Great** later picked up and developed). He particularly stressed the element of true faith leading to a deep desire of the heart for God, an affective spiritual tradition that made him an attractive and highly approachable Christian writer—aspects that still appear from engagement with his work. Only a few treatises can be singled out for special mention, such as *De doctrina christiana*, which laid out his biblical hermeneutical philosophy, or *De bono conjugali*, which argued (somewhat reluctantly) for the intrinsic holiness of sexuality in **marriage** (against **Jerome's** deeply hostile opinions). *De peccatorum meritis et remissione* and *De natura et gratia* both demonstrate why he thought **Pelagianism** so destructive of Christian religious experience. The *Enchiridion* is a summatic handbook of theology, composed for reference. His greatest exeget-

ical works are perhaps his *In Evangelium Johannis tractatus* and *De Genesi ad litteram* (commentaries respectively on John's Gospel and the book of Genesis). The commentary on the Psalms (*Enarrationes in Psalmos*) demonstrates his deep love for them as prayers. There is hardly a sermon, however, that is not an exposition of Scripture, or a serious theological reflection, in the manner he approaches it. Augustine's friend and monastic companion Possidius wrote a biography soon after his death, and made an invaluable list of all his writings, most of which are still extant. Augustine died as the Vandals were besieging his city on August 28, 430. One of his last instructions was to have his favorite psalms written in large letters around his walls so that he could read them as he died. Soon after his death, **Prosper of Aquitaine** began a process to lobby for Augustinianism as the standard theological system of the Latin West, a movement that slowly gathered momentum, culminating in Gregory the Great's enthusiastic endorsement of Augustine as preeminent Latin theologian in the late sixth century.

P. Brown, *Augustine of Hippo: A Biography* (Berkeley, Calif., 1967); H. Chadwick, *Augustine* (Oxford, 1986); A. D. Fitzgerald, ed., *Augustine through the Ages: An Encyclopedia* (Grand Rapids, 1999); F. van der Meer, *Augustine the Bishop* (London, 1961); P. Schaff, trans., *Works of St. Augustine* (NPNF; 8 vols.; Grand Rapids, 1887–1892); W. T. Smith, *Augustine: His Life and Thought* (Atlanta, 1980).

Baptism   The Greek word means to sprinkle with water, and was significant as the rite of initiating female converts in **Judaism**. The story of how baptism became the main ritual of Christian initiation is shrouded in obscurity, but it was certainly established as the primary ritual among the Hellenists of the first-century church, as seen in the account of Philip and the Ethiopian eunuch (Acts

8:26–40), and it was powerfully advocated by Paul, who supplied the first theological explanation of its mystical significance (appropriation into the mystery of Christ's *death* and *resurrection*) in Romans 6:1–11. The New Testament associates baptism with the forgiveness of sins and the gift of the **Holy Spirit** (Acts 2:38), incorporation into the body of the *church* (1 Cor. 12:13), and the entrance into *salvation* (1 Pet. 3:21). All of these themes are taken as standard by the earliest *patristic* writers (*Barnabas* 11; Shepherd of Hermas, *Vision* 3.3.1; idem, *Mandate* 4.3.3; idem, *Similitude* 9.13.3–6; Theophilus of Antioch, *To Autolycus* 2.16; Irenaeus, *Demonstration of the Apostolic Preaching* 3; ibid., 42; Clement of Alexandria, *Paedagogus* 1.6.25–32). Traditional *exegesis* also adopted several Old Testament types as primary symbols of Christian baptism, notably the flood (Gen. 6–9; 1 Pet. 3:20–21) and the crossing of the Red Sea (Exod. 14; 1 Cor. 10:1–2). The foundational text for Christian baptism was the Gospel account of the baptism of Jesus in the Jordan by John (Matt. 3:13–17; Mark 1:9–11; Luke 3:21–22). The Johannine account of the event represents all the paradoxical ways that Gospel sees the baptismal ritual, for it successfully conveys the tradition of the Johannine baptism of Jesus in words that carefully remove Jesus from the event of baptism altogether. For the Fourth Gospel, it is John only who baptizes with water, and Jesus who "baptizes with the Holy Spirit." Jesus is himself not baptized in the Fourth Gospel and does not practice the ritual of baptism (John 4:2). The evangelist makes a special point about insisting on this; only the disciples of Jesus instituted the rite, which is an odd insistence that speaks of an element of apologetic controversy already present in the church. The concept of the introduction of the ritual by the (later?) disciples is also conveyed by the Matthean account of the instruction to baptize as delivered by the risen Jesus in the terminal lines of the Gospel (Matt. 28:19). And yet the Gospel of John, which is ambiguous in its attitude to the ritual, is the same one that strongly advocates the necessity and practice of being "born of water and Spirit" (John 3:5). If the Gospel accounts generally seem embarrassed by the picture of Jesus submitting to John's baptism of cleansing (see the differences between the Markan and Matthean versions), it is possibly because they were under apologetic pressure from the continuing disciples of the Baptist. Many of Jesus' leading followers had originally been disciples of John, and if the same was true of Jesus himself (see the manner in which his praise of John is radically "toned down" in Matt. 11:11), a cleaner "separation" was perhaps desired by the first generation of the apostles than was actually the case historically. Even so, if John the Baptist's quintessential "prophetic sign" was the ritual use of water to signify cleansing and repentance, it is clear that Jesus' ministry (beginning after John's arrest) changed the focus and, accordingly, changed its primary "prophetic sign" from baptism in the river to the sharing of meals in the rural villages of Galilee (something that sufficiently disturbed John as to make him question what were Jesus' intentions: Luke 7:18–23). If immersion in water fitted John's theology of repentance, and was accepted by the endorsement of Jesus as the correct preparation for the preaching of the kingdom (Luke 7:24–30), then the sign of meals exactly fitted Jesus teaching on the reconciliation present at the "wedding feast" that accompanies the advent of the kingdom. So it was, one presumes, that both ritual remembrances, the **Eucharist** as meal of reconciliation (increasingly focused on the passion events because of the circumstances of the last week of Jesus' life) and the rite of baptism as penitent conversion of life, were destined to become the pillars of the Christian community's corporate identity. By the mid–first century both Eucharist and baptism were seen as mystical initiations into the mystery of the death and resurrection. From the second century baptism was prepared for by long prayers and fasting in the period leading up to Pascha (the origin of Lent in Christian observance). The candidates were given a series of moral instructions (*Didache* 7; Justin, *First Apology* 61), and in several places (notably **North Africa**) the *clergy* subjected applicants to a severe series of "scrutinies" that investigated many aspects of their moral attitude and previous conduct. When the clergy were satisfied that the request for baptism accompanied a sincere desire to change lifestyle, the candidates were admitted to baptism and thence to eucharistic communion. By the beginning of the third century, as instanced in **Hippolytus's Apostolic Tradition** and **Tertullian's** *De baptismo*, it seems that the period of instruction could be extended up to three years. By the mid–third century (as can be seen from elements of **Origen's** Lenten instructions to candidates in Caesarea, *Prayer*) the process of catechesis involved the explanation of basic biblical tropes, and the conveying of the creed and the Lord's Prayer so that they could be memorized. As baptism approached (usually on Pascha but by the fourth century also celebrated on days such as Pentecost and Epiphany) the candidates were exorcised. The significance of the ritual of exorcism related to the fact that most candidates at the time were adults who came into Christianity from an active involvement in Hellenistic religions, which were generally seen as "demonic cults" by the early church. As infant baptism became more popular after the fifth century (**Justinian** commanded it as a standard in the sixth century), the ministers of baptism became more and more the village *priests*, no longer the bishops in a single solemn ceremony as in earlier times. In the earliest accounts of baptismal ritual the prayers over the water are solemn and extended, petitioning the descent of the Holy Spirit into the waters. The candidates were liberally anointed with oil, entered the waters naked (females were

assisted by female deacons), and, confessing their faith, were immersed under the surface three times (Tertullian, *Against Praxeas* 26; Cyril of Jerusalem, *Catechetical Lectures* 17.14; Basil of Caesarea, *On the Holy Spirit* 15.35; Ambrose, *On the Sacraments* 3.1.1f.; John Chrysostom, *Catechetical Orations* 2.26; idem, *Homily on John* 25.2). They were then clothed (in white garments, hence the term *candidatus* or "dressed in white") and brought to the bishop, who anointed them with sacred *chrism* to signify the "seal of the Holy Spirit," laid hands on them, and in primitive times also led them to a symbolic meal of milk and honey. The congregation exchanged the kiss of peace and continued the liturgy with the celebration of the Eucharist (which had been paused so that the candidates could join in at the time of communion). The African church was much vexed by the question of whether baptism by heretics could be accepted as valid. **Cyprian of Carthage** and the Eastern churches were generally inclined to see it as invalid and so baptized *de novo* (though there were exceptions to this). In the West a more tolerant view prevailed after **Augustine's** struggle with the **Donatists**, allowing that heretical baptism was valid if conferred in the name of the **Trinity**, and heretics were often received into the church by the laying on of hands. In the seventh century Pope **Gregory I** expressed his opinion that although triple immersion was normal, a single immersion could also be permissible. Eastern tradition strongly defended the practice of threefold immersion under the waters, but Latin practice increasingly came to use a sprinkling of water on the head (also mentioned as a legitimate practice in **Didache** 7 if there was not sufficient water for immersion). In the fourth century there was a flowering of ritual and theological reflection around the practice of baptism. Several of the leading churchmen of the day, such as **Cyril of Jerusalem** (*Catechetical Orations*) and **Gregory of Nazianzus** (*Orations* 38–40), have left behind accounts of their catechetical preparations for the "awe-inspiring rites" of initiation. Gregory compares the baptismal experience to a deeper realization of all that the ancient mystery religions promised by their initiation ceremonies, and Cyril gives one of the clearest accounts of fourth-century sacramental practice we have. The writings of the fourth-century hierarchs, the last generation to preside over the solemn form of baptismal initiations, set the tone for most liturgical practice to follow, up to the medieval period.

J. H. Crehan, *Early Christian Baptism and the Creed* (London, 1950); A. Hamman, *Baptism: Ancient Liturgies and Patristic Texts* (New York, 1967); G. W. H. Lampe, *The Seal of the Spirit* (London, 1951); J. A. McGuckin, "The Sign of the Prophet: The Significance of Meals in the Doctrine of Jesus," *Scripture Bulletin* 16, 2 (summer 1986): 35–40; E. J. Yarnold, *The Awe-Inspiring Rites of Initiation: Baptismal Homilies of the Fourth Century* (Slough, 1972).

Baradeus   *see* **Jacob Baradeus**

Bardesanes (c. 154–222)   Also known as Bar-Daysan, Bardesanes was the first Syrian Christian poet, though none of this work survives except for some titles in Ephrem's reference to him in his *Hymns against the Heretics* 55. Fragments of his prose are preserved by later writers who censure him (from the perspective of fourth-century *Nicene* orthodoxy) for holding *gnostic* ideas. His system is represented in a surviving work, *The Dialogue of Destiny* (or *The Book of Laws of Countries*). Some scholars think that the apocryphal *Acts of Thomas* were written in his school. Astrology was important to his system, and he wished to discuss how personal freedom could be understood in the light of destiny. He argues against the common fatalism of the astrologers that Christ has counteracted the overwhelming force of the planets.

He is dualist in tone: evil is profoundly mixed with the good in this world, a theme he describes in Semitic form as a battle between light and darkness. *Ephrem the Syrian* in the fourth century claimed that Bardesanes understood Christ's *incarnation* as merely an appearance of human nature (*Docetism*). He was an interesting early example of palace theologian, a Christian philosopher-astrologer in the court of King Agbar VIII at Edessa.

H. J. W. Drijvers, *The Book of the Laws of Countries: Dialogue on Faith of Bardaisan of Edessa* (Assen, Netherlands, 1965); idem, *Bardaisan of Edessa* (Studia Semitica Neerlandica 6; Assen, 1966).

Barsanuphius and John (mid–sixth century)   Barsanuphius was regarded as one of the last of the classical tradition of *desert* saints and elders. He was an Egyptian by birth who lived as solitary ascetic in Gaza. His younger contemporary, John the Prophet, was a hermit who lived near him. Between the two men a series of literary exchanges took place later collected and disseminated under the title *Questions and Answers*. It was a series of queries posed to the elder, by John and other monks, possibly through John's mediation, that sought to elucidate the meaning of the *ascetical* life, and the ways to avoid common problems. The pithy dialogues sum up the desert tradition of the sayings of the fathers, at a time when monasticism was reacting strongly against *Origen's* speculative theology, and they had a profound impact on the later ascetical tradition during two important times of synthesis. The works influenced the important monastic teachers *John Climacus* and Dorotheos of Gaza shortly after their production. In a later period they also enjoyed a revival at Byzantium affecting such influential mystics as Paul of Evergetinos and Symeon the New Theologian. So it was they were preserved in the wider tradition of Eastern

Orthodox ascetical theology, as classics of hermit guidance on the need to quiet the soul and rise from purity of heart to the sense of the presence of God.

I. Hausherr, "S. Barsanuphe," in DSP 1 (Paris, 1937), cols. 1255–62; S. Rose, trans., *Saints Barsanuphius and John: Guidance toward Spiritual Life: Answers to the Questions of Disciples* (Platina, Calif., 1990).

Basilides (fl. 135–161) Nothing has directly survived of the work of this Syrian theologian, who was center of a *gnostic* school at *Alexandria*, and who composed some of the earliest Christian biblical commentary, including a gospel and a book of odes. Two traditions of his writing give significantly different pictures. In *Irenaeus's* account (*Adversus haereses* 1.24), Basilides' doctrine seems to be akin to the *Valentinian* gnostic system. The deity is beyond description, beyond existence, and emanated a series of intellective powers (Nous, Logos, Phronesis, Sophia, and Dynamis). The last two created the first heaven, initiating a series of other dyads making other descending hierarchies of heavens until the perfect number of 365 is completed (thus offering some form of metaphysical answer to the ubiquitous philosophical problem of reconciling the one and the many). Angels in this final and lowest heaven, led by the rebellious one the Jewish Scripture proclaimed as God, made the material cosmos, a work dominated by evil and oppression. Christ, embodying the spirit of Nous, was sent to effect liberation of souls from this gloomy bondage. He shifted shape with Simon of Cyrene, leaving Simon to be crucified while he ascended free, a passage Irenaeus finds scandalous in the extreme, but which probably signified originally the symbolic differentiation of the psychic "foolish" disciple, who lives a mimesis of Simon by a path of endurance and discipline, as distinct from the gnostic disciple, who seeks

after Nous and realizes the essential insignificance of the body and its affairs. In the account presented in *Hippolytus* (*Refutation of All Heresies* 7.20–27) and supported by references in other Christian writers, Basilides is said to have taught the cosmos existed as the high God's own all-inclusive "world-seed." Three sonships in a descending hierarchy (light, heavy, and defiled) derive from the seed. The first is an ascentive power; the second ascends with power from the Holy Spirit; the third is purified by assisting human souls to ascend. Two archons also derive from the seed, and both are accompanied by their sons. The first son leads his father and his realm (the perfect eight—or Ogdoad) to repentance, while the second son mirrors this process and teaches truth to his father and the realm of seven (the Hebdomad). The salvific light of the Ogdoad and Hebdomad was that which inspired Jesus, the enlightened one, who calls the elect back to God, healing the essential sinfulness of certain souls. *Origen* said Basilides taught the doctrine of transmigration of souls (*see* **Pythagoreanism**, **reincarnation**). The essential impact of his system was a principle of *soteriological* mediation that tried to meld the Christian *kerygma* with *philosophical* systems of cosmological mediation.

W. H. C. Frend, *Saints and Sinners in the Early Church* (London, 1985), chap. 2; R. M. Grant, "Place de Basilide dans la théologie chrétienne ancienne," REA 25 (1979): 201–16; W. A. Löhr, *Basilides und seine Schule: eine Studie zur Theologie- und Kirchengeschichte des zweiten Jahrhunderts* (Tübingen, Germany, 1996).

Basil of Ancyra (d. after 363) Basil of Ancyra was a leader in the fourth-century Arian controversy of the *Homoiousian* party, those who rejected the *homoousion* of *Council of Nicaea I (325)*, but were close to the general Nicene sense of the divine status of the Logos–Son of God. He was a leader of the Council of Sirmium in 351. After his death his party would eventually be reconciled with the Nicenes, under the leadership of *Meletius of Antioch*, and with the assistance of *Athanasius* at the Synod of Alexandria in 362 (who called for all people of good faith to come together despite differences of terminology), and that of the *Cappadocian Fathers* in the late 370s. The alliance was definitive in bringing an end to the Arian crisis in the Eastern church. Basil was elected bishop of Ancyra after the deposition of *Marcellus* in 336. The treatise *On Virginity*, attributed to *Basil of Caesarea*, is thought to be his work.

R. P. C. Hanson, *The Search for the Christian Doctrine of God* (Edinburgh, 1988); J. Quasten, *Patrology* (vol. 3; Utrecht, Netherlands, 1960), 201–3.

Basil of Caesarea (330–379)   Known even in his lifetime as "Basil the Great," Basil of Caesarea was the most dynamic and politically active of the *Cappadocian Fathers*, if not the most original of them. He was the son of a rhetorician, from a wealthy Christian family. He studied in Cappadocia (where he first met *Gregory of Nazianzus*), then in *Constantinople*, and finally for six years at Athens, where his friendship with Gregory Nazianzen was deepened into a lifelong alliance. In 355 he returned to Cappadocia and taught rhetoric for a year before he made his way (probably in the company of *Eustathius of Sebaste*) to tour the *ascetical* communities of *Syria*, Mesopotamia, Palestine, and Egypt. Basil was baptized on his return to Cappadocia and embraced the ascetical life under the influence of Eustathius and his own sister *Macrina*, who had already adapted their country estate at Annesoi in Pontus as a monastic retreat. Here he invited Gregory Nazianzen, though the latter found the style of monasticism not to his taste, preferring a more scholarly seclusion on his own estates. Gregory and Basil collabo-

rated in producing the *Philocalia* (a first edition of selected passages from Origen) as well as writings about monastic life. This early work of writing manuals for the ascetics gathered around them (especially Basil's *Asceticon*, though some see it as a work of Eustathius) had a historic impact in the form of the "Monastic Rules," which gave Basil the title of "father of Eastern monks." The *Moralia* came first in 358 (largely traditional ascetical maxims attached to their biblical proof texts) and were followed by the *Asceticon* c. 363 (which is what most refer to as the Rule). Ordained a reader in 360 and then priest for the church at Cappadocian Caesarea in 362, Basil was actively involved in the resistance of the radical Arian party led by *Aetius* and *Eunomius*. At first attached to the *Homoiousian* party, which was dominant in Cappadocia, he increasingly aligned himself with the defense of the Nicene creed (and the *Homoousian* party). He fell out with his bishop Eusebius, and retired to his estates until in 364 the threat of an installation of an *Arian* bishop of the entourage of Emperor Valens brought him back to the service of the Caesarean church. Gregory Nazianzen mediated that return, and the threat from Valens was deflected, though Basil had earned many enemies among the Caesarean clergy. In 368 he administered the church's relief effort for a great famine in the region and won the support of the people. In 370 he was elected bishop of his city, despite the opposition of the town curia and many bishops. Shortly afterwards, the great diocese of Cappadocia was divided in two, and to offset the influence of the new metropolitan Anthimus of Tyana, Basil desperately tried to fill small towns with episcopal appointments drawn from his circle of friends. This elevated Gregory of Nyssa and Gregory of Nazianzus to episcopal status but also caused rifts among his immediate circle, who felt his machinations were chiefly squabbles about revenues dressed up as theological conflicts. As he moved more and more to become the public face of the Nicene party, he stood in alliance with *Meletius of Antioch*, one of the old Nicene stalwarts. This alliance (which brought him into conflict with *Athanasius* and Pope *Damasus*) he saw as fundamental for the Nicene cause in the East, and he was faithful to it, even though it alienated his old friend and mentor Eustathius of Sebaste, who then went on to espouse the *Pneumatomachian* doctrine, denying the deity of the *Holy Spirit*. The public breach with Eustathius was marked by Basil's publication of a highly influential work: *On the Holy Spirit*, books 1–3, where Basil affirms the deity of the Son and Spirit and paves the way for the full *neo-Nicene* confession of the *Trinity*, which Gregory of Nazianzus would elaborate at the *Council of Constantinople* in 381. He died worn out with his labors in 379. Basil's letters are major sources of information about the life of the church in the fourth century. His *Hexaemeron*, or interpretation of the creation through the Genesis account, is a masterpiece of early Christian scriptural theology, and shows him as a moderate Origenist, with a fine feel for the moral power of Scripture. His treatise *Against Eunomius* was a major force revitalizing the Nicene resistance, and he did much in his time to persuade the Homoiousians that their position was in substance reconcilable with that of the Homoousians, a key element for the long-term success of the Nicene cause. His work in his church as teacher and public defender of his town (he instituted the building of one of the first major hospital sites staffed by Christian monks) made Basil a model for future Eastern bishops, and in Byzantine times he was designated along with Gregory of Nazianzus and *John Chrysostom* as one of the "Three Holy Hierarchs," the most important bishop theologians of the ancient period.

W. K. L. Clarke, *St. Basil the Great: A Study in Monasticism* (Cambridge, 1913); S. R. Holman, *The Hungry Are Dying: Beggars and Bishops in Roman Cappadocia* (Oxford, 2001); B. Jackson, *St. Basil: Letters and Select Works* (NPNF second series, 8; repr.; Grand Rapids, 1989); P. Rousseau, *Basil of Caesarea* (Berkeley, Calif., 1994).

Benedict of Nursia (c. 480–540) Regarded now as the veritable founder of Western monasticism, and impressing upon it a style and organized character that dominated all later Western ascetic experience, Benedict had, in his own time, only a small following and little other than local fame. It was his Rule, or plan for organizing a monastic community, that made him famous, along with Pope *Gregory the Great*'s praises of him in his widely influential *Dialogues*. Benedict came from the Apennine village of Nursia and studied as a young man in Rome. The city life disgusted him (Rome was also in serious political decline) and he retired to live a secluded life at Subiaco near the capital. Here he began to organize, with difficulty, small *ascetical* communities. He established a community at Monte Cassino, a safe hilltop settlement halfway between Rome and Naples, which served him and his monks well in the troubled times of war-torn Italy. He composed his rule by adapting earlier monastic regulations (especially the prototype called the *Rule of the Master*), but with particular stress of his own on the needful character of gentle paternal care, which should characterize the monastic abbot or leader. His monks were to find their salvation in obedience, and accordingly the abbot was to be a true pastor, a veritable Christ-figure to his charges. The stress in all his work, of course, was on monasticism understood as a matter of the common, or cenobitic, life. The chief function of the monastery was the Opus Dei— God's work of sustaining a constant rhythm of prayer and liturgy each day. Benedict looks to *Basil the Great (of Caesarea)* and *John Cassian* as spiritual masters for monks. His own Rule, however, was looked to as a marvelous example of humane moderation by his successors. His monks were forced from Monte Cassino by Lombard attacks in 570 and took refuge in **Rome**, from which center their rule became popularized. The Holy Roman Emperor Charlemagne insisted on Benedict's Rule as the standard of monasteries in his domains, and after the tenth century it achieved an increasingly normative status, giving to the entire Western church a cohesion and ecclesiastical organization that marked it deeply.

J. Chapman, *St. Benedict and the Sixth Century* (London, 1929); L. von Matt and S. Hilpisch, *Saint Benedict* (Chicago, 1961); J. McCann, *The Rule of St. Benedict* (London, 1952).

Bishops   *see* Episcopate

Boethius (c. 480–525)   Anicius Manlius Torquatus Severinus Boethius was a Roman aristocrat in the time of the Ostrogothic occupation of Italy. His studies took him through the traditional pattern of rhetoric and philosophy, but his lively mind developed on his formal training in a subsequent writing career that tried, with some originality, to synthesize in a Christian fashion the systems of **Neoplatonism** (*see* **Plotinus, Proclus**), **Aristotelianism,** and **Stoicism**. His Latin adaptations and translations of the Greek sources were influential. His philosophic career was interrupted when he entered into political service under the Ostrogothic King Theodoric. He was elected consul in 510 and in 522 he served as master of offices at the Ravenna court. Soon after, he was accused of entering into traitorous dealings with the Byzantine Emperor and was imprisoned at Ticinum (modern Pavia) and executed sometime between 524 and 526. The Catholic faith of Boethius allied to his symbolic value as a Roman patriot executed by an **Arian** king led to a local cult, and he is remembered at Pavia as Saint Severinus. He left behind treatises on the quadrivium—the medieval school curriculum of higher studies (music, arithmetic, geometry, and astronomy), which especially in the domain of logic had a pronounced influence on the medieval West. His understanding of **philosophy** was that all the schools could be resolved to a central corpus of doctrine, under the guidance of Christian faith. The faith itself could then be illuminated by rational enquiry. His concern was to probe the particular domains of **revelation** and reason, and in this he predated the medieval scholastics. In his theological writing he commented on the **Nicene** faith in **Christology** and **Trinity** (a brave thing in an Arian court) and made an enduring mark with some definitions of key terms that were to become classical—particularly *"person"* (an individual substance of a rational nature) and "eternity" (the simultaneous and perfect possession of a limitless life). His most famous work was the *Consolation of Philosophy*, written while he was in prison and wrestling very personally with the issue of social injustice and God's providence. It became one of the most beloved books of the Latin medieval world, a Christianized reaffirmation of the **Platonic** ideal that through fidelity to a philosophical way of life, the **soul** is made coherent and stable and prepared for the **vision** of God.

H. Chadwick, *Boethius: The Consolations of Music, Logic, Theology and Philosophy* (Oxford, 1981); G. O'Daly, *The Poetry of Boethius* (Chapel Hill, 1991); M. T. Gibson, ed., *Boethius: His Life, Thought, and Influence* (Oxford, 1981); V. E. Watts, trans., *Boethius: The Consolation of Philosophy* (Harmondsworth, U.K., 1999).

Burial   Christians generally seem to have followed the Jewish custom of burying the body (inhumation) rather than the widely practiced Hellenistic custom of incineration, although it is difficult to make hard-and-fast generalizations, as in the larger cities inhumation increasingly became the preferred option for the poor in the late empire, whether Christian or pagan. Christians adopted the term cemetery (*koimeteria*) or "sleeping ground" to connote their belief that death was a resting in the Lord and a transition to the immortal life into which Christ would induct his servants. It was in the second century that the first evidence arises for distinctive Christian practices in burial ritual. The *catacombs* in *Rome* provide the largest evidence, and there is much differentiation in burial style depending on the social class and wealth of the Christians who were interred. Burial places ranged from small niches (*loculi*) in towering subterranean walls that contained layers and layers of the dead, to larger mausoleum chambers (*cubicula*) with one wall fashioned into an archway over the tomb (*arcosolium*) that was often decorated with frescoes of such themes as the Orant (woman at prayer), or the good shepherd. At Rome, *North Africa*, and many parts of Asia Minor, the *cubicula* were also the site of commemorative meals (*refrigeria*) that the family would celebrate for the dead, a practice the Christians shared with their pagan neighbors. For the pagans the scent of meals and graveside sacrifices "refreshed" the ghost. Christians (generally) understood the meals as more of a commemoration, without the sense that the departed spirit needed anything other than *prayer*. It is notable that Christian graves universally abandoned the practice of the burying of gravegoods with the corpse. By the fourth and fifth centuries the practice of *refrigeria* was becoming increasingly rare, and *Ambrose* greatly surprised Monica, Augustine's mother, by his prohibition of it in the Milanese church. Increasingly the commemorations were relocated to the church, and the cultic use of the cemeteries waned. Earlier images of the persecuted church hiding in the catacombs and celebrating the *Eucharist*

there were much exaggerated, although certain sites in the catacombs, and across the world in other comparable places, were indeed specially venerated, namely the tombs of the martyrs. The Crypt of the Popes in the Catacomb of Saint *Callistus* in Rome is one such example, and the tombs of other martyrs frequently evolved from local shrines into the main church of the area, such as Peter's tomb in the Vatican necropolis that eventually became the Petrine Basilica. The central rites of Christian burial mainly adapted Roman custom. Psalms were recited through the time of dying by *deacons* and *clergy* (meant to suppress the older Roman practice of the keening and lamenting of the dead by professional mourners), and continued over the corpse after death. This is still the basic pattern of *funus* in the Eastern church. When *Augustine* felt death approaching he had the psalm texts (his favorite psalms of repentance) painted in large letters onto the wall of his room so that his dying eyes could follow them (Possidius, *Life of Augustine*). The dead person was formally called on by name to legally certify death had occurred (a rite still followed in the death of popes). The body was then washed and laid out by the women of the household, in the home on the evening before the burial (for *priests*, the washing was done by other ordained ministers, and the body was anointed with fragrant oil and laid on a bier, or *feretrum*, in the church). A funeral procession led by torchbearers conducted the deceased to the gravesite, followed by the mourners. The Christians generally discontinued the pagan practice of focusing the service around a portrait of the deceased, to which honors were given. Dirt was thrown onto the corpse and prayers were said. *Prudentius*, in one of the first Christian poems dedicated to burial ritual (*Cathemerinon* 10), mentions that white linen shrouds and myrrh were used on the body, and that flowers were also strewn in the grave. Two centuries earlier *Tertullian* had mentioned this custom with horror, that Christians could be so shameless as to celebrate the awesome passing to judgment with floral tributes. In general, the early Christian tradition sobered down, but did not completely dispense with, the Hellenistic practice of celebrating the person's life with speeches and compliments. *Gregory of Nazianzus* and *Ambrose* are among the first leading Churchmen in the fourth century to Christianize the Hellenistic practice of funeral encomia, and they judiciously balance the celebration of the deceased person's virtues (for the sake of edification) with the need to commend the soul of the deceased to God's mercy. The sense that the soul now stood before God chastened the Christian services considerably. From an early time names of the deceased were scratched onto the tiles that closed the *loculus*, and later this evolved into inscribed crosses, and in the post-Constantinian age, gilded glass medallions with Christian ciphers. Burial within the church building (unless the tomb was that of a martyr) was at first regarded as highly sacrilegious and much resisted, though it was clearly a custom that had already begun to creep in across the Christian world.

A. D. Nock, "Cremation and Burial in the Roman Empire," HTR 25 (1932): 321–59; G. F. Snyder, *Ante Pacem: Archaeological Evidence of Church Life Before Constantine* (Macon, Ga., 1985); J. M. C. Toynbee, *Death and Burial in the Roman World* (London, 1971).

Callistus of Rome (fl. 217–222)   A former *slave* who was subsequently *deacon* at *Rome* in charge of the *catacomb* on the Via Appia (now the San Callisto Catacomb), Callistus became pope after Zephyrinus in 217, and was probably martyred. During his administration he excommunicated the theologian Sabellius (*see* **Sabellianism**) for his **Monarchian** theology, but was himself accused by his rival **Hippolytus**, the **Logos theologian,** of being a "Patripass-ian" (a Monarchian who could not distinguish between the absolute Godhead and the suffering of the **incarnate** Logos), presumably because he held a less-than-enthusiastic view about Hippolytus's own theology. Callistus was also accused of moral laxity by Hippolytus because he had admitted back to communion those under censure for sexual sins (*see* **penance**), and because he had advocated legalizing marriage between noblewomen and slaves. His tomb is still venerated in the Trastevere district of Rome. He may possibly be the same as that Praxeas ("Busybody") attacked as a Monarchian by **Tertullian** in his treatise of that name.

G. L. Prestige, *Fathers and Heretics* (London, 1954), ch. 2.

Canon of Scripture   The word *canon,* in the sense of "rule" or standard of measurement, was adopted by the Christians to connote the definitive list of books that would be regarded by the church as inspired Scripture. The first Christian use of the term "Scripture" comes in the New Testament writings themselves (Matt. 21:42; 26:54; Mark 12:10; Luke 4:21; John 5:39; Acts 17:2; Rom. 1:2; 1 Cor. 15:3; 2 Tim. 3:16), and both here and in the *Apostolic Fathers* always signifies the Old Testament only. From the earliest times, however, the words and sayings of Jesus enjoyed immense authority in the Christian movement, and with the composition of the Gospels and Apostolic Letters in the mid–first century, the events of Jesus' life and the record of his sayings became the refractive lens for a whole realignment of the church's understanding of the scriptural panoply (Luke 24:27). In this sense the New Testament itself is a holistic commentary on Scripture, what the church regarded as the "fulfillment" (*teleiosis*) of the scriptural confession of Israel's faith in God. *Origen of Alexandria* in the early third century was to put this insight onto a systematic footing with his extensive exegetical writings, but it was a basic dynamic of Christian theology from the outset. It was the *gnostic* crisis of the second century that brought the issue of precisely defining the canon of recognized books into a sharp focus. Before that both the synagogue and the church had a looser idea of what were the definitive books of the Old Testament. For Christians this was not a critical matter since the texts concerned were not "primary law," but were celebrated for moral examples in the preaching tradition, and were never referred to in doctrinal controversies by any side. Already by the Christian era the central literature that would become our recognizable Old Testament had already been established, that is, the Law and the Prophets, but there were a variety of other texts that were less widely cited. Modern scholars have argued that the synagogue really did not definitively close its canon until well after the first century A.D. Christian patristic commentators generally took the Septuagint list (wider than the Hebrew canon) to be sufficient for the church's purposes, though *Origen* expressed some doubts about the full value of some of the Septuagint additions (appendages to Daniel such as Bel and the Dragon, or the Three Children in the Furnace—a story widely popular in the early church as a type of martyrdom, or the book of Tobit, also much loved for its image of protective angels). In the fifth century *Gregory of Nazianzus* and *Epiphanius of Salamis* shared Origen's doubts more openly. For the West, *Jerome* was an important biblical authority, and his negative attitude to the Septuagintal extra books was robustly expressed. He felt only those books that were extant in the Hebrew could be regarded as canonically definitive. *Ambrose* and *Augustine* shared the more traditionalist view that the Septuagint should be the church's Old Testament Bible, and they successfully tempered Jerome's views for the time being. The authority of Augustine made it the case that the later Latin church

agreed with the Greeks that all the books of the Septuagint were inspired Scripture. But Jerome's views had a long afterlife. Through the medieval era the West was careful not to cite the Septuagintal additions in a serious doctrinal case, sometimes regarding them as "deuterocanonical" (of the second rank), and using them mainly in liturgical services of prayer only. Jerome's restrictive view came back into favor at the Reformation, and most of the Protestant world relegated the non-Hebrew texts to the category of Apocrypha (where they are now listed in such modern Protestant Bibles as the NRSV). In regard to the definitive closing of the New Testament the issue was speeded up in a highly controversial dynamic of the church's conflict with *gnostics* and other theological groups that composed an abundant variety of gospels, Apostolic Letters, and apocalypses, all pseudepigraphical (retrospectively assigned to the name of a first-generation apostle). By A.D. 130 the four Gospels now recognized, and the thirteen Epistles of St. Paul, are all cited in patristic literature as apostolic tradition. By the end of the second century they were being cited as "Scripture" in the same sense as the Old Testament writings. The argument of *Marcion* (d. 160) that the Old Testament writings were incompatible with Christian values and ought to be excluded gave a decisive shock to the international body of Christians, and was probably the chief factor in making the various churches wish to insist on drawing up more formal lists of "what ought to be read in the church assemblies" (the liturgical imperative being the real dynamic that constituted the Christian canon of Scripture). After Marcion precipitated the rejection of radical exclusionism, the inclusive view of the canon was further challenged by gnostic groups that began in the mid–second century to compose a variety of "new gospels," many of which advanced gnostic *Docetic Christologies* and other factional views. Now the international reaction was to be less inclusive, and to set a limit on the number of New Testament books to be read in church. *Irenaeus* is much exercised in this period to argue the governing principles of canonical inclusion. He adopts a compromise governed by anti-Marcionite and antignostic strategies. Only that literature which has ancient, *apostolic*, and universally recognized authority can be accepted. So, for example, he argued that there could only be four Gospels, just as there are only four corners to the world (it had to be a self-evident thing, was his point, regardless of the unfortunate cosmology). Only those texts written by apostles or their immediate disciples could enter the canon. From this time on the requirement to assign important Christian literature to a recognized apostolic author (far from a self-evident thing) was an imperative. Hebrews was eventually admitted into the Pauline canon, the Fourth Gospel and book of Revelation (always regarded as suspect in the East) were assigned to John, as were the Johannine letters. Mark and Luke were rendered the immediate disciples of Peter and Paul respectively. Matthew (clearly a Greek text) was identified with the Apostle Levi-Matthew. This move to a strictly "apostolic canon" was not motivated by what we would regard as historical criteria, but it certainly manifested some historical sense to "close" the apostolic tradition against the claim of gnostic teachers that they preserved secret apostolic philosophy, unknown to the public traditions. Epistolary literature that was not Pauline had a slower passage towards general acceptance (self-evident canonicity in Irenaean terms). Lingering doubts were expressed for some time (still prevalent in *Eusebius of Caesarea* in the fourth century) in regard to Hebrews, Jude, 2 Peter, and 2 and 3 John. Some writings such as *Barnabas* or those of the Shepherd of Hermas were accepted as scriptural by some churches (the latter were included in the Caesarean canon up to the fourth cen-

tury, as can be seen from the Codex Sinaiticus), but not by most others, and they both eventually dropped out of the canon after the late fourth century. The first formal attempts to define a clear list of canonical New Testament books can be seen in the fourth century. Some time in the middle of the century a series of regulations (canons) were collected from recent synodical decisions. One of them is the so-called "Canon 60" of the Council of Laodicea, which lists and rebukes the variety of heretics that have so far troubled the church, before going on to make a formal list of what New Testament books can be read in church. The list is the same as that represented in the later–fourth-century "Apostolic Canons" (chap. 8.47 of the book *Apostolic Constitutions*), and represents the present state of the biblical canon with the exception of the book of Revelation and the Septuagintal additions (its Old Testament, in other words, follows the Hebrew canon). The first witness to the full canon of the Orthodox and Catholic churches is the paschal "Festal Letter" of Saint *Athanasius* for the year 367. The same list was affirmed by Pope *Damasus* in a synod at Rome in 382. It was reproduced by Pope *Gelasius* in 495 and is often called the Gelasian Decree. After the fourth century the matter was not raised again in patristic times. The canon of Scripture was always far larger than what might be called the "real Christian canon," or the "canon within the canon," that is, those biblical books which were the subject of serious and sustained scrutiny by patristic theologians, as represented by patristic biblical commentaries written about them. For the rest they featured largely in atomic proof texting; verses or small pericopes were often taken from them and used in teaching or liturgical contexts. In the patristic era, however, it was never the case that the affirmation of the wider canon simultaneously affirmed that all the books within that canon had equal weight and significance.

F. F. Bruce, *The Canon of Scripture* (Glasgow, U.K., 1988); E. E. Ellis, *The Old Testament in Early Christianity: Canon and Interpretation in the Light of Modern Research* (Tübingen, Germany, 1991); F. V. Filson, *Which Books Belong to the Bible? A Study of the Canon* (Philadelphia, 1957); B. M. Metzger, *The Canon of the New Testament: Its Origin, Development, and Significance* (Oxford, 1987); A. C. Sundberg, *The Old Testament of the Early Church* (Harvard Theological Studies 20; Cambridge, Mass., 1964).

Canons The word derives from the Greek for rule or standard of measurement. The *canon of Scripture* means the standard list, the definitive register, of those books that would be accepted as biblical. It has essentially the same meaning when applied to the creedal notion of the "Canon of Truth," the "Canon of the Mass," or the "canons of a cathedral" (the clergy listed in the ecclesiastical records as the chief ministers of the place). In the context of the early church the word in the plural signifies the list of rules or disciplinary decisions made by episcopal synods or local bishops. A body of decisions grew up in the fourth century, which were often appended to the conciliar acts. The first examples come from the Spanish Council of Elvira (306) and the Synod of Arles (314). The collection of conciliar canons was given its future shape by the early–fourth-century Asia Minor synods of Ancyra, Neo-Caesarea, Antioch, Gangra, and Laodicea. All kinds of disciplinary matters increasingly began to come under episcopal scrutiny. Most prestigious of them all was the international code of regulations appended to the *Council of Nicaea's* (325) doctrinal statements. The Nicene canons attempt to bring order and structure to a church that had long endured the disruptions of *persecution*. After this point reformatory canons, drawn up in this style, were regularly appended to conciliar acts, and collectively they grew to be the church's code of canon law. In the Eastern church they were never really rationalized, and to this day the ancient and more modern canons coexist, often haphazardly, and sometimes in mutual contradiction. In the West there were regular movements to streamline and update the system of canon laws, especially after the fifth century, and the laws of the Roman church came to have a wide circulation and influence. In the Western patriarchate the decisions of the pope, independently from conciliar legislation, came to have a powerful authoritative status (*see papacy*). These decretals much influenced the shape of canon law, whereas in the East the issuing of canons remained tied to synodical assemblies.

H. Hess, *The Canons of the Council of Sardica, A.D. 343: A Landmark in the Early Development of Canon Law* (Oxford, 1958); P. L'Huillier, *The Church of the Ancient Councils: The Disciplinary Work of the First Four Ecumenical Councils* (New York, 1995); J. Meyendorff, *Byzantine Theology* (New York, 1974); R. C. Mortimer, *Western Canon Law* (London, 1953).

Cappadocian Fathers (fl. fourth century) Cappadocian Fathers is the collective name given to the leading *neo-Nicene* theologians of Cappadocia who took on the direction of the Nicene movement after the death of *Athanasius of Alexandria*, several of whom were involved with the vindication of the Nicene cause at the *Council of Constantinople* (381). The leaders among them were wealthy rhetoricians, generally supportive of, and patronized by, *Meletius of Antioch*. They were all related either by family ties or close kin bonds, and are frequently called the "three Cappadocians" (the two Gregories and Basil), but are really a larger number including *Basil of Caesarea*, his sister *Macrina*, and his brothers *Gregory of Nyssa* and Peter of Sebaste, together with *Gregory of Nazianzus* and his cousin Amphilocius of Iconium. Basil and his family (perhaps not Macrina) moved from the **Homoiousian** position to the full confession of the **Homoousian** position, and acted as mediators to assist many other Syrians to come to harmony with the Alexandrian and Western Nicene party. Gregory of Nazianzus was more passionately an advocate of the *homoousion* of the **Logos** and of the **Spirit of God,** and his work laid down the major architecture of the neo-Nicene Christology and **Trinitarian** doctrine of later orthodoxy.

J. A. McGuckin, *St. Gregory of Nazianzus: An Intellectual Biography* (New York, 2001); A. Meredith, *The Cappadocians* (New York, 1995); idem, *Gregory of Nyssa* (London, 1999); P. Rousseau, *Basil of Caesarea* (Berkeley, Calif., 1994).

Cassia (c. 805–867) Cassia was an aristocratic Byzantine lady who founded a convent in **Constantinople** and entered it as its leader. She is the most famous of Byzantine women poets, composing her hymns and ethical verse instructions for her community's use in prayer. Letters exist from the great ninth-century saint, Theodore the Studite, which are addressed to his supporter Cassia the nun, and if this is the same as the poet, then she must have been active at a very high level in the **iconoclastic** controversy as a defender of the icons, and as a monastic reformer. Her most famous piece is the hymn on the repentant woman entitled "To the Harlot." It is a dramatic identification with the sinful woman who weeps over the death of Jesus as she brings myrrh. It has become an enduring part of Orthodox Lenten liturgy.

C. Trypanis, *The Penguin Book of Greek Verse* (London, 1971), 435.

Cassian   *see* **John Cassian**

Catacombs The *burial* places outside the city walls of ancient *Rome* (an area of soft tufa earth that was specially good for digging out burial niches) were originally referred to as being "by the hollows" (Latin: *ad catacumbas*), whence derived the name. The term first referred, probably, to the "hollow" of the quarry that was adjacent to the Catacomb of San Sebastiano, but by the third century it had become a generic description of any subterranean Christian cemetery (*see death*). The Roman Christians used catacombs from at least the second century, and began to construct their own subterranean chambers in the early third century. Then the catacombs soon received many of the bodies of the great martyrs and *saints* of the Roman church, thus becoming places of the veneration of saints, and the site of the celebration of the "meals of commemoration" (*refrigeria*). From this they have often been regarded as places of *prayer* and meeting of the Roman church during times of *persecution*. The popular image of the church hiding here to avoid the persecutors is an inaccurate one, but undoubtedly the cultic use of some of the grave chambers of the martyrs led to the catacombs being among the first places where Christian religious *art* has survived. Images of Christ and the apostles found here are among the earliest known iconic depictions, and themes of prayer (a woman with upraised hands—the "Orant") life and *paradise* (bucolic images, peacocks, and rivers) are also common, as are some of the earliest biblical depictions. The oldest of the catacombs is that which **Callistus** was appointed to administer when he was a *deacon* of Rome (later pope). It is the second level of the present San Callisto Catacomb in Rome. In this area (area 1 of level 2) is a plot that seems to date back to Roman Christianity of the second century (when it must have been owned by pagan administrators, but already Christians were using it as a collective grave site for their own purposes). Here can also be found the "Crypt of the Popes," which once housed the remains of several famous third-century popes.

Adjacent *cubicula* (the larger hollowed-out mausolea chambers, which denote important burials) of great significance are those of Pope Cornelius (d. 253) and the Crypt of Lucina, which contain important fresco illustrations. The extensive commitment of the Roman church authorities to the creation and extension of the catacombs manifests a profound concern for the sacred dignity of the body, expected to be caught up in the *resurrection* on the last day. It was a service the church offered to all its members, not simply the wealthy.

———

V. Nicolai, F. Bisconti, and D. Mazzoleni, *The Christian Catacombs of Rome: History, Decoration, Inscriptions* (Regensburg, Germany, 1999).

Catechumen   Catechumen is a term denoting a candidate for *baptism* who was in the process of receiving instructions for his or her initiation. That process, once inaugurated, could last as long as three years (*Apostolic Tradition* 17). But many Christians from the third to sixth centuries preferred to spend most of their lives as catechumens and receive baptism nearer death; this despite protests from such preachers as the *Cappadocian Fathers, John Chrysostom*, and *Augustine*. In the earliest period of the Syrian church, celibacy was often required of baptismal candidates, which also served as a strong force to restrict baptism there until the advance of old age. Infants seem to have been commonly enrolled as catechumens within fourth-century Christian families. The issue of a lifelong catechumenate passed away gradually, especially after the Byzantine emperor *Justinian* applied legal pressure in the sixth century to have infants baptized as a matter of course. Catechumens were admitted (by the rite of signing a *cross* on their head) if they passed scrutiny by the enquiring *presbyters* as to the circumstances of their motives, and their life situations (people living with concubines,

for example, were debarred, and so too were actresses, sellers of charms, gladiators, and some other professions). They were assigned a place within the body of the church so as to hear the liturgy up to the reading of the Scriptures; then they were dismissed by the deacons (a dismissal still extant in the Orthodox liturgies), and not allowed to witness the eucharistic mysteries until the night of their baptism. The group of catechumens who were in the final stages of preparation (during the Lent immediately preceding their initiation) were designated the "enlightened ones" (*photizomenoi*). Important examples of the material used by the early *bishops* to educate them can be seen in *Gregory of Nazianzus, Orations* 38–40, *Gregory of Nyssa's* Catechetical Oration (addressed to catechists to instruct them on how to teach), *Cyril of Jerusalem's* Catechetical Lectures, and *Augustine's* Catechizing the Uninstructed.

———

M. Dujarier, *A History of the Catechumenate: The First Six Centuries* (New York, 1979); R. M. Grant, "Development of the Catechumenate," in *Made Not Born: New Perspectives on Christian Initiation and the Catechumenate* (Notre Dame, Ind., 1976), 32–49.

Catholic   The word originally meant universal or holistic (*katholike, kath'olon*). In the late first or early second century it was used by *Ignatius of Antioch* (*To the Smyrnaeans* 8.2), who said: "Where Jesus is present there is the catholic Church." It is also found in *Polycarp* (*Martyrdom of Polycarp* 8.1; 16.2; 19.2), where it also connotes the *church* as a universally coherent mystery, the society of believers bonded together in the harmony of common allegiance to *apostolic* truth. *Clement of Alexandria* is the first to try to define the notion technically in this sense, though in a more overtly apologetic context. He says: "It is evident that these heresies, as well as those that are even more recent, are spurious innovations on the oldest and truest church. . . . Thus we say that the ancient and catholic church stands alone in essence, and idea, and principle, and pre-eminence." (*Stromata* 7.17.107). *Cyril of Jerusalem*, in the fourth century, gave one of the classic definitions when he wrote: "The Church is called catholic because it is spread through all the world; and also because it teaches universally and completely all the doctrines that we ought to know concerning things visible and invisible, heavenly and earthly; and also because it introduces all humanity to right worship, whether they are rulers or ruled, learned or unlearned; and finally because it universally treats and heals all manner of sins committed by soul and body, possessing within itself every conceivable virtue, whether in actions, or words, or spiritual gifts of every kind" (*Catechetical Oration* 18.22). The patristic use of "catholic," therefore, fundamentally signified the agreement of the church in faith and practice, as opposed to heretical or schismatic sectarianism, but also expanded to evoke the mystical concept of the "mystery of the church" as the communion of Jesus, the initiation of the kingdom of God on earth. As Cyril noted, the idea of effective reconciliation was a key constituent mark of catholicity. *Augustine*, in his argument with the rigorist *Donatists*, who claimed that they alone were the authentic and pure church, used the idea of catholicity to contrast the spiritually narrow and locally provincial character of Donatism, in comparison to the broad international communion of the truly "catholic" churches that professed an inclusive doctrine of forgiveness. In the West, after the seventh century, the idea of catholicity increasingly came to be referred to the test issue of communion with the supreme Western "apostolic see" of *Rome* (*see* *papacy*), and this eventually developed the word into a more narrow sense of those Christians in communion with the bishop of Rome (in this way it has been exclusively used by Latin Catholics after the Reformation). The

Eastern Christian world of the medieval period similarly began to prefer the concept of catholicity as Orthodoxy, and those terms, Orthodox and Catholic, now commonly describe adherents of churches. The original sense of catholicity, however, remains in the use of the notion to define one of the four "marks" of the church (one, holy, catholic, and apostolic), which were used as reference points to articulate the sense of communion in shared, universally valid perceptions of the Christian faith. Catholicity in patristic usage, therefore, is very closely associated to the idea of *apostolicity*.

P. M. Brek, "De vocis catholica: origine et notione," *Antonianum* 38 (1963): 263–87; J. N. D. Kelly, "Catholique et Apostolique aux premiers siècles," *Istina* 14 (1969): 33–45; R. P. Moroziuk, "The Meaning of *Katholikos* in the Greek Fathers, and Its Implications for Ecclesiology and Ecumenism," PBR 4 (1985): 90–104; idem, "Some Thoughts on the Meaning of *Katholike* in the Eighteenth Catechetical Lecture of Cyril of Jerusalem," SP 18 (vol. 1) (1985): 169–78.

Celibacy   Christian celibacy signifies the voluntary acceptance of a single life of chastity in order to dedicate time and energy to the demands of discipleship and Christian virtue (as based on Paul's dicta in 1 Cor. 7:25–28, 32–35). Celibacy was one of the central factors of the developing *ascetical* (monastic) movements in Christianity, and many fourth- and fifth-century patristic writers, such as *Athanasius, Gregory of Nazianzus, John Chrysostom, Jerome,* and *Augustine*, gave the single "virginal" life high praise, as the condition most conducive to the development of spiritual capacities. Athanasius in the *De incarnatione* spoke of *virginity* as a preeminent sign of the power of the *resurrection*, and Gregory of Nazianzus described it as a charism that reversed the natural order (comparing it to the fountains of *Constantinople* where water was made to run upwards), both writers thereby signifying that celibacy was primarily an *eschatological* witness in the life of the *church*. Jerome was so effusive in his praise of virginity that he regarded *marriage* as only good for one thing, the production of more potential virgins in the ascetical life. His views caused a furor in the church of *Rome* in his own day among the married aristocrats, which was partly responsible for him leaving the capital to settle in Palestine. *Pope Gregory I* was the writer who most influenced later Western theory, in defining the celibate "contemplative" life as the highest state a Christian could aspire to. This essentially monastic view was responsible for the long disparagement (despite many protests to the contrary) of marriage and *family* love in later Christian theology. The election of the single chaste life was regularly referred to the ascetical examples of Elijah, John the Baptist, and several of the other disciples of Jesus (especially John the apostle) who were given the command to abandon all for the sake of the kingdom, including wives and children (Matt. 19:27–29), and recommended to become "as eunuchs," again for the kingdom's sake (Matt. 19:12). The supreme example of celibate dedication, of course, was taken to be Jesus himself, universally understood to be the virginal son of a virgin. From New Testament times certain Christian women dedicated themselves as lifelong *virgins* in the service of Christ, following a retired life at home, specially dedicated to *prayer*. In the second-century churches, especially in Syria, the virgins began to evolve as a separate order, and were recognizable by the veils they wore standing together during church services. The order of *widows* (originally begun as a church assistance to widowed believers) also soon developed into a corporate body of those who dedicated themselves to prayer and celibacy after bereavement. By the fourth century both orders had more or less merged into the greater stream of monasticism, which from its earliest manifestations always represented both male and female partisans. Even though the adoption of celibacy was recognized to be a deeply personal and spiritual choice, it soon became the subject of church legislation. A movement at the *Council of Nicaea I* to demand celibacy of all the *clergy* was rejected, a decision that had determinative effect on Eastern canon law ever afterwards. Monasticism had at first been a flight from the city and the city churches, but by the end of the fourth century it had become so successful that it more or less subverted and co-opted the episcopacy, and after the fifth century bishops were almost universally monastic. Continuing pressure to make the other clergy (*priests*, *deacons*, and *subdeacons*) also celibate continued on and off until the Council in Troullo at Constantinople in 692 made the final decision for the Eastern church (Canon 13) that all bishops had to be celibate but priests and deacons could marry before *ordination*, although they were not allowed to marry afterwards. In the West the demand for the clergy to be celibate was more insistent, and was nurtured internationally by continuing pressure from the *papacy*. The Spanish Council of Elvira in 306 adopted Canon 33 to admit this position into formal church law: requiring higher clergy who had married before ordination henceforth to live as brother and sister with their wives. And in 386 Pope Siricius issued a decretal demanding celibacy of "priests and Levites" (priests and deacons) suggesting that it was already taken for granted that bishops should be celibates. This papal decretal had a limited effect but signaled that Rome would set a standard of clerical celibacy for other Western churches to follow. Pope Innocent I (402–417) repeated Siricius's demands, and comparable canons were introduced into the church of *North Africa*. It was not until the Lateran Council of 1139 (Canon 7) that celibacy was universally required of all Western clergy, a position that has applied to the present day in the Western Roman Catholic Church.

R. Cholij, *Clerical Celibacy in East and West* (Leominster, Mass., 1988); R. Gryson, *Les origines du célibat écclésiastique* (Gembloux, Belgium, 1970); H. C. Lea, *A History of Sacerdotal Celibacy in the Christian Church* (2 vols.; London, 1907); J. T. Lienhard, *Ministry* (Wilmington, Del., 1984).

Celsus (late second century)   Celsus was an important philosophical opponent of the Christian movement. His attack, published as *The True Word*, is the earliest considered set of objections to the church's theology. He was a Middle *Platonist* philosopher who studied the Hebrew Scriptures and (at least) the Gospels of Matthew and Luke. He was largely ignored by contemporary Christians but a century later his work was still regarded as so potent that *Origen* felt it necessary to compose a refutation, from which we derive our knowledge of his claims. Celsus, a prime example of the Hellenistic ascendant class, knew a variety of Christian factions such as *gnostics* and *Marcionites*, and generally regarded the Christian stories as feeble tales for the credulity of women and slaves. His constant exegetical notes turn on the idea that very little actually seems to have been fulfilled by the life of Jesus. This apologia served as a stimulus for much of Origen's reflections both in his book *Against Celsus* and in his more general exegetical theology.

M. Borret, "Celsus: A Pagan Perspective on Scripture," in P. Blowers, ed., *The Bible in Greek Christian Antiquity* (Notre Dame, 1997), 259–88; H. Chadwick, *Origen: Contra Celsum* (Cambridge, 1980); R. L. Wilken, *The Christians As the Romans Saw Them* (New Haven, Conn., 1984), 94–125.

Chiliasm (millenarianism, millennialism)   The doctrine of chiliasm was found in a variety of forms in some of the theologians of the first three centuries (it had a brief revival in the millenarianism of *Lactantius* in the fourth century but was very rare by that stage). It states that God would give to his saints a period of paradisiacal prosperity on earth before the final consummation of all things. The final state of earthly paradise would be the last age (of world history). The Greek term *chilias* (Latin: *mille*) denotes the thousand years that would symbolically represent this. The idea is found in a number of Jewish *apocalyptic* works, from which it probably came to the attention of Christian apocalyptic thinkers. In the church it is based on a close reading of Revelation 20:1–7, where Satan is held bound for a thousand years so that the suffering saints might have some respite, while the martyrs rise again to enjoy Christ's glory in *heaven*. All of this precedes the final *eschatological* battle (Rev. 20:7–10) that results in Satan's final defeat, the Last *Judgment*, and the making of a "new heaven and earth" (Rev. 20:2f.; 21:1f.). Christian millenarianism seems to have had its home in Asia Minor, from where the book of Revelation itself derived. It is not noticeable in the surviving oracles of *Montanism* although the whole movement was highly apocalyptic, but it can be traced in several other Asian authors. *Papias of Hierapolis* in Phrygia was an early—second-century chiliast who (in now-lost works) described the glorious time of the millennial paradise (cf. Irenaeus, *Adversus haereses* 5.33.3). *Irenaeus* says that this view was shared among the followers of the apostle John at Ephesus. On the basis of this authority Irenaeus himself (c. 185) was ready to accept the "hope" that the earthly restoration of Israel may not simply be an allegory (*Adversus haereses* 5.35), and he sees the purpose of the earthly paradise as part of the *apokatastasis*, God's bringing the creation back to a fulfilment of its initial design (*Adversus haereses* 5.32.1). At the same period as Papias (c. 100), the Asian theologian Cerinthus, perhaps one of the early *gnostics*, also seems to have been a millenarian (cf. Eusebius, *Ecclesiastical History* 3.28). Some theologians of the early church of *Alexandria* rejected the book of Revelation from the canon on the grounds that it had been written by Cerinthus, who used it to advocate his views on the millennial paradise (Eusebius, *Ecclesiastical History* 7.25). At the beginning of the third century, **Hippolytus** of Rome speaks about the end of the world as imminent, and relates the time of the end to a period five hundred years after the birth of Christ, which will also be the end of the sixth millennium of world history. After this, Hippolytus argues, there will come the sabbatical (seventh) millennium of rest, which has been promised in the book of Revelation (Hippolytus, *Commentary on the Book of Daniel* 4.23; 4.10). *Origen of Alexandria*, his younger contemporary, was a forceful voice who then put a stop to much millennial expectation, denouncing it as materialistically minded, and as a "Judaizing error" (Origen, *First Principles* 2.112; *Commentary on Matthew* 17.35). Origen's word carried great weight after him, and really set a term for millennial hopes in the early church. His own vision of the "rest of the saints" was one of spiritual transfiguration, not earthly beatitude. Methodius of Olympus, again a theologian of Asia Minor, was one of the last who publicly disagreed. He attacked Origen's overly spiritual view of the resurrection of the body, and added in to his apologia a revival of the old belief that the paradise to which the resurrected fleshly bodies of the saints will be directed is "a chosen spot upon this earth" (Methodius, *On the Resurrection* 1.55.1). In another book imitating Plato's *Symposium* (Methodius, *Banquet* 9.5), the earthly paradise is again connected with a millennial time of rest in the company of Christ on earth, before a final transfiguration into spiritual glory. The Latin *Commentary on the Book of Revelation* by Victorinus of Pettau, again from the beginning of the fourth century, also shows slight signs of millenarianism. Lactantius, writing at the same period, has extensive theories about millennial cycles in the seventh book of his *Divine Institutes*. His sources were a com-

bination of Virgil's *Fourth Eclogue*, the *Sibylline Oracles*, Hermetic wisdom literature, and the book of Revelation. His was one of the last instances of the appearance of millenarianism in the patristic period. After the fourth century it was progressively dismissed as a "Judaistic" archaism. *Eusebius of Caesarea* added his own comment on the ancient movement and opined that it was a sign of "smallness of intelligence" (*Ecclesiastical History* 3.39.13; 7.24.1). *Augustine's* eventual disapproval (*De civitate Dei* 20.7f.) more or less finished any hope it had for a later Western revival (where the book of Revelation was always favored far more than in the Greek world).

B. E. Daley, *The Hope of the Early Church: Eschatology in the Patristic Age* (New York, 1991); L. Gry, *Le Millénarisme dans ses origines et son développement* (Paris, 1904).

Chorepiskopoi   *Chorepiskopoi* is a Greek term for "village bishop," someone who had responsibility for the sparsely populated country areas (*chora*). It was an order of the *clergy* that could be seen in the East between the third and fifth centuries. By the eighth century, although the term is sometimes still used, it mainly refers to senior *priests* who act as episcopal vicars in remote areas. *Chorepiskopoi* are first mentioned in *Canon* 13 of the Council of Ancyra (314) and no less than fifteen were present at the *Council of Nicaea I* (325) who signed in their own right (though at the *Council of Chalcedon* in 451 they signed in the name of their superior bishops). It is presumed that they were originally bishops in the full sense, though in poor and obscure sees, but in the fourth century canons were passed at successive councils to restrict their role and rights, so as to bring them under the authority of the bishops of the nearest large cities. The Council of Ancyra (314) forbade them to ordain the three higher ranks of clergy, but allowed them to ordain the lower ranks (also Canon 10 of the Council of Antioch in 341). The Council of Sardica in 343 appealed for no bishop to be appointed to small country villages, so as "not to bring the title of bishop into disrepute." In the later fourth century the Council of Laodicea (c. 365) ordered the office to be discontinued, though it ran on for several more generations. In the Western church the *chorepiskopoi* were prominent chiefly among the Franks as missionary bishop-assistants. The concept of *chorepiscopus* was eventually mutated in the West into the idea of co-adjutor, assistant bishop. This, together with the reduction of the chorepiscopal rights in the fourth-century Greek church, was an erosion of the early *catholic* principle (first advocated by *Ignatius of Antioch*) of the *bishop* as the icon of Christ in a fully complete and perfected local church (whatever the size). It was one of the casualties of ecclesiology coming into collision with the Roman imperial system of ordering the political definition of a diocese.

H. Bergère, *Étude historique sur les chorévèques* (Ph.D. diss., Paris, 1905); F. Gillmann, *Das Institut der Chorbischofe in Orient* (Munich, 1903).

Chrism

The word (derived from the Greek *chrio*, to anoint) is most commonly used in the West to designate the holy oil made up from a synthesis of olive oil, balsam, and (at least in the Eastern church) fragrant perfumes. In the Greek church the term used is *myron*. The use of chrism in baptismal rites is attested from the time of *Tertullian*, and most of the liturgical commentators of the fourth century refer to it (*Cyril of Jerusalem, Theodoret, Ambrose*), symbolically linking it to the ritual of the anointment of *priests* and kings in the Old Testament as fulfilled in the royal priesthood conveyed by the *Holy Spirit* on illumined believers. In the Orthodox and Catholic churches it is used to anoint the newly *baptized* person, to convey the "seal of

the spirit." Orthodoxy also uses chrism to receive back lapsed Christians or Christians validly baptized in other communions who are entering the Orthodox church as adult converts. In the Western Catholic churches it is used for the same symbolic purpose at confirmation. In both East and West chrism is used for the consecration of churches and altars, or the anointing of Christian monarchs. In the West only it is applied at the ordination of priests (the anointing of hands). In the Western churches all diocesan bishops have the right to consecrate chrism (fourth century, second Council of Carthage, Canon 3). It is done usually on Maundy Thursday morning Mass. In the Orthodox Church the right to consecrate *myron* is reserved for patriarchs or heads of autocephalous churches. Each parish priest in Eastern Christianity preserves the chrism in a reserved place in the altar, or sanctuary, of the church. In the West, the chrism is usually kept in a safe depository in the sacristy.

M. Dudley and G. Rowell, eds., *The Oil of Gladness: Anointing in the Christian Tradition* (London, 1993); L. L. Mitchell, *Baptismal Anointing* (Alcuin Club Collection 48; London, 1966).

Christology

This modern term refers collectively to the study of the church's beliefs and teachings about the *person* and work of Christ. The study of the effects of Christ's redemption is more precisely described as soteriology (the doctrine of salvation), but modern studies of patristics have predominantly been concerned with both things, and rightly so, as the ancients never distinguished them, arguing in all forms of *patristic* Christology that the whole appearance of Jesus on earth was itself the divine plan of salvation for the human race. The key to all patristic thought on the issue and its inner dynamic, therefore, is that Christ himself is salvation *incarnate*.

Christology in the New Testament is remarkably fluid and poetically open-ended. It is advanced by a series of graphic images and analogies more than by systematic reflection. The images are represented in the numerous christological "titles" that are represented there, namely: Teacher (Mark 1:27), Prophet (Matt. 21:11), Son of David (Matt. 9:27), Messiah (Matt. 16:16), Servant of God (Matt. 12:17–18), Shepherd of Israel (Matt. 2:6), Beloved Son of God (Matt. 3:17), Apocalyptic Angel of Judgment (Matt. 8:29), Son of Man (Matt. 12:8), Lord (Matt. 14:30), Light of the World (John 1:9), Lamb of God (John 1:36), Exalted Serpent (John 3:13–14), Water-Bringer (John 4:10–14; 7:37–38), Bread of Life (John 6:35), Holy One of God (John 6:69), the One Who Is (John 8:58), Good Shepherd (John 10:2, 10), Gate of the Sheepfold (John 10:7), the Resurrection (John 11:25), the Way the Truth and the Life (John 14:6), the True Vine (John 15:1.), World Conqueror (John 16:33), King of Another World (John 18:36), Icon of God (Col. 1:15), Head of the Church (Col. 1:18), the Beginning (Col. 1:18), the New Adam (Rom. 5:12f.), High Priest (Heb. 5:1–10), Agent of Creation (Col. 1:15–17). This lists only some of the abundant range of christological acclamations, which clearly have not only a dogmatic intent but, more to the point, spring from a doxological, or confessional, motive. Christology in its inception is the church's confession and acclamation of Jesus as God's unique agent of salvation. It is the prayer of faith, before it is systematic teaching. The scriptural christological vision accumulates this variety of approaches to describe the once-for-all event of the restoration of the covenant of mercy through the teachings, death, and resurrection of the Master. However varied the approaches may be, this soteriological kerygma gives a coherent harmony to the whole scriptural proclamation of Jesus as Savior. In the earliest writings of the patristic era, typified in the Clementine literature for example, or the *Apos-*

tolic Fathers, it is mainly the continuance of the biblical terminology that directs thought and writing about Jesus, though with a progressive loss of titles, a narrowing of the range of acclamations used, so as to focus on the highest of them (Messiah, Lord, Son of God, Divine Agent of Creation). The use of Old Testament *typologies* also begins to be increasingly used (already present within the New Testament itself) to further embroider the sense of Jesus as the promised fulfillment of Israel's hopes (as can be seen, for example, in *Melito of Sardis's Treatise on Pascha*). In the *Apologists* of the second century a new dynamic can be seen to be operative, one that sets out to explain to the Hellenistic world, in language it would recognize, that this Jesus is no mere localized rabbinic teacher, but rather the central axis of world salvation. Philosopher-rhetoricians such as *Justin, Theophilus,* and *Tertullian* (it is to be taken to a pitch in the later theologians *Hippolytus, Clement of Alexandria,* and *Origen*) preached Jesus as the revelation of the divine Logos, the source and rationale of all inner harmony and meaning in the cosmos, the same who had now come in a particular historical incarnation to teach and gather together the elect "wise" of the world. As *Logos theology* took shape from its early and embryonic form in the Fourth Gospel, a whole nexus of related ideas would flow from it, and after the third century it would be the dominant voice of patristic Christology. But in the second and third centuries there were still a variety of other approaches being pursued. Some Jewish Christian groups (known later as the *Ebionites*) clung to the view that Jesus was a human rabbinic teacher whom God had exalted in the manner of a great prophet. These were not simply seen as alien to the profound sense of the second-century church that Jesus was a divine figure, but are already out of harmony with most of the New Testament writings, whose confessions and hymns demonstrate a very different sense already (see Phil. 2:6–11, a hymn already old when Paul quoted it). Some Hellenistic groups, by way of contrast, adopting the premise that the material world was utterly alien and opposite to divinity, saw Jesus as a spiritual epiphany of God, not a man at all. They have collectively been known as Docetists, from the Greek for "seemed to be human." The *docetic* christological imperative produced several apocryphal works in the second and third centuries that suggested Jesus' body was only an appearance. He was like a Greek god temporarily manifesting himself on earth in a phantasmagorical apparition. Other teachers, and they seem to have been more in the manner of individual speculative thinkers, such as *Paul of Samosata*, wondered whether Jesus had been an ordinary man who one day (usually the baptism of Christ is the moment chosen) was seized by God so profoundly that thereafter his life was taken over by the indwelling *Spirit of God*. Jesus was thus the Son of God in the sense that he contained the divine Spirit. As the Spirit "descended" on Jesus, so he was "exalted." The position has been called, in modern times, *Monarchianism*, because it was largely intended to preserve the full Christian stress on monotheism. If Jesus was God, he was not a second God, only God in the sense that the single divinity (the Father-Spirit) had elected him as his new manifestation (the Son was the Father). This view particularly clashed with the Logos theology, which placed all its emphasis on the idea of the divine Logos coming down into its own fleshly vehicle (not the exaltation of man into union with God), and also stressed the *hypostatic* distinctness of the divine Logos from the divine Father and Spirit. Modern commentators have often described these two early and archetypal movements of thought as "Christology from below" (Monarchianism in the manner of Paul of Samosata) and "Christology from above" (Logos theology in the manner of Hippolytus or Origen). But

while the terms may be helpful for a crude overview, they are ultimately anachronistic and have too often been overapplied, not recognizing how the various schemes of ascent and descent are already intimately paired (as for example in the Fourth Gospel). After the work of Hippolytus and Origen in the mid–third century, Logos theology was set to sweep the board in terms of all subsequent patristic Christology. It soon became the matrix of all reflection. The choice to emphasize the hypostatic distinctness of the persons in the deity (Father, Son-Logos, and Spirit-Paraclete) ensured that christological and *Trinitarian* thought would dominate the agenda of the Christian theologians for the next two centuries. The fourth and fifth centuries are overwhelmed by synodical attempts to clarify a christological settlement that could be accepted across all the communions. That story can be better told by studying the lives and works of some of the main contributors to the debate (*see Athanasius of Alexandria, Gregory of Nazianzus, Arianism, Apollinaris of Laodicea, Eusebius of Caesarea, Eusebius of Nicomedia, Diodore of Tarsus, Theodore of Mopsuestia, Nestorius, Cyril of Alexandria, Proclus, Eutyches of Constantinople, Leo the Great, Dioscorus of Alexandria*) and the chief councils at which a formal christological settlement was negotiated (*Nicaea I* [325], *Ephesus* [431], *Constantinople I* [381], *Chalcedon* [451], *Constantinople II* [553]). It may suffice here to give only the briefest of sketches.

At Nicaea the issue of the divinity of Christ, the incarnate Logos, had been affirmed, and more or less took hold as a major schema, despite long-running battles over the precise details. At the end of the century the Western bishops, with a party of determined Nicene theologians (Athanasius and the Cappadocians), had set as a basis for catholic consensus that the divine Logos was personally incarnate in the Christ, and was consubstantial (*homoousios*) with God (God of God and Light of Light). The issue of what this meant in terms of the incarnation was laid aside for the moment, as attention was chiefly focused on the way it affected Trinitarian relations, but as the fourth-century debates raged on, some of the problems inherent in ascribing the divine subject of the Logos to the human incarnation (Jesus or Christ) became increasingly apparent. How could a divine consciousness direct the human life of Jesus, for example? Could Jesus be ignorant of things if his mind was divine? If he had absolute knowledge of everything how could he be human in any meaningful way? Thinkers such as *Apollinaris of Laodicea* tried to resolve the problem by arguing that the divine mind (Logos) dispensed with a human mind and soul when it incarnated in Jesus. What need of the lesser when the greater supplied for it? So, using divine power the infinite reason of the Logos expressed itself, as and when appropriate, in the limited reasonings suitable to a first-century rabbinic teacher, allowing Jesus to sound like a man of his time. The idea, though ingenious, was not popular with anyone, as it was far too reminiscent of a revival of *Docetism*. Syrian thinkers in the fourth century (*Diodore* and his followers) made a robust attack on this Christology and argued that there were two person-centers in the Christ, namely the human soul and mind of Jesus, and the divine Logos. These two "personas" (not the same as "person" in the modern sense) were combined in a mutual harmony at the incarnation. The Son of Man was adopted by the Son of God, and acted in union as the Christ, the persona of christological union (the principle of how they came together). On the basis of the Syrian theory one could have no difficulty in seeing in Jesus a full and complete range of human psychic and intellectual responses (he did not know many things and he had human feelings and sufferings, for example), and also witnessing in Christ (for Jesus' human life was not the whole story) signs of the divine presence of the Logos. To the opponents of this school, the regular use

of the phrase "Two Sons" suggested too much of a dichotomous split. If there was a divine Son alongside a human Son, was it not blasphemous to worship Jesus (or call him Lord and God) since he was, at the end of the day, no more than "human"? At worst, it was feared, here was a reversion to the exaltation christologies (a man lifted up into association with the deity) of Paul of Samosata.

The full range of issues of the personal subjectivity of Christ came to a grand climactic moment in the early fifth century when two robustly stubborn exponents of the Alexandrian and Syrian approaches clashed head-on (Cyril of Alexandria and Nestorius). The resultant christological crisis was advanced through four important synodical meetings (the Councils of Ephesus [431], Ephesus [449], Chalcedon [451], and Constantinople II [553]). As a result, Syrian ideas were profoundly sidelined and the Alexandrian system of the divine Logos personally incarnate in Jesus carried the day. Jesus' consciousness was none other than that of the Word. The niceties of the reciprocity between the human and divine characteristics of Jesus' life were explained by a sophisticated and carefully guarded set of language formularies, and can be summed up in the doctrine of the hypostatic union and that of the *communion of properties*. Christ is possessed of two natures (human and divine), each perfect in its own regard, but united in a single divine hypostasis, which energizes and allows each nature to fulfill its appropriate functions. Each nature, though distinct, is so bonded by the single hypostasis, which realizes both simultaneously, that terms appropriate to each nature can legitimately be "crossed over" as applying, ultimately, to the selfsame hypostasis (or person). So traditional language such as the sufferings of God, or the *Virgin Mary* as the Mother of God (*Theotokos*), can be allowed and encouraged.

The detailed and complicated christological statements of the synods of the fourth and fifth centuries have often been dismissed by many modern commentators as scholasticism gone mad, but the synods were merely the dense synopses of larger christological arguments that were advanced in some of the most important patristic writing of that time, by leading theologians intent on being traditional in the most intelligent sense. These larger treatises, such as the christological writings of Cyril of Alexandria, for example, show clearly and without question that the motive for the christological niceties was always a profoundly strong doxological drive: the desire to confess Christ as the divine Savior who had humbled himself to share in the full reality of human life, motivated to such by pure compassion and philanthropy. Reading the wider context, rather than the synodical extracts (which are normally all that is presented in modern textbooks) one can still recognize in patristic Christology of the fourth and fifth centuries a legitimate and worthy heir to the religious spirit of the New Testament. Even most of the technical terms introduced in this period have biblical motivations and foundations when closely scrutinized. In the succeeding centuries, as christological controversy died away in the light of the imperial enforcement of the great synods, and as dissidents (such as the Syrians and Copts) were cut off from the main centers of the Byzantine and Latin worlds, patristic thought on the person and work of Christ developed a far more mystical and spiritual turn, such that can be witnessed in the writings of Pseudo-*Dionysius* and *Maximus Confessor*. The final stage of classical patristic Christology can be seen in the eighth-century synthesis of the synodical solutions as presented in *John of Damascus's* On the Orthodox Faith. The great achievement of patristic christological theory entered into the bloodstream of the church not merely in the dogmatic tradition, but simultaneously also through the formation of the classical liturgies that were reaching definitive stage at this same period, and in the spiritual monastic writings that were accumulating to give voice to the church's desire for mystical union with the Savior, more than merely exact knowledge about him.

R. H. Fuller, *The Foundations of New Testament Christology* (London, 1965); A. Grillmeier, *Christ in Christian Tradition* (vol. 1, 2d ed.; London, 1975); J. A. McGuckin, *St. Cyril of Alexandria and the Christological Controversy: Its History, Theology, and Texts* (Leiden, Netherlands, 1994); idem, *Cyril of Alexandria: On the Unity of Christ: That the Christ Is One* (New York, 1995); J. Meyendorff, *Christ in Eastern Christian Tradition* (Washington, D.C., 1969).

Chrysostom   *see* **John Chrysostom**

Church   The English term church (German *Kirche*) derives from the Greek *kyriakon*, which means "the Lord's belonging." The term has a primary significance in terms of a building, or sacred object, and the Anglo-Saxon concept of church invariably confuses the ideas of property and community, which were originally quite distinct in Christian thought. The ancient word for church as the society of believers was *ekklesia*, a term that denotes the "calling out" or election of a people. As such it is a profoundly important term in the New Testament writings used to signify the concept of the body of Christian believers as the newly constituted society of the covenant elect, the community of the new age, the mystical body of Christ. It was a word that had secular and biblical antecedents. It meant the assembly of citizens in a Hellenistic city (cf. Acts 19:39) and was the Septuagint word for the assembly (Hebrew: *qahal*) of the true Israel (cf. Deut. 23:3; Neh. 13:1; Acts 7:38). The word is rarely found in the Gospels or Acts (Matt. 16:18; 18:17; Acts 5:11) but is significantly used in the Pauline literature, which suggests it was a concept introduced by the Hellenist Christians to designate both the local community of believers (Gal. 1:2; 1 Thess. 1:1) and the idea of the world-wide fellowship of Christians (1 Cor. 12:28). Christian thinkers have often speculated on when the church was founded (at the calling of the disciples, at the institution of the *Eucharist*, at the *cross*, or at Pentecost), but the incipient signs of an organized community (albeit an *apocalyptic* one) are witnessed in Jesus' selection of twelve apostles to represent the missionaries to, and judges of, the twelve tribes of a new Israel (Matt. 10:1–16; 19:28). The Fourth Gospel sets the birth of the church as a mystery that can only unfold as a result of the saving death of Jesus (John 12:20–23), after he has breathed out his Spirit (John 19:30; 20:22–23). The earliest patristic reflection on the nature of the church is fragmentary, and little is known precisely about the institutional organization of church life in the first century. In the second-century literature the Pauline imagery of the church as the bride, the mystical body, or the temple of Christ comes to the fore (cf. *2 Clement* 14), and is joined with a newly developing sense of self-identity among the early Christians, something that probably developed apace as the conflict with the synagogue did not resolve, but became a deepening and permanent schism as more and more Gentile Christians entered the movement (*see Judaism*). *First Clement* is an important continuation of the Pauline sense of the regulation of "house churches" that have grown into something bigger. It gives a picture of ecclesiology and organization at *Rome* and Corinth in the early second century. Here the emphasis is on harmony and collegiality in the congregation of saints. The ministers should be obeyed, not overthrown (*1 Clement* 1). The church is the assembly of the elect, sanctified by God's will through the mediation of Jesus Christ (*1 Clement* 42). In the prologue of the *Martyrdom of Polycarp* (c. 156) an equally strong sense of a community at once manifested on earth in stability, and yet belonging to another order altogether, is manifested in the

words: "From the Church of God dwelling as a pilgrim at Smyrna, to the Church of God dwelling as a pilgrim at Philomelium, and to all the congregations of the holy and catholic church in every place." *Second Clement* already shows the signs of how greatly reflection on the church as a "mystery of salvation," much more than a sociological phenomenon, will predominate in patristic thought; as for example when he discusses the preexistence of *ekklesia*: "I know that you are not unaware that the Church is the Body of Christ. For scripture says: God made them male and female. Here the male is Christ, the female is the Church. Moreover, the sacred books and the apostles say that the Church is not of the present, but existed from the very beginning" (*2 Clement* 14). This teaching evoked the Hebraic sense that the Torah was eternal, but now reexpressed it to connote the church's apocalyptic reality. It preexisted in God's eternal plan, and in the mystical union it was destined to achieve in the *Logos*, who is its husband and Savior. In the work of the *Shepherd of Hermas*, written at Rome in the early second century, a similar idea of eschatological mystery is also prominent. Hermas has a vision of the church as an ancient woman: "Because she was created first of all, and for her sake the world was made" (Shepherd of Hermas Vision 11.4). *Origen* took up this idea of the preexistent church as the mystical society of those in communion with the Logos (*Commentary on the Canticle of Canticles* 11.8), and through him it would exercise a strong hold over Christian imagination afterwards, setting the tone for much later patristic ecclesiology (the concept of church) that managed to lift its head above the concrete problems of church unity. The *Apologists* mainly considered the church as the visible "community of salvation." In the Shepherd of Hermas one of the other visions (*Vision 3*) is the church as "an unfinished tower" to which stones were still being added, even though the time is nearing for the end. *Theophilus* describes the various churches as safe harbors where the shipwrecked can find safety (*To Autolycus* 2.14), and many of the other Apologists, such as the writer of the *Epistle to Diognetus*, *Aristides*, *Athenagoras*, *Minucius Felix*, *Tertullian*, and *Lactantius*, addressing an educated (and external) audience, liked nothing better than to point to the communities of Christians as ideal societies where morals and harmony reign supreme, as oases and beacons in a conflicted larger society. From the letters of *Ignatius* in the early second century to the glimpses *Justin* gives in his *First Apology*, it is clear that the system of liturgical assemblies and the ministers who govern them are important factors in the consolidation of an organized sense of the *ekklesia*. In Ignatius the dominant themes are the unity of the church as focused around the Eucharist and guaranteed by the unity the bishop brings to the assembly. As the second century ended the problem of church unity became more and more acute, and more concrete, and it is this idea that begins to dominate patristic ecclesiology through to the third century. *Irenaeus* found it remarkable that the church was a single community of mind and heart, however geographically disparate it might be. The unity of faith and practice was the "chief mark" of authenticity (*Adversus haereses* 1.10) and the root notion that explains how the idea of the "four marks" of the true church developed (one, holy, catholic, and apostolic). *Clement of Alexandria* and Origen took up the same idea of the mystery of unity as a mark of truth in their struggle with sectarian *gnostic* teachers. Following the lead of the Johannine Epistles they both defined the church as the united communion, from whose ranks sectarians declined, thereby losing any right to be called church. Clement put it in this way: "Clearly these older heresies, and others still more recent, are spurious innovations of the oldest and truest church. I think enough has been said to prove that unity is a characteristic mark of the true,

the really ancient Church" (*Stromata* 7.17.107). This gave birth to the powerful patristic conception that the church was one in the sense that it was indivisible. It could not be the case that a church could be divided and both sections still lay claim to the title. If a schism occurred, one group had de facto lost the right to be church. To decide which was church and which was the heretical or schismatic sect one had to look to the principles of tradition, apostolicity, and the general communion of other Christian authorities. In the mid–third century the *Novatian* dispute served to stimulate some extended thought on the issue of the church, and it is in this period that one finds the first systematic treatises dedicated to the theme. The presupposition had been, in simpler times, that one city would have one bishop, and that would largely guarantee the coherence of the Christian community. Now, as a result of disruptive *persecutions*, internal divisions in the community as to who was "worthy" to be admitted to the church severely split communities across the world. At Rome, in 252, the priest Novatian set himself up in opposition to Pope Cornelius, whom he denounced as a false bishop because of the latter's policy of reconciling those who had lapsed in the Decian persecution. Novatian shows how the idea of the church as the society of the pure elect was grating against the idea of the church as the community of the reconciled, a factor that would only be exacerbated after the fourth century when the church experienced an exponential surge in growth. Cornelius and his successor Stephen advocated for a church that was the earthly locus of the forgiveness of sins. The newly elected bishop in Carthage, *Cyprian*, was drawn into the dispute because his own church was conflicted in similar ways, with survivors of the persecution disputing his authority as bishop. Seeking advice from Rome, he asked Stephen (*Epistle* 72) if those who had received schismatic baptism among the Novatians ought to be rebaptized. It seemed logical to him that if they were a sect, they were not church, and could not dispense the sacraments of the church. Stephen advised that they ought not to be rebaptized, but Cyprian gathered support from other bishops to his standpoint, and composed one of the first dedicated treatises on ecclesiology (*The Unity of the Catholic Church*). Not surprisingly, its key theme is the necessity of unity. Cyprian's views were to enjoy great authority, but the dispute with Roman traditions had opened up a crack that revealed several problems in the notion of identifying who was in the church or out of it, especially when no matter of doctrine was involved (or even when it was, as in the case of the fourth-century *Arian* dispute that caused so much conflict). *Augustine*, in the early fifth century, would revisit Cyprian's unity issue again when he himself faced major troubles with the Donatist movement (who claimed that they were the true church and Augustine and the Catholics were invalid schismatics). In his anti-Donatist works (for example, the *Digest of a Dialogue with the Donatists*), Augustine turned the Latin tradition more expansively to the idea of the church as the community of reconciled sinners, not the domain of the pure. He exegeted the parable of the tares among the wheat to argue that God should be left to decide who was truly a Christian, since it was not obvious to human eyes. He thus gave an eirenic answer to many of the sectarian issues that have constantly dogged the heels of exclusivist ecclesiologies, but he did not really advance Cyprian's question as to how one recognized the schismatic who had ceased to be church from the authentic member of the church (an issue now at the very center of argument in the Donatist controversy). Augustine wanted to look to the larger scale of a nexus of ideas of traditional fidelity to *apostolic* doctrine, spaciousness in the conception of salvation, and communion with the wider Christian body on the international front. Yet he never resolved

the Donatist crisis, and in desperation he formulated his appeal to the emperor to suppress them forcibly, on the basis of the New Testament text: "Compel them to come in" (Luke 14:23, Vulgate). That was to sound a dark note for the medieval West after him. The fact of long-running schisms proved a thorn in the side of patristic theologians for several centuries, however, as their ideal vision of church as the harmonious society of peace was increasingly shaken by the reality of schism, national not merely local. In the West, after the fifth century, the *papacy* emerged more and more as the strong focus (both practical and theoretical) of church unity. Rome disseminated a principle of apostolic communion being guaranteed by the communion other sees had with their "apostolic see" (*see* Leo, *Epistle* 119), a theory that soon developed into the medieval doctrine of the papacy that underlies much Western Catholic ecclesiology. In the East, the cohesion needed for identifying the church was provided less by individual major sees than by the growing collation of synodical law supervised by the Byzantine emperor. Those who were not shown to be in harmony with apostolic authorities (increasingly including *patristic*) were synodically *anathematized* and excommunicated from the church. Where the secular power enforced the decision, it was a simple and clear process. Where such power did not extend (and increasingly that covered vast areas as Islam progressively diminished Byzantine rule), there was a major problem with this practical ecclesiology, and large areas such as the Christian communities of *Syria*, *North Africa*, *Armenia*, and *Ethiopia* fell away from the Byzantine communion, leaving the Eastern church with little practical idea how to go about effecting reconciliations.

G. Bardy, *La théologie de l'église de saint Clément de Rome à saint Irénée* (Unam Sanctam 13; Paris, 1945); idem, *La théologie de l'église de saint Irénée au concile de*

Nicée (Unam Sanctam 14; Paris, 1947); R. B. Eno, *Teaching Authority in the Early Church* (Wilmington, Del., 1984); R. F. Evans, *One and Holy: The Church in Latin Patristic Thought* (London, 1972); W. H. C. Frend, *The Donatist Church: A Movement of Protest in Roman North Africa* (Oxford, 1952); T. Halton, *The Church* (Wilmington, Del., 1985); R. Murray, *Symbols of Church and Kingdom: A Study in Early Syriac Tradition* (Cambridge, 1975); J. C. Plumpe, *Mater Ecclesia: An Enquiry into the Concept of Church as Mother in Early Christianity* (Washington, 1943).

Clementine Literature   *see* Clement of Rome

Clement of Alexandria (c. 150–215)

It was once thought Clement was a presbyter of the Alexandrian church and head of its catechetical school, though this is no longer generally accepted. It is far more likely that he was master of a private philosophical school, at a time when several other Christian philosophers (many of them gnostics) were also teaching in the city (*see Alexandria*). He began his studies in Greece and traveled to Italy, then through Syria and Palestine, before settling in Egypt as a philosopher. Clement's desire was to avoid the excesses of *gnostic* speculation, but still relate Christianity to the flow of Hellenistic *philosophy*. He spent time advising wealthy Christians on the right use of possessions and on correct social behavior. His higher philosophy seminars presented Christianity as the true aspiration of all the ancient wisdom traditions of Hellenism, and in this respect he was one of the early and most original Christian employers of the *Logos theology* witnessed in the biblical Wisdom literature, in *Philo*, and in the Fourth Gospel. His chief works compose a trilogy: *Exhortation to the Greeks* (*Protreptikus*), *Christ the Educator* (*Paedagogus*), and *Miscellanies* (*Stromata*). The contents of the three volumes present, in some form or another, an ascending curriculum. The first attracts students to the philosophic life. The second advocates a standard of ethical behavior consonant with the pursuit of wisdom, which finds in Jesus the supreme guide to conduct and the midwife of wisdom as Logos *incarnate*. The final volume (literally named a "carpet-bag") is a random set of aphorisms and teachings, highly enigmatic in nature, suggesting the curriculum that might be offered to advanced students of Clement who pursue the higher paths of esoteric seeking. Clement had a powerful influence over some of the most *mystical* thinkers of the later Christian tradition, but his independence from many of the mainstream concerns of the church in succeeding generations (he is the last great Christian theologian to exist in an environment uncontrolled by episcopal scrutiny) also sidelined him. His is a moderate gnostic Christianity (he affirms the value of the material world as a training ground given by God for mankind's good) that sees the Father-God drawing all humanity back to divine communion and angelic metamorphosis, through initiation in the Logos-Son. The Logos is the pedagogue, the shepherd, or the breasts of God, giving the milk of psychic nourishment to the initiate soul. Salvation is understood as largely a cosmic ascent to truth, and in this sense his master scheme of *salvation* theology displaced some of the earlier Christian *eschatology*, a movement that was to have a wider effect when taken up by *Origen* in the next generation.

E. F. Osborn, *The Philosophy of Clement of Alexandria* (Cambridge, 1957); S. R. C. Lilla, *Clement of Alexandria* (Oxford, 1971); A. Méhat, *Études sur les Stromates de Clément d'Alexandrie* (Paris, 1966).

Clement of Rome (fl. c. 96)

One of the *Apostolic Fathers*, Clement was leader of the Roman church c. 88–97 and is the author of an authentic *Letter to the Corinthians*, which is an important piece of evidence for the organization patterns of the early church communities. It was composed perhaps during the persecution of Domitian, and was still being read alongside the Pauline Letters at the church of Corinth in 170. In it Clement pleads for the restoration of peace in a divided community and supports the leaders who have been ousted. A second *Letter to the Corinthians* was also attributed to him in the fourth century. It is not authentically his, but still has great interest as, perhaps, the earliest surviving example of Christian homiletic from a liturgical context (based on Isa. 54:1). This text turns much on the idea of the election of the church and the need for repentance. Clement's name soon began to be a receptacle for much other literature from the early church that was seeking an authoritative home. Chief among this body of so-called Clementine literature are the *Clementine Homilies* and the *Clementine Recognitions*. In his legendary development in this early romance literature, Clement became seen as a major theologian whom the apostles used to transmit their teaching to the later churches. Clement of Rome was probably a freedman of the aristocratic clan of Flavius Clemens (*see* [Domitian] *Persecutions*).

B. Bowe, *A Church in Crisis: Ecclesiology and Paraenesis in Clement of Rome* (Philadelphia, 1988); K. P. Donfried, *The Setting of Second Clement in Early Christianity* (Leiden, Netherlands, 1974); J. B. Lightfoot, *The Apostolic Fathers* (London, 1890).

Clergy Clergy is the term for ordained Christian ministers derived from the Greek word *kleros*, those selected by lot. The term was already in standard use by the second century. *Tertullian* (*Exhortation to Chastity*) used it in contrast to "laity" (Greek term for "the people"), and it is also found in *Clement of Alexandria, Hippolytus,* and *Origen,* applied in a similar way. Tertullian is also the one (cf. *Monogamy* 12; *Exhortation to Chastity* 7) who speaks of "*ordination*" (entering an "order" derived from the Roman social idea of class rank) and he mentions the "priestly orders" of bishop, presbyter, and *deacon* (the "major orders"). By the late second century the concept of lower or "minor orders" had also emerged, and these offices were designated as "lower clergy"—lectors, subdeacons, porters, exorcists, acolytes, and so forth (cf. Tertullian, *Prescription against Heretics* 41; Hippolytus, *The Apostolic Tradition* 11; Cyprian, *Epistle* 7; idem, *Epistle* 69.15). The third-century pope Cornelius drew up a list of the clergy then serving at Rome. It amounted to 1 bishop, 46 presbyters, 7 deacons, 7 subdeacons, 42 acolytes, and 52 exorcists, readers, and porters combined (Eusebius, *Ecclesiastical History* 6.43.11). In the Eastern church the order of female deacons was more extensively known, at least after the third century, and lasted much longer than it did in the West. Most of the female deacons were single women, often drawn from the societies of *virgins* or *widows*. Attempts (often ideologically driven) to relegate the women deacons into the ranks of minor orders, as mere assistants at female *baptisms*, cannot be sustained from the evidence. By the fifth century the patristic theologians were attempting to find symbolic explanations for the term "clergy." *Jerome* said it derived from the fact that the Levites had no portion of land since the Lord was "their lot" (*Epistle* 52.5). *Augustine* (*Enarrations on the Psalms* 67.19) thought the term was reminiscent of the selection of the successor to the fallen apostle Judas as recounted in Acts 1:26. The drawing of lots from a short list of candidates was symbolic of leaving the selection to the divine will (a pattern still followed in some Eastern churches for the higher patriarchal offices). As far as can be told, however, ordination was always conveyed by the "laying on of hands." Fourth-century synods provide a large body of evidence about the continuing regulation of the clergy, which was a considerable rank in Byzantine times, carrying with it significant social and financial advantages (tax exemptions after the reign of *Constantine*). Early dispensations (such as 1 Tim. 3:2, 12; Titus 1:6) were supplemented by the Canons of Nicaea, forbidding the ordination of self-eunuchizers and newly converted. *Slaves* were subsequently debarred from orders, and increasingly those mutilated in any way. Clergy were required to have married suitably (that is, respectable virgins), and ordination was increasingly seen as a debarment from marriage. Although in the East ordinands could continue to live with their wives, Latin practice increasingly demanded that men ordained to major orders should henceforth live as brother and sister if they were married, a custom that devolved eventually into the current clerical practice of Catholic clerical *celibacy*. In 451 the *Council of Chalcedon* made the important requirement of "title" for ordination (no one could be legitimately ordained in the abstract, without having specific ecclesiastical duty in a specific community), and listed a number of professions that were forbidden to priests. The emperor *Justinian* in the sixth century put the seal of law on a practice that had been increasingly standard after the mid–fifth century, that all bishops should be celibate, which resulted in the current position in the Eastern church that only monastic clergy are ordained to the episcopate.

H. von Campenhausen, *Ecclesiastical Authority and Spiritual Power in the Church of the First Three Centuries* (Stanford, Calif., 1969); J. T. Lienhard, *Ministry* (Wilmington, Del., 1984).

Climacus   *see* **John Climacus**

Communicatio Idiomatum   *see* **Communion of Properties**

Communion of Properties (Communion of Idioms)   Also described as the principle of the "exchange of properties." The original Greek term was *antidosis idiomaton*. It is more commonly known in Western European theological textbooks in its Latin version as *communicatio idiomatum*. It was the Latin form that was in widest use, deriving from the *Tome of Leo*, the official document drawn up (from traditional statements by *Tertullian* and *Augustine*) by the papal Chancery under *Pope Leo's* instructions. This he sent to the *Council of Ephesus* in 449 to represent the official *christological* teaching of the Roman church. It was rejected by the conciliar president *Dioscorus*, who thought it contradicted the teaching of St. *Cyril of Alexandria*, which had been endorsed at the *Council of Ephesus* (431). The furor caused by Ephesus 449 led very soon to the calling of the revisionist *Council of Chalcedon* in 451. Here the imperial administration demanded that Leo's Tome be adopted alongside the teachings of Cyril, despite their differences in emphasis in approaching the concept of christological union. While Cyril wished to stress the organic unity of the divine person of Christ operating in a human body that had been fully integrated in the divinity, Leo wished to stress the authentic humanity, which never lost its own integral coherence even in its assumption by the divine Lord. The Tome of Leo, therefore, laid considerable stress on the plurality of "two natures," human and divine, which continued their respective operations under the presidency of a single divine person. When Jesus wept, the action was to be assigned to the humanity. When he raised Lazarus from the dead, the action was to be assigned to the divinity. Both actions were performed by the selfsame (divine) person. Cyrilline Christology regarded this as a defectively mechanistic view, but after Ephesus 431 both *Alexandria* and the church of *Constantinople* were anxious to make a harmonious liaison with Rome, and both Eastern churches agreed, eventu-

ally, that the Roman doctrine was essentially orthodox in that it assigned all the actions of Christ to a single person who was the *Logos* of God incarnate. To this extent the Alexandrians agreed that the redeeming factor about Leo's Christology (the one aspect of it which seemed to the Greeks to distinguish it from the *Nestorian* bi-polarism of an "integrally complete" man associated alongside the word of God, that is, two "discrete natures" instead of two natures that had become unified) was the dynamically unifying concept of the communion of idioms. The *idiomata* signify the things which are "proper or peculiar to a nature." So the *idiomata* of the humanity would be mortality, hunger, weakness, and so forth. The *idiomata* of divinity would be immortality, infinite power, and so on. How could the two be reconciled in the single person of Christ? Alexandrians had long been accustomed to refer the two *idiomata* indiscriminately as a mark of their strong support for the single-subject Christology. Thus, Cyril often spoke of the "sufferings of the divine Word" and such. A similar style of christological language was also traditional in *Rome*, but strongly resisted in *Syria*. Leo suggested that in Christ both the divine and the human *idiomata* must always be attributed to the selfsame person, the divine Word who had become flesh. In this way the hunger of Christ was a human act of the divine Word, just as the walking on the water was a divine act of the Word in his human body. The Communion of Idioms thus became the basis of common agreement between Latin and later Byzantine christological thought as to the viability of the Chalcedonian scheme of the "single divine person in two complete natures."

A. Grillmeier, *Christ in Christian Tradition*, vol. 1, 2d ed. (London, 1975), 452–53, 534–37.

Communion of the Saints The

term signifies the spiritual, familial bond between believers that exists on account of the church's collective and individual union with God through the mediation of Christ. It is thus a dynamic evocation of the theology of the church's communion (ecclesiology). It has two distinct associations. The first is the communion of saints that exists on earth. From New Testament times, "the saints" was a designation of Christians, and a popular term of reference in Paul. John also expresses this sense of the ecclesial communion most distinctly when he says: "What we have seen and heard we declare also to you, so that you also may have communion (*koinonia*) with us, and our communion may be with the Father, and with his son, Jesus Christ" (1 John 1:3; also cf. 1:7). The second, and related, aspect is the manner in which this communion (or fellowship) extends beyond the visible community of the faithful to embrace the saints and angels before the time of Jesus, and the *saints* who have passed through death to the heavenly communion. The communion of saints in this sense connotes the concept of the heavenly support that Christians receive in the course of their discipleship. In Colossians 1:12 the communion-fellowship of the saints on earth is affirmed with those who have gone before: "We give thanks to God the Father who has made us worthy to share in the lot of the saints, in light." From the earliest times Christians prayed for the assistance of angels, the martyrs (who were believed to be especially ready to defend the members of the local church they had left behind; cf. Rev. 6:9), and above all the *Virgin Mary*, a fact that can be attested by numerous church graffiti from the late second century onwards. Many early Christian burial grounds show evidence of "clustering" around a martyr's grave, marking the hope of the early believers that at the *resurrection* of the dead their proximity to the martyrs (who could plead for them) would assist them in the *Judgment*. Similarly, the church on earth was always conscious that it ought to remember and venerate the martyrs, not merely symbolically, but by specific names and dates (thus instituting the liturgical commemoration of their executions). Soon the practice of praying more extensively for the dead grew out of the martyr cult, as an expression that the communion of the saints was not disrupted by death, or constricted by time or space, since it was first and foremost a communion of the resurrection. Just as the earthly church could expect the assistance and prayers of the great saints in *heaven*, so it was believed that the prayers of the faithful on earth, especially if offered in the course of the public liturgy (when the resurrection transected time and space in the earthly congregation), could help the souls who had to stand before God in judgment after death. The actual term, "Communion of the Saints," was first developed in Latin writing by Nicetas of Remesiana in the early fifth century and was introduced into the last article of the (Roman) Apostles' Creed in the West after the early sixth century. The idea, however, was universally present in the Latin and Greek churches until the time of the Reformation, when it became a highly disputed notion for the West. It continued to be developed in Byzantine theology as a primary mode of conceiving the church as a mystical communion in the resurrectional life of Jesus, a bond of *koinonia* that was established in time and space, but destined to transcend it. It marks most Eastern Christian ecclesiology with a strongly mystical character, in distinction to the more institutional context of much Western ecclesiology.

J. N. D. Kelly, *Early Christian Creeds* (3d ed.; London, 1972); R. I. Benko, *The Meaning of Sanctorum Communio* (Studies in Historical Theology 3; Oxford, 1964).

Confession—Confessor In the New Testament and patristic era "confession" meant primarily the confession (*exomologesis*) or public witness of the faith (1 Tim. 6:13; 2 Cor. 9:13). The title is

used in this sense of acclamation of the glory of God as a public witness, in the famous text of **St. Augustine**, *Confessions*. Confession of faith was an integral part of the baptismal ceremony (**Tertullian**, *De spectaculis* 4; **Cyril of Jerusalem**, *Catechetical Orations* 2.4) and is represented in the creedal confessions. When infant *baptism* became more common, it was still required that someone should speak the confession on behalf of the child (Hippolytus, *Apostolic Tradition* 21). The close association of confession and witness made it a term that after the third century came to be closely associated with that most particular witness (*martyria*) that the Christian was expected to give when arrested and scrutinized by magistrates who were seeking a denial of the faith. The confession at trial, of course, usually secured the fate and status of a martyr for the person so confessing. Those who survived trial and imprisonment and returned back to the community of the church in the times of peace after the *persecutions* enjoyed great positions of honor and status. They were called "confessors." Up to the early fourth century (when this idea was restricted), the act of having confessed the faith under persecution was regarded as an equivalent of ordination (so theorizes **Hippolytus**). Confession is also a term that ordinarily denotes the tomb of a martyr. The confession was the small tomb itself, or more often, after the fourth century when the cult of the martyrs was widely extended, the small edifices that were built over the grave inside the church. The "Confession of Saint Peter" (the deep depression in the nave floor in front of the high altar) is one example of an ancient confession still in use at a martyr's tomb in the Vatican Basilica of St. Peter's. After the fourth century (noticeable first as a process in **Ambrose** and **Gregory of Nazianzus's** funeral encomia) the acclamation of the sanctity of martyr-confessors was increasingly extended to include other categories of holy men and women: especially ascetics and hierarchs. These non-martyr saints were commonly called confessors (as in the famous title conferred in 1161 on King Edward the Confessor, one of the last Saxon kings of England). *Tertullian* is one of the first, in the late second century, to relate the idea of confession to a public penitential admission of faults before the priests and people: "This confession (*exomologesis*) is a disciplinary act of great humility. . . . it teaches the penitent to cast himself at the feet of the presbyters, and to fall on his knees before the beloved of God, and to beg of all the faithful to intercede on his behalf" (*On Penance* 9). With the rise in popularity of private *penance* in the medieval era (a practice encouraged by monastic traditions of the telling of the heart's secrets to a priest or monastic leader), the term confession more generally came to denote the act of penitent ascesis, the confessing of one's sins. The hearer of that confession (at first often simply a spiritual elder, then later only a priest) also became known as one's "father confessor."

O. Cullmann, *The Earliest Christian Confessions* (London, 1949); E. Ferguson, *Early Christians Speak* (Abilene, 1987), 23–32; O. D. Watkins, *A History of Penance*, 2 vols. (London, 1920).

Constantine the Great (c. 275–337)

Constantine is commonly regarded as the first Christian Roman emperor (although that was probably Philip the Arab, 244–249). Constantine's rise to power simultaneously marked a monumental change in the fortunes of the Christian church, bringing it from an environment of sporadic and often savage persecution into the status of a favored religion. Within seventy years of Constantine's first official patronage of the church, Christianity would be proclaimed as the state religion of the Romans. Constantine was the son of a Roman general, Constantius Chlorus, who had been promoted as Diocletian's junior emperor (Caesar) of the West. On

this promotion Constantius's wife, Helena, was retired and dismissed. She was, in all probability, a Christian, and her lowly origins were considered as unsuitable. Helena may have introduced Constantine to Christianity early in his life. She would be brought back to high prominence and proclaimed Augusta in her son's reign, at which time she gained a reputation as a profound benefactor of Christians in her own right. In 293 Constantius's son was brought for his education to Diocletian's capital at Nicomedia, a form of hostage-taking. Here he was possibly educated in rhetoric by the Christian philosopher *Lactantius*, beginning a long association between Constantine and subsequent Christian advisers (especially *Hosius, Eusebius of Nicomedia*, and *Eusebius of Caesarea*). Knowing that the emperor Diocletian intended to pass him over in rearranging the succession to the imperial throne, Constantine fled from the capital and joined his father at the military camp in York in 306. As his father lay dying, the troops there acclaimed his son Augustus, and so the civil war began that would result in Constantine's inexorable rise to supreme power in both parts of the empire. He soon executed both his Western rival emperors, Maximian (his father-in-law) and Maxentius. His defeat of Maxentius at the Battle of the Milvian Bridge at *Rome* in 312 was heralded by Constantine (and publicized by Lactantius and Eusebius of Caesarea) as being foretold by a great sign of divine deliverance. He told how he had seen a strange symbol in the skies (in Lactantius's account it is a dream visitation) and had the sign painted on his soldiers' shields before the decisive battle. The sign (the *labarum*) was closely related to the Christian chi-rho (the first two letters of the name of Christ), and thus began the public association of the rise of Constantine to supreme power with an act of the blessing of the "new god" Jesus. Much discussion of the vision of Constantine (and its role in the ongoing apologia of the rise of the church in the fourth century) has distracted commentators from the reality that almost all Roman emperors in the field were expected to receive divine intimations before battle, and it is not unexpected for Constantine to speak in such terms as *summus pontifex*. Passing through Gaul a little while before, he was reported to have experienced Apollo's particular favor, and for many years after his public alliance with the Christians, Constantine depicted his favored divine symbol, the Unconquered Sun, on coins of his dominions. His religiosity, therefore, was profoundly central to his policy but equally a typical late antique syncretism of cults, in his case the sun cult and (then increasingly) Christianity. His religious opinions generally focused around encouraging a moralistic monotheist consensus within his empire. When in 324 he defeated his last surviving rival, the Eastern emperor Licinius, he undoubtedly felt the divine hand had raised him to sole power as a reward for his vigorous pursuit of monotheism. Oceans of ink have been spilled debating whether Constantine used the church or the church used him, and doubtless both are true. By the mid–third century Christians were a force to deal with in the empire, and had shown their resistance to all official attempts to check their progress. From as early as 306 Constantine gave Christians protected status in his dominions, and in 313 he persuaded his coemperor Licinius (the Edict of Milan) to restore Christian property lost during persecutions. The myth that the church was richly endowed at this time masks that fact that the restoration did not match what had been lost, but the giving of reparations (and an increasing series of tax exemptions) certainly put the church on the path to becoming a major land- and property-owning corporation, and this ensured its permanent political influence in the structural affairs of the empire ever afterwards. Constantine began to build a new capital of world empire, a new Rome, soon after his defeat of Licinius in 324, and it

was dedicated as *Constantinople* in 330. The city would soon become the center of Christian affairs in the East. As early as 314 Constantine had received an appeal from *North African* bishops concerned about the divisive social effects of the *Donatist* schism. He intervened personally at first, then referred the case to a court presided over by the bishop of Rome acting as imperial legate, and finally (when he realized how disruptive they were) again acted by private judgment against them. So began a long history of the Christian emperors intervening in church policy and affairs. The hierarchs of the time deflected his desire to intervene absolutely by emphasizing their traditional practice of convoking governing synods of bishops. After conquering the Eastern territories, Constantine determined to use the church as a major substructure of governance, and so set about to repair the ruinous effects of years of *persecution*, which had allowed dissensions to all but destroy Christian consensus. He was especially concerned to put a stop to the *Arian* controversy and so summoned a great "worldwide" (Oecumenical) Synod to meet at his palace at *Nicaea* in 325. Here he followed the advice of Bishop *Hosius* of Cordoba and imposed a creedal amendment to form a consensus around the Christology of *homoousion*, finding in favor of the Alexandrian church and against Arius. The Nicene faith soon appeared to him as not a broad enough consensus, and Constantine progressively abandoned it for a vaguer "Arianizing" policy, dictated to him by Eusebius of Nicomedia. His successors largely followed this tendency almost to the end of the fourth century. His building of the capital at Constantinople allowed for the development of a more focusedly Christian center of political life (such as Rome could never be), and in the process of beautifying it Constantine took many of the major cult statues from all over the ancient world and erected them in the streets—an interesting policy of secularizing pagan cult objects, which Christians energetically followed in the missionary expansion of the church over the next two centuries. Constantine ordered for himself a mausoleum Church of the Holy Apostles, and seems to have been buried in the central sarcophagus, surrounded by porphyry tombs symbolizing the Twelve, a suggestion that he may have seen himself, in his old age, as a kind of new Logos or Iso-Christos. The church rhetors happily applied praises of the Christian emperor, the "bishop of those outside the church," but at the same time carefully deconstructed his pretensions, allowing him only the title of thirteenth apostle, while deleting his self-referential "theologies" from the record. On his deathbed he received baptism from Eusebius of Nicomedia, and departed this life in 337, in typical ambivalent style, wearing white robes— traditional dress both of the newly baptized and of the pagan emperors of Rome who were undergoing apotheosis. His career began the age of Christian Byzantium, and without question marked a watershed, establishing policies that would mark and form the church for centuries to come.

T. D. Barnes, *Constantine and Eusebius* (Cambridge, Mass., 1981); A. H. M. Jones, *Constantine and the Conversion of Europe* (repr.; Toronto, 1985); H. A. Drake, *Constantine and the Bishops: The Politics of Intolerance* (Baltimore, 2000); O. Cullmann, *The Earliest Christian Confessions* (London, 1949); E. Ferguson, *Early Christians Speak* (Abilene, Tex., 1987), 23–32; O. D. Watkins, *A History of Penance* (2 vols.; London, 1920).

Constantinople   After gaining absolute control of the Roman Empire in the civil war of 324, *Constantine the Great* marked his victory with the foundation of a city that would bear his name. The locus of the administrative center of the empire for a long time had already been drifting eastward. Constantine's awareness of the strategic defects of *Rome*, and the hostility to his rule that was deeply seated there in the traditional pagan aristocracy, induced him to invest this new foundation with a dynastic and strategic importance that allowed Constantinople soon to become the dominant capital of the newly Christianized empire. Its role as a great Christian city, situated at the gate of Europe and Asia, and poised on the axis point between the Slavs and the Semites, gave it from the very start an immensely influential role in the dissemination of ideas within the wider church. Constantine conducted a foundation ceremony on November 4, 324. He chose the site of the colony of Byzantium (from which derives the adjective "Byzantine"), attracted there because of the town's commanding geographical position, its strong defense capability, and its excellent potential as a trade port. His building program favored the erection of Christian churches. By 328 the walls on the only side of the city exposed to land attack had enclosed three square miles, and in 330 he presided at the dedication ceremony. To glorify his new capital, Constantine commandeered the greatest of the ancient world's sacred and secular statuary, and it induced Saint Jerome's trenchant remark: "Constantinople dedicated: all the world stripped bare." The siting of these venerable works in the open streets may be read as one of the first essays in the desacralization of the old religion, a program that would continue apace under Constantine's Christian successors. Constantinople's early fortunes as a ecclesial center were inauspicious. It was dominated by the more important ecclesiastical centers of *Alexandria* and Ephesus in the south, and *Antioch* to the north. In the time of the *Arian* crisis it allied itself with anti-Nicene factions, and in the time of *Theodosius* almost all its churches had to be forcibly reappropriated by troops and given back to the tiny Nicene party under the administration of *Gregory of Nazianzus*. In the *canons* of the *Council* *of Constantinople I* in 381 the first efforts were made to ensure the city's independence from Alexandria and Rome, which had been vying to control it. By the early fifth century the see of Constantinople had risen in power by association with the imperial court, and in the time of its charismatic bishop *John Chrysostom* it was awarded a large ecclesiastical "territory" encompassing much of Asia Minor. Chrysostom's political downfall was partly orchestrated by provincial synods resistant to his claims to extend Constantinople's jurisdiction. Not until the late fifth century and into the sixth century did the city finally establish itself as the undisputed ecclesial center of the East, much to the disadvantage of Alexandria and the constantly expressed dissatisfaction of Rome. At the *Council of Chalcedon* in 451 the ambiguously phrased Canon 28 was added to the acts conferring on the city a preeminence after Rome. Constantinople understood that to mean a successor's parity with Rome, while Rome reluctantly took it to mean immediate subordination. Therein lay the seeds of much bitter dispute between the churches for years ahead and ultimately of the division between the Eastern and Western churches. In the sixth century the bishops of the imperial city claimed the title "Oecumenical Patriarchs," meaning the chief bishops of the "civilized (Roman) world." The claim was advanced on the notion that church jurisdictional power ought to reflect the civil imperial divisions of administration, a principle of Eastern church governance in place from the time of Valens in the fourth century. The city enjoyed the benefits of the recovery of the empire in the sixth century under *Justinian*. There followed a magnificent phase of new building, including the still-surviving churches of Hagia Sophia, Hagia Eirene, and Saints Sergius and Bacchus. Hagia Sophia was then the world's largest cathedral, and even today in its denuded condition creates a stunning evocation of the lost glories of Byzantium. After Justinian, the finances

and political stability of the empire moved into a long winter. Constantinople remained the center of all Eastern ecclesiastical affairs, however, and as the Byzantine empire increasingly lost control of territories, the city's role was amplified even more. It was undoubtedly the center of monastic life in the Eastern church, and even Stylites set up their pillars there and had a following among the aristocracy, who were always ready to patronize and protect those with a reputation for sanctity. Many of its bishops and patriarchs in the patristic period represented the leading intellects of the age, especially *Gregory of Nazianzus*, John Chrysostom, *Nestorius*, *Proclus of Constantinople*, and *Flavian*. The monasteries that had been established in the large suburban hinterland from the fourth century had with the course of years been absorbed into the city proper, and the many monastic theologians who congregated there added to the theological vitality of the capital. By the sixth century there were approximately eighty-five monasteries in the city, some specializing in manuscript production (such as in the Stoudium) and others offering hospital care to the local inhabitants. In the ninth century, minuscule writing is thought to have originated at the Stoudium, making transcription cheaper and facilitating the transmission of both Christian and antique classical texts to later generations. Constantinople's role in passing on the heritage of classical antiquity cannot be overestimated. From the late fourth century onward the city was the locus of the great *christological* controversies that formed the agendas of the Oecumenical councils, including the seventh, *Nicaea II*, which was called to articulate a theological answer to the *Iconoclasts* of the imperial court. The close proximity of a strong monastic party within the capital, together with the clerical staff of the Great Church gathered around the patriarch and the imperial court, created the vital synthesis between monastic patterns of *prayer* and a splendid imperial liturgy that was to form the future character of Eastern Christian church services.

D. Buckton, ed., *Byzantium: Treasures of Byzantine Art and Culture* (London, 1994); G. Every, *The Byzantine Patriarchate 451–1204* (London, 1962); P. Hetherington, *Byzantium: City of Gold, City of Faith* (London, 1983); R. Janin, *Les Églises et les Monastères de Constantinople* (Paris, 1953); R. Krautheimer, *Three Christian Capitals* (Berkeley, Calif., 1983).

Councils—Conciliarism   It is often said that the meeting of the apostles (Acts 15) to discuss whether circumcision was required of Gentile converts was the primary model of the church's practice of leaders' meetings for debate and resolution of problems, but the example of the "Council of Jerusalem" is not alluded to in patristic writing until the fifth century. It is more likely that the Hellenistic world (organized as a chain of cities in dependence on the emperor) provided a ready example of the necessity of provincial leaders to establish common policies by meetings of town councils and occasions when delegates could represent the town to the provincial governor concerning regular fiscal and political affairs. The first example of Christian bishops conferring with one another is provided in the practice of extending letters of communion (*eirenika*) and recommendations for Christians traveling between various city churches (a common event in the vast network of trade relations that composed the Roman Empire). *Tertullian* is one of the first to mention that the Asia Minor bishops had a custom, already in place before the second century, that the church leaders of their large area would meet occasionally to discuss controversies (*On Fasting* 13). It was the *Montanist* crisis that put this practice on the public map as a highly efficient way of resolving church problems, and one that did not rely on the single authoritative voice of a leading see (cf. Eusebius, *Ecclesiastical History* 5.16.10). Pope Victor's treatment of the Montanists had been seen by many as too severe, and an alternative system of church order as provided by a larger gathering of bishops proved popular across a wider area of the church in both East and West. In response to Pope Victor's call to settle the date of Easter coherently (the **Quartodeciman Controversy**), a series of councils was convoked across the Christian world (Eusebius, *Ecclesiastical History* 5.23.2–4), and this internationalized the Asia Minor synodical practice. In the mid–third century, in the later part of *Origen's* life, he had been called by the collective of Palestinian bishops as a theological specialist (*Dialogue with Heracleides*) to help them resolve several problems of theological interpretation (on the significance of blood, and on the nature of resurrection). His records of the meeting show that the gathering (Greek: *synodos*) was a genuine dialogue seeking common agreement and consensus through study. At the end, the dissident bishop is reconciled to the majority by admitting he had been convinced by the evidence. Only later did the councils, or synods, assume the character of "trials" of dissidents. By the third century the principle of annual meetings of the bishops of a province became common. *Cyprian* shows that the *North African* bishops met regularly to decide disciplinary matters in their churches (Cyprian, *Epistles* 55; 67.1). This established councils (at least in the Eastern church) as the supreme source of *canon* law. The disciplinary decisions they published became known simply as "the canons." After the fifth century the *papacy* increasingly issued law as from the Roman see, witnessing an increasing friction between the idea of authority vested in the *Apostolic* See of Rome, or authority vested in the wider collective of bishops of the Western Patriarchate (the medieval Conciliarist controversy). Pope *Leo I* issued a set of guidelines in several letters explaining how the authority of councils was vested in the inspiration of the *Holy Spirit*, in the foundation of Scripture, and in harmony with universal tradition. He also went on that the council to be authentic had to agree with its predecessors, be popularly received (the consensus of the faithful) and be approved by the Holy See (Leo, *Epistles* 13; 14; 106; 119; 129; 145–147; 162; 164; 166). Apart from the last item the East concurred entirely. If the idea of conciliar authority being the final court of appeal was conflicted in the West, because of the extraordinary rise of the power of the papacy, it was not so in the East. The council was always given precedence in authority over the bishop or patriarch. From the beginning, the synod of bishops was expected to manifest a "common mind." It was presumed that when the senior hierarchs gathered they should "know the faith," not be groping like novices to define what it was. Thus, when a crisis arose over a point of doctrine or discipline, the collective mind and faith of the bishops should be able to recognize immediately and acclaim authoritatively the true line of the tradition. It is clear, therefore, that the bishops were regarded as endowed with prophetic and priestly charisms. The conciliar outcome was not to be decided by majority vote, and so there was always great pressure to ensure that the final vote, when taken, was always unanimous. If this could not be achieved (certainly more common after the fourth century), the dissidents who refused to sign the conciliar acts were denounced by the synod as not having the "mind of the church," and thus *anathematized* as having become heretics. By the fourth century the nature of synodical debates was already giving way to become more and more an issue that had been prejudged by the collection of authoritative voices from the ancient authorities (the beginning of the use of *"patristic"* authors as definitive witnesses to authentic *tradition*). Even so, and despite the advantage afforded to the particular episcopal chancery that was able to take charge of the collection and

arrangement of the texts, all the large synods remained governed by Roman conventions regarding debates (the process of the senate was taken as a model), and by Hellenistic ideas about how philosophical ideas could be exchanged (more propositional than informative). After *Constantine* had achieved supreme power in the empire, he determined that the Christians should be a force for cohesion, and his religious policy strongly advocated this. He encouraged a much wider assembly of bishops, based on the model of the senatorial gatherings of the emperor's advisers. The first example of this "international" kind of meeting (Greek—*oecumenical* or worldwide, thus giving rise to the notion of an Ecumenical Council) was the Council of Arles in 314 called to resolve the *Donatist* crisis. It failed to do so. Constantine tried again in the East, this time to settle the *Arian* crisis. He called an "ecumenical synod" together at his palace in Nicaea in 325 to mark the occasion of his twentieth anniversary of reign. This determined that a provincial council of bishops should be held in every local area at least twice a year (Canon 5). Its theological decisions would later become the determinative standard of orthodox *Christology*, and it also established the rule that the emperor was the one who should convoke an Ecumenical Council; but in the aftermath of Nicaea, as its decisions were highly controverted and a whole series of councils held throughout the fourth century conflicted with one another, the Arian crisis continued to play out in full spate. At the *Council of Chalcedon* in 451 the assembled bishops looked back and retrospectively declared that of all these numerous synods, only three had hitherto been truly "ecumenical": those of *Nicaea I* (325), *Constantinople I* (381), and *Ephesus I* (431). After that point only momentously significant councils have earned the designation Ecumenical (or Oecumenical). These comprise a total of seven in the patristic era, all in the Greek Christian world, and have been commonly regarded as the supreme authority, under God, for settling matters in the Christian Oecumene. Given the embarrassment that numerous synods had publicly manifested conflicted views within the international episcopate, the principle of synodical inspiration took something of a battering in terms of popular faith and increasingly, after the fifth century, the synods mutated into a collection of patristic evidences, after hearing which the bishops passed a sentence of agreement with the standard authorities of the past. By this stage the earlier idea of the synod as an open sharing of ideas had largely passed, and it took on a forensic character, although at no stage was the idea abandoned that a synod's decisions were especially governed by the Spirit of divine inspiration.

P. R. Amidon, "The Procedure of St. Cyprian's Synods," VC 37 (1983): 328–39; L. D. Davis, *The First Seven Ecumenical Councils: Their History and Theology* (Wilmington, Del., 1987); G. Florovsky, "The Authority of the Ancient Councils and the Tradition of the Fathers," in G. Muller and W. Zeller, eds., *Glaube, Geist, Geschichte* (Leiden, Netherlands, 1967); J. A. McGuckin, *St. Cyril of Alexandria and the Christological Controversy* (Leiden, Netherlands, 1994); idem, "Eschaton and Kerygma: The Future of the Past in the Present Kairos. The Concept of Living Tradition in Orthodox Theology," SVTQ 42, 3–4 (winter 1998): 225–71.

Council of Chalcedon

Council of Chalcedon   The Council of Chalcedon was called by Empress Pulcheria and Emperor Marcian to resolve the continuing *christological* crisis that had been simmering from the time of the *Council of Ephesus I* (431), and had been recently greatly embittered by *Dioscorus of Alexandria*'s presidency at the *Council of Ephesus* in 449, where he had exonerated *Eutyches*, castigated the Syrian theologians, slighted Pope *Leo*, and censured *Flavian of Con-*

stantinople. The emperor Theodosius II had not been willing to reopen the discussion even though Dioscorus's behavior had greatly enraged opinion in Syria, Constantinople, and Rome, but immediately following the former's sudden death the new administration was determined to effect an eirenic reconciliation of the Byzantine, Syrian, and Roman traditions of Christology, and rein in the Egyptian church (and its tradition so deeply indebted to *Cyril of Alexandria*), which had hitherto been highly dominant. Although Chalcedon was designed as a council of reconciliation, its results caused much future unrest in the Eastern provinces, occasioning deep divisions (the *Monophysite* controversy) that have not been healed to the present day. The emperor was determined that business at this synod should be kept under the closest supervision of the military, so it was located in the suburb of *Constantinople*, in the imperial palace on the Asian shore, at Chalcedon. The refusal of Dioscorus to admit the Tome of Leo at Ephesus 431 was an urgent item on the agenda, and the council is notable for the way in which the imperial commissioners kept insisting that the (apparently reluctant) bishops should adopt the *Tome* (a classical synopsis of Western dual-nature Christology, drawn largely from *Tertullian* and *Augustine*) as their central statement. The bishops were very reluctant indeed to accede to the preference of Leo over Cyril, and after several stalled sessions, a compromise was eventually adopted which combined elements of the Cyrilline theology (strongly insistent on the unification of natures into a seamless *henosis*) with the clarity of the Leonine demand to affirm "one (divine) person and two natures in Christ." The first session on October 8 was taken up by demands from the commissioners for the deposition of Dioscorus. Agreement could only be secured for his censure for use of violence (thus the majority refused to condemn his theology), and his exclusion from the chamber was only a small victory, for the subsequent appearance of *Theodoret of Cyrrhus* (one of the strongest theological enemies of the Egyptians who had been deposed at Ephesus 449) occasioned storms of protest. The second session, two days later, turned to an exposition of the faith. Traditional documents such as the Nicene Creed and the Second Letter of Cyril to *Nestorius* (which had been read at Ephesus 431) were again endorsed. So too was the statement of reconciliation (*Let the Heavens Rejoice*—also known as the *Formula of Reunion*) adopted by John of Antioch and Cyril in 433, to signal the reconciliation of Syria and Egypt. But when Leo's *Tome* was brought forward for official endorsement, many of the bishops acclaimed it "as in harmony with Cyril" (a subtle hermeneutic of subordination) and some from Illyricum and Palestine actually expressed doubts about it, as being redolent of "Nestorian" tendencies to divide the union into two personal centers. The *Tome*, of course, was far removed from Nestorianism, but it clashed to a real degree with Cyril's unwavering insistence that any talk of "two natures" after the union demonstrated lack of belief in that union. In resisting Leo, many bishops, not just the Egyptians, felt they were defending the tradition of Ephesus 431. Their attempt to conclude business there and then by simply censuring the violent behavior at Ephesus 449 was a ploy the imperial officers themselves resisted. By session four on October 17, the Roman papal delegation (the small contingent of Western bishops and priests present) were encouraged by the emperor to assert their demands. They set forth a view of christological orthodoxy that described the two extreme poles as those represented by Nestorius and Eutyches. It also listed the authentic line of councils: Nicaea, Constantinople I, Ephesus 431, finally culminating in Leo's *Tome*, the supposed perfectly balanced median position of christological orthodoxy. This became a classically accepted view of conciliar pedigree for the orthodox churches, but the implied position of the Roman delegates that Chalcedon should now endorse the *Tome* as its own theological statement met with passive resistance (although the *Tome* was ever after accepted in the West as the definitive christological resolution, and the synopsis of what Chalcedon stood for). After much backroom maneuvering a plan was presented to the fifth session on October 22 that drew up a new synthesis of elements from Cyril's writings as well as selected excerpts from Leo, all supplied with an explanatory gloss that read them in a Cyrilline manner. It was thus hoped that the many supporters of the Cyrilline tradition would not be alienated, a hope that proved fruitless in the long term. The Egyptian bishops refused to participate in the decree, claiming that as they had lost their patriarch, Dioscorus, they could not vote. The central paragraph of the Chalcedonian statement of faith read as follows: "And so, following the holy fathers we confess one and the same our Lord Jesus Christ, and all teach as one that the same is perfect in Godhead, the same perfect in manhood; truly God and truly man; the same of a reasonable soul and body; consubstantial with the Father in Godhead and the same consubstantial with us in manhood; like us in all things except sin; begotten before the ages of the Father in the Godhead; the same one in these last days, and for our salvation, born of Mary the Virgin *Theotokos* in the manhood; one and the same Christ, Son, Lord, unique; recognized in two natures, unconfusedly, unchangeably, indivisibly, inseparably; the difference of natures being by no means taken away because of the union, but rather the distinctive character of each nature being preserved, combining in one person and hypostasis; not divided or separated into two persons, but one and the same Son and Only Begotten God, Word, Lord Jesus Christ; as the prophets of old, and the Lord Jesus Christ himself, have taught us in his regard, and as the creed of the fathers has handed down to us." It had all the enforced clarity of a commit-tee statement intended to bring an end to discussion. It succeeded in that aim in the West. In the East matters simmered on until *Council of Constantinople II* in 553, but still the sought-after reconcilia-tion could not be found in Byzantium. One of the unintended effects of the Chalcedonian language was to make *Christology* primarily a matter of "bal-ance," instead of an expression of the restless energy of God's mystery of sal-vation, and as Chalcedon was the last word for many years, much of late patristic Christology suffered, to a degree, from bureaucratic overload.

L. D. Davis, *The First Seven Ecumenical Councils: Their History and Theology* (Wilmington, Del., 1987); P. T. R. Gray, *The Defence of Chalcedon in the East: 451–553* (Leiden, Netherlands, 1979); A. Grillmeier, *Christ in Christian Tradition* (vol. 1, 2d ed.; London, 1975), 520–57; E. R. Hardy, *Christology of the Later Fathers* (Philadel-phia, 1964); J. A. McGuckin, *St. Cyril of Alexandria and the Christological Controversy* (Leiden, Netherlands, 1994); R. V. Sellers, *The Council of Chalcedon: A Historical and Doctrinal Survey* (London, 1953).

Council of Constantinople I

The Second Ecumenical Council, Council of Constantinople I, was held in the East-ern capital in 381. The *Arian* party had retained a dominant hold in the Eastern church through the patronage of the emperors for most of the fourth century, but in 378 the last Arian emperor, Valens, suffered a decisive defeat in war with Gothic refugees, and was killed by an enemy scouting party. The shock to the Roman Empire, and the immediate anx-iety it caused about Goths crossing the Danube, caused the Western emperor Valentinian to send over a replacement Augustus quickly, and he chose Theodo-sius I as an experienced soldier who could pacify the Goths and secure the borders. *Theodosius* was a devoted Latin Nicene Christian and so, from

early in 379, it was clear that as he made his progress to Constantinople the impo-sition of *Nicene* faith would be one of his priorities in his own capital. To take advantage of the situation, the eastern Nicene bishops under the leadership of *Meletius of Antioch* encouraged *Gre-gory of Nazianzus* to take up residence in the capital. He converted his cousin's house into a small chapel and began preaching a series of *Orations* in defense of the Nicene faith and in defense of the divinity of the *Holy Spirit*, the kernel of the doctrine of the coequal *Trinity* (see esp. *Orations* 27–31). When Theodosius entered the capital in 380 he confirmed Gregory in office as the city's bishop (exiling the Arian Demophilus). He also decreed that a general council should be summoned for May of 381, to repair two outstanding problems that were putting Eastern church affairs into disorder: the question of the legitimate succession at Antioch (the *Meletian Schism*) and the definitive endorsement of Nicene theol-ogy in the East (together with plans for the suppression of the Arians; *see* Sozomen, *Ecclesiastical History* 1.7.7; Socrates, *Ecclesiastical History* 1.5.8). His policy in relation to the former was clear when he appointed Meletius of Antioch himself as the conciliar president. The affair of the schism was thus settled by acknowledging Meletius of Antioch as the rightful bishop. Gregory's election at the capital was also endorsed. Then, to the surprise of all, Meletius died sud-denly and the presidency transferred to Gregory. The intention to proclaim a generic affirmation of christological orthodoxy (the affirmation of the Nicene *homoousion*) was suddenly taken a step further by this consummate theologian, and under his presidency the ascription of the *homoousion* to the Holy Spirit was also attempted. It was a doctrine that he had argued for in his *Orations*, but one that struck many of the bishops present as "untraditional." There were, apart from 150 bishops who were ardent sup-porters of Nicene theology, another 36 bishops also present who were followers of Macedonius, and who were more to the Arian than the Nicene side, though the emperor hoped that their public reconciliation might open the way for his Nicene policy to be more universally palatable. Gregory's powerful defense of the deity of the Holy Spirit alienated this faction (later called the *Pneumatomachians*—since they "fought against the Spirit" of God). Gregory's efforts thus increasingly met with raised eyebrows from the emperor, and with great resistance from the other bishops, and ultimately were rejected. His further proposal to follow the intentions of Meletius and allow the rival Nicene bishop at Antioch (greatly supported by the Western church) to succeed "officially" to that see (thus ending the schism definitively) met with furious protests from the younger Syrian bishops who formed Meletius's entourage. It was this that stalemated the council and more or less forced Gregory's resignation (*see* Gregory, *Orations* 39–40; *Letters* 88–90, 95–97, 99–100, 128–29, 153, 157). In later poems describing the events (see especially *On His Life* vv. 1506–1918, PG 37), he bitterly described the whole affair as "the quacking of angry geese" and swore that he would never again trust a synod of bishops. It is thought that a *creed* was issued from this council (one is certainly associated with it but may have been retrospectively assigned), but it was a meeting that did not have official acts that survived, and so it is difficult to tell exactly what happened. Gregory, who in his poetry describes the council's course in detail, was not there, of course, for the final statements. The Constantinopolitan Creed affirms the Nicene *homoousion*, and adds to the shorter Nicene statements extra clauses in relation to the divine Spirit: "We believe in the Holy Spirit, the Lord and Giver of Life, who proceeds from the Father. Together with the Father and Son he is worshipped and glorified." This pneumatology was an important synodical recognition of the deity and coequality of the Holy Spirit, first declared at

Athanasius's Council of Alexandria in 362. It avoids the pneumatological use of *homoousion,* and does not explicitly acclaim the Spirit as God (the two things Gregory had demanded), but it admits the Spirit's direct divine procession, and in its use of divine titles (Lord and Life-Giver) as well as in its admission of the appropriateness of worship (conglorified with the Father and Son) it implicitly affirms the Christian doctrine of Trinity (though in terms more redolent of *Basil of Caesarea* than Gregory of Nazianzus). The Creed was adopted later as a statement to be read at eucharistic services, and thus became so popular that it is most generally referred to today (at least liturgically) as the Nicene Creed, though it should not be confused with the creed issued in 325. Despite his setback, and his disappointment with the council's theology, Gregory did not give up. His final years in retirement were spent in massive literary efforts to explain the theological intention of the synod's pneumatology. It was his exegesis of the council (as provided in his account of the synod, as well as in his *Orations* on the subject of Trinitarian theology) that finally won an international hearing, regardless of the fact that the synodical members balked at his advice on the day. The series of canons attached to this council were meant to strengthen church discipline and organization. The first canon drew up a list of heresies that were to be universally condemned, including Arianism and *Apollinarism.* Canon 2 restricted the rights of Alexandria (it had been making many resented interventions in the process of the episcopal elections at Constantinople), and Canon 3 reassigned orders of precedence in the East (elevating Constantinople over Alexandria, and thus making it a strong rival to *Rome's* precedence as an ecclesiastical court of appeal). This especially caused Rome to refuse to acknowledge this council for many years. When it did receive it, it continued to reject its canons (an anomalous position) until well into the seventh century. At Chalcedon 451, the synod of 381 was retrospectively given Ecumenical status as the Second Ecumenical Council.

L. D. Davis, *The First Seven Ecumenical Councils: Their History and Theology* (Wilmington, Del., 1987); R. P. C. Hanson, *The Search for the Christian Doctrine of God* (Edinburgh, 1988), ch. 23; J. A. McGuckin, *St. Gregory of Nazianzus: An Intellectual Biography* (New York, 2001).

Council of Constantinople II

The Second Council of Constantinople was the Fifth Ecumenical Council, held in the Eastern capital. There were 165 Eastern bishops in attendance, along with Pope Vigilius (who did not come to the sessions) and Patriarch Eutychius of Constantinople. The council was convoked at Hagia Sophia by the emperor *Justinian* to try to make a christological settlement that would reconcile the several Eastern church factions that regarded the Chalcedonian two-*nature Christology* as a betrayal of the Cyrilline vision of christological union, as exemplified in his theological writings and (at least as understood to be so in many parts of Syria and Egypt) at the Council of Ephesus in 431 (*see Monophysites*). The anti-Chalcedonian parties were united in one thing, which was to read the true line of christological development as passing from the *Council of Ephesus* 431 through *Ephesus* 449, and radically excising the Tome of Leo, which for them was tantamount to *Nestorianism*, not so much that it split the person-centers of Jesus into two (as Nestorius was thought to have done) but that it attributed each nature's sphere of operation separately to the divine person, thus counteracting the dynamical movement "into one" that the christological union was believed to have seamlessly effected. In other words, Leo, for all his close and detailed precision, avoiding "confusion" and concepts of "merging" in the two natures, was a fig-ure of great contention in the East, and Chalcedon was generally regarded as a forced synod (under heavy military supervision) that would not otherwise have accepted the Roman two-nature Christology in that form. The anti-Chalcedonian Easterners were willing to accept the statement that the one Christ came "out of two natures" (insofar as it acknowledged the perfect authenticity of the divinity and humanity in Christ), but not that he subsisted "in two natures" (insofar as this suggested that the christological "union" did not "do anything in particular," that it did not lit-erally "render one" the natures it was supposed to have united). To the Roman and Chalcedonian position that "union" was compatible with the continued claim that there subsisted two natures in Christ, the anti-Chalcedonians replied that this could be true only if one really meant "association" instead of "union" (a point *Cyril of Alexandria* had first made). It was a highly charged position since it was the *Syrian* thinkers, *Diodore*, *Theodore Mopsuestia*, and *Nestorius*, who had used "association" as their pri-mary christological idiom, and the latter had been condemned for it at Ephesus 431. As a theologian himself, Justinian was convinced that the reconciliation of the Eastern pro- and anti-Chalcedonians was possible on the basis of a strong emphasis on the Cyrilline theology they both shared. In separate decrees in 543 and 551 he condemned the *Three Chapters*, writings of three earlier Syrians most opposed to the thought of *Cyril of Alexandria* (Theodore Mop-suestia, *Theodoret of Cyrrhus*, and *Ibas of Edessa*). Many of the Syrian hierarchs had, since the days of Nestorius, come over to a radical Cyrilline position them-selves. All that was necessary was to keep the Romans in the dialogue, and they were firmly determined that nothing should shake Chalcedon's supremacy and (at least in the Western perspective) the *Tome of Leo*, which they felt to be at the heart of it. Accordingly, the West was generally hostile to the condemnation of the Three Chapters, sensing it as recidivist revisionism. Previous emperors after 451 had tried to circumvent Chalcedon with various personal statements (such as the *Henoticon* or the *Ekthesis*). Justinian now intended to arrange a grand-scale council to rephrase Chalcedon in a much more clearly pro-Cyrilline manner, without abandoning that synod (but implicitly moving as far away from the *Tome's* language as he could). It was imperative, therefore, to secure the involvement of the *papacy* in the council affairs. Pope Vigilius, reluctant from the outset, was dragged to the capital and forced to be an involved agent. He vacillated continuously but was eventually compelled to sign the acts and agree to the condemnation of the Three Chapters, much to the disgust of the Western church leaders who eventually received the news. The council affirmed the previous great councils as ecumenical (Nicaea, Constantinople I, Ephesus, and Chalcedon) but also strongly signaled its radical rejection of Nestorianism by condemning the Three Chapters again. Its eleven *capitula* decisively reject the Syrian "Christology of duality" (which was where the unspoken critique of Leo's *Tome* lay). Its fifteen anathemas also attacked the problem of Origenism. In *Anathema* 11 the name of *Origen* himself appears as a heretic. Modern scholarship has since argued that the name was inserted as a later interpolation into the conciliar acts to justify the burning of his books (though many propositions from *Evagrius* and the Origenist monks of the desert were certainly condemned here). Milan and Aquileia broke communion with Vigilius because of his acceptance of this council, and its acts were not accepted as "ecumenical" in the whole West until the end of the sixth century (at Aquileia not until the end of the seventh century). The christological statement observes the clarity and precision of the Chalcedonian settlement but makes no mention of Leo and returns to affirm the strongest of Cyril's christological statements (the *Twelve Anathemas* attached to the *Third Letter to Nestorius*), which had been passed over at Chalcedon in favor of the Roman texts. Thus the vivid language of Theopaschism (God suffered in his own flesh) was admitted into the conciliar tradition. The council was a bold attempt to reconcile the Syrian and Egyptian monophysites, on the basis of Cyrilline theology, retaining Chalcedon, but glossing it so as to reduce the impact of *Leo's Tome*. It failed, in the end, to achieve what was hoped for, largely because Egypt and Syria were soon lost to the Byzantine world through Islamic invasion. It has, in modern times, been the subject of renewed interest for an ecumenical rapprochement between the Byzantine, Latin, Coptic, and *Armenian* traditions, which were separated after Chalcedon because of the Monophysite controversy. The Byzantine tradition has always preferred the tenor of christological theory represented in the intellectual trajectory of Ephesus 431 culminating in Constantinople 553. In the West, Christology has always been predominantly interpreted through Chalcedon 451 as read through the lens of the *Tome of Leo*, and very little notice has, accordingly, been given to Constantinople II.

W. H. C. Frend, *The Rise of the Monophysite Movement* (Cambridge, 1979); P. T. R. Gray, *The Defence of Chalcedon in the East: 451–553* (Leiden, Netherlands, 1979); A. Grillmeier, *Christ in Christian Tradition* (vol. 2, part 2; London, 1995); E. R. Hardy, *Christology of the Later Fathers* (Philadelphia, 1964), 378–81; M. Kalamaras, *He Pempte Oikoumenike Synodos* (Gk. text; Athens, 1985).

Council of Constantinople III

Constantinople III was the Sixth Ecumenical Council, held in the eastern capital between 680 and 681. The council was called by Emperor Constantine IV. It was opened with the agreement of Pope Agatho (who sent a three-person Roman delegation) and arranged under the presidency of Patriarchs George of Constantinople and Macarius of Antioch (then resident at the capital). It was convened in the Domed Hall (Troullos) of the imperial palace and is, accordingly, sometimes known as the Council in Trullo (a name also given to the so-called "Fifth-Sixth Council" [the *Quinisext*]), which was a synod called in 692 to supply a list of reformatory canons, retrospectively, to the Fifth and Sixth Ecumenical Councils). More than 164 bishops were in attendance. At Constantinople III it was hoped to bring an end to several controversies then prevalent in the Eastern church that related to the interpretation of *Christology*, namely *Monothelitism* (the doctrine that Christ only had one *will*), and *Monoenergism* (the catch-all doctrine that was proposed as a sidestepping of the previous issue), so that Christ could be seen as constantly motivated by a single power (*energeia* or *dynamis*), and that a divine one, wherein the humanity was thoroughly caught up into the remit of the Word's activity and presence. Both Monothelitism and Mono-Energism were attempts to reconcile the *Monophysite* crisis by circumventing the two-*nature* theology of the *Council of Chalcedon,* and both had run into strong opposition from the West for many years previously. By 680 it was also clear to the Byzantine emperors that their policy of trying to suppress christological arguments in the East, or of controlling them by imperial dictat, had utterly failed. The council was a serious attempt to think through and resolve some of the problematics still remaining. In this sense it was the last gloss, or rationale, offered to the prior conciliar christological tradition. It has attracted very little study in later times, which is unfortunate, for the issues raised extend very deeply, and were one of the few times Christian theologians of antiquity considered the dimension of personal freedom and psychological identity. The council extended over eighteen sessions, the first eleven of which were presided over by the emperor in person. Macarius of Antioch insisted that the admission of

two wills in Christ was tantamount to a revival of *Nestorianism*. The majority of bishops followed the teachings of *Maximos the Confessor* (d. 662), who had argued strongly that to deny a human will to Christ was to render his humanity specious. Likewise, to see Christ merely as a single divine "force" betrayed the previous conciliar tradition that accepted that the Single Christ performed acts both divine and human, according to the humanity and according to the divinity, and thus exercised two energies of life, both of which were perfectly harmonized in his divine person. In other words Mono-Energism implied that the christological union should be posited in the concept of force; whereas Maximos argued it had to be posited in the concept of a free and gracious person. Christology was thus a mystery of personal engagement (God's salvation of his created people through love), not a simple manifestation of abstract power. Macarius of Antioch was deposed from office. In the final session the names of previous supporters of the Monothelite and Mono-Energist positions were also anathematized: one of the rare occasions a pope (Honorius) was posthumously condemned as a heretic. Thus the doctrine of Christ having two wills (a divine and human) perfectly harmonized in his divine person, just as the person perfectly harmonized the operation of his two natures, was affirmed. This is known as Dyothelite Christology.

L. D. Davis, *The First Seven Ecumenical Councils: Their History and Theology* (Wilmington, Del., 1987).

Council of Elvira   see **Anathema, Canons, Celibacy, Sexual Ethics**

Council of Ephesus I   The First Council of Ephesus was the Third Ecumenical Council, convoked by Emperor Theodosius II. It was held at Ephesus in 431 under the presidency of *Cyril of*

Alexandria to resolve the christological crisis that had flared up between Cyril and *Nestorius of Constantinople*. Soon after Nestorius's appointment as archbishop of Constantinople in 428, he began a series of reformatory sermons and other measures that were bent on introducing the disciplines and teachings of his own native Syrian church into his new see. In the course of this energetic reform campaign his tactless behavior made him many enemies, notably the empress Pulcheria, the Byzantine military aristocracy, popular factions (Nestorius had banned erotic entertainments), and not least the many monks and clergy at *Constantinople*, who traditionally looked to *Alexandria*, its archbishop, and its theological traditions to inform their practice. When Nestorius found that many in his capital favored the Alexandrian christological custom of indiscriminately associating, in the strongest language, acts appropriate to the Godhead and humanity respectively, he was determined to instruct those whom he regarded as ignoramuses. It concerned statements such as Mary as the "Mother of God" (*Theotokos*). Nestorius argued she was "properly speaking" the Mother of Christ, or of Jesus, not the Mother of God who had no mother. Another example was the much-favored custom of making strong "paradox pairs," such as speaking about the "God bound in swaddling bands," or "God bleeding on the *cross*." Nestorius found these kinds of statements highly objectionable. The problem was that they were not merely popular pieties expressing the sentiment that Jesus was divine, but also deeply embedded in the formal christological tradition of *Alexandria*. It was Nestorius's misfortune to censure this kind of language at a time when Alexandria was governed by one of its most powerful political, as well as intellectual, archbishops. Cyril responded to growing complaints from a number of clergy who found that Nestorius's theology alarmingly separated the divine Word from

the human Jesus. Nestorius did not himself believe that there was a merely human man Jesus, in whom there was also present the divine Word (which would have been a revival of *Paul of Samosata*), but his language was that of his *Syrian* teachers, *Diodore of Tarsus* and *Theodore of Mopsuestia*. Long beforehand, *Gregory of Nazianzus* had censured Diodore for speaking about "Two Sons" (the Son of God and the Son of Man), and when Nestorius revived this style of language in Constantinopolitan Greek, rather than his native Syriac, he was heard in very different ways from those he had intended. To his claim that Mary was not "strictly speaking" the Mother of God, Cyril countered with the statement that "If Mary is not, strictly speaking, the Mother of God, then he who is born from her is not, strictly speaking, God." So battle lines were drawn. Cyril on the one side regarded Nestorius's language of two personal reference zones (*prosopa*) that were overlapped in a third zone as tantamount to a Christology of schizoid separation. Nestorius felt that one could make statements first about the human being Jesus, or second about the divine Word, or third about the two as they were associated together, · which latter would be statements about the Christ, or the Son of God, or the Lord (these terms being the only ones appropriate to convey the other two zones). So Jesus (or the Son of Man) suffered thirst, the *Logos* raised Lazarus, and the Christ (or Son of God) walked on the water. But God did not bleed on the cross (Jesus did), and Jesus did not heal the sick (the Son of God did). This strict propriety of personal attribution, as far as the Alexandrians were concerned, belied the central mystery of the *incarnation*: that God had united flesh to himself so that the human nature itself was appropriated, in Christ, so as to become the "very flesh of God," something Cyril saw as the source of all salvific blessing. For Cyril, if Christ, and Jesus, and divine Word were not synonymous referents, and the single subject of all of the incarnate acts, then a union of God and humanity had not occurred in the incarnation, and the acts of Jesus were not universally potent. In other words the death of a human being, Jesus, could not have the fundamental salvific effect the church understood by the notion of the "death of God enfleshed" for the salvation of the world. Nor could the incarnation itself be the ontological reconciliation of Godhead and humanity in the person of Jesus, and through him as a *grace* to his church. The council was first convoked to meet at the capital, and envisaged (at least by Nestorius) as a trial of Cyril's own language (which Nestorius had claimed was *Apollinarism* revived). Someone (we might suspect Pulcheria) changed the venue to Ephesus in Asia Minor. This greatly inconvenienced all of Nestorius's supporters from Syria. Cyril assumed the presidency (on the right of his ancient see) as soon as he arrived, much to the fury of Nestorius, who claimed it was meant to be a trial of Cyril. He refused to attend any of the sessions. Cyril proceeded anyway, even before the Syrians had arrived, and on the basis of several visiting *bishops* having heard Nestorius claim that it was "impossible" to call a small baby "God" (presumably he meant the issue of the "Logos in swaddling bands"), they denounced him as a heretic and deposed him. There is no doubt that he did not receive a fair hearing. It is also true to say that his *Christology* was deeply confused and rejected not simply because Cyril was determined to sink it, but more so because it so severely clashed with the traditional piety represented by the majority of bishops present at Ephesus. When the Syrians finally arrived they sided with Nestorius and deposed Cyril. Matters fell into a long stalemate while the emperor heard appeals at the capital, putting all the protagonists under house arrest at Ephesus. Finally (mainly because of riots against Nestorius in the city, although "gifts" were also distributed by Cyril to allow his party to access the emperor more regularly) Theodosius

decided in favor of Cyril and exiled Nestorius to his home in Syria (later he would be exiled to Petra in Arabia, and then to the Great Oasis in Egypt since he refused to accede to his condemnation). Cyril's writings were afforded the status of conciliar orthodoxy, and the title Theotokos was formally endorsed; but the triumph was not complete since the Syrian church refused to enter into communion with him. Two years later, a reconciliation was moderated by the palace, and Cyril and John of Antioch signed a joint agreement (the *Formula of Reunion*) that set out a christological statement combining elements of the Syrian and Alexandrian confessions, and agreeing to the personal unity of Christ. This formal rapprochement did not end the smoldering resentment of the Syrians to the way in which Egypt had railroaded the conciliar events, and indeed all of Cyril's writings after he signed the agreement continued to denounce the greatest Syrian teachers (Diodore of Tarsus and Theodore of Mopsuestia) as "Nestorians" uncondemned. It also masked the issue that had not been settled at the council, which was the manner in which the "two natures" were combined. Was Christ a single union "out of two natures" (Cyril's preference) or was he a single person existing "in two natures" (the preference of Rome and Syria)? Cyril was persuaded not to persevere in his attacks on the Syrian tradition, but his disciples were not so easily won over, and after Cyril's death in 444, *Dioscorus* his successor determined to take up the struggle again, a move that resulted in the *Council of Ephesus II* (449).

L. D. Davis, *The First Seven Ecumenical Councils: Their History and Theology* (Wilmington, Del., 1987); J. A. McGuckin, *St. Cyril of Alexandria and the Christological Crisis: Its History, Theology, and Texts* (Leiden, Netherlands, 1994, and New York 2004).

Council of Ephesus II   The council held at Ephesus in 449 was convoked by

Theodosius II to settle the controversy that had arisen at Constantinople under *Patriarch Flavian* concerning the priest-monk *Eutyches*, who had been condemned by Flavian's local synod for holding views that Dioscorus (wrongly) thought were those of Cyril. Dioscorus thus believed that in the condemnation of Eutyches, Nestorianism was being admitted once more into the capital, and his own Alexandrian tradition was under attack. He so violently seized the initiative at Ephesus, using monks as roughnecks to enforce his views, that he gained the presidency of the council, which he then turned into a trial of Flavian and an exoneration of Eutyches. The Roman delegates present tried on numerous occasions to have the *Tome of Leo* read and entered into the official minutes as their church's formal contribution to the christological debate. After Dioscorus had read it, he felt it so clashed with Cyrilline theology that he vetoed it, to the great anger of the Romans. It was this that determined Pope *Leo* to have the *Tome* entered as official acts at any forthcoming council that would review this one (which would be two years later, at the *Council of Chalcedon*). Flavian was so roughly treated after his deposition that he later died from the shock. The Syrian theologians were roundly condemned, and *Theodoret of Cyrrhus*, who had passionately denounced *Cyril of Alexandria* ever since Ephesus 431, was also deposed. The council's affairs were widely seen as disgraceful. Pope Leo wittily called it the "Latrocinium" (the Brigandage of Ephesus, or Robber Council; cf. Leo, *Epistle* 95), a name that has stuck in many textbooks. Even so, in the East most of Dioscorus's theological arguments were felt to be largely in agreement with the *Council of Ephesus I* (431), and the emperor Theodosius II refused to reopen the issue or review complaints. However, after the latter's sudden death from a horse-riding accident in 450, the empress Pulcheria and the newly appointed emperor Marcian agreed to

Roman demands to review the affair, and at Chalcedon in 451 Dioscorus was deposed for his behavior (though pointedly not for his doctrine). Several textbooks (somewhat reductively and anachronistically) regard this council as the beginning of *Monophysitism*.

L. D. Davis, *The First Seven Ecumenical Councils: Their History and Theology* (Wilmington, Del., 1987); S. G. F. Perry, trans., *The Second Council of Ephesus* (Dartford, 1881).

Council of Nicaea I   The first of the Ecumenical Councils, the First Council of Nicaea was summoned by *Constantine the Great* to his palace at Nikaia in Bithynia, in 325 on the occasion of his twentieth anniversary of reign. It was presided over by *Hosius of Cordoba*, with *Eustathius of Antioch* and Alexander of Alexandria (the latter was attended by his deacon, *Athanasius the Great*). As soon as Constantine had assumed total monarchical control over the East he determined to settle the disputes troubling the Christian provinces there in the aftermath of a long series of wars and persecutions; most particularly he wished to settle the high feelings that were being stirred up by the *Arian* dispute. His theological advisor, Hosius, had arranged a council in Antioch in 324, and here several aspects of Arianism were condemned. Hosius took this as something of a rehearsal for Nicaea. Following Constantine's advice to seek a broad reconciliation among the bishops, a traditional baptismal *creed* (probably that of *Jerusalem*) was agreed on, but a series of insertions were added to emphasize the anti-Arian agenda and affirm the eternal divinity of the Son of God. To these insertions describing the status of the Son (Light of Light, True God from True God) was added one that for the first time used nonbiblical terms to define the Son's relation to God: "of one substance with the Father" (*homoousios*). This was to become the distinctive cipher of Nicene theology. To make matters abundantly clear a series of explicitly anti-Arian *anathemas* were also attached to the end of the creed, refuting the view that the Son was born from nothing as a creature. Athanasius was not immediately taken by the vague idea represented by the *homoousion* ("of the same stuff as God"), but later saw that it had a usefulness in marking off Arian opponents, and so spent his later career, as archbishop in Alexandria, clarifying and fighting for the principle of the Son's eternal essential identity with the Father (one in essence, and that the same essence). The Nicene Creed, the *canons*, and a synodical letter are all that exist from the council itself, as no acts have survived, and we only have accounts of it from partisans. Athanasius (*Ep. Afr.* 2) says that 318 bishops were present (a symbol based on Gen. 14.14); modern scholars have revised this to probably between 220 and 250; all except 8 Western delegates were Easterners. The twenty genuine canons of Nicaea attempted to restore a common discipline in the aftermath of serious civil and ecclesiastical disruptions. They became seen as the matrix of later canon law and many councils subsequently emulated them. The canons set up a system for determining the date of Easter, and regulated the precedence of sees and other matters. Theologically the council proved highly controversial. Although all signed on the day, Constantine himself soon drew back from the *homoousion* policy he himself had proposed, and many of the bishops demonstrated throughout the remainder of the fourth century a great vacillation in regard to the Nicene doctrine. In many instances the Nicenes were a minority in the East, but were sustained by support from the West, and eventually carried the day at *Council of Constantinople I* in 381. The council was also important for establishing the pattern of church governance for future major controversies (*see Councils*): a synodical gathering now modeled on the pattern of a senatorial

assembly (with force of law to its decrees), summoned by the emperor, at which theological matters were debated and resolved. Nicaea was retrospectively regarded as an "Ecumenical Council," but it was indeed the event that transformed the ancient synodical process into something far more significant for a Christian world now under Christian emperors.

R. P. C. Hanson, *The Search for the Christian Doctrine of God* (Edinburgh, 1988); J. N. D. Kelly, *Early Christian Creeds* (3d ed.; London, 1972); C. Luibheïd, *The Council of Nicaea* (Galway, 1982); C. Stead, *Divine Substance* (Oxford, 1977). 223–66.

Council of Nicaea II   Nicaea II was the Seventh Ecumenical Council, convoked by the empress Irene in the Church of the Holy Apostles at *Constantinople* in August 786, with Patriarch Tarasius of Constantinople presiding. The council was an attempt to bring the *iconoclastic* controversy to a definitive end (though it would run on until 843). Pope Hadrian and the Eastern patriarchs sent delegates. No sooner had the council opened than the garrison of troops stationed in the capital raided the church and drove off the bishops, a testimony both to their iconoclastic loyalties (as maintained by the former emperors) and their hostility to Irene, who had assumed power violently. Biding her time, the empress quietly transferred the iconoclastic troops on active patrol far away from the capital, and then rearranged the council. This time it met in September 787 at the town of Nicaea, to give it a symbolic weight by reference to *Nicaea I.* The letter of Pope Hadrian to Irene was endorsed, which defined the veneration (respectful and honorific) that could be given to icons (*aspasmon kai timetiken proskynesis*) as distinct from the adoration (*alethine latreia*) that could only be given spiritually to God. The writings of *John of Damascus* and Germanos of Constantinople were elevated as authentic guides to the theological issues involved in icon and relic veneration (later Theodore Studite would be added to the list). Worship of the icons (that is, "veneration," for the modern term "worship" occludes the ancient distinctions) is something that was defined as passing on through the medium of the image, the *cross*, or the *relic* directly to the person of the one who was represented in it (Christ, the *Virgin Mary*, or the *saints*) and *sacramentally* rendered present by it. Devotional acts such as incensing or bowing before an icon of Christ were not idolatrous, because they had reference to the material image only as a medium to the presence of the holy person it represented. To the charge of the Iconoclasts (literally the "icon-smashers") that no material image could ever represent God, the Iconodules (the venerators of icons) replied that veneration of the material image as a valid manifestation of Christ was a confession of the principle of the incarnation of God in the flesh. By this connection, established beforehand in the writings of the main Iconodules, the Second Council of Nicaea has been regarded as the last of the Ecumenical Councils concerned with *Christology.* It is important not only for the practice of later Eastern Orthodoxy, and for the history of Christian *art,* but also for establishing principles of sacramental mediation in Christian thought. For the Orthodox Christian world this synod brought an end to the series of Ecumenical Councils, since no other was held before the Great Schism of the East and West. In the Latin world the popes continued to call international councils and designated them as "Ecumenical" on many occasions.

L. D. Davis, *The First Seven Ecumenical Councils: Their History and Theology* (Wilmington, Del., 1987); P. J. Henry, "Initial Eastern Assessments of the 7th Ecumenical Council," JTS 25 (1974): 75–92; K. Parry, *Depicting the Word: Byzantine Iconophile Thought of the 8th and*

9th Centuries (Leiden, Netherlands, 1996); D. J. Sahas, *Icon and Logos: Sources in Eighth Century Iconoclasm* (Medieval Texts and Translations 4; Toronto, 1986).

Creeds   The term derives from the Latin *credo,* "I believe," which often began the formal recitation of the truths that the believer accepted and confessed. The creeds grew up originally as very short statements of faith. Several of the earliest protocreeds can be seen still embedded in the later parts of the New Testament as short confessional prayers and hymns, mainly *christological* in nature (cf. Phil. 2:6–11; Col. 1:15–20; 1 Tim. 3:16). In the second century the growing conflicts among Christian communities, in the context of the gnostic crisis, made church leaders more wary of what new converts actually believed about the basic truths. Periods of instruction were instituted, with statements of faith increasingly required of candidates at *baptism*. These began with the confession that one God and Father was the creator of heaven and earth (thus renouncing *Gnosticism*) and confessed the central facts of the redemption given by the descent of God's Son to an earthly ministry, suffering, resurrection, glorification, and eventual return in judgment. The statement of belief in the *Holy Spirit* was also present, usually to state that the divine Spirit inspired all of Scripture (thus renouncing the *Marcionites* and gnostics who attacked that principle). Other creedal clauses (such as belief in the single efficacy of baptism, the holiness of the church, and resurrectional life) were also inserted in the third century. The creeds underwent intense development in the fourth century as they were increasingly used as traditional "standards of belief" in times of doctrinal crisis. Because they were, generally, very broad in character, they were often rewritten to make them specifically appropriate to contemporary matters. A prime example of this is the expansion of the Jerusalem church's baptismal creed to become the doctrinal creed of *Nicaea*, or the expansion of the Nicene Creed itself at the First *Council of Constantinople* (381) to clarify the deity of the *Holy Spirit* as a *hypostasis* within the *Trinity*. Before the fourth century there were many local varieties of creeds. After that time, the Apostles' Creed (in the West) and the Nicene-Constantinopolitan Creed (in the East) became the only ones in use at baptisms. The Western church also greatly favored the Athanasian Creed (Quicunque Vult), which synopsized christological and Trinitarian belief. After the fifth century the creed was introduced into the Eastern liturgy, where it is still recited at each *Eucharist.* In the early eleventh century the practice was also introduced at *Rome,* and spread through the medieval Western churches.

J. N. D. Kelly, *Early Christian Creeds* (London, 1950); P. Schaff, *The Creeds of Christendom* (New York, 1877).

Cross   The cross is one of the most universally potent symbols of the Christian religion, being the instrument on which Jesus was executed by the Roman authorities. Christian fascination with the cross is witnessed from the beginning of the proclamation of the *kerygma*. The passion narratives demonstrate a clear and sober narrative of the brutally casual execution of Jesus, knowing that crucifixion was the much-feared death reserved for slaves and insurgents. The passion narratives focus not so much on the cross (or other incidents of the sufferings) but unwaveringly on the constancy of Jesus, who thus becomes a model of martyrs. At first Christian theology demonstrates mainly a horrified sense of awe that the powers of wickedness could treat the Lord in such a way (Acts 2:22–35). But the tone was decidedly that God's glorification of his servant Jesus far outweighed the dishonor that the powers of darkness tried to inflict. Peter, in his speech to the people

of Jerusalem, sums it up in the words: "God has made this Jesus whom you crucified, both Lord and Christ" (Acts 2:36). There is a regular contrasted pairing of the ideas of humiliation (in the cross) and exalted glorification of Jesus by God (because of the faithfulness to the point of crucifixion), such as can be seen in the ancient hymn that Paul quotes (Phil. 2:6–11) as well in the schemes of ascent (*anabasis*) and descent (*katabasis*) that structure the Fourth Gospel's theology of crucifixion and glorification (cf. John 3:13–15). Paul took a decisive step when he made the cross not merely a scandal to be explained away but a mystery of faith and God's love that ought to be celebrated (Gal. 6:14) as pivotal. The cross in Christian use was already shifting away from a thing of shame to a sacrificial covenant of reconciliation (Eph. 2:16; Col. 1:20; Heb. 12:2). In the early *Apologists* and *Apostolic Fathers* the cross is rarely mentioned (cf. *Ignatius of Antioch, To the Ephesians* 9.1; 18.1; *To the Trallians* 11.2; *To the Philadelphians* 8.2). But popular devotion to it as a confident symbol of Christian victory over the powers of this world was growing, as can be seen in the appearance from the second century of the cross-shaped monogram *fos-zoe* (light and life in the cross). After the dedication of Constantine's new Basilica of the Anastasis at Jerusalem in 335, marking the site of Christ's death and resurrection, devotion to the cross took on a new and international impetus. Although there are recorded cross inscriptions from the middle of the second century, after the Constantinian era the appearance of the cross as a Christian cipher became more and more common. In 395 *Ambrose of Milan* recounts the story that Helena, mother of *Constantine*, discovered the True Cross of Jesus. *Cyril of Jerusalem* also attests it was discovered (not naming Helena) during Constantine's reign. The "invention" (or finding) of the cross at the site of Calvary is probably to be associated with the extensive excavations undertaken on the site when the Anastasis church was being prepared (*see Jerusalem*). Egeria in the account of her visit to Jerusalem in 380 records the elaborate ceremony of the veneration of the cross that was practized there. The traditional version of the story of the invention recounts how the True Cross was found in the quarry with other remains of crosses and the local bishop laid a paralytic on each to see which one cured him. The Feast of the Invention was celebrated first only locally at Jerusalem (and then throughout the Eastern world) on September 14. The same day was later chosen as the Feast of the Exaltation of the Cross, to mark the occasion (originally in the spring of 629) when the emperor Heraclius returned the great relic of the True Cross to the church at Jerusalem after recapturing it from the Persians, who had taken it away as spoils of war in 614. Heraclius took the occasion to transfer many relics of the True Cross to Constantinople, and from there relics were sent to *Rome* and other important sees as prized gifts of the Christian emperors. The Roman Pontifical also claimed that *Constantine* himself had given relics of the cross and passion to the Basilica of Santa Croce in Gerusalemme, where they are still venerated today. Christian *art* greatly developed the theme of the cross, and numerous different "types" are found still in use. The Latin cross, for example, is longer in its length than its arms, whereas the Greek cross is a cross-in-square, which also eventually came to be the dominant form of all Byzantine churches. The crucifix (depiction of the body of Jesus on the cross) was developed more in the West than the East. The Byzantine church painted Christ crucified in a sinuous shape (reminiscent of Moses exalting the serpent on the stick, as in John 3) and as a divinely calm redeemer. Byzantine church crosses in metal usually did not have a corpus. With increasing devotion to the sufferings of Jesus, and a renewed sense of desiring to empathize with them, Western medieval examples of the crucifix

depicting Jesus in realistic sufferings on the cross became introduced in the church. The old mockery that all the relics of the True Cross put together would be enough to build a wooden ship was disproved by De Fleury, who mathematically estimated that all surviving fragments amount to one-third of a typical Roman cross. Relics of the cross, wherever they are held in churches, are usually a central feature of the service of the veneration of the cross on Good Friday.

———

J. W. Drijvers, *Helena Augusta: the Mother of Constantine the Great and the Legend of Her Finding of the True Cross* (Leiden, Netherlands, 1991); R. de Fleury, *Mémoire sur les instruments de la Passion* (Paris, 1870); A. Frolow, *La Relique de la Vraie Croix: Recherches sur la développement d'une culte* (Archives de L'Orient 7; Paris, 1961); G. de Jerphanion, *La représentation de la Croix et du Crucifix aux origines de l'art chrétien* (Paris, 1930).

Cyprian of Carthage (c. 200–258) Cyprian was one of the most important of the early Latin theologian-bishops. He was a distinguished rhetorician at Carthage, who was converted (c. 245) to Christianity by the presbyter Caecilius, and shortly afterwards gave up most of his estate for the benefit of the poor and became a presbyter. Soon (c. 248) he was elected bishop of Carthage by public acclamation, but had some opposition within the ranks of his clergy who regarded him as insufficiently experienced. Immediately after his election the church was thrown into disarray by the Edict of Decius (250) demanding that all citizens should offer sacrifice to the gods (*see persecutions*). Cyprian withdrew from the city to avoid arrest. Many Christians quickly conformed, either by offering sacrifice or by obtaining certificates to show that they had done so. The initial danger having passed, Cyprian determined to readmit them only after a suitable time of penance, but dissident presbyters subverted his leadership and using the authority of *confessors* (those who had survived earlier persecutions and enjoyed enhanced authority within the community) allowed them to be readmitted. Threat of a new persecution in 251, under Gallus, made Cyprian change his mind and call for general reconciliation. At this time the Roman church was itself caught up in factional fighting between the rigorists (represented by the antipope *Novatian*) and those more open to reconciliation of the lapsed (Pope Cornelius). Cyprian became involved in this factional fight, and so was his own church, to such an extent that a group of presbyters chose a new bishop, Fortunatus, to stand against him. From 255 to 257 Cyprian was involved in a war of letters with the Pope Stephen concerning whether or not sacraments administered by heretical and schismatic clergy were valid. Cyprian took the conservative view that they were not, and was censured for it. In 257 the emperor Valerian issued a new edict demanding public sacrifice. This time Cyprian was exiled, and the following year brought back to Carthage since he had refused to accede to any of the terms of the new laws. He was tried in Carthage in 258 and, confessing his faith, was beheaded under the proconsul Galerius Maximus. His theology was learned on the job and demonstrates a lively mind seeking to acquaint himself with the full character of his new religion. So, apart from some works of general apologia for Christianity (*To Donatus* and *To Demetrian*), we have specific treatises: *The Lord's Prayer*, *Works and Almsgiving*, *The Dress of Virgins*, and *To Quirinius*, which is a collection of Scripture passages (using ancient traditional formularies) that can be used to demonstrate various points in preaching. His bitter experiences of disunity led him to write two very influential volumes, *The Lapsed* and *The Unity of the Catholic Church*. The latter work would become a classic in the construction of a catholic theology of the *church* (or ecclesiol-

ogy). His letters are priceless historical resources for understanding church life in the early third century.

M. A. Fahey, *Cyprian and the Bible: A Study in 3rd Century Exegesis* (Tübingen, Germany, 1971); P. Hinchcliff, *Cyprian of Carthage and the Unity of the Christian Church* (London, 1974); M. M. Sage, *Cyprian* (Cambridge, Mass., 1975).

Cyril of Alexandria (c. 378–444)

Cyril is one of the most important theologians on the *person* of Christ in all Greek Christian writing. He was the major figure, both intellectually and politically, in the great crisis of *Christology* in the international church of the fifth century, and presided over the *Council of Ephesus I* (431) where the teaching of *Nestorius* was condemned and Cyril's Christology was adopted that affirmed the single subjectivity of the divine Logos personally present in Jesus. Cyril's teaching went on to determine the agenda of three following Ecumenical Councils up to the seventh century. He was a native of Egypt, and when his uncle *Theophilus* became the archbishop of Alexandria in 385, he brought the young man to *Alexandria* for advanced studies. In 403, when he was twenty-five years old, Cyril was ordained lector, and in the same year attended Theophilus at the notorious Synod of the Oak, which deposed *John Chrysostom*. At his uncle's death in 412, after a tumultuous election, Cyril was consecrated archbishop. His early years were marked by several major conflicts between the Christians and both the pagan and Jewish factions of the city. At the same time he was using the monastic movement to advance the Christian evangelization of a country where the old religions still held considerable sway (*see* *Shenoudi*). After 428 Cyril was increasingly drawn into conflict with the new archbishop of Constantinople, Nestorius, who conceived of two centers of operation simultaneously present in the life of Christ: one human and one divine, with one sometimes predominating over the other. Cyril denounced this as heretical, insisting that Jesus was wholly and completely divine, thus only one single person, and that person God. For Cyril, everything that Jesus did, whether it was a human act such as sleeping or a powerful act such as raising the dead, was equally a work of the single divine Lord, now embodied within history. The divine power present in the humanity was also an archetype of how God had intended to "divinize" the human condition in the act of incarnation. Thus Christ is the pattern of the world's salvation. The process of *deification* is best exemplified in the reception of the *Eucharist*, the "life-giving blessing" of the divine flesh that immortalizes the believer. It was a dynamic Christology that eventually came to represent the classical statement of the Christian East, but not without major resistance on the way, especially from theologians in *Rome* and *Syria*. The Council of Ephesus, where Cyril was judge and jury simultaneously, caused great bitterness in its aftermath, and the emperor's negotiators had to work for several years to restore church communion, especially between Alexandria and *Antioch.* Eventually in 433 a compromise was agreed on (the Formula of Reunion) where important points of the Antiochene position (Christ had two authentic natures—both human and divine) could be reconciled with Cyril's insistence that Christ was a single reality, one divine person, but the precise ramifications of that agreement still needed much clarifying debate, and in default of this it was inevitable that the whole argument would soon break out again. It did so with great force in the following generation. Cyril died on June 27, 444, a little short of his seventieth year.

J. A. McGuckin, *St. Cyril of Alexandria and the Christological Controversy: Its History, Theology, and Texts* (Leiden, Netherlands, 1994); N. Russell, *Cyril of Alexandria* (London, 2000).

Cyril of Jerusalem (c. 315–387)

Cyril was *priest* and then *bishop* (from 349) of the Jerusalem church at a time when its liturgical ritual, celebrated in the splendid new buildings that *Constantine* had endowed there, was achieving wide attention. He is most famous for his twenty-four lectures on the church's sacramental life, which were his homilies given in the process of admitting candidates for *baptism.* The first of these was a *Protocatechesis* delivered before Lent began, the next were *Eighteen Catecheses* delivered to candidates during Lent, and the final five were *Mystagogic Catecheses* (which some attribute to his successor John of Jerusalem) delivered in Bright Week, immediately following Pascha. The *Catecheses* reveal a great deal about early Christian liturgical practice, theology, and discipline. The main series of eighteen catecheses are substantially a commentary on the *creed,* stanza by stanza, and the mystagogic lectures explain the symbols and mystical significance of the baptismal rituals of immersion, anointing, and *chrismation,* as well as the *eucharistic* mysteries that immediately followed. During his time as bishop Cyril was generally a supporter of the *Homoiousian* position and was thus regarded with suspicion by both the Nicenes and the *Arians.* Acacius, the *Homoian* Arian bishop of Caesarea, his earliest patron, turned against him for personal and theological motives and, using charges of financial maladministration, succeeded in having him exiled in 357. He was exiled, in all, no less than three times. After the last occasion, under Valens, he was forced to be absent from Jerusalem for almost ten years. When he returned in 378 he became a senior figure welcomed into the policies of the *neo-Nicene* restoration of orthodoxy, especially after *Gregory of Nyssa* visited Jerusalem and reported favorably on his theology. At the Council of Constantinople in 381 Cyril possibly recited the Creed of Jerusalem (containing the *homoousios*) to indicate his acceptance of the full Nicene theology. This may account for the establishment of that creed in the records associated with the council, and for its subsequent international ascendancy (ousting the original form of the Nicene Creed) across the Christian world.

F. L. Cross, *St. Cyril of Jerusalem's Lectures on the Christian Sacraments* (London, 1951); E. H. Gifford, *St. Cyril Archbishop of Jerusalem: The Catechetical Lectures* (NPNF, series 2, 7; repr., Grand Rapids, 1989); R. Gregg, "Cyril of Jerusalem and the Arians," in *Arianism: Historical and Theological Reassessments* (papers from the Ninth International Conference on Patristic Studies, September 5–10, 1983, Oxford, England; ed. Robert C. Gregg; Cambridge, Mass., 1985).

Cyril of Scythopolis (b. c. 525)

Cyril was a native of Scythopolis (Beth Shan) in Palestine, whose parents administered a guest house for traveling monks. He was much attracted by the life and achievements of St. Sabas (d. 532), and set off as a young man, in 543, to become an *ascetic* himself. He spent some time at *Jerusalem* with the monastic leader John the Hesychast, and then tried the life of a solitary in the monastery of St. Euthymius. When the Origenist controversy severely disrupted life here, Cyril moved in 557 to become a monk at St. Sabas's monastery near Bethlehem. The date of his death is unknown. His major work was the composition of the *Lives of the Palestinian Monks*. He is a major hagiographic historian of Palestinian monasticism during the Origenistic crisis. His writing is full of lively detail, and set a standard for much Byzantine *hagiography* to follow.

R. M. Price, trans., *Cyril of Scythopolis: Lives of the Monks of Palestine* (Kalamazoo, Mich., 1989).

Damasus of Rome (c. 304–384)

Damasus, one of the chief *deacons* of *Rome*, became pope in 366 after a violently contested election. The public riots in its wake were resolved only by imperial intervention when Valentinian I endorsed Damasus as bishop. The struggle is an interesting marker of how important and powerful the office of Roman bishop had now become. Damasus used that office to the full, establishing the standard of Nicene doctrinal orthodoxy both at home and internationally. He frequently invoked the help of imperial legislation to back up his synodical decrees. Presiding over a council in Rome in 382, he established an official *canon* of the recognized books of the Bible, and also commissioned *St. Jerome* to produce a pure Latin text of the Scriptures, a "Vulgate," which was to have immense influence on the subsequent Latin world. Damasus worked diligently to order the archives of the Roman church and restore its ancient monuments and *martyr*-shrines, and was one of those who laid the foundations for a greatly expanded sense of the office and significance of the *papacy* (establishing the terminology of Rome as the "Apostolic See"). His interventions in the affairs of the Eastern church were less happy. He had an enduring suspicion of *St. Basil the Great*, and refused to recognize the legitimacy of *St. Gregory of Nazianzus* as bishop of *Constantinople*. By supporting the claims of Paulinus in the divided church at Antioch (against *Meletius of Antioch*), Damasus added to the confusion of the leading *neo-Nicene* theologians in the East. The *Tome of Damasus* is the synopsis of *Trinitarian* and *christological* orthodoxy Damasus wished Paulinus to establish in the East (anathematizing the *Apollinarists* and the *Pneumatomachians*) and prefigures a style of later interventions on the part of Rome, not least that of the *Tome of Leo* at the *Council of Chalcedon* (451). When *Theodosius* assumed imperial control in 380 he decreed that the faith of Damasus of Rome and Peter of *Alexandria* (the Nicene Creed) would henceforth be the official *orthodoxy* of the empire.

M. A. Norton, "Pope Damasus," in J. Marique, ed., *Leaders of Iberian Christianity* (Boston, 1962), 13–80; J. Taylor, "St. Basil the Great and Pope St. Damasus I," DR 91 (1973); 186–203, 262–74.

Deacons   The title signifies servants or ministers (Gk. *diakonoi*). It is one of the three (major) orders of Christian priesthood (bishops, presbyters, and deacons). Originally it seems to have been a title of the church leaders of the Hellenist Christians, in distinction to the term "apostle" (one sent), which Jesus applied to his first missionaries, and which was later taken as a title of honor in the apostolic organization of the Jerusalem church of the latter half of the first century. The Hellenist deacons included among their number powerful theologians such as Stephen and Philip. As twelve was regarded as the symbolic number of apostles (although it was always exceeded in the ancient listings of "apostles"), so seven was first taken as a symbolic number of deacons (see Acts 6:5). Luke, in his account of conflicts in the Jerusalem church between Hellenists and Hebrew Christians, gave his own (massively simplifying) version of early institutional ministerial development, which was to be determinative for all later perspectives. He reconciled the history of conflicting origins of institutional leadership structures by subordinating the diaconal order to the apostolic order in his tale of how the apostles instituted the diaconal office, so as to serve as distributors of dole while they preached the word (Acts 6:1–6). Luke's account became commonly accepted as the Hellenist movement was absorbed into early catholic Christianity by the end of the first century, and deacons spread in the churches as officers who were chiefly concerned with the administration of practical charity. Paul mentions that there were women deacons (Rom. 16:1), and Pliny the Younger tortured two deaconesses in the time of Trajan (*Epistulae*

10.96.8; *see* **persecutions**). The origins of a specific order of women deacons in the main church (they were already prominent in the clerical structures of **Montanism**) only separates clearly from the orders of *widows* and *virgins* later in the fourth century. From earliest times the office of deacon was attached to the episcopate as an administrative helper (Phil. 1:1; 1 Tim. 3:8). In the *Letters of Ignatius* they appear for the first time as the third office in the triad of ministerial offices. At **Rome** and other great cities, the deacons were powerful clergy who often rose to become the popes. At the *Council of Nicaea I* (325) their powers were defined and limited (Canon 18), and in the seventh century the Council of Toledo (633) and the Synod in Troullo (692) both acted to restrict their growing influence. Deacons were not allowed to celebrate the *Eucharist* except as assistants to the bishops and presbyters. They were given special liturgical functions, however, such as the singing of the Gospel, the proclamation of the prayers of the people (the litanies), the reading of the diptychs, the care of the eucharistic vessels, the administration of the Eucharist (with the officiants), and the general regulation of conduct in the church buildings. Their stole of office worn long over the shoulder was wrapped around them at various times, to signify their symbolic representation of the angels at the liturgy. Women deacons developed strongly as an ordained order in the third and fourth centuries. Their functions are outlined in the *Apostolic Constitutions* and the *Didascalia*. The latter demands that they be at least fifty, a requirement reduced to forty at the *Council of Chalcedon*. The motive was to put them past child-bearing age, and often they were ordained out of the ranks of the ascetics, the widows and virgins, though several married female deacons were known, not least the wife of St. *Gregory of Nyssa*. Women deacons did much the same as their male counterparts, especially taking charge of dole to the poor women, baptismal anointings of women, and the supervision of the women's galleries in the great churches (many female deacons were on the staff of Hagia Sophia at **Constantinople** in the sixth century). The male and female deacons were both ordained within the course of the liturgy, and invested with the stole, and both celebrated at the altar. The office of female deacons went into decline first in the West in the sixth century. Here, the Councils of Epaon (517) and Orléans (533) ruled to abolish the female diaconate, though it survived elsewhere in the West until the eleventh century, and later than that in the Eastern churches (to the late nineteenth century among the **Armenians**). In both cases monastic clerical pressures were probably the root cause of hostility to the female order. The **ordination** rite, however, still survives in the service books of the East. The male diaconate continued with much vitality in the Eastern churches, where it is often a lifelong ministry. In the West the male order of deacons also decayed, to becoming predominantly a stage on the path to priesthood.

J. N. Collins, *Diakonia: Re-Interpreting the Ancient Sources* (New York, 1990); J. Colson, *La fonction diaconale aux origines de l'Église* (Paris, 1960); J. Daniélou, "Le ministère des femmes dans l'Église ancienne," *La Maison Dieu.* 61 (1960): 70–96; R. Gryson, *The Ministry of Women in the Early Church* (Collegeville, Minn., 1976); A. G. Martimort, *Deaconesses: An Historical Study* (San Francisco, 1986).

Death   In Christian reflection death is far more than the simple cessation of bodily life on earth. It is a highly charged *eschatological* mystery, and has always been a central part of patristic theological reflection on the gospel. The Old Testament writers largely see death as the fundamental sign of creaturely status, the ultimate powerlessness of the human being (Ps. 6:5; 89:48). The Fourth Gospel show a distinctly new Christian emphasis that Christ will give to his disciples a gifted destiny of Life (John 11:25). Paul set the tone for most of patristic thought on the "mystery" of death when he described death in personalist terms as a tyrant who had captured humanity through humanity's foolish venture of sin (Rom. 5:12–14). Sin was an enslavement to the tyrant who exacted death as a price (Rom. 6:23). But Christ's victory over death had liberated humanity and given back the potential for life through the mystery of the *resurrection* (Rom. 6:9; 1 Cor. 15:26, 54–56). Following on this Pauline theme, many patristic writers (esp. *Gregory of Nyssa*) saw in the Genesis accounts of Adam walking hand in hand with God in the garden an intimation that death was never part of the original human constitution, but rather one of the penalties imposed by God on account of the sin of Adam (*see* Wis. 2:23). So, for several significant patristic thinkers, Adam was conceived as originally designed as an immortal creature, who lost that immortality in the collapse of the order of his being brought about by the slavery to sin. In the *De incarnatione* Athanasius described how the turning back to divine contemplation could restore the inner divine image, which in turn would restore immortality to human beings. This restoration was primarily effected by the *incarnation* of the *Logos* who, in his own body, brought about the breaking of the power of death and the end of the tyranny of the prince of the world, who had captured all the human race in the bonds of death and corruption. *Athanasius* takes the diminishment of the fear of death among Christians as a vital sign of this hope (*De incarnatione* 27.2). The hymns of *Romanos* in the sixth century, celebrating the paschal victory of Christ, use the imagery of the roots of the *cross* breaking through the roof of *hell*, with Satan and Death (personified) feeling sick to the soul as the risen victor liberates the *souls* of the righteous dead from their grasp ("Hymn on the Victory of the Cross"). The image is expressed in later icons of the resurrection, where Christ breaks the gates of hell and pulls Adam and Eve from their tombs. From earliest times Christians showed a great care for the dead (*see* **burial**) and were also concerned about praying for the good estate of the dead, a practice in which they knew they were innovating without much biblical precedent (Tertullian, *The Crown* 4.1; cf. 2 Macc. 12:40–45). Church **prayers** were specially offered each year on the "death-day," which Christians in the second century had already replaced as a commemoration instead of the more usual observance of the "birthday" (*see* Tertullian, *The Crown* 3.3; *Exhortation to Chastity* 11.1; *Monogamy* 10.1). Christian feasts (*refrigeria*) in memory of the dead continued for a very long time, despite some clerical disapproval; most of these feasts had a theme of conviviality, as many frescoes in the **catacombs** show. One of the dominant ideas of Christian attitudes to death is hope in the resurrection (John 6.40), and hope in the power of remembrance (anamnesis): that of the church on earth who prays for the dead, but above all that of the risen Lord who continues his care and mindfulness of all disciples living or dead. As Jesus insisted, in relation to the divine remembrance of the ancient patriarchs: "He is God not of the dead, but of the living" (Mark 12:27).

E. Lash, trans., *St. Romanos: On the Life of Christ (Kontakia)* (London, 1997); H. M. Luckock, *After Death: An examination of the testimony of primitive times respecting the state of the faithful dead, and their relationship to the living* (New York, 1886); F. S. Paxton, *Christianizing Death: The Creation of Ritual Process in Early Medieval Europe* (London, 1990).

Deification   Deification is the process of sanctification of Christians whereby they become progressively conformed to God, a conformation that is ultimately demonstrated in the transfiguration of the just in the heavenly kingdom. Deification (Gk. *theosis, theopoiesis*) was a bold use of language, deliberately evocative of the pagan language of apotheosis (humans, especially emperors, being advanced to the rank of deity), although that precise term was strictly avoided because of its fundamentally pagan conceptions of creatures transgressing on divine prerogative. The notion is first found in 2 Peter 1:4 (becoming "participants of the divine nature"), and the **Alexandrian** theologians, **Clement, Origen, Athanasius,** and **Cyril,** took the idea to new heights, relating it to the incarnation of the **Logos,** wherein the divine Logos assumed flesh so that all humankind could be lifted up into the mystery of his divinity. It is a common term in Dionysius the Areopagite (cf. *Ecclesiastical Hierarchy* 1.3), and after him becomes commonplace in most Eastern writers to connote the transformative effects of salvation. The meaning of deification turns around the idea that what the Logos was by nature is given "by participation," as a "grace of union," to his faithful (see Irenaeus, *Adversus haereses* 5 *praef.*; Athanasius, *De incarnatione* 54.3; *Orationes contra Arianos* 1.39; *De decretis* 14; Gregory of Nyssa, *Catechetical Oration* 25). Athanasius conceived the **incarnation** in and of itself as a concretely physical atonement, a mystical reconciliation of the hitherto disparate natures of God and humanity. Cyril of Alexandria pressed and clarified his implications further. That which could not happen, that is, the "natural" (we might today say ontological) reconciliation of divinity and humanity, had in effect been demonstrated in the incarnation of the Logos as the God-man Jesus Christ. Cyril further argued that this whole mystical transaction "in the natures" came about not merely in the person of Christ or for Christ's sake, but rather for the human race, and as no less than the divine re-creation of the foundations of human nature. Greek patristic thought thus conceived the incarnation as having reconstituted the human person as a divinely graced mystery: *deification* was the term chosen to represent this. This dynamic approach of incarnational theology was soon diffused in the Christian mainstream. Cyril particularly connects it with eucharistic theology. The language of deification was never quite as dominant in the West, where it did not carry the main burden of redemption theory as it did with the Greek Fathers, but it is a term found in parts of *Augustine* (*Sermon* 192; *Enarrations on the Psalms* 49; 146) to denote the transformative effects of *grace*.

D. Balas, *Metousia Theou: Man's Participation in God's Perfections According to St. Gregory of Nyssa* (Rome, 1966); G. Bonner, "Augustine's Conception of Deification," *JTS* 37 (1986): 369–86; M. Lot-Borodine, *La Deification de l'homme selon la doctrine des pères grecs* (Paris, 1970); J. Gross, *La Divinisation du chrétien d'après les pères grecs* (Paris, 1938); V. Lossky, *The Vision of God* (London, 1963).

Desert   Biblical paradigms first in use among the Christians suggested the desert was primarily the place where Israel rebelled against God. None of those who first entered the desert would enter the promised land (cf. Num. 14:22f.). It became a symbol of sterility and sin, therefore, an image that (especially in Egypt) was confirmed by the Isis religion, which saw the desert regions as inhabited by Set, the enemy of gods and humans. When Jesus withdraws into the desert after his baptism (Matt. 4:1), it is above all the place where he wrestles with Satan, and is tempted once more as Israel was. There were a few resonances in Scripture to suggest it was also the place where God spoke his secrets to his beloved. In Hosea the desert is the place God recalls wandering Israel so that he can renew its love (Hos. 2:14f.), and after his withdrawal to the desert mountain Elijah hears the voice of God speak to him in the quiet breeze (1 Kgs. 19:12). After the busy time of the missionary

tour, it is also into a deserted region that Jesus leads his disciples to refresh them (Matt. 20:17; Mark 6:31). After the fourth century however, when the *ascetical* movement flourished in the desert regions of Egypt, Syria, and Palestine, the desert became a new symbol of paradise regained. *Athanasius* drew many parallels in his *Life of Antony* with the monastic life in the desert as a mimesis of the gospel. It thus became especially the place where the ascetic imitated the struggle of the Lord (*Life of Antony* 47f.). Those hermits who achieved conformity with Christ (known generically as the Desert Fathers and Mothers— Abbas and Ammas; *see Antony, Macarius of Alexandria, Syncletica*) were like the innocent first parents who walked harmoniously in the world: and so, many stories about hermits dealing intimately with wild animals began to be recorded (cf. *Cyril of Scythopolis, Life of Euthymius* 23.4; *Gregory the Great, Dialogue* 1.3). *Jerome's Life of Paul the Hermit* painted a romantically idealized vision of the desert as a place of quiet (*otium*) where the affairs of the heart and soul could flourish, where the scrub land had broken into bloom, and where empty wildernesses had become new civilizations of ascetics; and it was this image that became immensely popular in later Christian rhetoric and art.

G. J. M. Bartelinck, "Les oxymores desertum civitas et desertum floribus vernans," *Studia Monastica* 15 (1973): 7–15; D. J. Chitty, *The Desert a City* (Oxford, 1966); A. Louth, *The Wilderness of God* (London, 1991); B. Ward, *The Desert Myth: Reflections on the Desert Ideal* (Kalamazoo, Mich., 1976).

Diadochus of Photike (fl. mid–fifth century)   Diadochus was bishop of Photike in Epirus, Greece. He was the author of an important ascetical work called *Gnostic Chapters* that became very influential for later Byzantine theologians (especially *Maximus Confessor*, and the medieval Hesychasts). He set out to combine the (Origenian) spiritual tradition of *Evagrius of Pontus* (with its emphasis on intellective unknowing, an imageless approach to the transcendent Godhead) with the Syrian tradition (as manifested in Pseudo-Macarius—*see Macarius the Great [2]*) of the distinct sensibility of the Spirit's indwelling as light and warmth in the human heart. The synthesis became constitutive of most Eastern Christian spirituality thereafter. He is one of the early representatives of the tradition of reciting the name of Jesus, time and time again, as a recollective mystical prayer, a custom that also developed extensively in later years to become the Orthodox tradition of the Jesus Prayer.

J. A. McGuckin, *Standing in God's Holy Fire: The Byzantine Tradition* (London, 2001), 62–66; G. Palmer, P. Sherrard, and K. Ware, trans., "Diadochus of Photike: The Hundred Gnostic Chapters," in *The Philokalia* (vol. 1; London, 1979), 252–96; K. Ware, "The Jesus Prayer in St. Diadochus of Photike," in G. Dragas, ed., *Aksum-Thyateira: A Festschrift for Archbishop Methodius of Thyateira and Great Britain* (London, 1985), 557–68.

Didache   The Greek word means "teaching" and is the abbreviated title of a very important book of church discipline rediscovered only in the late nineteenth century: *The Teaching of the Lord through the Twelve Apostles to the Nations.* It comes from the late first to mid–second century, and is more in the style of a compilation of practices for a group of churches than the work of a single theologian-author. The *Didache* is the first of a long series of church order books that claimed the authority of the apostles. Its own context shows it originated, probably, in *Syria*, but some scholars think that conditions mentioned also evoke the church in Egypt. In the fourth century it was still highly regarded, but was increasingly becoming obsolete (it survives today only through a single manuscript). *Eusebius of Caesarea* mentions it as a venerable book, but one that was not canonical scripture (H.E. 3.25.4); *Clement of Alexandria* thought it was Scripture, and **Athanasius** specifically recommends it as a useful text to serve as a guide for catechumens (*Festal Letters* 39). The *Didache* had a strong influence on another church order (of the late fourth century), namely the *Apostolic Constitutions*, which reproduces much of it in its own book 7. The *Didache* gives a picture of a church still closely bonded to Jewish religious thought and practice. The communities, however, have some pagan converts, and these they are anxious to instruct. The early books (chaps. 1–6), presented as an example of moral catechesis for baptismal candidates, speak of the two ways (life and death) that stand before the believer. This is a form of paraenesis (moral exhortation) that is typical of late Jewish literature, and has parallels with the *Shepherd of Hermas* and *Barnabas*. One of the few specifically Christian elements of this material is an extended interpretation of Jesus' commandment to love (*Didache* 1.3–2.1). Chapters 7–10 give instructions on *baptism*, *prayer*, *fasting*, and the *agape*, or common meal. The church's fast days are set as Wednesday and Friday. Baptism is to be generally by triple immersion (effusion is permitted in cases where no deep water is available). Prayer is to be offered in the form of the *Lord's Prayer* every day. The eucharistic prayers in the book (chaps. 9–10) are based on Jewish table blessings. It is still not universally agreed whether they reflect a Christian agape (love feast) or a *Eucharist*, or a combination of both. In chapter 14 the *synaxis* of the Lord's Day is mentioned, and reconciliation among the community is given a high priority as the proper eucharistic preparation. The churches to whom the book is addressed still witness what must have been an ancient pattern of ministerial order, insofar as they are visited from time to time by itinerant "apostles and prophets," who are "your chief priests." The local ministers are instructed to give way to the prophets for a short time, but the prophets are not to linger in one church for more than a few days. Chapter 15 gives a very early instruction on the election of *deacons* and *bishops*. It ends in chapter 16 with a warning about the coming of the antichrist and the imminent *Parousia*.

S. Giet, *L'Enigme de la Didache* (Paris, 1970); C. N. Jefford, *The Sayings of Jesus in the Didache* (Leiden, Netherlands, 1989); R. A. Kraft, *Barnabas and the Didache* (The Apostolic Fathers: A New Translation and Commentary; New York, 1965); F. E. Vokes, "The Didache: Still Debated," *CQ* 3 (1970): 57–62; A. Voobus, *Liturgical Traditions in the Didache* (Stockholm, 1968).

Didascalia Apostolorum

Didascalia Apostolorum is an early–third-century **Syrian** book (originally written in Greek but surviving complete only in Syriac, and partially in other Latin and Greek versions). It is one of the series of "Apostolic Orders," which is a combination of moral exhortation and rules for church discipline. It is aware of, and uses, parts of the *Didache*, the *Shepherd of Hermas*, and the *Letters* of *Ignatius of Antioch*. It bears the title in Syriac: *Catholic Teaching of the Twelve Apostles and Holy Disciples of Our Savior*, but is more generally known by the shorter reference above. The text argues that only the moral prescripts of the Old Testament remain binding for Christians. The office of bishop is prominent as the source of church order, and instructions are also given about *family* life. The structure of ministers in the church reveals that *widows* and *deaconesses* were active. It advocates a six-week Lenten *fast* before Pascha. In the book's baptismal instructions the practice of anointing in the name of the *Trinity* takes place before the immersion; even a twofold anointing, a common practice in Syria at this time. The doctrine of the church's for-giveness of all sins (even adultery, apostasy, and idolatry) is advocated, except for the "sin against the *Holy Spirit*," which is left unclear. The work was incorporated into the first six books of the *Apostolic Constitutions*.

J. V. Bartlet, *Church Life and Church-Order During the First Four Centuries With Special Reference to the Early Eastern Church-Orders* (Oxford, 1943); R. H. Connolly, *Didascalia Apostolorum: The Syriac Version Translated and Accompanied by the Verona Latin Fragments* (Oxford, 1929).

Didymus the Blind (313–398)

Didymus was a leading exegete and intellectual disciple of *Origen* at the church of *Alexandria*. He was first appointed to his theological position by *Athanasius of Alexandria*, and possibly taught *Cyril of Alexandria* when the latter was being prepared for ordination by his uncle the archbishop *Theophilus*. He was blind from childhood and demonstrated amazing gifts for memorization and extemporization, which he put to good use in a lifelong study of the Scriptures. He dictated many works to scribes, and was thus a prolific theological writer. His treatise *On the Holy Spirit* has been preserved in its Latin translation, made by *Jerome*. It argues for the *Nicene* theology and the full divinity of the *Holy Spirit*, representing the range of ideas Athanasius would defend in his *christological* writings and his *Letters to Serapion*. One of his greatest works in antiquity was his treatise *On the Trinity* (now generally thought to be lost; though some have claimed to see most of it in an anonymous treatise *On the Holy Spirit* surviving in an eighteenth-century manuscript). The writings of Didymus were anathematized at the *Council of Constantinople II* in 553, as he was one of the most favored writers of the Origenist monks whom *Justinian* was determined to suppress. After that point they were dissipated and lost. In 1941 a cache of papyri was discovered at Toura in

Egypt, and several fragments of Didymus's exegetical works were found among it. These are badly damaged but show him to have developed Origen's allegorical exegesis even more elaborately. Some scholars attribute to Didymus the fourth and fifth books appended to *Basil of Caesarea's Against Eunomius*.

G. Bardy, *Didyme l'Aveugle* (Paris, 1910); J. H. Tigcheler, *Didyme l'Aveugle et l'Éxégèse allégorique: Étude sémantique de quelques termes exégétiques importants de son commentaire sur Zacharie* (Nijmegen, Netherlands, 1977).

Diodore of Tarsus (d. c. 390)   Diodore, a native of Antioch, was a student at Athens. He returned to Syria and became head of a monastery near Antioch. He was active in the struggle against *Arianism* in that city, part of the group loyal to *Meletius*. He administered the see of Antioch during Meletius's exile. After the fall of Valens the Meletian party began an active campaign to secure Nicene ascendancy in the East, and Diodore was appointed in 378 as bishop of Tarsus. He was one of the leading theologians at the *Council of Constantinople I* in 381, where he had a major falling out with *Gregory of Nazianzus* over the succession for Meletius, who died during the council. The dispute led to Gregory's resignation, and the ill will was manifested in the following years when Gregory's verse autobiography appeared containing the first criticisms of Diodore's *Christology*—his apparent teaching that Christ was "Two Sons": the Son of God (the Logos) and the Son of Man (Jesus). Gregory is the first to suggest Diodore is the other extreme of Christology from *Apollinaris*, and equally censurable. Diodore was one of the greatest biblical interpreters the Syrian church had ever produced. In his own lifetime, and for a long while following it, his reputation was in the ascendant. It was the fate of

his pupils that changed this situation detrimentally. Diodore taught both *John Chrysostom* and *Theodore of Mopsuestia*. But, as Theodore (posthumously) and the latter's disciple, *Nestorius*, became embroiled in the christological controversy at the *Council of Ephesus I* 431, so too Diodore was posthumously drawn into the debate, and his works were again censured (especially by *Cyril of Alexandria* and thus the whole Eastern Orthodox tradition) as the precursors of the Nestorian heresy of double subjectivity in Christ. This was somewhat anachronistic, but fatal to the text tradition of his works. In his own time Diodore established the pattern of the Antiochene style of exegesis—a constant preference for literal and moralistic exegesis of the Bible, especially disapproving of *Origen's* enthusiasm for allegorical readings. The relation of the Old to New Testaments was conceived as a cycle of *typological* (more than straightforwardly prophetic) fulfillments. Now only fragments remain of his work. Recently scholars have reconstructed his *Commentary on the Psalms*.

R. Abramowski, "Untersuchungen zu Diodor von Tarsus," ZNTW 30 (1931): 234–62; idem, "Der theologische Nachlass des Diodor von Tarsus," ZNTW 42 (1949): 19–69; M. Brière, "Quelques Fragments syriaques de Diodore évèque de Tarse c. 378–394," ROC 30 (1946): 231–83; J. M. Olivier, *Diodori Tarsensis Commentarii in Psalmos* (CCSG 6; Louvain, Belgium, 1980); M. Richard, "Les Traités de Cyrille d'Alexandrie contre Diodore et Théodore et les fragments dogmatiques de Diodore de Tarse," in *Mélanges dédiés à la mémoire de Félix Grat* (vol. 1; Paris, 1946), 99–116. Reprinted in M. Richard, *Opera Minora* (vol. 2; Turnhout-Louvain, 1977).

Diognetus, Letter to   This document is an anonymous second-century Greek apology for Christianity (*see Apologists*) addressed to one Diognetus (thought by some to be either the tutor of the emperor Marcus Aurelius [161–180] or a high-ranking Alexandrian magistrate mentioned in papyri [c. 167–203]). Because of its address, it was mistakenly thought, when it was rediscovered in modern times, to be a letter. It had survived, apparently, in only one thirteenth-century manuscript, which itself was afterwards destroyed in Strasbourg in 1870. The text begins (chaps. 2–4) with arguments why Christianity is superior to paganism and *Judaism* (the one being idolatrous, and the other being too ritualistic). Its most famous section is chapters 5–6, which give a very eloquent encomium of the Christian faith (Christians live spiritually detached in the world as its very *soul*). Chapters 7–8 argue that the new religion appeared so late in time because God wished to demonstrate the unarguable need of salvation to the human race, which had utterly gone astray. It ends with chapter 10 inviting Diognetus to become a Christian. The final sections in the manuscript (chaps. 11–12) seem to be from a separate treatise, written by an early *Logos theologian*. They describe the gathering together of the *church* of God as the reconstitution of *paradise*.

P. Andriessen, "The Authorship of the Epistula ad Diognetum," VC 1 (1947): 129–36; L. W. Barnard, "The Epistle Ad Diognetum: Two Units From One Author?" ZNTW 56 (1965): 130–37; R. H. Connolly, "The Date and Authorship of the Epistle to Diognetus," JTS 36 (1935): 347–53; idem, "Ad Diognetum 11–12," JTS 37 (1936): 2–15; J. A. Kleist, trans., *The Didache, the Epistles and Martydom of St. Polycarp, the Fragments of Papias, and the Epistle to Diognetus* (ET; ACW 6; New York, 1948), 125–47.

Dionysius of Alexandria (d. 264)

Dionysius was a wealthy pupil of *Origen* and after being head of the catechetical school in the city (c. 233–248) became the bishop of *Alexandria* c. 248. He was a learned and capable leader of a church in a city greatly disturbed by *persecutions*, civil war, famine, and plague. He took to flight during Decius's persecution (was arrested and escaped), and was again subsequently banished during Valerian's persecution. In the aftermath of the persecutions he took a strong stand for a measured policy of reconciliation of the lapsed. To this effect he sided with Cornelius of Rome against the rigorism of *Novatian*, and he took the part of Stephen of Rome against *Cyprian* when the latter advocated the need for rebaptizing heretics and schismatics. However, he would not agree to breaking communion with those who did rebaptize. In the tradition of Origen's *Logos theology*, Dionysius attacked *Monarchianism*, both in the theological monism of Sabellius and in the guise of the *adoptionism* of *Paul of Samosata*. In the process of attacking Monarchianism Dionysius used terminology (the inapplicability of the term *homoousios*, and the existence of three *hypostases* or persons in the Godhead) that seemed to Dionysius of Rome to be teaching a tritheist doctrine. He expressed his meaning in a subsequent *Refutation and Apology* that demonstrated his agreement with early Western Trinitarianism. His theology (now only preserved in quoted fragments) was defended as orthodox by *Athanasius* (*De sententia Dionysii*), who was at pains to point out that Dionysius had eventually agreed to use the term *homoousios*, but Dionysius was always held in suspicion by *Basil of Caesarea*. Apart from establishing moderate teachings on Eastern church discipline, Dionysius is important mainly for laying down an early form of Trinitarian terminology (the Son is the brightness of the Father's light, the river from his fountain; the Spirit is inseparable from the One who sends and the One who brings him). Dionysius was clearly also a careful and interesting biblical exegete in the school of Origen. He is recorded as having noted the stylistic differences between the Fourth Gospel and the Apocalypse, concluding that they cannot have been from the same hand.

W. A. Bienert, *Dionysius von Alexandrien zur Frage des Origenismus im dritten Jahrhundert* (Berlin, 1978); C. L. Feltoe, *The Letters and Other Remains of Dionysius of Alexandria* (Cambridge, 1904); S. D. F. Salmond, *The Works of Dionysius: Extant Fragments* (ANF 6; repr.; Grand Rapids, 1971), 77–120.

Dionysius of Rome (fl. first half of the third century)   Dionysius was a *priest* in Rome who eventually succeeded to the *papacy*, two years after the death of Xystus II. During his papacy (c. 260–268) he reorganized the Roman church, which had been heavily disrupted by the Valerian *persecution*. Even before his election he had received correspondence from *Dionysius of Alexandria* to solicit his agreement to a policy that those who received *baptism* from heretics should not be rebaptized. As bishop he wrote two other significant letters to *Alexandria* (recorded by *Athanasius*): one against the *Monarchianism* of Sabellius, and another a censure of what he thought was the *subordinationism* of *Dionysius of Alexandria*, who was stimulated by this epistle to articulate his views on the relationship of the Son and *Holy Spirit* to the divine Father. Dionysius of Rome was opposed to the doctrine of God in three *hypostases*, which he (misleadingly) called *Marcionitism*. This Roman opposition to the terminology of three hypostases in the *Trinity* would lead to significant confusion between the Latin and Greek churches in the following century, until it was agreed that both churches had apparently "reversed" technical terms but agreed fundamentally on the same doctrine (three divine *persons* and a single divine *nature*). In other words, *hypostasis* (the semantic equivalent of the Latin *substantia*, substance or essence) actually meant what the Latins intended to connote by *persona* (person), and not "essential being" at all.

J. F. Bethune-Baker, *An Introduction to the Early History of Christian Doctrine* (Lon-

don, 1942), 113–18; G. C. Stead, *Divine Substance* (Oxford, 1977).

Dionysius the Areopagite (early sixth century)   Dionysius the Areopagite is the pseudonym of an unknown Syrian bishop or *priest ascetic* who was a leading theologian of the early sixth century. Four relatively short treatises of Dionysius (and ten letters) are among the most important of early church literature dealing with mystical prayer. They represent a profound attempt to express the evangelical spirit of divine communion in language that would be recognizable to the Hellenistic (especially Neoplatonist; *see* **Platonism**) philosophical tradition. The writings are clearly influenced by the work of *Plotinus* (d. 270) and *Proclus* (d. 447). It is possible that they were offered to Byzantine society at the time when the last Hellenistic philosophy schools (especially the academy of Athens) were being closed by *Justinian* (529), as an example of missionary outreach. This may explain why the author chose to describe them (pseudepigraphically) as the works of Dionysius the Areopagite, a companion and disciple of St. Paul in Athens. Although the subterfuge was not taken seriously when the texts surfaced in Byzantine theological dialogues (*Severus of Antioch* first mentions them in 533), they nevertheless soon established themselves as "*apostolic*" literature, and with this label went on to have a profound influence for centuries to come, especially on *Maximus the Confessor* and *Andrew of Crete* in the East, and Pope *Gregory the Great*, John Scotus Eriugena, Bonaventure, and Albert the Great in the West. They were the main inspiration behind the later medieval mystical revival of the West, as evidenced in the *Cloud of Unknowing* and in such mystics as Meister Eckhart and Tauler. The *Divine Names* discusses the attributes of God, teaching that deity is beyond any direct knowing and relates to creation through the saving dynamic of divine emanation. The book introduces the influential concepts of kataphatic (affirmative) and apophatic (speech-transcending) theology. The *Celestial Hierarchy* describes how nine ranks of angelic beings mediate between God and the creation. The book teaches the influential view that evil is unreal in itself; the absence of the good. The *Ecclesiastical Hierarchy* shows how the principle of emanations continues to provide the substructure of the mystical church of Christ. Here three orders of priests (bishops, priests, and *deacons*) mediate three mystical orders (*baptism, Eucharist,* and *chrismation*) to the three orders of Christians (monks, laity, and *catechumens*). The system of mediation and emanation is dynamically conceived as a process (as in *Origen of Alexandria*) whereby the *soul* ascends to the divine Presence, which stoops down to the creation as Savior and healer. The treatise *Mystical Theology* describes the soul's ascent to *deification*, in a transcendence of all sense and utterance (encountering the divine darkness of unknowing). In Dionysius the system of the soul's rising up to God is marked by a triadic character of purification, illumination, and perfection of union. This scheme had overwhelming authority with the subsequent Christian mystical tradition.

A. Louth, *Denys the Areopagite* (Wilton, Conn., 1989); C. Luibheid, *Pseudo-Dionysius: The Complete Works* (CWS 54; New York, 1987); P. Rorem, *Biblical and Liturgical Symbols within the Pseudo-Dionysian Synthesis* (Toronto, 1984).

Dioscorus of Alexandria (d. 454)

Dioscorus was archbishop of *Alexandria* after *Cyril*, and an uncompromising theologian insisting on Cyril's *christological* settlement to the exclusion of all other voices. He unraveled the delicate negotiations, which Cyril himself had agreed to, between the Alexandrian and Antiochene christological traditions in the aftermath of the *Council of Ephesus I* (431). He presided over what had initially been designed as the *Council of Ephesus II* (449) to settle the dispute between *Flavian of Constantinople* and *Eutyches*. Here he took Eutyches's side, demanding that all "two nature" language should be excluded from *Christology*. At Ephesus his rivals were so badly mishandled that the Christian world was scandalized, and it became commonly known as the Latrocinium, or Robber Synod. He was summoned to the *Council of Chalcedon* (451) and deposed there. His fall marks the beginning of the long division of the Oriental Orthodox churches over the christological issue. For the so-called *"Monophysite"* churches (the non-Chalcedonians, especially the Copts and *Ethiopians*), Dioscorus remained a hero of the faith.

R. V. Sellers, *The Council of Chalcedon* (London, 1953); W. H. C. Frend, *The Rise of the Monophysite Movement* (Cambridge, 1972).

Docetism

Docetism, deriving from the Greek *dokesis*, to seem or to appear, is a term first used by Serapion the bishop of Antioch (190–203) (cf. Eusebius, *Ecclesiastical History* 6.12.6) to defend his view that the flesh of Jesus was "spiritual." It now generally denotes the view held by some in the first two centuries that Jesus was a spiritual power of God who only "seemed" to have flesh and humanity, but in reality was a pure spirit, emitting a fleshly epiphany on earth. The idea is most dramatically seen in the apocryphal Acts (especially visible in the gnostic writings from Nag Hammadi), which often speak of the epiphanic, not fleshly, body of Jesus (*First Apocalypse of James* 5.31.1–26; *Second Treatise of the Great Seth* 7.55.9–56; *Letter of Peter to Philip* 8.139.15–29; *Acts of John* 97–104). *Ignatius of Antioch* is very concerned in his writings to attack a group at Antioch who seem to have been Docetic in their *Christology* (Ignatius, *To the Smyrnaeans* 2.1–8.2; *To the Trallians* 10). He set the tone for much patristic thought that followed in the manner in which he stressed the physical actuality of Christ's sufferings and *death* (*To the Ephesians* 1.1; *To the Romans* 6.6), as well as the fundamental need of a real body, for Christ to work within it the process of redemption on behalf of the human race (*To the Trallians* 9.2; *To the Smyrnaeans* 7.1). Who the Docetists were is generally a matter that can not be answered with precision, and it was probably more a tendency of *gnostic*-oriented communities rather than an organized group or school. Serapion of Antioch and Cerinthus are among the few people actually named as Docetists. Elements of the Christology of the New Testament hymns (for example, read Phil. 2:6–11 in the light of asking what manner of "form" Christ has as his own) show traces of what would later be called Docetism. And the group attacked in 1 John 4:3 and 2 John 7 seems to have had similar views, denigrating the flesh in the cause of exalting the spiritual significance of Jesus. A chain of *patristic* commentators attacked the Docetic thinkers as undermining the whole principle of the redemption of flesh and blood in the person and work of the incarnate Lord. *Irenaeus* and *Tertullian* both mock them as being as "unreal" as their Christ (Irenaeus, *Adversus haereses* 4.33.5; Tertullian, *Against the Valentinians* 27.3). There was much disapproval expressed against one of the main Docetic ideas, that the spiritual Lord could not possibly suffer in the flesh. Their attempts to explain away the "scandal of the *cross*" in terms of a ploy by the Lord to fool the demons into thinking the Savior was simply another mere mortal, disposed of by their plot to crucify him, was regarded by Irenaeus and others (Irenaeus, *Adversus haereses* 1.7.2; 1.26.1–7; 3.16.1–5; 3.18.6; 4.33.5; Hippolytus, *Refutation of All Heresies* 8.1–4; Tertullian, *The Flesh of Christ* 3–5; idem, *Against Marcion* 1.19) as making void the central point of the *kerygma* of *salvation*.

G. Bardy, "Docétisme," in *Dictionnaire de Spiritualité* (vol. 3; Paris, 1957), cols.

1461–68; A. Grillmeier, *Christ in Christian Tradition* (vol. 1; London, 1975), 78–79; W. R. Schoedel, *Ignatius of Antioch* (Philadelphia, 1985), 220–46.

Donatism This schismatical movement in *north Africa* was named after one of its early episcopal leaders, Donatus. It took its origin immediately after the Great *Persecution* (303–305) and divided the African church for the next two centuries, only declining when the imperial authorities finally decided, in response to lobbying from *catholic bishops* such as *Augustine*, that the alternative hierarchy he represented was the authentic one, and the Donatists ought to be subjected to heavy legal penalties. The movement continued in north Africa until the eventual overwhelming of the whole region by the Muslim invasions of the seventh century. The schism first arose because many *clergy* during the persecution handed over sacred books to the authorities. These *traditores* (the word is the origin of "traitor") were denounced by a group of imprisoned *confessors* who declared (with the great authority then afforded to confessors in the African church) that only those who acted bravely in the persecution would be given a heavenly reward (*Acts of Saturninus* 18). Their attitude, however, was censured by the archdeacon of Carthage, Caecilian, who was (later) said to have punished them by reducing their dole of church food. In 311 Caecilian was elected as bishop of Carthage in a contested consecration, and in the following year the primate of Numidia held a *council* of seventy bishops at Carthage that deposed Caecilian and elected another. Caecilian refused to give way. That same winter Constantine's armies occupied north Africa, and Caecilian was accepted into his administration as the leading bishop to serve as his representative in Africa. *Constantine* gave moral weight and a large income to Caecilius, and threatened his rivals with legal penalties if they did not come round to his communion. After many continuing protests Constantine referred the dispute between Caecilian and the Numidian bishops to the hearing of Pope Miltiades, who again decided in favor of Caecilian. The rivals were now led by Bishop Donatus, who arranged another appeal to the emperor, alleging that one of Caecilian's consecrators was a *traditor*, and thus the whole ordination was invalid. Constantine decided to refer the matter once more to a larger synod to adjudicate it; the synod took evidence about the circumstances of the original consecration. The council met at Arles in 314. The decision again went against Donatus, and the verdict was reaffirmed by imperial decree in 316. In 320 a trial before the governor of Numidia revealed that many of Caecilian's opponents in the Numidian hierarchy had themselves been *traditores* in the persecution. Even so the movement did not lose momentum. The Donatist protest gained its greatest allegiance in those provinces of north Africa which were the least Romanized (Numidia and Mauretania Sitifensis), suggesting its popularity was closely related to anticolonial protests. By the latter half of the fourth century Donatism probably represented the majority of churches in north Africa, but it was always regarded as a very "local" schism, with provincial views on theology, and the rest of the Christian world looked to Caecilian as the true bishop. After his death the "Caecilianist party" disappeared, and the issue became seen as a *schism* between the "Catholics" and the Donatists. In the day-to-day administration of north Africa, by the end of the fourth century, the imperial authorities were slowly accepting the reality of the Donatist majority and increasingly admitting them to civil rights when some of the leaders of that party allied themselves with Count Gildo, who rebelled against the empire in 397–398. His downfall once more brought about a long-term suspicion of the whole Donatist movement, and from that point on the moral influence of the Catholics far outweighed their numbers. It was really Augustine's arrival on the scene as an African bishop of the Catholics that turned the tide. Between 399 and 415 he wrote a series of treatises against the Donatists, which inestimably advanced the looser ecclesiologies that had hitherto been operating. Augustine isolated as the chief points of his argument first that the initial charge against Caecilian had been wrong; second, that the Donatist movement was a local sect, obviously not in communion with the rest of the Christian world, and thus could not lay claim to catholicity (universality), which was a fundamental mark of the true *Church*; and third, that they had lapsed into heresy by insisting on the rebaptism of converts from the Catholic church (a practice instituted by Donatus, who rebaptized *clergy* who had lapsed in the Great Persecution) knowing that *baptism* is unrepeatable. In 405 Augustine and Aurelius of Carthage succeeded in persuading the emperor Honorius to ban the Donatists as heretics, and strong pressure began to be inflicted on them. They were forced to attend a conference at Carthage in 411 (286 Catholic hierarchs and 284 Donatist), after which the imperial tribune issued a decree condemning them as a separate hierarchy. They dwindled dramatically after that point, but never completely disappeared as long as north Africa remained Christian. The Donatists generally regarded the church as the society of the pure elite. If serious sin was manifested it denoted a lapse from membership of the church. Clergy who lapsed rendered all their sacraments void. They heavily depended on the writings of *Cyprian* to illuminate their view on the rightness of rebaptizing heretics. Augustine, in attacking them, advanced the theory that the church is the ark containing saints and sinners (or the field containing wheat as well as tares). God would sort out the goats and sheep at his *Judgment,* but the "church of the pure" was a contradiction of the church Christ wished to institute, which was more of a general hospital than a sanitized isolation ward. His work was heavily influential on later Latin ecclesiology and sacramental theology. The manner in which Augustine needed to stress the communion with *Rome* and the internationality of his catholicity, over and against the localized sense of communion operative among the Donatists, had a long influence in the later Latin theology about catholicity as assured by communion with the Roman see. The Donatists were a group strongly charismatic, and aware of the inalienable sense of equality of all Christians. They frequently attacked rural landowners and forced them to trade places with their slaves (one of the reasons the imperial authorities did not like them). They also held high the ideals of martyrdom and voluntary poverty. The rigorism that characterized their views on ecclesiology was part of a general outlook of a "resistance" church that had little trust in the attitudes of the emperors, whether or not these now claimed to be Christian. One of Donatus's most celebrated remarks was: "What has the emperor to do with the church?" (Optatus of Milevis, *Against the Donatists* 3.3).

W. H. C. Frend, *The Donatist Church: A Movement of Protest in Roman North Africa* (Oxford, 1952); R. Markus, *Saeculum: History and Society in the Theology of St. Augustine* (Cambridge, 1970); G. G. Willis, *St. Augustine and the Donatist Controversy* (London, 1952).

Dreams   Dreams were commonly regarded in antiquity as means of the divine communicating with humans. Scripture gave the Early Christians several paradigms of the positive appreciation of dreams as a revelatory medium (cf. Gen. 28:12; 31:11, 24; 40:9). In the apocalyptic literature, for example, prophets such as Daniel (Dan. 7:1) are seen caught up in dreamlike visions during which important truths are communicated to them. Jacob and Joseph were other famous "dreamers." In the New Testament literature Joseph the husband of Mary is warned in a dream, as are the magi (Matt. 1:20; 2:12) and the wife of Pilate "suffers much in a dream" because of the trial of Jesus (Matt. 27:19). Joel speaks of the renewal of charisms of prophecy in Israel under the figure of dreams (Joel 2:28). At the same time, however, the Scriptures (like ancient men and women generally) also knew that dreams were largely nonsense: recycled desires and anxieties of the day. They were spoken of as specious vanities in several biblical texts (Job 20:8; Ps. 73:20; Jer. 29:8; Eccl. 5:3, 7), and on occasions the magicians or folk shamans who divined dreams (Dan. 2:2) were ordered in Israelite law to be censured or even put to death for impiety if they proclaimed a heterodox doctrine (Jer. 23:32; Deut. 13:1–5). The Roman Empire in the early Christian period had a very hostile attitude to popular divination and *magic*, and often acted violently against its proponents (who were very numerous). The early church inherited all these conflicted attitudes. It was very cautious indeed about the multitudes of dream-diviners and astrologers who formed the chief ranks of a lively folk religion in late antiquity, and it generally regarded them as idolaters who were suffering the delusions of demons they had themselves summoned (Hippolytus, *The Apostolic Tradition* 16). In several Christian apologetic texts the miracles associated with Hellenistic shrines and the accuracy of dream interpretations associated with pagan cults were not explained away, but rather affirmed as a result of the successful invocation of these demons (the Hellenistic pantheon), who could partially exercise a range of powers of foresight superior to humans (Lactantius, *The Divine Institutes*). Dreams were not a major part of Christianity's own scriptural writings. Their occurrence in the infancy narrative is very much an exception in the

Matthean Gospel. Moreover the category of dreaming was commonly despised in superior, "philosophic" literature of the time, and the early Christians were generally very cautious about associating their faith and doctrines with visionary experiences or basing them on the authority of dreams. Peter's dreamlike trance at Jaffa is, of course, a very important exception, and in that account the authorization of a whole Gentile Christianity hangs on a revelatory trance (Acts 10:9–16). In the second century the publication of the *Dream Book* of the Hellenist sophist Artemidorus of Ephesus shows something of a revival of the dream as a "respectable" subject of learned discourse. In the same period the dream vision functioned prominently in the healing cults of Aesculapius and Isis, two of the most powerful religions of the time. The association of dreams with pagan therapeutic cults was at first another negative aspect as far as Christian thinkers were concerned. **Origen** and **Tertullian** both treat that archetypal biblical dreamer, Jacob, as a type of the "man of knowledge." For Origen he is quintessentially the meditative and introspective visionary who understands God (*Commentary on Canticles, Prologue* 3). For Tertullian he is a type of prophet. Neither of them is interested in his function as a "dreamer" as such. Tertullian in *De anima* 45.4 simultaneously dismisses dreams as emotional nonsense, yet also thinks that, in the main, for Christians they can be a source of much insight into the divine realm (*De anima* 47.2), thus implicitly invoking the common Christian distinction between a revelatory dream (what **Gregory of Nazianzus** would distinguish as a "waking dream") and insignificant brain fantasies during sleep. In the **Shepherd of Hermas**, who commanded a high authority up to the third century, the central prophetic narrative is advanced by means of the dream revelations the author receives. It should be noticed, however, that the dream sequence in the visions Hermas narrates begins with his walking down the road, where he is seized by something akin to the "waking trance" narrated of Peter at Jaffa (Shepherd of Hermas, *Vision* 1.1.3–1.2.2). In the early third century the dream diary of **Perpetua**, the north African martyr, also did much to bring the idea of prophetic dream back into the heart of Christian interests (*Passion of Perpetua* 4–10; see also *Martyrdom of Polycarp* 5.2). It has sometimes been suggested that the interest in revelatory dreams here betrays some **Montanist** influence. The dream narratives in the *Passion of Perpetua and Felicity* have all the vividness of authentic firsthand accounts, and generally relate to the young martyr's anxieties about her coming ordeal, as well as interest over the nature of **paradise**. Increasingly, by the fourth century, attitudes were changing. Many of the leading patristic writers of the period see dreams as proof positive that the soul is immortal and not tied to the body (**Athanasius**, *Contra gentes* 2.31; **Augustine**, *On the Literal Interpretation of Genesis* 12; Synesius of Cyrene, *De Insomniis* 3–5). Gregory of Nazianzus regards dreams in a very positive light: especially if the dreamer is ascetically prepared, and has made his or her spirit receptive to divine promptings. He refers to his own dream of heavenly beings to explain his youthful choice to become an ascetic, and he regularly and approvingly refers to dream visions among his family as a sign of their spiritual election. In the fifth century the shrine of St. Thecla at Seleucia was actively functioning as an incubationary healing center, where sick Christians would sleep in the shrine and some would experience visions of the saint coming to heal them (a close appropriation of the ancient Aesculapian practices). **Cyril of Alexandria** also appears in this period as a dreamer who can communicate with the saints, as well as being a hardheaded leader of his people. And in his own dream of martyrs Cyril devises a strategy of setting up the saints (with a relic shrine to Saints Cyrus and

John) as a successful "opposition" to the great temple of Isis at Menouthis. By the fifth century the dream communication between ancient *saints* and Christian leaders was a common theme, with the saints often revealing the places of their lost relics. Ascetics such as *Jerome* describe several of their dreams, most famously Jerome's dream of Christ telling him he was not really a Christian but rather a Ciceronian, for his love for literature was too excessive (Ep. 22). In Jerome, by and large, the dream is reinterpreted as an aspect of the conscience, not a prophetic charism as it is in Gregory. The treatment of dreams throughout the early Christian period shows this ambivalent fascination in the literary sources. In popular religiosity, however, and it is especially true of the Byzantine church, revelatory dreams were part and parcel of common Christian religious experience, and the same can be said of the experience of early Christian *Ireland* and (increasingly) of the African literature, as for example in the late *desert* stories where visions, which had formerly been rarely narrated and generally disapproved of, come more to the fore as a mark of psychic advancement. In the *Ladder* of *John Climacus*, for example, the elders often see the figures of ancient prophets walking by, or have conversations with other saints whom their disciples cannot see (as in the *Life of Shenoudi*). The ambivalent interest in dreams as a divine medium thus remained in Christianity for centuries to come.

P. Cox-Miller, *Dreams in Late Antiquity* (Princeton, N.J., 1994); E. R. Dodds, *Pagan and Christian in an Age of Anxiety* (Cambridge, 1965), 37–68; R. Lane-Fox, *Pagans and Christians* (London, 1988), 102–67; J. A. McGuckin, *The Influence of the Isis Cult on St. Cyril of Alexandria's Christology* SP 24 (1992): 191–99; idem, *St. Gregory of Nazianzus: An Intellectual Biography* (New York, 2001), 62–76; H. Musurillo, *The Acts of the Christian Martyrs* (Oxford, 1972), 107–31 (ET of *The Passion of Perpetua and Felicity*).

Dyothelitism   see **Council of Constantinople III**

Ebionites   The name "Ebionite" derives from the Greek transliteration of the Aramaic word for the "poor ones." It is used in patristic texts to refer to the surviving remnants of Judeo-Christianity, before the virtual refounding of the Palestinian church in the Constantinian age. *Irenaeus* is one of the first to mention them (*Adversus haereses* 1.26.2), and *Origen* explains the significance of the name (*First Principles* 4.3.8; *Against Celsus* 2.1) but cannot resist the pun that it refers now to their "intellectual poverty." It may well have been originally a self-designation of the *Church* as the *anawim* of God, the "poor saints." Later antiheretical writers such as *Hippolytus* (*Refutation of All Heresies*) and *Tertullian* (*Prescription against Heretics* 4.8) imagined they were a sect founded by a person called Ebion (by then a heresy had to have a heresiarch). According to Irenaeus their movement was distinguished by their rejection of the writings of St. Paul, whom they regarded as an apostate Jew who illegitimately separated the gospel from the Torah. In relation to the universally emerging *canon of Scripture*, they accepted only the Gospel of Matthew, retained all the observances of the law, and denied the virginal birth of Christ, generally regarding him as Messiah, but prophetic and human, not divine (Tertullian, *The Flesh of Christ* 14). Origen adds that they observed Passover as the ultimate festival, and that at least one group among them did accept the traditions of the virginal birth. This suggests that they were known to him, both in *Alexandria* and Caesarea, as a real body of Christians. *Epiphanius of Salamis* (*Against the Heresies* 30.16.7–9) provides further information, including excerpts from their writings that include what has been recently identified as the *Gospel of the Ebionites*. It is difficult to know whether they were a continuation of the earliest circles of the **Jerusalem** church, dating back to James the Brother of Jesus (cf. Eusebius, *Onomasticon*, ed. De Lagarde, 138: though Eusebius opines the same about the Nazoraean sect), who were cast into obscurity by the effects of the Roman-Jewish war, and were an isolated (and apparently odd) group once the wider church caught up with them again (as Bauer imagines); or whether they were simply one of the most "unusual" groups among a wider body of Jewish Christians in Palestine, who by the third century had already become "curious" in the eyes of the vastly gentile church.

B. Bagatti, *L'Église de la circoncision* (Jerusalem, 1965); W. Bauer, *Orthodoxy and Heresy in Early Christianity* (Philadelphia, 1971), 241–85; L. E. Keck, "The Poor Among the Saints in Jewish Christianity and Qumran," ZNTW 57 (1966): 54–78; A. F. J. Klijn and G. J. Reinink, *Patristic Evidence for Jewish-Christian Sects* (Leiden, Netherlands, 1973), 19–43.

Ecclesiology   *see* Church

Economic Trinity   A modern term
for an ancient and somewhat embryonic position on the divine *Trinity*. It particularly focuses on the relation of the supreme God to the divine *Logos*, envisaging God's "extrapolation" of the Logos purely for the purposes of the creation of the cosmos. In some schemes the further extrapolation of the **Holy Spirit** could also be envisaged as a corresponding part of this "economy," or purposeful activity, for the *salvation* of the world. The distinction drawn by the Apologist **Theophilus of Antioch** between the Divinity complete in himself, with his Word and Wisdom immanently contained (*logos endiathetos*) in his own being, and then the Logos being "uttered" by God for the purposes of the

creation (*logos prophorikos*) suggests this scheme. The whole conception is based within the standpoint of pre-Nicene **Monarchianism**. God is ultimately one, and only became "threefold" for the purposes of creation and redemption. Since the Trinity is thus an "action of salvation" (*oikonomia*) rather than three distinct and permanently coexistent persons (hypostases), it is a scheme that can be called "economic Trinitarianism." It differs from **Modalism** insofar as it was an implied position, not a fully worked-out theology (hence it is a modern retrospective to designate it so clearly), and because it sees the Trinitarian persons as perhaps more permanent realities in God than Modalism did. Economic perspectives, in varying trace degrees, mark the thought of **Tertullian**, **Novatian**, and **Paul of Samosata**. In **Marcellus of Ancyra** it made one of its last appearances, already being seen as an archaism in the early fourth century. Marcellus pressed the notion to suggest that God the Father would finally draw back into his immanent life the **hypostases** of the Son and Spirit in the final consummation of all things. To denounce his ideas the christological phrase "whose kingdom will have no end" was added to the Nicene Creed. The church's public rejection of Marcellus was one of the factors that led to the elaboration of a full-blown Trinitarian theology after **Nicaea**, which was initiated by **Athanasius of Alexandria**, and accomplished in the **Cappadocian Fathers, Basil of Caesarea, Gregory of Nazianzus**, and **Gregory of Nyssa**. In the middle of the twentieth century it was a theory resurrected by some theologians to attempt to underpin a "suffering God" theology. In antiquity the theory was regarded as highly defective in that it confused the activity of God (*energeia*) with the essence of God (*ousia*), blurring a critical distinction between the Creator and the creative act manifested within the parameters of created time and space. The supposition that God as revealed in the economy of salvation was synonymous with God-in-himself was radically rejected by the Cappadocian Fathers, who stated the classical patristic position that God was revealed partially in the economy of salvation, but remained wholly unknown in his own essence to all except the other hypostases of the Trinity (cf. Gregory of Nazianzus, *Orations* 37–41).

G. L. Prestige, *God in Patristic Thought* (London, 1936), 97–111; H. A. Wolfson, *The Philosophy of the Church Fathers* (London, 1970), 177–23; B. Bobrinskoy, *The Mystery of the Trinity* (New York, 1999) 197–219.

Economy   *Oikonomia* (Latin: *dispensatio*) was a term used in the late Pauline literature (Eph. 1:3–14, esp. 1:10; 3:9; Col. 1:25–26) to connote a panoramic sense of the divine plan for the redemption of the cosmos. It is designated in the scriptural texts the "mystery of the economy" of salvation. This was an encouragement the patristic writers took up enthusiastically, for the concept of economy had been used beforehand by Stoic religious philosophers to designate the principles of order within the world that manifested providence to the reverent observer. In patristic writing after *Origen of Alexandria,* who made the connection extensively, "economy" became a keyword denoting the system of salvation (*soteriology*) that God has put into effect through the *incarnation*, death, and *resurrection* of Christ. In the *christological* controversies of the fourth and fifth centuries it was customary for theologians to stress the contextual difference that had to be noted when considering who God was and how God acted. *Cyril of Alexandria*, for example, accused *Nestorius* of not realizing that all God-statements made about the human Christ (such as whether it was legitimate to designate Jesus simply as "God," or whether it made sense to talk about the "divinity of Jesus of Nazareth") could be affirmed only in the context of the economy. For Cyril what was true of the preexistent

Logos could not simply be affirmed of the Christ, without regard for the different context inaugurated by the economy of the incarnation. It was thus legitimate "according to the economy" (*kat' oikonomian*) to speak about the "sufferings of the divine Word," a phrase that would have been blasphemous "according to the deity" (*kata theoteten*), that is, if stated outside the economic context of the Word's incarnation in history. A distinction thus developed between theology proper (*theologia*) on the one hand, which referred to statements about the nature of God (the divine *ousia*) and had to resolve into affirmation of transcendent mystery since that *ousia* was ultimately unknowable, and on the other hand in relation to the economy, soteriological statements (such as about Christology, pneumatology, or ecclesiology), which described how God revealed himself in the world through redemptive acts. In modern terms this would mean that the *patristic* writers generally regarded all the theological disciplines, apart from the doctrine of God per se, as economy. After the late fourth century, first noticeable in the *Cappadocian Fathers* (Basil, *Epistle* 199; *Gregory of Nyssa,* Catechetical Oration 34), the term also started to acquire a more specific ecclesiastical meaning in terms of the administration of the *sacraments*, and how tolerant one could be in reconciling dissidents to full communion. This sense, that what was strictly not permissible could be tolerated in order to effect a compassionate reconciliation or healing of a defective situation, was something that developed apace in Byzantium and became an important aspect of church discipline (*canons*) in the East.

J. Ruemann, "Oikonomia as Ethical Accommodation in the Fathers, and Its Pagan Background," TU 78 (1961): 370–79; A. Grillmeier, *Christ in Christian Tradition* (vol. 1, 2d ed.; London, 1975), 112–13, 443; J. A. McGuckin, *St. Cyril of Alexandria and the Christological Controversy* (Leiden, Netherlands, 1994).

Ecstasy The word derives from the Greek *ekstasis* and literally means "standing outside oneself." Its cognate (*exesti*: or being outside oneself) is used as a hostile criticism of Jesus in the Gospels (cf. Mark 3:21) implying that he was out of his mind (and thus dispossessed of himself—a charge editorially related to the accusation of the scribes in the adjacent section of the Gospel that Jesus was demonically possessed; cf. Mark 3:22). In Hellenistic religious experience the ecstatic dispossession of a worshiper was certainly not unknown, and the very term "being God-filled" (implying an ecstatic state) was later to become very well known in Christianity as "enthusiasm" (*enthousiasmos*). At first this was most closely associated with Dionysiac religion. In this context the consumption of much wine was a religious act that assisted the advent of the state of being God-filled. The Pythian priestess at Delphi was also known to utter, while under a state of drug-induced intoxification (the smoke of laurel leaves), the (gibberish) oracles that were later turned into beautiful poetry by the priest-scribes. Most of the earliest Christian attitudes, however, mirror the sobriety of Jewish religious approaches: presupposing that the advent of the divine Spirit to the soul emphasizes its moral human characteristics (rationality, awareness, and obedience) rather than wiping out its human consciousness in a state of ecstatic mindlessness. To this extent, the "prophetic" typology of most of the Scripture envisaged the drawing near to God as a state of great awe, but one in which the creature was expected to be instructed. This was the dominant archetype of early Christianity, and it probably explains why the church generally regarded ecstatic experiences with something akin to hostility. The first-century church at Corinth clearly knew ecstatic experiences of the Spirit (such as speaking in tongues) but Paul, while not censuring them exactly, determinedly subordinates these quasi-ecstatic gifts to the "rational" gifts of the interpretation of tongues, or the teachers and prophets who could usefully instruct the congregation (1 Cor. 12:7–16; 14:1–32). Even when he subordinates ecstatic religion, however, he is well aware that claims for spiritual authority on this basis were far more "appealing" in a Hellenistic environment and so he returns to the issue in 2 Corinthians, where he too claims to have had a rapture to the third heaven that can outrank any of his opponents' experiences. In this instance it is again clear that he relegates ecstatic experience (even when he overtly seems to prioritize it), for he again implies here that the purpose of the rapture "beyond human words" was to instruct him in the manner of an *apocalyptic* prophet (2 Cor. 12:1–6), and although he does not communicate that wordless vision, he certainly communicates his authority in the many words of his Epistle. Paul's dictum carried much weight for later ages: "Prophets can always control their prophetic spirit, since God is not a God of disorder but of peace" (1 Cor. 14:32). The rise of the *Montanist* movement in Asia Minor in the second century marked a change in this, for Montanus and the prophetesses who shared the early leadership of the movement with him did advocate ecstatic possession by the Spirit as a mark of the true charism of inspiration. Yet theirs was a mixture of ecstasy and didactic instruction, for their oracles too were collected and listed for edification (books of Montanist *Testimonia* have recently been reassembled from their citation by opponents and from the other surviving fragments). It is often thought that the wave of opposition raised among the larger congregations of Christians against the Montanists caused a further hardening of attitudes toward ecstasy among Christian theologians generally. It is not until the late fourth century that some of those attitudes began to change, and then only slightly. The alteration is noticed in the ascetical writings on prayer of the early monks. It first comes in the Syrian ascetics. Pseudo-Macarius (*see* **Macarius**

the Great II) begins to speak in quasi-Dionysiac terms, of the "drunken sobriety" of the soul when it experiences God at first hand (a term also found in *Philo*). The Evagrian tradition of prayer advocates ecstasy as the highest form of perception of the divine. But in this there is a subtle change from earlier Hellenistic religiosity, for the ravishing of the intellect (*harpage*—as in Nilus, *Ad Magnum* PG 79.1004) is understood in the Origenian school as a transcendence of earthly wisdom and imagery, but by no means an overriding of reason, insofar as it is a communion with the divine *Logos* (reason itself). This has been called technically not ecstatic but "katastatic" (the rapturous vision of God is the fulfillment of the structure of human wisdom as the icon of God). In harmony with this broad tradition of *Origen* and *Evagrius*, *Gregory of Nyssa* described the highest state of divine perception as a mystical darkness in which the soul went out of itself (*ekstasis*) in order to be raised to God's very presence "on the wings of love." The medieval mystical writer of the *Cloud of Unknowing* precisely summarized this Origenian tradition (by means of [Pseudo] *Dionysius the Areopagite*, who had greatly popularized it) when he wrote: "By Love God may be gotten and holden, but by thought, never."

H. Crouzel, *Origène et la connaissance mystique* (Paris, 1961); R. S. Kraemer, "Ecstasy and Possession: The Attraction of Women to the Cult of Dionysus," HTR 72 (1979): 55–80; A. Louth, *The Origins of the Christian Mystical Tradition: From Plato to Denys* (Oxford, 1981); J. A. McGuckin, *Standing in God's Holy Fire: The Spiritual Tradition of Byzantium* (London, 2001); T. Spidlik, *The Spirituality of the Christian East* (Kalamazoo, Mich., 1986), 71–86, 339–40.

Education   Ancient Graeco-Roman society had fixed and traditional views on the system of education (Greek: *paideia*) for the young, and Christianity,

when it had attained sufficient social standing that an educational program for youth began to matter to it (that is, by the end of the fourth century), made little change to that overall structure, except to see to it that the multitude of references to pagan cult in the old *canon* of literary classics (heavily based on Virgil and Homer and the other poets) would be suitably excised, and the many "immoral stories" related to the lives and loves of the old gods would be avoided. This, however, was easier to state than to effect, and some patristic writers tried to create a new school curriculum that was more heavily focused on paraphrases of the biblical text. *Origen* is one of the first important theorists to see how a Christian school could function as an important missionary outreach for the church. Both *Clement* and he had served as professors at *Alexandria* before this, probably with small numbers of private fee-paying pupils. Clement's educational program has survived in his *Paedagogus* and the *Stromata*. He made an important foundational argument for the Christians: that true philosophy ("our philosophy" the fathers later designated their religion) had to be rooted in justice and worship before it could be a preparatory education in the things of the Spirit (*Stromata* 1.7.37). In the mid–third century, Origen moved to Caesarea and began there an important new venture, founding a Christian *schola* with a library that would last for centuries. The curriculum theory Origen espoused here is praised by one of his graduating pupils (*Theodore's Address of Thanks to Origen*). Here there is sketched out a theory that begins with grammatical studies, and progresses through the natural sciences to rhetoric and finally theology. It would be a model that would have great long-term influence. *Apollinaris of Laodicea*, his father, and *Gregory of Nazianzus* all responded to the emperor Julian's *Edict on the Professors*, in the mid–fourth century, which banned Christians from the higher levels of academic posts, by preparing their own dossiers of materials for a Christian school. Gregory's work has survived in the form of numerous biblical paraphrases written up in the varieties of Greek metrical forms, so that children could simultaneously learn the basics of their biblical heritage while memorizing examples of classical versification. Gregory, however, also illustrates the hit-and-miss character of this plan, for Julian's proscription was very brief indeed, and had little general effect. Although Gregory is one of the most eloquent of the Fathers in denouncing immoral Hellenistic paideia (though see also Tertullian, *De praescriptione* 7.1–13), he is also, without question, the single patristic writer most thoroughly steeped in classical literature. His own correspondences cite the poet Sappho and most of the other classical authors of the Hellenistic canon. The difference lay in his episcopal sermons, where the Bible has replaced those authors. His theory of education was to turn to the classics and "clip the roses of their thorns" (as his cousin Amphilokius put it), while providing a foundational base of biblical stories to illustrate moral cases. Classical education remained, for most of the educated classes of the fourth-century church (exactly that class who would soon occupy the episcopal sees as bishop-teachers), very much a personal preference. In the patristic writers generally we see a division between those who had little prior education (especially monastic writers in the East) and those who were clearly educated over long years in the best Hellenistic schools. The greatest orators and rhetoricians were perhaps Apollinaris, the *Cappadocian Fathers*, and *John Chrysostom*, but the *Syrian* teachers *Diodore* and *Theodore* also show the results of long years of rhetorical study. By the fifth century highly educated clerics such as *Cyril of Alexandria* are showing that the Christian church has now extensively influenced the general program of studies for Christians. These writers cite hardly any of the old classics, and instead are heavily based within biblical paradigms. *Basil of Caesarea*, in his *Address to the Young*, took up a phrase and idea first coined by Origen when he described giving Christian youth a classical education as something worthy of the church's efforts (Clement of Alexandria had long before mentioned the opposition to the whole idea in his local community). Basil said the process could be seen as the biblical "despoiling of the Egyptians," when the Israelites took from their captors gold and silver, from which they later fashioned the sacred vessels of God's altar. Just so, the Cappadocians argued, a Christian school could select from the whole array of Greek culture and take the best, rededicating it to the service of God. *Augustine* in the fifth century would be the one to take this idea to a pitch and draw out a program of how the spoliation of the Egyptians could take place. His works themselves soon became a veritable canon of *philosophy*, Scripture, and rhetoric from which later Western theologians did not feel it was necessary to deviate greatly. Monastic traditions generally had an ambivalent view of classical education, despite their work in preserving that heritage for subsequent generations. Jerome dreamed that Christ denounced him because of his continuing love for classical authors. He tells in *Epistle* 22 how Christ told him he was "not a Christian but a Ciceronian," and in the later educational programs of the Western church, increasingly Christian authors came to displace the Hellenistic canon. In Byzantium, for the élite schools, the canon of the ancient classics continued to be studied well into the Middle Ages much as it had been done in late antiquity, but even here the spirit of the appropriation of that literature (one that melded its artistic, moral, and religious insights and imperatives) was radically different. The Christians read the old classics for their antique and venerable beauty, for the charming turn of phrase, or for the erudite allusion. There is something of an antiquarian's interest in how all except the philosophers were approached. In the areas of religious speculation and poetic composition it is clear from the Byzantine writers that the new ideas and new spirit of Christianity eventually had to produce a new canon of literature (*patristic* homilies in the moral domain, and liturgical *hymns* in the poetic) to correspond to its new interests and passions. From its earliest beginnings (with the catechism given to new converts) the church has, nonetheless, been deeply engaged in the processes of education, and generally seen it to be fundamental to its task of preaching the advent of the divine Wisdom in the world.

G. Buckler, "Byzantine Education," in N. Baynes and H. Moss, eds., *Byzantium* (Oxford, 1948), 200–220; H. I. Marrou, *St. Augustin et la fin de la culture antique* (Paris, 1958); idem, *A History of Education in Antiquity* (Madison, Wisc., 1982); W. Jaeger, *Early Christianity and Greek Paideia* (Cambridge, Mass., 1962).

Egeria (fl. late fourth century)   Egeria was a wealthy Christian lady, quite possibly a leader of a community of women *ascetics* in Spain. Shortly after 381 she embarked on a three-year voyage to the holy places of the Christian East. Beginning with a voyage to Egypt (*Sinai* and the sites associated with the exodus), she moved to the Holy Land, and then northeast to Edessa, through Asia Minor and finally to *Constantinople*. She left a travel journal of the many out-of-the-way places and communities she visited, which is of immense interest, for both her lively style and her eye for telling details. Often she was guided by local hermits to the sites the various churches had already identified with the holy places of biblical history. She was particularly concerned to record details of the liturgical customs of the churches she visited (probably for the reference of her own community in the West). Egeria was present for the Feast of the Nativity in

Egypt and *Jerusalem* (January 6), for the Epiphany at Bethlehem (where a night vigil was kept), and for Holy Week and Pascha at Jerusalem. She took part in the daily and Sunday liturgical offices, as well as the special services she describes, such as the procession with palms to the Mount of Olives and the Veneration of the *Cross*. She speaks of six chief churches in the Jerusalem region: the Holy Sepulchre, the Church of Zion, the Imbomon and the Eleona on the Mount of Olives, the Nativity Church at Bethlehem, and the Church of Lazarus at Bethany. On her return journey she also stayed in monasteries at Constantinople and Seleucia. To this extent she was an important transmitter of the Eastern ascetical culture to Western Europe before the ascendancy of Benedictinism. The single anonymous manuscript containing the work (missing the beginning and the end) was rediscovered only in 1884; its ascription to Egeria (sometimes Aetheria) was made later in the early decades of the twentieth century and further substantiated by P. Devos (*Analecta Bollandiana* 85 [1967]: 165–94).

G. Gingras, *Egeria: The Diary of a Pilgrimage* (ACW 38; Washington, 1970); H. Sivan, "Who Was Egeria? Piety and Pilgrimage in the Age of Gratian," HTR 81 (1988): 59–72.

Egypt   see **Alexandria, Antony the Great, Arianism, Asceticism, Athanasius of Alexandria, Cyril of Alexandria, Dionysius of Alexandria, Evagrius of Pontus, Macarius of Alexandria, Nitria, Origen of Alexandria, Scete, Syncletica**

Encratism—Encratite   A radical *ascetic* attitude, often tied in with early *Syrian* theology of the first three centuries. Encratism particularly regarded sexuality as hostile to spiritual liberation and discouraged, even forbade, *marriage* to the initiated members of the Christian community. They were generally vegetarian and non–wine-drinking. The movement was often allied with a strongly polarized view of the "Two Ways" (light and darkness, good and evil; *see* **Didache**) that held the world to be profoundly corrupt, and saw the **Church** as the body of pure elect withdrawn from it. Among the Encratites a large body of apocryphal writings of the first three centuries seem to have originated. (*See* **Antioch, Sexual Ethics, Tatian, Virginity**.)

L. W. Barnard, "The Heresy of Tatian: Once Again," JEH 19 (1968): 1–10; R. Cecire, *Encratism: Early Christian Ascetic Extremism* (Ph.D. diss., University of Kansas, 1985); R. M. Grant, "The Heresy of Tatian," JTS 5 (1954): 62–68.

Enhypostasia Enhypostasia in Greek patristic writing generally meant nothing more than being "hypostasized" (*see* **hypostasis**), that is, having a concrete personal identity or subsistence. In some twentieth-century textbooks the term was heavily overtranslated and read back into Byzantine theology as signifying quite precisely "having a hypostatic existence within another hypostasis." This made sense in reference to a precise theological context, that of the post-Chalcedonian *christological* controversies in the late fifth and sixth centuries (*see* **Council of Chalcedon**). The term can be found partly referring to this issue in the writings of Leontius of Byzantium and **John of Damascus**, when the defenders of the Chalcedonian Council attempted to address some of the perceived philosophical deficiencies of the synodical decree. The Chalcedonian settlement had imposed on the Byzantine and Latin churches the confession that Christ was comprised of one *person* (*hypostasis*) and two *natures* (*ousiai*). The person was divine and eternal, and since the divine person was single, the divinity present in Christ was necessarily synonymous with the divine Word, the eternal Son of

God before the ages. According to contemporary presuppositions of philosophy, existent being needed to be grounded in a precise concrete form. In other words, a being could not simply exist but had to exist as something particular: any abstract *ousia*, to be real, had to be hypostasized in its proper concrete form (a divine *ousia* demanded a divine hypostasis, a human *ousia* a human hypostasis, an animal *ousia* an animal hypostasis, and so on). In terms of the Chalcedonian vision of Christ as one (divine) person and two natures (one of which was divine and the other human), the theologians of the late fifth century retrospectively saw great problems. In the Chalcedonian Christ, the divine nature was perfectly well concretized in the divine hypostasis of the *Logos*. Having a divine nature concretized by the divine hypostasis made the Son of God "perfectly real" and perfectly present in the specific reality and existence of Christ. The human nature of Christ, however, did not have a corresponding hypostasis to concretize it, to make it real. Without a human hypostasis corresponding to the abstract human nature, the humanity of Christ appeared to be very much "less than real." Christ's humanity was, then, apparently only an abstraction not a concrete reality, a position that ran immediately in the face of everything the Gospels affirmed about the real humanity of Jesus. Even if one admitted that such *"Docetism"* was only apparent, not intended, it still left the Chalcedonian settlement paradoxically affirming that while Jesus was fully human (that is, possessed of an authentic human nature), he was by no means a human being (a human person). Indeed the latter aspect was one of the necessary corollaries of the Chalcedonian insistence that Jesus was divine, and was a compromise settled on in order to rule out *Adoptionist* or *Nestorian* conceptions that there was in the composite "Christ" a divine Logos in some form of association with a certain human being called Jesus. If one came at the Chalcedonian settlement from this angle, it could be interpreted as a diminution of the very humanity of Jesus that the council had set out to defend. The response of the pro-Chalcedonians was to argue that while the human *ousia* in all other human beings definitely needed to be rendered concrete (hypostasized) in a specifically human hypostasis, in Christ alone the divine hypostasis, that is, the Logos himself, personally hypostasized the human nature. The human nature of Christ, in short, was rendered concrete by a special act of divine energy. It was "hypostasized in" or "hypostasized by" the Logos directly and immediately as a perfect representation of the generic *ousia*: in other words, by the divine hypostatization, Jesus was not only perfectly human, but more to the point, a "perfect" exemplar of humanity. This meant that the human nature of Christ was created by direct divine intervention from the moment of conception in the *Virgin Mary*, and was sustained in being by the divine Word, who had adopted it as "his own human nature." The theory had the benefit of restating much of the original christological vision of *Cyril of Alexandria* (a favored motif of later Byzantine theology was to interpret Chalcedon strictly in accordance with the terms of Cyril's writings). Enhypostasia was, therefore, something of an emergency retrospective repair of the council, and testifies to the somewhat artificial nature of the Chalcedonian settlement in and of itself. In the East a more enduring christological settlement was reattempted at the *Council of Constantinople II* in 553, which returned to the more organic christological conceptions of Cyril of Alexandria. The Western church, on the other hand, clung assiduously to Chalcedon and neglected the terms of the later Greek conciliar developments. By routing the understanding of Chalcedon through the narrowest of channels, the *Tome of Leo*, with its mechanistic view of person and nature, Latin Christology further exacerbated the problem of the "abstrac-

tion of humanity." Accordingly many twentieth-century theologians (themselves apparently understanding the Council of Chalcedon to be synonymous with Leo) lamented the Chalcedonian "diminishment" of the humanity of Jesus, and thought that reviving the concept of enhypostasia might go some way to resolving the issue.

A. Grillmeier, *Christ in Christian Tradition* (vol. 1, 2d ed.; London, 1975), 437–39, 459–61, 481–83, 495f., 521–23.

Ephrem the Syrian (c. 306–373)

Ephrem was a deacon and ascetic of the church of Nisibis. He was the most important of the early Syrian Nicene theologians and the most significant representative of Syrian hymnography, with numerous extant *hymns* and poem-homilies, through which he strove to disseminate Nicene teaching by the liturgical medium of the biblical song. His work is deeply Semitic in character, using scriptural symbols in cascades of allusions rather than following the linear schematic sequence of Greek thought. It results in Ephrem having a decidedly original approach to theology, even though his life's aim was consciously apologetic, determined to rebut the numerous heretical movements he saw affecting the Syrian Christian experience (especially *Manicheism, Gnosticism, Arianism,* and astrology [*see* Bardesanes]). His works were translated into Greek at an early stage (attracting many forgeries into the Greek textual tradition) and influenced later Byzantine midrashic styles of liturgical poetry, especially that of *Romanos*. In recent times, following a renewal of Syriac studies, they have also seen new English editions, which have stimulated interest in Ephrem as a theological thinker. When the Roman empire ceded Nisibis to the Persians in 363, he moved with the refugees to Edessa. Here he led a school of theology and wrote many hymns for the community of female ascetics resident there. He died ministering to plague victims in Edessa in 373. Tales of other journeys (to Nicaea with his bishop, to Cappadocia, or Egypt) are not generally accepted today. Biblical *typology* (where a figure or event in the Old Testament is read as a redactive lens over the New Testament mystery to which it relates) forms the structure of much of Ephrem's thinking. He sees the visible creation as a great scheme of symbolic mysteries, which faith can interpret. The central key to understanding it is the *incarnate* Word of God, who plays on "three harps": namely, the two testaments and the book of *nature*. That the Word has reestablished the lost path to paradise for his faithful is a perennial theme for Ephrem. His most famous works are the *Hymns on Faith, Hymns on Paradise,* and *Hymns of Nisibis.*

S. P. Brock, *The Harp of the Spirit* (2d ed.; London, 1983); idem, *St. Ephrem the Syrian: The Hymns on Paradise* (New York, 1990); idem, *The Luminous Eye: The Spiritual World Vision of St. Ephrem* (Cistercian Studies 124; Kalamazoo, Mich., 1992); K. McVey, *Ephrem the Syrian: Hymns* (*On the Nativity, On Faith, Against Julian*; Classics of Western Spirituality; New York, 1989).

Epiclesis Literally "calling down upon," *epiclesis* in Christian theology refers to prayer in general, and most particularly the solemn invocation of the **Holy Spirit** in the most sacred part of the **eucharistic** liturgy, after the words of institution ("This is my body") so that the eucharistic gifts might be consecrated and transformed. The *epiclesis* was a feature of almost all ancient liturgies from the third century onwards, first exemplified in the *Liturgy of Addai and Mari* and the **Apostolic Tradition** of **Hippolytus**. It received commentary in the fourth-century *Mystagogical Catecheses* of **Cyril of Jerusalem**, a fact that gives testimony to a higher awareness throughout the fourth century (especially after the definition of the deity of

the Spirit at the *Council of Constantinople I* (381) of the consecratory and sanctifying power of the divine Spirit. The apparent absence of an *epiclesis* in the Roman rite was noticed as a peculiarity, and the liturgical reforms of the twentieth century restored it to the Mass. In the Byzantine liturgy the *epiclesis* reads: "Again we pray you: Send down your Holy Spirit upon us and upon these gifts here offered, and make this bread the precious body of your Christ, and that which is in this cup the precious blood of your Christ; making the change by your Holy Spirit. Amen. Amen. Amen." The medieval Latin church generally regarded the consecration of the Eucharist as taking place after the dominical words of institution. In the East the liturgical consecration was generally regarded as effected by the special operation of the Spirit (although all operations of God are from the single and undivided Trinity), and according to the teaching of **Gregory of Nyssa** (*Catechetical Oration* 96–97) and **John Chrysostom** (*Homily 1 on Judas' Betrayal*, para. 6), as occurring only after the prayer of *epiclesis*. To this day, in Orthodox ritual, it is not until that moment that the *clergy* and people fall down in worship before the sacrament.

B. Botte, "L'epiclèse eucharistique dans les anciennes liturgies," MSR 3 (1946): 197–206; M. Jugie, *De forma eucharistica, de epiclesibus eucharisticis* (Rome, 1943).

Epiphanius of Salamis (c. 315–403) One of the most noted writers and political bishops of ancient Cyprus, Epiphanius is now most famous for his compendium listing the varieties of heresies he had found prevalent in the church, which he published in an attempt to "name and shame" all the divergences from the Nicene orthodox faith of which he was a vigorous champion. Epiphanius was born in Palestine and studied in *Egypt*, where he became involved in the *ascetic* movement.

When he returned to Palestine in 335 he founded his own community in Judea and was the superior there for thirty years. His fame as a dynamic and pastoral leader led to his invitation to become bishop of Constantia (modern Salamis) in 365. He gained international fame as a vigorous voice denouncing theological compromises. He especially stood against the *Homoiousian* theology then favored by the imperial administration, and often advocated the policy favored by the bishops of *Alexandria* and *Rome*. All through his long monastic life he was an opponent of the Origenist style of spirituality and theology (thinking that it encouraged *Arianized* forms of *Christology*), preferring a simpler and more biblically literalist approach to the faith. *Jerome* encouraged him in his anti-Origenist stance, and Epiphanius's visit to Jerusalem in 394 led to much bad feeling between himself and the local bishop John. In the year 400 *Theophilus of Alexandria* summoned him to *Constantinople* and tried to involve him in the trial of *John Chrysostom*, but realizing the issue was about politics more than faith, to his credit, Epiphanius abandoned the proceedings. He died on the sea journey making his way back to Cyprus. His heresiological book has been variously called the *Medicine Chest* (*Panarion*) or the *Refutation of All Heresies* (*Haereses*). He also published the *Ancoratus*, which is a more positive exposition of Nicene orthodoxy. His minor works, still extant, include a treatise *On Weights and Measures* and another *On the Twelve Gems*. There are also surviving letters and notes on scriptural passages.

P. R. Amidon, *The Panarion of St. Epiphanius Bishop of Salamis* (New York, 1990); J. F. Dechow, *Dogma and Mysticism in Early Christianity: Epiphanius of Cyprus and the Legacy of Origen* (Patristic Monograph Series 13; Louvain, Belgium, 1988); F. Young, *From Nicaea to Chalcedon* (Philadelphia, 1983), 133–42, 347, 383f.; idem, "Did Epiphanius Know What He Meant by Heresy?" SP 17 (1982): 199–205.

Episcopate "Episcopate" derives from the New Testament term *episkopos*, or overseer, an office first mentioned in the Pastoral Epistles, in reference to one who has oversight of the Christian community (Phil. 1:1; 1 Tim. 3:1–7; Titus 1:7; 1 Pet. 2:25). The Saxon term "bishop" became its standard translation. In 1 Peter the title is connected with the "pastoral" office of being a shepherd of souls. And in Philippians the office is closely connected with the *deacons* of the church. This primitive association was strengthened after the third century when the council of presbyters (originally celebrating with the bishop) left the cathedral church for the villages in a large expansion of the church, and the deacons became especially seen as episcopal attendants. First Timothy establishes the basic qualifications of an *episkopos*, that he should only have been married once, that he should be a good administrator of his own household, not a neophyte, a good teacher, and an upright and hospitable character generally. The very earliest structures of the Christian ministerial offices are shrouded in obscurity, but by the second century there emerged a triadic form of *episkopos*-bishop, *presbyteros*-elder (which was rendered by the Old English "Priest"), and *diakonos*-deacon. This more and more replaced a range of other offices that had characterized the earliest church (such as apostolic missionaries, wandering prophets, exorcists, and didaskaloi-teachers) and became established by the end of the second century as a common pattern in most Christian communities. The Pastoral Letters of the New Testament and the *Apostolic Fathers* (especially *Ignatius of Antioch* and the Clementine literature) give a testimony to the rapid growth of this pattern. More or less by the middle of the third century, the office of the episcopate underwent a further elaboration.

Cyprian in the West refers to it extensively in terms drawn from the Old Testament literature of (Aaronic) priesthood (Ep. 63.14; Ep. 3; *On the Unity of the Church* 17). For Cyprian, the bishop is the *sacerdos*: the high priest of the Christian community. In the East, particularly the large cities such as **Alexandria**, other changes were also in progress to make the bishop stand out more and more clearly from the larger ranks of the presbyters. Although **Jerome** can still protest in the fourth century that the bishop and presbyter are really the same thing (and there is some ground to think this may have been so originally as the terms are interchangeable in the New Testament: Acts 20:17, 28; 1 Peter 5:1–4; Titus 1:5–7; and **Clement of Rome** uses the term in the plural [1 Clement 42; 44] to refer to the *clergy* of Rome), nevertheless his argument was already falling on deaf ears by his day. The bishops of great cities, and Rome is a prime example, were able to develop the role and function of their office considerably because of the prestige of their see. In the East, Demetrius of Alexandria, in the first quarter of the third century, was one of the first to insist on the clear demarcation of the bishop from the presbyters, and he emerges as a strong monarchical leader. A sense of monarchical authority (the bishop is the icon of Christ in the church and subject to no other authority) is witnessed as early as Ignatius (*To the Magnesians* 6.1), but the actualities of the latter's governance of Antioch should probably be contextualized in a nexus of other church "authorities" that included teachers and **confessors**. Clement of Rome (whose writings show a position at Rome where the bishop was an important spokesman and president for the council of presbyters) in his *First Letter* to the Corinthians notes that even though the community elects its bishop, that does not give the community the right to overthrow him. From that time onward election seems to have been an important element in the choice of all new bishops. The right of election already

features in **Didache** chapter 15. Such communal power dwindled in Byzantine times to a mere consultation of the people (often they were expected to "acclaim" the new leader), but even so there were many instances of a bishop being unable to assume duties because of the hostility of a local church who felt their wishes had been overlooked (such as the case of Proclus of Constantinople). By the end of the second century one finds lists of bishops being drawn up (first by **Hegesippus**) as a form of "pedigree" for a church's purity of faith. This devolved from Irenaeus's argument that the way the bishop succeeded the apostles (**Apostolic Succession**) was a guarantee of authenticity of teaching (*Adversus haereses* 3.3.1–3). For all Cyprian's insistence on his right to single episcopal authority, his own church wavered greatly over whether he, or the assembled presbyters, or the confessors had the higher standing. Inevitably with the bishop assuming the presidency of the services, especially **baptism** and **Eucharist**, his office predominated as the director of all the clergy. In the earliest times, it was a particular function of the bishop to be able spontaneously to compose the great eucharistic prayer of a church, and to this extent the ministerial role was assigned to the most charismatically gifted, and was often seen as a direct extension of the prophetic charism. It is only later that administrative duties sometimes outweighed these essentially hieratic functions. In the Irish church experience, as can be seen in the instance of St. Cuthbert, the bishop was chosen from the renowned ascetics, as a holy man, and the administrative duties of the diocese were arranged by other clergy. This pattern was already archaic in its day. After the fourth century when Constantine favored the bishops and encouraged them to administer local justice for Christians of the area, the office rose even higher in prestige and legal power. The fourth century shows many examples (not least **Athanasius of Alexandria**, the **Cappadocian Fathers**,

Eusebius of Nicomedia, and George of Cappadocia) of bishops who commanded immense powers, locally and internationally. Their ranks begin to include internationally renowned rhetoricians and philosophers, even relatives of the imperial family. The ability of a bishop to bring an emperor to admit fault, as was the case with *Ambrose* and *Theodosius*, marks a veritable high point in the prestige of the office. After the fourth century the Christian emperors increasingly honored the episcopate, and a tension can be noticed between its original conception as an office of liturgical president and teacher and its new functions as magistrate and administrator for a large diocesan area. The bishops of powerful cities in the empire came to have a greater influence than their colleagues from small towns, although the primitive principle of the equality of all bishops as icons of Christ was maintained. Even so, the bishops of the large cities came to rank as "metropolitans" and commanded the governance of larger matters such as episcopal ordinations and the care of synods. The really great cities, after the time of *Justinian*, claimed the title patriarch (Jerusalem was added for honor's sake) and a Pentarchy of Patriarchates was thus evolved (*Rome, Constantinople, Alexandria, Antioch*, and *Jerusalem*) whose bishops enjoyed particular respect in international affairs. The fact that Rome was the only patriarchate in the West contributed significantly to the evolution of the papacy. Augustine's definition of the bishop as "the servant of the servants of God" (Ep. 217) remained a constant reminder of the pastoral nature of the office, even after the phrase was taken by Gregory the Great (Ep. 1.1, 36; 6.51; 13.1) to become a particular designation of the Roman popes (*see papacy*).

A. Cunningham, *The Bishop in the Church: Patristic Texts on the Role of the Episkopos* (Wilmington, Del., 1985); G. Dix, "Ministry in the Early Church," in K. E. Kirk, ed., *The Apostolic Ministry* (London, 1946), 185–303; E. Ferguson, "Church Order in the Sub-Apostolic Period: A Survey of Interpretations," RQ 11 (1968): 225–48; E. Hatch, *The Organisation of the Early Christian Churches* (London, 1888); E. G. Jay, "From Presbyter-Bishops to Bishops and Presbyters," TSC 1 (1981): 125–62; W. Telfer, *The Office of a Bishop* (London, 1962).

Eschatology   The word means the study of the last things (Greek: *ta eschata*). It is a modern designation introduced by biblical scholars to attempt to cover a whole nexus of ideas that were prevalent in ancient theology, especially *apocalyptic* thought, and which represented the concept of God's indefectible dominion over human creaturehood, particularly in his manifested dominion of human times and empires. The rise and fall of human destinies, envisaged in cosmic terms or like the fall and rise of nations in great battles, was integral to the late flowering of prophecy in the apocalyptic literature of Judaism (now only witnessed in the Old Testament in parts of Ezekiel, Isaiah, and Daniel, but marked throughout the New Testament (cf. 1 Thess. 4:13–5.11; 1 Cor. 15; 1 Pet. 4:7–19; and especially in the book of Revelation). It is a scheme of thought also greatly in evidence in the apocryphal books of the intertestamental and the very early Christian periods (*Apocalypse of Peter, Ascension of Isaiah, Sibylline Oracles* 7–8). Just as the elevating of Israel to the status of elect nation was central to the biblical covenant theology, so too the constant collapse of Israel before the armies of hostile world powers was a major shock and threat to that theology of covenant. If God had intended the world for the sake of Israel, why had so much of that plan fallen into ruins before the force of the Assyrians, Babylonians, Persians, Greeks, and Romans? Apocalytpic literature was an attempt to give an answer to that problem of Providence theology. In apocalyptic thought the prophet is typically lifted up from the earth to "see" the reasons: God has allowed evil to flourish but only for a time, a season of his own judgment. The overturning of world order (the "covenant order" where the elect were meant to be free from the attacks of the evil) was only a short space of purification and testing of the just. Soon God shall return in force to effect true judgment and vengeance for the suffering saints. The return in judgment is often considered as a "new heaven and a new earth." The image of that new creation is clearly manifested in the book of Revelation, itself written after that recent shock to the system of the early church in Asia Minor, of the death of many believers in a persecution by Roman authorities (the "whore" of the great beast). Apocalypticism gave birth to an extended and pervasive *eschatological* sense in the theology of the Christian Fathers. The notion of God's relation to the world as primarily one of judgment and vindication is elevated as a chief presupposition of much early Christian writing. The "last things" of death, judgment, heaven, and hell thus became powerful forces in shaping and sharpening a highly ethical teleological worldview, which contemporary Hellenist thought (with the exception of some *Stoics*) and religions (with the exception of some of the Greek mysteries) did not share. For Hellenism in general, death was a sad dwindling away into a land of sorrowful shades. For the Christians it was the shared hope of participating in the *resurrection* of Christ, that supreme eschatological inbreaking of God into the historical order. The later New Testament literature, as already evidenced in the *christological* hymns of Ephesians, Colossians, and Philippians, shows that apocalypticism in the late first century was already being subsumed as a subset of Christology. That trend continued in the *Apostolic Fathers* of the second century, and a new form of patristic eschatology emerged, born of Jewish apocalyptic, but firmly fixed now on the issues of Christ's resurrection as a gift to the church (a "new creation" of the fundamentals of human *nature*, which had formerly been tied to corruption), and on the implications of his second coming (*Parousia*) as the key to that "moment of judgment" when Christ would be "all in all." By the late second century, apocalyptic revivals were still common in the church as the *Montanist* crisis demonstrates. *Tertullian* also shows a worldview permeated by a similar hope for an imminent judgment that would usher in a *millennial* time of peace (*Adversus Marcionem* 3.24). By the time of *Eusebius of Caesarea* in the fourth century, such millennial expectations (still witnessed, as for example, in the elaborate millenarianism of *Lactantius's Divine Institutes*) were dismissed as crudely archaic (Eusebius, *Ecclesiastical History* 3.39.13; 7.24.1). By the third century an intellectualist revision of apocalyptic themes, harmonizing them in line with hopes of a soul-communion with God, had already begun to appear. Eusebius was one of its defenders. The *Cappadocian Fathers* would be its ultimate synthesizers and disseminators. Its origin took place in *Alexandria*. *Clement* retranslated apocalypticism in this way (*Stromata* 7.11.63.1f.; 7.2.12.2f.; 7.6.34.4; 7.12.78.3). *Origen* himself was well aware that the eschatological scheme of death, resurrection, judgment, *heaven*, and *hell* was part of the traditional *Regula Fidei* given to *catechumens*. He presents it, however, as a valid vision of things (*PArch. Praef.* 5–7), but one that is suited for the "little children," those of literalist faith who have not thought deeply about reality. He suggests that the real cosmic scheme of God is far more comprehensive than this simple program allows: that the whole of the cosmic order is in a long process of return to communion with God, which this Christian eschatology simply symbolizes. Similarly the resurrection of the body was more of a symbol of spiritual transcendence than a real corporeal resuscitation. When Origen comments on the apocalyptic warnings Jesus gives in Matthew 24:3–44, for instance (Origen, *Ser Mt* 32–60), he reinterprets them in ways that emphasize Jesus' cosmic domination on a vast scale, his presidency of the souls of all creation ascending to God in purity of intellectual vision. Both Clement and Origen thought hell could not be eternal, but had to be a corrective process whereby God restored sinners to a proper focus on the deity. Not all the Fathers shared Origen's *soul*-centered cosmology; even fewer shared his view of the resurrection, but most of them followed his path toward a profoundly christological exegesis of the "last things." In the West, *Augustine* synthesized the several varied strands of Latin eschatology, and even though many of his contemporaries thought the fall of Rome was the sign of the end, he remained cautious about an imminent Parousia (*Epistle* 199). Even so he gave support to a more literally grounded eschatological scheme than was being argued among the Greek Origenists (*On the City of God* 20–22). His "simplicity" was deeply rooted in a highly sophisticated theology of time: contrasting the swift passage of human destinies with the timeless condition of God and the divine judgments. Eschatological fulfilment, for Augustine, was an issue of the admission of the creature into the timeless condition of God (*On Psalms* 101.10; *On the Gospel of John* 31.5; *Confessions* 13.37). Augustine's great popularizer, Gregory the Great, in the seventh century, though he personally thought the end would be in his own time, still prepared a full-scale pastoral program for his church (*The Pastoral Rule*) as if it had a long journey yet before it. Eschatological thought thus began with the church's birth, and continued throughout the patristic age to give a dynamic pulse to most Christian reflection on human nature and the social condition, even when much of the original apocalyptic stimulus was creatively refashioned in christological mysticism or ascetical ethics.

B. E. Daley, *The Hope of the Early Church: A Handbook of Patristic Eschatology* (Cambridge, 1991); G. Florovsky, *Creation and Redemption* (vol. 3 of the *Collected Works*; Belmont, Mass., 1976), 243–68; R. M. Grant, *Christian Beginnings: Apocalypse to History* (London, 1983); G. W. H. Lampe, "Early Patristic Eschatology," in W. Manson, ed., *Eschatology* (London, 1953), 17–35; J. Pelikan, *The Shape of Death: Life, Death, and Immortality in the Early Fathers* (Nashville, 1961); A. J. Visser, "A Bird's Eye View of Ancient Christian Eschatology," *Numen* 14 (1967): 14–22.

Ethiopia   Ethiopia (sometimes called "*India*" by the patristic writers, and "Abyssinia" by writers of the early twentieth century) is one of the oldest Christian civilizations. Its geographical isolation, later exacerbated by the collapse of the *Nubian* church in the later Middle Ages (which cut it off from the Nile passage down to *Alexandria*), was made even more critical by the relentlessly advancing pressures of Islam (moving to it from the immediate east). Eventually Islamic power would cut off the Ethiopians from their possession of the coastal strip, forcing them into the highlands and in the process further "sealing off" their Christianity from the rest of the Christian world. The Byzantine forms are very important to the Ethiopians (who are generally classified today as one of the Oriental Orthodox churches), especially as these were mediated by the more or less constant presence of Coptic influence from the church of Alexandria (which provided Ethiopia's archbishops for centuries), but other influences marked the Ethiopian church in unique ways. The pervasive influence of Jewish ritual practice has been much debated: whether it is an early medieval influence or represents an ancient and indigenous form of Christianity that never adopted the more stringent synagogue-church separation that entered Latin and Byzantine

Christianity in the rest of the Mediterranean world. The Ethiopians, for example, observe both circumcision and *baptism*; both Shabbat and Sunday; and they also preserve books in their *canon* that were not only never accepted anywhere else, but that fell from existence everywhere else. The rediscovery in Ethiopia of the *Book of Enoch* proved a major event for modern biblical scholarship. The origins of the church are quite possibly traceable to the first century, although Ethiopian legends themselves place the foundation in the celebrated encounter between Solomon and the queen of Sheba, who is said to have brought the ark of the covenant back with her to the highlands of Ethiopia (the Solomonic legends tend to date from the thirteenth century). The reference to the Ethiopian eunuch in Acts, however, is a more certain historical incident. The apostle Philip (Acts 8:26–39) is shown baptizing the chief eunuch of the administration of the Ethiopian kandak, or queen (her title is misunderstood in the New Testament as a personal name: Candace). The author of Acts inserts this story to symbolize the spread of the gospel to the furthest corners of the world. Already in Greek literature the Ethiopians had been classified as the gentlest but most remote people on earth. Philip's encounter, however, is significant in that it suggests the first Christians of Ethiopia were constituted from the "God-fearers" who regularly traveled to *Jerusalem* and took part in the festal celebrations of the temple. The *trade routes* to the holy city from Ethiopia (the eastward Indian land and sea route) were well traveled in antiquity, and there is no reason to doubt a historical connection from the earliest times: a connection that has remained a vital and dominant part of Ethiopian church life ever since, exemplified today by the manner in which they have retained a small chapel at the rear of the Holy Sepulchre aedicule and a monastic community on the roof of the same church. Historical traditions relate that the church was given a second foundation by St. Frumentius (c. 300–380; Rufinus, *Church History* 1.9f.; Socrates, *Church History* 1.19; Sozomen, *Church History* 2.24; Theodoret, *Church History* 1.22). Frumentius and his brother Aedesius had been Roman youths, trading in Ethiopia during a time of war, when they were captured and forced to serve the Ethiopian king Ezana. Their rise in the court led to the adoption of Frumentius by *Athanasius of Alexandria*, who ordained him bishop when he visited Alexandria, and commissioned him to institute churches and services in the Alexandrian manner (cf. Athanasius, *Apology to Constantius* 31). In the late fifth century Ethiopian traditions speak of the arrival of the "Nine Saints." These appear to have been wandering Syrian missionaries and monks. Their impact on the Ethiopian church was inestimable, giving it the strongly monastic, *ascetical*, and *apocalyptic* character it bears to this day. The "third founders" established Christianity in a way that coincided with the rise of the Christian king Caleb. He rose to power by destroying the armies of the African-Jewish king Dhu Nuwas, who had slaughtered Christians in his dominions. Caleb's dynasty instituted Aksum as a center of Christian civilization, and inaugurated the first great period of the church's flourishing. During this era the Bible and many patristic writings were translated into Ge'ez. After that time the rising power of Islam overshadowed the church and pushed it into a slow retreat into obscurity. The numerous wars and raids that devastated Ethiopian Christianity played havoc with its written sources: but there was also always a preference for the oral tradition, which today makes ancient Ethiopian Christianity difficult to reconstruct around its many legends. Clearer knowledge of the church only becomes available again after the rise of the Zagwe dynasty of kings (1137–1270), one of whom (Lalibela) is thought to have ordered the construction of the amazing rock-carved churches of Roha-Lalibela. In this later period of the thirteenth and fourteenth centuries, another phase of Christian expansion, led by the monastic missionary Tekla Haymanot, extended the church to the south, and began a further period of translation of Christian texts from the Arabic: a time when many Western sources entered the literature; most notably causing a great upsurge of devotion to the Mother of God. The church's later history was marked by a cycle of encounters with Portuguese Catholicism and destructive wars with Islam. Through the church's historic outposts at Jerusalem and Alexandria, the higher Ethiopian clergy always managed to keep an eye on developments elsewhere in the Christian world, while maintaining the distinctive character of their ancient traditions. The Ethiopian church shares a profound *patristic* heritage with the Copts and the Orthodox. Like the Copts it rejects the christological tradition of the *Council of Chalcedon* in favor of the single divine-human reality of the Christ (*see Monophysitism*).

A. Grillmeier, *The Church of Alexandria with Nubia and Ethiopia after 451* (vol. 2, pt. 4 of *Christ in Christian Tradition*; London, 1996), 293–392; J. M. Harden, *An Introduction to Ethiopic Christian Literature* (London, 1926); A. Hastings, *The Church in Africa: 1450–1950* (Oxford, 1994); M. Heldman, ed., *African Zion: The Sacred Art of Ethiopia* (New Haven, Conn., 1993); H. M. Hyatt, *The Church of Abyssinia* (Oxford, 1928).

Eucharist The Greek term (*eucharistia*) means a "giving of thanks," and from early times designated both the generic act of spiritual thanksgiving (as in Origen's *De Oratione*, where he cites the necessity to give thanks regularly to God as one of the fundamental duties of the Christian at *prayer*) and also the specific and central act of corporate Christian prayer, the celebration of the eucharistic rite, the memorial of the Lord's body and blood as instituted at the Last Supper (or the "Mystical Supper," as it is called in Eastern Christianity). While the first reference to the communion ritual seems to have been "the breaking of the bread" (*klasma*), the designation Eucharist was in use at least as early as Paul. The first records of Jesus' prayer at the Last Supper focus quite explicitly on the context that the Lord took bread and wine "and gave thanks" to God (1 Cor. 11:24; Matt. 26:27). Second-century writers such as the *Didache* (9.1), *Justin Martyr* (*First Apology* 66), and *Ignatius of Antioch* (*To the Philadelphians* 4; *To the Ephesians* 13.1; *To the Smyrnaeans* 7.1; 8.1) all demonstrate that Eucharist has already become a technical word for the ritual of Holy Communion. It was originally parallel with anamnesis, a word used regularly by Justin Martyr to describe the ritual as the "remembrance" of the Lord. In later Byzantine writing "Eucharist" was regularly used alongside the designation "the *Mysteries*," which also embraced the other sacraments such as *baptism* and chrismation. In patristic writing the Eucharist is above all a "sacrifice of praise and thanksgiving" rooted in the memorial of the Lord's saving passion and resurrection. The celebration of the eucharistic mysteries was approached *eschatologically*: the consecratory power of the *Holy Spirit* who once again made present the Lord of Glory in the eucharistic forms (*see epiclesis*) opened up a timeless window within the time-bound earthly church whereby believers, both individually and collectively, were caught up into the single redemptive work of Christ that had been accomplished within history but now applied beyond all time and history. The Eucharist celebrated the Christ who through his sacrifice (as re-presented in the church's mystery) restored life to the faithful. Eucharistic worship, in all the ancient rites, shows this deep sense of eschatological presence and expectation. *Irenaeus* described the sharing of eucharistic bread as an anticipation of "the mystery of the final harvest"

(*Adversus haereses* 4.17–18). The first account of the Christian Eucharist was given by Justin Martyr in his *First Apology* (65, 76), when he describes (generically) the Sunday rituals of a typical Christian assembly. By the third century church writers were beginning to turn their attention more specifically to the matter (beforehand they had more or less "presumed it" as a basic element of church life) and *Cyprian of Carthage* was the first to devote a small treatise to the subject (*Epistle* 63). His central themes are the joy and spiritual inebriation one experiences at Christ's meal, and how the mystery associates the entire church in the saving work of the passion of the Redeemer. The collection of numerous grains of wheat into a single loaf becomes for him (as for the *Didache* and many other patristic writers) a meaningful sign of how the Christian Eucharist is first and foremost a symbol and efficient cause of unity within the church. In the fourth century, after the church had emerged into the light of imperial favor and expanded its public rituals, the eucharistic rites were the subject of several extensive liturgical and spiritual treatises by patristic writers, most notably *Cyril of Jerusalem, John Chrysostom, Ambrose, Augustine, Cyril of Alexandria, Dionysius the Areopagite,* and *Maximus the Confessor.*

M. Goguel, *L'Eucharistie des Origines à Justine Martyr* (Paris, 1910); R. P. C. Hanson, "Eucharistic Offering in the Pre-Nicene Fathers," PRIA 76c (1976): 75–96; D. J. Sheerin, *The Eucharist: Message of the Fathers of the Church* (vol. 7; Wilmington, Del., 1986); G. Wainwright, *Eucharist and Eschatology* (London, 1978).

Eunomius of Cyzicus (c. 325–395)

Eunomius was a Cappadocian rhetor who rose to prominence from the lower classes, and was a constant critic of the aristocratic *Cappadocian Fathers.* It was his work, in particular, that largely stimulated the Cappadocians to advance their thought on the future of the Nicene synthesis. Eunomius and *Basil of Caesarea* were bitter opponents throughout their ecclesiastical careers, but *Gregory of Nazianzus* also composed his famed *Five Theological Orations* in a deliberate attempt to refute Eunomius, who was then living near him in *Constantinople.* Eunomius studied at Constantinople, *Antioch,* and *Alexandria,* where he met with the charismatic logician and rhetor *Aetius,* to whom he attached himself for the rest of his life. Aetius was the leader of the radical movement of protest within the Arian movement that wished to denounce the Homoians, the *Homoiousians,* as well as the *Homoousians.* As a result he advocated a position that the Son of God was "completely unlike" the Father (*Anhomoios*) and the school was subsequently known as the Anomoeans despite their own preference to be called Heterousiasts (Different Essencers). The Aetian-Eunomian party (for Eunomius's energy soon secured the virtual leadership of the group) laid great stress on the need for strict logical method in theological teaching. God was quintessentially the One who was ungenerated. Ingeneracy was posited as the primary character of God, such that the Son and the *Holy Spirit* (as well as all other generated beings) were clearly not-God, however close to the Absolute Ingenerate they might be. In addition, words were seen as having essential revelatory force. Names, that is, revealed essences. In regard to the Scriptures the titles Son and Father denoted different essences, not simply different persons. The Cappadocians were forced by this sophisticated logical attack on the simple fideism of many of their movement to articulate deeper answers. The titles in Scripture, for example, were argued by them to be relations not essences, largely because of reaction to Eunomius. Similarly the *neo-Nicene* insistence on mystical insight as the primary mode of theology was elevated, at first, as a precise attack on Eunomius's prioritization of logical syllogism in the elaboration of his teaching. The surviving Cappadocians secured Eunomius's final exile in Cappadocia in the time of *Theodosius* the Great. Eunomius's *Apology* survives, as does his *Confession of Faith*, and numerous sections of his *Apology for the Apology* are cited in *Gregory of Nyssa's* defense of Basil from Eunomius's attacks.

M. V. Anastos, "Basil's Kata Eunomiou," in P. J. Fedwick, ed., *Basil of Caesarea: Christian, Humanist, Ascetic* (Toronto, 1981), 67–136; E. Cavalcanti, *Studi Eunomiani* (OCA 202; Rome, 1976); R. P. C. Hanson, *The Search for the Christian Doctrine of God* (Edinburgh, 1988), 598–636; T. A. Kopecek, *A History of Neo-Arianism* (vols. 1–2; Cambridge, Mass., 1979); R. P. Vaggione, *Eunomius: The Extant Works* (Oxford, 1987); L. R. Wickham, "The Date of Eunomius' Apology: A Reconsideration," JTS 20 (1969): 231–40.

Eusebius of Caesarea (c. 260–340)

Eusebius is the most important of the early Christian writers of church history, and he set the tone of most subsequent Christian historical writing for centuries after him. He was the disciple of Pamphilus, the theologian and devoted Origenian, who headed the Christian school at Caesarea Palestina. After Pamphilus's martyrdom in 310, Eusebius fled to Tyre, then Egypt, where he was imprisoned for the faith. By 315 he had been elected to the episcopate at Caesarea and he led the theological school there, with energetic scholarly efforts to enlarge the great library begun by *Origen*. His church became an important center for manuscript transmission. At the beginning of the *Arian* controversy he defended Arius, and this caused his condemnation at the Council of Antioch in late 324. At the *Council of Nicaea I* (325) he successfully defended his orthodoxy and was rehabilitated at *Constantine's* command. Eusebius shared his teacher's devotion to Origen and was always regarded with deep suspicion by the Nicene party, mainly because he regarded

the concept of *ousia* as inappropriate when referred to the transcendent deity, and so he could not sincerely support the *Christology* of *homoousion*. Several times he found himself in alliance with *Eusebius of Nicomedia* to damage the career of *Athanasius*. He became a favored rhetorician of Constantine, whose reputation as a Christian benefactor Eusebius heavily propagated. Eusebius was the chief rhetorician who delivered the *Tricennalian Oration*, to praise Constantine on his thirtieth anniversary of accession, in 336. He is regarded by many as the theologian who did most to foster the Byzantine view of a providential "symphony" between the (now Christian) emperor and the church. His historical writings often contain deductive speculation confidently delivered as fact, and are sometimes erroneous in their chronologies and sequencing of events. His worth, however, is inestimable because of his high and honest regard for the ancient documents (many of which he could immediately reference from his own excellent church library) and also his habit of including many of them wholesale in his account. His work needs to be used with caution, but it is a major authority for the whole prospectus of Christianity up to the early fourth century. Apart from the *Ecclesiastical History* he wrote works of biblical interpretation and apologetic. His *Life of Constantine* is a court panegyric, blatant official propaganda of the Constantinian dynasty, but is also a major source of information for imperial Roman history.

T. D. Barnes, *Constantine and Eusebius* (Cambridge, Mass., 1981); R. M. Grant, *Eusebius as Church Historian* (Oxford, 1980); C. Luibhéid, *Eusebius of Caesarea and the Arian Crisis* (Dublin, 1981).

Eusebius of Nicomedia (d. 342)

Related to the imperial family, and welcome among them through his close association with Constantine's sister

(Licinius's wife Constantia), Eusebius was patronized by the pro-Christian dynasties of the early fourth century and was the *bishop* who performed the *baptism* of the dying *Constantine* (a fact often overlooked given Eusebius's theological ideas and his lifelong championing of the cause of *Arius*). Eusebius was bishop of Beirut until 317, when the emperor Licinius transferred his capital to Nicomedia, and Eusebius was given charge of the see. He exercised great influence as a royal court theologian, becoming Constantine's own adviser when the latter also moved to Nicomedia. At the end of his life, in 339, he was appointed bishop of the new city of Constantinople, after Constantine had determined to move the capital to the Bosporus. Early in his dispute with Bishop Alexander, Arius had appealed to Eusebius's protection (they had been fellow students of *Lucian of Antioch*) and had received assurances of support. At the *Council of Nicaea I* Eusebius accepted the *Homoousian* creed, but refused to subscribe to the condemnation of Arius himself, for which cause Constantine deposed and banished him. He was recalled within two years, however, and became the emperor's close confidant. Constantine wished to move to a consensus theology that could be established in the East, and Eusebius represented this recidivist move away from Nicaea, much to the annoyance of the old Nicenes such as *Athanasius*, whom Eusebius managed to depose at the Arianizing Synod of Tyre in 335. He also secured the deposition of other leading opponents, including *Eustathius of Antioch* and *Marcellus of Ancyra*. In 341 Eusebius presided over the Dedication Council at Antioch, an event that marked the ascendancy of official Arianism for the next generation in the East. His political acumen gave a coherence to the Arian movement, more so than Arius himself ever provided, through much of its early development. His party were often called the "Eusebians" by their Nicene opponents.

G. Bardy, *Recherches sur S. Lucien d'Antioche et son école* (Paris, 1936); C. Luibheid. "The Arianism of Eusebius of Nicomedia," ITQ 43 (1976): 3–23.

Eusebius of Samosata (c. 310–380)

A much respected leader of the Eastern *Nicene* party, Eusebius was bishop at Samosata from c. 360. He was a close friend and supporter of *Meletius of Antioch*. He was also a friend and supporter of *Basil of Caesarea* and *Gregory of Nazianzus*, and he influenced them both in his policy of rapprochement with *Athanasius* to establish a wider base of internal Nicene agreement. He criticized Basil's dereliction of Gregory in Sasima, and was instrumental in recommending, at the Council of Antioch in 379, Gregory's historic mission to *Constantinople*. Eusebius had been exiled for his resistance of Valens in 374 and made a triumphant return under Gratian in 378. While making his way through *Syria*, installing pro-Nicene bishops wherever he could, he was murdered by an Arian woman who dropped a heavy house tile on his head while he was passing below. His last act, as he lay dying in the street, was to make his entourage swear they would not take revenge on the captured woman.

F. Halkin, "Une Vie grecque d'Eusèbe de Samosate," AB (1967): 5–15; H. R. Reynolds, "Eusebius of Samosata," DCB 2 (1880): 369–72.

Eustathius of Antioch (fl. 325)

Eustathius was a native of Side in Pamphylia, who became bishop of Beroea (Aleppo) and was then transferred to become bishop of the great city of *Antioch* in 324. A year later he played a prominent part at the *Council of Nicaea I*, as the main theological voice condemning *Arius*'s theology. After the council Eustathius actively prosecuted Arian sympathizers in the Syrian diocese.

From that time on he was marked out as an enemy by *Eusebius of Nicomedia*. The latter's associate *Eusebius of Caesarea* (whom Eustathius had denounced as an Arian) accused him in return of being a Sabellian and secured his deposition on administrative grounds at a synod at *Antioch* in 327. For the rest of his life Eustathius appears to have continued work as a writer and apologist in Thrace (Trajanopolis). It is difficult to fix any subsequent dates for him. The historians *Socrates* and *Sozomen* speak of him as being in the vanguard of the anti-Arian fight in *Constantinople* as late as the 370s. His theology seems to have been of a vaguely *Monarchian* type. He affirms the one divine nature and the distinct *prosopa* of Father and Son, which are, however, basically modes of the presentation of the divine nature. At Nicaea he argued against Arius on the point of contention that his *Christology* implied the *Logos* merely inhabited a vehicle of (soulless) flesh, whereas Christian faith demanded that the Logos dwelt within a true human being. He is thus one of the earliest representations of the Antiochene Christology that would become more prevalent in the late fourth century with *Diodore, Theodore of Mopsuestia*, and *Nestorius*. Eustathius was a lifelong critic of Origen's theology and exegetical style. His one surviving homily *On the Witch of Endor* was a rallying cry to beware of excessive allegorization. *Jerome* lists other (lost) works including the treatises *Against the Arians* and *On the Soul*.

***

R. V. Sellers, *Eustathius of Antioch* (Cambridge, 1928).

Eustathius of Sebaste (c. 300–380)

Son of *Bishop* Eulalius in Sebaste, Eustathius was educated in *Alexandria*, possibly as a student of *Arius*, when the latter was still active as a *priest* there. He returned home to the *Armenian* diocese and his father's church, enthusiastically endorsed the growing *ascetic* movement, and was soon recognized as the charismatic head of ascetics for all his region. This potential fraction line between ascetic and episcopal authority led to his censure by his own father. Eustathius's monasticism was of a radical character and insisted on equality of status among monastics. This attack on the social hierarchy of classes, and the validity of the status of *slavery* (he also seems to have demanded vegetarianism, and resisted the legitimacy of *married clergy*) alarmed many of the hierarchs of his day. *Eusebius of Nicomedia* opposed him for supporting his rival Macedonius for the throne of *Constantinople*, and denounced him to the Armenian bishops as an unbalanced zealot. The reaction to Eustathius can also be gauged from the acts of the Council of Gangra (c. 340), which censured him, although he was ordained that same year to the priesthood in Caesarea. The synodical condemnation allowed Eusebius to secure his deposition at the Council of Antioch in 341. Eustathius became an adherent of the *Homoiousian* school and, as newly elected bishop of Sebaste (357), he attended the Homoiousian Synods of Ancyra (358) and Lampsacus (364). At Sebaste he initiated the building of a hospice that was influential on *Basil of Caesarea's* subsequent vision of monastic bishops, a radically new departure for Christianity. Eustathius was an important role model for Basil, and initiated him into his ecclesiastical career, when they both were allies in attacking *Eunomius*. Even in antiquity it was thought that Basil's monastic rules (especially the *Asceticon*) were heavily representative of the thought of Eustathius (if not by Eustathius). His connection with Macedonius was a long-lasting one, however, and Eustathius and Macedonius shared the belief that the Holy Spirit could not be properly classed as divine. As Macedonius became party leader for the Pneumatomachians (Spirit-fighters, as the Nicenes gathered round *Meletius of Antioch* called them), the growing rift between the *Cappado-*

cian Fathers (who also supported Meletius) and Eustathius could not be hidden, much though Basil tried, and eventually there was a bitter falling out between Basil and his former friend, partly forced by Gregory of Nazianzus, who pressured Basil to admit openly the doctrine of the deity of the Spirit and his consubstantiality with the Father and Son. Basil's treatise On the Holy Spirit represents his parting of the ways with Eustathius, who is represented in it as dialogue partner. Some scholars think that the monastic tradition of Eustathius was maintained by Macrina, Basil's sister, and can be discerned today as represented in the spiritual writings of Pseudo-Macarius (see Macarius the Great 2). No directly attributed works have survived, and Basil's family and friends assiduously covered up Basil's connection with Eustathius after his death, to distance themselves from someone they now regarded as blatantly heretical.

J. Gribomont, "Le monachisme au quatrième siècle en Asie Mineure: de Gangres au Messalianisme," in K. Aland and F. L. Cross, eds., Studia Patristica (TU 64; 1957), 400–415; idem, "Eustathe le Philosophe et les voyages du jeune Basile de Césarée" RHE (1959): 115–24; idem, "S. Basile et le monachisme enthousiaste," Irenikon 53 (1980): 123–44; R. P. C. Hanson, The Search for the Christian Doctrine of God (Edinburgh, 1988), 683–85.

Eutyches of Constantinople (c. 378–454) Head of an important monastery in Constantinople and heavily involved in the christological arguments that occurred after the controversial Council of Ephesus I (431), Eutyches fell into conflict with Flavian, his archbishop, who was negotiating an international reconciliation between Syria and the other Eastern sees that would be acceptable to Rome. Flavian, with Pope Leo's support, censured Eutyches for leading the hard-line party that insisted on adherence to Cyril of Alexandria's thought to the exclusion of all Syrian influence. The christological doctrine of the "Two Natures" was central to the reconciliation, and it was this that Eutcyhes most resisted. Eutyches received support from the aristocracy in Byzantium and from Dioscorus of Alexandria, Cyril's successor. His ecclesiastical trial unraveled to become the major Council of Ephesus II (449), which, to the great anger of the Syrian and Roman churches, vindicated him and condemned Flavian instead. The bitter protests of the Romans led to the summoning of the revisionary Council of Chalcedon in 451, which condemned both Eutyches and Dioscorus. Eutyches is more important as a catalyst of great events than as a theologian. He represented the early "One Nature" (mia physis) theology of Cyril, but taken to an unacceptable pitch, which even Cyril had warned against in his lifetime. Eutyches's misfortune was, eventually, to alienate all his friends, for he finally tried to emphasize the transcendent deity of Jesus by teaching that his humanity was not consubstantial (homoousion) with that of ordinary human beings—an idea that shocked the rest of the pro-Cyril movement in the Egyptian churches, and led them to abandon him as a heretic just as decisively as did Constantinople and the West. (See Eutychianism, Monophysitism.)

W. H. C. Frend, The Rise of the Monophysite Movement (Cambridge, 1972); J. A. McGuckin, St. Cyril of Alexandria and the Christological Controversy (Leiden, Netherlands, 1994).

Eutychianism The heresy of Eutychianism was one that was largely packaged for wider consumption by Pope Leo I, wishing to elevate an easy target that he could then denounce and parody. In castigating and hereticizing Eutyches as a "foolish old man," Leo offset the christological opposition to his own see, and its clear "two nature" Christology, which was already being regarded as seriously defective by large sections of the Greek-speaking churches. The constant reference of the Leonine Christology to two natures coinhering within the single person, but subsisting intact after the incarnation, seemed to many a direct rebuttal of the vision of St. *Cyril of Alexandria* (expressed at the *Council of Ephesus I* [431], and in his treatise *That the Christ Is One*) of two natures being "made one," or united, by the dynamism of the incarnation, so that One Lord resulted, who was both God and man. For some of the hard-line Cyrillians, the Latin vision of one person possessed of two natures was barely indistinguishable from *Nestorianism* (it was miles apart, given Leo's insistence on the singleness of the divine person and the mutual reference of the natures). Eutyches seemed to have shared that view, and so argued for a theology he thought was Cyrilline, but which was in reality less carefully envisioned, and weak on the central aspect that had become critical in the generation after Ephesus 431, that is, the manner in which the integrity of humanity and divinity in Jesus could be clarified and equally stated in a christological confession. Eutyches seemed to wish to return to a vague and confused "mixture" of divinity and humanity. His piety made him draw back from admitting that Christ had "a humanity like ours," which to less friendly ears suggested he thought Christ's humanity was either deficient, merely apparent, or a hybrid (so possessed by the divinity that it had been absorbed and utterly changed from common humanity). In the brunt of the attack, as he was brought through synodical trials censuring him in *Constantinople*, then vindicated at the *Council of Ephesus II* (449), and then condemned at the *Council of Chalcedon* (451), the more he had to leave his role as anti-Latin agitator and become an articulate spokesman of international theology, the more he buried himself in obscurities. He thought he was a Cyril of

Alexandria, but his acuity was nowhere near the brilliance of his teacher. It would not be until the appearance of *Severus of Antioch* that the anti-Nestorian, anti-Latin, and anti-Chalcedonian party found a theologian who could effectively articulate why Cyril had thought the "two nature" language was a mistake. Eutychianism is often (improperly) used as a derogatory reference to *Monophysitism*. The Monophysite theologians of his time, however, condemned Eutyches for denying the humanity of Christ was consubstantial with that of the human race. His heresy is best understood as an attempt to argue a vision of incarnate unity wherein the divinity so thoroughly absorbs the humanity of Jesus that he is not so much "God and man" but "deified man"; fully God, certainly, but human only in a way that has transcended anything that we think of as normal humanity, and thus human only in a qualified sense. (*See Eutyches of Constantinople.*)

R. Draguet, "La Christologie d'Eutychès d'après les Actes du Synode de Flavien (448)," *Byzantion* 6 (1931): 441–57; W. H. C. Frend, *The Rise of the Monophysite Movement* (Cambridge, 1972); J. A. McGuckin, *St. Cyril of Alexandria and the Christological Controversy* (Leiden, Netherlands, 1994).

Evagrius of Pontus (345–399) Evagrius was a rhetoric student of *Gregory of Nazianzus* and was ordained *deacon* by *Gregory of Nyssa*, who took him to *Constantinople* for the great Council of 381, where he probably assisted Gregory of Nazianzus in the composition of the *Five Theological Orations*. He remained in Constantinople as deacon and adviser to Gregory's successor Nektarius, but had to flee from the city, probably as a result of falling for an aristocratic lady and rousing the family's fury against him. He made his way to *Jerusalem* and was counseled in the monastery of the

Mount of Olives by **Melania the Elder** and the Origenist scholar Rufinus. Here he continued his studies of **Origen's** works. In 383 he moved to the great Egyptian center of ascetical monasticism at **Nitria** and spent two years there before moving on, in 385, to Kellia, where he stayed until his death. At Kellia he joined a community of monks of the intelligentsia under the leadership of one Ammonius (*see* **Tall Brothers**). They were soon called the household of Ammonius and Evagrios, and later simply the "House of Evagrios." In the desert he met the leading ascetics of the day, including the two **Macarii** and **Palladius**, and he became a chief architect of the early monastic movement's intellectual spirituality. His works had a decisive effect on almost every great monastic theorist who followed: **John Cassian, Maximus the Confessor**, and **John Climacus** among them. Most later writers reduced his explicit Origenist views, especially his metaphysic that each soul was once part of a divine unity, but fell through sin to an earthly existence, and could use ascetical endeavor to purify the spiritual intellect so as to ascend once more to union with God. His writings not only demonstrate a great *stress* on the path to imageless *prayer* that transcends thought, but also offered very practical levels of advice to ascetics on the controlling of psychological states, the taxonomy of virtues and vices, and the discernment of spirits. By the sixth century his Origenism led to his posthumous condemnation (*see* **Council of Constantinople II**), and the surviving works were either preserved in Syriac or reassigned, pseudepigraphically, to other obscure writers (such as St. Nilus). The late twentieth century witnessed a revival of his writings and a just renewal of interest in a theologian who should rightly be regarded as one of the founders of Christian mysticism.

J. E. Bamberger, *Evagrius Ponticus: Praktikos and Chapters on Prayer* (Cistercian Studies Series 4; Kalamazoo, Mich., 1972, 1989); G. Palmer, P. Sherrard, and K. Ware, eds., *The Philokalia* (vol. 1; London, 1979), (*Select Works of Evagrios*. pp. 29–71); S. Brock, trans., *The Syriac Fathers on Prayer and the Spiritual Life* (Kalamazoo, Mich., 1987); A. Louth, *The Origins of the Christian Mystical Tradition* (Oxford, 1981), 100–113; J. A. McGuckin, *Standing in God's Holy Fire: The Byzantine Spiritual Tradition* (London, 2001), 37–54.

Evagrius Scholasticus (c. 535–600)

A *Syrian* who came to Antioch to practice law, Evagrius Scholasticus decided to produce his own *Church History* in emulation of the earlier writers **Eusebius, Socrates, Sozomen**, and **Theodoret**, whom he had read and admired. His own *Church History*, which he began c. 593, covers the period from 428 to his own day, and is thus an important source for the *christological* issues devolving from the **Council of Ephesus I** (431) through the **Council of Chalcedon** (451) and its aftermath. He is not deeply informed about theological controversy, but shows a lively interest in hagiographical stories, and has passages where he criticizes the defective historiography of some historians, such as the Monophysite Zacharias the Rhetor, and the pagan apologist Zosimus. He follows Eusebius's master idea that God's providential plan for human society was consummated in the Christianizing of the Roman Empire.

P. Allen, *Evagrius Scholasticus, the Church Historian* (Louvain, Belgium, 1981); G. F. Chesnut, *The First Christian Histories: Eusebius, Socrates, Sozomen, Theodoret, and Evagrius* (2d ed.; Macon, Ga., 1986); E. Walford, trans., *Evagrius: The Ecclesiastical History* (London, 1846).

Excommunication

Excommunication is the disciplinary exclusion of a believer from the reception of the *sacraments* and, by implication, from communion in *prayer* and society with the congregation of believers, until such time as *penance* has been performed and the offender can be readmitted to the life of the Christian assembly. It originally had a therapeutic intention, but increasingly came to be a disciplinary and juridical sanction. It grew out of the biblical conception of the *church* as the "pure Israel," whose sacred society could tolerate no element within it of cultic defilement. Although the notion clashed in many respects with the tolerance of Jesus' preached doctrine of reconciliation, the Old Testament paradigms of the exclusion (*herem*) of sinners from Israel influenced Christian mentalities considerably (*see anathema*). The Johannine Letters already speak of the exclusion of dissidents from the church, the *ekklesia*, not merely the local community. In a tightly argued point, the dissident schismatics are shown to have left because they were not members in the first place (1 John 2:19) for "if they had belonged" they would not have left. So the Johannine literature and later catholic epistles defended the unity of the church against a context of increasing doctrinal and lifestyle diversity in the age of *Gnosticism.* Appeal was made to the example of Paul, who had temporarily excommunicated ("handed over to Satan") a member of the church who had transgressed marital regulations (1 Cor. 5:1–7; see also 2 Cor. 2:10–11). Such a one had been "excluded" from the new Israel until repentance had been shown. A similar attitude is also shown in Jesus' instructions to his disciples (Mark 6:11) that they should shake off from their sandals the dust of villages that had not listened to their proclamation. This purification ritual was observed by pious Jews returning to Israel from Gentile territory, so that they would not bring the defiled dust of pagans into the Holy Land; and so those who had not received the message of the apostles, by implication, had lapsed from Israel, and were given a sign of their excommunication. A similar concept of exclusion is manifested in Matthew 18:16. In the early centuries of

the church the practice of excommunication did not register prominently, though it is often witnessed in episcopal correspondences (such as that of *Basil of Caesarea*) relating to local and personal matters. But after the fifth century the more centralized power of the *episcopate*, presiding over eucharistic worship and doctrinal teaching in a more focused and city-wide manner, made the penalty of excommunication more politically effective as an episcopal censure. The highest form of excommunication was that applied by the episcopal synods. The Ecumenical *Councils* had the weight of an imperial judgment and incurred exile and confiscation of goods. Inflicting such a sentence, even in a local episcopal tribunal, came to have increasing "weight" as the church could command more legal influence, and would eventually carry serious penalties relating to possession of goods and rights at law for the person who was excommunicated.

W. Doskocil, *Der Bann in der Urkirche: Eine rechtsgeschichtliche Untersuchung* (Munchener theologische Studien 3; Munich, 1958); J. Gaudemet, "Notes sur les formes anciennes de l'Excommunication," RSR 23 (1949): 64–77.

Exegesis   The term "exegesis" derives from the Greek (*ex hegesthai*) "to bring out," and was intended to connote the drawing out of the implications of a text. As such it can be contrasted with eisegesis (the reading-in of materials or meanings into a text that were not there in the first place). The whole subject of exegesis has become of peculiar interest in recent years following on structuralist and postmodernist theories of meaning in narratives, but the ancient Hellenist rhetors had already advanced exegetical theory considerably at *Alexandria,* in the course of establishing a canon of sacred classics from the mythic poets (chiefly Homer), and the main philosophers (chiefly *Plato* and *Aristotle*). At the Great Library of Alexandria the concept of a *canon* that demanded careful exegetical skills both in establishing a critical text and in elevating scientific methods of interpretation was carefully elaborated by a series of learned scholar-directors. The intellectual climate of the city was such that it encouraged religious thinkers to see how the ancient truths of religion (mythically conceived) could be harmonized with scientific and philosophical advances. Hellenist thinkers were much occupied in trying to "translate" the old poetic tales of the deeds of the gods into a cosmologically and ethically coherent narrative. The first great intellect to apply such scientific process to the *canon of Scripture* was *Philo* of Alexandria. His work was to have immense influence on Christian exegetes that followed him. At first the Christian fathers were content largely to continue a piecemeal citation of the Scriptures, in the form of proof-texting, or small citations that supported various points they wished to make, either establishing doctrines or illustrating points of church order and discipline. The very New Testament books, particularly the Gospels, had this piecemeal character in regard to the ancient Scriptures. Not all the narrative of the Hebrew Bible was addressed; highly selected texts were taken out and shown as "fulfilled" in its Jesus narratives. Even the structures of those first Christian narratives of Gospel and Letters were built up from small units (the subject of modern form and redaction criticism) or were occasional writings stimulated by local problems rather than being grand-scale treatises. Most of the use of Scripture in the *Apostolic Fathers* to the end of the second century retains this ancient character of proof-texting. Books were even composed illustrating how passages could be excised from the Scripture and applied to Christian preaching. One example of such an ancient *Book of Testimonies* has survived, now attributed to *Cyprian* (*Ad Quirinum*). By the third century, however, intellectuals such as the

early *gnostic* writers had seen that the Christian religion had elevated a whole set of cosmological and *anthropological* statements that required a deeper and more holistic form of harmonization. To this end they set about interpreting Christian *soteriology* (the pattern of salvation) through an often elaborate set of mythic accounts of *fall* and salvation. It was among the early gnostics that the Hellenist forms of secular exegesis of literature first began to be popularized (even though elements of Hellenistic forms such as *allegory* and typology can be found in Paul and other early writers). Allegorical reading of texts, whereby something a text claimed could be reinterpreted in purely symbolic fashion (one thing symbolically standing for another thing) allowed the gnostics to connect their doctrines with the simpler evangelical and apostolic writings. It caused considerable alarm among the early patristic witnesses, and was one of the reasons *Irenaeus* denounced the whole gnostic scheme in his *Adversus haereses*, arguing that their symbolical style of interpretation cut Christianity adrift from its historical moorings. Irenaeus made a boast of being "simpler" and more *"apostolic,"* and certainly more tied to the historical sense of Scripture. But his work already shows a sophisticated awareness that scriptural texts are not simply self-explanatory, and need to be set in context, explained for their many obscurities, and symbolically related to other parts of the Scripture; in short, approached like all other literary forms, with a careful view to interpretative consistency on the part of the exegete. Irenaeus, however, established an important principle for all Christian exegesis to follow, which was that the interpreter had to follow the "mind of the author." In the case of Scripture that author was an apostle, writing out the truths that God had communicated. Fidelity to the original (apostolic) meaning, therefore, became a proof of the continuing apostolicity of the church, and the primary way the exegete was faithful to the supreme author of the Scripture, God himself. It was *Origen of Alexandria* who really laid the foundations for the Church's exegetical practices for centuries to come. In his *Book of First Principles (De principiis)* he carefully set out a whole range of exegetical problems (the contradictions within the Gospel narratives, the many "impossible readings" within Scripture, the problem of the correlation of the Old and New Testaments, the questions of establishing correct texts, the many ethically dubious passages seemingly commended as righteousness), and laid down a system for approaching the Christian Scripture as a coherent whole. He saw that all Scripture had been given by God to the "illumined mind" of the believer (especially the great initiates such as Paul and John). An illuminated believer could see the hidden meanings of the ancient narratives through the "key," which was Christ. This christocentric analysis of the entire Scripture was critical to this thought. By means of a thoroughly christocentric reading Origen established that all Scripture led to Jesus, and continued to lead to him, now in his glorious state as the divine *Logos* presiding over the return of all *souls* to divine communion through intellectual enlightenment. Even passages in the New Testament (that lens whereby the dark mirror of the "Old" Testament was "clarified") were subject to progressive enlightenment in the hands of Christian exegetes. Just as Jesus spoke certain things in valleys, on plains, or on mountains, so the Scripture, Origen said, gave messages to the simple, to the learned, and to the mystically advanced. The simple should not presume to claim that a literalist meaning is all that Scripture contains. It bears such a message only for them, at their impoverished state of understanding. Scripture has several levels of reality just as a human being does; with soul, and body, and psyche. Thus, Origen simultaneously took the Bible extremely seriously as history and

text, and also was able to move out from the Scripture in a highly speculative cosmological theology. He seemed to have formed a synthesis of the gnostic and antignostic theologians over the question of how historically binding was the biblical text. His exegetical system was preserved by the *Cappadocian Fathers Gregory of Nazianzus* and *Basil* in their *Philocalia* (preserving many parts of the *De principiis* on their own authority) and thus became "orthodox" even when the rest of his corpus suffered greatly in the anti-Origenist reaction of later centuries. Many Syrian writers from the fourth century onward (*Eustathius of Antioch, Diodore,* and *Theodore* chief among them) found his "excessive allegorization" distasteful (especially as it was pressed to extremes in later disciples such as *Didymus*), and argued for a more simple historical and moral reading of the texts. Even so, they themselves often used allegory, which was by then an established method of reading any narrative, in their interpretations. Origen's exegetical work was massively influential on the Western world. *Ambrose* and *Jerome* were heavily indebted to him, and introduced him as a staple element of Latin exegesis even when the exegetes themselves might never have known they were reproducing Origen. *Augustine* carefully and courageously approached critical problems of biblical interpretation in his own age, often rising to great heights from an immediate or local controversy. He approached the problems associated with a literal interpretation of Genesis (*On the Literal Interpretation of Genesis*) and the critical problems associated with the harmony of the Gospel narratives (*On the Harmony of the Evangelists*), and in his book *On Christian Doctrine* he summarized and set out a set of rules governing scriptural interpretation (drawn in part from the *Donatist Tyconius*), which set scriptural exegesis as the supreme foundation for all Christian teaching. After Augustine (comparable in his authority to Origen for the East) the Latin church always had a healthy resistance to fundamentalist literalism in its reading of the Bible. *Gregory the Great* set the terms of most Latin exegesis to follow in his *Great Moralia on Job* and his *Pastoral Rule*, where he drew up (on the basis of Augustine and Origen) a grand theory of how the preacher ought to approach the text "ascentively" from a historical, moral, and then mystical viewpoint, being careful to lead up his listener, as he expounded the sacred text, through all the levels to a spiritual perfection. Exegesis in the patristic writings is the main avenue of theological speculation. Most of the great fathers after the fourth century were primarily biblical exegetes. In modern times their works have more often been quarried for dogmatic propositions relating to theological controversies. In their own time, even the controversialists were first and foremost biblical theologians. It is a fact that is increasingly coming back into focus in contemporary patristic research. For centuries patristic exegesis was looked down upon, from the narrow viewpoint of nineteenth-century liberalism, as being historically defective. It too is now receiving increased attention.

R. P. C. Hanson, *Allegory and Event* (London, 1959; repr. Louisville, Ky., 2002); B. de Margerie, *Introduction à l'histoire de l'exégèse* (vol. 1; Paris, 1980); M. Simonetti, *Biblical Interpretation in the Early Church* (Edinburgh, 1994); F. M. Young, *Biblical Exegesis and the Formation of Christian Culture* (Cambridge, 1997).

Exorcism   From the Greek *exorkizo*, "I adjure" (cf. Matt. 26:63), "exorcism" became a term prominent in early Christianity from the early second century onward (cf. Justin, *Dialogue with Trypho* 76.6; 85.2) as the casting out of devils. In ancient exorcism rituals the command (adjuration) to the demon was a central part of the casting-out process, something that was common to Hellenist (cf. Philostratus, *Life of Apollonius*), Judaic

(Acts 13:6; 19:13; Josephus, *Antiquities* 8.46–49), and early Christian practice. The Gospel narratives of the exorcisms of Jesus are the archetype of all reflection on Christian exorcism, and scholars have posited that the exorcism narratives (cf. Matt. 9:32–34; 12:22–29, 43–45; 17:14–20; and parallels) are themselves among the earliest sections of the Gospel structures. In the New Testament, Jesus' divine authority (*exousia*) is at the heart of his almost effortless casting out of demonic oppression from Israel. The Gospels always depict the exorcism as an act of manifesting the approaching kingdom of God (Luke 11:14–22), a sign greater than the immediately local "cure" of the demoniac. Jesus is described as "throwing out" (*ekballein*) the demons, and the epiphany of divine power that he demonstrates customarily produced "great awe" (*thauma*) among the witnesses. His ease and power of command is in contrast to the great number of surviving magical papyri from antiquity where exorcists are typically shown having considerable difficulty finding the exact word of command required to control the demon. It is probable that in the earliest preaching of the Christian *kerygma* in the first century, exorcists were an important part of the evangelization techniques in ancient cities, serving as a prelude to the preachers by demonstrating concretely and effectively the "power of the name of Jesus" over the possessed and the sick. The disciples are described from the beginning of the preaching ministry as continuing the practice of exorcism (Luke 9:49f.; 10:17; Acts 16:18). The practice of Christian exorcism drew down much controversy, with contemporary Pharisees apparently claiming that Jesus' ability as an exorcist showed he was a demoniac himself (Matt. 12:24). Celsus in the second century also continued that charge (thereby showing that Christians were still associated with exorcisms), when he accused them of being involved in *magic* (a serious crime in the late empire). Several of the patristic writings are concerned to distance Christian exorcism from therapeutic magic as it was then widely practiced. And most of the apologetic writing this charge occasioned focuses on the manner in which Christians are different from other peoples insofar as they only use the name of Jesus (not elaborate rituals) and employ prayers and Scripture readings for this cause (Justin, *Dialogue with Trypho* 76; Tertullian, *Apology* 23; Origen, *Against Celsus* 7.4; 7.57; *Commentary on Matthew* 13.7). There is clear evidence, however, that Christians were very interested in the proper conduct of exorcisms, which is why the Gospels are careful to preserve the exact Aramaic words of Jesus in the case of some of his exorcisms. The ritual survived prominently in the **baptismal** initiations (Hippolytus, *Apostolic Tradition* 20–21), which involved the anointing with oil, the laying on of hands, making the sign of the *cross* over the candidate, reading the Scriptures, and "blowing in the face" (exsufflation). The Pseudo-Clementine treatise *On Virginity* (1.12) preserves one of the first explicit accounts of exorcism. *On Virginity* also mentions the laying on of hands, and anointing with blessed oil, as part of the ritual. Up until the third century the exorcists were a regular part of the church's **clergy**, and Pope Cornelius lists them as such (Eusebius, *Ecclesiastical History* 6.43.11). After that point the ministry fell into relative abeyance, surviving mainly in the baptismal rituals, and in the monastic penitential accounts, which attributed temptation to demonic activity. The formal ritual of exorcism was still occasionally invoked for special needs. In later times it was practiced by bishops and **priests**, using the sign of the cross, blessed oil, the invocation of the holy name, and the laying of the Gospels on the head of the afflicted person. In the Orthodox service books the prayers of exorcism attributed to **Basil the Great** are still in use, for common as well as particular cases of need. In the Latin church the rite of exorcism is now very rarely used, and then only with episcopal permission. The exorcism prayers continue the ancient association of sickness and blight with demonic activity, and the blessings of beasts and fields in the Orthodox service books to this day make a regular pairing of the ideas.

L. Delatte, *Un office byzantin d'exorcisme* (Athos. Ms. Lavra. 9.20; Academie royale de Belgique, Classe de Lettres, Mémoires; Collection in Octavo; 2d series no. 52; 1957); E. Ferguson, *Demonology of the Early Christian World* (New York, 1984); H. A. Kelly, *The Devil at Baptism: Ritual, Theology, and Drama* (Ithaca, N.Y., 1985); E. Sorenson, *Possession and Exorcism in the New Testament and Early Christianity* (Tübingen, Germany, 2002); G. H. Twelftree, *Jesus the Exorcist: A Contribution to the Study of the Historical Jesus* (Tübingen, Germany, 1993).

Facundus of Hermiane (fl. 540–570)

Facundus was a **north African** theologian and bishop. During the **Monophysite** controversy following the **Council of Chalcedon** (451) he was a passionate opponent of **Justinian's** policy to condemn the **Three Chapters**, and so made his way to **Constantinople** to argue for the theological orthodoxy of all three writers concerned: **Theodore Mopsuestia, Theodoret of Cyrrhus**, and **Ibas of Edessa** (though he had doubts about Theodore). His first apology composed in 547–548 was entitled *In Defense of the Three Chapters*. Facundus's chief anxiety was that **Justinian's** policy to reconcile the Monophysites by condemning the Three Chapters was tantamount to a denial of the balance of Chalcedonian **Christology** (which was his main interest). After the condemnation of the Three Chapters was reconfirmed at the **Council of Constantinople II** (553), Pope Vigilius censured him for his continuing opposition, causing him to write two further works in self-defense: *Against Mocianus the Scholastic* and *A Letter on the Catholic Faith: In Defense of the Three Chapters*. Apart from being an acute theologian, Facundus supplies important historical perspectives on the Council of Constantinople II.

R. B. Eno, "Doctrinal Authority in the African Ecclesiology of the 6th century: Ferrandus and Facundus," REA 22 (1976): 95–113.

Fall   The concept of a fall from an originally purer and greater state of humanity, a first condition or creation that was devoid of harmful and noxious elements, is common to many religions, but was fundamental to the structure of Christianity, which gave great prominence in the construction of its metaphysics, cosmology, *anthropology*, *soteriology*, and ethics to the Book of Genesis, widely interpreted among the Christian exegetes as a historical and "foundational" part of Scripture. Genesis 3:1–24 narrates the transgression of Adam and Eve, their disobedience that results in their expulsion from *paradise*, and the "sentencing" to a life of laborious difficulty on earth. *Patristic* theologians were highly influenced by Paul's prior use of Adam *typology* in his writings, especially his connection of *sin* and *death* (Rom. 5:12f.). As Adam sinned, Paul had argued, he brought sin into the creation and through sin entered death. Christ, the new Adam, would similarly reverse that bondage to mortality by his profound obedience to God (a contrast to disobedient Adam; cf. Phil. 2:6–11), and this righteousness introduced the principle of *resurrection* back to the race. God, who in his anger and just *judgment* has banished mankind from life and the divine presence, had now been reconciled in Christ, and readmitted the race to the benefits of the divine heritage: divine "sonship." Later patristic writers, especially *Origen*, were more attuned to the idea that the real fall was a premundane reality, first witnessed among the angels. The idea could easily be, and often was, harmonized with the Genesis account, as the serpent was readily identified with

Satan as one of the leading fallen angels of God, intent now on spreading the fall to the human race. Origen developed an extensive account of the premundane fall, discountenancing the literal interpretation of the Genesis account and offering instead a version of how the original and pure creation had been entirely spiritual. Some of the spiritual powers (*noes*) grew careless in their contemplation of God, and fell into corporeality: a state of corrective penitential discipline God had prepared for them to serve as the spur to their eventual return, as pure spirits, after their time of earthly suffering had been fulfilled. His ideas caught the imagination of the East, although they were much corrected and emended by *Athanasius* and the *Cappadocian Fathers,* who reduced his stress on the nature of the premundane fall and connected the idea of psychic lapse with a more literal acceptance of Genesis. It was Paul's connection of sin and death, however, that dominated most patristic thought on the fall and its consequences. Adam and Eve were seen as having first been created as "almost" immortal, given the human *proprium* of walking hand in hand with God in the garden. For Origen, Athanasius, and *Gregory of Nyssa* this signified the communion of divine contemplation, which humanity was given as the icon of God on earth (*see image of God*). When this internal icon of God was lost, through the neglect of contemplation, Adam and all the human race after him progressively wandered into alienation from God, and even ignorance of God, in which false cults grew up enslaving the religious sense of the race. As the alienation and ignorance deepened, so did humanity increasingly lose its hold on life, and grow ever more "corrupt" (*phtharsia*) in mortal fallibility and decay (Athanasius, *On the Incarnation* 3–5; Gregory of Nyssa, *On the Making of Man* 17.2–5; John Chrysostom, *Homily on the Statues* 11; ibid. 12; *Homily 16 on Genesis* 5; Ambrose, *On Paradise* 42; 53). The dynamic corollary of this apparently pessimistic scheme of fall into deep loss was (much as it was with Paul) that it served to introduce a very positive and optimistic view of evil and redemption. In the first place evil is extraneous, not part of the creation designed by God, and not "natural" to humanity, but rather a sad mistake that can potentially be corrected. All evil exists as a result of the moral weakness of creatures (Justin, *Second Apology* 5; *Dialogue with Trypho* 88; Tatian, *Oration to the Greeks* 7–9; Theophilus, *Ad Autolycum* 2.27; Origen, *De Principiis* 3.2.2; *Contra Celsum* 4.65–66). In the second place the **incarnation** by Christ is seen as more than simply a reversal of the corruption introduced into the world, but a veritable new creation, where the divine benefits are even greater than before. In the treatise *On the Incarnation* Athanasius sees the resurrection of Christ as being the dynamic principle that reintroduces life and immortality back to the race in a veritable second making of the human species. Athanasius argues that if humanity looks inward once more, cleans the darkened mirror of the **soul** in contemplation of God, the soul will rise once more to an eternal life lost by the first parents. Later patristic theologians such as **Cyril of Alexandria** connected this principle of immortalization with the reception of the **sacraments**, especially the **Eucharist** as the "medicine of immortality" (*pharmakia tes athanasias*). In the West, **Augustine** speculated extensively on the nature of Adam's sin. He was much motivated to oppose what he saw as a deeply wrongheaded optimism on **Pelagius's** part that humanity could free itself of the effects of the fall through moral effort. Augustine thought that the original human condition had been a fallible one, but one that was spiritually elevated and stabilized by the capacity of Adam and Eve to eat of the fruit of the Tree of Life (*On the Literal Interpretation of Genesis* 8.4.8–8.5.11; 11.18.23–24). The real sin that caused the fall, as Augustine saw it, was not an accidental lapse, but a spiritual rebellion, a deliberate preference of human pride to the law of God (Augustine, *Enchiridion* 45; *On the City of God*

14.13; *On the Literal Interpretation of Genesis* 11.41.56f.), which then became endemic to the human race. Sin was transmitted through the very lusts and weaknesses (through concupiscence, that is) that immediately sprang up to terrorize humanity in the moment of the fall from grace. This was not simply sin as a voluntarist lapse, but "Sin" that was in the very bones of the race, as it were, transmitted to the species as a whole: original sin. It was the power of the resurrection that countermanded it, and the function of **baptism** to purge it, although the rest of the Christian life remained a constant struggle of **grace** against the effects of actual sin that threatened to make humanity a "damnable mass." Augustine's domination of the later Latin tradition made his perspective very prevalent. In the East there was, perhaps, a more optimistic sense (taken from **Irenaeus** and Origen in the main) that the effects of sinfulness were not so damaging or structurally prevalent, and that the incarnation more than repaired its deficiencies spiritually, although the many sorrows of earthly life remained as a continuing part of God's punishment for sin. Nowhere in the patristic writing (since so much of it was designed to offset **gnostic** determinist theories of the fall as a result of a divine mistake) is there any indication that the fall had been "necessary" for the salvation that was to come in Christ; but there is a general sense that the fall brought with it many benefits (as well as the undeniable sorrows of existence) in teaching the race humility and a fervent desire for the good of heaven in contrast to the sorrows of this earth (cf. Irenaeus, *Adversus haereses* 3.20.1–2; Gregory of Nyssa, *On the Making of Man* 21; *Catechetical Oration* 8). The Genesis account of the angel standing with a fiery sword to keep out Adam and Eve from **Paradise** becomes a symbol of great hope and beauty in **Ephrem the Syrian's** *Hymns of Paradise*: for he sees the sufferings and victory of Christ as having reintroduced paradise even now in the church's experience.

H. Crouzel, *Origen* (Edinburgh, 1989), 205–18; E. V. McClear, "The Fall of Man and Original Sin in the Theology of Gregory of Nyssa," TS 9 (1948): 175–212; V. MacDermot, *The Fall of Sophia: A Gnostic Text on the Redemption of Universal Consciousness* (Great Barrington, Mass., 2001); F. R. Tennant, *The Sources of the Doctrines of the Fall and of Original Sin* (Cambridge, 1903); N. P. Williams, *The Ideas of the Fall and of Original Sin* (London, 1927).

Family   The writers of the Apostolic period (cf. *First Clement*) often continued a theme that had already permeated much of the Pauline and Pastoral Letters of the New Testament, which was to inculcate the "household code," a social ideal, or trope, of the late Roman Empire. In this ideal home, the father ruled a serene and obedient family, where everyone knew and kept to their ordered place. It was a marked contrast to Jesus' apocalyptic attitude to "family values," where he often seemed to call for their subversion (cf. Mark 3:31–35; 10:28–30; Matt. 10:35, 37–38). In the Apostolic literature this common Hellenistic image of an ordered society in the household was regularly applied to the *church*, and mainly used to advocate good order and discipline in urging the faithful to obey their leaders. The earliest Christian experience based the development of churches on the pattern of the extended Roman family, and probably continued to meet in private homes for purposes of worship until well into the second century. Paul bears witness to this origin of the mission of Christianity when he frequently sends or receives greetings from various households (Rom. 16:10; Phil. 4:22). He speaks of whole households having been converted in one instant (presumably as the head of the household adopted the new faith; cf. 1 Cor. 1:16; Acts 16:15). Paul also uses the image of the "household of faith" (Gal. 6:10) and the "household of God" (Eph. 2:19) to designate the elect church. Much earlier Hellenistic thought had sketched out the form of the household code, especially in terms of how society had "fixed places," which were almost predetermined by God. To upset the social order was not a commendable thing. This may explain why, despite its advocacy of profound new freedoms and equalities (Gal. 3:28), Christianity was very slow in seeing the immoral nature of *slavery*, so fundamental a support for the very household code it advocated. Centuries of Greek thought had made it almost axiomatic in antiquity that women (generally) ought not to be educated, and should keep to the interior world of the house and domestic affairs, while the man kept to the "exterior" worlds of politics, rule, rhetoric, public business, and social gatherings. The idealized image of the paternal ruler of the house (rarely at home) with a modest and docile wife and children to support him, though sometimes evoked by patristic writers (cf. Syriac *Didascalia*) and advocated as a divinely appointed scheme to heal the "more natural proclivity of females" to frivolous enterprises (Clement of Alexandria, *Pedagogue* 2.33.2; *Letter of Aristeas* 250) was always more a rhetorical trope than any serious analysis, let alone description of, social realities in the early Christian world. The domestic condition of Christian households must have been more or less like the several references that are found outside the bourgeois rhetorical texts, especially in the comedies of antiquity, where a more realistic range of characters is encountered. Even so, the Pauline texts that had indicated women ought to obey their husbands carried considerable weight among the early writers (Titus 2:5; Eph. 5:21–25; 1 Pet. 3:1; Ignatius, *To Polycarp* 5; Irenaeus, *Adversus haereses* 4.20.12; 5.9.4). And this can partly be accounted for given the widespread ancient custom of older men marrying much younger, and uneducated, wives. The patristic reflection on the value of family was taken up in large part with writings on the nature of *sexual ethics*, primarily advocating a severe

Stoic-orientated approach that regarded sexual activity as permissible only when directed at procreation (cf. Lactantius, *Divine Institutes* 6.23). After the fourth century (cf. Synod of Elvira) sexual behavior increasingly came under the scrutiny and attempted control of increasingly ascetic bishops. Christian patristic writing consistently and fiercely condemned infanticide and *abortion*, and strongly advocated monogamous fidelity, all of which were factors in stabilizing Christian households in comparison with pagan ones, and doubtless in raising the fecundity, proliferation, and survival rates for Christian women and families. The rise of *asceticism* as a strongly advocated value after the fourth century affected women as much as men. *Macrina*, the sister of *Gregory of Nyssa*, who testifies to her powerful influence over the whole family (including *Basil*, who ignores her in his writings), is a case study in how the ascetical life afforded new possibilities of freedom and self-determination in the church. Women who were wealthy, by electing *virginity* or *widowhood* (rather than remarrying as state pressure had earlier demanded), were able to keep control of the finances they could regularly inherit (from their much older husbands). Female ascetics such as *Melania the Elder* demonstrate the idea remarkably. In the Byzantine era women ascetics, allied to the aristocracy, were able to exert considerable pressure on church policies and exercised their own rituals of association, often related to vesperal services, common meals, and patronage of the poor. As often as social developments extended the range of women's influence in the church, however, times of military insecurity could set them back. By and large, given the ascetical domination of most patristic writing and the social conditions of the late empire, it is not surprising, though nonetheless disappointing, that patristic reflection on the family did not extend to the consideration of more of the theme of mutual love and support and inti-

mate community that could have been expected of it.

P. M. Beagon, "The Cappadocian Fathers, Women, and Ecclesiastical Politics," VC 49, 2 (1995); V. Burrus, *Chastity as Autonomy* (Studies in Women and Religion 23; Lewiston, N.Y., 1987); E. A. Clark, *Women in the Early Church* (Message of the Fathers of the Church 13; Del., 1983); S. Dixon, *The Roman Family* (London, 1992); S. Elm, *Virgins of God: The Making of Asceticism in Late Antiquity* (Oxford, 1994); H. Moxnes, ed., *Constructing Early Christian Families: Family as Social Reality and Metaphor* (London, 1997); G. Nardin, *Famiglia e società secondo i Padri della Chiesa* (Rome, 1989); J. M. Petersen, *Handmaids of the Lord: Contemporary Descriptions of Feminine Asceticism in the First Six Centuries* (Kalamazoo, Mich., 1996); M. Sheather, "The Eulogies on Macrina and Gorgonia, Or: What Difference Did Christianity Make?" *Pacifica* 8 (1995): 22–39; P. Veyne, ed., *A History of Private Life: From Pagan Rome to Byzantium* (Cambridge, Mass., 1987).

Fasting The early church adopted the practice of fasting mainly from *Judaism*, although it was not unknown in other Hellenist religions of the time. The practice of the fast had long been established in the Old Testament as a sign of repentance or mourning, particularly fitting for a time of crisis or special need that demanded heartfelt prayer for the mercy of God (2 Sam. 12:16; 1 Kgs. 21:9; 2 Chr. 20:3; Ezra 8:21; Jonah 3:5; Jer. 36:9; Ps. 109:24; Luke 2:37). The later rabbinic practice (as demonstrated in the story of Honi the Circle-Drawer in the Mishna who fasted until he "forced God's hand" to take pity on Israel) illustrates the idea that fasting redoubles the force of earnest prayer and attempts to call down God's pity and ready hearing. The disciples of the Baptist followed their teacher's tradition in observing several fasts (Mark 2:18) and seem to have been scandalized by the fact that the disciples of Jesus did not fast at all. Jesus defended their practice by observing that fasting was inappropriate for the "attendants of the bridegroom." But then the text goes on to indicate that a time would come when fasting would be observed among his disciples. This has been interpreted in contemporary scholarship to suggest that fasting was not a mark of the earliest disciples, but by the latter part of the first century had become a distinctive practice of the church as it conformed more to Jewish practice. The reference to fasting in the cure of the demoniac, when Jesus told them explicitly, "this type can only be cast out by prayer and fasting," depends on a late textual interpolation (Mark 9:29). The earliest version does not mention fasting: another indication it came later into the tradition. From the beginning, the church sought a reason for its fasts, and as Mark 2:18f. shows, that was first and foremost lamentation for the death of the Master, a factor that has always associated fasting in Christian practice with the memory of the Passion, thus marking Wednesdays and Fridays as "stational" days of fasting from as early as the time of the *Didache* (ch. 8; cf. *Didascalia* 21; Tertullian, *On Fasting* 14; Augustine, *Epistle* 36.16.30). Perhaps the great Lenten Fast before Pascha began as an extension of the fasts that prepared for *baptism*, but it soon became focused as a long memorial of the Passion and was practiced from as early as the second century, as *Irenaeus's* letter to *Pope Victor* demonstrates (Eusebius, *Ecclesiastical History* 5.24). Jesus began his ministry with fasting (Matt. 4:2), a form of intense *prayer* that the evangelist associates with the symbol of Israel's passage through the *desert* with little food. The burden of Jesus' preaching, however, soon turned to the sign of feasting as a mark of the approaching kingdom of God. His ready reference to the wedding feast in his parables, as another sign of the kingdom he preached, also explains why he may have said fasting was inappropriate for his immediate disciples. Jesus' doctrine of God's prodigal mercy given to the repentant sinner sat a little

uneasily with the older Jewish doctrine of fasting to persuade God to hear the repentant sinner. After the events of the Passion the church felt it more suitable to fast for the memory of the suffering bridegroom, and indeed the very term "bridegroom" became a particular designation of the suffering Lord in the Eastern church. By apostolic times fasting was used to mark special occasions of solemn prayer such as the laying on of hands (Acts 13:3), a practice which still attends the reception of great *sacraments* in the church such as baptism (the minister and candidate are instructed to fast; cf. *Didache* 6.4; Justin, *First Apology* 61; Tertullian, *On Baptism* 20), *Eucharist* (noted after the fourth century), or anointing. The *Didache* is anxious to distinguish Christian fasting from Jewish practices, a problem it solves by instructing the Christians to observe the "different" fast days of Wednesday and Friday (Pharisees fasted Mondays and Thursdays). Fasts were normally marked by an avoidance of all food from morning to sunset (later by a restricted intake of food during the day). Some fasts could be xerophagic ("dry food," that is, vegetables without oil), or "abstinence," which meant the avoidance of meat and wine. The rise of *Montanism* in the second century gave an impetus to the more regular appropriation of fasting as a spiritual exercise in Christianity, and Tertullian dedicated a treatise to the subject (*On Fasting*; see also Augustine's tract, *On the Utility of Fasting*). After the fourth century the general rise of *asceticism* (advocated among the monks as a strong form of control over the passions) also encouraged fasting to become a matter of general Christian observance (Epiphanius, *Against Heresies* 65.6; *Exposition of the Faith* 22). At the *Council of Nicaea* the practice of a forty-day pre-Paschal fast was established, and in later centuries the number of those periods of fast increased (there are now several smaller Lents observed in the Eastern church before Christmas, and Feasts of the Apostles and the Virgin). The custom of fasting was thus connected with three foundational principles: the first, as mentioned in several church orders (*Didascalia* 21; *Apostolic Constitutions* 5.3), is that prayer, fasting, and alms-giving can obtain the forgiveness of *sins* (Tobit 12:8). In other words fasting is a primary sign of repentance. Second, fasting is a spur to the concentration necessary for prayer. It is a form of sincere and heartfelt prayer appropriate for times of urgent need and crisis. Third, it is a devotional form of *memoria passionis*.

W. L. Johnson, "Motivations for Fasting in Early Christianity to AD 270" (Th.M. thesis, Southern Baptist Theological Seminary, 1978); J. A. McGuckin, "Christian Asceticism and the Early School of Alexandria," in *Monks, Hermits, and the Ascetic Tradition* (Studies in Church History 22; Oxford, 1985), 25–39; idem, "The Sign of the Prophet: The Significance of Meals in the Doctrine of Jesus," *Scripture Bulletin* 16, 2 (summer 1986): 35–40; H. Musurillo, "The Problem of Ascetical Fasting in the Greek Patristic Writers," *Traditio* 12 (1956): 1–64; J. F. Wimmer, *The Meaning and Motivation of Fasting According to the Synoptic Gospels* (Rome, 1980).

Felicity   *see* **Perpetua and Felicity**

Filioque   The Latin word *filioque* means "and from the son" and refers to that clause, added into the creed of the Second Ecumenical *Council of Constantinople* (381) by the Latin church in the early medieval period, which qualified the manner in which the **Holy Spirit** of God proceeded from the Father. The creed originally stated its belief in the Spirit's procession in the words: "And [we believe] in the Holy Spirit, the Lord and Giver of Life, who proceeds from the Father, who together with the Father and Son is worshiped and glorified." The *filioque*, added after the word "Father," made the creed subsequently read: "who proceeds from the Father and from the Son." This was known also as the doctrine of the "double procession" of the Spirit. The original text of the creed was jealously guarded by the Eastern church, who saw in the Latin addition an incipient **Trinitarian** heresy, or at the least an unwarranted intrusion into the dogmatic record and statement of an ecumenical council. From the time it first appeared as a common element of Latin theology, mainly from the Carolingian period, it became a matter of sharp controversy between the Greek and Latin churches, and remains so to this day despite several attempts formally to reconcile the difference. The Eastern theology of the single procession of the Spirit, articulated by **Gregory of Nazianzus**, followed the dogmatic statement of John 15:26: "the Spirit of truth who comes from the Father." Gregory argued that "procession" is the *proprium* of the Spirit, just as Sonship is uniquely characteristic of the Son's *hypostasis*. The Son issues from the Father by manner of generation, just as the Spirit issues from the Father by manner of procession. Both Son and Spirit come from the selfsame Father, and have the nature of that Father as their own nature. There is thus one single nature of Godhead in the divine Trinity (none other than the divine nature of the Father) with three hypostases expressing it characteristically: the Father expressing his own nature as the unique Uncaused Cause of Godhead (*Aitia*); the Son expressing the Father's nature (now his own) as filiated hypostasis, and the Spirit expressing it as processed hypostasis. The single procession of both Son and Spirit from the Father alone thus preserved the Christian sense of one supreme Godhead. For the Greeks the association of the Son with the causation of the divine hypostasis of the Spirit (a factor not always or necessarily intended by the Latin profession of the *filioque*) was a disruption to the very coherence of the doctrine of the Trinity, and was regarded as a very serious matter, a perspective not generally shared in the West. The Latin theologians were aware that many of the earlier Fathers had linked the Spirit to the Son most intimately. *Athanasius* and others called him the "Spirit of the Son" (Athanasius, *To Serapion* 1.24; 3.1; Gregory of Nyssa, *Against Eunomius* 1.378; Basil of Caesarea, *Epistle* 38; John of Damascus, *On the Orthodox Faith* 1.12). In this the Fathers were generally referring to the mission of the Spirit within the saving economy, whereas the creedal statement was referring to the emanation of the hypostases within the eternal life of the Godhead. Even so the concept of the Spirit proceeding from the Father "through the Son" was known in the East. It was included in the statement of faith sent by Tarasius, Patriarch of Constantinople, to the other Eastern patriarchs in 784 (and endorsed by John of Damascus in his *summa* of theology, *On the Orthodox Faith* 1.8). This statement was implicitly acknowledged by the second *Council of Nicaea* (787), which examined it. Again, the context here ought to be understood as the soteriological mission of the Spirit in the Church and the world. In 867 the patriarch *Photius* came across the *filioque* in the context of a dispute with Latin missionaries in Bulgaria. He examined the doctrine and at a council in Constantinople in 879–880, with delegates present from Pope John VIII, the notion was condemned. Photius composed a synodical letter on the subject (PG 102, 793–821) as well as a specific treatise (*The Mystagogy*) attacking Western views. The notion of the double procession of the Spirit, however, was an element of Latin speculation from an early time. It first appears in *Tertullian*, an important architect of Latin systematic thinking on the *Trinity* (*Against Praxeas* 4.1). *Hilary* also argued that the Spirit is an expression of Trinitarian unity, or bonding, because "He receives from both the Father and the Son" (Hilary, *Historical Fragments* 2.31; cf. also Victorinus, *Against the Arians* 1.13; and Ambrose, *On the Holy Spirit* 1.11.120). In all these cases the immediate context is of the soterio-

logical mission of the Spirit, but there is clearly a sense of speculation present about the immanent relations of the Trinity too, and this trend was strengthened further by *Augustine's* monumental work, his highly influential book *On the Trinity*. Here he clarified that the Father was the principal source of the Spirit, but that "by the Father's gift" the Son also serves as a source of the Spirit's procession such that there is a "common procession" of both (*On the Trinity* 15.26.47). It was only a matter of time before these influential theologians of the Latin church impacted on the public liturgy and declarations of faith. The term *filioque* is first encountered in the acts of the Third Council of Toledo (589), and defended by Paulinus of Aquileia at the Council of Friuli (796). Pope Martin first alarmed the Easterners by referring to the doctrine of double procession in a synodical letter to *Constantinople* in 694. The *filioque* clause was introduced into the liturgically chanted creed at the court of Charlemagne, and from there, in 807, Latin monks introduced it into their liturgical practice at their monastery on the Mount of Olives. The patriarch of *Jerusalem*, alerted by monks from St. Sabas, immediately protested the practice to Pope Leo III, maintaining that it was an unauthorized change to a conciliar statement, that it professed dubious doctrine. Carolingian theologians under the pope's instruction considered the question and reported that the Greeks were in theological error, and that changes were only forbidden to conciliar statements in terms of orthodox thought, not matters of exact words. The pope issued a decision defending the orthodoxy of the *filioque* doctrine, while diplomatically dropping any charge against the Greeks. He also refused to allow the addition of the clause in the Roman liturgy and advised the Frankish and Spanish churches gradually to discontinue their innovatory practice. The Frankish court continued unabashed, however, and by the early eleventh century the *filioque* finally made its way into

Roman liturgical custom too. There were several historical attempts to resolve the controversy. Greek theologians at the Council of Lyons II (1274) and Ferrara-Florence (1439) agreed on the orthodoxy of the *filioque* (though not on the legitimacy of its addition to the *creed*), but in both cases those councils were strongly disavowed afterwards by the Greek clergy and people.

G. C. Berthold, "Maximus the Confessor and the *Filioque* Controversy," SP 18 (1985): 113–18; J. P. Farrell, *St. Photios: The Mystagogy of the Holy Spirit* (Brookline, Mass., 1987); R. Haugh, *Photius and the Carolingians: The Trinitarian Controversy* (Belmont, Mass., 1975); J. N. D. Kelly, *Early Christian Creeds* (London, 1972), 358–67; L. Vischer, *Spirit of God: Spirit of Christ: Ecumenical Reflections on the Filioque Controversy* (London, 1981).

Flavian of Constantinople (d. 449) Flavian was an archbishop of the Eastern capital who tried to reconcile the Roman and Syrian *christological* traditions with the theology of *Cyril of Alexandria* as promulgated by the *Council of Ephesus I* in 431. Cyril's successor *Dioscorus* used the occasion of Flavian's trial of *Eutyches* to demand the emperor convoke a major synod (*Council of Ephesus II* [449]) at which Flavian himself was deposed. His treatment at the hands of Dioscorus was so rough he died as a result, and the scandal initiated a major change of policy that resulted in the *Council of Chalcedon*.

H. Chadwick, "The exile and death of Flavian of Constantinople: A prologue to the Council of Chalcedon," JTS n.s. 6 (1955): 17–34; R. V. Sellers, *The Council of Chalcedon* (London, 1953).

Fortunatus *see* **Venantius Fortunatus**

Fulgentius of Ruspe (467–532) A *north African* bishop and theologian,

Fulgentius came from a wealthy family and was well educated in Greek and Latin (becoming a bilingual scholar unusual for that period). At first he administered the estates of his widowed mother, but then decided, against much family opposition, to become a monk. The Vandal administration of north Africa was then actively sponsoring *Arianism*, and Fulgentius became known as an ardent *Nicene*, involving him in much wandering to avoid arrest. He was once beaten soundly by an Arian priest to convince him of his errors. He became *priest* and then bishop at Ruspe (Byzacena) in 507. The Arian king Thrasamund exiled him and other *Catholic clergy* to Sardinia. When Fulgentius was recognized as the leader of the group, Thrasamund recalled him for a public theological debate in Africa, but soon exiled him again as he was actively encouraging Nicene dissidents. On Thrasamund's death in 523 Fulgentius returned to Africa and resumed his office as bishop. Fulgentius enjoyed great status in the church of his time both as a theologian and a *confessor* for the faith. The Scythian monks known as the Theopaschites appealed to his support, and so he entered into the series of christological discussions that were ardently being pursued in the aftermath of the *Council of Chalcedon*. His *Christology* is a reflective defense of the unity of subject in Christ, but also of the validity of the two-nature language of the *Tome of Leo*. He sees the Latin church as occupying a balanced middle between *Nestorianism* and *Monophysitism*. He also wrote in defense of *Augustine's* theology of *grace*, in opposition to the work of Faustus of Riez who had attacked it. Fulgentius was deeply convinced of Augustine's view of the corruption of the human will, and perhaps even transmitted a deepened sense of Augustinian pessimism to Roman north Africa. He also revived Augustine's belief in predestination as a solution to the problem of grace and salvation. His *Trinitarian* writings are a moderated form of

Augustine's insights, but have a freshness coming from the way his apologetic work in this area had been stimulated by an unexpectedly sharp encounter with a late form of Arianism.

J. A. McGuckin, "The Theopaschite Confession (Text and Historical Context): A Study in the Cyrilline Reinterpretation of Chalcedon," JEH 35, 2 (1984): 239–55; W. G. Rusch, *The Later Latin Fathers* (London, 1977); S. T. Stevens, "The Circle of Bishop Fulgentius," *Traditio* 38 (1982): 327–41.

Gelasius I (late fifth century) Gelasius was bishop of Rome from 492–496 and, in the course of the Acacian Schism that had arisen between *Rome* and *Constantinople* over the issuing of the Henoticon of the emperor Zeno (an attempt to resolve the *Monophysite* crisis in the East by underplaying the importance of the *Council of Chalcedon* [451]), he developed a strong line on papal primacy (*see* **papacy**) that was to have influence in the Western churches for many centuries to come. He is the first to advance the theory of the "Two Swords" that would become constitutive of medieval papal theory: that Christ had intended (by the symbol of the two swords mentioned in the narrative of the garden of Gethsemane) that the emperor should wield a sword to govern the secular world, but that the pope had the sole charge of the spiritual sword, that is, all affairs relating to the church and the expression of the Christian faith. Gelasius was the first pope to change the traditional title of the Roman bishops from Vicar of St. Peter to Vicar of Christ; also part of his general policy to advance the significance of the papal office. His policy at home was marked by the abolition of the last pagan festival at Rome (the *Lupercalia*) and the suppression of the *Manicheans* and *Pelagians* who still survived in Italy. Important liturgical and canonical texts (the *Gelasian Sacramentary* and the *Gelasian Decretals*) are not by him.

J. Taylor, "The Early Papacy at Work: Gelasius I (492–96)," JRH 8 (1974–1975): 317–32; A. K. Ziegler, "Pope Gelasius I and His Teaching on the Relation of Church and State," CHR 27 (1942): 412–37.

Gnosticism The term derives from the Greek word for knowledge (*gnosis*) understood as secret insight into spiritual truth. It is probably what the generic religious word "enlightenment" would mean today. It is used to describe a broad trend of late Hellenistic religiosity that embraces a large variety of movements and different sects. Over the last century the origins of the gnostic movement have been much studied, and its pre-Christian roots are now generally admitted. It appears in Iranian religion and parts of *apocalyptic* (and other forms of) Hellenistic *Judaism*. It was, however, also dear to many Hellenistic philosophical schools, which had, several centuries before the appearance of Christianity, adopted a strong "otherworldly" tendency, with a desire both to theorize about the entrapment of the spiritual principle within a hostile material cosmos and to envisage the flight of the soul to the realms of transcendent spiritual freedom. One common factor in all the gnostic systems, therefore, is a profound suspicion of materiality, a dichotomous view of matter and spirit; and thus a tendency to moral and religious duality following after that (a good God, and an evil or defective world-making God; goodness being pure spirit; evil being flesh and ignorance). The world of Hellenism in the two centuries before and after the appearance of the early church was an ideal ecoculture for the rapid transmission and mutual interpenetration of such a nexus of ideas, and it is thus not surprising that even after so many years of profound study of the gnostic movements (aided by the rediscovery in the middle of the twentieth century of the Nag Hammadi collection of Christian gnostic literature), there is still no common consensus about Gnosticism as a whole, or even how far the generic term is helpful anymore. *Manicheism*, for example, is probably the most successful form of Gnosticism in Christian form, though it is doubtful whether it can be easily classified either as Christian or as gnostic. Christian Gnosticism, in the sense of groups who claimed to represent the true "inner" meaning of the gospel, is not much easier to resolve, historically speaking. One problem is that the various gnostic teachers proved their own insight and grasp of gnosis by elevating their own secret revelations as dogmatic constructs (or at least mythopoiesis). Thus the concept of a school dedicated to transmitting the thoughts of an earlier master intact, through successive generations, was not highly valued. It was for this reason, among others, that the early Christian bishops (such as *Irenaeus*) found the system of teachings so alarming in its capacity to "lose" the authentic Jesus tradition within a very short time. By using extensive spiritual *allegorization* of texts (before the larger body of the church thought it proper to adopt such a technique) Christian gnostics were able to render Jesus into an honorable savior-figure within their largely independent schemes of cosmic *fall* and spiritual ascent. The physically concrete details of Jesus' teaching on Torah, or the matter of his sufferings on the *cross* and bodily *resurrection*, rarely fitted in to the gnostic schemes, however (many of which were fundamentally *docetic*), and accordingly most of the antignostic Christian theologians (especially Irenaeus, *Adversus haereses*; *Hippolytus*, *Refutation of All Heresies*; and *Tertullian*, *On the Prescription of Heretics; Against Marcion*) were able to denounce them on the basis of their lack of respect for "*apostolic* tradition" and their refusal to admit the centrality of the death of Jesus in the Christian redemptive scheme. These two points, along with the constantly reiterated criticisms of their cosmological and theological dualism and their propensity for dissolving history into myth, made a clear and cogent target against which the antignostic theologians could marshal their efforts. Thus, Gnosticism was probably much more clear and defined as far as the Christian heresiologists were concerned than ever it was in the realities of history. Christian Gnosticism seemed to have flourished from the latter half of the first century through to the latter part of the third. It was at its strongest when advocated by private rhetoricians in the large-city environments where citizens would pay for independent classes. Its leading and best-known exponents were *Valentinus*, Ptolemy, *Basilides*, and *Heracleon*. By a variety of methods, the *patristic* theologians of the first two centuries opposed Christian gnostic teachers vigorously, and in the process developed the structure of early catholicity. Their antignostic program included elevating a strong principle of apostolic tradition against it; organizing the role and office of the communal episcopate over and against the private religious-philosopher; setting the history and sufferings of Jesus in a clear focus as elements that had to be transmitted intact from generation to generation; and using techniques such as creedal formulae to make a clear and nontechnical form of the common Christian belief (*see* **creeds**). Gnosticism was one of the most important factors in making the church of the first two centuries articulate its character and quality as an independent religious movement.

J. Behr, *The Way to Nicaea: The Formation of Christian Theology* (vol. 1; New York, 2001); H. Jonas, *The Gnostic Religion* (Boston, 1963); B. Layton, *The Gnostic Scriptures* (Garden City, N.Y., 1987); P. Perkins, *The Gnostic Dialogue: The Early Church and the Crisis of Gnosticism* (New York, 1980); K. Rudolph, *Gnosis: The Nature and History of Gnosticism* (San Francisco, 1983).

Grace   The idea and theological concept of grace (Greek: *charis*; Latin: *gratia*) has been so heavily developed in Western Christianity after *Augustine*'s clash with *Pelagius* in the fifth century that most Christian conceptions of the idea, both in medieval and modern thought, are heavily conditioned by the Augustinian system (especially as it was more scholastically applied and developed in the medieval West), with a major distinction being made between grace understood as God's salvific presence (uncreated grace) and grace as varied forms of God's philanthropic assistance to human beings on the path to salvation (created grace). *Patristic* thought before Augustine, especially among the Greeks, was not so scholastically hemmed in, but was much more diffuse in its understanding of the concept and its correlated nexus of ideas. The pre-Augustinian Latin ideas on grace were more discrete and "transactional." Augustine stood within this tradition, and although his thoughts all grow immediately out of a very local controversy with Pelagius, he passed on the terms of this approach authoritatively to the wider Latin world. The Greek Fathers, by contrast, did not see the transactional paradigm as so dominant, and applied a wide diversity of terms to approach the same idea. Grace in Greek Christian writing could be *charis*, the divine gift of a whole range of benefits and assistance from God, or could be God's generic favor (*eudokia*) and kind regard (*philanthropia*) for a human being, or the manner of loving condescension (*synkatabasis*) in which God reached out to save and deliver the creation at every point. Little distinction was made, perhaps purposefully so, between the God who saved from his own inner being and presence, and the power (*energeia*) that he communicated to the believer to assist that salvation. Moreover, the Greek East consistently resisted a growing distinction, which marked much Latin thought, between the world of *nature* and the world of supernature. In the one there was seen to be a regular order of natural laws; in the other God intervened to

make a believer rise out of temptations and corruption in order to "transcend nature by grace." Grace in the Western approach thus became more and more of a "supernatural" commodity. For the Greeks, nature itself was a transcendent miracle of God's providence. There could thus be no "purely natural" phenomenon that was not already profoundly graced. The human being within the natural world stood as a sacred priest of God's designs and intentions. *Athanasius* described it in the *De incarnatione* as a question of a human being rediscovering the perfect *image of God* within the *soul* by cleansing the (doubtless corroded, but nevertheless perfectly intact) mirror within. Western thinkers such as *Tertullian* and *Augustine* were more drastic in their conceptions of how seriously the soul had fallen, but Greek ascetical thought (and it is dominantly underscored in *Origen*) saw no problem in conceiving grace as a synergy, a close cooperation, between God and the soul. While God was always the source of all life, natural and spiritual, the vocation he constantly gave to the soul to ascend had to be reciprocated in a free assent. *Maximus the Confessor*, in the sixth century, expressed it in his distinction between gnomic and true (natural) *will*. He was developing on Athanasius's vision in the *De incarnatione* (5; 11; 54) that even when Adam was a natural being (*physei*) he had a direct vision of God, to which Christ's work has more splendidly restored the race. Gnomic will, as Maximus explained it, was what remained to fallen human beings: it was damaged and not always capable of instinctively directing a human being to the choice of the good and the free and unerring election of divine realities (the original design of natural will, which Christ alone now retained from all humanity). Nevertheless, by Christ's saving work, divine grace formed a human gnomic will, and trained it to choose the good habitually (even when its original instinct for good had been confused).

The choice for God "divinized" the soul. In fact the progress of the believer into deepening mystical union with God was a *deification* that affected both body and soul in an indissoluble synergy. The Greeks largely expressed this sense of progressive divinization through their *soteriological Christology*. Grace in the Greek Christian conception, therefore, is a basic way of connoting the divine energy present in the christological mystery that effects the world's restoration and deification. It has a primary rootedness in these theological base concepts before it is applied to the moral and mystical process of entering deeper communion with God, that is, to the *ascetical* domain. Partly because of this, the Greek East always had difficulties with Augustine's apparently narrower perimeters of argument, and the manner in which grace was seemingly contrasted with nature understood as a thoroughly corrupted force.

Of course the negative strand in Augustine's theology of grace grew immediately out of his local context of argument with the overly optimistic moralizing preacher *Pelagius*. Some of the latter's statements seem to suggest that if everybody could only "pull themselves together" a complete moral transformation would result. Augustine knew humanity better than that, and had, as an ascetic himself, searched the conscience more agonizingly. His understanding of grace in his own writings was a radiant doxology, a confession of praise, to the God whose philanthropy and restless plan to embrace all in salvation he felt most vividly in his own life's story. His stress on the complete prevenience of God (which the Greek East also affirmed), was set in relief by a corresponding stress on the defectibility of human effort. The Latin tradition, before and after him, also had a tendency to use transactional imagery for conceiving its ideas of redemption ("redemption" itself being a preferred term, referring to the buying back of commodities). Natures were seen as "possessions" of persons, rather than the organic aspect of human psychic condition. There was, therefore, a certain rigidity that led to grace being seen predominantly as the external assistance God gives to the salvific process. *Tertullian* had been one of the first (*De anima*) to set the basis of psychological scrutiny that would always attend Latin reflection on grace. His chief terms, "making satisfaction" and "gaining merits," also underscored the character of voluntarist moralism that would be the immediate context of most Latin thought to follow. It was Tertullian who first made the strong distinction between nature on the one hand and grace on the other (*De anima* 21.6). Augustine was stimulated to treat the problem with a major retrospective largely to defend two primary apologetic fronts. The first was a defense of freedom of will against *Manichean* pessimism and fatalism. The other was giving a rationale for the local custom of Africa in baptizing infants, against Pelagius's and Caelestius's more simplistic moralizing attacks. Augustine needed to show why a pre-moral infant needed the sacrament of forgiveness par excellence. Because of these immediate rhetorical contexts his great and expansive work in reflecting on the internal processes of salvation was channeled through fixed and somewhat narrow forms. When his work was further scholasticized after *Gregory the Great*, and so passed on to medieval Christianity, an even greater contrast between the Greek and Latin patristic ways of reflecting on salvation was erected, which has endured to the present. Nevertheless, there is a remarkable uniformity about Christian reflection on grace, and both Greek and Latin traditions concur in attributing to God an overwhelming power of philanthropic love that motivates a ceaseless search to restore divine communion with and within his creation. This grace, this "giftedness," is both the means and the goal. The grace of God, in the end, serves to bring all life into the presence of the God of grace.

J. P. Burns, "Grace: The Augustinian Foundation," in B. McGinn and J. Meyendorff, eds., *Christian Spirituality* (New York, 1985), 331–49; B. Drewery, *Origen and the Doctrine of Grace* (London, 1960); P. Phan, *Grace and the Human Condition* (Message of the Fathers of the Church 15; Wilmington, Del., 1988); A. Vanneste, "Nature et grace dans la théologie de S. Augustin," RecAug 10 (1975): 143–69.

Gregory of Nazianzus (329–390)

Gregory was the son of a wealthy landowning bishop in Nazianzus, Cappadocia (also named Gregory). He received the finest local schooling, and then (with his brother Caesarios) was sent to *Alexandria* and finally to Athens, where he spent ten years perfecting his rhetorical style and literary education. He was the finest Christian rhetorician of his day, and certainly the most learned bishop of the early church. His sea journey to Athens in 348 was interrupted by a violent storm and, fearing for his life, Gregory seems to have promised himself to God's service, a vow he fulfilled by accepting baptism at Athens and beginning his lifelong commitment to the ascetical life. It was a dedication he saw as entirely consonant with the commitment to celibacy required of the serious philosopher. Gregory did much to advance the theory of early Christian *asceticism*, but always with the stress on seclusion in the service of scholarly reflection. He regularly described Christianity as "our philosophy." At Athens he shared lodgings with his close friend *Basil of Caesarea*. Returning to Cappadocia in 358, Gregory's plans to live in scholarly retirement on his family estate were rudely interrupted by his father, who forcibly ordained him to the priesthood in 361. Gregory fled in protest to Basil's monastic estates at Annesoi, where he edited the *Philocalia* of *Origen*. He soon returned to assist in the administration of his local church, and in 363 Gregory led the literary attack against Julian's imperial policy of bar-

ring Christian professors from educational posts (*Invectives against Julian*). In 364 he negotiated Basil's reconciliation with his bishop, and eventually in 370 assisted him to attain the episcopal throne at Caesarea. Thereafter began their long alienation. Basil accused him of pusillanimity, and Gregory regarded Basil as having become too high and mighty. In 372 Basil and Gregory's father conspired against his will to appoint him as bishop of Sasima; Gregory found himself dropped in a miserable frontier town, at the center of a row over church revenues, and refused to occupy the see. He assisted his father as suffragan bishop of Nazianzus instead, and began his series of episcopal homilies, all of which were taken down by scribes, and edited at the end of his life for publication as a basic dossier of "sermons on every occasion" for a Christian bishop. In this guise they enjoyed an immense influence throughout the Byzantine centuries. From the outset Gregory stood for the Nicene cause of the *homoousion*, and advanced it to the classic *neo-Nicene* position of demanding that the *homoousion* of the Holy Spirit (with the Father) should also be recognized (thus becoming the primary architect of the classical doctrine of the coequal *Trinity*). He constantly pressured Basil to make his own position clear and led him, eventually, to break with *Eustathius of Sebaste* and declare openly for the deity of the Spirit of God. On his father's death in 374 Gregory retired to monastic seclusion, but was summoned, after Valens's death gave new hope for a Nicene revival, by the Council of Antioch (379) to assume the task of missionary apologist at *Constantinople*, where he had high-ranking family in residence. He began, in 379, a series of lectures in Constantinople on the Nicene faith (*Five Theological Orations*), and was recognized by the leading Nicene theologians, *Meletius of Antioch*, *Eusebius of Samosata*, and Peter of Alexandria (though not by Pope *Damasus*), as the true Nicene bishop of the city. When *Theodosius* took the capital in 380 Gregory's appointment was confirmed when the incumbent (Arian) bishop Demophilus was exiled. In 381 the *Council of Constantinople* was held in the city to establish the Nicene faith as standard in the Eastern empire, and when its president, Meletius, died, Gregory was elected in his place. His mild and reasoned leadership (and also probably his prosecution of the doctrine of the *homoousion* of the Spirit) soon brought the council into crisis, and resignation was his only way out. He retired to his estates and composed a large body of apologetic poetry, which gives crucial information on the controversies of the time. In his final years he composed large amounts of poetry (some of it very good) and prepared his orations for publication. In the Byzantine era Gregory was the most studied of all the early Christian writers. His theological works against *Apollinaris* were cited as authorities at the *Council of Chalcedon*, where he was posthumously awarded the title Gregory the Theologian. His writing on the Trinity was never rivaled, and he is the undisputed architect of the church's understanding of how the divine unity coexists in three coequal hypostases as the essential dynamic of the salvation of the world.

J. A. McGuckin, *St. Gregory of Nazianzus: An Intellectual Biography* (New York, 2001); F. W. Norris, *Faith Gives Fullness to Reason: The Five Theological Orations of Gregory of Nazianzus—Text and Commentary* (Leiden, Netherlands, 1991); R. Ruether, *Gregory of Nazianzús: Rhetor and Philosopher* (Oxford, 1969); D. F. Winslow, *The Dynamics of Salvation: A Study in Gregory of Nazianzus* (Philadelphia, 1979).

Gregory of Nyssa (c. 331–395)

The younger brother of *Basil of Caesarea* and friend and supporter of *Gregory of Nazianzus*, his elder contemporary, Gregory of Nyssa was a leading member of the group of *Cappadocian Fathers*, who advanced the *Nicene* cause in the van-

guard of the triumph of Nicene doctrine at the *Council of Constantinople* in 381. In recent times his work has enjoyed a popular revival for his interest in *apophatic* mystical theology as, for example, in his *Life of Moses*, where he depicts the achievement of divine communion in the manner of entering a dark cloud of unknowing. His *exegesis* is influenced by *Origen's* sense of the *soul* always driven onward to seek communion with the *Logos* (*Commentary on the Song of Songs; On the Christian Manner of Life; On Virginity*). He is the most openly "Origenian" of all the Cappadocians, teaching that souls preexisted, and that even souls in *hell* would eventually return to God (*see Apokatastasis*). His disciple and *deacon, Evagrius of Pontus*, later did much to disseminate Origen's influence on the Christian theory of *prayer* and *asceticism*. Gregory was brought up and educated by his sister *Macrina*, who tried in vain to enroll him as an ascetic in the monastery she had founded on their familial estates in Pontus. Macrina was more successful in her influence over Basil, who committed himself decisively to the ascetical life. Though Basil never admitted her influence, Gregory the younger brother always looked to Macrina with deference and eventually composed a *Life*, depicting her in the manner of the dying Socrates. Gregory was pulled into church politics by Basil, who ordained him in 371 to a small episcopal see in Cappadocia, from which the *Arians* orchestrated his removal in 376 on grounds of financial mismanagement. He regained control of Nyssa on the death of Valens in 378. After Basil's death in 379, Gregory took up the literary cause against the Arian movement with renewed force, especially in his attacks on *Eunomius*, who continued to denigrate Basil posthumously. Along with Gregory of Nazianzus, Gregory was commissioned by the Council of Antioch in 379, and was a leading protagonist at the council in the capital in 381. Afterwards he was commissioned by the emperor **Theodosius** to be one of the arbiters of Nicene orthodoxy for bishops in the region of Pontus. Favored by the court, he was specially called for to deliver the state orations for the funerals of Princess Pulcheria and Empress Flacilla. Apart from his works on asceticism and anti-Arian apologetic, he also wrote on the full humanity of Jesus (attacking **Apollinaris**), and left numerous works. His *Catechetical Oration* was designed to serve as a guide for the deacons who instructed **baptismal** candidates. It is a fascinating introduction to *sacramental* theology and basic doctrinal themes from the fourth-century Nicene perspective.

D. F. Balas, *Metousia Theou: Man's participation in God's perfections according to St. Gregory of Nyssa* (Rome, 1966); V. E. F. Harrison, *Grace and Human Freedom According to St. Gregory of Nyssa* (New York, 1992); A. Meredith, *Gregory of Nyssa* (London, 1999); H. Musurillo, ed., *From Glory to Glory: Texts from Gregory of Nyssa's Mystical Writings* (New York, 1961).

Gregory of Tours (538–594)   Bishop and historian of the Frankish nation, Gregory was the thirteenth member of his family to be the bishop of Tours. His access to state documents as an advisor to the king makes his most famous book, his ten-volume history of the Franks (*Historia Francorum*), a work of the highest importance. He also wrote extensively on the witness of the miracles of Christ and the saints (especially the saints of his native Gaul), and his *hagiography* had a wide influence.

S. Dill, *Roman Society in Gaul in the Merovingian Age* (London, 1926); M. Heinzelmann, *Gregory of Tours: History and Society in the 6th Century* (Cambridge, 2001); E. James, *Gregory of Tours: Lives of the Fathers* (Liverpool, U.K., 1991); W. C. McDermott and E. Peters, eds., *Monks, Bishops and Pagans: Christian Culture in Gaul and Italy 500–700. Sources in Translation: Including the World of Gregory of Tours* (Philadelphia, 1975); L. Thorpe, *Gregory of Tours: The History of the Franks* (Harmondsworth, U.K., 1974).

Gregory Thaumaturgos (c. 213–270) Gregory Thaumaturgos is thought to be the same as the student of **Origen of Alexandria**, Theodore, who dedicated a speech of thanksgiving to Origen when he graduated at Caesarea Maritima in c. 240. He was thus a wealthy pagan from the city of Neo-Caesarea in Pontus, whom Origen converted to Christianity. When Gregory (which is generally presumed to be his baptismal name) returned to his native city he was made its bishop and became famed as a great evangelizer. Numerous tales of his signs and wonders (**exorcisms, healings,** and **visions**) later gave him his title of "thaumaturge," and he posthumously became one of the pillars of the Cappadocian church, to whom the later **Cappadocian Fathers** looked back to for authority. Gregory was one of the bishops present for the Synod of Antioch in 264–265, which censured **Paul of Samosata**. His main theological works are the *Canonical Letter*, which demonstrates the state of church discipline in the early third century, and his *Ekthesis on the Faith*, which is an attempt to plot a balanced **Trinitarian** theology between the polarities of **Monarchianism** and Tritheism. His thought is heavily determined by Origenian premises.

R. Lane Fox, *Pagans and Christians* (1986), 516–42; W. Telfer, "The Cultus of St. Gregory Thaumaturgus," HTR 29 (1936): 225–344.

Gregory the Great (c. 540–604) Important bishop of **Rome**, political administrator, and theologian, Gregory belonged to an aristocratic Christian family in Rome at a time when the fortunes of both Italy and the ancient city were in decline because of **Justinian's** wars of reconquest and later (from 586) raids from Lombardian brigands. His father was a senator, and in 573 Gregory himself became the prefect of Rome (the highest civic office possible). Soon afterward he announced his retirement from public life and dedicated his extensive properties in Rome and Sicily to the cause of Christian *asceticism.* His large villa on the Caelian hill, near the Colosseum, became his Monastery of St. Andrew (still functioning), where he lived a life of scholarship and prayer with companions. Pope Pelagius II soon ordered him to resume public service for the church, and so he was ordained *deacon* and sent as papal representative (*apocrisarius*) to **Constantinople**, where he lived from 579 to 586, engaging in dispute with the patriarch **Eutyches**. He began one of his greatest works in this period, the *Magna Moralia in Job*, designed as an ascetical commentary on the text of Job for the use of his monastic companions. After resuming his duties as papal secretary in Rome, Gregory administered the church during the time of plague in 590, and on Pelagius's death in that year, he was elected pope (much against his inclination) as Gregory I. He rallied the city with extensive penitential processions to ask for God's mercy. Later tales spoke of a vision of an angel putting away his sword over Hadrian's mausoleum (Castel San Angelo), where today the statue of the same is a familiar Roman landmark. Gregory began a highly efficient administration in Rome, a symbolic end to a long decline of the Roman church. He profoundly monasticized the Roman administration, despite protests of the *clergy,* so beginning a long tradition along these lines that would mark Western Catholicism ever afterward. His successful leadership over Rome and its province led to his *papacy* becoming almost a paradigm of how the papal office could develop in the future. Gregory, realizing the futility of the local Byzantine administration at Ravenna, independently negotiated peace with the Lombard invaders. Many later reforms (such as the liturgical

changes that came to be called Gregorian chant) were retrospectively fathered on him. His writings on theological matters were chiefly pastoral, biblical, and *hagiographical.* His extensive biblical *exegesis* and theological comments were a moderated and simplified form of *Augustine*, and Gregory did more than any other (except perhaps **Prosper of Aquitaine**) to elevate Augustine's influence over the whole Western church, giving a theological preeminence to the doctrine of *grace* and adding his own view on purgatorial purification, a view that eventually grew into a distinctive Roman doctrine (*purgatory*). His *Pastoral Rule* (written largely for himself soon after he assumed the papacy) was designed as a guidance manual for a bishop. It became a standard text in Western church schools. He sees the bishop above all else as a pastor of *souls*, a leader and expositor of the divine word of Scripture. Gregory's exegetical works also standardized the Western view of biblical exegesis as the three stages of house-building, where the foundations were the exposition of the literal and historical sense of the text; followed by the roof and walls of the allegorical sense, which interprets higher Christian mysteries present within the old narratives; and finally the beautiful decorations that perfect a building, in the form of moral counsels designed to elevate the lives of the hearers. His insistence that a preacher should pay attention to all three aspects of a text proved determinative for the later Middle Ages. His *Dialogues* were also immensely popular. In these four books Gregory recounts the lives of Italian ascetic saints. The miraculous element abounds, marking an important stage in the development of the cult of the *saint* at a time when, both in Byzantium and the West, the fundamental idea on how to access the divine presence and favor was undergoing radical reconstruction and local democratization. In the second book of *Dialogues* Gregory popularized **Benedict**, the hermit of Nursia, thus providing an enormous impetus to the spread of Benedictinism as a paradigm of Western monasticism. His spiritual writings had a similarly determinative effect on the Latin Middle Ages insofar as he prioritized the monastic life as the "perfect" way of contemplation, excelling the lay married state.

F. H. Dudden, *Gregory the Great* (2 vols.; London, 1905); G. Evans, *The Thought of Gregory the Great* (Cambridge, 1986); R. A. Markus, *From Augustine to Gregory the Great* (London, 1983); J. Richards, *Consul of God: The Life and Times of Gregory the Great* (London, 1980); C. Straw, *Gregory the Great: Perfection in Imperfection* (Berkeley, Calif., 1988).

Hagiography The term literally means writings about *saints*, and designates a genre of Christian literature that proliferated after the fourth century. It was first and foremost a celebration of the life, deeds, and teaching of a Christian hero, held up for public emulation. Hagiography was present in *Judaism*, first noticeable in the great interest in Moses as an idealized figure, or in the Elijah-Elisha cycle of stories (1 Kgs. 17–2 Kgs. 13) about the great prophets. It was also present from the earliest times in the Christian movement. The Gospels are, of course, in a certain sense a hagiography of the Lord, carefully recounting his deeds and teachings. In this sense they have certain correspondences with other Hellenistic "lives of the heroes" that had already accumulated around the characters of great sophists and sages. The Gospel served as an archetype for most Christian hagiographies that followed, often providing episodes in which the saint would parallel certain episodes from the Gospel. The writer of the book of Sirach devotes several passages to the hagiographic record of the great heroes of the Bible (Sir. 44–50), with an invitation ("Now let us praise famous men," Sir. 44:1) that Jerome later took as his inspiration for a large book listing the literary heroes of the Christian movement (*On Illustrious Men*). Within the New Testament there were already short sections narrating the achievements of great heroes such as Stephen (Acts 6:8–7.60) and Paul (Mark 13:9–13; Acts 9 and passim). The genre of hagiography was further developed by the interest the Christians took, in the second and third centuries, in carefully recounting the passions of their martyrs. Examples can be seen in the *Acts of the Scillitan Martyrs*, *The Martyrdom of Polycarp*, or the *Passion of Perpetua and Felicity*. Martyrologies highly developed the form of narrating the "glorification" of the great Christian saints. Indeed the martyrs were the first category of saint commonly and clearly believed to have passed from this life to present glory in heaven. There was thus an important impetus in preserving their renown and honoring their memory, as their intercession could be hoped for and sought after by the church remaining on earth. The cult of the martyr, and the martyrological record, thus was the immediate prelude to the great flowering of hagiography that occurred in the fourth century when the categories of sainthood were expanded to include the ascetics of the church. The first example of the new genre was Athanasius's highly popular *Life of Antony*. This produced a veritable explosion of saints' lives in the Latin and Greek churches thereafter (cf. Palladius, *The Lausiac History*). **Gregory of Nazianzus** developed the genre through the medium of the Funeral Oration, and **Gregory of Nyssa** presents an early ascetical *Vita* (a shorthand term for saint's life that is often used) in his *Life of Macrina*, even though the latter is more in the form of a philosophical dialogue than a genuine account of his sister. A classical set of Byzantine saints' lives can be found in **Cyril of Scythopolis's** *Lives of the Fathers*, which recounts the hagiographies of the founders of Palestinian monasticism, Theodosius, Euthymius, and Sabas. In later Byzantine times the hagiographic text was read out on the saint's feast day, and so the genre continued to be produced as part of the Eastern church's canonization process. In the Western church, hagiography was just as popular, though not so many instances were composed as in the East. Martin of Tours was one of the early and lively sources of hagiographic tales, and so too *Benedict*. *Augustine's Confessions*, first designed as an internal scrutiny of his *soul* before God, also became one of the great sources of his hagiography and wide popularity in the early Middle Ages. Many of the hagiographies began to expand on the miraculous elements of the saint's life, and even to outdo one another with such elements. For a long time historians tended to regard the multitude of Christian hagiographies as wholly unreliable sources of information. In recent years there has been renewed appreciation of how valuable these texts are, not merely for relating details of a particular veneration of a saint, but for the incidental light they shed on conditions of late medieval society in the various regions of the world they reflect; and many new editions and translations of hagiographies have begun to appear.

P. Brown, *The Cult of the Saints: Its Rise and Function in Latin Christianity* (Chicago, 1981); E. Dawes and N. Baynes, *Three Byzantine Saints* (London, 1977); H. Delehaye, *The Legends of the Saints: An Introduction to Hagiography* (Norwood, 1974); A. G. Elliott, *Roads to Paradise: Reading the Lives of the Early Saints* (London, 1987); S. Hackel, ed., *The Byzantine Saint* (2d ed.; New York, 2001); S. Wilson, *Saints and Their Cults: Studies in Religious Sociology, Folklore, and History* (New York, 1984).

Healing   The Gospels show an intense interest in the healing ministry of Jesus (Mark 1:29–34; 1:40–2:12; 3:1–6; 5:21–43; 6:53–56; 7:24–37; 8:22–26; 10:46–52) and it was a concern that followed on into the early church, and has been present in varying degrees for the rest of Christianity's history. In the context of first-century Hellenistic religions, healings were often seen as epiphanies of the power of the gods. The cults of several deities were particularly associated with healings, notably Isis (especially at the great temple at Menouthis near *Alexandria*) or the several shrines of Aesculapius, the god who visited worshipers who came for incubational rest in his temples and there received healing ministrations from the priests as well as visitations in *dreams*. The accounts of these healings are often found inscribed on the walls of the ruined sites. The Christians, not denying their veracity, often attributed them to demonic power intent on confusing the witness of Jesus' divine healings. The symbol of Aesculapius as the serpent entwined around the staff (today still a symbol of doctors and hospitals), and the close association of this with Jesus in John 3:14 is more than coincidental. So too, perhaps, is the shrine of Aesculapius the healer discovered within Jerusalem at the excavations of the pool of Bethzatha, the site of Jesus' cure of the paralyzed man in John 5:1–18. Within the Gospels, the healings of Jesus, like the exorcisms he performs, are presented as manifestations of the advent of the kingdom. He is not a healer per se, but rather presents healings as a "sign" of his authority (*exousia*, Mark 2:11), and a manifestation that is meant to elicit wonder and faith. For *Judaism* and early Christianity, sickness was a manifestation, if not of demonical possession, at least of demonical assault. This is why the exorcisms and healings are placed in such proximity in the Gospel accounts, and why the early church always associated healing with a necessary attitude of repentance on the part of the sick person. The earliest continuations of the healings of Christ, as can be seen in the accounts of the apostolic healing miracles (Acts 3:1–10; 9:36–42; 14:8–18), run on in the same manner of presenting healings as signs to validate and empower the earliest preaching of the kerygma of the kingdom of God. They are signs meant to elicit faith in their agent and his message (1 Cor. 2:4; 2 Cor. 12:12; Acts 2:43; 3:6–10; 5:12–16; 9:32–35; 14:3; *Acts of Paul* 50–55; *Acts of John* 38–45). In the earliest missionary expansion of Christianity, healings "in the name of Jesus" were a part, just as *exorcisms* were, of the *kerygmatic* preaching process. Paul lists healings as one of those charisms expected in the church as the community of the new age (1 Cor. 12:9; see also Justin, *Second Apology* 13; idem, *Dialogue with Trypho* 17; ibid. 30; Irenaeus, *Adv. haereses* 3.18.4; 4.20.2; 5.3.1f.; Origen, *Against Celsus*, 7.32; Cyprian, *Epistle* 74.2; 76.2). But, more and more, it seems, the healing ministry was restricted to the elders of the community, a tendency that is first witnessed in the Epistle of James 5:14–16, where healing is **sacramentally** conceived through the form of anointing by the **presbyters**. By the second century, however, the attitude toward healings had reverted more to the generic attitude found in the Psalms and other parts of the Old Testament, where frequently the psalmist prays for deliverance from affliction (Ps. 6:1–10; Pss. 31–32, 38) or asks the intercession of the prophet or holy man of God (Isa. 38:1–20; 1 Kgs. 17:22–24; 2 Kgs. 5:1–14). Healings were expected by the Christian faithful from those who were about to receive martyrdom, a sign of their proximity to the kingdom (Eusebius, *Martyrs of Palestine* 1.1; *Passion of Perpetua and Felicity* 9.1; 16.4; *see* **Acts of the Martyrs**), and soon the charism of healing was widely transferred to the ascetic saint, whose intercessory powers worked wonders, like the prophets of old (Athanasius, *Life of Antony* 80; Gregory of Nyssa, *Life of Gregory the Wonderworker* PG 46, 916; Jerome, *Life of Hilarion* 8.8). The pagan apologist **Celsus** dismissed Christianity's claim to offer healings as another example of its reliance on tricks to support its religious claims (Origen, *Against Celsus* 3.52), and it was a charge that Origen was careful to refute. He does not deny that the church frequently witnessed healings as part of its regular life cycle, but he is most anxious to distance the practice from the "magical" invocation of healing that was widely used in contemporary religions (Origen, *Against Celsus* 1.46; 3.71f.). In the third century there were still those who had the charism of healing who were not ordained elders (**Hippolytus** says that they ought to be acknowledged for their gift but not enrolled in the *clergy* because of it; *Apostolic Tradition* 1.5); but more and more the gift of healing was appropriated by the presbyters, and reference to the charism of healing is found in the early **ordination** prayers (**Apostolic Constitutions** 8.16, 26). From the late fourth century onward this double pattern of healings became normative. In the first place healing was accepted as a continuing part of God's manifested mercy in the church understood as the harbinger of a new creation, and it was thus regarded as something that should be readily available as a ministration of prayer or through the sacraments (anointing and **Eucharist** were the normal channels) by means of presbyteral invocation. Thus there were many rituals of healing available in the church's service books from ancient times. In the second place, however, the act of healing was still regarded as a wondrous phenomenon, a particular inbreaking of the kingdom of God for the special end of manifesting an epiphany or of eliciting faith. This aspect is emphasized in the hagiographies, and taken as a mark of great sanctity on the part of the agent of healing. The healings of the saints were soon attributed to their relics and were at the center of the experience of pilgrimage from its very inception. From the late fourth century the church became increasingly involved with the provision of hospitals and other centers of healing ministry. *Gregory of Nazianzus's Oration* 14 served as an important fundraiser and theological rationale for **Basil of Caesarea's** leprosarium, built with imperial funds, and from the time of **Justinian** onward, the episcopal oversight of hospitals was more and more common an aspect of diocesan organization.

H. Avalos, *Health Care and the Rise of Christianity* (Peabody, Mass., 1999); D. Constantelos, *Byzantine Philanthropy and Social Welfare* (New Brunswick, 1968); E. Frost, *Christian Healing: A Consideration of the Place of Spiritual Healing in the Church of Today in the Light of the Doctrine and Practice of the Ante-Nicene Church* (London, 1940); R. M. Grant, *Miracle and Natural Law in Graeco-Roman and Early Christian Thought* (Amsterdam, 1952); H. C. Kee, *Medicine Miracle and Magic in Early Christian Times* (Cambridge, 1986); S. V. McCasland, *By the Finger of God* (New York, 1951).

Heaven   Christian theology significantly changed earlier Jewish speculation on the nature of heaven, largely by simplifying and democratizing it, and certainly by routing all speculation about it through the *eschatological* understanding of the *resurrection* of Christ. Biblical thought had conceived the heavens as the proper dwelling place for God and his angels. Jacob looked up and saw the passage of the heavenly beings from the heavenly regions to earth (Gen. 28:12), and God could be conceived as "coming down" from heaven to Sinai (Exod. 19:18–20). Jesus passed on this general conception to his church, as for example in the way he habitually "looked up to heaven" in order to pray (Mark 6:41; John 17:1) and addressed God as "Our Father in the heavens" (Matt. 6:9). Jewish thought at the time of the New Testament had envisaged seven layers to heaven. In the highest heaven was God alone surrounded by the seraphim, who veiled him from all other creation. Their proximity to the divine majesty was so intense that they had burst into flame as they circled the divine glory. In the lower heavens were the cherubim and archangelic powers. The first heaven was that heavenly domain visible to mortal perception, not exactly the skies, but rather the upper sphere where the angels still battled all the hostile spiritual powers who congregated there to influence earthly destinies. It was one of the powerful early Christian claims that Christ's resurrection victory had been felt in that sphere, the overcoming of hostile energies (Eph. 1:10–11; 4:7–9; Phil. 2:9–11; Col. 1:15–20), a victory that meant the spiritual liberation of the souls of the just, and a "safe passage" won for them in the time when their own souls had to make the awesome journey from this earthly sphere to the heavenly regions. This journey of the *soul* was a central cause of concern in Hellenistic religions too, especially the mystery cults, and part of Christianity's great appeal in the earliest generations was that it democratized the possibility of access to heavenly life, in Christ. Paul refers to this scheme of a variety of heavens incidentally when he mentions "the man" caught up into the third heaven, where he received divine inspirations (2 Cor. 12:1–4). And it was also used as vivid testimony to the unique significance of Christ's risen glory that he had thereby ascended beyond all the heavens (Eph. 4:10). The earliest catacomb art shows Christians imagined the entrance of the just into heaven as a *refrigerium*, and an enjoyment of *otium*, a pleasantly cool enjoyment of delights such as the paradisiacal banquet (the messianic banquet mentioned in the parables) and especially rest from labor. Paradise was frequently evoked as an image of heaven that appealed to the restoration of the beautiful "garden of delights" lost to Adam. Scenes of children are common, where they play in a carefree way in peaceful meadows. Third-century funeral inscriptions speak of the dead as "living now in Christ" or "refreshed and joyful among the stars." The tension exhibited in several of the earliest Christian sources between a judgment immediately after death (cf. Luke 16:19–31; *1 Clement* 5.4–7; 6.1–2; 50.3–4; *Martyrdom of Polycarp* 17.1) and one in the distant future (Rev. 20:11–15) was generally reconciled (certainly after the fourth century) by a common belief among the Christians that the just would be welcomed by Christ soon after their death. In parts of the early Syrian church the dominant belief in the future resurrection was taken to mean the dead would lie in a dreamless sleep until the last day, when they would be called to *Judgment* before being admitted to paradise or consigned to Hades. The two concepts (survival or final restoration of consciousness) were generally reconciled by the fourth century, and Augustine's synthesis of them (an individual judgment anticipates the Last Judgment) became standard in the West after the fifth century (*Enchiridion* 109–110; *Commentary on John* 49.10; *On the Literal Interpretation of Genesis* 12.32). The Christians (following Paul in 1 Cor. 15) were generally insistent, against contrary *gnostic* teachings, that the body was good and would have a part in the risen life in heaven (*Epistle of Barnabas* 5.7; 21.1; Irenaeus, *Adv. haereses* 1.10.1; 3.9.1; 5.13.2–3; 5.20.1; *1 Clement* 49.6; *2 Clement* 9.1–5; Justin, *Dialogue with Trypho* 80; Tertullian, *On the Resurrection of the Flesh*). Even *Origen* taught that traditional doctrine of a risen body (*De principiis, praef.* 5), which would be identifiable with this present one (*De principiis* 2.10.1–2), although elsewhere (*Against Celsus* 5.18–23) he maintained a more "spiritualizing" view of the transfiguration involved in heavenly life. The body in heaven would not be the same as this corporeal body but emanate from it as wheat did from germ (Origen, *De principiis* 2.10.3). After the decisive rejection of Origen's ideas on a radically spiritualized heavenly body in the fourth century and again in the sixth century, the church generally presumed a greater corporeality of the heavenly *saints* than Origen had envisaged, though Paul's paradoxical image of the "spiritual body" in 1 Corinthians 15 always served as a brake on those who wanted to make it a thoroughly corporeal vision (*see chiliasm*). Notions of the ongoing perfection involved in the heavenly life, transitions "from glory to glory," and the potential-

ity of an ever higher communion with God were dominant in the *Cappadocian Fathers* and other later "Origenians" such as *Maximus the Confessor*; and so they never wholly left Christian speculation on the heavenly life. The precise details of what constituted the heavenly life were supplied often by popular preaching, but theological speculation had been cautioned by Paul from an early time, and Christians took it to heart, that it was fundamentally "What no eye has see, no ear heard, no mind conceived, what Godhas prepared for those who love him" (1 Cor. 2:9).

D. W. Lotz, "Heaven and Hell in the Christian Tradition," RIL 48 (1979): 77–92; C. McDannell and B. Lang, *Heaven: A History* (London, 1988); U. Simon, *Heaven in the Christian Tradition* (New York, 1958); J. D. Tabor, *Things Unutterable: Paul's Ascent to Paradise in Its Greco-Roman, Judaic, and Early Christian Contexts* (London, 1986).

Hegesippus (c. 110–180) *Eusebius of Caesarea* used the Palestinian historian Hegesippus as a source for his own *Ecclesiastical History*, particularly relying on his *Memoirs Against the Gnostics*. This work recounts how Hegesippus travelled to *Rome* via Corinth, and was impressed by the unanimity in doctrine of the many bishops he met. The extant parts of his *Memoirs* deal with the conflicted history of the Jerusalem church and its sects. *Epiphanius* (*Refutation of Heresies* 27.6) is thought to reproduce the list of the earliest popes of Rome from Hegesippus. Because of his knowledge of Hebrew and of unwritten rabbinic traditions, Eusebius deduced that Hegesippus must have been a convert from *Judaism* (*Ecclesiastical History* 4.22.7). Hegesippus is an advocate for the view that Christian orthodoxy can only be sustained and guaranteed by the church's most gifted bishops continuing the *apostolic* preaching, and this theology of charismatic succession, or *tradition* (*diadoche*), lies behind his care to record the lists of the Roman and *Jerusalem* churches.

G. Bardy, *La Théologie de l'Église de saint Clément de Rome à saint Irenée* (Paris, 1945), 196–98; N. Hyldahl, "Hegesippus Hypomnemata," ST 14 (1960): 70–113; M. J. Routh, *Reliquiae Sacrae* (vol. 1; Oxford, 1846), 207–84; W. Telfer, "Was Hegesippus a Jew?" HTR 53 (1960): 143–55.

Hell   The early Christian concept of hell combines two ideas from the New Testament, connoted by the terms Hades and Gehenna. Hades was synonymous in Hellenistic religion with the realm of the dead (named after the god of the underworld; Homer, *Odyssey* 4.834), but was also the common Septuagintal translation of the biblical term Sheol. In the Hellenistic sense, Hades was a sad realm of fading shadows. Early Hebrew thought shared some of those associations (cf. Ps. 89), the concept of *resurrection* and afterlife not being generally extensive until much later. The falling into Hades was often a synonym for being mortally sick, and it appears often in this way in the psalms that pray for a release from the jaws of death, or the "pit of the earth." It was imaginatively conceived as lying somewhere in the middle regions of earth (Ps. 28:1; Matt. 11:23; Luke 10:15). Gehenna was originally the Valley of Hinnom, adjacent to the temple mount in *Jerusalem*. It had once been the site of human sacrifices to the god Moloch (2 Kgs. 16:3) and was regarded as a place of abomination, a site where God's anger would fall (Jer. 19:6; cf. Josh. 15:8). The valley was later used as the refuse dump for Jerusalem. Its permanently stinking fires were evoked by Jesus when he too referred to it as a sign of God's judgment and definitive rejection of evil (Matt. 5:22; Mark 9:47–49), and so began the long association of hell as a fiery place of torment. The combination of ideas of judgment of souls with an afterlife had not been widespread in Hellenistic religion, but was well known in Egyptian mythology, and was increasingly part of the Jewish and early Christian experience in the *apocalyptic* era, when ideas of resurrection and afterlife as reward or punishment came more to the fore. Gehenna soon was associated with the more graphic symbols of Jewish and early Christian apocalyptic *judgment*, such as the fiery abyss (Matt. 13:42) and the lake of fire (Rev. 20:10). And early Christian imagination filled in the details of the topography of hell accordingly. The old ambivalence between Hades as a place where all human life was destined to go (not necessarily a place of horror but a place of fading away) and Gehenna as a place of the punishment of the wicked was replaced in one sense by a new Christian vision of afterlife as a sharply discriminating matter of judgment: the passage of the elect to *heaven* and the wicked to hell (only much later did the intermediate state of *purgatorial* purification arise). But the ambivalence continued, in another sense, in the manner in which there remained confusion in the wider *patristic* tradition about whether the *souls* of the just went to paradise after *death* or had to linger in Hades until the general resurrection on the last day. *Irenaeus* regarded the gnostic belief that the souls of the righteous could go straight to heaven (*Adversus haereses* 5.31.1–2; Justin, *Dialogue with Trypho* 80) as not corresponding to the pattern revealed by Jesus: that he lived on earth, then descended into the house of Hades for three days, and only then rose to heavenly glory. Irenaeus thought that the elect would rest in Hades until the day of resurrection when they would finally rise to glory. Thus part of Hades was reserved for the consolation of the just, while another part contained the wicked who were punished for their crimes. This image is reflected in the parable of Dives and Lazarus (Luke 16:19–31). Other strongly held views in the early church maintained that the souls of the martyrs and the elect *saints* would pass straight to paradise (Luke

23:43; 2 Cor. 5:8), and thus Hades only contained penitent sinners and the wicked. In the late second century *Hippolytus* filled the gap by writing one of the first "travel guides" to the afterlife (*On the Universe* 1). Here the righteous are taken by angels by the right gate to a light-filled pace in Hades called "Abraham's Bosom," while the wicked are taken in by the left gate to a dark and smoky place, from which they can make out the fiery lake of Gehenna, which is currently unoccupied but which awaits them in the future judgment. *Tertullian* believed that the general occupation of Hades (in differentiated places) was the fate of the church with the sole exception of the martyrs who could bypass Hades and go straight to heaven as a result of their extraordinary virtue (*On the Soul* 55). He saw the time of the just in Hades as a period of postdeath purification (Tertullian, *On the Soul* 58; *Against Marcion* 4.34), and that of the wicked as a punishment in body and soul (*On the Resurrection of the Flesh* 16). Before him, *Justin* had also strongly maintained that the punishment of fire was eternal, and had been prepared for demons, but would now be delayed in its execution so that the souls of wicked humans could be included on the last day (Justin, *First Apology* 8.28.52). *Origen*, however, regarded the notion of endless punishment as unworthy of a God who always sought to correct and save. He regarded the postdeath correction of the soul in Hades as purely remedial punishment, which would have a logical terminus when its goal had been achieved (*CCels* 6.25; *De principiis* 3.6.5). His theory of the *apokatastasis*, when all souls will one day be restored to communion with God, created much controversy in the later church, and as a result of it there was a hardening of patristic speculation on salvation and judgment after the late third century. Origen's close reading of 1 Corinthians 3:12–15, however, made him stand against the old view that Hades would contain both just and wicked, and his *Homily on 1 Samuel*

28.3–25 specifically refuted Irenaeus's thought that all Christians were destined to follow Jesus into Hades. After Origen, most Christian teaching imagined the descent to Hades as part of Christ's definitive liberation of the souls imprisoned there, so that the just could thereafter enter heaven to "be with the Lord," as Paul had expressed it. *Gregory the Great* agreed with this latter idea, and popularized it in the Latin Church after him (*Moralia in Job* 12.13). Most of the Latin Fathers after the fourth century believed that the punishment of the damned fell upon them immediately after death (Hilary, *On Psalms* 51.22; 57.5; Jerome, *Commentary on Joel* 2.1; Augustine, *On the Predestination of the Saints* 24). It was an idea Gregory the Great authoritatively affirmed (*Dialogue* 4.38). He and *Augustine* were largely responsible for the later common teaching that the prayers of the living were of no avail in saving a soul once it had fallen into hell (Augustine, *Enchiridion* 109; *On the City of God* 21.9, 16–27; see *Perpetua and Felicity* for a contrary older view), though the Eastern church never quite made its mind up about this, and while it generally held to that view, its solemn "kneeling prayers" on the day of Pentecost specifically call on God in the name of the whole church to alleviate the sorrows of the lost souls. The tale of Abba Sisoes (who dug up bones of a dead pagan who spoke to him and asked for his prayers to alleviate the sorrows of hell) was also a popular story from the Desert Fathers that encouraged prayer of this type. With the development of the doctrine of purgatory, the West became ever more specific about the state of the afterlife. In the Eastern church more ambiguity remained. Here it was thought that the just soul passed through various regions and levels of instruction by angels after death (for which various liturgies were assigned to cover the first forty days). Several of the church's prayers for the dead evoke a state of "green pasture and refreshment" reminiscent of the repose of the righteous in

Hades, but more and more the belief in a transition to paradise became standard, as in the West.

R. H. Charles, *A Critical History of the Doctrine of a Future Life in Israel, in Judaism, and in Christianity* (London, 1913); H. Crouzel, "Hades et la Gehenne selon Origène," *Gregorianum* 50 (1978): 291–331; G. L. Prestige, "Hades in the Greek Fathers," JTS 24 (1922): 476–85.

Heracleon (fl. 145–180)   Heracleon was one of the leading disciples of *Valentinus*, the Christian gnostic teacher. According to *Hippolytus* (*Haer.* 6.35.5–7), Heracleon and Ptolemy constituted the nucleus of the Roman Valentinian school in the late second century. *Clement of Alexandria* and especially *Origen* have preserved parts of his great work, *The Commentary on John*, which seems to have been one of the earliest commentaries on a New Testament book ever written. Heracleon follows the form of the Valentinian myth of the cataclysmic *fall* of spirits which, through the descent of Christ, become aware of their heavenly origin and can ascend once more, liberated from this oppressive world and the demonic forces that try to keep them in the bondage of ignorance. Heracleon used the Gospel of John to expound the vision of Christ trying to lead *souls* out from the Demiurge's domain of the material cosmos, applying *allegory* extensively to make his point. His work elicited (and partly influenced) Origen's refutation, written almost a century later, which became the latter's own magnum opus, *The Commentary on John*. Some scholars also see Heracleon as the author of the Nag Hammadi gnostic text *The Tripartite Tractate*.

A. E. Brooke, *The Fragments of Heracleon* (Cambridge, 1891); E. H. Pagels, *The Johannine Gospel in Gnostic Exegesis: Heracleon's Commentary on John* (SBL Monograph Series 17; Nashville, 1973).

Heresy   *see* **Orthodoxy, Patristics, Schism**

Hermas (fl. 90–150)   One of the *Apostolic Fathers*, Hermas is the writer of *The Shepherd*, a treatise that at one stage was considered for inclusion in the New Testament *canon*. The work gains its title from the character of the Angel of Repentance, who appears in the guise of a shepherd to guide Hermas's understanding. Another figure, an old woman who becomes progressively younger, is one of the first female characterizations of the *ekklesia* or **church**. The oldest part of the work is a free-standing *apocalypse* written c. 90 (*Visions* 1–4), and the apocalyptic character is never far absent from all the later materials. Its author was a *slave* in Rome who rose to high prominence in the Roman Christian community. He was probably a Palestinian, and possibly one of those brought in captivity to **Rome** after the fall of the temple (some have hypothesized a former *priest*). Some scholars have identified him with the author of the *First Letter of Clement*. He was certainly contemporary with him. Hermas's owner was the wealthy Roman matron Rhoda, who eventually freed him. He was ruined in a *persecution* (probably that of Domitian) and denounced by his own family. He determined, in the course of receiving *revelations*, to adopt a penitent *ascetic* life. The book was composed over a considerable period. It describes a series of *visions* that serve as vehicles for his teaching to the wider church community. It is divided triadically: 5 Visions; 12 Mandates; 10 Similitudes. The writer is grappling with the problem of postbaptismal *sin* among Christians, and he is moved, almost reluctantly, toward the conclusion that God has finally allowed (by means of special revelations to him as a prophet) the possibility of a second, and final, repentance. He writes, probably, in the context of encouraging the church not to delay *baptism* until the deathbed, which was the pastoral result of the earlier belief that baptism was a once-for-all (unre-peatable) purification. The tone of the work is rigorist despite its advocacy of a theology of reconciliation (not rigorist enough for *Tertullian*, who denounced it as the "shepherd of adulterers"), and it opens an important window on the earliest Roman church. The writer seems to be functioning as a Christian prophet in the ecclesial structure (such as we meet with in the *Didache*), and here we see the main character of that office as moral paraenesis. Hermas's *Christology* is archaic: he identifies the *Holy Spirit* with the preincarnate Son, and suggests that the Trinity came into being after the ascension.

D. E. Aune, *Prophecy in Early Christianity and the Ancient Mediterranean World* (Grand Rapids, 1983), 299–310; L. W. Barnard, "The Shepherd of Hermas in Recent Study," HJ 9 (1968): 29–36; C. Osiek, *Rich and Poor in the Shepherd of Hermas: An Exegetical-Sociological Investigation* (Washington, 1983); J. N. Sparks, *The Apostolic Fathers* (Nashville, 1978).

Hilary of Poitiers (c. 315–367)

Hilary was the leading defender of *Nicene* theology in the Western church. He seems to have converted to Christianity, impressed by the lofty character of the Scriptures. He was a married man with one daughter when he was elected as bishop in Poitiers c. 350. He stood for the *homoousion* policy of the Nicenes, and so began drafting what became his main work, a large-scale defense of Nicene faith entitled *De Trinitate*. Because he would not consent to the condemnation of *Athanasius*, he was censured at the Synod of Béziers and exiled by the emperor Constantius to Phrygia, where he became acquainted with many aspects of Eastern Christian life, not least *hymn*-singing. He became one of the earliest Latin hymnographers (three fragments surviving). In Phrygia he finished the *De Trinitate* in twelve books and from his acquaintances in the *Homoiousian*

movement (anti-Arian but also anti-Nicene) he gained a deeper appreciation that *orthodoxy* was a larger concern than the simple ascription to the Nicene Creed (a lesson Athanasius himself would learn only much later in 372). In consequence, he completed an account (*De Synodis*) of why so many Eastern councils had been held, setting out for Western readers why the term *homoousion* was so controversial for the Greeks. Hilary appeared with the Homoiousians at the Council of Seleucia in 359. He made his way back to Gaul (though not allowed to resume duties at Poitiers), and there he organized the anti-Arian party. At the Council of Paris in 361 he succeeded in having a theology promulgated that reconciled the Homoousian and Homoiousian interests. He last appears in 364 with Eusebius of Vercelli, trying to expel the *Arian* bishop Auxentius. Hilary also produced an *Opus Historicum* preserving the texts of Arian creeds, and a blistering *Apology against Constantius*, whom he designates as the antichrist. Two significant *Tractates* on Scripture are extant, on Matthew and on the book of Psalms, which show that Hilary had studied *Origen*, one of the benefits of his enforced Eastern exile when he learned Greek. Hilary is an unusually thoughtful and eirenic theologian. He emphasizes the distinction of Father and Son, but conceives their unity as a mutual interpenetration (*perichoresis*) where no difference remains except the manner of origination: the Father communicates his entire self to the Son, and the Son receives all that is the Father, except that the one remains Father and the other is Son. To meet Arian *christological* arguments that the sufferings of the *Logos* incarnate demonstrate his nondivine status, Hilary proposed a Christology where Christ's body was indeed real, but also heavenly; where Christ could feel the impact of the crucifixion, for example, but not the pain of it (*see Eutyches*). His pneumatology is relatively undeveloped; he certainly thinks the *Holy Spirit* is divine, contrary to the

Arians, but conceives it as a dynamic power of God more than a distinct person or *hypostasis*.

C. F. A. Borchardt, *Hilary of Poitiers' Role in the Arian Struggle* (The Hague, Netherlands, 1966); P. C. Burns, "Hilary of Poitiers' Confrontation with Arianism 356–357," in R. C. Gregg, ed., *Arianism* (Cambridge, Mass., 1985), 287–302; E. P. Meyering, *Hilary of Poitiers on the Trinity* (Leiden, Netherlands, 1982).

Hippolytus of Rome (c. 170–236)

Hippolytus was an important *Logos theologian* and philosophical presbyter of the Roman church. *Origen* traveled to hear him lecture. Several Eastern sources describe him as the bishop of *Rome*. If this is accurate he must have broken away from the communion of Pope Zephyrinus (198–217), or (more likely) *Callistus* (217–222), whom he regarded as theologically heretical and morally lax. It is often thought that Hippolytus thus became one of the first antipopes. Because of this history, and also because he wrote in Greek (common among the theologians of Rome at that period), his reputation and his text tradition suffered neglect until the modern era. The early Roman tradition was that both Hippolytus and Pope Pontianus (230–235) were arrested in 235 and condemned to be worked to the death in the salt mines of Sardinia. In their exile they were reconciled, and Pope Fabian (236–250) had both their bodies brought back as revered martyrs to the cemetery on the Via Tiburtina. In 1551 excavations in the same area brought to light a statue of Hippolytus, prepared in his own lifetime, which is now in the Vatican collections. His chief work (though a minority does not attribute it to him) was a *Refutation of All Heresies*, which derives all Christian heresies from the corruption of mystery religions or Hellenistic *philosophy* prioritized over the gospel. He wrote an attack on *Sabellian Christology* as represented by the teacher *Noetus*

(*Contra Noetum*) and composed an *Apostolic Tradition,* a discussion of how the community's worship ought to be conducted, with extremely important examples of *prayers* that the presiding bishop ought to offer. Scholars have recently been able to abstract this writing from the various liturgical collections in which it was later incorporated. It now stands as one of the earliest and most important sources for knowledge of early Christian *ordination* rituals, the ordering of various ministries, the *catechumenate, baptism*, and the praxis of the early *Eucharist*. Hippolytus also wrote works of biblical commentary. The *Commentary on the Book of Daniel* survived complete in Slavonic. His *Benedictions of Moses* and *Benedictions of Isaac and Jacob* are also extant, as is a work *On Christ and Anti-Christ*. As a theologian Hippolytus stood for a vision of the *church* as the community of the pure elect, and strongly resisted the trend he deplored in Callistus (*see penance*) to advance a theology of reconciliation (a church of sinners following the path of repentance). He follows the earlier *Apologists* in his understanding of the Logos as having been extrapolated from the divine Monad for the purpose of creation and salvation (*see Theophilus*). The Logos was at first immanent in the divine Monad, then became the emitted Word in the process of creation, and finally was the incarnate Word in the economy of salvation. Hippolytus thought Callistus was a *Monarchian* in his Christology, a proponent of *Sabellianism,* for which he had a lifelong aversion; but Callistus in turn thought Hippolytus's own distinction between the Word and the Father was so underscored (the *Refutation* also lacks explicit reference to the *Holy Spirit*) that he must be a ditheist. In his spacious understanding of soteriology, Hippolytus follows Irenaeus's concept of salvation as *recapitulation,* whereby Christ assumes flesh to reverse the damage caused by Adam and restore immortality to the human race.

R. Butterworth, trans., *Hippolytus: The Contra Noetum* (London, 1977); G. Dix, trans., *The Treatise on the Apostolic Tradition of St. Hippolytus of Rome* (London, 1968); C. Osborne, *Rethinking Early Greek Philosophy: Hippolytus of Rome and the Pre-Socratics* (Ithaca, N.Y., 1987); D. L. Powell, "The Schism of Hippolytus," SP 12; TU 115 (1975): 449–56.

Holy Spirit   Throughout the Old Testament the term "spirit" (Hebrew: *ruach;* Greek: *pneuma*) is used to signify the inner life force of a being (Gen. 7:22; Job 15:13; 17:1; Ps. 51:10; and passim), not least the manifestations of that force in extraordinary and godly skills (Exod. 31:1) or strength (Judg. 14:6). It is most intimately associated with God as the giver of the breath of life (Ps. 104:29–30; Eccl. 12:7) and is generally the chief term for the inner essence of a *person,* the life force. It would later be regarded in Christian writing as intimately related to the idea of soul, but as something more theologically weighty than the *soul,* particularly so as Paul advanced a tripartite *anthropology* in many of his writings, describing the human composition as being that of body, soul, and spirit (*soma, psyche, pneuma*). In several parts of the Hebrew Bible interest turned to the concept of the Spirit of God, that dynamic life force which was God's own. In most instances it was a generic designation of God himself, but perhaps God seen especially as animator and life-giver, and as the rouser of the spiritual force within his servants, particularly the prophetic witnesses (Gen. 41:38; Num. 24:2; 1 Sam. 10:10; 2 Chr. 15:1; 24:20). In the opening words of Genesis, God's Spirit moved over the waters and gave form to the chaos (Gen. 1:2), a vivid image of the supreme archetype of energy, creation, skill, and life. The precise term "Holy Spirit" is not found extensively in the Old Testament. It appears only in two instances (Ps. 51:11; Isa. 63:10–11), both of which are generic references to God. The psalmist prays:

"Do not take your Holy Spirit from me." In this case we could render the sense as referring to the presence of God's favor. Again, in Isaiah, the term Spirit of God is simply a synonym for God's holiness. The much greater interest in the idea of spirit (and divine Spirit) in the New Testament can be gauged from the fact that this far smaller body of literature has twice as many references to the notion than are found in the entire corpus of the Old Testament.

Many of the New Testament passages are generic, in the same form as the majority of the Old Testament texts. The Spirit of God inspires the disciples with what to say under trials (Matt. 10:20; Acts 2:4); it inspires the prophecies of David (Matt. 22:43) and directs Jesus in the beginning of his ministry (Matt. 4:1; Luke 2:27), descending upon Jesus to mark him as the chosen Son of God (Mark 1:10; John 1:32–33). In the ongoing life of the *church,* the Spirit continues to direct and energize the apostles (Acts 8:29; 10:19; 21:4). It is the writings of John and Paul, however, that mark a clear development in the understanding of the Spirit of God understood in a particular sense: what later generations of Christian thinkers would be able to articulate with precision (because the *patristic tradition* provided a vocabulary that was not yet in existence in the scriptural era) as a "*hypostatic*" sense, that is, the Spirit considered as a distinctly personal characteristic (or characterization) of God. It is too early yet to say a "distinct person" of God (for that theology can only emerge in the light of elaborated reflection on the doctrine of the *Trinity*), but the sense of Spirit as a distinct manifestation of God (not just a generic synonym for God) is clearly present in the Johannine account, which has Jesus speaking about the Spirit that he would reveal (John 7:39): a text that markedly sets its own (evangelist's) comment about that revelation of the Spirit "retrospectively," noting that "as yet the Spirit had not been manifested." This important Johannine passage encouraged

Christian theologians to see the revelation of the Spirit of God as a primary aspect of the *resurrectional* glorification of Jesus. It is already sketched out in this way in the Johannine *pneumatology,* where Jesus prays for the "other" Paraclete to be sent after his passion and glorification (John 16:7–14). It is also implied in the pregnant Johannine phrases that Jesus "gave up his spirit" in the moment of his *death* (John 19:30), and "breathed out his spirit" (John 20:22) onto the apostles on the day of his resurrection. Paul's theology was also intensely aware of the importance of the Spirit of God, and it too brought the church a long way down the road toward understanding the Spirit as a distinct hypostatic manifestation of God (a proto-Trinitarian theology). In Paul's thought, Jesus is manifested as Savior, and glorified as Son, "in the Spirit" (Rom. 1:4; 8:11; 1 Tim. 3:16), and his Spirit is poured out on the church to be the essential "inspiration" (the inbreathing) of Christian life: something Paul can talk about as "walking in the Spirit" (Rom. 8:1, 9; Gal. 5:16) and as the dynamic of "spiritual" communion in the church (1 Cor. 6:17; 1 Cor. 12:4; 2 Cor. 4:13) bonding the disciples together with the Lord in the mystery of the presence of the Resurrected One. Paul habitually, and familiarly, speaks of the Spirit's indwelling in the Christian, as the interior energy of prayer and illumination (Rom. 8:16f.; 1 Cor. 2:10–15). With Paul begins a long tradition in Christian theology associating the Spirit preeminently with the divine power of sanctification.

In the patristic age that followed, the doctrine of the Spirit was slower than *Christology* to reach a full and energetic articulation, probably because of the range and complexity of the ideas expressed about the divine Spirit within the foundational texts. Controversy also fastened on the issue of Christology at an early stage, and nothing so sharpens Christian discourse as much as passing through a bitter dispute. It was not until the late fourth century that the *Arian* crisis would bring pneumatology, in its own turn, to crisis point, and demonstrate then that a dynamically renewed vocabulary was called for. On that occasion the work of *Athanasius* and the *Cappadocian Fathers* would be decisive. In the earlier period, much of the reference to the Holy Spirit within patristic writing progressed slowly along the path of a growing sense of the specific *nature* of the Spirit of God as a character of the divine presence. The image of the descent of the Spirit in the distinct (and separate) form of a dove while the Father speaks approbation over the Son in the Jordan (Matt. 3:16–17) gave Christians a fixed sense that it was appropriate to designate God's Son and Spirit separately (despite some texts that associated the Lord and the Spirit [cf. 2 Cor. 3:18; Phil. 1:19; Rom. 8:9; Gal. 4:6]). Increasingly theologians began to seek out how to specify the various "operations" of the Son and Spirit, noting that the Spirit effected the incarnation of the Word (Luke 1:35), energized his command to the spirits (Matt. 12:28), and inspired the prophets and *saints.* The gift of the Spirit was especially seen to be given at *baptism,* and so the whole dynamic of the church's sense of consecration, of matter and persons, was particularly seen to be the work of the Spirit: indwelling and energizing the *sacramental* rites that renewed the holiness of the church's members (though, curiously, the special invocation of the Spirit over the *Eucharist* would not be common until after the fourth century—*see* *epiclesis*). These traditional associations of the "operations" of the Spirit would be later summed up in the fourth-century Constantinopolitan creedal description of all that the church had earlier professed: that the Spirit was "Lord, and Life-Giver, who proceeds from the Father, and together with the Father and Son is worshiped and glorified: who spoke through the prophets" (*see* **Council of Constantinople I** (381). This summatic statement was the culmination of three centuries of rather sporadic patristic reflection on the nature of the Spirit's work. As Swete (1912, 159) put it succinctly: "The worship of the Trinity was a fact in the religious life of Christians before it was a dogma of the Church."

The *Apostolic Fathers* up to the time of *Irenaeus* continued mainly the biblical insights, without much specific addition. The context of all thought on the issue is that of the dynamic of salvation: the revelation of God brought in Jesus, and the power of the Spirit sent into the world through the church as a result of Jesus' saving *atonement* (*see soteriology*). *First Clement* 48 alludes to the Spirit as the "bond of communion," in the Pauline manner, and appeals to the unity that the Spirit brings as a reason church order ought to be observed carefully at Corinth and elsewhere. Clement calls upon the "witness of the Living God, the Lord Jesus Christ, and the Holy Spirit, who are at once the faith and the hope of the elect." His main emphasis on the work of the Spirit, however, is as the "inspirer of the Scriptures" (*1 Clement* 13; 16; 45; and passim). From his time onward Trinitarian invocations become more common (cf. the baptismal form suggested by Matt. 28:19–20; Ignatius, *Epistle to the Magnesians* 13; *Martyrdom of Polycarp* 14.1; *Didache* 7.1.3). Ignatius graphically describes the harmony of the soteriological process, referring to God's salvation as a hoisting up of the people of God to be stones of a new temple. The Father hoists the stones using the *cross* of Jesus as the lifting machine, and the Holy Spirit as a rope (*Letter to the Ephesians* 9). The *Shepherd of Hermas* is much concerned with the role of the Holy Spirit in the inspiration of the prophetic visions and insights he offers to the early Roman community. The power of the Spirit is self-authenticating and manifest (Shepherd of Hermas, *Vision* 1.1.3; 2.1.1; *Mandates* 11.2, 5, 7, 12). The author of the Shepherd is also very conscious of the indwelling of the Spirit of holiness in the Christian (Shepherd of Hermas, *Similitudes* 5.6.5) and he urges

the church to be holy for the sake of retaining the presence of the holy Sanctifier (so too Tatian, *Against the Greeks* 16; 20). Hermas advises Christians to put aside any depressed anxiety: "For the Holy Spirit that is given to you is a cheerful Spirit," and he thinks that if a soul is too full of grief it will cause the Spirit to ask God to depart from such a poor dwelling (Shepherd of Hermas, *Mandates* 10.2.1; 3.1.2). This concept of "grieving the Holy Spirit" by sin and causing it to withdraw from its indwelling of the elect soul becomes a common theme of later patristic writing (especially the monastic *ascetical* writings: *see Macarius the Great II*). Hermas seems at times to confuse the Son with the Spirit (Shepherd of Hermas, *Similitude* 5.5.2), a reductionism (known as Binitarianism) that is also witnessed in *2 Clement* 9.5. In *Justin Martyr* there is found one of the first attempts to articulate the place of the Holy Spirit in the Trinity. He envisaged the Son and Spirit as parts of a descending hierarchy: "We give the second place to Jesus Christ, our Teacher, and assign the third rank to the Spirit of prophecy" (*Apology* 1.13). This "subordinationist" scheme would become marked in most of the pre-Nicene writers to follow. Justin also sees the Spirit of God, who descends on the *Virgin Mary*, as none other than the *Logos* of God who is himself a divine Spirit (*Apology* 1.33).

The second-century *Montanist* crisis brought the question of the person and role of the Holy Spirit into the full light of day for the early church theologians. Montanus, Prisca, and Maximilla claimed to have experienced afresh the outpouring of the Spirit of prophecy in the last days. As part of the larger reaction against their movement, there was increased attention to the nature of inspiration, and the character of the Spirit's influence within the church. One result of that was a general insistence that the Spirit of God elevated and refined human spiritual capacities, rather than "overcame" or dispossessed them in *ecstasies* and raptures. At this time

Irenaeus demonstrated a more wide-ranging interest in the person and work of the Holy Spirit. He repeated the "traditional" faith of the church, citing the names of the three divine persons, and listing the *proprium* of the Holy Spirit as to be the inspirer of all the prophecies concerning Jesus (*Adversus haereses* 1.10.1; 4.33.7). So far this is a *summa* of the general nature of second-century thought, but he also went on in the *Demonstration of the Apostolic Preaching* to extend the Rule of Faith to add a strong emphasis on the Spirit's primary role in the sanctification of the world. He also describes the Son and the Spirit as "the two hands of God," an image that again reflects the soteriological impetus of his thought (*Adversus haereses* 4, preface 4; see also ibid. 4.20.1; 5.6.1.28). Irenaeus lays a noticeably greater stress on the role of the Spirit as coagentive (with the Son) in making the fabric of the cosmos, following the lead of the Wisdom literature (Prov. 3:19; 8:22) (*Adversus haereses* 4.20.3.4; 2.30.9). He thus clearly implies a certain coequality of significance, as salvific powers of God, between the Son and the Spirit; and there is far more differentiation of persons in his writing than there was in the case of Justin Martyr. Irenaeus says: "The Father anoints the Son. The Spirit is that anointing" (*Adversus haereses* 3.18.3; *Demonstration of the Apostolic Preaching* 47). Through the anointing of the Christ, the anointing of the human race with the gift of the Spirit was enabled (*Adversus haereses* 3.17.1), and all the church's apprehension of Christ and his saving work was mediated through that Spirit (*Adversus haereses* 3.17.2–3; 3.24.1; 4.20.5; 5.8.1; 5.36.2; *Demonstration of the Apostolic Preaching* 7). Irenaeus advanced the concept of the Holy Spirit considerably, but his general context of withstanding gnostic emanationist theories of the divine perhaps explains why he did not employ the concept of Trinity. He envisages the work of the "two hands" of God primarily as an expression of the internal life of God, expressed *economically* in the created order.

It was only after the **Monarchian** clash with the Logos theologians of the third century that the stage could be set for another movement in Christian pneumatology. With the prevalence of Logos theology, the concept of the Word as a hypostasis of the divine being was secured. The idea inevitably threw a clearer light on how to proceed with the articulation of the nature of the divine Spirit. The leading thinkers in this era were **Tertullian, Novatian, Hippolytus** (who strongly fought against Monarchian presuppositions), and **Origen.** Hippolytus gave the most explicit teaching yet that the Father, Son, and Spirit were "three distinct realities, and yet one single power of Godhead, manifested in a threefold economy of salvation" (*Against Noetus* 8). His near contemporary Novatian was also emphatic that the Spirit is the same one who inspired prophets, apostles, and the contemporary church, where he continues the work of sanctification by invigorating the sacraments and sanctifying believers (*On the Trinity* 16[24]). Origen was able to pick up on Hippolytus's clear hypostatic language and accumulate it into the basic and classical architecture of the Christian Trinity: one God in three divine persons, whose economic activity leads from the Father to the world, and leads the world back, by the Spirit and the Word, to communion with the Father. He frequently uses the term "venerable Trinity" (*Commentary on John* 6.33.166; *Commentary on Romans* 1.16; see also *Commentary on John* 10.39.240; *Commentary on Matthew* 15.31; *On First Principles* 1.4.3), and never fails to notice the Trinitarian implications of his Old Testament texts (*Homily on Genesis* 2.5; *Homily on Numbers* 21.2; *Homily on Jeremiah* 8.1; *Commentary on Matthew* 12.42; 17.4). Origen provided the Greek church with the basic formula, "One Substance (*Ousia*) and Three Persons (**Hypostases**)" (*Commentary on John* 2.10.75; *Commentary on Matthew* 17.14), but not without some fumbling over the appropriate terminology (a process that would go on for another 150 years in patristic theology), for he also labored under the philosophical difficulty of not having a sufficient semantic basis to distinguish *hypostasis* and *ousia*. This explains why in some cases, taking the terms as synonyms, and generally meaning to differentiate the person-hypostases, he asserted the Son and Spirit were "different" in *ousia* or subsistence from God (*On Prayer* 15.1: *heteros kat' ousian kai hypokeimenon*). In the West, Tertullian had performed a similar service of establishing a technical vocabulary describing the place of the Spirit in the divine Triad, as he offered a powerfully cogent argument for the understanding of the divine monarchy (one single power and nature of Godhead) as a single nature (*natura*) expressed in three divine persons (*personae*). His formulary would become standard for all the West. It subsequently guided important Latin treatises on the Spirit and the nature of the Trinity, including *Hilary* (*On the Trinity*), *Ambrose* (*On the Holy Spirit*), and not least *Augustine* (*On the Trinity*), who added to his predecessors the highly influential vision of the Spirit as the very bond of unity between the divine persons. After a short period of confusion between the Greeks and Latins (exemplified in the correspondence of *Dionysius of Alexandria* and *Dionysius of Rome*), when *hypostasis* was taken for a translation of substance (*substantia*), it was soon resolved that the formula "one God, one divine *nature* (*ousia, natura*), and three divine *persons* (*hypostases, personae*)" was common to the universal *catholic tradition*.

The full-scale crisis that affected Logos theology in the fourth century, in the form of the *Arian* dispute, resolved, in the hands of the *Nicene* theologians, to a sense of the necessity of confessing the full and coequal deity of the Word of God. It was this Nicene christological solution that led to the final significant stage of reflection on the Holy Spirit in patristic theology. *Athanasius of Alexandria* was one of the first Nicenes

to see that the implications of Christology passed on inevitably to the doctrine of the Holy Spirit (*see also Didymus the Blind*). In the fourth century, liturgical catechesis was one of the avenues of a deeper reflection on the nature of the Spirit as sanctifier. The tendency can be seen in *Cyril of Jerusalem* (*Catechetical Lectures* 16–17), but is taken to a pitch in Athanasius and the Cappadocian Fathers. In his *Letters to Serapion* Athanasius attacked those (*Tropici*) who said that the Spirit was simply another way of referring to God, another mode of reference to the Father or the Son, or else it was a supreme angel of God, but nonetheless a creature, not divine. He stressed the point that the Spirit was hypostatically distinct and fully divine, and he used the liturgical tradition to demonstrate his point: that the one who freely gives sanctification and regeneration cannot himself be other than the source of holiness and life. If the Spirit deifies mankind, it follows he must be God (*To Serapion* 1.25) and, moreover, consubstantial (*homoousion*) with God (*To Serapion* 1.27). *Basil of Caesarea* elaborated Athanasius's argument extensively in his own treatise *On the Holy Spirit*, though he moved away from the direct attribution of the term "consubstantial" to the Spirit, a prudent economy he argued, surrounded as he was by Arian leaders wanting to find an excuse to depose him, but nevertheless a falling back for which *Gregory of Nazianzus* criticized him, himself affirming in his highly influential *Theological Orations* (*Orations* 27–31; esp. 31) that the Spirit had to be consubstantial and coequal with God just as the Logos was. This high pneumatological theology of Athanasius and Gregory was not exactly what was affirmed at the *Council of Constantinople I* in 381, whose creedal *summa* we have already noticed. The terms affirmed there certainly expressed the full sense of the divinity of the Spirit of God, but omitted reference to the *homoousion* of any but the Son. Nevertheless it was Gregory of Nazianzus's patristic *exegesis* of that creed that won the day, and marked the Council of Constantinople as the definitive rejection of **Pneumatomachianism** (those who "fought against" the divinity of the Spirit) and in a sense the high-water mark of patristic reflection on the role and the coequal divine status of the Holy Spirit.

After Constantinople I in the East and Augustine in the West, the patristic doctrine of the Spirit was little more developed in formal dogmatizing. Reflection on the Holy Spirit was more fully invoked in the liturgical texts and in the monastic ascetical writings on prayer, where the abiding presence of the Spirit was especially a point of focus (most interestingly seen in the writings of Pseudo-Macarius; *see* **Macarius the Great [2]**). The church's Christology was more rapidly expressed, perhaps, than its pneumatology, and certainly with more controversial force; but while the Christian theology of the Holy Spirit was slower in coming to a formal statement, it was nevertheless just as intimately woven into the very fabric of the early church as was the faith in Jesus, and it is an example of a theology that expressed itself, in the end, largely through the more diffuse, but nonetheless fundamental, Christian doxological tradition of prayer and sacraments.

C. K. Barrett, *The Holy Spirit and the Gospel Tradition* (London, 1947); G. Bonner, "St. Augustine's Doctrine of the Holy Spirit," *Sobornost* ser. 4 no. 2 (1960): 51–66; S. M. Burgess, *The Spirit and the Church: Antiquity* (Peabody, Mass., 1984); J. P. Burns and J. M. Fagin, *The Holy Spirit* (Wilmington, Del., 1984); R. P. C. Hanson, *The Search for the Christian Doctrine of God* (Edinburgh, 1988); A. I. C. Heron, *The Holy Spirit* (Edinburgh, 1983); J. A. McGuckin, *St. Gregory of Nazianzus: An Intellectual Biography* (New York, 2002); C. R. B. Shapland, *The Letters of St. Athanasius Concerning the Holy Spirit* (London, 1951); H. B. Swete, *The Holy Spirit in the New Testament* (London, 1910); idem, *The Holy Spirit in the Ancient Church* (London, 1912).

Homoians   The word derives from the Greek *homoios*, meaning something that is "like" something else. The Homoians were a theological party of the fourth-century church. They are designated as such by modern scholars who note the formula they proposed at the Council of Sirmium in 359, that "Christ is like the Father in all things, according to the Scriptures." They were the mainstream **Arian** faction resistant to the **creed** and theology of Nicaea. While the **Council of Nicaea I** (325) had advocated that the Son of God be regarded as "the same substance" as God (**homoousios**), a large party of revisionists after the council ended, led particularly by **Eusebius of Nicomedia**, had lobbied for the abandonment of the twin terms "same" and "substance," and the adoption instead of a much wider and broader term of reference, that is, the Son's "likeness" to God. This movement was advocated by the emperor Constantius, and did not long outlive him. The Homoian profession avoided even apparent ascriptions of material substance to the divinity (that is, God did not have "substance" in the way two apples possessed and could be said to have the same substance); and it also protected the divine monarchy by insisting that the Son and the Father were not at all the "same thing." Of course, it also had the political advantage of being a much vaguer catch-all policy for a church hierarchy that was deeply divided by the Arian debate. The Nicene party, led by **Athanasius of Alexandria**, rallied to the defense of the **homoousion** doctrine in order to expose the Homoians as Arians who were bent on dismantling the Council of Nicaea that had ruled against them. The Arian Homoian camp was itself further divided as the fourth century progressed into two other separate parties. The first was called the Homoiousians (a compromise between the Nicene party and the Homoians, who refused sameness, but admitted likeness, and yet insisted on the ascription of "substantial" likeness between the Son and the Father; *see* *homoiousianism*). These alienated both the Nicenes and the Homoians but eventually made common cause with the Nicenes to bring the Arian crisis to a resolution. The second was the Anhomoians (or Anomoeans, the "Not-Likers"). These were radical Arians who denied even a likeness existed between the Son and Father. Both were disparate beings. One was divine and one was not divine. The Anhomoians were detested by Nicenes, Homoians, and Homoiousians alike, and were never a large party, though they included some acute thinkers and logicians such as *Eunomius* and *Aetius*, and their apologetic writings served as a spur for all that the *Cappadocian Fathers* wrote on the subject.

R. P. C. Hanson, *The Search for the Christian Doctrine of God* (Edinburgh, 1988).

Homoiousianism

Homoiousianism is the affirmation, sustained by a considerable party of fourth-century Eastern bishops in the time of the *Arian* crisis, that the Son of God is "like in substance" to the Father. It is a deliberate step back from the Nicene confession that the Son is "the same substance" (*homoousios*). It was meant to be a median position between the *Homoians* (the Son of God is like the Father) and the Homoousian Nicenes. The Homoiousian party was, as a whole, very much opposed to the Arian premise that the Son of God was not divine. Accordingly, the tendency of the older textbooks to describe this party as "Semi-Arian" was not particularly helpful and is now generally avoided. The Homoiousians regarded themselves as traditionalists, among whom were many acute theologians in the Origenian tradition (who regarded the very notion of substance as too materialist a conception to apply to the deity). They found the Nicenes distasteful in polity (many were deeply hostile to *Athanasius of Alexandria*) and too boldly innovative in their desire to force the whole church to a confession of the *homoousion* (neither a scriptural term nor one that had been widely used in Christianity before the *Council of Nicaea I* [325]). The chief intellectuals among the party were *Eusebius of Caesarea, Basil of Ancyra,* George of Laodicea, and *Meletius of Antioch.* After the death of the pro-Arian emperor Constantius in 362, when Athanasius of Alexandria made a concerted effort to bring the Homoiousians round to his side (recognizing their substantial agreement over the critical issue of the full divinity of the Son of God), a new front was opened up by the alliance, which was the harbinger of the *Neo-Nicene* settlement (brokered by Meletius and the *Cappadocian Fathers, Basil of Caesarea, Gregory of Nyssa,* and *Gregory of Nazianzus*) that brought an end to the Arian crisis in the late fourth century. The Cappadocians particularly expended themselves to argue for the intellectual synonymity of Homoiousianism and Homoousianism (a feat in itself). Their work was of major significance not only in resolving the Arian dispute, but in setting the terms for the classical doctrine of the *Trinity* of three *persons* in one substance or *nature*.

R. P. C. Hanson, *The Search for the Christian Doctrine of God* (Edinburgh, 1988).

Homoousion

Homoousion is the doctrine espoused at the *Council of Nicaea I* (325) that the Son of God was consubstantial (of the same substance) as the Father. It was first suggested, at the prompting of *Constantine* the Great, by *Hosius of Cordoba,* who stage-managed the council. Hosius and Constantine thought that it would be effective as a confessional "addition" to the traditional *baptismal* creed, which would serve to rally together all the Eastern theologians who had been so divided over the Arian question during the time of *persecutions*. As soon as Constantine had assumed monarchical power over the Eastern and Western halves of the empire in 323, he determined to end the troublesome conflict decisively. His introduction of the *homoousion* was controversial. It was not a traditional term nor was it found in Scripture. To assert that the Son was consubstantial (what the Father was, so essentially was the Son), however, was to him a simple way of making the statement that the Son of God was fully and completely divine, and worthy of worship. For Constantine it probably meant little more, and when he saw in the years ahead that his term had not commanded the wide consensus he had wished, he showed himself ready to abandon it—hence his anger against *Athanasius of Alexandria*, who refused to allow the term (and the Council of Nicaea) to slip quietly into obscurity. At first the Alexandrian theologians were glad for the term, as a way of ostracizing Arius (who refused to subscribe to it since he felt material terms such as "substance" were far too crass to apply to God), but they were not passionate advocates. Athanasius preferred to describe the Son as "of an identical essence as the Father" (*tautotes ousias*), which avoided any sense (widely feared among the opponents of Nicaea) that the *homoousion* affirmed the numerical identity of the Father and Son in a manner reminiscent of old-style *Monarchian* modalism. Athanasius only attached himself to the *homoousion* when he realized that the imperial policy was only interested in a bland consensus on *Christology*, and if necessary the Nicene Creed would be abandoned in favor of more moderate *Arian* confessions (the imperial policy for Constantine's last years and those of his son Constantius). Athanasius was the rallying leader of the Homoousians in the east, along with *Marcellus of Ancyra*, whose problematic views on *Christology* confirmed many bishops' worst fears. If it had not been for the dogged support of the Western bishops, who consistently clung fast to the *homoousion* doctrine, it is doubtful Athanasius would have won the day, to the extent that the creed and doctrine of

Nicaea became the standard confession of *Trinitarian* and christological *orthodoxy*.

J. F. Bethune-Baker, *The Meaning of Homoousios in the Constantinopolitan Creed* (Texts and Studies 7.1; Cambridge, 1901); R. P. C. Hanson, *The Search for the Christian Doctrine of God* (Edinburgh, 1988); C. Stead, *Divine Substance* (Oxford, 1977), 190–266.

Hosius (Ossius) of Cordoba

(c. 256–357)   Important symbol of the original *Nicene* faith for the Western bishops during the *Arian* crisis, Hosius was also adviser to the emperor *Constantine* from 313 to the time of the *Council of Nicaea I* (325). Shortly afterward he lost his role to *Eusebius of Nicomedia*, and Constantine abandoned Hosius's ecclesiastical ideas and policy. Hosius was bishop c. 295 and was a *confessor* in Maximian's persecution. Because of his high reputation, Constantine sent him as a personal delegate to *Alexandria* to investigate the dispute between *Arius* and Alexander of Alexandria. His report became the basis for the arrangement of the Council of Nicaea. The tone was set in advance by an anti-Arian synod at Antioch in 325 where Hosius presided. He was an important speaker at Nicaea, and is thought by many to have originated the idea of inserting the term *homoousion* into the creed. Hosius presided over the anti-Arian Council of Sardica in 343, and refused to assent to the condemnation of *Athanasius*, for which he himself was exiled to Sirmium by Constantius in 355. Among his very few surviving fragments (no major theological work exists) is a letter he wrote to Constantius in 356 advocating (on the basis of Matt. 22:21) that the emperor should not interfere with ecclesiastical affairs. In 357 the Arian Council of Sirmium forced the extremely old man to sign the creed it issued (the so-called "Blasphemy of Sirmium") and soon after he was allowed to go home to

Cordoba. According to Athanasius (who is the only one to mention it), he repudiated his signature before he died. Western Nicenes reacted violently to what was clearly the Arian abuse of a confused old man, and news of his signature only hardened their resolve.

H. Chadwick, "Ossius of Cordova and the Presidency of the Council of Antioch 325," JTS n.s. 9 (1958): 292–304; V. C. De Clercq, *Ossius of Cordova: A Contribution to the History of the Constantinian Period* (Washington, 1954).

Hymns   "Hymn" derives from the Greek term (*hymnos*) for religious songs or odes. Christians sang songs to Christ in their common gatherings from the earliest days. Pliny's report to Trajan (98–117) testifies that he had made investigations and found that Christians "Sang a hymn (*carmen*) to Christ as if to a god" (*Epistle* 96.7). Many of those earliest hymns are still traceable in the text of the New Testament (Luke 1:46f.; Rev. 15:3–4; 19:1f.; Acts 16:25; Eph. 5:19; Phil. 2:6–11; Col. 1:15–20; 1 Tim. 3:16), and are increasingly regarded as significant vehicles for the character of the earliest Christian theological **confessions**. The practice of singing to God was well established in Jewish cult, not least in the Psalms, the book of temple worship, but also in many other parts of the Old Testament (Exod. 15:1f.; Judg. 5:3–5; Job 5:9–16; 12:13–25; Isa. 42:10–12; 44:23; 52:9–10; Sir. 39:14–35; 42:15–43:33). By the third century, papyri start to witness to the existence of commonly known Christian hymns. One of the earliest of these, and still central to the rite of Orthodox Vesperal prayer, was the Phos Hilaron, which celebrates Christ as the "cheerful light of God the Father's glory," and which was sung in churches and in private homes at the time the first lamps of evening were brought in. Greek hymn writers were quick to see the application of the genre to catechism, and in the fourth century *Arius* of Alexandria used metrical forms to advance his apologia, a factor that made the orthodox quick to reply in kind. Writers such as *Clement of Alexandria* with his famous hymn to "Christ the Shepherd" at the end of his *Pedagogue* and Synesius of Cyrene developed the Christian hymn as a high literary and philosophical form. It was taken to a pitch by some of the most elevated and skillful of the Christian poets, notably *Prudentius* in the West (*The Cathemerinon*) and *Gregory of Nazianzus, Romanos the Melodist,* and *John of Damascus* in the Eastern church. Many of the greatest hymns have long since found their way into the offices and service books of the Latin and Greek churches. A vast body of other Christian hymns in *Armenian, Ethiopian,* Coptic, and other Christian languages remains to be discovered by the larger world. Most hymns, however, were not high literary or theological masterpieces, but solidly robust meters designed for communal use. In this genre *Ambrose* was the most significant Latin hymn writer. Fourteen of his original hymns have survived, but he also fathered a massive number of imitators (and pseudepigraphers) after him. The Christian poetry of the Greek and Latin Middle Ages is generally less theologically intense than the great patristic hymns, but nonetheless charming in its elegance, humanity, and fine eye for detail.

W. Christ and M. Paranikas, *Anthologia Graeca Carminum Christianorum* (Lepizig, Germany, 1871); A. Fitzgerald, *The Essays and Hymns of Synesius of Cyrene* (Oxford, 1926); J. A. McGuckin, *St. Gregory of Nazianzus: Selected Poems* (Oxford, 1986, 1989); idem, *At the Lighting of the Lamps: Hymns of the Ancient Church* (Harrisburg, Pa., 1997); J. T. Sanders, *The New Testament Christological Hymns* (Cambridge, 1971); H. Waddell, *Medieval Latin Lyrics* (5th ed.; London, 1975).

Hypostasis   The Greek word literally means "that which stands underneath something." Its direct equivalence in Latin would be "subsistence" (*subsistentia*) or individual entity. It could also be rendered as "substance" (*substantia*), and for some time in the third-century theological exchanges between the Greek and Latin churches over *Trinitarian* theology there was no small degree of confusion caused by the rendering of *hypostasis* as *substantia*, for where the Greeks argued for three hypostases in the Godhead within a single *ousia* (three subsistences within one nature), the Latins heard them as teaching three divine natures, which was tantamount to Tritheism. The word *hypostasis* was perhaps one of the first and most important of the technical terms that increasingly began to enter Christian theological vocabulary from the third century onward. It had a role to play in the *christological* and Trinitarian debates with differently nuanced meanings. At first it was a Hellenistic scientific term connoting the sediment precipitated in a liquid. In the Epistle to the Hebrews, however, it already assumes the significance of how Christ could express the being of God (Heb. 1:3), connotes the concept of the "individual personhood" of Christ (Heb. 3:14), and stands simply as a term for "substance" (Heb. 11:1). Thus it entered the late New Testament christological vocabulary as both a referent for distinct personal existence (individuant) and essential concrete reality. In the third century, following the lead of *Origen* (*Against Celsus* 8.12; *Commentary on the Gospel of John* 2.10.75), the word became the preferred term to combat *Sabellianist Monarchianism,* and the distinct identities of the three *"persons"* of the Godhead were designated the *hypostases*. Three *hypostases* in one *ousia* was a technical formula to which *Athanasius* gained common assent at the Synod of Alexandria in 362, thus allowing the Eastern churches space to focus on a solution to the crippling christological problems of the *Arian* period. It was at this juncture that *Apollinaris of Laodicea* returned the word to the christological

arena, using it to assert his strong views on the single reality of the divine Jesus. The many anti-*Apollinarists* (not least in the *Syrian* church) from that time onward always associated the term with a theory of confused divino-humanity that coalesced to make a single-substanced God-man, and even into the late fifth century many of the enemies of *Cyril of Alexandria* (who took the word to a new pitch of refinement) pretended to (or perhaps really did) hear him in the antique manner. Where Cyril argued that Christ was a single hypostasis (meaning subsistent person) his enemies accused him of teaching a single *nature* (*Monophysitism*). It seemed that once again the double signification of the word (a substantial fundament, or an individual reality) was confusing the field of debate rather than clarifying it. It was *Gregory of Nazianzus* (following on Athanasius's *Letter to Epictetus*) who rescued the word from Apollinaris and clarified how it ought to be used by the orthodox: insisting that in Trinitarian and in christological contexts the word had opposite meanings. In Trinitarianism it was the principle and dynamic of distinctness (the threeness), whereas in Christology it was the principle and dynamic of union (the oneness). In Trinitarian theology one must confess three hypostases. In Christology one must confess only a single hypostasis (*Letter 101 to Cledonius*). Cyril of Alexandria took the word a stage further in the great christological conflict with *Nestorius* beginning in 428, and running through the debates of the *Councils of Ephesus I* (431) and *Chalcedon* (451). Cyril wished to avoid Nestorian language of two sons (a divine son of God and a human son of man) and was determined to fashion a strong language of christological unity. Beginning with a preference for the formula "the single incarnate nature of the divine word" (*mia physis*), which he thought (wrongly) carried an Athanasian provenance, he soon discarded this terminology when he realized its Apollinarist pedigree, and thereafter stuck consistently throughout the Ephesine debates to the formula "the single hypostasis of the divine Word" as the principle and dynamic of the christological union. In other words in Christ there was no other personal subject than the divine *Logos* (the second hypostasis of the Trinity). Thus, at the same moment all of Christ's actions (even the human ones such as weeping) were "divine" because they were the acts of the Word, and yet were nonetheless "authentically human" because they were the acts of the Word in his own human body (thus his own human tears). For Cyril the theory of the single hypostasis confirmed and articulated enough of the christological mystery as was necessary for the correct interpretation of the Scriptures. Further than this he did not wish to go. The Councils of Ephesus and Chalcedon confirmed this terminology of the single (divine) hypostasis. In the end, and it was something that could be seen incipiently with Cyril but grew in the Byzantine writers, the two significances of *hypostasis* grew together, and marked a monumental change in philosophy that is perhaps one of the distinctive contributions of Christianity to the history of *philosophy*. For the first time in Hellenistic thought the concept of the individual existent (what was distinctive or personal) was given "substantively" concrete signification. One of the hypostatic realities of the triune Godhead (the Logos) was affirmed as the concretizing principle of a human life. In this synergetic union, individuation (which had always been understood by the Greeks to be accidental or peripherally significant) was brought to the center stage of revelation of true being (the restoration of the fallen being of humanity). In a sense, with the introduction to Christology of the word *hypostasis*, individual being was given a new ontological significance in the history of Western thought.

J. A. McGuckin, *St. Cyril of Alexandria and the Christological Controversy* (Leiden,

Netherlands, 1994), 212–22; M. Richard, "L'introduction du mot hypostase dans la théologie de l'incarnation," MSR 2 (1945): 5–32, 243–70.

Hypostatic Union The theory developed out of the *Christology* of St. *Cyril of Alexandria,* and was active in the conciliar Christologies of the *Councils of Ephesus I* (431), *Chalcedon* (451), and *Constantinople II* (553). It affirms the divine *Logos* is the sole personal subject (*hypostasis*) of the Christ. As the single divine hypostasis, the Logos personally concretizes, that is, existentially realizes (in Greek hypostatizes), the humanity of Christ (the human *ousia*). The hypostatic union means that the two natures are brought together as one in the single subjectival *person*. According to the terms of the hypostatic union, the acts of the human *nature* (eating and sleeping for example) and the acts of the divine nature (omniscience and immortality for example) can both be legitimately and fully referred to the same subject. Thus is it permissible to speak about Christ using terms such as "God's death," or "the Word of God in swaddling bands," or call the *Virgin Mary* the "Mother of God" (*Theotokos*). It was a theory taken to refined levels in the Byzantine christological and mystical writers to symbolize the *deification* of humanity effected by the *incarnation* of God in human history.

J. A. McGuckin, *St. Cyril of Alexandria and the Christological Controversy* (Leiden, Netherlands, 1994), 212–22; G. L. Prestige, *God in Patristic Thought* (London, 1952), 162–90.

Ibas of Edessa (fl. 435–457) Ibas was a highly intelligent *Syrian* bishop caught in the midst of a major international conflict between the *christological* traditions of *Alexandria* and Syria. He was deeply involved in the unfolding of the crisis as it moved from the

Council of Ephesus I (431), where *Cyril of Alexandria* enforced a condemnation of *Nestorius* and an implicit indictment on the whole Syrian church, to a resolution (of sorts) at the *Council of Chalcedon* (451), and he even featured posthumously as a significant symbol at the *Council of Constantinople II* (553). He was bishop of Edessa from 435 to 449, until he was condemned at *Dioscorus*'s *Council of Ephesus I* (449), and was later restored to his see after Chalcedon, to occupy it again from 451 to his death in 457. The translations he made at this period of the works of *Theodore of Mopsuestia* into Syriac ensured their long-term survival. Ibas wished to make a moderate compromise between the dualism he felt Nestorius had admitted into Christology through a careless exposition of the Syrian tradition and what he felt to be dangerous *Monophysite* tendencies present in Cyril's thought. He was, in short, one of the school who advocated the considered Syrian rapprochement after the Council of Ephesus 431, presided over by John of Antioch. Ibas worked with *Theodoret of Cyrrhus* to propose an agreement that Cyril himself accepted in the Formula of Reconciliation that he signed in 433. Dioscorus of Alexandria regarded this post-Ephesine settlement with the Syrians as a lapse of judgment on Cyril's part, and the renewed emphasis on the one nature (*mia physis*) Christology that he instigated made Ibas and Theodoret the two chief targets for a renewed attack after Cyril's death in 444. The depositions of both were secured at Ephesus 449, though reversed at Chalcedon two years later, when Dioscorus himself was deposed. In private writings both Theodoret and Ibas expressed a more strident distaste for Cyrilline Christology (Ibas called it "obnoxious"), and Ibas's *Letter to Mari* was brought forward as proof of an unregenerate (allegedly Nestorian) attitude. Despite the Chalcedonian rehabilitation, Ibas was posthumously used as a sacrificial victim to placate the Monophysite Cyrilline party at Constantinople II. His was one of the *Three Chapters* condemned (the posthumous hereticization of Theodore, Theodoret, and himself), which resulted in the total destruction of all his writings except for the offending epistle, which was preserved in the conciliar *Acta*.

A. d'Ales, "La lettre d'Ibas à Marès le Persan," RSR 22 (1932): 5–25; P. T. R. Gray, *The Defense of Chalcedon in the East*, 451–553 (Leiden, Netherlands, 1979).

Icon   *see* **Art, Iconoclasm, Image of God**

Iconoclasm   The word derives from the Greek for "the smashing of images." It refers to a major disruption of the life of the Byzantine Christian world in two periods. The first iconoclastic era was instituted by the Syrian imperial dynasty (by Leo III and his son Constantine V, Copronymos) and lasted from 726 to the accession of Leo IV (775–780), when it began to abate. After Leo's death his wife Irene became regent for their son (Constantine VI), and in the face of much court opposition she began to reverse the iconoclastic policy, culminating in her arrangement of the *Council of Nicaea II* (the Seventh Ecumenical Council) in the time of Patriarch Tarasius, which she summoned at *Constantinople* in 786 and then transferred to Nicaea in the following year. This set out a dogmatic statement explaining the legitimacy and necessity of the veneration of icons of Christ, the Virgin, and the saints, whose images served as channels to transmit the veneration of the church to the "prototypes" represented by those icons. Adoration and worship of God (*latreia*) was strongly distinguished from all veneration of saints and holy things (*proskynesis, douleia*), though the latter too were decreed as fitting recipients of Christian respect and veneration. At Nicaea II the works of *John of Damascus* (*In Defense of the Holy Images*) and Patriarch Germanos, the chief anti-iconoclastic theologians, were afforded *patristic* status. John outlined the chief arguments against the iconoclastic claim that icon veneration was idolatrous and unbiblical by clarifying the distinction between idol worship and the Christian honor given to the Savior through the medium of his icon in churches (*see art, image of God*). He also demonstrated from the Scriptures the number of times God commanded images to be made for the process of worship (the imagery on the ark of the covenant or Temple curtains, for example), and made the point that it was idolatry that was forbidden, not image-making per se. In an unenlightened age the two might have been seen as synonymous, he argues, but in the time after the advent of God in the flesh, the icon is a suitable theological medium for expressing belief in the sacramentality of matter. As Christ's body was *deified*, and deifying, so the icon too becomes a material *sacrament* of a divine presence. For John, hostility to the principle of icons serving as sacramental forms manifested an aversion to the fundamental principles involved in the authentic *revelation* of God enfleshed. Thus, icon veneration was not really an "indifferent" matter, but actually central to the *orthodox* faith. Iconoclasm was, therefore, not merely a rigorist puritanism, but more precisely a *christological* heresy. The second period of Iconoclasm was revived by Emperor Leo V of the Byzantine Armenian dynasty and lasted from 814 to 842. The second phase of the attack against icons and their supporters (the "Iconodules") was again centered in the court and the army, and again resisted by the monks. It was probably more violent than the first. It ended with the death of the emperor Theophilus in 842. After that point the empress-widow Theodora elevated the Iconodule theologian Methodius to the patriarchal throne and together they instituted a great festival to coincide with the first Sunday of Lent. This great "triumph of the icons," involving the street procession of the sacred images of Byzantium, was immensely popular and marked a definitive end to the iconoclastic tendencies of the army, whose dissident forces were dissolved. In the second period of Iconoclasm the leading theologians representing the legitimacy of icon veneration were Theodore the Studite and Patriarch Nikephoros. The celebration of the "restoration of orthodoxy" was afterward institutionalized in the Byzantine liturgy for the first Sunday of Lent, and is now known as the "Feast (or Triumph) of Orthodoxy," when all ancient heresies are liturgically anathematized, culminating in the Iconoclasts. It was this, perhaps, that led to the radical "slowing down" of the notion of holding ecumenical councils, a belief that Nicaea II had capped the whole series. It was a tendency which was exacerbated by the imminent rupture between the Latin and Greek churches in the immediately following centuries.

M. Barasche, *Icon: Studies in the History of an Idea* (New York, 1995); A. M. Bryer and J. Herrin, *Iconoclasm* (papers given at the Ninth Spring Symposium of Byzantine Studies, Birmingham University, 1975; Birmingham, 1977); J. M. Hussey, *The Orthodox Church in the Byzantine Empire* (Oxford, 1986), 30–68; A. Louth, trans., *Three Treatises on the Divine Images (St. John of Damascus)* (New York, 2003); J. A. McGuckin, *The Theology of Images and the Legitimation of Power in Eighth-Century Byzantium* (SVTQ 37, 1 [1993]: 39–58; C. P. Roth, trans., *On the Holy Icons (St. Theodore the Studite)* (New York, 1981).

Ignatius of Antioch (c. 35–107)

Ignatius was the bishop of the *Antiochene* church. Some time late in Trajan's reign (98–117) he was arrested for his profession of Christianity and taken to *Rome* under a guard of ten soldiers. On the way to his trial he composed a series of letters to the leaders of the Christian churches he was passing by. He was received at Smyrna by *Polycarp*, who arranged his reception by leaders of the local Asia Minor churches. From Smyrna, Ignatius wrote three letters of encouragement to the churches of Ephesus, Magnesia, and Tralles, and a fourth to Rome, asking them not to prevent his chance of *martyrdom*. He was then taken by his guards to Troas, and while there he wrote another three letters: to the churches of Philadelphia and Smyrna and to Polycarp personally. Other letters than these seven were apocryphally added to the corpus in the fourth century (it is thought by the author of the *Apostolic Constitutions*). It is generally presumed that his journey to the capital ended in his execution—so *Origen* and Polycarp—for his reputation as a martyr was very high in the ancient church. Accounts (*Acta*) of his death were composed later without much historical foundation. Ignatius's letters, first collated by Polycarp and preserved archivally by *Eusebius of Caesarea*, are a very important source for the state of the church at the beginning of the second century. They demand comparison with the manner in which the collection of Paul's letters were assembled, but they also reflect (and greatly assisted the establishment of) a monarchical model of episcopacy in the international Christian communities. Ignatius, along with the deutero-Pauline letters, is a strong advocate of the single bishop of the community holding the status of Jesus in the church. The bishop is elevated as the efficient symbol (the sacrament) of the unity of the *church*, and is the chief legitimator of the sacraments of *marriage* and *Eucharist*. His authority devolves directly from Christ. Ignatius warns against *docetic Christology*, which denied Jesus' fleshly reality and so disconnected him from history. Ignatius is a strong advocate of Jesus' divinity coterminous with his humanity, referring to the Savior as "Our God, Jesus the Christ." His eucharistic theology is dynamic and realist: "That flesh which suffered for our sins," and he sketches the mystical connection between the believer and Christ as established in the

Eucharist, not least when he refers to his own impending martyrdom in the image of himself being ground (like bread) in the jaws of the lions, just as Jesus was eucharistically the sacrifice of *salvation*. As confessor martyr and as bishop, Ignatius both sees and designates himself as God-bearer (*theophoros*). In the next generation *Irenaeus* would bring his sketch of monarchical episcopate to complete fruition in his theology of the *apostolic succession*.

L. W. Barnard, *Studies in the Apostolic Fathers and Their Background* (Oxford, 1966), ch. 3; R. M. Grant, *Ignatius of Antioch* (Philadelphia, 1985); W. R. Schoedel, "Polycarp: Witness to Ignatius of Antioch," VC 41 (1987), 360–76.

Image of God   The idea of the human being as the "image" of God is a theme that is small enough in the Hebrew Bible, but becomes profoundly important to later *patristic* interpreters, so much so that it evolved as a fundamentally constitutive element of much Christian *anthropology*, *Christology*, and *soteriology*. Genesis has two references to the creation of "man" (Hebrew: *adam*) as an image (Gen. 1:26, 27–28), which some of the Fathers elaborated into a mystical typology of "two creations." Paul had already made a positive connection between the ideas of humanity as generic and individual, so that the sin of the first father, Adam himself, could be undone in the new or second Adam, Jesus the Christ (Rom. 5:14f.; 1 Cor. 15:22f., 45). Conceiving of Adam simultaneously in personalist and corporately representative terms had served as an important avenue of Pauline redemption theory (the hymn in Phil. 2:5–11 may find its force in the contrast between the two Adams, one disobedient and the other obedient to death). Paul had also initiated the idea, which ran on into the later New Testament christological hymns, that Christ was himself the "icon" or "image of the unseen God" (2 Cor. 4:4; Col. 1:15; Heb. 1:3; see 1 Cor. 11:7). The theme of the "image of God," which combined these biblical, soteriological, anthropological, and christological premises, ran on to serve as a deep foundation for soteriological thought in *Irenaeus.* He was one of the first to notice (*Adversus haereses* 5.6) that in the Genesis accounts the text made a distinction, first describing the making of humanity as "in the image and likeness of God" (Gen. 1:26) and then noting that humanity was made "in the image of God" (Gen. 1:27–28). He and *Origen* (and *Cyril of Jerusalem* later in *Catechetical Orat.* 14.10) regarded the status of being "image" as referring to man's first condition (before the *fall*), destined to be superseded by man's final state, the consummation of becoming the "true likeness" (cf. 1 John 3:2). *Clement of Alexandria* developed that pattern of *exegesis* after Irenaeus (*Stromateis* 2.38.5; *Protreptikos* 12), and so it came to Origen, who developed the theme extensively (*PArch* 3.6.1; *CCels* 4.30; *Com Rm.* 4.5) and thus brought it into the mainstream of patristic theology. Origen stressed the point that the "image of God" (*eikon*) in humanity was a natural affair. It was not a matter of bodily imagism (*PArch* 4.4.10), but a pattern of the *Logos* (who had first made humankind) left in the human nature somehow, and shared equally among all the race. The "likeness" of God (*homoiosis*) Origen saw as something particularly reserved for those initiated believers who had approximated to God in deeper mystical and noetic communion. If the image was what all humanity began with, the likeness was what enlightened humanity aspired to. This Origenian ascetical and mystical theme was extensively developed in the later Alexandrian and *Cappadocian* theologians, who generally dropped the earlier distinction between image and likeness (Athanasius, *Contra Gentes* 34; *On The Incarnation* 13; Didymus, *On the Trinity* 2.12). It was a theme particularly favored in the monastic ascetical theology after

the fifth century. In the Greek tradition, the image of God par excellence was Christ himself. Man was thus the image and likeness of the "archetypal" Image. *Gregory of Nyssa* (echoing Origen) thought the image was a more static ontological foundation, and the likeness was a dynamic moral force in mankind. In this way the whole concept of being the image caught up humanity in a christologically centered process of *deification*. Closer and closer assimilation to the Logos-Image, through the grace of the *incarnation* and the ongoing transformative processes of the *Eucharist* and other *sacraments*, rendered the Christian disciple into a more exact "likeness" (a true image) of God, what Paul expressed by being "conformed" to the image of Christ (Rom. 8:29). Several of the Greek Fathers noted the connection in Genesis between the image and humanity's "naming of the animals," and concluded that somehow or other being the image of God was related to mankind's dominion over the created order (Eusebius, *Demonstration of the Gospel* 4.6; Gregory of Nyssa, *On the Making of Man* 4; Diodore of Tarsus, *Commentary on Genesis* 1.26; Chrysostom, *Homily on the Statues* 7.3; Cyril of Alexandria, *Glaphyra on Genesis* 1; idem, *Letter to Calosirius*; Theodoret, *Questions on Genesis* 20; Ambrosiaster, *Questions on the Old and New Testaments* 127). In the Western church Augustine gave the theory of the image of God a new impetus and a new direction. The concept of Christ as the supreme archetypal image was somewhat sidelined (possibly because it was felt to be too *subordinationist*: Christ was not so much the image, as God himself). Instead the image of God was referred specifically to man, and concretely located in the *soul* (a common theme among the Greeks who also saw the image to be especially located in the *nous* or logos of humanity). For Augustine, the soul, in turn, manifested the image of the *Trinitarian* deity in its threefold structure: memory, understanding, and will. In this Augustine mediated in the long-running battle between pro- and anti-Origenian factions in the church: fighting as to what extent the image of God in humanity had been lost or destroyed through sin. The general position was that the image had been to some extent damaged and needed restoration (Irenaeus, *Adversus haereses* 3.18.1; 4.38.4; 5.16.2; Origen, *Commentary on Canticles* 3.8; *Homilies on Genesis* 1.13; Hilary, *On the Trinity* 11.49; Basil, *Ascetical Discourse* 1; Cyril of Alexandria, *Commentary on John* 1.9; 9.1; 11.11; *On the Trinity* 6; Leo, *Sermon* 12.1). *Epiphanius*, however, had argued strongly against Origenian influence that the image remained intact in Adam (Jerome, *Epistulae* 51.6–7). Augustine moderated in the dispute, arguing his theory of "vestiges of the Trinity" remaining in the soul (*The Trinity* 14.4; *Retractations* 1.25).

R. Bernard, *L'Image de Dieu d'après S. Athanase* (Paris, 1952); W. J. Burghardt, *The Image of God in Man According to St. Cyril of Alexandria* (S.T.D. diss., Catholic University of America, Washington, D.C., 1957); D. Cairns, *The Image of God in Man* (London, 1953); T. Camelot, "La Théologie de l'Image de Dieu," RSPT 40 (1956): 443–71; H. Crouzel, *Théologie de l'Image de Dieu chez Origène* (Paris, 1956); J. T. Muckle, "The Doctrine of St. Gregory of Nyssa on Man as the Image of God," *Mediaeval Studies* 7 (1945): 55–84; J. E. Sullivan, *The Image of God: The Doctrine of St. Augustine and Its Influence* (Dubuque, Iowa, 1963).

Incarnation   Incarnation is the concept of the eternal Word of God (the *Logos*) "becoming flesh" within history for the *salvation* of the human race. Incarnation does not simply refer to the act itself (such as the conception of Jesus in the womb of the Virgin, or the event of Christmas); it stands more generically for the whole nexus of events of the life, teachings, sufferings, and glorification of the Lord, considered as the earthly, embodied activity of the Word. As such the theological concept of incarnation is a profoundly *soteriological* term: it always has reference to the dynamic effects of God's involvement in the cosmos. It is also an obviously christocentric way of approaching the concept of salvation. As was always true in Christian history, when one approaches a theology of salvation through the medium of the incarnation of the Logos, one soon finds the argument turns into the profoundly related areas of the *Trinitarian* doctrine of God and transfigured anthropology. The word incarnation derives from the Latin "in the flesh." It would thus be a translation of the Greek "made flesh" (*sarkothenta*). This, however, is only one part of the overall scheme of incarnational theology. To envisage that the Word of God enters the "flesh" of Jesus of Nazareth is often called in modern textbooks a "Logos-Sarx" Christology. It implies something of a fundamental contrast between categories of "divinity" and "flesh" (standing in for "God" and "creature"). This Logos-Sarx theology was witnessed in early *christological* schemes, ranging from *gnostic Docetics*, who could not accept any fundamental connection between the Logos and a "fleshly" reality, which they saw as profane. Logos-Sarx thinking can also be seen vividly in *Apollinaris of Laodicea*, who thought that the intellectual power of the Logos of God "stood in" for the human powers of reason in Jesus. When the Logos entered flesh, therefore, it had no need of a human mind or soul, itself providing for those basic functions. Apollinaris thought that this was a useful way of insisting on the single personality of the divine Word in the figure of the incarnate Christ, but his opponents such as the *Cappadocian Fathers* soon answered that it was a highly defective Christology since it rendered the humanity of Christ mindless and soulless (cf. Gregory of Nazianzus, *Epistle 101 to Cledonius*). From the beginning, Christian acceptance of the scheme of incarnation was widespread, with several variants in early times. Most writers before the third century do not think about it in great detail, concerned only when extremes appeared, such as the denying of the full reality of either the human or divine character of the Christ. After the third century the particular issues of incarnationalism become more and more specified, and turn mainly on the issue of the problem of a coherent subjectivity: in what way could a divine being (the Logos) be a human being? The Greek Fathers generally used a broader range of terms than incarnation and thus the English word commonly falsifies their sense. They generally speak of the incarnation as the "enhominization" of the Word of God (*enanthropesis*), a broader and more inclusive notion (the Greek term for "man" in this instance being seen as the genus, as well as being a biblicism directly evoking "the man" or new Adam). The mainstream christological tradition (and it is something that applies to the Greeks and Latins alike) was adamant that the humanity was not merely an empty suit that the Word "put on" (even though this Pauline image of "putting on" clothes was heavily used), but a genuine human life that the Word of God used as his primary medium of living on earth. *Origen* had tried to insist on the authenticity of both the Logos and the earthly Jesus, in the face of several alternatives (such as the *Gnostics*, who argued for an apparitional Christ, or the *Adoptionists*, who argued that the Spirit of God possessed a man temporarily), by his own complex theory of the Word dwelling in the great preexistent *soul* Jesus who had become human within history. The scheme never quite managed to work, for it never saw Jesus as synonymous with the Word incarnate. Later theologians such as *Athanasius* (*On the Incarnation*) set out a fuller elaboration of the Word as the single psychic subject of the Christ. His work was taken to a pitch by *Cyril of Alexandria* (*That the Christ Is One*), who argued against *Nestorius* that a single subjectivity in the incarnate Lord meant that flesh and spirit, God and man, previously alien and disparate categories, had finally been reconciled in the mystery of the Christ. This mystery of communion, which belonged to Christ naturally, was passed on to the church as a *grace*. Thus the incarnation of the Word became the paradigm for the *deification* of the race. Its previous inevitable subjection to corruption and *death* had now given way to the potential for immortalization and divine communion. Cyril argued that nowhere was this more vividly seen than in the deifying grace of the *Eucharist* and the *sacraments*, which ensured the immortality of the Christian. The Alexandrian incarnation (enhominization) theology became standard in the church through its adoption and promulgation by the fourth- and fifth-century ecumenical councils.

A. Grillmeier, *Christ in Christian Tradition* (vol. 1; London, 1975); J. A. McGuckin, *St. Cyril of Alexandria and the Christological Controversy: Its History, Theology, and Texts* (Leiden, Netherlands, 1994); idem, *St. Cyril of Alexandria: On the Unity of Christ* (New York, 1995); R. A. Norris, *The Christological Controversy* (Philadelphia, 1980); F. M. Young, *From Nicaea to Chalcedon* (Philadelphia, 1983).

Incense   Incense is made from the fragrant resinous balsam from trees and bushes, mixed with spices and powdered stone. Laid on burning charcoal, pellets of the soft resin slowly melt and produce a fragrant smoke. The burning of incense to perfume the houses of the rich was common in antiquity, and from ancient times it was also burned in temples to stand as an offering to the gods. The ritual of the Jewish temple used incense; first to burn in the tabernacle (Exod. 30:34–38) and then in the temple at Jerusalem, where the priests are instructed to mix frankincense in with the cereal offerings (cf. Lev. 2:2), to produce a "pleasing odor to the LORD." In the Exodus account the detailed recipe for preparing the incense is given, and the result is described as something that "shall be for you most holy." The people are forbidden to burn this mixture in their own tents. In the later temple ritual, on the Day of Atonement, the high priest entered the Holy of Holies with copious incense before sprinkling the blood on the mercy seat of the ark. The offering of incense here seems to have evolved in its symbolic significance, so as to connote the cloud that veils the divine presence (the Shekinah); thus the incense is at once an evocation of the presence of the Holy One in the inner sanctum (as he once inhabited the pillar of cloud in the desert) and the protecting veil that masks the eyes of the mortal high priest from the awesome and dangerous vision of the Lord (Exod. 33:20). The early Christians were at first in two minds about the use of incense in ritual. On the one hand, the ubiquitous pagan custom of offering incense to the gods was a practice they wished to be distanced from (see Tertullian, *Apologeticus* 30; Augustine, *Enarrationes in Psalmos* 49.14). In the time of *persecutions*, it was a common ploy for the authorities to make suspected Christians throw grains of incense into the dishes of charcoal burning in state buildings, or before the entrances to temples, in honor of the gods of *Rome*; and this the church regarded the quintessence of idolatry, the act of offering incense (a mark of divine honor) to mere "demons." But the memory of the importance of incense in the service of the true God, from the biblical temple rituals, was also known to them. So too was the instructive phrase in the book of Psalms (141:2), "Let my prayer arise like incense before you," which eventually became constitutive of early Christian evening prayer. The rite of vespers, celebrated when twilight first appeared, turned around the symbols of the lighting of the evening lamp and the offering of incense to symbolize the prayer of the church rising in the presence of God. The priestly prayer for the blessing of incense before it is burned on the altar, as used in the Eastern

eucharistic liturgy, reveals the whole symbolic purpose: "Incense we offer you, O Christ our God. Receive it on your heavenly throne, and send down upon us in return the grace of your all *Holy Spirit*." The date when the use of incense in Christian worship became widespread is not exactly known. It probably became common in the fourth century, when the prayer offices were being structurally established. But in Revelation 8:3–5 the burning of incense already symbolizes the prayers of the saints, and may reflect its use in church life in the immediate postapostolic era. The Syrian church regarded it as so important that a *Eucharist* could not be celebrated without it, an attitude that soon pervaded the entire Eastern church. Incense was also used in Christian funeral rituals as early as the time of Tertullian (*Apologeticus* 42). *Constantine* gave a gift of several incense burners (thuribles) for the use of the Basilica of St. John Lateran in Rome, and *Egeria* also mentions the custom of the Anastasis Church at *Jerusalem* to burn incense in the Christian temple. In both cases it may well be a matter of perfuming a large church that contained crowds of (malodorous) visitors. In Byzantine court ritual, the censing of dignitaries and visiting crowds was a basic part of social etiquette (magistrates had the right to walk the streets with a thurible of incense burning before them), and the church adopted this too. *John Chrysostom* and *Dionysius the Areopagite* both mention incense as part of the normal rituals of the church in their day. In fifth-century church practice the incensing of the altar and the eucharistic gifts was taken, in the biblical sense, to be a strict "offering" to the glory of God, a form of worship, unique and proper to the divinity. In his conflict with the emperor Constantius, *Athanasius* described the latter's intrusion into church life as being as obviously invalid as a lay person offering incense to God, and thus saw the act of incensing as one of the distinctive marks and offices of the priesthood. But incense was also "offered" to the congregation as a mark of respect in Eastern Christian ritual; to signify their status of equality as brothers and sisters of the One Lord, and also their religious value as living "*images of God.*" This censing of the people usually followed after, and quite distinct from, the offering of incense at the altar of God. After the *iconoclastic* crisis, the censing of the people was distanced from the offering of incense on the altar by the intermediary juxtaposition of the incensing of the icons in church. Today all Eastern Christian liturgical ritual uses incense, and many forms of Latin Catholic ritual do so also, although in antiquity it was the Latin custom to use incense only on the most solemn occasions. Most Eastern Orthodox will also offer incense to God as part of their evening devotions, before the household icons, laity using a small hand censer, as the use of the thurible is reserved to the ordained clergy.

G. C. F. Atchley, *A History of the Use of Incense in Divine Worship* (Alcuin Club Collections 19; London, 1909); M. Righetti, *Manuale di storia liturgica* (vol. 1; Milan, Italy, 1964), 390–94.

India   Some of the ancients used the term "India" to refer to what we would today call *Ethiopia*, and thus the first appearances of Christianity on the Indian continent proper are not clearly known. The first solid reference in the *patristic* literature is that of the sixth-century Byzantine writer known as Cosmas Indicopleustes (the word means "the sailor to India"), who made trade voyages out of *Alexandria* to the East and recorded his observations in his treatise *On Christian Topography*. He remarked that the Christian church was established in India long before the mid–sixth century. The presence of a strong community of Christians in the southwest of India (they later spread outwards from this original locus to be a strong evangelizing movement), with

many *Syrian* characteristics in its church life, suggests that Syria was indeed the ecclesiastical source (as it was with Ethiopia in parts of its early history), and thus a missionary outreach in the fourth to fifth centuries when that church was still at the height of its powers might be imagined. The Christian communities of India have a lively tradition of their own that they were founded by the apostle Thomas (Didymus), but the figure of that apostle, as a symbol of *Encratite* teaching, was already rooted in the ancient traditions of the Syrian church, and so the Thomas tradition may have come to India via Syria as well.

S. C. Neill, *The Story of the Christian Church in India and Pakistan* (Grand Rapids, 1970); idem, *The Beginnings to AD 1707* (vol. 1 of *History of Christianity in India*; Cambridge, 1984).

Ireland   Christianity may have come to Ireland before St. *Patrick* (some random archaeological Christian finds from the fourth century have been discovered), but it is with the mission of *Palladius* and then Patrick that the first recorded origins of the church can be dated. According to Prosper of Aquitaine (*Chronicle: for the year 431*), Pope Celestine sent one of his deacons to be a bishop "for the Irish believing in Christ." This suggests that an existing church was already there, probably based in the south of Ireland; but further knowledge of Palladius and his activity is lost in obscurity. The various *Lives of St. Patrick* (which are concerned with pushing Palladius aside) tell of his martyrdom or that he went back to Britain (though he had not come from Britain) and are generally not reliable for definite information. Nevertheless, as Palladius was one of the personal *deacons* of the pope, this Irish mission is not insignificant. The real apostle of Ireland, however, was indisputably Patrick. He was a British Christian who had been captured and enslaved by Irish pirates and made to work as a shepherd. He escaped and shortly afterwards entered the monastic life, finally returning to Ireland as a missionary bishop. His field of work was in the north of Ireland, and for more than thirty years he developed a dramatic and dangerous traveling mission among the pagan lords of the north. The churches that he founded all flourished and grew. He learned Irish and the many stories associated with him suggest that he attacked pagan *magic* head-on with thaumaturgal acts that outdid the Irish shamans. His mission was attacked by British clergy who thought he had infringed their rights and in response he produced his famed *Confessions* to justify his apostolate. His *Letter to Coroticus*, the British king, bravely threatened the Christian warlord with *excommunication* for having enslaved Irish Christians during a raid (*see slavery*). Both writings are the earliest known documents written in Ireland, and they present a vivid picture of a courageous man, filled with a sense of his apostolic destiny. After Patrick there is a paucity of historical sources until the late sixth century, when a series of monastic saints (Columba, Brigid, Brendan, and Columbanus) demonstrate the highly *ascetical* and penitential character of the Irish church, which remained characteristic of it until modern times. During the seventh century there was considerable internal conflict in the Irish church between the conservators (who wished to retain the Celtic characteristics of their church) and the "innovators" (who wanted to adopt liturgical and institutional forms that brought Ireland into line with Roman traditions). The controversies led to the formation of numerous small colleges, and were responsible for the rise of the reputation of Irish church leaders as among the most learned in Europe. The tensions were generally settled at the end of the seventh century when the Romanists succeeding in having the Roman computation of Easter adopted generally; and the Celtic party succeeding in retaining the monastic

organization of churches rather than a metropolitan system of bishops as elsewhere. Only after the ninth century did cities play a part in Irish church organization. In the sixth and seventh centuries Irish scholars (rooted equally in the Celtic spirit and in the forms of Latin literature) wandered far and wide in Gaul and Germany and Italy, taking their literary and artistic skills with them. Writers such as Sedulius Scotus (*Scotus* being the original Latin form for "Irishman") took the Celtic influence into the heart of the Carolingian domain. The Irish writers of the patristic period were chiefly important as transcribers of manuscripts, and made numerous copies of the Scriptures as well as preserving the works of the Latin Fathers for western Europe in a period when the infrastructure of the Western Roman Empire had effectively collapsed. Irish Christian poetry is one of the jewels of early medieval literature.

D. O. Croinin, *Early Medieval Ireland: 400–1200* (London, 1995); J. F. Kenny, *Ecclesiastical* (vol. 1 of *The Sources for the Early History of Ireland*; Records of Civilisation 11;. New York, 1929, 1966); L. de Paor, *St. Patrick's World: The Christian Culture of Ireland's Apostolic Age* (London, 1993).

Irenaeus of Lyons (c. 135–200)   An important theologian from Smyrna (he tells us he had known *Polycarp*), Irenaeus studied at *Rome* before becoming a *presbyter* of the church at Lyons. In 177 the church sent him on a mediating mission to appeal to Pope Eleutherius for tolerance of the *Montanists* and while he was there persecution broke out at Lyons, claiming the life of Bishop Pothinus, whom Irenaeus succeeded on his return. In 190 he returned to Rome to plead with Pope *Victor* (189–198) on behalf of the Asia Minor bishops (*Quartodecimans*) who celebrated Easter at a different date from that being advocated as standard by Rome. A late tradition suggests he was martyred. Irenaeus is one of the major voices opposing the *gnostic Christologies* of his time. His apologia established patterns of thought and administration that became constitutive for later *catholic orthodoxy*. He is an interesting theologian who influenced *Origen* and the later Alexandrian tradition in significant ways. His major work is the five-volume tractate *Against Heresies* (*Adversus haereses*). Here he reviews gnostic theological systems, especially that of *Valentinus*, which he seems to know best. Until the Nag Hammadi discoveries of several of the original gnostic treatises in the mid–twentieth century, Irenaeus was one of the most comprehensive sources for knowledge of Christian *Gnosticism*. Discovery of some of the originals shows that while he was a hostile witness and frequently a distortive quoter (as were almost all the ancients), his characterization of the gnostic systems was not inaccurate. His hostility to gnosis was expressed in the mind-set of a benign pastoral authoritarian. He does not wish to set up an alternative "orthodox gnosis" in the way *Clement of Alexandria* and Origen later dealt with the issue, but he seeks to apply "commonsense rules" to prevent his community from being led astray by teachers whose popularity clearly threatened the administration of the early Christian bishops and their status as authoritative theologians. To this end Irenaeus emphasized the unity of God and his profound involvement with the material order as the dynamic principle of salvation. The One God is the good maker of heaven and earth. The initial clauses of the creeds were probably formed at this same era to refute the fundamental gnostic premise of the difference between the "Father" of Christ, and the wicked demiurgic god of this material cosmos (the god gnostics saw in the Old Testament). Irenaeus affirms the sacramentality of the world axiomatically in his thought and sets out a theory, based on Paul, of the *recapitulation* (*anakephalaiosis*) of human destiny in the *person* (and body) of Christ. As Christ sums up the whole cosmos in his divine and human person, so mankind is liberated from *sin* and *death*, and restored to a divine destiny. His system is a major *patristic* elaboration of the theology of *deification* (*theosis*), which will be so important later. Irenaeus's cosmology becomes seamlessly integrated with his soteriology. Such is his primary, and most impressive, argument against gnostic dissidents. He also used as many other antignostic arguments as he could muster. Chief among them were a ridiculing of their ideas of multileveled cosmic mediation. Like many ancient rhetors he pressed the implications of his opponents' positions until they yielded nonsense, for which he then berated them. Irenaeus believed that the intellectual heritage of the Jesus tradition was best protected by the authority of the bishop, and to this end he greatly developed on *Ignatius's* ideas of monarchical episcopate. For Irenaeus, the bishop is the linear didactic successor of the apostles and the embodiment of the direct continuing tradition of a simple *apostolic* faith (as distinct from sophisticated gnostic esoteric doctrines that innovate). The *tradition* of apostolic Christianity, deriving immediately from Jesus' teachings, is demonstrated in the Scriptures (he asserts the fundamental unity of the Old and New Testaments, and their constant Christ-orientation) and also in the traditional practices (especially *creeds* and liturgies) of the church, all of which make up a Rule of Faith (*Regula Fidei*). It is this Rule that can be used to test bishops (to demonstrate their harmonious fidelity and mutual consonance), as well as the variety of gnostic professors (who contradict the tradition and diverge from one another). Irenaeus is a major figure developing the idea of the Scriptures as a normative theology of consonance, and insists that they are a closed *canon*, thus ruling out the many gnostic Apocrypha that were being produced. In the early twentieth century a lost work of his was discovered in *Armenian* translation, the *Demonstration of the Apostolic*

Preaching. It is a book that relates the Old Testament texts to the coming of Christ. Once more, acting as a major apologia against the gnostic separation of the Testaments, it also serves as a handbook to be used in the instruction of *catechumens.*

J. Lawson, *The Biblical Theology of St. Irenaeus* (London, 1948); J. T. Nielsen, *Adam and Christ in the Theology of Irenaeus of Lyons* (Assen, 1968); G. Wingren, *Man and the Incarnation: A Study in the Biblical Theology of Irenaeus* (Edinburgh, 1959).

Isaac of Nineveh (seventh century) Isaac was a monk of the Chaldean church from Beit Quatraye, possibly Qatar on the Persian Gulf. He was appointed bishop of Nineveh sometime before 680, but after a few months in the position resigned his charge and returned to the solitary life. In later life he became blind from his scholarly labors. His spiritual authority and the beauty of his writings on *prayer* and mystical experience made his works cherished by both the rival *Monophysite* and *Nestorian* factions of the Persian church of his time. In the ninth century they were translated from the Syriac into Greek and Arabic versions and came to Byzantium shortly after, where they had a large impact on the developing hesychastic spiritual theology. Isaac lays great stress on the sensibility of the grace of God in the heart (see also *Macarius the Great II*), and is one of the most mature and gentle authors on the spiritual life from Christian antiquity. In recent years lost works have been rediscovered, and by virtue of new English translations he is once again becoming known as one of the great masters of early Christian spirituality.

D. Miller, trans., *The Ascetical Homilies of St. Isaac the Syrian* (Boston, 1984).

Jacob Baradeus (c. 500–578)   Jacob "the Ragged" (from the traveling dis-guise of a beggar that he used to avoid detection by the imperial police) was an important missionary bishop, strongly anti-Chalcedonian, who, by his indefatigable travels and organization of resistance communities, set the *Monophysite* movement on its way to permanent establishment in *Syria.* His name was later attached, by their opponents, to the anti-Chalcedonian churches, which were known for a time as "Jacobite." He was the son of a *priest,* became a monk at Nisibis, and in 527 went on a delegation to seek for tolerance of the anti-Chalcedonians at the court of *Justinian.* There he received the patronage of the empress Theodora. He spent fifteen years at the capital before becoming (without imperial consent) the bishop of Edessa in 542. From this vantage point he energetically consecrated bishops and numerous priests from his own anti-Chalcedonian party, in as many vacant sees as he could. His *christological* position is essentially that of *Severus of Antioch.*

E. W. Brooks, trans., *John of Ephesus: Lives of the Eastern Saints* (PO 18; 1924), 690–97; (PO 19; 1926), 153–58.

Jacob of Serugh (c. 450–520)   Jacob was one of the greatest of the Syriac theologians, and one of the last teachers from the final period of independence in the *Syrian* church, when it was still dynamically related to the Syro-Hellenistic cultural medium. He came from the district of Serugh near Edessa, and became a priest there. He was a prolific poet and earned the title of "Flute of the Spirit." Jacob was a strong follower of *Cyril of Alexandria's Christology* in a church that was torn apart by the crisis initiated at the *Council of Ephesus I* (431), and exacerbated by what his party saw as the "betrayal" forced on the churches at the *Council of Chalcedon* (451). He was a disciple and friend of *Severus of Antioch* and like him was a moderate force in trying to bring the so-called *Mono-*

physite party to an alignment with Cyrilline (not *Eutychian*) thought. He was consecrated a bishop in 519, just before his death. He was famed as a vivid poet in his lifetime and his sermons are classic examples of the *memre*—the Syriac rhythmic (metrical) sermon. *Romanos the Melodist* (another Syrian) is a classic example of this form as it was transmitted in Greek to Byzantium and thereafter became the substrate of the Byzantine *kontakion* (liturgical hymn). Jacob, however, authored masterpieces of literature only extant in Syriac (736 *memresa* are attributed to him in the textual *tradition*), and thus suffered the same fate of obscurity as his native language in the subsequent affairs of the church. Only today are his poems and sermons beginning to be translated. He is a treasure largely still locked in a chest.

R. C. Chesnut, *Three Monophysite Christologies* (Oxford, 1976).

Jerome (c. 347–420)   One of the most argumentative *ascetics* of the fourth century, Jerome was perhaps the most important biblical scholar of the early Western church. He was born in the town of Stridon on the Dalmatian border of the empire, and studied Latin grammar before coming to *Rome* around 360 to study rhetoric with Aelius Donatus, one of the leading *littérateurs* of the day. Here he polished his brilliant Latin style. In 366 Jerome converted to Christianity and, after staying for a while in Trier, moved in the company of friends including Rufinus to Aquileia, where he adopted the ascetic lifestyle. About 372 he decided to live as a hermit in the East, and so he advanced his study of Greek at *Antioch* before moving to the *desert* of Chalcis in Syria for about five years, where he also learned Hebrew. Bishop Paulinus (*see Meletian Schism*) ordained him *priest* at Antioch but he is never known to have exercised that office, and his alliance with Paulinus won him many enemies. It was in Antioch at this period that he heard the lectures of *Apollinaris,* and had a famous dream in which Christ denounced him for being "a Ciceronian not a Christian," a psychic warning he took seriously, turning his attention to theology and biblical interpretation as the main focal points of his restless energies thereafter. He came to *Constantinople* with Paulinus and *Epiphanius* for the Council of 381, and there listened to *Gregory of Nazianzus* and *Gregory of Nyssa,* whom he admired. Traveling to Rome to secure Pope *Damasus's* assistance for Paulinus's claims, Jerome stayed on and acted as private secretary to the pope between 382 and 385. In this period Damasus gave him the commission to prepare a good Latin version of the Gospels from the Greek, a project that eventually grew into the Vulgate, an attempt to make a fluent and accurate translation of all the Bible to replace the rather crude *Itala* or Old Latin versions that had been in use beforehand. During his time in the capital Jerome attracted a group of wealthy ladies to his side, acting as spiritual father to them. They included Marcella, Paula, and her daughter Eustochium, who subsequently became his patronesses. After Damasus's death, the Roman *clergy* (among whom he was generally unpopular) actively encouraged him to leave, and he returned to Antioch, visiting Egypt and eventually settling at Bethlehem, in the episcopal domain of John of *Jerusalem.* He had antagonistic relations with John, barely acknowledging the latter's ecclesiastical rights. At Bethlehem, with Paula, he founded a double monastery of men and women. But John's attachment to Origenian ideas allied the bishop more to *Melania* and Rufinus (who had themselves established a monastery on the Mount of Olives), and from this time onward Jerome's friendship with Rufinus turned to bitter resentment. From having been a devoted Origenian scholar and translator himself, Jerome began to denounce *Origen* as a baneful influence (while still continuing to use vast amounts of unacknowledged exegetical material). Throughout the 390s Jerome sought and gained the support of the Roman and Alexandrian churches to offset his enemies in Antioch and Jerusalem. He was a most touchy character, but not unsuccessful in his political trafficking. Toward the end of his life he had a cautious encounter with **Augustine**, whom he seems to have gruffly admired (they shared a hostility toward **Pelagianism**). His greatest work is the translation of many sections of the Bible into elegant Latin, using Hebrew and Greek skills that were in his day almost unheard-of in Western ecclesiastical writers. He anticipated the Hebraic *canon* (as later advocated by the Reformers). He had made a thorough study of all the earlier Latin theologians, although his own scholarly gifts lay elsewhere than in the creative application of a synthesis. He was passionately **Nicene**, passionately pro-Western, and unfailing in his advocacy of an ascetical and scholarly lifestyle. His translations of **Origen** ensured the survival of important materials after the latter's condemnation by the Fifth Ecumenical **Council of Constantinople** (553), and he more or less established Origen's influence over most of later Western *exegesis* (despite his own public U-turn over his former hero). Jerome spent years producing biblical commentaries, especially on Genesis, the prophets, Psalms (the latter preserves Origen's lost *Selecta in Psalmos*), Matthew, Mark, as well as Revelation and select Pauline letters. His reputation as exegete is overstressed in the Western church (at least if we look for originality) but served to establish canons of good style and (Origenian) subtlety in much subsequent Latin exegesis that looked to him as a model. Jerome deliberately sought to continue the historical work of **Eusebius of Caesarea** with a most important handbook: *On Outstanding Men* (*De viris illustribus*), which gives important details of Christian writers up to his day (culminating in himself). His apologetic works against individuals often lacked moderation and charity. In later life he wrote several treatises in praise of ascetical virginity in which he disparaged sexuality and marriage in a pessimistic and extremist fashion (*Against Helvidius* and *Against Jovinian*), thus setting a precedent that cast a gloom over subsequent centuries of Christian (clerical) attitudes (*see* **sexual ethics**). His numerous surviving letters show him to be a brilliant, witty (and extremely prickly) correspondent.

J. N. D. Kelly, *Jerome: His Life, Writings, and Controversies* (London, 1975); H. F. D. Sparks, "Jerome as Biblical Scholar," in P. R. Ackroyd and C. F. Evans, eds., *The Cambridge History of the Bible* (vol. 1; Cambridge, 1970), 510–41.

Jerusalem Jerusalem has always been regarded as the "mother church" of Christianity, although it has never been significant at all (other than as a pilgrimage destination) except for two periods. The first was in the apostolic age when the "pillars of the church," Peter, James, and John, were based there, and later James the brother of Jesus was the leader of the Jerusalem Christians. The second was from the fourth to sixth centuries, when the church functioned as a center of liturgical and monastic life that came to a wide notice because of the pilgrimage traffic. The story of the conflict between James's vision of a church where the stress on observance of the law was high and that of Paul where a vision of a universal mission to the Gentiles predominated is sketched out in the Pauline Letters as well as in Acts of the Apostles. It was Paul's argument that won the day, not simply because of his forceful personality and the pressures of the expansion of Christianity into Gentile communities, but also because the war armies of Rome devastated Jerusalem in A.D. 70 and destroyed the temple. Overnight, from being the veritable center of Jewish liturgy and doctrine for a **Judaism** built around a highly organized priesthood, Jerusalem became a small provincial town, with no more independent revenues flowing into it from the temple tax, and hardly any population left on site. In the time of Hadrian a last desperate revolt from Jewish Zealots was crushed with implacable Roman determination and at that time, in 135, Hadrian decided to refound the city under the name of Aelia Capitolina. He issued a decree banishing all Jews from the city. Jewish Christians were still known to be located in the Decapolis, Transjordanian region, but what remained of the Jerusalem church was then purely a Gentile phenomenon. Tradition has it that in order to defile the site of Jesus' tomb the Romans built a temple to Aphrodite over it. Only after the empress Helena's visit to the Holy Land in 326 did Jerusalem begin to revive again. Her endowment of the church there encouraged its flourishing as a center for Christian pilgrimage. The stories of the finding of the True *Cross*, as well as numerous other relics of the apostles and martyrs that went on apace for the next century, marked a strong connection between the energetic building that was going on here and the people of *Constantinople* and *Alexandria*, who were increasingly eager to see the holy sites associated with Jesus. Both capitals had lively sea routes to the Holy Land, and the splendid Constantinian Church of the Anastasis (now known as Holy Sepulchre) functioned as a great center of liturgical ceremony that soon was being copied all over the Christian world. In the time of *Origen*, the church had a scholarly bishop, Alexander, who had studied at Alexandria and had inaugurated a library at Jerusalem for the advancement of Christian studies. But for all the period up to the *Council of Chalcedon* in 451, Jerusalem was a dependent church attached to Caesarea, which was the real intellectual center of affairs. One of its priests, later to become the bishop, *Cyril of Jerusalem,* has left a remarkable series of liturgical sermons that show how the church by the fourth century had become famed for its ritual ceremony. During the *Arian* crisis the Jerusalem *baptismal creed* was often used as a "standard of orthodoxy" in the conciliar attempts to settle the dispute. In the fifth century Juvenal of Jerusalem lobbied for the church to become a patriarchate at the Council of Chalcedon, but it was a titular honor in the main. That century saw the remarkable rise of Palestinian monasticism, as exemplified in the lives of Euthymius and Sabas, whose achievements are chronicled by *Cyril of Scythopolis*. In Palestine the new form of lavriotic monasticism (a family of small eremitical communities along a valley) became popular. Increasing border raids as the Byzantines lost control of the Holy Land and the rise of Islamic power in the seventh century led to the long eclipsing of Jerusalem once more, although it remained a constant source of attention as a pilgrimage center, and the Byzantine emperors regularly negotiated safe passage for Christian visitors in the age before the Crusades.

E. D. Hunt, *Holy Land Pilgrimages in the Later Roman Empire, AD 312–460* (Oxford, 1982); R. L. Wilken, *The Land Called Holy: Palestine in Christian History and Thought* (New Haven, 1992).

John Cassian (c. 360–433)   John Cassian was a Scythian (Romanian) by birth whose travels finally brought him to the West, where he established important monasteries and had a foundational influence on the theology of *ascetical* experience. He came as a young man to adopt the monastic life at Bethlehem. Shortly after he moved to Egypt to study asceticism there, and was deeply influenced by *Evagrius*, whose thought he moderated and disseminated through his own writings. In 404 he was at Constantinople and served as a *deacon* to *John Chrysostom*, who sent him on a mission to Pope Innocent I. Here he met and became friends with *Leo*, who would later become pope himself. John seems to have settled in the West after this point, founding two monasteries at Marseilles in 415. It was for these communities he wrote his most famous two books, *The Institutes*, which describe the eight chief vices that hinder monks, and where he dictates the regimen (food, dress, times of *prayer*) that directs a monk's lifestyle; and also *The Conferences*, which relate the many conversations he had with monastic elders in the East. Both works had a deep impact on monasticism as it was beginning to expand in the Western church. His *Institutes* in particular affected the form of many Western monastic rules, and were adapted as a substructure by the Benedictine family. John had a typical Greek dislike for *Augustine's* ideas on grace, and in *Conferences* 13, he attacked his ideas by presenting the teaching of John Chrysostom (so earning the designation semi-Pelagian in the Western church afterward, though in the Eastern church he is regarded as a saint). In the course of the lead-up to the *Council of Ephesus* in 430, Pope Celestine asked Cassian for an official adjudication on the doctrine of *Nestorius*, and so he made a study of *incarnational* theology that eventually issued in his *Seven Books on the Incarnation of the Lord*.

C. Luibheid, *John Cassian: The Conferences* (CWS; New York, 1985); P. Munz, "John Cassian," JEH 9 (1960): 1–22; P. Rousseau, *Ascetics, Authority, and the Church in the Age of Jerome and Cassian* (Oxford, 1978).

John Chrysostom (c. 345–407)   His name means John "Golden Mouth," in honor of the brilliant oratory and pure style of the many sermons he delivered while archbishop of *Constantinople*. His works were so highly valued by the Eastern churches that they were canonized as paradigms of homiletic. He was equally influential over the West, where his high ethical tone made him a model moralist and social reformer. John was a native of *Antioch* and son of a civil ser-

vant in the administration of the military governor of the Syrian province. His mother, Anthusa, was widowed at twenty but secured the highest level of education for her son, who probably studied under Libanius, the greatest sophist of the age. He studied theology with *Diodore*, the great Syrian biblical theologian, and was baptized in 368, after which he began a course of scriptural study with *Meletius*, the bishop. In all his subsequent writing he represents the Antiochene school at its zenith, moderating those polarities that would later bring that tradition into crisis in the fifth-century *christological* controversies. In 371 he was ordained lector, and spent some time in seclusion with an aged monk. From 373 to 381 he returned home in poor health, and lived with his mother as a monastic recluse. In 381 he was ordained *deacon* by Flavian, the newly appointed archbishop of Antioch, and then priest in 386, when he was given the charge of preaching regularly in the cathedral. His sermons on the scriptural passages he interpreted during this period are both extensive and of the highest quality. He uses his Syrian exegetical training to make a close connection with the historical and contextual meaning of the narrative, and highlights the moral significance of the text without elaborate allegorism or speculation. For this reason he has been much appreciated by modern readers (*see exegesis*). In 387 after a riot in Antioch had destroyed statues of the emperor, threatening to bring down destructive military punishment on the city, John delivered a series of passionate appeals for clemency (*Homilies on the Statues*), and his reputation was established. In 398 he was chosen by the emperor Arcadius to replace Nektarios as archbishop of Constantinople, and he determined to reform his city church as soon as possible. His ascetical and severe attitude alienated many of the court and *clergy*, and especially the empress Eudoxia, who took personally his remarks about the venality of the vacuous rich, who would not lift a finger to help the poor. She began to hound John and press for his dismissal. *Theophilus of Alexandria* saw his opportunity to assert dominance over the capital when John gave shelter to the *Tall Brothers*, the monks whom Theophilus had censured and exiled from Egypt because of their Origenism. Theophilus came to Constantinople and, at the Synod of the Oak at Chalcedon in 403, he tried and deposed John for canonical irregularities. The royal court, conscious of John's growing popularity with the ordinary people of the capital, endorsed the sentence and exiled him for a short time, presuming that this would be enough to ensure his future behavior. As soon as he was recalled he renewed his reform program with even greater zeal, earning the bitter enmity of the empress. He was exiled again, on the specious grounds that he had resumed his see after synodical condemnation and without canonical authorization. International appeals from Rome were to no avail. Sent back at first to Antioch, his punishment was increased by a second enforced winter march to the Black Sea, which had the intended effect of hastening his death. John's fame rests on his reputation as a fearless martyr bishop, who saw his task as the defense of the poor against the depredations of the rich. He is also believed to have instituted liturgical reforms, which later caused the attribution of the Constantinopolitan form of the eucharistic liturgy (demonstrating Syrian origins) to be attributed to him. This liturgy is now the standard rite of the Orthodox churches and both as liturgical doctor and preacher John has become one of the central *patristic* authorities. In Antioch he engaged in a polemic to stop local Christians from attending Jewish religious festivals (apparently a common practice), and his language is often harsh. In later times, applied in different contexts, it provided a dangerous paradigm for anti-Semitic rhetoric among Christians (*see* **Judaism**). Historically he is of immense importance for ensuring the enduring impact of the Syrian theological tradition on developing Byzantium. His manuscript tradition became a ready depository over the centuries for numerous works not by him, not least several sermons by *Nestorius* (on the high priesthood of Jesus).

C. Baur, *John Chrysostom and His Times* (2 vols.; London, 1960); J. N. D. Kelly, *Golden Mouth: The Story of John Chrysostom: Ascetic, Preacher, Bishop* (Ithaca, N.Y., 1995); M. Lawrenz, *The Christology of John Chrysostom* (Lewiston, N.Y., 1996); J. H. W. G. Liebeschuetz, *Barbarians and Bishops: Army, Church, and State in the Reign of Arcadius and Chrysostom* (Oxford, 1990); R. L. Wilken, *John Chrysostom and the Jews: Rhetoric and Reality in the Late Fourth Century* (Berkeley, Calif., 1983).

John Climacus (c. 575–c. 650)

John of *Sinai* (where he lived most of his life), or John "of the Ladder" (*Klimakos*), takes his name from his most famous book: *The Ladder of Divine Ascent*. It was a work summating the desert tradition in its late golden age, and became a standard manual for the direction of Eastern monastics. In 591, aged sixteen, John came to Sinai from an unknown origin and attached himself as a novice to Abba Martyrius. When he was about twenty years of age his elder died and John continued living alone as a cave hermit more or less for the next forty years. His growing fame as a wise counselor attracted disciples, but some members of the neighboring Sinai monastery also voiced criticism, which he answered by returning to complete solitude. Soon after, he was elected as the new superior of the Sinai monastery and must have returned to the cenobitic motherhouse in about 635. In his final years he composed his practical manual of guidance for monks. It is a traditional collection, based on materials John had assembled over decades of monastic experience and teaching. He composed it on the eve of the devastation of Christian Egypt. His book is designed in thirty sections, the supposed steps of a ladder to heaven. The first twenty-three explain the vices that are dangerous for *ascetics*, and sections 24–30 interpret the virtues that ought to define a monk. John's teaching simplified the spirituality of the Gaza school, that of *Barsanuphius* and Dorotheus, and his synthesis would deeply influence Athonite monasticism and thus the Orthodox East to the present day. His work teaches that the simplification of *nature* (its quieting down into spiritual Hesychasm), which the monk required to advance his prayer, would be assisted by the constant repetition of a sentence concentrating the mind (for example, the name of Jesus, and its salvific power): so-called monologistic prayer. The great Christian tradition of the Jesus Prayer grew out of this.

D. Chitty, *The Desert a City* (Oxford, 1966), 170–75); C. Luibheid and N. Russell, trans., *John Climacus: The Ladder of Divine Ascent* (CWS; New York, 1982).

John Malalas (c. 490–575) His name signifies "the Rhetor." He is the author of a *Chronographia* in eighteen books, charting universal history from the creation to 563 (the years to 565, which were in the original, seem to have been lost). Written at *Constantinople*, nine books precede the incarnation and nine take up the story of the church. His *Chronographia* is a mixture of sources, some now lost, often unreliable in its own understanding of history, but important for information about the age of *Justinian* and especially affairs in *Antioch*, where he seems to have lived for a time.

E. and M. Jeffreys and R. Scott, trans., *The Chronicle of John Malalas: A Translation* (Melbourne, Australia, 1986).

John Moschus (c. 550–619 or 634) A monastic traveler and spiritual writer, John Moschus in 575 became an *ascetic* at the monastery of St. Theodosius near *Jerusalem,* and in 587 made a famous journey (in the company of his friend and disciple Sophronios, who later became patriarch of Jerusalem), traveling to see as many monastic institutions as he could (in Egypt, *Sinai, Syria,* Cyprus, and *Rome*). He edited his travelogue into a collection of tales about the monastic saints entitled *The Spiritual Meadow* (*Pratum Spiritale*). The stories were immensely popular in the Byzantine world.

N. H. Baynes, "The Pratum Spiritale," *OCP* 13 (1947) 404–14; repr. in idem., *Byzantine Studies* (London, 1955), 261–70; H. Chadwick, "John Moschus and His Friend Sophronius the Sophist," *JTS* n.s. 25 (1974): 41–74; J. Wortley, trans., *John Moschus: The Spiritual Meadow* (Kalamazoo, Mich., 1992).

John of Damascus (c. 655–750) John of Damascus (Yanan ibn Mansur) was a member of a high-ranking Christian family, and followed his father in holding office at the court of the Islamic caliph at Damascus, probably representing Christian affairs there. John resigned his post around 725, probably because of political pressures, and became a monk at Mar Saba monastery near Bethlehem, where he was ordained priest. During the first *iconoclastic* crisis under Emperor Leo (726–730) he wrote three *Discourses* in defense of the icons, which became standard works on image veneration. He was *anathematized* by the iconoclastic synod of 753, but Palestine was then out of the reach of the Byzantine court. The icon venerators (Iconodules), who were eventually victorious, hailed him as a heroic confessor at *Council of Nicaea II* in 787. His correlation of the theology of icon to *incarnational Christology* was a notable aspect of his apologia. John also began a systematic presentation of the patristic teachings on all aspects of faith. This became his most important work: *The Fountain of Knowl-*

edge. It has the hallmark of a scholastic compendium comprised of three parts: *On Philosophy, On Heresies,* and *On the Orthodox Faith.* The last section soon assumed the status of a one-volume authority on Orthodox theology, and also exerted a massive influence on the medieval Western church, not least because it was a primary source for Aquinas in his *Summa Theologiae.* John, who had extensive firsthand experience of Islam, categorizes it as a heretical deviation of Christianity, rather than a new religion (and as such a partner for potential religious dialogue). He also composed a collection of texts relating to the ascetical life, the *Sacra Parallela* (now preserved only in fragments). John's practice of *hymn*-writing (in company with his kinsman Cosmas the Melodist) set an example for liturgical writing in the East, and many are still used in the churches to this day.

D. Anderson, trans., *St. John of Damascus: On the Divine Images* (Crestwood, N.Y., 1980); J. A. McGuckin, *The Transfiguration of Christ in Scripture and Tradition* (Lewiston, N.Y., 1987); J. Nasrallah, *St. Jean de Damas: Son époque, sa vie, son oeuvre* (Paris, 1950); M. O'Rourke-Boyle, "Christ the Eikon in the Apologies for Holy Images of John of Damascus," *Greek Orthodox Theological Review* 15 (1970): 175–86; D. J. Sahas, *John of Damascus on Islam: The "Heresy of the Ishmaelites"* (Leiden, Netherlands, 1972); S. Salmond, trans., *St. John of Damascus: On the Orthodox Faith* (NPNF 2d ser., vol. 9; Grand Rapids, 1899); F. H. Chase, trans., *St. John of Damascus: The Fount of Knowledge* (Fathers of the Church 37; Washington, D.C., 1958).

John of Gaza   *see* **Barsanuphius and John**

Jovinian (d. c. 406)   Jovinian was a monk in Milan who, although dedicated to the monastic life, was alarmed at the manner in which the *ascetical* movement in the West was developing detrimental views on *marriage* and *sexuality.*

He wrote a book to argue that ascetics and married had an equal spiritual status in the church. He also expressed doubts (following the writer Helvidius) over the perpetual virginity of the Mother of God (*see* **Virgin Mary, Theotokos**). His views stirred up a veritable storm of protests from leading Western theologians such as **Ambrose** (who condemned him at the Synod of Milan in 393), **Augustine** (who wrote *The Good of Marriage* and *Holy Virginity* against him), **Pelagius**, and **Jerome** (*Against Jovinian*). Jerome's castigation of Jovinian was felt to be so extreme that it did not gain a good reception in **Rome**, but the protests nevertheless secured Jovinian's imperial exile and the burning of his book. **Gregory the Great,** later summarizing Augustine's views, ensured that the exact opposite view to Jovinian's (the superiority of the spiritual status of celibacy over married life) would triumph as standard orthodoxy in the Western church.

J. N. D. Kelly, *Jerome: His Life, Writings, and Controversies* (London, 1975), 180–87.

Judaism, the Church and   The relationship between Judaism and Christianity has been marked by such longstanding hostility from the earliest times that it is difficult, though important for many reasons (not least because of the many pogroms and persecutions that have historically been committed against the Jewish people in the name of Christian zeal), to find some historical balance that would show it was not always a "dangerous" hostility operating between the two, and that such a hostility is not a necessary part of interreligious relations. The very foundational documents of the church, its Gospels and Letters, demonstrate that a tension already existed between the "church" and the "synagogue." Jesus is depicted in the Gospels almost as if he were in constant tension with the Pharisees, whom he generally censured as hypocritical, and also in bitter dispute with the priests, whom he regarded as corrupt (and who eventually orchestrated his murder). There is no doubt that this represents some of the picture in relation to Jesus, but more acutely portrays a sharpening of apologetic between the nascent Christian movement of the mid– to late first century on the one hand and the deeply conservative guardians of Jewish Law on the other, against whom it felt it was having much friction in the course of its missionary expansion. Many of Jesus' teachings, such as on *resurrection*, on *grace*, on angels, and on inner purity, were far more resonant of Pharisaic doctrine than they were opposed to it. If Jesus is often depicted as a pugnacious foe to the Pharisees, it is because he too adopted common rabbinic forms of theologizing, heavily based in the exchange of controversial propositions. This form of ancient argumentation appears much more hostile in the written record than on many occasions it actually was: comparable perhaps to witnessing a dialectical debate between Buddhist monks in a dharma school, where the outside observer often thinks that the exchange may come to blows at any moment, though in fact the vigorous exchange of dialectic is orchestrated in such a manner as a matter of course. This is not to say there were no points of disagreement between Jesus and the other schools of contemporary Judaism of his day, for indeed there were, but it makes a very crucial distinction that these conflicts cannot be elevated as a clash between Christianity and Judaism per se. Even in the apostolic generation, when we see Paul's mission having many points of friction with Jewish authorities in *Jerusalem* and the Diaspora synagogues, it is still not true to say these represent anything more than local apologetic problems. Paul had as many issues with the "Jewish Christians" of James's circle in Jerusalem, but this was not to say Paul was any less a "Jewish Christian" himself. To make him a paradigm of Gentile Christianity just as James was of Judeo-Christianity is simply to falsify the record in the light of the later increased separation of rabbinic Judaism and post–second century predominantly Gentile Christianity in the Hellenistic towns. For the first three formative centuries of early Christianity, the Christians (increasingly witnessing a Gentile membership who did not observe all the legal commands, or observed them in a thoroughly reinterpreted way) lived and moved in a hellenized city culture that immersed them in the communities of the other "God-fearing ones" whom they recognized: the Jews and the monotheists of ethical lifestyles (such as the sects of Hypsistarians in Cappadocia). This was especially true in areas where Christians and Jews lived in very close proximity, in significantly large community groups, such as in *Rome, Alexandria, Antioch,* and Asia Minor (all places where the foundational fabric of Christian theology was fashioned). *Aphrahat* the Persian and *Melito of Sardis* give us examples of theologians who are simultaneously in an argument with Jewish sages, yet who also demonstrate profound points of contiguity. Well into the third century the Christian clergy had to insist that their flocks should stop observing Jewish feasts and prayers alongside Christian rites, a series of prohibitions (such as found in *Origen of Alexandria*) that only has relevance if it is presumed to have been a common occurrence. The same complaint that the community of Christians eagerly observes Jewish religious feasts is found in *John Chrysostom*, and in *Cyril of Alexandria* in the fifth century. Both patristic theologians have several passages of harsh polemic against the Jews, using bitter language about the Jewish people's "betrayal" of Christ, that would become common in medieval Christianity, even entering its liturgical tradition and forming a mentality of hardened opposition that was all the more dangerous because the world of Hellenistic city life, where the Christian and Jewish communities were cheek by jowl together, soon passed away into memory. In the Byzantine era, or in the cities of the Latin world, it increasingly became the case that the Gentile church knew less and less about the religious life of its Jewish neighbors, and increasingly was content to substitute its own narrow apologetic for any real exchange of views. The regular pressures put on Jewish communities in the Byzantine era by emperors who demanded conformity made the Jewish journey "eastwards," to Baghdad or Damascus, more and more appealing. In the early Christian era, the strongest Jewish communities were in Rome, Syria, Palestine, and Egypt. What was a common cultural environment in the second century became a climate of ignorance on the part of the church, where the old intra-Jewish scriptural apologias were sharpened out of context into dangerous new absolutes. One example is the use of the regular criticisms of the *Iudaeoi* in the Fourth Gospel. Here the evangelist has harsh words to say about the Judeans who rejected Christ. His immediate context is that of a time when missionaries of his community appear to have been ejected from the synagogue. It may well reflect the period in the late first century and early second when Judaism was beginning to organize itself on rabbinical lines after the debacle of the Roman conquest. Yet, the evangelist who attacks the *Iudaeoi* so robustly is himself outraged because of the exclusion from the synagogue of those who confess Jesus (a context manifested in the narrative of John 5), and he spends much time in his Gospel arguing that Jesus is the fulfillment of the liturgical and spiritual life of Israel, by no means its termination, or "obsolescence." This too is a point strongly maintained by Paul, who, for all his theology of Jesus as the fulfilled hope of Israel who now liberates from excessive attachment to the old prescripts, still does not advocate a doctrine of the "supersession" of Israel by the church (cf. Rom. 11:1–32). The community of the

Fourth Gospel appears to have been vested in Samaria, as perhaps illustrated by the missionary narrative in John 4, and it was hostile to the temple cult in Jerusalem (cf. Acts 7, which narrates the death of Stephen, one of the leaders of this "Hellenist" school). To forget this obvious context of why the bitter apologia is present, and to render the "Judeans" of the Fourth Gospel simply into "Jews" for the new contexts of a universalized Christianity of the Byzantine era, was a root cause of fostering an identity on Judaism as "the other," an intellectual and social movement that soon degenerated into the "oppressed other." So, while the *patristic* writings up to the fifth century, however hostile they might have been in their rhetoric, were not exactly "anti-Jewish," in the sense that their sharpness can more or less always be explained on the basis of two large communities grinding against one another locally, they nevertheless laid down a basis that soon developed into anti-Jewish sentiment in a later age when scriptural texts and patristic rhetoric was increasingly absolutized out of its historical context and original milieu. The many accounts of Jewish hostility to the first wave of nomadic Christian missionaries that penetrated the synagogues of Asia Minor took on another resonance among Christians as the tale entered the canon of Scripture as the book of the Acts of the Apostles, and was elevated to an "archetypal" religious significance. Some of the most hostile of the early Christian-Jewish material was designed for the "war of converts" that was going on between the two communities. Among Jewish circles at least one slanderous biography of Jesus was composed to offset the attractions of the church. It survives in basic form in the medieval *Sepher Toledoth Yeshu*. Melito of Sardis (d. 190) was equally concerned to show potential converts from Judaism that Christian liturgy preserved the best of all that was in Jewish tradition (*On the Pascha*), but now expressed in a more universally appropriate form. Melito was actually writing to encourage a Christian community that was numerically and socially much inferior to the Jewish community. This general apologetic, that Judaism had been gentilized and internationalized as the destined mission of Israel to the world, was a powerful factor in drawing converts to the church, and was met with equal force in arguments that focused on the "illegitimacy" of Christianity's forms of interpretation. An outline of such an exchange can be discerned in the remarkable notes the Greek-Samaritan *Justin Martyr* kept and used to write up his *Dialogue with Trypho*, which records his apologetic exchange with a Jewish thinker in the first half of the second century. Justin (*Dialogue with Trypho* 16.4) incidentally notes that the Tannaitic "tightening up" of Judaism in his day had introduced an anti-Christian curse in the synagogue service. This argument, about church as an "internationalized" form of the covenant, was at its highest pitch intellectually in the time of **Origen** at Caesarea, from the mid–third century onward, where he worked very close to the important rabbinic academy. Origen's apologia sharpened matters considerably by setting out a vast scheme of biblical *exegesis* that would soon dominate all forms of Christian thinking. In it he elaborates very strongly the notion of the "shadowy time" of the "Old Testament," which had now given way to the clear light of the New (*see* **allegory**). After his time supersessionism (the argument that the arrival of the church has rendered all of Judaism obsolete) became more and more common a way of approaching the problematic relation of the two religious systems from the Christian standpoint. Christians of the fourth century found themselves favored by the imperial power, and little time passed before conciliar enactments, now given force in Roman law (*see* **councils**), began to demand a greater social and legal separation between the two religious communities. In the sixth-

century Code of Justinian the social disabilities lifted up against the Jewish communities of the empire began to be added to with political and financial disabilities. Novella 146 even intervened in an internal Jewish dispute to demand that those practices be followed as authoritative in Jewish services and doctrines which most closely resembled Christian practice. It was the beginning of a long decline in relations that the advent of a new religious force, the aggressively rising star of Islam, did nothing to alleviate. Even so, the regular production of apologetic texts between the two communities, especially the number of treatises *Against the Jews* that were written in Byzantine and early medieval times, testifies to the long continuation of a strange mutual attitude of attraction as well as repulsion: for such texts would certainly not have been so passionately written (with laborious proof texts from Scripture, as well as demonstrations that the church is the universal expansion of the Old Israel), or composed in such numbers, if the communities had been indifferent intellectually and religiously to one another. Once the original Hellenistic context of close proximity could no longer be presupposed, that is, after the fifth century, what was once a robustly apologetic exchange was set more and more on the road to become the seeds of anti-Jewish xenophobia.

S. Krauss, "The Jews in the Works of the Church Fathers," JQR 5 (1893): 122–57; N. de Lange, *Origen and the Jews: Studies in Jewish-Christian Relations in 3rd Century Palestine* (Cambridge, 1976); J. Neusner, *Aphrahat and Judaism: The Christian-Jewish Argument in 4th Century Iran* (Leiden, Netherlands, 1971); idem, *Judaism and Christianity in the Age of Constantine* (Chicago, 1987); J. Parkes, *The Conflict of the Church and the Synagogue: A Study in the Origins of Anti-Semitism* (New York, 1974); A. F. Segal, *Two Powers in Heaven: Early Rabbinic Reports about Christianity and Gnosticism* (Leiden, 1977); M. Simon, *Verus Israel: A Study of the Relations*

Between Christians and Jews in the Roman
Empire (135–425) (Oxford, 1986); R. L. Wilken, John Chrysostom and the Jews: Rhetoric
and Reality in the Late 4th Century (Berkeley, Calif., 1983); A. L. Williams, Adversus
Judaeos: A Bird's Eye View of Christian
Apologiae Until the Renaissance (Cambridge, 1935).

Judgment The concept of God's
judgment of the world, and of the individual *soul*, holding both accountable
for individual sins against the divine
code of mercy, and for collective trans-
gressions against the divine principle of
order and destiny meant for the cosmos,
is a concept that permeates the entire
New Testament as well as the *patristic*
writings on matters of ethics and *eschatology*. To make judgment the sharp
point of a theological perspective, and its
inner dynamic, was a religious vision
first seen in the biblical writers (as in the
words of Ps. 58:11: "surely there is a God
who judges on earth") and most acutely
in the classical prophets (cf. Isa. 30:18),
who raised Israel's consciousness of collective and corporate sin by their passionate preaching for justice on every
level—a justice that would be based
within the divine call for covenant
mercy, but would be vindicated by
divine vengeance if that code was
ignored. Part of that prophetic message,
and clearly seen in Isaiah and Jeremiah,
for example, took the invasions of Israel
by foreign armies as a clear sign of the
divine correction that had been called
forth by Israel's sins (Isa. 1:4–9; Jer. 4:6).
In the immediate centuries before the
birth of Christianity, the *apocalyptic*
movement took the concept of divine
judgment to a particular new pitch
of intensity. The classical apocalyptic
schema of theology had the seer taken in
rapture by God to a part of the heavenly
court where times past, present, and to
come were revealed to him. The overarching theme of the seer's cosmic visions
was generally that of the increasing hostility of the nations of the earth, harrying

the elect nation Israel and constantly
frustrating God's plan to establish it as
the kingdom of God on earth, where the
kingdom values would be nurtured in
the observance of the covenantal code.
In the apocalyptic genre (it can be witnessed scripturally throughout the book
of Daniel, and in the New Testament
book of Revelation, which is written in
the same form) the crushing of the
earthly foes of God is part of the divine
judgment that is predicted and called
upon as a hope for the *saints* on earth, as
their vindication and relief (*see persecutions*). The New Testament writings in
their turn witness both the prophetic
and apocalyptic senses of a theology of
judgment, but also testify to a newly
sharpened sense of individual Judgment, where the souls of all men are destined to be judged by God in accordance
with their individual record of good or
evil on earth (Matt. 12:36–37; cf. Heb. 6:2;
9:27). The later New Testament texts also
attribute the Judgment to the Son (cf.
John 5:22, 27; 9:39) as a specific part of his
exaltation glory. He would especially
return in glory to exercise that cosmic
judgment at the *Parousia* at the end
of time (Matt. 25:31–46). This third
aspect of Judgment became increasingly
marked in patristic writing, and envisaged as a matter of postdeath scrutiny by
the angels of God, and before the judgment seat of Christ, which then determined the place of the soul in the
afterlife, either in Hades (*see hell*) or in
paradise. In this "Last Judgment" the
individual and collective senses were
still retained, a notion that led in later
times to the distinctions of the "general"
and "particular" Judgment, which was
also refined into a Christian concept that
the immediate after-death judgment of
an individual soul would give way, at
the last day, to a general judgment
of mankind, when the definitive judgment of God would be effected. Most
of the earliest patristic writers repeated
the biblical doctrine of judgment without much addition (1 Clement 16; 28;
Ignatius, To the Ephesians 16.2; idem, To

Polycarp 2; *To the Philippians* 2; ibid. 7; *Didache* 16; *Shepherd of Hermas*, *Vision* 3.8.9; 4.3; ibid., *Similitude* 9.18.2; 9.27.3). Many later patristic writers, however, also developed a lively sense that is equally witnessed in the Psalms and other early writings of Israel, that God would also express his judgment on the wicked in the present life. So, the sins of an individual or a nation could call down the divine displeasure. In Christian writers this judgment of God was most commonly seen in terms of sickness, natural disasters, or defeats by enemy forces. A classical example of the patristic theological response to this can be seen in *Gregory of Nazianzus*'s *Oration on His Father's Silence in the Time of Famine* (*Oration* 16), where he establishes a Christian perspective on the "mercy" of divine judgment in the light of the biblical tradition before him and expounds with great sensitivity on the manner of interpreting difficulties of life in a manner that balances a sense of repentant openness to divine correction with an unwavering hope in a perennially philanthropic divine providence and mercy.

J. A. Baird, *The Justice of God in the Teaching of Jesus* (London, 1963); S. G. F. Brandon, *The Judgment of the Dead: An Historical and Comparative Study of the Idea of a Post-Mortem Judgment in the Major Religions* (London, 1967); E. Schüssler Fiorenza, *The Book of Revelation: Justice and Judgment* (Philadelphia, 1985); J. G. Griffiths, *The Divine Verdict: A Study of Divine Judgement in the Ancient Religions* (Leiden, Netherlands, 1991).

Julian of Eclanum (c. 386–454)   He was the son of an Italian bishop, and married to a bishop's daughter. His father's circle was in friendly relations with *Paulinus of Nola* and *Augustine*. After his *ordination* as a *deacon* in 408, Augustine wrote to him inviting him to visit. In 416 he was consecrated as bishop of Eclanum in Apulia. Julian was alarmed at the hostility which Pelagius

had attracted for his simple moral message, and refused to accede to Pope Zosimus's synodical condemnation of the monk in 417, for which cause he was deposed from his see and banished. He spent the rest of his life traveling, attempting to secure a fair hearing for his case. He spent time with *Theodore of Mopsuestia*, and from 429 with *Nestorius of Constantinople* (the presence of Julian as a guest at the capital was one of the reasons *Cyril of Alexandria* secured the whole-hearted support of Pope Celestine when in 430 he began to attack Nestorius's *Christology*). Julian's case was reviewed at the *Council of Ephesus I* (431) and he was again condemned. It is thought that he ended his life teaching rhetoric in Sicily. Julian found much in the *Syrian* theology that resonated with his own thought, and tried to make the case that this, and not the *North African* theology represented by Augustine, was a more truly Latin tradition. He deeply distrusted Augustine's theological style, seeing it as puritanical, and (with the possible exceptions of *John Cassian* and Faustus of Riez) his was the only authoritative voice of the Western church that questioned the wisdom of the triumph of Augustinianism. Julian thought the pessimism manifested in Augustine's view of human nature was a residue of his *Manichean* past, and wholly agreed with *Pelagius* that human nature was a graced reality and not corrupted by sin at its source. But Julian was a better theologian by far than Pelagius. He especially disliked Augustine's theory of original sin transmitted through sexual concupiscence, which he felt was untraditional, a denigration of the beauty of human sexuality, and elaborated mainly in defense of the unnecessary practice of infant *baptism*. His works that have survived (composed in the period 418–426) are 4 *Books to Turbantius* and 8 *Books to Florus*. Sections of his writings also appear in the refutations Augustine made of them. He is thought to be the translator of the Latin version of Theodore's *Commentary on the Psalms*.

P. Brown, "Sexuality and Society in the 5th century AD: Augustine and Julian of Eclanum," in E. Gabba, ed., *Tria Corda: Scritti in onore di A. Momigliano* (Athenaeum I Como; 1983), 49–70; A. E. McGrath, "Divine Justice and Divine Equity in the Controversy Between Augustine and Julian of Eclanum," DR 101 (1983): 312–19.

Justinian (482–565) Flavius Petrus Sabbatius Justinianus was one of the most powerful of the Byzantine emperors, and his reign marked a revival of the Roman imperium after long years of decline. He studied law and theology before his elevation to power, patronized by his uncle Justin, a military commander who assumed the throne after the death of Anastasius in 518. He directed policy in his uncle's administration, already conscious of the need to bring internal unity to eastern provinces racked by *christological* dissensions resulting from the *Council of Chalcedon (Monophysitism)*. He married Theodora, a noted actress, who became a skilled partner in his rule (they are depicted in a famous mosaic in Ravenna). In 527 he succeeded to the throne. In 537 the Nika revolt fomented by aristocrats almost brought his life to an end, but his wife's coolheadedness brought about his victory. The widespread damage to the capital in the aftermath inaugurated Justinian's major building campaign. He had already constructed the magnificent church of Sts. Sergius and Bacchus, but now he amplified his ambitions to produce the greatest church in the world, the magnificent St. Sophia, whose denuded condition today still evokes wonder. This had a dynamic effect of making the eyes of the whole Christian world turn toward *Constantinople* and its *art*, liturgy, and theology for many centuries to come. Having concluded a peace settlement with Persia, Justinian was able to turn his attention to the western territories long lost to *Arian* German tribes. His western wars were to last over twenty years: *North Africa* was reclaimed from Vandals in 534; Italy from Ostrogoths in 555; Spain from Visigoths in 555. The ancient boundaries of Roman imperium were almost restored but the cost of overextension was too great and the restoration did not last, and perhaps even served to diminish the idea of a single Romano-Christian polity for the future. Justinian inaugurated a major review of Roman law that, in 529 (again in 534), was issued as the Codex Justinianus. A collection of *Digests* was issued in 533 along with the *Institutes*. All three collections became the *Corpus of Civil Law*, which was to have determinative effect on later European (and Islamic) civil law as well as on the church's canon law in both East and West. Justinian was the most proactive of the Christian emperors in terms of regulating church life. He was not just a guardian but a prosecutor of *orthodoxy*, summoning *councils* as well as deposing bishops and popes where necessary. He was deeply opposed to the Origenist monks, though not much successful in suppressing *Origen's* influence despite his orchestration of a posthumous synodical condemnation of 543. His chief ecclesiastical policy was aimed at the reconciliation of the Monophysite schism, and so he tried to moderate the authority of Chalcedon, without alienating *Rome*, by making *Cyril of Alexandria's* authority preeminent once more. The *Council of Constantinople II* in 553 was his design, and issued severe condemnations of the *Syrian* theologians Cyril had fought against a century before (*see* **Three Chapters Controversy**). In the long term it did not so much reconcile as serve to mark the differences in tone and character between the Syrian church (soon to leave the Byzantine political orbit), the *Alexandrian* and *Ethiopian* churches (who denounced Chalcedon and did not find Constantinople II to be sufficiently radical), and the Byzantine and Roman churches, which held to Chalcedon in significantly different styles. Justinian actively suppressed paganism with legal penalties. He closed the last School of Athens in 529, and suppressed Samaritan and Jewish worship in Palestine. He commissioned the missionary bishop John of Ephesus to organize mass-conversion expeditions among the pagans of Asia Minor, and reports of 70,000 baptisms were recorded. His empire, especially Constantinople, was set back severely on two occasions by the appearance of bubonic plague. Estimates of upwards of 20 percent population loss have been advanced, a factor that set in process the resumption of the slow decline of the Eastern Empire after his death.

G. P. Baker, *Justinian* (New York, 1931); R. Browning, *Justinian and Theodora* (New York, 1971); G. Downey, *Constantinople in the Age of Justinian* (Norman, Okla., 1964); J. Meyendorff, *Imperial Unity and Christian Divisions* (New York, 1989), ch. 7; K. P. Wesche, *On the Person of Christ: The Christology of the Emperor Justinian* (New York, 1991).

Justin Martyr (d. c. 165)   One of the leading *Apologists*, Justin Martyr was a highly important source for the life, theology, and worship of the church in the second century. Justin was a Palestinian from Nablus. He seems to have been a pagan who made a restless tour of the various philosophical schools (*Stoics, Peripatetics, Pythagoreans*, and *Platonists*) until as a mature adult, in about 132, he discovered the teachings of the Christians through an encounter with an old sage, and thereafter became a fervent convert. He had been deeply impressed by the courage he had seen from Christians who held to their philosophy despite any threat to their lives. He records how the old sage showed him the meaning of the Old Testament texts and their fulfillment in the life and teachings of Jesus. Justin describes the experience in words reminiscent of the disciples on the road to Emmaus:

"Immediately a fire was kindled in my heart . . . and I embraced Christianity as the only safe and wholesome philosophy" (*Dialogue with Trypho* 8). He habitually wore the traditional cloak of a philosopher and began to teach Christianity as a way of life, alongside the other itinerant sages typically found in the *agora* of the ancient Hellenistic cities. Justin moved to Ephesus around 135 and engaged in debate with a Jewish teacher named Trypho. He then traveled on to open a school at *Rome,* where *Tatian* was one of his pupils. He taught during the reign of Antoninus Pius (138–161), publishing the *First Apology* (c. 155) to make a case for the defense of Christians being persecuted by unjust laws. At the same time he published his Ephesian debate as *A Dialogue with Trypho the Jew*. Soon after Marcus Aurelius assumed power (161), Justin issued a *Second Apology* addressed to the senate of Rome. One of his philosophical rivals, the Cynic Crescens, denounced him to the authorities along with several of his students. When they refused to offer sacrifice they were scourged and beheaded. The record of their trial was taken down by eyewitnesses, and still survives. Justin is one of the most interesting of the Christian Apologists. He refuted the usual charges made against the Christians (immorality, seditious intent, hatred of humanity), but also set out to show to open-minded hearers the essential character of the new movement. He describes the church as the community of those devoted to the *Logos,* or reason of God. The creative Logos had put a germinative seed of truth (*Logos Spermatikos*) in all hearts, and in the person of Jesus, had *incarnated* within history to reconcile all lovers of the truth in a single school of divine sophistry. For Justin, Christianity is the summation and fulfillment of all human searching for truth. Christians are monotheists, and believe that the Logos is God, in second place to the supreme God. His *Dialogue with Trypho* was important in establishing a view of the Christian Gentiles as the

New Israel. The Old Testament is used in a thoroughly christocentric way. His *First Apology* is one of the earliest and most authoritative accounts of the primitive Christian liturgies of *baptism* and *Eucharist*.

L. W. Barnard, *Justin Martyr: His Life and Thought* (Cambridge, 1967); H. Chadwick, *Early Christian Thought and the Classical Tradition* (Oxford, 1966), 1–30; E. R. Goodenough, *The Theology of Justin Martyr* (Jena, Germany, 1923); R. Holte, "Logos Spermatikos: Christianity and Ancient Philosophy According to St. Justin's Apologies," ST 12 (1958): 109–68; D. Trakatellis, *The Pre-Existence of Christ in Justin Martyr* (Missoula, Mont., 1976).

Juvenal *see* **Jerusalem**

Kenosis The Greek term . means "emptying out." In older textbooks it is referred to by its Latin translation as "exaninition." It derives from the *christological hymn* in Philippians 2:5–11, especially verse 7a, which says Christ "emptied himself, taking the form of a slave." In christological thought, especially in the great controversies of the early fifth century, it was used by such theologians as *Cyril of Alexandria* to connote the manner in which the divine *Logos* was able to assume all the conditions of human nature while retaining his full divinity coterminously. To the criticism that this concept made his ideas of the Word's assumption of humanity "artificial" (for example, if the Logos knew he was immortal by nature, the prospect of death would not "really" have been so terrifying as it seems to have been to Christ in the garden of Gethsemane), Cyril answered that the assumption of the human *nature* implied the complete adoption and embracing of all the corresponding qualities, limitations, and proper characteristics of that human nature (sin only excepted—which Cyril insisted was not

proper to humanity anyway), and this meant such experiences as confusion, fear, and sorrow. Since these were not necessarily proper to humanity per se, the experiencing of such things by the divine Logos was a freely chosen implication of his assumption of the human nature, and was effected by the Word's special "self-emptying" in compassionate solidarity with the human race.

J. A. McGuckin, *St. Cyril of Alexandria and the Christological Controversy* (Leiden, Netherlands, 1987), 221–22.

Kerygma In Hellenistic Greek the word meant simply a message or an announcement. In the New Testament it emerged as one of the key terms of the Christian movement, signifying the "proclamation," the essential content as well as the act of proclaiming the saving gospel. Jesus and John the Baptist are regularly described as proclaiming (*kerussein*) their message to the people, a verb that contextually carries the force of a divine imperative. The Pauline literature begins to specify the fundamental structure of the kerygmatic proclamation, the first lineaments of what will subsequently emerge as the *creeds*. Peter and Paul are depicted, in several instances, delivering outline versions of the ancient kerygma (Peter: Acts 2:14–36, 38–39; 3:12–26; 4:8–12; 10:34–43; Paul: Acts 13:16–41). In all these cases the proclamation of the *death* and *resurrection* of Jesus is rendered as synonymous with the "good news" of salvation. There are also more mystical accounts of the kerygma in other parts of the New Testament (Phil. 2:6–11; Col. 1:15–20; 1 Cor. 8:6; 2 Cor. 8:9; Rom. 10:6–9; Heb. 1:2–4), which poetically depict the historical ministry of Jesus within the wider cosmic arc of divine condescension and exaltation. A distinction was made (seemingly from the time of the earliest apostolic missions) between hearing the kerygma and being saved by it (as in 1 Cor. 1:21; 2:4), and between the ongoing need for *didache* (teaching), which would be continued in the day-to-day life of the church. In the *apostolic* age kerygma was used to signify the totality of the "Christ mystery" (Shepherd of Hermas, *Similitude* 8.3). Hermas also refers to *baptism* as the "seal of the kerygma" (*Similitude* 9.16). In his argument with the *gnostics*, *Irenaeus* began to attempt a more concise description of the kerygma, and approached it as "apostolic doctrine" concerning the twofold fundamentals of Christian faith; first, the doctrine of God as Father, Son, and *Holy Spirit*, and second, the concept of the *economy* of *salvation* (subdivided into the human birth, passion, and death of Jesus, the resurrection, ascension, *Parousia, anakephalaiosis* of all things, the resurrection of the human race, and the ultimate *Judgment* of all) (Irenaeus, *Haer.* 1.10.1). From the time of *Origen* onward, the concept of kerygma is partly divided in *patristic* literature. One theological track develops the notion of the "content," focusing on the concept of the rule of faith and extrapolating the *creeds* especially in times of crisis. The other crucial aspect of kerygma as the proclamation of life through the saving economy of the death and resurrection is more extensively developed in the *christological* and spiritual writers. *Athanasius* in the fourth century made a remarkable attempt, in his *De incarnatione*, to explain to a new intellectual environment the kerygmatic implications of the incarnation, death, and resurrection of Jesus. His treatise was twinned with a preceding work in which he denounced the idolatry of paganism (*Contra gentes*), which suggests that the ancient pattern of kerygmatic proclamation as the church's basic structure of (prebaptismal) missionary preaching was still more or less intact. After "demonic cult" had been assailed (*see exorcism*), the fundamentals of the Jesus proclamation were delivered (*kerygma*), and then those who had been "marked for salvation" came forward to receive the moral and doctrinal instruction that would induct them into the church (*didache*). The fourth-century

bishop is probably doing it much as the apostolic missionaries of the late first century did.

_____

C. H. Dodd, *The Apostolic Preaching and its Development* (London, 1936); J. I. H. McDonald, *Kerygma and Didache: The Articulation and Structure of the Earliest Christian Message* (Cambridge, 1980).

Lactantius (c. 250–325)　　Lucius Caecilius Firmianus was a leading though late *apologist* and one of the earliest Latin writers to attempt a systematic exposition of the Christian faith in his *Divine Institutes.* He was a native *North African,* who was summoned as court rhetor and professor of Latin to Nicomedia by the emperor Diocletian. It was probably here that he first encountered, and possibly taught, the young *Constantine,* whose adviser he later became. In the *persecution* of 303 he resigned his post and soon left the city. He ended his days at the imperial court in Trier, as tutor to the Caesar Crispus. Throughout the *Institutes* and his other works (especially the *Poem on the Phoenix*) Lactantius shows a lively interest in hermetic mysticism, which he thinks is a sign of natural *revelation* being brought to a fulfillment in Christ. His open religiosity is very akin to that of the early Constantine. Lactantius poses the thesis that the ancient world was frustrated in its civilized progress because its religion was divorced from wisdom and its wisdom traditions were hostile to religion. The adherents of the common cults were uninformed polytheists and the adherents of the schools were religious relativists. He describes Christ, the incarnate wisdom of God, as the high priest who is simultaneously the true philosophical teacher of the world, and he advances the Christian movement as the exemplification of a new society that is religiously humane and that finds its *philosophy* in a cult of wisdom that gives social unity and direction under the aegis of justice. His antipagan apologia was the most sustained, and reasoned, of all the early Latin writers (with the possible exception of *Tertullian*). The date of Lactantius's conversion has been much discussed. His knowledge of Christianity and his wide citation of Scriptures and other hermetic literature suggest someone who knew Christianity intimately from an early stage. His theology, however, is archaic for someone writing on the eve of the *Council of Nicaea.* He was a *chiliast,* presents an angel *Christology,* and was a Binitarian in his doctrine of God. He evidences no interest at all in liturgical or other common matters witnessed in other contemporary writers except insofar as they are transmuted into his vision of a new universalized religion that will gather in all nations to a philosophical cult of the divine Wisdom. For this reason he returns again and again to the primacy of a theology of justice. His accounts of the persecutions (*The Deaths of the Persecutors*) and the era in which the church was rising to ascendancy make him one of the most important historical sources of the early fourth century. His account of Constantine's "dream" before the battle of the Milvian bridge became immensely famous in Christian literature, and his style was always highly admired among the Latins. The Renaissance divines later called him the Christian Cicero.

M. F. McDonald, *Lactantius: The Divine Institutes* (Fathers of the Church 49; Washington, D.C., 1964); idem, *Lactantius: The Minor Works* (Fathers of the Church 54; Washington, D.C., 1965); J. A. McGuckin, "The Non-Cyprianic Scripture Texts in Lactantius' Divine Institutes," VC 36 (1982): 145–63; idem, "Spirit Christology: Lactantius and His Sources," *Heythrop Journal* 24 (1983): 141–48; idem, "Lactantius as Theologian: An Angelic Christology on the Eve of Nicaea," *Rivista di Storia e Letteratura Religiosa,* 22, 3 (1986): 492–97.

Leo the Great (fl. 440–461)   Leo was one of the most capable bishops of *Rome* in the fifth century. Very little is known

of his life before his election to the *papacy,* except that he was a *deacon* assisting the administration of his two predecessors (Celestine and Xystus III). He was closely involved in the *christological* crisis concerning the *Council of Ephesus I* (431) and commissioned his friend *John Cassian* to make a close study of the issues involved in the dispute between *Cyril of Alexandria* and *Nestorius.* The preparation made Leo an important and direct contributor to the christological crisis as it renewed itself again at the *Councils of Ephesus II* (449) and *Chalcedon* (451), where his intervention was highly significant. His energetic regulation of the Roman church immensely increased the prestige of the papacy, and Leo set down ideas that were to have a major development in future centuries, for he saw the preeminence of his see as being based in the Scriptures, and so set the Roman *theologoumenon* of the primacy of Peter's Vicar on its way to being a determinative idea of Western Catholicism. He secured from Emperor Valentinian III a rescript that formally acknowledged his jurisdiction over all Western provinces, and he greatly increased the papacy's political weight by persuading the invading Huns to withdraw beyond the Danube and by making a settlement with the Vandals, who captured Rome in 455. The Eastern patriarchs remained, as usual, unconvinced of the Roman ideas on primacy, but Leo was soon drawn very decisively into Eastern Christian affairs when he was appealed to by Flavian of Constantinople, who had condemned the Christology of the monk *Eutyches* and called down the fury of the church of *Alexandria* on his head. Leo's delegates to the Council of Ephesus (449) were completely ignored by *Dioscorus,* who presided there, and who was shocked by the dossier Leo sent (*The Tome of Leo*) setting out a standard two-nature christological settlement, drawn up from classical statements of venerable Latin theologians such as *Tertullian* and *Augustine.* Leo was determined to have this document at the center of the agenda for the subsequent Council of Chalcedon in 451, and although the bishops assembled there found it disturbingly different from the Cyrilline theology they had adopted at Ephesus 431, they were pressured to accept it reluctantly. From that point onward Western theologians usually interpreted the significance of Chalcedon as a triumph of *Leo's Tome*, whereas Eastern writers more or less disregarded the *Tome*, seeing its acceptance only as a subsidiary affirmation of Cyril of Alexandria's thought. The difference came out once again at the *Council of Constantinople II* (553). Leo's Christology is perhaps more mechanical and bipolar than that of Cyril, which stresses more the mystical unity of the divine Christ incarnated in a new mode of humanity, whereas Leo sees *natures* as legal properties inhabited by *persons.* But his traditional Latin schema set out in simple terms of one person (divine) and two natures (one human and one divine) a Christology that could be easily transmitted in catechesis. Meant, perhaps, as a settlement of the controversy, the Leonine elements in Chalcedon initiated centuries of further conflict, resulting in ecumenical division in the Eastern churches that to this day are not healed.

Henry Bettenson, trans., *The Later Christian Fathers: A Selection from the Writings of the Fathers from St. Cyril of Jerusalem to St. Leo the Great* (London, 1970); T. G. Jalland, *The Life and Times of St. Leo the Great* (London, 1941); W. Ullmann, "Leo I and the Theme of Papal Primacy," JTS n.s. 11 (1960): 25–51.

Leontius of Byzantium (d. c. 543)

Leontius was a monastic theologian (probably the same as the Leontius mentioned as an Origenist in *Cyril of Scythopolis's Life of St. Sabas*) who strongly defended the *Christology* of the *Council of Chalcedon* (451) against both *Nestorian* and *Monophysite* opponents. He

was sent c. 531 to *Constantinople* on a mission from his Palestinian monastery, and represented the Chalcedonian monks of the Holy Land at synods in the capital in 532 and 536 (though some see the Leontius present at the latter meeting as a different person). Leontius occupied an interesting median position in the christological argument, at first interpreting the Two Natures doctrine of Chalcedon by means of the theological works of *Diodore of Tarsus* and *Theodore of Mopsuestia,* though he abandoned this attempt as it became clear that these theologians would never be the basis of an international consensus. He resisted the increasing attempt to suppress Origenism in the monasteries, seeing in the anti-Origenists evidence of a dangerous tendency in the church to suppress intellectualism. Two important works, *Against the Monophysites* and *Against Nestorius*, have been attributed by some scholars to (a different) Leontius of Jerusalem. Some scholars think he may be the author of the treatise *Against the Frauds of the Apollinarists.* The *Apollinarists* were circulating "One Nature" christological writings under the names of ancient orthodox Fathers. If he is the author of that exposé, he was a skilled literary analyst.

B. E. Daley, *Leontius of Byzantium: A Critical Edition of His Works, with Prolegomena* (D. Phil. diss., Oxford University, 1978); idem, "The Origenism of Leontius of Byzantium," JTS n.s. 27 (1976): 333–69; idem, "A Richer Union: Leontius of Byzantium and the Relationship of the Human and Divine in Christ," SP 24 (1993): 239–65; D. B. Evans, *Leontius of Byzantium: An Origenist Christology* (Washington, D.C., 1970).

Liturgy

The word derives from the pre-Christian Greek term for public works (*leitourgia*), which could connote civic good deeds, political service, or the formal recognition of a divinity's benefactions. It had already been adopted into biblical usage by the Septuagint translators to designate the (civic) worship of God in the Hebraic state cult, and thus it made its appearance in the New Testament writings to reflect the sense of the service of Christ (Heb. 8:6), or of Christians one for another (Phil. 2:30), or the ministry of church leaders (Acts 13:2; cf. *Didache* 15.1), or the heavenly worship conducted by the angels (Heb. 1:14). *Clement of Rome* is the first *patristic* writer to use the term to contrast the cultic practices of the Old Testament with the worship services that characterize the church (*1 Clement* 40–41; 44). *Hippolytus* defined a Christian minister as one who has been *ordained* for the service of the Church's *leitourgia*, and it is this meaning, liturgy as public worship, that soon gained the predominance. The Latin equivalents were ministry, or divine office (*ministerium, officium, munus*). To this day the Latin church includes the divine office (services of psalms for the hours of the day) in its broad conception of liturgy, whereas the Eastern church restricts the meaning of the word to the *sacramental* rites of the church, most particularly the "divine liturgy," that is, the *eucharistic* service. Christian liturgy in this sense of the development of specific worship services has a complex and very profound history. It was hardly ever controversial, very different from the history of doctrinal matters, and because of that liturgical history progressed in quiet incremental style over the centuries. The great rites of the Christians developed in stages: first the rituals of Eucharist and *baptism*, then other sacramental rites, and finally the services of monastic prayer that turned into the "divine office," services of psalmody and intercessory prayers that marked off the hours of the day. By the ninth century the generic shape of all the liturgies of the ancient Christian churches were more or less formed, and had an immense staying power, as liturgical change was usually very slow after that point. There were times of lively development in the patristic era, and this is particularly true of the fourth and fifth centuries, so much so that most of the ancient Roman rite and the current liturgies of the Byzantine and Oriental churches are still profoundly steeped in patristic thought forms, theological imagery, and language.

Christian liturgy began with the adoption of the Jewish practice of morning and evening *prayer* (Mark 1:35; 6:46; Luke 10:17). The rites of baptism and Eucharist were also quickly adopted internationally (though their precise protohistory is still shrouded with obscurity because of paucity of textual information). In both cases the intellectual foundations for the ritual acts was provided in the New Testament apostolic writings. Other sacramental rites (such as *marriage* or ordination) also found their inspiration in Jesus' acts (such as the wedding at Cana or the selection of the apostles), but in such cases the symbolic "start" provided in the New Testament archetypes really had to be filled out quite extensively by patristic reflection on the nature of the mysteries. So, for example, the ordination rituals took some time to take a definitive shape, although they were universally based around the New Testament pattern of the "laying on of hands." A fuller form of ordination rite can be found in the *Apostolic Tradition* (2–3; 7–8; and the version as practiced east of the Jordan in the second century can be seen in the Clementine Epistles, *Hom.* 3.60–72). It was not until the early fourth century that marriages were considered something that should be brought before the bishop to bless in the name of the church. The rituals of crowning (in the East) and veiling (in the West) were civil practices the church simply adopted and adapted. The book of Revelation and the Letter to the Hebrews are two early and important texts that demonstrate how extensively a cultic, or liturgical, spirituality had already permeated the Christian imagination. The principle enunciated in both these texts, that the events of the liturgy in heaven are mirrored by the heavenly liturgy of the church on earth, was formative on Christian liturgical theology. By the end of the second century, the church's eye was set on the liturgical books of the Old Testament, and it increasingly took the temple rituals as a form of archetypal instruction, even though there was always a lively awareness of the differences between Christian "spiritual" worship on the one hand (by which they meant moral awareness and the "offering" of prayer) and the notion of physical sacrifice on the other hand (a common enough experience not only in Judaism but throughout antiquity). Christian aversion to physical sacrifices marked off the church distinctively from the earliest times, but incense and prayer offerings were given notable stress, particularly in the early *Syrian* church. The origins of Christian liturgy seem to derive from the custom of meeting for Eucharist on the first day (Sunday) of each week (Acts 20:7–11; *Didache* 14.1). *Justin Martyr* is the first patristic witness to give an account of such a Sunday eucharistic service (*First Apology* 65; 67). Other accounts of the pre-Nicene liturgy can be found in several other places (*Apostolic Tradition* 4; *Didache* 9–10; *Anaphora of Addai and Mari*; *Anaphora of St. Mark*). The pattern of the Eucharist from the fourth century onward is more widely attested, with many more specifically "liturgical treatises" being composed, such as *Cyril of Jerusalem's Catechetical Lectures*, which sets out to explain to neophytes the rites of their new faith. There is also an early–fourth century bishop's altar book that survives in the form of Serapion of Thmuis's *Euchologion*. It seems to be the case that early eucharistic prayers, and other formularies probably, were composed by the presiding bishop, only becoming more fixed as they were written down later. The third and fourth centuries witness more and more legislation restricting the principle of spontaneous composition of liturgical prayers. The eucharistic rites as they were celebrated

in Syria had a special impact on Eastern forms of liturgy, and can be seen (in developed form) in the liturgies still commonly used in the Eastern world: of *Basil the Great,* and the Liturgy of Saint *John Chrysostom.* There were numerous "families of liturgies," and much modern scholarship has been concerned with drawing out the relationships between them all, both Eastern and Western. The main divisions can be listed as the liturgical traditions of *Alexandria* (Coptic); *Jerusalem* and *Antioch* (Eastern and Western Syrian respectively); Cappadocia (*Armenian*); and *Constantinople* (Byzantine)—the last one predominating in the long period when the city was a world capital, and synthesizing many of the other Eastern forms. In the West, the main liturgical path of development was more coherent, less varied, but local traditions are certainly noticeable in the churches of *Rome,* Milan, Spain, Gaul, *North Africa,* and the Celtic western islands. The annual cycle of Christian feasts took some time to establish. It began with the observance of Pascha (Easter). It is first noticed in Asia Minor (Melito's *Peri Pascha* gives much information) and from there spread internationally very quickly so that by the middle of the second century it was a universal aspect of Christian observance. The *Epistle of the Apostles* (135–140) gives a very early account and attributes the feast to a divine commandment. Early paschal festivals were based around an all-night vigil during which extensive scriptural readings demonstrated the link between the exodus experience and the Christian Passover of Jesus' death and glory. A Eucharist celebrated at daylight on the Sunday of Pascha inaugurated fifty days of rejoicing afterwards. Some communities wished to celebrate not on the Saturday-Sunday, but on the 14th of the month of Nisan (April) in memory of the Lord's day of execution. This caused a crisis in many communities as the Roman church, under Pope *Victor,* exercised its influence to suppress the practice in the interest of common observance (the **Quartodecimans** controversy). By the late fourth century the basic shape of a "liturgical year" was in evidence, namely, a Pascha preceded by forty days of Lenten observances and followed by feasts celebrating Ascension and Pentecost. In the fourth century the East followed Western practice in observing Christmas on December 25, and the West in turn took on the feast of Epiphany from the Eastern church. Christmas was soon preceded by another smaller Lent, called Advent, and the last element to be added was the cycle of great feasts of the Lord and the Virgin, and the multitude of martyrs' festivals and other saints' festivals. The practices of the Jerusalem church were widely copied from the fourth century onward. The forms of early baptismal ritual are witnessed in *Didache* 7.1–2; Justin Martyr, *First Apology* 61; Hippolytus, *The Apostolic Tradition* 15–21. The fourth-century fathers also extended their comment on baptismal practice quite extensively and several catechetical lecture series (those of **Cyril of Jerusalem, Theodore of Mopsuestia, Ambrose of Milan**) describe the ritual, with many liturgical sermons also preserved (including some fine examples from **Gregory of Nazianzus,** John Chrysostom, and **Augustine**). The fundamental rites were preliminary exorcisms, immersion (affusion was allowed only for emergencies but later became standard in the West) three times in the name of the triune God, with anointings (oil and *chrism*) to symbolize the laying off of *sin* and the reception of the "seal of the Spirit." Only in Syria did the chrismation precede the baptism itself.

P. Bradshaw, *The Search for the Origins of Christian Worship* (Oxford, 2002); T. Carroll and T. Halton, *Liturgical Practice in the Fathers* (Wilmington, Del., 1988); L. Deiss, *Early Sources of the Liturgy* (London, 1967); C. Jones, G. Wainwright, and E. Yarnold, eds., *The Study of Liturgy* (Oxford, 1978); J. A. Jungmann, *The Early Liturgy to the Time of Gregory the Great* (Notre Dame, Ind., 1959); H. J. Schulz, *The Byzantine Liturgy* (New York, 1986); J. S. Srawley, *The Early History of the Liturgy* (Cambridge, 1947); R. Taft, *The Byzantine Rite: A Short History* (Collegeville, Minn., 1992).

Logos Theology

Logos Theology Logos theology is a modern term to designate the development of a school of early *christological* thought that stood in opposition to *Monarchianism*. It was developed by the later *Apologists*, especially *Theophilus, Athenagoras, Justin,* and *Tertullian,* and came to a fuller development in the third century with *Hippolytus, Clement of Alexandria,* and *Origen.* After Origen the schema of Logos theology entered so profoundly into the mainstream that it formed the substrate of all christological and *Trinitarian* thought thereafter. It takes it point of origin from the (very few) references in the Fourth Gospel prologue to the Logos of God, which was "with God in the beginning" (John 1:1) and which "became flesh and dwelt amongst us" (John 1:14). The connection of the idea of Logos (reason, inherent structure, creative pattern, or spoken word) with the biblical tradition of the Word of God (cf. Isa. 55:11), particularly that word, as uttered throughout the Wisdom literature, for the ordering of the cosmos in wisdom and grace struck the early *patristic* writers as a highly useful term of reconciliation between the Greek philosophical traditions of cosmogony and the biblical understanding of God as personal creator. The Stoics had already applied the term "Logos" to connote the principles of divine order within the cycles of cosmic generation. In applying the concept of Logos to denote God's wise energy in creation, through his Word, and finally (in the last times) through that Word as manifested in the life and teachings of Jesus, the Apologists made every effort to communicate the Christian message to contemporary culture. It was the first serious attempt of Christian theologians to universalize the gospel for the Greeks, and to explain how the life and teachings and death of a human teacher, Jesus, could be a matter of supreme moment simultaneously to the history and to the destiny of the universe. In its potential range, covering matters of fundamental interest to *Stoicism* and *Platonism* (the creative demiurge of the *Timaeus* was soon absorbed into the range of the Christian meaning of Logos), it was a brilliant conception; and as it developed it was clear that it was more than a simple hellenization of the gospel truth (as Harnack had once complained) because the driving force of the program of reconciliation of languages was always its biblical inspiration. In the process of adapting the biblical concept of the word, the Christians synthesized the notions of the divine Word (Logos) and Wisdom (Sophia) (cf. Ps. 33:6–9; Prov. 8:22; 9:1–2). Before the third century, within the church at large, possibly one could say within the church as it spoke to itself (in distinction to the work of the Apologists, who elaborated a message for communication on a wider front), not everyone was enamored of the Logos scheme. Often a simpler, less coherent, and biblically based pattern of language was used. Phrases from Scripture were applied as the substrate of the earliest forms of prayer to God, and the supreme image of the unique and single Father with his obedient Son predominated. By the time of the third century the sophisticated advances of Christology based on the Wisdom literature and Logos terminology (already prefigured in the christological hymns of the late Pauline texts of Colossians and Ephesians) made such earlier simplicity seem archaic. Increasingly, traditionalists who resisted Logos theology were pressed to explain how the Son of God was a "son" in the times before his historical birth, when embodiment could not apply. It was the genius of the Logos scheme to be able to connect the eternal (immanent) life of God with the *economy* of salvation, and its utility in the apologetic domain gave

it a double advantage. By the late third century Monarchianism had increasingly given way to a deepening sense of the *hypostatic* (personally subsistent) reality of the Logos, and soon of the *Holy Spirit* too. The implications of the development of third-century Logos theology (rooted substantially in the concept of the Word's role in the creation and redemption of the cosmos) came to a pitch in the fourth century when the *Arian* crisis questioned its fundamental premises. Emerging victoriously from that crucible of theological debate, Logos theology went on to be increasingly refined in the form of the conciliar Christology of the fourth century, and it reached its apex in the formal doctrine of the *Trinity* of three hypostases in the single deity, when the last vestiges of the inherent "*subordinationist*" presuppositions of the schema were finally eradicated.

A. Heron, "Logos, Image, Son: Some Models and Paradigms in Early Christology," in R. McKinney, ed., *Creation, Christ, and Culture* (Edinburgh, 1976), 43–62; W. Kelber, *Die Logoslehre von Heraklit bis Origenes* (Stuttgart, Germany, 1976); D. C. Trakatellis, *The Pre-Existence of Christ in Justin Martyr* (Missoula, Mont., 1976); H. A. Wolfson, *The Philosophy of the Church Fathers* (Cambridge, 1964).

Lord's Prayer The Lord's Prayer (Greek: *Proseuche Kyriake*) is the *prayer* Jesus taught his disciples (Matt. 6:9–13; Luke 11:2–4), otherwise known as the Pater Noster or Our Father, from its opening invocation. The prayer exists in two forms in the New Testament; that of Luke shows signs of adaptation for use by a Gentile congregation. The Greek forms are evidently translations from Aramaic, and the Lukan sense of "daily bread" (hyperousial, supersubstantial) is obscure in the Greek. The prayer can also be fragmentally observed in the account of Jesus in Gethsemane given by Mark in his Gospel. It is partly based on the Jewish evening Kaddish, in which the kingdom of God was prayed for, to come speedily, even in the lifetime of the present generation. The fact that it is partly recognizable as a common Jewish prayer formula is no reason to suppose that it did not originate from Jesus himself. The opening verses are full of a sense of the glorification of the holy name through the manifestation of the kingdom of God, a central element in Jesus' own preaching, which is equally true of the subsequent petitions for forgiveness and sustenance from the fatherly care of God (according to the mercy given out "so will the mercy be given"), and for deliverance from "trials" (now commonly interpreted as temptation but originally referring to times of persecution and hardship that could deflect the courage of a believer) as they were stirred up by the evil one. In the early church (certainly by the early third century) the Lord's Prayer was communicated to *catechumens* in the prebaptismal Lenten instruction and was expected to be learned by heart (a catechetical practice that has marked the church ever since). The prayer was only allowed to be recited by believers, and was expected to be recited daily, and sometimes advocated to be said three times a day. The earliest *patristic* commentaries on the Lord's Prayer (a fine example is preserved in *Origen's* treatise *On Prayer*) originate from the catechetical process. *Tertullian* was the first to write an explanation of it (*On Prayer*), designating it "the epitome of the entire Gospel." *Cyprian* too commented on it (*On the Lord's Prayer*), and *Augustine* devoted an extended section to it in his *Sermon on the Mount* (2.15–39). Among the Greeks, *Cyril of Jerusalem* spoke of it (*Catechetical Lectures* 7), and *Gregory of Nyssa* devoted five sermons to the exposition of the prayer (*Sermons on the Lord's Prayer*). By the fourth century it was commonly recited at the *Eucharist* (Cyril of Jerusalem, *Catechetical Lectures* 23.11). In the Western Ambrosian rite, it followed the breaking of the bread and preceded the kiss of peace and communion; and Pope *Gregory the Great* instructed that it should also occupy this place in the Roman rite, which more or less reflected its position in the Byzantine liturgy as a preparatory communion prayer. This eucharistic context made later patristic commentaries on the Lord's Prayer focus strongly on the spiritual aspect of the "daily bread" (a fine example is the *Commentary on the Lord's Prayer* by *Maximus the Confessor* in the seventh century).

R. E. Brown, "The Pater Noster as an Eschatological Prayer," TS 22 (1961): 175–208; F. H. Chase, *The Lord's Prayer in the Early Church* (Cambridge, 1891); J. Petuchowski and M. Brocke, eds., *The Lord's Prayer and the Jewish Liturgy* (New York, 1978); R. L. Simpson, *The Interpretation of Prayer in the Early Church* (Philadelphia, 1965).

Lucian of Antioch (d. 312)

A *presbyter* of the *Antiochene* church and one of the leading sophists of his age, Lucian was the teacher of *Eusebius of Nicomedia* and *Arius*. He is presumed (because of this) to have taught a *subordinationist Christology* that was also rumored to be the source of the Arian controversy, but his martyr's death and his reputation for sanctity (along with the complete loss of his theological writings) ensured his reputation was preserved more or less intact. Alexander of Alexandria attacked him as the teacher of Arius and claimed that he was a disciple of *Paul of Samosata*. This was once taken seriously, but now is generally seen as a rhetorical ploy, without foundation. Lucian was a famed biblical scholar who revised the Septuagint Old Testament text and the Greek text of the Gospels. His Gospel version became the standard (Textus Receptus) of the Byzantine era, and that of the Septuagint became the standard in *Constantinople* and *Syria*. He was tortured to death at Nicomedia in the Great *persecution*.

R. P. C. Hanson, *The Search for the Christian Doctrine of God* (Edinburgh, 1988), 79–84.

Macarius of Alexandria (d. c. 394)

One of the early hermit monks who lived in the vicinity of *Antony the Great*. In 355 he was ordained priest to serve the monastic communities at Kellia (*see Nitria, Scete*), and gained a great reputation for his sanctity and wisdom as an elder among the Desert Fathers. Along with *Macarius the Great I* (not to be confused with Pseudo-Macarius: *see Macarius the Great II*), he is often known as one of the "Two Macarii," symbols of the theology and praxis of the Desert Fathers.

E. T. Meyer, trans., *Palladius: The Lausiac History* (New York, 1965), chap. 18; A. J. Festugière, ed., *Historia monachorum in Aegypto* (Brussels, 1961), chap. 29.

Macarius the Great I (c. 300–390)

The "real" Macarius the Great (as distinct from the "Pseudo-Macarius" who later took over his identity in the textual tradition: *see Macarius the Great II*) was the monastic founder of the colonies of *Scete* (Wadi el Natrun—*see Nitria*) in the Egyptian wilderness south of *Alexandria*. He was a supporter of *Athanasius the Great*, and a leading Desert Father who features in the collection of *desert* wisdom known as the *Sayings of the Fathers* (*Apophthegmata Patrum*). The monastic historians *Palladius* and *Rufinus* speak a little about him, but basically next to nothing was recorded of his life; a fact that made him an ideal candidate for the subsequent attribution of important monastic texts that were not really his.

E. T. Meyer, trans., *Palladius: The Lausiac History* (New York, 1965), chap. 17; Rufinus, *History of the Monks* chap. 28.

Macarius the Great II (Pseudo-Macarius) (fl. late fourth century)

Macarius the Great is also the pseudony-mous name for a *Syrian* writer who was an important monastic leader of a circle that had earlier been criticized for certain excesses in its spiritual theology. Some have identified him as Symeon of Mesopotamia (named as the group leader by *Theodoret*), and he is now often known as either Macarius-Symeon or Pseudo-Macarius. The criticism of his monastic heritage begins to be discernible from the 370s onwards. Sources call his adherents Messalians (a corruption of the Syriac word for "people of prayer"—*MshLni*). In some Greek sources they were known as the Euchites, but later heresiologists add to the confusion by thinking they were founded by a certain Messalius (who never existed). Even the objectionable element of the movement was not clearly understood by those criticizing it, and *Epiphanius*, who attacked the Messalians in his *Refutation of All Heresies* in 377, can only find their "lack of discipline" as grounds for censure. Other critics claimed they held that *baptism* was not sufficient for a Christian life, which had to be constantly supplemented and sustained by *prayer*, a doctrine that could be heretical or not, depending on how it was received, by enemy or friend. The movement was condemned at a session of the *Council of Ephesus I* (431), which cites passages from a key work, *Asceticon*. It is clear that elements of this text were taken from the homilies of Pseudo-Macarius. There are, however, certain themes that, whether "Messalian" or not (and the relationship of Pseudo-Macarius to any precise Messalian movement is still a dubious contention), do seem to be constitutive for the circle of *Syrian ascetics* for whom he was writing. These are the idea that *sin* dwells in a human heart like a serpent and the human being has a tendency to spiritual dissolution that needs to be offset by constant prayer and inner attentiveness. The school also advocated the abandonment of traditional monastic ideas of hard labor as a form of ascesis, advocating instead a wandering lifestyle, that focused more on spiritual withdrawal and recollection (probably why local *bishops* disliked them). Another typical theme seems to be the strong stress on the sensible consciousness (*aesthesis*) of the working of the *Holy Spirit* in the innermost heart. This monastic family taught that if a person was not deeply conscious of the Spirit's presence, then that person was clearly unregenerate. Those possessed of the Spirit could often feel the presence as a vision of light or warmth. Pseudo-Macarius himself shows signs of all these elements; indeed, the spirituality of the attentive heart and the constant invocation of *penthos* ("joy-making mourning") are major contributions that he makes to the development of international Christian spirituality. There is little indication that he takes any of these ideas to an objectionable extreme. His work, chiefly the *Great Letter* and the *Fifty Spiritual Homilies,* influenced *Gregory of Nyssa's* ascetical theology, and went on in latzer Byzantium to be a major source of the hesychastic renewal from the eleventh century onward.

J. Gribomont, "Monasticism and Asceticism," in B. McGinn and J. Meyendorff, eds, *Christian Spirituality: Origins to the 12th Century* (New York, 1993), 89–112; W. Jaeger, *Two Rediscovered Works of Ancient Christian Literature* (Leiden, Netherlands, 1965); G. Maloney, *Ps. Macarius: The 50 Spiritual Homilies and the Great Letter* (CWS; New York, 1992); J. Meyendorff, "Messalianism or Anti-Messalianism: A Fresh Look at the 'Macarian' Problem," in *Kyriakon. Festschrift. J Quasten.* II (Munster, Germany, 1971), 585; S. Tugwell, *Ways of Imperfection* (London, 1984), 47–58; idem, "Evagrius and Macarius," in C. Jones, G. Wainwright, and E. Yarnold, eds., *The Study of Spirituality* (Oxford and New York, 1986), 168–75.

Macedonianism   *see* Pneumatomachianism

Macrina (c. 327–380)

Macrina was an ascetic in Cappadocia. She was the elder sister of *Basil of Caesarea* and *Gregory of Nyssa,* and granddaughter of Macrina who had been the disciple of *Gregory Thaumaturgos,* the great Origenist theologian whose authority was almost "patronal" in Cappadocia. Betrothed, and soon "widowed" while only twelve years of age, she appealed to church laws that equated betrothal with a wedding to block her father's plans to have her married again, and instead lived as an *ascetic* at home, teaching her brother Gregory of Nyssa while Basil was away studying rhetoric. On her father's death Macrina transformed their country estate in Pontus (Annesoi) into a familial monastery. There Basil was won over to asceticism (it has often subsequently been attributed as his idea), and it was the site of *Gregory of Nazianzus's* and Basil's construction of the rule of monasticism (the *Asceticon* attributed to Basil), which had great subsequent influence in the Eastern churches. Macrina established a community, where it is possible she followed *Eustathius of Sebaste's* radical ideas about monastic life, such as invoking social equality among monastics. The men of the family do not appear to have agreed with this leveling of social ranks. Macrina may also have retained an attachment to Eustathius, who was condemned by the family because he resisted the Nicene confession of the *homoousion* and the deity of the *Holy Spirit* of God. As a result, Basil condemned his sister to a literary annihilation, although Gregory of Nyssa wrote a moving *Life of Macrina* as a testament to her ascetical philosophy. In *Letter* 19 he speaks of her, and in his treatise *On the Soul and the Resurrection* he presents her, like the dying Socrates, musing on the immortality of the soul from her deathbed.

V. W. Callahan, *Gregory of Nyssa: The Life of Macrina* (FOTC 58; Washington, D.C., 1967), 161–191; idem, *On the Soul and the Resurrection* (FOTC 58; Washington, D.C.), 195–272; S. Elm, *Virgins of God: The Making of Asceticism in Late Antiquity* (Oxford, 1994); J. Laporte, *The Role of Women in*

Early Christianity (New York, 1982), 80–88, 103–5; P. Wilson-Kastner, "Macrina: Virgin and Teacher," AUSS 17 (1979): 105–17.

Magic   Magic is a vast category, and its definition varies widely. Christians were quite sure that most of Hellenistic religion consisted of magical practices that were sponsored by demonic powers and gained their force from demons. Such was a lively charge against Hellenism that is found in most of the early *Apologists*. For their part the ancient world saw Christianity either as yet another magical sect or as a form of religion that frequently employed magical practices in its *healing* rituals and invocatory prayers. The Christians were determined to draw a sharp line between religion and magic, an aspect that has been sustained in all later forms of Christian theology. In this context magic would be an attempt to coerce the daimonic earthly powers to perform deeds or reveal truths that could be beneficial to the practitioner (cf. Justin, *First Apology* 26.1–3; 56.2; *Dialogue with Trypho* 120.6). Religion on the other hand would be the obedient service of God, and any attempt to secure God's benefits would be pursued with humility and without "bargaining," which would be offensive to the belief in God's overarching parental providence. Such a precise delineation, however, would also have been approved by many parts of Hellenistic religion, but it can serve as a preliminary working definition, for the word "magic" normally connoted the popular aspects of folk religion (astrology, curse rituals, petitions for sexual or business favors, and such like) that were looked down on by Christian and Hellenist religious philosophers alike but nevertheless played a considerable part in ordinary lives in antiquity, and were often subject to scrutiny and control by later bishops, who often tried to uproot them from Christian experience. Suetonius, the Roman historian, classed the Christians he knew as devotees of *Malefica*, the classic Roman legal definition of obnoxious magic. It was a serious charge that drew with it strict legal penalties. Roman legislation treated magic most severely, fearing the "evil eye" that could be unleashed by occult practices. The church was very anxious indeed in the times of persecution to distance itself from any association with magic. Early rabbinic apologetics tried to discredit Jesus by portraying him as just another magus (magician) who practiced healings based on demonic powers (a charge that turns up in the New Testament itself: Mark 3:22–24). It was a fine line to insist on the essential difference: and the early Apologists were much occupied in making that case in the face of the prevalence of the accusation among Jewish and Hellenist writers (Justin, *Dialogue with Trypho* 69.7; 108.2; *First Apology* 30; *Clementine Recognitions* 1.58; Origen, *Against Celsus* 7.69; Tertullian, *To His Wife* 2.4.5; Lactantius, *The Divine Institutes* 5.3.19; Socrates, *Church History* 3.13.11–12). The central argument was that the bending of demonic powers was a far different thing from the manifestation of the power of the supreme God at work through his servant Jesus, and continued in his church by the grace of the *Holy Spirit*. *Augustine* was one of the last to formulate the response (*De doctrina christiana* 2.35–36). But from the beginning Christians at the popular level believed that the very sign of the cross bore spiritual power, as did the *relics* of the dead *martyrs*, or the elements of the holy *Eucharist*, or the very words of the Scriptures when used in invocations (the phrase "The Word was made flesh" was often used as an invocation to protect from lightning strikes). For sickness, or to mark the passage of the *soul* from the body, there was often the extensive reading of the Psalter. To outside observers in antiquity, the use of material elements (especially the bones of the executed dead) and the employment of prayer rituals had all the esoteric marks of common magic. To Christian theologians, however, they were *sacramental* media of grace. Yet, even the *patristic* theologians wanted to discourage the popular use of amulets. Christians generally replaced pagan ones for their own: wearing neck crosses, or amulets that contained dust from the tomb of Jesus, or lockets with biblical verses inscribed on them (cf. Chrysostom, *Homilies on the Gospel of Matthew* 8.3). In Egypt there are several examples found of scarabs (the ancient good luck charm) with the cross inscribed on its back. Similarly the ankh sign of life could be reworked to become a resurrectional cross. To this day one of the most popular good-luck charms in Greece is the eye sign (the eye of God) that counteracts the "evil eye," which at first was simply an apotropaic aversion ritual that received a Byzantine Christian makeover. The common scholarly charge of "superstition" for these folk practices of Christianity (implying they were quasi-magical) is manifestation of a certain lack of awareness of the deep sentiment among the ancients that the world was full of spiritual powers, malign as well as good. It is probably more useful to draw an intellectual line not merely between Christian religion and magic, on the one hand, but also between genuine expressions of Christian piety and prayer and superstitious reliance on "amulets" or fetishes, a line that depends for its relevance on the degree of incorporation of the religious practices into the overall lifestyle of the participants. In other words, when one finds a mixture of pagan and Christian religious symbols it is a different matter from the prevalence of personal cult objects in a thoroughly Christianized environment. Otherwise there tends to be a prejudice among scholars favoring elements of religion that were those of the intellectual classes (eucharistic theology, or ecclesiastical liturgical symbolism) and against those of the ordinary people (Christian jewelry, grave signs, and other aspects of domestic cult).

D. E. Aune, "Magic in Early Christianity," ANRW 2.23.2 (1980): 1507–57; P. Brown, "Sorcery, Demons, and the Rise of Christianity: From Late Antiquity to the Middle Ages," in *Religion and Society in the Age of St. Augustine* (London, 1972), 119–46; E. V. Gallagher, *Divine Man or Magician? Celsus and Origen on Jesus* (Decatur, 1982); H. C. Kee, *Medicine, Miracle, and Magic in New Testament Times* (Cambridge, 1986).

Malalas   *see* **John Malalas**

Manicheism   The movement was once immensely popular, and for a time vied with *catholic* Christianity for the title of principal evangelizer of the ancient world. It originated with the teacher Mani (Latin Manichaeus), who was born near the capital of the Persian empire, Seleucia-Ctesiphon, and lived c. 216–276. He was brought up in the strict Judeo-Christian sect of Elkesaites, and felt compelled to adapt the teachings of the apostle Paul to proclaim a view of religion more universal in significance and liberative in principle. His Paulinism was strongly influenced by contemporary currents of *Gnosticism* and elements of Buddhism, as well as Zoroastrian religion, which was indigenous to Persia. His religious *visions* began at age twelve, when he spoke of seeing his "heavenly twin" who enlightened him, and thereafter he experienced a series of visions that he attributed to the Paraclete. His career as a religious preacher and wandering philosopher (deliberately emulating Paul as a new apostle for a new age) commenced in 240, and he gained numerous disciples in a wide range of territories in the East. Returning to the Persian capital in 242, he was at first supported by the ruler, Sapor I, though with increasing opposition at court. Sapor's successor Bahram I eventually arrested him and had him flayed alive, hanging his stuffed skin from the walls to deter his followers. His movement (known as the "Body" of Mani) nevertheless spread both eastward and westward. It traveled to China where it was still active in the tenth century (perhaps even into the seventeenth century). In the West it became known at *Alexandria* in the third century, and at *Rome* from the beginning of the fourth. From Rome it spread to *North Africa*, where it gained a large following in the later fourth century. It is in its Western manifestations that it chiefly became known to the *patristic* writers, who were often unsure whether it was simply *Gnosticism* or a heretical form of Pauline theology. It was generally classed in patristic writing as a Christian heresy, and thus it gained the concerted opposition of the hierarchs. The young *Augustine of Hippo* was one of many who were drawn to it. Manichean doctrine emphasized the perennial cosmic and religious battle between light and darkness, good and evil. The Evil Lord had stolen particles of divine light and imprisoned them in human consciousness within a material world, which was always antagonistic to any true spirituality. Religion and wisdom was a matter of releasing the divinity within, through a whole series of *ascetical* acts and ritual harmony with the cosmos. The Milky Way was the ladder of light back to heaven; and the phases of the moon were manifestations of the entrapment and release of spiritual lights in the material cosmos. Sexual abstinence was required (those who could not accept that requirement were listed in a second category of discipleship, the "hearers"), as was strict vegetarianism. Sexual conception was just another process of the many forms of the entrapment of souls in matter, and Mani's biography even records how he heard the agonized screams of vegetables as they were cut by thoughtless humans. In his doctrine of No-Harm, he is close to the Indian principle of ahimsa prevalent in Jainism and Buddhism. Mani regarded himself as the latest in a series of spiritual masters who had been sent into the world to proclaim the doctrine of spiritual liberation. His predecessors, he taught, included Buddha, the Jewish prophets, and Jesus. The Manichean movement encouraged its elect to be so detached from the "world of harm" that they depended entirely on the material support of the hearers, who provided a strong social network in the early empire that rivaled that of the catholic Christian congregations (Augustine owed his chair in rhetoric in Milan to Manichean patronage). The combination of *episcopal* opposition in the Christian empire, together with the decline of the class of hearers, probably accounted for the severe decline of Manicheism in the Greek and Latin churches after the sixth century, although some have claimed to see its revival in the forms of medieval Bogomilism and Albigensianism.

P. Brown, "The Diffusion of Manichaeism in the Roman Empire," JRS 59 (1969): 92–103. Repr. in idem, *Religion and Society in the Age of St. Augustine* (London, 1972), 94–118; F. C. Burkitt, *The Religion of the Manichees* (New York, 1978); R. Cameron and A. Dewey, eds., *The Cologne Mani Codex: Concerning the Origin of His Body* (Missoula, Mont., 1979); S. N. C. Lieu, *Manicheism in the Later Roman Empire and Medieval China* (Manchester, U.K., 1985); K. Rudolph, *Gnosis* (San Francisco, 1983), 326–42.

Marcellus of Ancyra (c. 280–374)

A bishop and controversial theologian, Marcellus of Ancyra was one of the strongest opponents of the *Arian* movement but caused great concern, both in the minds of his opponents and in the ranks of the Nicenes, for he sustained views that increasingly made many of the Nicene party wish to distance themselves from him. *Eusebius of Caesarea* was one of the first to attack Marcellus, insinuating that he was a Modalist *Monarchian*. He based this critique on Marcellus's work (now lost), *Against Asterius*. In this treatise Marcellus seems to have argued that the *Logos* was identical with the Father, one monad, which was consubstantial (*homoousios*) as a single concrete reality (hypostasis). The differentiation between Father and Son occurred only for the purpose of the *economy* of salvation within history (*see Theophilus*). At the end of time the Son would deliver all things back to the Father, and would reenter completely undifferentiated union, so that God would be "all in all." He based this view on 1 Corinthians 15:24–28. Marcellus was everything that the Arians most hated, and as his neo-Modalist theology increasingly became an embarrassment to the main Nicene party they worked to refine the precise meaning of the *homoousion*, which they wished to defend, as distinct from his kind of archaic monism. He was condemned by several synods in the East, but presented an acceptable statement of the faith at *Rome*, where Pope Julius exonerated him along with *Athanasius* as defenders of the *Council of Nicaea*, in a synod in 340. He was again exonerated by Western bishops meeting at the Synod of Sardica in 343. By this stage Athanasius was most anxious to distance himself and the cause of the *homoousion* from Marcellus and his extreme interpretations. Isolated from the main Nicene party, Marcellus's *Christology* increasingly began to take on the *subordinationist* character associated with his pupil Photinus. At the *Council of Constantinople* (381), he was condemned along with *Photinianism,* and the christological phrase "Whose kingdom will have no end" was deliberately inserted into the *creed* to refute his doctrine of the Son being finally absorbed back into the divine monad at the end of time.

J. T. Lienhard, *Contra Marcellum: Marcellus of Ancyra and Fourth Century Theology* (Washington, D.C., 1999); T. E. Pollard, "Marcellus of Ancyra: A Neglected Father," in J. Fontaine and C. Kannengiesser, eds., *Epektasis* (Paris, 1972), 187–96.

Marcion (d. c. 154)   A theologian from Pontus, son of a bishop, Marcion made a fortune in shipping and came to *Rome* to study c. 140, where he gave massive donations to the local church. He became a disciple of Cerdo, a *gnostic* teacher, and soon developed his own school on the basis of gnostic speculations. The Roman church, alarmed by his unusual views, excommunicated him in 144 (returning his money at the same time). He then organized an alternative community with the same rituals and patterns as the Roman church, which lasted for many centuries as a minority alternative church, though one that was increasingly taken over by *Manichean* views. Two hundred fifty years after Marcion's death *Cyril of Jerusalem* thought it important to warn his *catechumens* (*Catecheses* 4.4) not to enter a Marcionite church when traveling, in mistake for an orthodox one. Marcion was not much interested in the descending hierarchies of emanations that were common to many gnostic theological systems (accordingly he is not certainly classified as a gnostic), but he was, like them, convinced that the God of the Old Testament was something completely different from the God and Father of the Lord Jesus. He wished to make a radical separation between the two Testaments and advance an extreme supersessionist view (*see Judaism*) where the law had been finally abolished and replaced with the religion of Christ's *grace.* The Old Testament, for him, spoke only of an incompetent demiurge who involved all of humanity in the oppression of *sin* and *judgment.* The true God was revealed by Jesus: a God of love who contrasted with the vengeful demiurge of the Jewish texts. Marcion believed that only Paul had correctly understood the message of Jesus (though he either does not know or rejects the Pastoral Epistles). The other apostles were still caught up in the delusions of the law, and thought that the Christ of those texts was one and the same as Jesus, whereas the Jewish

Messiah they spoke of was meant to bring the Jewish nation back from exile, an event that Marcion argued still clearly belonged to the future. Marcion's Bible was further reduced by the progressive abandonment of the Gospels other than Luke, a process of simplification he based upon Galatians 1:8–9. Passages within Paul that contradicted his view of the covenantal dispensation were rejected by Marcion as later interpolations. He also deleted the genealogy and infancy stories from Luke as having been infiltrated by Judaizers. Marcion stood against *allegorism* in any form, and resisted any attempt to connect Christian thought to the fulfilment of Old Testament *types* or traditions. Because of this he was often an object of ridicule for later Christian writers (Irenaeus, *Adversus haereses* 1.27; 4.8, 34; Tertullian, *Prescription against Heretics* 30–44; Clement of Alexandria, *Stromata* 3.3–4; Origen, *Against Celsus* 6.53), especially in Tertullian's dedicated apologia *Against Marcion*. His major interest in textual tradition, however naïve it was, made Marcion the first Christian ever to set about compiling a catalogue (a *canon*) of what ought to be regarded as the authoritative "biblical" texts that should command the attention of the church. Although his version of that canon was completely rejected by the wider church community, his canonical concept was to prove immensely influential, and come to an international resolution in the fourth century. Marcionism entirely faded away by the fifth century, but it set views on the "supersession" of Judaism that had a long posthistory in Christianity.

E. C. Blackman, *Marcion and His Influence* (London, 1948); A. von Harnack, *Marcion: The Gospel of the Alien God* (Durham, N.C., 1990; ET of 1921 original); R. J. Hoffmann, *Marcion: On the Restitution of Christianity* (Chico, Calif., 1984); R. S. Wilson, *Marcion: A Study of a Second Century Heretic* (London, 1933).

Marriage   Marriage in the Christian community, as the conception was laid down in the *patristic* era, clearly derives most of its characteristics from a synthesis of biblical paradigms within a matrix of Roman law. The major scriptural imperatives were the sayings of Jesus about marriage (Matt. 5:32; 19:1–9; Mark 10:1–12; Luke 16:18), which themselves were based in the Genesis account of mutual harmony between the sexes (Gen. 1:27; 2:24). Jesus taught that marriage was a divine ordinance rooted in the creational institutions of God, not merely arising from societal customs. To that extent, his argument ran on, the dissolving of marriage as if it were a mere legal formality ran counter to the fundamental covenant between God and Israel, his elect nation. His immediate context was a pharisaic argument of the first century, which discussed whether Moses' law of divorce applied only for serious offenses such as adultery, or whether it could be invoked for small failings on the part of the woman (only in Roman law could a woman initiate divorce, not in Mosaic law). Jesus' response not only startled his rabbinical opponents, it puzzled his disciples, and the marks of that wonderment are already there in the records of the later first century when the Gospels were assembled (cf. Matt. 19:10–12; Mark 10:10–12). Paul seems to have found the marriage dictum one of the "hard sayings" of Jesus, and repeats it in his own marriage legislation in 1 Corinthians 7. Here, he clearly makes the distinction between what he himself has to offer as regulation on the subject and what the Lord had ordained (1 Cor. 7:12). But the context of the Gospels, whose editors evidently take the issue Jesus is raising to be a matter of the legitimacy of divorce, witness a certain slippage from Jesus' primary point, which was not really about "divorce" (except to say it was a countersign of the covenant comparable to adultery) but quite precisely about "marriage." In other words, when he was asked about the pure keeping of the covenant, in relation to divorce, he turned the argument around and spoke about the pure keeping of the covenant in regard to marriage. The subsequent history of the Christian church has been so obsessed with divorce legislation that it has often missed this critical point, except in rare cases such as *Gregory of Nazianzus,* to whom we shall return shortly. If one were to posit the original purpose of Jesus' teachings on marriage as a sure bond, a reliable sign of the covenant, it could be suggested they should be interpreted (along with most of his other dicta) as sayings illustrating the kingdom of God. That is, Jesus elevates marriage as a sign of the kingdom, and discusses it in relation to the advent of the kingdom. In this sense it corresponds to the frequent allusion to the wedding feast that one finds in Jesus' parables and sayings. The wedding feast is the preeminent sign of the advent of the kingdom; the rejoicing and reconciliation it brings into society are harbingers of the kingdom that Jesus' preaching and deeds usher in to Israel: similarly a time of reconciliation and forgiveness. The approach is reminiscent of other prophetic utterances, not least from Hosea, who describes Israel's relation to God as that of an errant wife, whom the Lord still does not set aside (Hos. 3:1). To lift up divorce (as the Pharisees in the Gospel seemed to wish to) as a matter of theological interest in the scrupulous observance of the covenant is to Jesus a profoundly misguided thing. Divorce is adultery, he says. We might add, just as faithlessness is. The original context of Jesus' sayings on marriage go on *in situ* to advocate perfect continence, to be "as a eunuch" for the sake of the kingdom. In this he alludes to the missionary disciples he has gathered to stand with him in his task of preaching the advent of the kingdom. This advocacy of eunuchism (Matt. 19:10–12) is not separate from the marriage-divorce sayings, but seems integral to

them (although some form critics have argued that they derive from disparate occasions). In other words there is a strong implication from Jesus that the true response to the kingdom ethic is either a pure devotion to marriage (such that one's love can be elevated as a sign of God's fidelity) or a devotion to celibacy (such that one's faithfulness to Christ) can be absolute, and amount to that complete leaving behind of family ties and responsibilities that he advocates on several other occasions (Mark 10:28–30; Luke 18:28–30). It is not that Jesus is inconsistent in commanding perfect security for marriage at one moment and then insisting his followers leave wives and children on another occasion. Rather, that he is elevating pure commitment as a fundamental virtue, what we might translate as that basic element of the kingdom ethic: faith (*pistis*) or complete abandonment to God's will. The apostolic writers, however, lifted the marriage saying out of that context of the kingdom parables, and applied it straightforwardly as one of the few times Jesus seemed to have legislated, as if for the Christian community of the future. Paul is the first to apply the rule in the ongoing life of the church, and this marked an early involvement of Christian leaders in the issue of marriage approached and understood in a narrow and forensic way. A similar interest is observed in *Ignatius of Antioch, To Polycarp* 5, where he says: "Marry only with the bishop's approval." This was to grow more and more to be an expected church requirement, certainly after the fourth century; yet from the beginning, and for many centuries, there was not actually any Christian service to mark marriage. The giving of crowns in the East or the veiling and hand-joining ceremony of the West were parts of the civic rite of contracting marriage under Roman law (the common context of all regions of the early church). As far as ceremonies went, the Christians were noticeable only in having a desire for their *priests* and bishops to bless the nuptial union, instead of offering an animal sacrifice to mark the occasion (cf. *Paulinus of Nola, Carmen* 25). There is also a body of literature advocating that Christians should be less riotous in their celebrations afterwards. Within the civil law of the late empire, marriage was envisaged more or less entirely as a contract between two people (or families) based upon goodwill, and certainly as a thing fundamental to law and good order as it was rooted in conceptions of property. As much as the wife was man's partner, in the Greco-Roman mind-set she was also partly his possession. If the church accepted most of this unreflectively, as its immediate intellectual ambience, it did bring in some changes. Most particularly, the idea of marriage as a sacred sign of God's covenant with his people survived, in the best of the Christian reflections. Marriage was not simply seen among the Christians as a property contract (though of course it was seen as that) but as a theologically charged mystery, which was meant to be a bond of love (*vinculum amoris*) comparable to that which existed between Christ and the church (Eph. 5:21–33). It was, on Christ's authority, also seen as a creation ordinance (Gen. 1:27; 2:24). It was this above all that saved a Christian theology of marriage (however embryonically) from being wholly absorbed by negative emphases: notably the **gnostic** movement, which often regarded marriage as a sign of deep evil insofar as it was connected with sexuality, a paradigm of material enslavement to the demiurge who had created an evil world; or the **Encratite** movement, which in early Syria taught that only the celibate could be admitted to **baptism**; or the rising **ascetical** movement, which after the fourth century became more and more obsessed with **virginity** and monastic renunciation of sexuality. The patristic texts often make depressing reading on the subject of marriage and sexuality. They are often joyless, and to such a degree rooted in **Stoic** middle-class literary presuppositions about shame, self-control, and purposeful procreation (Hellenistic attitudes to **sexual ethics** that contrasted with the joyful Hebraic sense of sex as a divine charism) that they are chiefly focused on the issue of the legitimacy of marriage considered as a series of sexual acts; barely at all on the question of marriage as a wondrous symbol of the kingdom. Sexual intercourse is generally advocated as "permissible" only for the purposes of direct procreation (cf. Origen, *Homilies on Luke* 6; Lactantius, *The Divine Institutes* 6.23). The patristic writers of the pre-Nicene age are generally writing about marriage as a veiled discourse for recommendations on domestic order, or on sexual ethics. In both cases their chief interest is to represent Christianity as comparable to (even better than) Stoicism and other forms of Hellenistic *sophrosyne*, that philosophical detachment that a wise man has from the world. This is why the literature is entirely androcentric and anxious to show that Christians were remarkable for their sexual sobriety. After the fourth century, when the bishops increasingly were elected from among the monastic renunciants, their theology was (much as could be expected) still focused on marriage as a "concession" (virginity became the true life of perfect discipleship) and as a "control of lusts." Both the pre-Nicene philosophic tradition of writings and the post-Nicene ascetical context were singularly ill-suited to a rounded theology of marital love. Theologians such as **Jerome** were particularly unbalanced in regard to their views. His understanding of marital love reduced it to the level of defilement (*To Jovinian* 1.7–8; though see also Rev. 14:4). **Origen** and **Augustine** also thought that marital sexual relations were always a defilement, but only of a type of "venial sin" (Origen, *Commentary on Matthew* 17.35; Augustine, *On Marriage and Concupiscence*). Augustine's views combined both the philosophical and the ascetic tendencies of Christianity and compounded them. His early statement on marriage sets a tone: "I think there is nothing I should avoid as much as a marriage. There is nothing I know which brings the manly mind down from the heights more than a woman's caresses, and that 'joining of bodies' without which one cannot have a wife" (*Confessions* 1.10.17). Augustine, however, did set up some resistance to Jerome's even more gloomy views, and his doctrine of the various "goods" of the married state (procreation, alleviation of lust, mutual fidelity, and the spiritual symbolic value of love) had a constitutive effect on later Western thinking. Jerome and Augustine between them weighed in so heavily against their opponents (*Jovinian* and *Julian of Eclanum*, respectively), who were rare voices raised for the cause of marriage and sexuality as religious values, that there were hardly any others afterward who wished to follow in the steps of the disgraced "decadents." The philosophers and the ascetics, of course, were the rhetoricians too. Only they had easy access to textuality. That left the vast body of Christians, who were ordinarily married, one presumes, in perfect silence. How much they paid attention to these teachings of ascetical rhetors in their church is a matter of pure speculation. But as the centuries advanced, the church attempted to exert more and more control over married sexual life, often through the penitential process (*see confession*), still without developing any noticeably profound appreciation of marriage (cf. the fourth-century *Acts of the Synod of Elvira*). One exception to the overarchingly legalistic and rigorous approach of patristic writing to the issue is the extraordinary case of *Gregory of Nazianzus*. He too was as philosophical and as ascetical as the other fourth-century writers, and in his poetry has many dismissals of sexuality as "defilement and flux" in a high sophistic style. But when he was elevated as archbishop of *Constantinople* in 380, the emperor Theodosius consulted him about marriage legislation, for he had noticed in

taking his eastern capital that the east-Roman Christian law allowed remarriage while former partners were alive, while the west-Roman law was strict in its forbidding of Christian remarriage under any circumstances. Theodosius takes for granted that church and civil law cannot diverge in a Christian empire. Gregory was called upon, seemingly, to advise for a strict application of church law, in line with the West (to make Western church law replace the looser civil law). What he produced instead was an elegantly written document that justified the practice of allowing divorce and remarriage within the church. Christ, Gregory says, was the consummate law-giver. But for every interpretation of law in times of doubt, recourse must be made not to the letter but to the "spirit and intentionality of the lawgiver." Christ, he argues, was in such a position when the Pharisees asked him about the matter, and he returned to the intentionality of the original lawgiver, not Moses but God. So now, when faced with similar issues of Christian marital law: what would be the intentionality of Jesus? Gregory goes on to argue that as Christ's constant concern was compassion for the poor men and women who "swim as fishes in a sea of misery," it would be contrary to the mind of the merciful lawgiver to apply a rigorous prohibition of subsequent marriage. Gregory argues that a first marriage should be taken as a theological sign of the kingdom (it ought to be for life). But a second marriage can be allowed as a concession for the sinfulness of the world. A third marriage is even permissible, but ought to be criticized more heavily. A fourth marriage, he says, is "fit only for pigs" (Gregory of Nazianzus, *Oration* 37). This doctrine of the permissibility of three marriages, passing from joyous to increasingly penitential in liturgical tone, is the standard practice of the Eastern church to this day. It is surprising that Gregory, such an ascetic himself, can see beyond the legal issues to the issues of the heart that illuminate the interior of the mystery. Others did not seem able to do so. His younger colleague *Gregory of Nyssa*, who was himself married, wrote a treatise *On Virginity*, wishing out loud that he had followed that path himself. From such a tradition of overarching sophistic expectation we can not look for deep illumination on the subject.

D. S. Bailey, *Sexual Relation in Christian Thought* (New York, 1959); P. Brown, "Sexuality and Society in the 5th Century AD: Augustine and Julian of Eclanum," SP 6 TU 81 (1962): 303–14; idem, *The Body and Society: Men, Women, and Sexual Renunciation in Early Christianity* (New York, 1988); E. Clarke, ed., "Anti-Familial Tendencies in Ancient Christiánity," JHS 5 (1995): 356–80; eadem, *St. Augustine on Marriage and Sexuality* (Washington, D.C., 1996); S. Laeuchli, *Power and Sexuality: The Emergence of Canon Law at the Synod of Elvira (4thC)* (Philadelphia, 1971); K. Stevenson, *Nuptial Blessing: A Study of Christian Marriage Rites* (London, 1982).

Martyrs   *see* **Acts of the Martyrs, Confession, Persecution, Saints**

Mary   *see* **Virgin Mary**

Maximilla   *see* **Montanism**

Maximus the Confessor (c. 580–662)   One of the most important Byzantine theologians, Maximus was a masterful synthesizer of the Origenian theology, who combined it with a powerful ascetical theology of prayer (much of it drawn from *Dionysius the Areopagite*) and who (like *Gregory of Nazianzus* before him, whom he explicitly emulated) moderated *Origen's* legacy in the aftermath of his condemnation by *Justinian* and saved the best insights of the ancient teacher for a wider Christian reception. Maximus was an aristocrat in the service of the emperor Heraclius. In 614 he entered the monastic life at Chrysopolis. The disruptions of the Persian War (626) caused him to move to Crete, Cyprus, and finally *North Africa.* In 654 the Greek monastery at Carthage became the site of a debate between Maximus and Pyrrhus, the exiled patriarch of *Constantinople* who was advocating the *Monothelite* compromise in *Christology* favored by the imperial court: a policy that tried to sidestep the Two Nature Christology of the *Council of Chalcedon* by teaching that Christ possessed only a divine will that was the religious and psychic focus of his subjective unity. This Monothelite theology was opposed by an opposite party (*Dyothelitism*) that taught two wills, one human and one divine, each corresponding to the two natures, and each presiding over what was proper to its own remit. Maximus regarded the Monothelite position not only as a betrayal of Chalcedon in the (forlorn) hope of reconciling the *Monophysites,* but also as a dangerous heresy that implicitly evoked a less than fully human Savior; a Christ who was not possessed of a true human *will.* For him Monothelitism was a vision of the Savior's humanity that verged on the mechanical. The Western bishops encouraged Maximus, fearing the undermining of Chalcedon by the emperor's policy. In the course of the debate Pyrrhus declared himself convinced that Maximus was correct (he would later change his mind). Several African synods soon condemned Monothelitism as a heresy, and *Rome* followed suit, with Pope Martin anathematizing the doctrine in the Lateran Council of 649. The emperor Constans II was determined, however, to press the Monothelitism of his *Typos* and, in 653, arrested and brought both dissidents to Constantinople. Martin died en route, but on his refusal to sign the *Typos* Maximus was exiled. He was recalled in 658 and 661, and on his final refusal he was tortured. Tradition has it that his tongue and right hand (which had continued to defy the emperor) were cut off (hence his title *Confessor*). He died soon after in exile in Georgia. His many works attack the

Monothelite Christology, advancing a powerful doctrine of the freedom of the human person, which is assured by the incarnation of Christ. The *incarnation,* seen as the high point of all human history, is the dynamic method and means of the *deification* of the human race, a spiritual re-creation of human nature that allows individuals the freedom needed to practice virtue, since all humans were formerly enslaved by passions. Maximus seamlessly combines his theological teachings with a mystical vision of the Christian life as an ever-deepening communion with God. His ascetical writings (*The Ascetic Life,* and the *Chapters on Charity*) and his theological commentaries on difficult subjects (*The Ambigua, Questions to Thalassius*) are profound works that have increasingly attracted attention in recent decades. His liturgical studies (*Mystagogia* and *Commentary on the Our Father*) show a powerful intellectual who is also capable of writing lyrically on *prayer.*

G. Berthold, trans., *St. Maximus the Confessor* (CWS; New York, 1985); A. Louth, *Maximus the Confessor* (London, 1996); L. Thunberg, *Microcosm and Mediator* (Lund, Sweden, 1965).

Melania the Elder (c. 342–410)

A wealthy Roman matron who became an *ascetic* after her husband's death around 365, in 372 Melania left her young child in *Rome,* moved to Egypt to study the monastic life, and became a patron of Origenist theologians. Settling in *Jerusalem* in 379, she established a double monastery on the Mount of Olives, with *Rufinus of Aquileia,* and it became a center of Origenian learning, thus earning the disapproval of *Jerome.* At her monastery she advised *Evagrius* to adopt the ascetical life when he took refuge with her after his flight from *Constantinople.* In 400 she returned to Italy and visited with *Paulinus of Nola.* Escaping the devastation of Italy by the Goths in 408, she returned to Jerusalem

and was buried in her monastery. Traces of it possibly remain in the grounds of the modern shrine of Dominus Flevit on the Mount of Olives. She was the grandmother of *Melania the Younger.*

F. X. Murphy, "Melania the Elder: A Biographical Note," *Traditio* 5 (1947): 59–77.

Melania the Younger (c. 385–439)

Melania the Younger was a vastly wealthy Roman lady. Her early desires to be a *virgin ascetic* were frustrated by her parents (her father was that infant child whom *Melania the Elder* had left behind in order to become an ascetic in Palestine). Accordingly she married, but soon persuaded her husband, Pinianus, to adopt the ascetical lifestyle, and they became generous patrons of the churches and the ascetics. Like her grandmother she and her husband traveled east. They fled from Italy during the Gothic invasion, and in 410 settled with other refugees on their estates in *North Africa,* founding two monasteries at Thagaste, where they made the acquaintance of *Augustine.* In 417 they moved to Palestine and stayed with *Jerome* at Bethlehem. After Pinianus's death in 431, Melania founded a monastery of her own on the Mount of Olives, near the one that her grandmother (*Melania the Elder*) had founded. She visited *Constantinople* before her death at *Jerusalem* in 439. The priest Gerontius, who took over charge of her monastery, wrote an account of her life soon afterward.

E. A. Clark, *The Life of Melania the Younger: Introduction, Translation, and Commentary* (New York, 1984).

Meletius of Antioch (d. 381)

Meletius was one of the most important of the Nicene theologians in the early fourth century, but also a "sign of contradiction" who caused much dissension among the Nicene ranks and hindered the cohesion of the Nicene community until late in the century. He began his ecclesiastical career in 360 as bishop of Sebaste, sponsored by the *Arians*, but when he was transferred to Antioch soon after he transferred his own allegiance to the Nicene party, and his inaugural address (explaining Prov. 8:22 in a Nicene manner) led to his immediate dismissal by Emperor Constantius. He was able to return to *Antioch* in 362, though he was banished again in 365–366 and 371–378. Meletius earned the lasting enmity of the Arian party, and could never fully secure the trust of all the Nicenes, especially *Athanasius*, whose hostility toward him (a mutual dislike) communicated itself to the West. Meletius had strong support in Cappadocia and among the wider Antiochene diocese especially in his later years from the leading generation of younger Nicene theologians, such as *Diodore*, *Basil of Caesarea*, *Gregory of Nyssa*, and *Gregory of Nazianzus*. Along with *Eusebius of Samosata*, Meletius acted as a much respected mentor for the neo-Nicene generation. The pro-Western party at Antioch, still attached to the memory of their earlier (Nicene) bishop *Eustathius*, arranged in 362 for the consecration of a Nicene antibishop, Paulinus, who was supported by the Westerners. This so-called *Meletian Schism* (not to be confused with the Melitian Schism of Egypt; *see Melitius of Lycopolis*) deeply troubled the international unity of the Nicenes and prevented Eastern and Western alliances for over a generation. After Valens's death in 378 Meletius arranged an influential synod of Nicenes at Antioch and commissioned Diodore and the two Gregories to spearhead a movement that finally resulted in the *Council of Constantinople I* (381), the definitive triumph of the Nicene cause made effective by *Theodosius*. Meletius was the president of the council of 381 but died in the early weeks of its sessions, passing on his presidency to Gregory of Nazianzus. It was continuing agitation over the issue of the resolution of the Meletian Schism that pressured Gregory to resign as president of the Council in 381.

R. P. C. Hanson, *The Search for the Christian Doctrine of God* (Edinburgh, 1988), chap. 20; W. A. Jurgens, "A Letter of Meletius of Antioch," HTR 53 (1960): 251–60; J. A. McGuckin, *St. Gregory of Nazianzus: An Intellectual Biography* (New York, 2001).

Meletian Schism (mid– to late fourth century)   The Meletian Schism in the church of *Antioch* (after 362) divided the Nicene Eastern party from the West through much of the critical fourth century. It was occasioned by the uncanonical ordination of Paulinus as bishop of Antioch by Lucifer of Cagliari, as a protest against *Meletius of Antioch's* early *Arian* tendencies. Even after Meletius gave his allegiance to the Nicene cause (providing dynamic Nicene leadership in the East), *Athanasius of Alexandria* and the Western sees would not give him their trust. Meletius brokered an attempted settlement of the schism at the Synod of Antioch in 379, a prelude to the *Council of Constantinople I* in 381, where his death as president, during the early sessions of the council, threw the whole negotiation into turmoil. *Gregory of Nazianzus*, who succeeded him as president, attempted to solve the international problem by acknowledging the rival incumbent candidate at Antioch (who was already recognized by the West). This caused such fury among the majority party loyal to Meletius that Gregory was forced to resign from Constantinople. The council elected another member of Meletius's entourage, and the schism lasted a while longer (though no longer as damagingly, since the Nicene cause had been triumphant under *Theodosius's* patronage) before eventually dying out. It ought not to be confused with the *Melitian Schism* (*see also Melitius of Lycopolis*), which divided the church of *Alexandria* during the episcopacy of Athanasius of Alexandria.

R. P. C. Hanson, *The Search for the Christian Doctrine of God* (Edinburgh, 1988), 382–84.

Melitian Schism   *see* Melitius of Lycopolis

Melitius of Lycopolis (fl. early fourth century)

Melitius of Lycopolis was a *priest* of the *Alexandrian* church who took a rigorist view of the readmittance of lapsed Christians during the *persecutions* of 303–311 and, as a result, renounced his allegiance to Bishop Peter of Alexandria. He was deposed by an Egyptian synod in 306 and led a *schismatic* movement of *clergy* that endured through the tenures of Peter's successors, Achillas and Alexander. Alexander brought the matter for settlement to the *Council of Nicaea I* (325), which allowed clergy ordained by Melitius (reportedly twenty-eight *chorepiskopoi*, or country bishops) to continue as junior clergy of Alexander, but deprived Melitius himself of episcopal status. When *Athanasius* was elected to the see of Alexandria (328), the schism was renewed again under the encouragement of *Eusebius of Nicomedia*, one of the leading *Arians* of the day, who hoped it would undermine Athanasius's authority. The schism was a constant distraction to Athanasius, and a source of several attempts to have him deposed or exiled. The Melitians increasingly came to be seen as the tools of Arian politics, but the schism endured for many centuries and was still a matter of concern to *Cyril of Alexandria*, especially in the regions of Upper Egypt. The Melitian Schism ought not to be confused with the *Meletian Schism* occasioned by the uncanonical ordination of Paulinus as rival bishop to *Meletius of Antioch* in the same period.

W. Telfer, "St. Peter of Alexandria and Arius," AB 67 (1949): 117–30; idem, "Meletius of Lycopolis and Episcopal Succession in Egypt," HTR 48 (1955): 227–37; R. Williams, "Arius and the Melitian Schism," JTS n.s. 37 (1986): 35–52.

Melito of Sardis (d. c. 190)

One of the bishops of Asia Minor who belonged to the *Quartodecimans* group (celebrating Pascha on the 14th of the month regardless of the Sunday) (*see Irenaeus*). He was described as "one of the great lights of Asia" in an early source. His only surviving work was rediscovered in 1932, a sermon *On the Pascha*, but he is said to have written seventeen books in all on subjects as varied as apologia (to the emperor Marcus Aurelius), biblical interpretation (a discussion of the book of Revelation), and liturgical matters. He traveled as a pilgrim to the Holy Land (the first Christian known to have done so) in order to gain a deeper understanding of the places where the acts of Christian salvation were first accomplished (*see soteriology*). He also wished to gain exact information as to the books that comprised the "Old Testament" (Melito is again the first Christian writer to use that term). His sermon *On the Pascha* shows a lively conception of the divinity of Christ, and is sharply focused against Jewish objections to Christianity. The work is a fine example of *typological exegesis*. The Passover episodes all find their fulfillment in the redemptive mystery of Christ.

L. H. Cohick, *The Peri Pascha Attributed to Melito of Sardis: Setting, Purpose, and Sources* (Brown Judaic Studies; Providence, R.I., 2000); S. G. Hall, *Melito of Sardis: On Pascha and Fragments* (Oxford, 1979); F. W. Norris, "Melito's Motivation," ATR 68 (1986), 16–24; A. Stewart-Sykes, *The Lamb's High Feast: Melito, Peri Pascha, and the Quarto-Deciman Paschal Liturgy at Sardis* (Leiden, Netherlands, 1998).

Messalians   *see* Macarius the Great II (Pseudo-Macarius)

Millenarianism   *see* Chiliasm

Minucius Felix

A late–second- and early–third century *apologist*, Minucius Felix was a *North African* Latin rhetorician who composed a dialogue entitled *Octavius*, which describes a conversation between a Christian, Octavius, and a pagan respondent, Caecilius (from Cirta in Numidia, the town where *Lactantius* would later come from). The work was addressed to pagan readership of **Stoic** persuasion, and while it avoids most references to Scripture or church practice, it makes a strong case for the superiority of Christianity in terms of its rationality (Lactantius took much of his later attacks on the absurdities of pagan cult from Minucius), its moral integrity, its universal monotheism, and its advocacy of divine providence and the immortality of the **soul**. It is a matter of dispute whether **Tertullian** used the *Octavius* or Minucius himself borrowed from the *Apology* of Tertullian, but there is a dependence between the writings. At the end of the *Octavius*, Caecilius declares himself to have been convinced of the arguments for the church, and wishes to become a Christian. The work is an indication of the buoyant optimism that characterized North African Christianity at this period.

H. J. Baylis, *Minucius Felix and His Place Among the Early Fathers of the Latin Church* (London, 1928); G. W. Clarke, "The Literary Setting of the Octavius of Minucius Felix," JRH 3 (1965): 195–211; idem, "The Historical Setting of the Octavius of Minucius Felix," JRH 4 (1967): 267–86.

Miracle　The word derives from the Latin *miraculum*, which signifies a wondrous thing, and is a close semantic parallel to the word that predominates in the New Testament and later Greek church: *thauma*, or awesome wonder. The original intent of the words in earliest Christian usage was to point to the essence of a "miracle" as a sign given to indicate to the witness to, or the participant in, the wonder that the presence of God was moving among humankind. The Christian sense of miracle thus always originally had a purpose, a significance that opened up for another end, not merely the fact of presenting the wonder for its own sake. For the church, the archetypal form of a miracle story was laid down by the Gospel accounts of the wondrous deeds of Jesus. His teachings, exorcisms, cures, and raisings of the dead are all presented in the evangelical accounts as deeds of power that caused awe (*thauma*) in the onlookers and often stimulated the question: "What manner of man is this?" (Mark 4:41). In later **patristic** writing the treatment of miracle extends in two ways. The first is to approach the "wondrous sign" more in the manner of an action that contradicts the laws of the world and less in the manner of a sensibility of the presence of God in the community of faith. Second, the miracle comes to be treated first and foremost as a "proof" of Jesus' divine status (his otherworldly power), as a **christological** vehicle. This is related to the New Testament usage (for already the evangelists manifest a christological motive) but also marks a departure: for Jesus intended the wonder to be a sign of the kingdom, and incidentally of his authority (*exousia*), whereas later Christian theologians interpret it as an indication of the unique character of his **person**. In **apostolic** times, as well as in the later classical patristic era, there was never any doubt expressed about the ability of Jesus to perform wondrous deeds. They were not explained away, even when they were given a highly symbolic reading by **allegorical** biblical interpreters. Thus when Tertullian argued that Jesus' cure of the blind man was really symbolic of his enlightenment of the Jewish people (*Against Marcion* 4.36.13), he did not mean to imply that the cure did not actually take place. Symbolic allegorism existed in harmony side by side with a general acceptance of the *thaumata* of Jesus. From apostolic times the mighty deeds of the Lord were expected to be represented also in the life of the church (cf. John 14:12; 2 Cor. 12:12; Rom. 5:19), and the book of Acts is full of accounts of the apostolic preaching being validated by continuing "mighty works." The church was most concerned that it should not be confused with the practitioners of *magic,* not least because of the dangerous legal penalties that attached to that association. In external opinion, in antiquity, the miracles of Jesus were generally not denied (although some such as *Celsus* questioned the poor witnesses available for the *resurrection*), as much as attributed to low-level magic. There was some late patristic reflection on the issue of miracle and the abrogation of natural law, though it was not extensive. *Augustine* (*On the Literal Interpretation of Genesis* 6.13.24) suggested that miracles were not so much deeds that contradicted natural laws (instituted by God himself), but rather acts that contradict what humans know of natural laws in their limited perspective of reality (*see grace, nature*). By the later fourth century the association of wonders with the standard pattern of Christian evangelization had clearly fallen off considerably (at first exorcisms and healings had been part of the *kerygmatic* proclamation), so much so that *John Chrysostom* tries explain the lack of miraculous deeds in the church of his day by suggesting that such things were needful for the age of missionary expansion, not for the age when the church was established. A great interest and continuing interest in the phenomenal is abundantly witnessed, however, in numerous *hagiographies* (lives of the saints) that appeared from the fourth century and through to the end of the patristic era. Miracles of holy men and women, such as those recounted in *Cyril of Scythopolis's Lives of the Monks of Palestine,* show a careful concern to correlate the deeds of the saints with those of Jesus as recorded in the Gospels. Miracles were increasingly expected of the *saints,* living and dead, in the latter case from their *relics.* In hagiographies from the seventh century onward (the change can be noticed in *Gregory the Great, Dialogues* 1.1–5), the miraculous element increases and becomes more and more "extraordinary." Issues such as intercessions to avert natural disasters or to invoke healings, however, were never relegated to the domain of the extraordinarily miraculous within Christian understanding, but were kept to the forefront of experience in the normal rituals of the church, and can be witnessed in the service books, which deal on many occasions with healing prayers. This is one aspect of how the patristic era never completely forgot the original connection of the *miraculum* as a regular (validating) sign of the preaching of the kingdom, a reminder of wonderment in the sensed presence of God among men and women: a presence that was doubtless miraculous in itself, but not to be regarded as a contradictory aspect of natural life, rather a dawning fulfillment of a life already lifted up transcendently.

P. Brown, *The Cult of the Saints: Its Rise and Function in Latin Christianity* (Chicago, 1981); R. M. Grant, *Miracle and Natural Law in Graeco-Roman and Early Christian Thought* (Amsterdam, 1952); J. A. Hardon, "The Concept of Miracle from St. Augustine to Modern Apologetics," TS 15 (1954): 229–57; H. Hendrickx, *The Miracle Stories of the Synoptic Gospels* (London, 1987); H. C. Kee, *Miracle in the Early Christian World* (New Haven, Conn., 1983); R. M. Price, trans., *Cyril of Scythopolis: Lives of the Monks of Palestine* (Kalamazoo, Mich., 1991).

Modalism   see Monarchianism

Monarchianism   (*See also adoptionism, Callistus of Rome, Paul of Samosata, and Valentinus.*) The term is an ancient one (first used by *Tertullian* in his classic treatise attacking the movement [*Against Praxeas* 10.1]). It also had a modern revival, especially in Harnack's analysis of the early church, and is commonly used to describe the general theological tendency of two schools of early–second-century Roman theology.

Monarchianism concerns one of the first formal attempts to reconcile a profound sense of biblical monotheism with the church's developed instinct in the divinity of Jesus. The juxtaposition of the two ideas could present either a major intellectual problem to the early church (especially to accurate theologians), or no problem at all (to popular piety for instance). It could, for example, not be a problem if Jesus' divinity was popularly regarded as applying in a merely "honorific" sense. In that era the ascription of divine honors to a multitude of humans was certainly not unknown. Such a reference to Jesus as divine figure would, however, represent a radical Hellenism that was hardly in keeping with the strict sense of the absolute unicity of the God of Israel. To envisage Jesus' divinity as a matter of his spiritual exaltation among the heavenly hosts (for example as a preexistent Great Angel of God) was a path that had already been taken, already suggested in the Philonic doctrine of *Logos.* The Logos could be envisaged as God's angelic power of governing the world, and in that image (aided by the Wisdom literature of the Old Testament) the Logos theologians indeed found a useful path toward helping them articulate the role of Jesus within the divine unity: as a distinct agent of God, graced with divine glory, yet not the same as the God who sent him. The problem was that all of this subtle theology of ascribing similarity of status (power, or essence, or glory) while affirming distinctness of person (or function, or rank) was something that as yet had no linguistic infrastructure. It would take until the end of the fourth century before Christian theologians would elaborate a clear theology of a *Trinity* of divine *persons* sharing the selfsame essence or *nature.* In the early decades of the second century the issue was at once simpler and cruder: Was Jesus God? If so, how could this cultic confession be reconciled with the unicity of the Godhead described in biblical faith? Monarchianism generally tried to answer this prob-lem by stressing the unity of God as a single power (a monarchy). The theologians who represented this movement fell into two categories. In the first (more influential) group were Noetus (c. 200), Sabellius (early third century), Pope *Callistus* (217–222), and perhaps Praxeas, if the latter is not merely Tertullian's nickname for Callistus, as the word can mean "Busybody." They were grouped in *Rome,* and had a dominant influence over the affairs of the Roman church, as can be seen by the manner in which Pope Callistus regarded the defense of the Monarchian cause as simply the preservation of the integrity of the ancient Roman tradition in the face of new innovations from the Logos theologians (especially *Hippolytus*). Hippolytus's treatises *Against Noetus* and the *Refutation of All Heresies* (9.1, 5–6) focus on the issue. His view was that Callistus was simply an ignoramus elevating his lack of knowledge into the canonicity of tradition. Their group has often been called the Modalist Monarchians. Their attempt to resolve the problem of unicity and diversity in the Father-Son relationship was based on the idea that the Father was a distinct mode of operation of the single God when addressing the world as Creator. The Son was another mode of operation of the selfsame God when addressing the world as Savior; and the *Holy Spirit* was a third modality when working within the world as Sanctifier. The Father, Son, and Spirit are thus all three different *"economic"* faces of the same God in different modalities of salvation-encounter. Tertullian and Hippolytus were among the early Logos theologians who poured ridicule on this primitive attempt to reconcile unicity with a confession of Jesus' divine status. Tertullian mocked the whole enterprise as "Patripassianism," that is, tantamount to teaching that the Father was crucified, since he was synonymous with Jesus (*Against Praxeas* 27–29). In turn the Monarchians called the Logos theologians "ditheists." The second group of Monarchians were attempting to reach the same goal, but by significantly different means. This included the two scholars who worked in Rome c. A.D. 190, **Theodotus the Cobbler** and Theodotus the Banker, his disciple (cf. Hippolytus, *Refutation of All Heresies* 7.23–24). In a later phase it also included *Paul of Samosata* (censured at a synod in 268; cf. Eusebius, *Ecclesiastical History* 7.27–30) and Artemon his contemporary, who lamented that the ancient Monarchian-adoptionist tradition had been crushed illegitimately by Logos theology (cf. Eusebius, *Ecclesiastical History* 5.28.3). These theologians followed the path that the divinity was one and undistinguishable, but was manifested in different modes of operation in the Christ (hence they have been called Dynamic Monarchians), namely, the concrete elevation of Jesus of Nazareth into the divine ambit (his radical "possession" by the power of God) for his earthly ministry; and the more diffuse expression of the divine power, by the Spirit of God at work in the world. Jesus could thus be called "God" and even worshiped, in accordance with Christian tradition, but was not thereby confused with the supreme God and Father. After Jesus' death he was exalted into heaven as a reward for his fidelity. But the "divinity within" Jesus was always that of the Father alone. Strictly speaking, there was no plurality of divine beings, only the supreme Monarchy of the Father, employing different economic channels. Both schools of Monarchians found a strong wall of opposition to them elevated very quickly in the form of the Logos theologians (Tertullian, Hippolytus, *Clement of Alexandria*, and *Origen of Alexandria*). In many ways they served as a whetstone for the rapid advancement and sophistication of the early Logos school, which soon displaced Monarchianism and claimed the place of the major mode of theological thinking in the church after the end of the second century. When Origen was asked to address a synod in Arabia in the mid–third century to persuade bishop Heracleides that his Monarchian position was theologically defective (Origen, *Dialogue with Heracleides*), his success demonstrated the resolution of the problematic on unity of divine power within the Logos scheme of distinctness of *hypostases*. When Heracleides the Monarchian finally agreed with Origen the Logos theologian that the Father was God, and the Son was God, but there was only one power of deity between them, then the stage was set for the progression through the fourth century to the classic doctrine of *Trinity*.

H. J. Carpenter, "Popular Christianity and the Theologians in the Early Centuries," JTS 14 (1963): 294–310; J. N. D. Kelly, *Early Christian Doctrines* (London, 1978), 115–26; G. La Piana, "The Roman Church at the End of the Second Century," HTR 18 (1925): 201–77; G. L. Prestige, *God in Patristic Thought* (London, 1952).

Monasticism   *see* **Asceticism**

Monoenergism   The term signifies a belief that the dynamic of union between the divine and human *natures* of Christ can best be described as a matter of single energy (monoenergistic activity), whereby the one Christ, simultaneously man and God in an ineffable and mysterious way, acted within human history in a single divinohuman energy. The approach was popular with a wide range of Byzantine monks because of its mystical potentiality, and because it coincided with much of the theological "tone" of *Cyril of Alexandria's Christology*, as exemplified at the *Councils of Ephesus* 431 and 449. It was a theory adopted by the Byzantine administration of Heraclius under Patriarch Sergius to attempt a resolution of the Great Schism between the Chalcedonians and anti-Chalcedonian *Monophysites*. It was thought that if the idea of a union involving "natures" as the key term was avoided, the idea of energy (*energeia*) as the common bond could resolve the *christological* impasse in the Eastern church. The imperially sponsored rapprochement was opposed by Sophronios, the patriarch of Jerusalem, and *Maximus the Confessor* as a veiled attempt to abandon the significance of the *Council of Chalcedon* (451). Sophronios argued that the concept of life-energy derived from *nature* (*ousia*), not from *person* (hypostasis), and thus if Christ had two natures, he must also have two energies: one human and one divine. Accordingly Monoenergism was simply Monophysitism in another disguise. Having adopted the theory as a way forward in the early 630s, the emperor decided to ban all discussion of the idea when it became clear Rome was not favorable. He then turned his hopes to the alternative solution of positing one *will* in Christ, one principle of moral action and intentionality (what we today would call spiritual consciousness). Again, this move was taken in the understanding that this new central term of will (*thelema*) would oust the language of one or two natures that had been so divisive. This approach (*Monothelitism*) again proved to have no better a fortune than its predecessor. Maximus the Confessor argued even more fiercely that to deny Christ a human will voided the entire purpose of a salvific *economy* of *incarnation,* where Christ adopted a human will in order to *heal* and save it, since it was within and by the will that the human race first fell from *grace*. Emperor Constans II in 648 finally despaired of the use of the latter scheme of rapprochement and issued a *Typos* in 648 banning any discussion in the empire either about single will or single operation. In response, Pope Martin called a synod at the Lateran in Rome in 649, where he anathematized both the Monothelitic doctrine and the emperor's audacity in trying to control theological discussion of the faith. In his turn the emperor acted violently against both the pope and Maximus the Confessor. The controversy was not resolved until

680–681, when the Sixth Ecumenical Council (*Council of Constantinople III* [680–681]) condemned both Monoenergism and Monothelitism and affirmed that just as Christ had two natures, so he had two wills and two energies (human and divine), which were in perfect accord and harmony with one another, and whose mutuality provided the model and dynamic goal for all Christians to aspire to: the perfect alignment of human life with the divine presence and will.

———

L. D. Davis, *The First Seven Ecumenical Councils: Their History and Theology* (Wilmington, Del., 1987); C. Laga, ed., *After Chalcedon: Studies in Theology and Church History* (Louvain, Belgium, 1985).

Monophysitism The term Monophysitism (from the Greek: "one nature") designates those who rejected the theology of the *Council of Chalcedon* (451), with its insistence on two perfect *natures* (human and divine) harmonized without confusion or separation in the single (divine) *person* of Christ. As the Chalcedonian theology was Diphysite (two nature) so, by implication, the rival party were increasingly called "Monophysites." Many Chalcedonians, past and present, have erroneously gone on from the basis of this hostile and rather simplistic summation of their opponent's beliefs to conclude that such a single nature of the Christ must, of necessity, be a hybrid or "mingled nature" of God-manhood. The implications of this, forcefully expressed in many earlier *patristic* studies, are that Dyophysite thought represents *christological* clarity where the one divine person of the incarnated *Logos* presides directly over two distinct natures, whereas Monophysitism represents muddy thinking where deep piety (affirming Christ's unquestioned divine status) underestimates the full authentic range of his human experiences. Some of the opponents of Chalcedon undoubtedly did follow a line of thought that paid less than sufficient attention to Christ's human actuality. Following in varying degrees in the steps of *Apollinaris of Laodicea,* they often believed that to affirm human limitation was a disservice to the divine Christ. Thinkers such as Julian of Halicarnassus and *Eutyches of Constantinople* represented this kind of confused piety. There were others, however, such as *Philoxenus of Mabbug, Timothy Aeluros* (the "Cat"), and *Severus of Antioch,* whose sophisticated theology can not be reduced to this level. The major argument, if hostile apologetics can be cleared away, turns around two closely related issues: first, that *Cyril of Alexandria* (who had become a towering authority on Christology in the East) had used certain terms simultaneously in two senses; and second that the Council of Chalcedon, for the sake of clarity, wished to move toward one agreed technical vocabulary and had vetoed some of his early expressions. His followers (not least the entire Egyptian church) refused to accept such a veto. Cyril had spoken of the seamless union of divine and human activity in a single Christ under the party slogan: "one *physis* (*mia physis*) of the Word of God incarnate." Here he applied *physis* in the antique sense of "one concrete reality," which was more or less a synonym for the central idea of his (and Chalcedon's) Christology that there was only "one hypostasis" in Christ. Unfortunately, even by his day the word *physis* was coming to be taken as a synonym for *ousia,* or nature understood not as a concrete reality (a subjective presence), but more as a set of (natural) properties or attributes (such as "human nature" and "divine nature"). Thus, to describe Christ as one single *physis*-nature, in this sense, was generally taken by non-Cyrillians to be advocating for a new form of hybrid nature (divinohuman synthesis) in Christ. Cyril felt such graphic language of *physis* unity was necessary, for he was worried that those parties who ostensibly wished to defend

the authenticity of human experience in Christ, and the differentiated spheres of human and divine actions in his life (the Syrian church), had actually strayed into such a polarization that the incarnation had become artificial; a disunion rather than a union of God and man. Cyril's followers, alienated after the Council of Chalcedon by the condemnation of *Dioscorus,* were more and more labeled as Monophysites and accused of teaching the doctrine of a confused hybrid of natures (*Eutychianism*). They themselves saw their defense of the "union of natures" as a last stand for the belief in the *deification* of the human race that came from the dynamic of the *incarnation* of God. In their turn they regarded the Chalcedonians as no better than defenders of *Nestorianism.* In this they were quite wrong (just as their opponents were wrong to see them as Eutychians), but the semantic confusions made the controversy run for centuries, and after the Islamic seizure of Syria and Egypt in the seventh century, the possibilities of reconciliation with the Byzantine and Roman traditions became increasingly slight. The best of the so-called Monophysites actually represent the *mia physis* formula of Cyril's early theology (before his reconciliation with John of Antioch after the *Council of Ephesus I* [431]). The anti-Chalcedonians consistently rejected any Two Nature language as both a betrayal of Cyril (hence of Ephesus 431) and of the belief that the incarnation was a dynamic of unity; as such they were increasingly prosecuted by the imperial government. It is one of the great tragedies of the patristic era that so many attempts to reconcile the dissidents failed, when clearly the central issues (integrity of humanity and divinity in the Christ, who is but a single divine person) were agreed on both sides. Political and ethnic factors played a considerable part in this.

W. H. C. Frend, *The Rise of the Monophysite Movement* (Cambridge, 1972); A. Grillmeier with T. Hainthaler, *The Church of*

Alexandria with Nubia and Ethiopia after 451 vol. 2, part 4 of *Christ in Christian Tradition* (London, 1996); A. A. Luce, *Monophysitism Past and Present: A Study in Christology* (London, 1920); J. Meyendorff, *Christ in Eastern Christian Thought* (New York, 1975).

Monothelitism   *see* **Council of Constantinople III, Monoenergism, Maximus the Confessor**

Montanism   Montanism is the name their opponents gave to the movement the protagonists called "New Prophecy." Montanus was a controversial early Christian prophet who began a charismatic revival movement in Phrygia (Asia Minor) between 155 and 160. Appearing suddenly as a Christian preacher (some stories say that he had only been recently converted from paganism), he traveled in central Asia Minor with two female prophets, Maximilla and Prisca (Priscilla). The latter are significant (though little is known about them) as two of the most significant female prophetic leaders of early Christianity. Montanus claimed that he was the mouthpiece of the *Holy Spirit*, and that the Paraclete who had been promised in John 16:7 was now incarnate in him. His context is probably a protest against the declining apocalyptic expectation among the early communities and a corresponding adjustment of organized church life to an urban environment. Some have thought that the ecstatic element of his religion was more a carryover from his pre-Christian adherence to oracular cults, and that this is the context in which we need to see his reliance on prophetesses to deliver oracles. Others see the female leadership (it remained in the Montanist communities but not in the *catholic* communities) as something that reveals a wider pattern of early Christian offices than that which survived after the Montanist controversy. Montanus represents one of the last attempts in the patristic era to revi-

talize a thoroughly apocalyptic worldview, claiming that the present end times had initiated the need to renew church life under the leadership of his ecstatic prophetic circle (*ecstasy* was thought to characterize Spirit inspiration, and speaking in tongues [glossolalia] was encouraged). Our knowledge of the movement comes mainly from indirect and antagonistic sources (Eusebius, *Ecclesiastical History* 5.14–19; Epiphanius, *Refutation of All Heresies* 48f.), both of whom were fourth-century writers who drew upon the earlier anti-Montanist writings. Several of the original Montanist formulas have thus been preserved (edited by Heine). *Irenaeus* (himself a native of Asia Minor) found them to be an admirable group, and he defended their cause at *Rome.* His own form of millenarianism (*Adversus haereses* 5) may reflect the Phrygian tendency to apocalyptic prophecy (*see chiliasm*). The three inner-circle prophets claimed no less than the direct authority of God. They regarded the ecclesiastical established authorities (the early bishops are their first organized opposition) as having no authority to teach or lead if they opposed them, or did not accept their prophetic words as equivalences to the body of Scriptures. (It was the magnitude of this claim that really caused questions to be raised against them.) Bishops might organize in the churches, but never in opposition to the authority of the prophets. They taught that the end times were imminent, and in preparation for the cataclysm Christians had to adopt a rigorously ascetic lifestyle. Marriage was banned (later this was relaxed only to a ban on remarriage); regular and severe fasting was encouraged; so too was substantial almsgiving. Martyrdom was encouraged, flight from *persecution* forbidden as an apostasy (another reason urban bishops disliked them as an endangerment to the wider Christian community). At the end, the new Jerusalem promised in the Scripture (Rev. 21:1–10) would physically descend from heaven at Pepuza (Timione), a tiny village in Phrygia. Here true believers would have to gather together before the Lord's coming. To a large extent, however, Montanism was a movement uninterested in "doctrine" as such. It accepted the *resurrection* of the flesh (a notion that was usually in contention among secessionist Christian groups) and interpreted many points of Scripture with simple directness (not too far removed from the majority among the contemporary early Christian communities). Its fundamental impetus seems to have been renovationist, following the inspiration of the ancient *apocalyptic* strand of early Asia Minor Christianity. The attack on local church leadership caused some difficulties in concrete situations, but the movement obviously had a popular appeal. Several bishops of early communities actually adopted the message and advocated for it. The lack of objectionable doctrinal elements caused church authorities considerable difficulties in deciding what, if anything, was wrong with it. The movement spread to the West, where for a time between 177 and 178 the Roman church was thinking of recognizing it as an official aspect of church life. From Rome it moved to *North Africa,* where it had a second life (called Stage Two Montanism). The rigorist Christian theologian *Tertullian* passed from being a critic to an enthusiastic adherent late in his life. It is thought by some that the leading *Monarchian* theologian, *Theodotus the Tanner,* was also closely associated with the Montanist movement, although Tertullian (*Against Praxeas* 1) tells us that the Monarchian Praxeas was instrumental in having it banned at Rome. In the later form of Montanism, as it took root in North Africa in the late second and early third centuries, many of the original highly charged apocalyptic elements had been smoothed out. The function of ecstatic prophecy was then given a lighter stress, and the urgency of the imminent *Parousia* seemed to have receded. It is thought that the Montanist movement was clearly involved in the

production of the *Passion of Perpetua and Felicity,* that classic *martyr* narrative where *dream-vision* and prophetic apocalypticism play dominant roles. The strong advocacy of martyrdom as the supreme Christian destiny remained characteristic of Montanism to the end, and flavored the Christianity of North Africa. The greatest of all proto-Montanist texts, of course, is the book of Revelation itself, which also emanates from Asia Minor and probably represents generic tendencies of the church of that area that took a particularly sharp form in the rise of Montanism. The movement dwindled away by the fourth century, except in the small village of Pepuza, which had by then become the sect's headquarters. It was a movement that made Christianity reflect seriously on the nature of prophetic inspiration. In reaction to the Montanist stress on ecstasy, the patristic writers generally envisaged the workings of the *Holy Spirit* within the soul as an enhancement of rational consciousness, rather than the suppression of it. This would have a long-term determinative effect on Christianity. The early bishops in Phrygia also reacted to the perceived threat of the movement as a community-destabilizing force by arranging to meet together in "assemblies" (synods) to discuss the crisis and come to a common episcopal resolution (Eusebius, *Ecclesiastical History* 5.16.10). This is probably the first time that episcopal *councils* (which would soon become a standard way of organizing churches) are witnessed in Christian history. Very quickly the synodal "mind of the bishops" would claim the prophetic authority that had been wrested from the Montanists. The resolution of the crisis also marks the rapid obscuring of the ancient office of Christian prophet in favor of an ascendant role for bishops and presbyters.

D. E. Aune, *Prophecy in Early Christianity and the Ancient Mediterranean World* (Grand Rapids, 1983); T. D. Barnes, "The Chronology of Montanism," JTS 21

(1970): 403–8; J. A. Fischer, "Die anti-montanistischen synoden des 2–3 jahr-hunderts," AHC 6 (1974): 241–73; R. E. Heine, ed., *The Montanist Oracles and Testimonia* (Macon, Ga., 1989); F. C. Klawiter, *The New Prophecy in Early Christianity: The Origin, Nature, and Development of Montanism, AD 165–220* (Ph.D. diss., University of Chicago, 1975); idem, "The Role of Martyrdom and Persecution in Developing the Priestly Authority of Women in Early Christianity: A Case Study of Montanism," *Church History* 49 (1980): 251–61; J. Massingberd-Ford, "Was Montanism a Jewish Christian heresy?" JEH 17 (1966): 145–58; C. Trevett, *Montanism: Gender, Authority, and the New Prophecy* (Cambridge, 1996).

Montanus   *see* **Montanism**

Moschus   *see* **John Moschus**

Mystery   The Greek term *mysterion* derives from the verb *muein*, "to be silent." From antiquity it had a profound religious connotation, mainly signifying the so-called "mystery religions" of Hellenism, in which candidates were admitted to a secret initiation with the god or goddess, one that involved an intense emotional and psychic charge. At the culminating point of the initiation the sacred regalia of the divinity were "shown" to the initiate and the sacred kerygma was passed on. In many cases this involved secret words or incantations that would assure the initiate's safe passage through the heavenly spheres after death, thus assuring the soul of an immortal destiny. One of the most sacred obligations that fell on the initiate was to "keep silence" about what had been shown and told. Mystery was thus a matter of profound revelation of secrets and faithful observance of trust. It was not a religious psychology that greatly interested the more corporate religious sensibility of the Hebrew Bible, but in the time of late *apocalyptic Judaism* it assumed some religious force as a term connoting the revelation of "final age" mysteries. The apocalyptic prophet (typically rapt to the higher heavens, where he could see the destiny of ages unfolding below him) saw a condensed plan of God's "mystery for the ages," the hidden providential plan woven into earthly affairs. In the early Christian era it is this usage which has an impact on the church through the example of St. Paul, who recognized in the apocalyptic *kerygma* of the gospel many aspects that could be compared to the mystery cults in order to gain a wider foothold in apologetic communication to the Greek world. The stress on personal devotion, initiation through the *death* and *resurrection* of Christ, and the gift of immortal life could all be expressed in the manner of the *revelation* of mysteries. Paul, of course, makes a deliberate play on this terminology (rather than merely adopting it) because he is concerned with "speaking out the mystery," which would have been a contradiction to a contemporary Hellenist (Rom. 16:25; 1 Cor. 2:7; Eph. 1:9; 6:19; Col. 1:26–17f.). For later Christians the mystery became the synopsis of the Christ experience, or the *economic* salvation Christ offered. In Mark 4:11 the whole kerygma is summed up as the "mystery of the kingdom," which only those on the path of salvation can discern, since to others all is foolishness and obscurity. In 1 Timothy 3:16 it has almost become a creedal synopsis of the "faith." In later *patristic* writing Paul's idea of the hidden plan of God revealed in the pattern of Christ's life is taken up and enthusiastically developed in several related ways. After *Origen*, the Scripture (especially as it is itself a pattern of shadows and revelations) is seen as a corporate "mystery of salvation." From the fourth century onward, through the example of *Athanasius*, *Cyril of Jerusalem*, and *John Chrysostom*, the word mystery becomes a cipher for the Christian sacraments, especially *baptism* and *Eucharist.* In these mysteries Christ is seen to be present, powerfully transforming his community. Some writers, such as *Clement of Alexandria*, Origen (in part), *Evagrios,* and the later

Byzantine writers such as *Dionysius* and *Maximus the Confessor,* followed the example of Paul (1 Cor. 14:2), who had hinted at the "mysterious knowledge" of the soul in a transcendent state. This was the beginning of the Christian use of "mystical," a term that is first applied to theology by *Dionysius the Areopagite* in the sixth century. It had been presaged from the earliest times (but only by the fourth century brought into clearer focus) that the soul's acuity could know God only by being admitted (though limited and creaturely) into an immortal condition. The true perception of the divine, if communicated to the soul, was an experience that could neither be explained nor appreciated except by another initiate. Origen and many after him compared it to the special state of *vision* and knowing that enabled the disciples on the mountain to see Jesus transfigured and to recognize the immortal prophets, even though natural knowledge would not have sufficed for such things. The Byzantine spiritual writers stressed that this transcendent *theoria* was a veritable anticipation of the kingdom, and a "manner of knowing" that was more purely spiritual than intellectual. This is the beginning of "mysticism" as commonly understood today, although the early theologians never had a discrete category for it. Throughout the Byzantine era the title "mystic" signified simply a "private secretary."

L. Bouyer, "Mystique: Essai sur l'histoire d'un mot," VSp 3 suppl. (1949): 3–23; H. Crouzel, *Origène et la connaissance mystique* (Paris, 1961); H. A. A. Kennedy, *St. Paul and the Mystery Religions* (London, 1913); V. Lossky, *The Mystical Theology of the Eastern Church* (London, 1957).

Natural Law   *see* **Nature, Sexual Ethics, Stoicism**

Nature   The modern term generally connotes two things in theological language: the natural environment, or more simply "the world" understood as a creation of God, and then the condition of the creature, or, in other words, "human nature." In *patristic* thought the issue is approached entirely from the perspective of the divine power of the creator. The concept of nature as creation is covered by the term "world" (*kosmos*). Most of the biblical underpinning of the concept of "the world" conveys the sense that it is a major manifestation of the power and dominion of the creator God who continues to direct the affairs of the world order he made (Ps. 24:1; 50:1; 90:2). In the New Testament the word signifies the forces in the world that are still hostile to the dominion of God. This is why, in the Fourth Gospel, for example, the "world" regularly appears in such a pejorative way, something resistant to God (John 17:14, 25; 14:17; 15:18) or at best something passively needing God's salvation (John 1:29; 3:16; 6:51; 12:47), something still discernible in the Christian contrast of the kingdom of God with the "secular" attitudes of those not committed to the kingdom. "Secular" (*saecularis*) in this sense is the exact Latin equivalent of the Greek *kosmos,* meaning all that belonged to the "present age" in distinction to the "age that was to come." In patristic writing the second- and third-century conflicts with the gnostics, who generally regarded the world as a profoundly negative phenomenon, sobered up the earlier apocalyptic manner of drawing a contrast between God and the world, and set the basis for a much more theologically positive consideration. *Irenaeus* was one of the first significant theologians to affirm the beauty of the creation as a primary manifestation of God's *grace* and glory. *Origen* described God's making of the world as a therapeutic gesture, a training ground for fallen souls. Though still influenced by many gnosticizing trends, Origen was highly influential for the manner in which he insisted on the full biblical inheritance among Christians, understanding the world as a place of divine beauty and revelation.

The second- and third-century *apologists* assumed much from *Stoic* religious writing, and Christianized their argument that the world was a schoolroom for God's activity, a plain lesson in providence for those who could see it. *Athanasius of Alexandria* set the tone for much of the later patristic thought to follow in his early work *Contra Gentes*. In this, the world became an apologetic starting point for innumerable instances of divine providence but was also envisioned as having been integrally restored by the enfleshment of the divine Word within it. St. *Basil* provided one of the finest examples of this genre of theologizing from the world to the philanthropy of God who constituted it in his *Sermons on the Hexaemeron* (the six days of the Genesis creation account), which he delivered to workers of his diocese, drawing in simple but elegant language the connections they instinctively knew from their own workshops between the design of the world and the mind of the designer. Because of this, a profoundly optimistic strand remained in Greek patristic thought in regard to the world of nature. Athanasius described the *fall* in his *De Incarnatione* as a matter of the original "mirror" that was the human soul becoming corroded and obscured to the point that many could no longer see God in the world or in their own lives. His remedy, however, was to scour the image once more (through *baptism*, repentance, and *prayer*) so that it could function again as it was designed to do. The Greeks never favored that streak of pessimism that dogged the steps of Latin Christian thought, culminating in Augustine's severe *North African* view of the wholesale corruption of the world and human nature after the fall, such that only supernatural grace could repair the extensive structural damage. The Greek patristic tradition never fully accepted Augustinian grace theory, and thereby resisted the implications of a scheme that inserted a radical division between nature and supernature. In Greek patristic thought all of nature was a divinely graced mystery, even if fallen, and one in which the symbiosis of the divine presence within the material form was frequently and luminously manifested (most sublimely and archetypally in the *incarnation* of God himself as man).

The other primary use of the term "nature" in Christian thought was as a reference to the "limiting natures" that constituted the entire *kosmos*. Reflection on the specific nature (*ousia, natura*) of the human being turned on the idea of delimitation. A nature, in this sense, was the "limit of being" assigned to a creature as part of its fundamental destiny within the creation. Patristic thought on human *ousia* turned much on the human *problema* of a synthetic nature that contained so many disparate tendencies: an immortal soul, a sensual body, and a transcendentally aspiring spirit. The human composite (*to syntheton*) was approached by most patristic writers in pedagogical terms. The human had to learn to orientate him- or herself back toward God by subordinating the lesser elements of the synthesis to the guidance of the higher elements. Such a difficult and lifelong task was regarded as the *asceticism* necessary for a truly human life. God's nature was regarded as essentially inconceivable. While all other created natures were delimiting ontologies (natures thus set a limit around being), God's nature was limitless, and thus did not fit within conventional terms describing natures as sets of attributes. *Gregory of Nazianzus* in his *Theological Orations* (*Orats.* 27–31) eloquently describes how much of ordinary cosmic "nature" transcends the human mind, and how all the more so does that of God. As a result of these strands of reflection, patristic thought found the close juxtaposition of the ideas of human nature and divine nature particularly troublesome in the late third century onward, when *Christology* and its relation to *Trinitarian* theology came to be at the center of controversial debate. In Christology the idea of *person* and nature dominated the scene. Latin thought tended to approach the issue of nature in this context as a "set of attributes possessed by a person," but the balance proved unsatisfactory when it came to imagining how the divine person of Christ could simultaneously possess two complete and discrete natures. Greek Christology preferred to leave behind the static idea of "possession of natures" in favor of the concept of the synergy of natures: the dynamic "coming together into union" that Christ symbolized and realized. Although a common form of words (one person in two natures) was agreed at the *Council of Chalcedon,* there remained a fault line between the wider christological imaginations of the Latin and Greek churches precisely because of the more fixed or more fluid understandings of "nature" operative in the respective traditions.

D. S. Wallace-Hadrill, *The Greek Patristic View of Nature* (New York, 1968); H. A. Wolfson, *The Philosophy of the Church Fathers* (London, 1976), 364–493.

Neo-Arianism   (*See Aetius, Arianism, Eunomius.*)

Neo-Arianism was one of the late forms of the *Arian* movement, attacking and attacked by the Nicene *Cappadocian Fathers* in the latter part of the fourth century. It was called, largely by its opponents, Anomoeanism (or Anhomoianism: the Un-Likers) from the school's controversial resolution of the key Arian question: Was the Son of God the same (*homos*) as the Father or simply like (*homoios*) the Father? They proposed that the Son was wholly "unlike" the Father. Their radical dissolution of the terms of the larger Arian syllogism caused them as many enemies among the Arian camp as among the Nicenes. Their own preferred self-designation was Heterousiasts, reflecting their central statement that the Son was of a different essence or nature (*ousia*) from the Father. *Aetius* and *Eunomius* were the leading neo-

Arian theologians. Both were trained in syllogistic method and strictly applied the rules of logic to theological discourse, resisting the view that theology was a matter of "mysteries," and often coming up with surprisingly challenging views, such as that which argued that God is entirely knowable (in the scriptural syllogisms we find a perfect revelation of theological actualities: so, for example, "sons" are clearly not the same thing as "fathers"). The theology of the Nicene Cappadocians was much sharpened by their encounter with the neo-Arians. *Gregory of Nazianzus* designed his *Five Theological Orations* (*Orations* 27–31) as a direct answer to Eunomius; and there also survive treatises *Against Eunomius* from *Basil of Caesarea* and his brother *Gregory of Nyssa.* Gregory of Nazianzus attacked their central syllogism by arguing that Son and Father are not terms that designate natures, but relations, and that the issue of the *incarnation* is more a *mystery* than a *revelation* and cannot be deduced by simple logic, but is more like poetry, requiring spiritual illumination and refined sensitivity to make sense of it (all of which he denied to the neo-Arians). In the course of his argumentation Gregory immensely developed the Christian doctrine of Trinity. The neo-Arians were a major target of *Theodosius's* antiheretical policy after the *Council of Constantinople I* (381), and they died away as a group after Eunomius's exile to Cappadocia shortly after the council.

M. V. Anastos, "Basil's Kata Eunomiou," in P. J. Fedwick, ed., *Basil of Caesarea: Christian, Humanist, Ascetic* (Toronto, 1981), 67–136; G. Bardy, "L'héritage littéraire d'Aétius," RHE 24 (1928): 809–27; E. Cavalcanti, *Studi Eunomiani* (OCA 202; Rome, 1976); R. P. C. Hanson, *The Search for the Christian Doctrine of God* (Edinburgh, 1988), 598–636; T. A. Kopecek, *A History of Neo-Arianism* (vols. 1–2; Cambridge, Mass., 1979); R. P. Vaggione, *Eunomius: The Extant Works* (Oxford, 1987);

L. R. Wickham, "The Date of Eunomius' Apology: A Reconsideration," JTS 20 (1969): 231–40; idem, "The Syntagmation of Aetius the Anomoean," JTS 19 (1968): 532–69; idem, "Aetius and the Doctrine of Divine Ingeneracy," SP 11 (1972): 259–63.

Neo-Nicenes A recent scholarly designation of that party of Eastern bishops in the late fourth century who continued Athanasius's defense of the Nicene doctrine of the *homoousion* of the Word of God, in his later years (especially after the Synod of Alexandria, which he organized in 362), and in the time immediately after his death. The neo-Nicene party is largely represented by the *Cappadocian Fathers*: *Gregory of Nazianzus, Basil the Great, Gregory of Nyssa,* and *Amphilokius of Ikonium.* The term mirrors the depiction of parts of the later *Arian* movement as "Neo-Arianism," another recent designation of the radical Anhomoian school (*Aetius* and *Eunomius*), who were deeply disliked by the Cappadocians, who wrote several treatises against them. Neo-Nicene theology reflects a focus on the concept of "same substance" as meaning "coequality" of essence, and also reflects a growing interest in the concept of a coequal *Trinity* of divine persons. For Gregory of Nazianzus, at least, this implied that the **Holy Spirit** was consubstantial with the Father and the Son (cf. Gregory of Nazianzus, *Oration* 31).

R. P. C. Hanson, *The Search for the Christian Doctrine of God* (Edinburgh, 1988); J. A. McGuckin, *St. Gregory of Nazianzus: An Intellectual Biography* (New York, 2001).

Neoplatonism *See* Platonism, Proclus

Nestorianism (*See* **Council of Ephesus I (431), Cyril of Alexandria, Nestorius.**) The doctrine, ascribed to *Nestorius of Constantinople,* that there were two separate *persons* in Christ, one human and one divine. Nestorius himself did not actually teach this, but in antique rhetorical argument the positions that could be logically extrapolated from an opponent's original position statements were often assigned to that speaker, whether they had actually maintained them or not. Nestorius thought that he was representing the traditional *Christology* of *Syria* as exemplified in *Diodore of Tarsus's,* and *Theodore Mopsuestia's christologies,* where both thinkers had stressed the need to preserve the distinct integrity of the two *natures* (human and divine) in the Christ. Syrian language had traditionally used images such as the high priesthood of Jesus to connote his elevation by, and ascent to, God (a marked contrast with traditional *Alexandrian* Christology, which had long preferred to speak of the descent of the heavenly *Logos* to earth and his adoption of humanity, but not a human person). Syrian thought also liked (especially in Diodore) to refer to the "Two Sons," meaning the divine Son of God and the human Son of Man. This was originally no more than a poetic way of connoting what later Christology would mean by the "Two Natures"; but in the early fifth century it seemed to many Alexandrian thinkers (especially Cyril) that it was a blatant way of teaching that a man, Jesus of Nazareth (the Son of Man) was associated in the work of salvation along with the true Son of God (the Logos). Cyril relentlessly pushed this point. If there are two Sons, he thought, there must be two subject centers in Christ: and who then was this human son? Cyril castigated the theology of two persons in Christ as a betrayal of the fundamental belief in the union of Godhead and humanity in the single Christ. The drama and clarity of his Christology of the single person contrasted sharply with Nestorius's looser and more intellectualist theology. Nestorius also alienated many bishops at the *Council of Ephesus I* in 431 by losing his temper with traditional statements of piety (such as "My God wrapped in swaddling bands") and telling some hierarchs present that "I cannot call a baby of two or three months old my God" (he was already known to have thought the *Theotokos* title was foolish). This seemed to confirm that Cyril's worst suspicions of him had been true, and soon afterward he was condemned as a heretic who taught two persons coexisted in Christ. In his later exile he tried to justify himself with a *Treatise to Heracleides* (wrongly known in earlier decades as the *Bazaar*), but it had little circulation. It was rediscovered in the early twentieth century, and a fuller sense of his intentionality was then apparent. The condemnation of Nestorius in 431 was the beginning of a wholesale attack on the Christology of the church of Syria across the next two centuries in ecumenical synodical process. The great controversies that then resulted in Christology led to major disruptions in the life of the Eastern churches that have still not been doctrinally resolved.

G. Driver and L. Hodgson, trans., *The Bazaar of Heracleides* (Oxford, 1925); F. Loofs, *Nestoriana* (Halle, Germany, 1905); J. A. McGuckin, *Cyril of Alexandria and the Christological Controversy* (Leiden, Netherlands, 1994), chap. 2; idem, "Nestorius and the Political Factions of 5th Century Byzantium: Factors in His Personal Downfall," in J. F. Coakley and K. Parry, eds., "The Church of the East: Life and Thought" (issue title), BJRUL 78, 3 (1996): 7- 21.

Nestorius of Constantinople (c. 381–452)

Nestorius of Constantinople was a monk from *Antioch* and a disciple of *Theodore of Mopsuestia*, famed for his preaching, who became archbishop of *Constantinople* in 428 and immediately attempted to impose a *Syrian* theological vocabulary on the populace. He caused such controversy that within three years he had involved every major Christian see in one of the greatest *christological* arguments ever witnessed. He especially roused against himself the

redoubtable *Cyril of Alexandria,* who was to bring about his eventual downfall at the *Council of Ephesus I* (431). Cyril had secured the agreement of the Roman see to the censure of Nestorius's teaching, and arranged an Egyptian synod in 430 to threaten him with deposition if he would not recant. The emperor Theodosius II determined that the christological issue should be debated at a major synod, at first planned for Constantinople. Early in 431 the venue was changed to Ephesus, where Cyril took charge of affairs and, despite a lot of support for Nestorius from the Syrian bishops (present only after much delay), Nestorius and his teachings were anathematized and the Christology of Cyril was affirmed as a standard of orthodoxy. The emperor reserved judgment to himself and arranged for the arrest of both Cyril and Nestorius, but after street riots demonstrated the unpopularity of the latter, the sentence against him was confirmed. Sent back in exile to Syria, he was moved to Arabian Petra and his writings were burned in 435 because he continued to protest the injustice of his trial at Ephesus. Soon afterwards he was sent to a lifelong exile in the Great Oasis of Upper Egypt, the most remote penal colony of the Byzantine world. He died, believing that the *Council of Chalcedon* had vindicated him, soon after 451. Nestorius emphasized in his teaching that Jesus had two distinct centers of operation in his life. He was human, and was divine. These two circles of operation, however, must not be confused, otherwise the resultant vision of Christ would be muddied and confused: someone who was properly neither God nor man. For Nestorius exact language was very important in this process of keeping to a pure faith. The Godhead, present in Christ, worked signs of great power, such as the raising of the dead, while the humanity in Christ showed the usual signs of weakness and need (hunger, thirst, and so on). The Word of God was the proper grammatical subject of the divine acts; the man Jesus was the subject of the human acts, and if one wished to connote the mysterious way the Scriptures spoke of the "union" of the two factors, one should use the grammatical subject "Christ." He was specially vehement in denying the legitimacy of common phrases that evoked the union, such as Mary as the Mother of God (*Theotokos*), or Christmas hymns that spoke of "God in swaddling bands" and so on. Since these things were the strong staple of popular piety in Constantinople and elsewhere, he was bent on trouble. Many of those who heard him took him to be suggesting that there were two personal subjects in Christ, a man and a god, and so they denounced him as if he had revived the ancient heresy of *Paul of Samosata* (a man Jesus who had been "possessed" by the divinity). It was by no means what he meant, but it was how a large section heard him, and has become, ever after, the popular (if inaccurate) meaning of the heresy of *Nestorianism*: the doctrine that a man, Jesus, dwelt simultaneously alongside the divine Word in the person of Christ. His own vocabulary resisted Cyril's talk of a concrete (physical) union between the natures (such that they became as one in the single divine person of Jesus) and spoke instead of an association (*synapheia*) of natures constituted by the divine grace or favor (*kat' eudokian*). Nestorius was the significant catalyst of a major Christian disputation on the subjectival unity of Jesus that endured from this time onward until the middle of the following century (*see Council of Ephesus, Council of Chalcedon, Council of Constantinople II*). Although most of his writings were destroyed, excerpts have survived in the Acts of Ephesus 431, and some sermons on the high priesthood of Jesus under the name of *John Chrysostom.* The *Book of Heracleides*, where he attempted to clarify his christological thinking in the time of his exile, was rediscovered in the late nineteenth century.

F. Loofs, *Nestoriana* (Halle, Germany, 1905); G. Driver and I. Hodgson, trans.,

The *Bazaar of Heracleides* (Oxford, 1925); J. A. McGuckin, *Cyril of Alexandria and the Christological Controversy* (Leiden, Netherlands, 1994), chap. 2; idem, "Nestorius and the Political Factions of 5th Century Byzantium: Factors in His Personal Downfall," in J. F. Coakley and K. Parry, eds., "The Church of the East: Life and Thought" (issue title), BJRUL 78, 3 (1996): 7–21.

Nicene *see* **Christology, Council of Nicaea, Neo-Nicenes**

Nitria A desert region near *Alexandria*, to the west of the mouth of the Nile, Nitria was near ancient *Scete* (the modern Wadi al Natroun) and was a center of intellectual life for Egyptian desert monasticism (*see asceticism*). The settlement was founded by Ammonius, one of the so-called *Tall Brothers*, who were later hounded by *Theophilus of Alexandria* because of their Origenism. Ammonius also exercised leadership over settlements at nearby Kellia (to the north of Scete). *Evagrius of Pontus* entered monastic life under the guidance of Ammonius; living first at Nitria from 383 to 385, and then settling permanently at Kellia. The settlements were often associated with the mystical spirituality of the Origenian-Evagrian school.

D. J. Chitty, *The Desert a City* (London, 1977); H. G. Evelyn-White, *History of the Monasteries of Nitria and Scetis* (3 vols.; New York, 1932).

Noetus of Smyrna *see* **Monarchianism**

North Africa The northern littoral of the African Mediterranean coast was significant to the Christian movement from the very beginning. The coastal strip, especially eastward from Alexandria to the modern territory of Libya, was occupied in Roman times by a series of trading towns with large Jewish communities in most of them, many of whose inhabitants took part in the regular traffic to the *Jerusalem* temple before the Roman War of A.D. 66–70. One of those little communities, Cyrene, sent an otherwise unknown Jewish pilgrim called Simon, whose name was ever after celebrated in the Gospels as the man who helped Jesus to carry his *cross*. Simon's sons, Rufus and Alexander, were sufficiently known to the church for whom Mark wrote his Gospel (Mark 15:21) as to need no further introduction. The great metropolis of *Alexandria* at the Nile Delta was always a Greek-speaking Hellenistic capital, but the further east one traveled the country changed dramatically: for the northwestern coastal strip was profoundly Latin-speaking and looked to *Rome*, not Alexandria, as its cultural and trade partner. This is the territory of Roman North Africa proper (today it covers the territory of the western part of Libya, Tunisia, Algeria, and part of Morocco). Most of the important events of the North African church in its period of energetic flourishing (from the second to the sixth centuries) have to be contextualized in the light of this intimate relationship. The first Christian text from Africa is the account of the *Passion of the Scillitan Martyrs* in 180. The African church fiercely venerated its *martyrs*, and from the earliest times is characterized by a strong spirit of "resistance to the world" notable in its martyr cult and severe approach to church discipline. The *Montanist* movement found a ready welcome here, although in moderated form, after its migration from Asia Minor, and the other great African martyr narrative, *The Passion of Perpetua and Felicity* (A.D. 200), shows some Montanist influence in its lively interest in revelatory experiences. The first great theologians of the church were *Tertullian* and *Cyprian*, although earlier *apologists* such as *Minucius Felix* had tried to explain the moral attractions of the new religion for a pagan literary audience. Tertullian set the basis for much of Latin Christianity's vocabulary in fundamental theological areas such as *trinity* and *Christology*. Other significant African apologists would be Optatus of Milevis, Arnobius, and *Lactantius*. The latter was an important adviser to *Constantine* the Great, and in his *Divine Institutes* represented the first attempt at a Latin systematic theology (although it was never popular and was soon overshadowed by *Augustine's* work). The third century was a period of growth for the African church with Carthage as its chief center. The Council of Carthage in 256 was attended by eighty-seven Latin African bishops. A clearer picture of the church is provided by the *Letters* of *Cyprian* the bishop of Carthage in the mid–third century. His difficult episcopate tried to deal with the numerous problems caused by the *persecution* of Decius, and in the course of his administration he wrote significant works on the nature of ecclesiology and church *penance*. During Cyprian's episcopate, tensions with the Roman administration of Pope Stephen, arising when Cyprian refused to accept the Roman judgment that the baptisms of heretics were valid, led to the African church asserting an increasing independence. The persecution of Diocletian in 303–305 once again disrupted the life of the North African church in ways that endured longer here than almost anywhere else. Internal conflicts between hard-liners and reconciliationists over who had lapsed and how they ought to be regarded in the restoration of peace led to the splitting of the North African church into the *Catholic* party (a minority in the fourth century) and the Donatists. The social fact that most of the Latin Catholic church was Roman, and thus colonial, asserted itself during the controversy, with the *Donatist* movement gaining considerable local support from the lower classes, whom it championed. Donatist theologians such as *Tyconius* developed important rules of biblical exegesis, which influenced even Augustine. Augustine of Hippo, in the fifth century, was the single greatest Latin African theologian. His episcopacy was deeply involved with the Donatist and *Pelagian* controversies, but his extensive works provided the Latin church with a veritable dossier of theology ever afterwards, and through Augustine many aspects of the severe African tradition (not least its views on original *sin* and divine *grace*) moved to become central to the "Roman" tradition as such, especially so after they were championed and disseminated by Pope *Gregory the Great.* In 439, shortly after Augustine's death, the Vandal king Gaiseric captured Carthage, and Roman Africa passed into the control of *Arian* occupiers. *Justinian* took North Africa back into the imperial fold in the campaign of 534–535, and for a brief time catholic Christianity flourished again with theologians such as Vigilius of Thapsus, *Fulgentius of Ruspe,* and *Facundus of Hermiane* producing interesting works on Christology. After the fall of Carthage to Islamic armies in 698, Christianity in Roman North Africa faded away into the gloom of powerlessness and ultimately to insignificance.

W. H. C. Frend, *The Donatist Church: A Movement of Protest in Roman North Africa* (Oxford, 1952); P. Monceaux, *Histoire littéraire de l'Afrique chrétienne* (Paris, 1901–1923); B. H. Warmington, *The North African Provinces* (Cambridge, 1954).

Novatian   *see* Novatianism

Novatianism   Novatianism was a dissident and rigorist church movement deriving from Novatian, a Roman *presbyter* (Cyprian, *Epistles* 30, 32, 55; Eusebius, *Ecclesiastical History* 4.43.13) who lived during the time of the Decian *persecution* (249–250). He had enjoyed a reputation as a leading theologian (already having written a significant work, *On the Trinity*) and during the time of persecution, when Pope Fabian was martyred, he assumed a strong leadership of the presbyters, demanding that standards in the church be stepped up and not relaxed in any way. After the persecution, he was passed over in the election for a new pope, and strongly disliked the new choice of Cornelius (251–253). Cornelius was already facing much opposition from the rigorist party of the Roman church, who wanted to forbid the return to communion of those who had recently lapsed under pressure. Cornelius wished to institute some form of a process of penitential return (*see penance*). He was supported in this by the higher *clergy* at Rome and Carthage (where *Cyprian* was also undergoing similar problems, and whose letters give us our information on the crisis), but Novatian dramatically took the side of the rigorists and became their figurehead. He was consecrated *bishop* (the first known antipope) by three Italian bishops, and also got them to ordain to the episcopate other sympathizers in an attempt to set up a rival hierarchy. When he understood that Cyprian also shared rigorist attitudes, he abandoned his earlier hostility to him. Novatian represented a vision of the church as the society of the pure elect, whose boundaries could tolerate no defilement from those who renounced their baptismal commitments and were thus no better than pagans. Apart from this rigorist and exclusivist ecclesiology, the Novatians were traditional in regard to all other theological forms and liturgical practices. They were widely admired for their strictness even by their opponents, and were always regarded as a major "schism" in the patristic era rather than a heresy as such. At the *Council of Nicaea* in 325 Constantine personally rebuked one of the leading Novatianist bishops (Acesius) for wanting to "climb to heaven by himself." Canon 8 of that council set the terms required of those who wanted to return to orthodox communion from the Novatianists. They survived well into the fifth century as a small sect. Their attitudes have often been revived in the course of later church history (often after times of persecution, when suffering parties are not inclined to any form of lenient restorationism). The conflict between Cyprian and the rigorists of his own church at Carthage, while he was aware of the Novatianist problem, led him to reflect on the nature of ecclesiology (*On the Unity of the Catholic Church*) and the reasons that would necessitate the (re)baptism of apostates. *Augustine* later developed a broader view of the *church* as a "dragnet of different fishes" or a field "full of tares and wheat," contrasting in several respects to that of Cyprian. The fracture line of these *patristic* ecclesiologies (an exclusivist or an inclusivist attitude) still marks the Catholic and Orthodox communions; but historically, Novatianism and later *Donatism* were the causes of considerable patristic reflection on the nature of the church as the community of *salvation*.

A. d'Alès, *Novatien: Étude sur la théologie romaine au milieu du troisième siècle* (Paris, 1924); H. Gulzow, *Cyprian und Novatian* (Tübingen, Germany, 1975).

Nubia The ancient church of Nubia, once (excepting *Ethiopia*) the only sub-Saharan example of indigenous Christianity in the ancient world, is now thoroughly forgotten. It is a tragic example of a church that flourished in the *patristic* period with a lively connection to both Byzantium and Ethiopia through the *trade route* of the Nile, by means of the gateway of *Alexandria*. With Alexandria's fall to Islamic power in the seventh century, Christian Nubia was effectively cut off from easy communication with the wider Christian world, and its subsequent record was (like that of Ethiopia) one of constant battle for survival. The Nubians and Ethiopians both have an extraordinary number of warrior *martyrs* in their calendars, a testimony to the bitter experience of their church history. The Nubian church existed for nine hundred years. It was comprised of the three African Christian kingdoms of Nobatia, Makurrah (or

Makuria), and Alwah (or Alodia), and occupied the fertile land around the Nile from the first cataract (Aswan) to the borders of Ethiopia. The territory is now largely located in northern Sudan. The church began with a mission to Nobatia from Alexandria sponsored by Empress Theodora in the sixth century. By 580 all three kingdoms had become extensively Christian in line with their kings. The three kingdoms were allied with the Byzantine court after their Christianization, but belonged to the anti-Chalcedonian (the so-called *Monophysite*) *christological* tradition, which Theodora seems to have advocated. The events of the mission to the Nobatian court in 542 are described by John of Ephesus. In the early eighth century the three kingdoms were united in the person of King Mercurius of Nobatia. The Arabic Christian text *History of the Patriarchs* describes the events briefly, and also speaks of the Christian court's diplomatic relations with the Islamic caliphate at Baghdad and the emirate at Cairo. During this time Nubia served as an important political patron and defender of the Coptic Christians of Egypt. During the ninth and tenth centuries the Nubian church enjoyed considerable peace and prosperity, but the encroaching power of Islam and its own vulnerable strategic position led to its invasion and rapid collapse in the fifteenth century. As quickly as it had arisen, so did it decline when its kings at Dongola adopted the Islamic religion. In 1960, when the Aswan dam was going to inundate northern Nubia, rapid excavations demonstrated the extent and quality of the Christian civilization that had once flourished there. Its main churches were at Dongola, Qasr Ibrim, and Fars (where wonderful tenth-century Afro-Byzantine frescoes have been discovered). Although its highest church leaders were appointed from Alexandria, the frescoes clearly show that they were sub-Saharan African archbishops, not, as had often been presupposed, imported Coptic clergy from Egypt.

W. Y. Adams, *Nubia: Corridor to Africa* (Princeton, N.J., 1977); A. Grillmeier, *The Church of Alexandria with Nubia and Ethiopia after 451,* vol. 2, part 4, *Christ in Christian Tradition* (London, 1996), 263–94; P. L. Shinnie, "Christian Nubia," in J. D. Fage, ed., *The Cambridge History of Africa* (vol. 2; Cambridge, 1978), 556–88; J. Vantini, *The Excavations at Faras: A Contribution to the History of Christian Nubia* (Bologna, Italy, 1970).

Olympias (c. 365–410)   Olympias was an aristocratic Byzantine woman in *Constantinople.* She was a distant cousin of *Gregory of Nazianzus* and her family was instrumental in supporting his invitation to the city as missionary bishop in 379. Olympias was married to Nebridius, prefect of Constantinople in 386, and on his sudden death soon afterward, she refused to remarry (despite pressure to do so from the emperor *Theodosius* I). Dedicating herself to the ascetic life, she used her immense wealth in the service of developing a women's community adjacent to the Cathedral of Hagia Sophia, which became a center of charitable work. She supported her friend the aristocrat Nectarius, who was elected to replace Gregory of Nazianzus as bishop of the capital, and was ordained (aged thirty) as deaconess by him. She was also a close friend and patron of *John Chrysostom,* and had several others of her community ordained *deaconess* by him. Several of his letters to her from his exile survive in his correspondence. Olympias was caught up in the fall of Chrysostom in 404, and was herself fined and exiled to Nicomedia, where she later died. Her work gave a model for the several communities in the capital later led by women aristocrats and ascetics who exercised considerable patronage through their charitable works (and thus extensive sway over the affairs of the church). Her life was written in the middle of the fifth century, and pseudonymously attributed to Chrysostom.

E. A. Clark, *Jerome, Chrysostom, and Friends: Essays and Translations* (New York, 1979).

Ordination   Ordination is the conferring of ministerial "orders" on a person. In Greek it is signified by the term "the laying on of hands" (*cheiorotenia*). It primarily designates the major orders of Christian ministry (bishop, *priest,* and *deacon*) and the minor order of subdeaconate. Other ranks of the clergy such as readers, acolytes, or doorkeepers were admitted to their office by a blessing (*cheirothesia*) of the bishop, which was distinguished from ordination as such. *Ordinatio* in the Latin usage derives from the subsequent "listing" (*ordinatus*) of the candidate in the ranks of the church's *clergy.* The hereditary priesthood of the Old Testament was decisively abandoned in the early church for a vision of the unique and single high priesthood of Christ. The Letter to the Hebrews developed the distinction of priesthood "according to Melchizedech," which was that of Jesus, as distinct from the old law's priesthood according to Aaron. The election and commissioning of the apostles (Matt. 10:1–5) along with their *eucharistic* initiation and consecration at the Last Supper (John 14:26; 15:16–20; 17:5–26) and their illumination at Pascha-Pentecost (John 20:19–23; Acts 1.8; 2:1–4) were seen as the prototypical narratives of Christian ordination. In the church of the late first century the ritual structuring of ministerial appointment was more and more regularized, and in Acts the process of appointing elders (presbyters) or overseers (*episkopoi*) is attributed to Paul (Acts 14:23; 20:17). In the Pastoral Letters there emerge clear signs of the regular appointment of ministers by the laying on of hands (1 Tim. 3:1–13; 4:14; 5:22; 2 Tim. 1:6). The elders are at first seemingly synonymous with the overseers (Acts 20:28). Patterns of ministry, which were originally varied in the ancient church (presbyters, deacons, teachers, prophets, and exorcists), soon accumulated into the simpler pattern of a council of presbyter-elders, and deacons as their assistants who were charged with the practical administration of church affairs (based on a paradigm taken from Acts 6:1–6). The episcopacy seems to have arisen as a monarchical president elected from the council of elders. The *Letters of Ignatius of Antioch* and the *Clementine Letters* from *Rome* are among the first to witness the rise of the single episcopate. In certain large cities such as Rome, *Antioch*, and Alexandria, this movement towards a single "overseer" happened more quickly than elsewhere, but by the middle of the third century it was becoming the standard in all the Christian churches. *Cyprian* in the West did much to advance a theology of priesthood that drew from Levitical and temple typology in the Scriptures. After the fourth century deacons became especially attached to the service of the bishops, and presbyters came more and more to have charge of smaller churches separate from the cathedral (at first the rule had quite literally been "one city, one church"). Women were enrolled among the deacons from an early time. In the Greek church they were important in the baptismal rituals of other women, but also served at the altar in the eucharistic ritual. In the Western church the female diaconate fell out of use relatively early. In the East it was still prominent until after the ninth century, and the ordination ritual still exists. It is probable in both cases that monastic pressures caused the decline of female ministry in the major orders.

P. F. Bradshaw, *Ordination Rites of the Ancient Churches of East and West* (New York, 1990); B. H. Streeter, *The Primitive Church: Studied with special reference to the origin of the Christian ministry* (New York, 1929).

Origen of Alexandria (c. 186–255)

The most influential of all Greek theologians, Origen was the architect (whether his opinions were followed or were explicitly rejected) of most of the substructure of Christian dogma and biblical theology in the late antique period of Christianity. His influence was as great as that of *Augustine* in the West, although in the Greek-speaking world the variety of other major thinkers moderating and redirecting the channels of his thought (such as *Gregory of Nazianzus* or *Maximus the Confessor*) ensured that his intellectual legacy would be more creatively received and developed. When he was seventeen, in 202, the Great *Persecution* broke out in Alexandria and his father Leonides was arrested and executed. Origen's mother prevented her son from trying to join him in his confession. Afterward he received some form of sponsored position from the local church, probably appointment as a catechist. His father had been a grammarian, and Origen also supported the family by carrying on privately instructing pupils. He himself followed advanced courses in philosophy with some of the leading intellectuals of his day and began to develop his own school, living an *ascetical* life as a philosopher-sage. It was an example that would subsequently have great impact on the early development of the monastic movement, which always retained a special place for Origen's view of theological wisdom as fundamentally an ascetic ascent to communion with God. When he was about twenty he sold his father's library in exchange for a small pension that would allow him independence to pursue philosophy single-mindedly. At this time his ascetical life was rumored to be the result of a decision to have himself castrated. It was a story reported a century after his death by *Eusebius* in book six of his *Ecclesiastical History*, but it is highly unlikely, as Origen himself speaks of those who interpret the Gospel text on castration (Matt. 19:12) in a literal way as little better than fools. Eusebius wishes to use the story as a reason to explain the local bishop's protest at Origen's *ordination* by others (castration was a canonical irregularity in the fourth century) and thereby distract attention from the fact that Origen had probably been accused of heterodoxy in his own lifetime. Origen's guiding star in his intellectual life was the belief that the highest goals of philosophy were reconcilable with the mysterious plan of the divine wisdom (the *Logos*) and that in the sacred Scriptures, the gift of *revelation* and the human quest for enlightenment would meet, a symbolic rapprochement that was mystically witnessed in the *incarnation* of the Logos within history. From the time he devoted himself to *philosophy,* he deliberately dedicated all his life to biblical *exegesis.* He followed the highest traditions of contemporary literary analysis as exemplified by the scholars of the Great Library at Alexandria, and set out rules of interpretation that would be massively influential on all Christians who followed. His approach was governed by the notion that the Scripture was a single reality, a coherent corpus emanating from one mind, that of the divine Logos. Its apparent multiplicities were but the masking of the eternal revelation under the illusory appearances of history and relative conditions. A text, therefore, had several layers of meaning. It had a historical import (such as Israel taking possession of the promised land from the Canaanites), a moral meaning (the story of the fight for the promised land "more significantly" connoted the individual's constant battle for control of his or her own psyche in the face of passionate desires), and a mystical meaning (the "real meaning" or the highest significance of the entry to the promised land would be the soul's communion with God in the kingdom, which is to come after this earthly cosmos passes away). This meant that *allegorical* (or spiritual) interpretation was constantly his preferred method. Texts that had an "impossible" meaning (obnoxious moral tales in the ancient Testament, or stories that were clearly unhistorical, for example) were like special page-markers left in the Scriptures by the Logos, designed to make intelligent souls stop and realize that a deeper mystery lay buried like a treasure in the field. For Origen, those who stayed only with the literal meaning of the text were unenlightened souls who had not realized that Jesus gave some of his teaching in the valleys and some on mountain tops. Only to the latter disciples, those who could ascend the mountains, did Jesus reveal himself transfigured. In 212 Origen travelled to *Rome* and heard *Hippolytus* lecture. His fame was already beginning to travel before him, as *Jerome* records that Hippolytus stopped and pointed out the presence of their distinguished visitor to the assembled lecture room. Back in Alexandria he published his first major work, *On First Principles*, ambitiously designed as an introductory summatic to Christian faith, with a vast scope, trying to relate how the Christian philosophy embraces cosmology, philosophy, and religion, and attempting to offer a definitive answer to the major issues raised by all other schools before him. His vision was certainly highly missionary in its design. Its explicit preference for *Platonic* metaphysic (not least the preexistence of *souls*) also drew down on his head the wrath of his local bishop, the ambitious Demetrius who, at that period, was extending the office of the bishop of Alexandria in a most powerful manner toward monarchical government. Demetrius grew very wary of Origen, fearing that he was becoming another of a long series of independent Didaskaloi, gnostic teachers who had already been seen in Alexandria and Rome. In fact, though adopting many of the most brilliant insights of the *gnostics*, Origen was a consistent critic of their system. Government authorities began to invite Origen on international lecture tours. He took the opportunity (and the money earned) to begin to gather the nucleus of a large research library. When he finally settled in Caesarea in Palestine, it became the core of the world's first Christian university. When he left Alexandria in 215 to escape Caracalla's punishment on the university professors, the bishops of Palestine invited Origen to address the churches at Caesarea and *Jerusalem.* His own bishop was infuriated and recalled him by messenger to his tasks of catechizing. He obeyed the summons and quietly resumed his work, inspired by ancient texts he had found and bought at Jericho (they sound suspiciously like early exemplars of the Qumran finds). So he began a massive project called the *Hexapla:* six columns of text listing the various versions of the Old Testament, written for comparative research. It was the first time a Christian school had undertaken biblical exegesis in such a scientific manner, and gives to Origen the undisputed title of "father of Christian exegesis." Soon afterward he was invited by no less than the empress Julia Mammaea to discourse at her court in *Antioch.* This honor gave him financial independence as well as increasing confidence that perhaps the hostile church climate of Alexandria was not the best place to be. One of his students, an immensely wealthy former gnostic named *Ambrose,* commissioned him to compose a major *Commentary on the Gospel of John.* He began the work but friction from his bishop over the issuing of the *First Principles,* and his apparent denial that the **resurrection** body would be material (in his *Stromata*) caused him to abandon the early chapters and take refuge in 231 in the Palestinian church, where the scholarly bishops of Jerusalem and Caesarea were delighted to have him among them. In Palestine he was ordained priest, and in addition to his more learned treatises, composed a large body of homiletic, which offers us an unrivaled window into the Sunday and weekday preaching customs of the third-century church (albeit from the pulpit of a great genius). *Extempore* delivery of interpretations seems to have been common, and regarded as an extension of the *clergy's* "prophetic" role. He

completed his *Commentary on the Gospel of John* here, and it remains one of his masterworks. So too his wonderful *Commentary on the Song of Songs.* At Caesarea Origen founded a new school around his library and classroom and opened his doors to all comers. One of his students, later to become **Gregory Thaumaturgus,** the great missionary bishop of Cappadocia, has left behind a *Panegyric,* describing his own love for Origen as an inspiring teacher and outlining the broad comparative curriculum followed in his school. Origen's labors made Caesarea the veritable intellectual center of Christianity within his generation. There was hardly a biblical book that did not receive his attention, but above all he loved the Johannine Gospel and the Pauline letters, seeing them in his own system of biblical hierarchies as "the firstfruits among the firstfruits." Demetrius of Alexandria and his successor Heraclas continued to pursue Origen from a distance, and sought the assistance of Rome in securing his condemnation. It was a distraction that made him produce several apologetic writings, but his Palestinian bishops supported him, and his prestige was such that he became the leading theologian of the church of his day, speaking at several synods in Arabia, usually on the need for careful exegesis in the establishment of Christian doctrine. As priest at Caesarea Origen also composed his *Treatise on Prayer,* which shows him pastorally explaining the nature of the **Lord's Prayer,** probably to a group of **catechumens,** and (typically) rising from the simplicities of childlike prayer to questions about cosmic providence. In 235 the persecution of Maximin the Thracian threatened him and so he went into hiding, composing a most moving treatise, *Exhortation to Martyrdom,* for those of his friends who had been captured. Restoration of the peace allowed him to make another journey to Athens (between 238 and 244) to gather books and teach in the city. He was back in Caesarea when the death of the pro-Christian emperor

Philip the Arab unleashed a new storm of hostility against the Christians of Palestine under the sponsorship of Decius. This time Origen was carefully sought out and the governor ordered him to be tortured slowly (so that he would not die before he had denied the faith). He was set in the iron collar and stretched over "four spaces" (ratchet marks in the rack), which would more or less have permanently crippled him. His courage outlasted his persecutors, and in the restoration of peace in 253, he was taken into convalescence by the church, and spent a year dying. Eusebius tells us that he was most concerned that those who had suffered in the trials might not be discouraged, and so he wrote a series of letters to them: "After these things Origen left many words of comfort, full of sweetness, to those who needed assistance, as can be seen abundantly and most truly from so many of his epistles" (*Ecclesiastical History* 6.39.5). This literature is now lost. He died aged sixty-nine with a martyr's honor, if not a martyr's crown. If he had possessed that status formally his works might not have suffered the depletions that have reduced them over the centuries. His writings were ordered to be burned after many years of controversy in the sixth century, when *Justinian* arranged for their condemnation in 543. (*See* **Council of Constantinople II.**) But even so, a massive amount of writing has survived. There is hardly a major thinker of the Greek (or Latin) church who is not deeply indebted to Origen. From the middle of the twentieth century, focused scholarly symposia (issuing a four-yearly series of studies entitled *Origeniana*) have once again begun to study and critically expound the rich Origenian legacy.

G. W. Butterworth, trans., *Origen: On First Principles* (London, 1936); H. Chadwick, trans., *Origen: Against Celsus* (London, 1953; repr. 1986); H. Crouzel, *Origen* (Edinburgh, 1989); R. Heine, trans., *Origen: Commentary on the Gospel of John* (FOTC 80, 89; Washington, D.C., 1989, 1993); C. Kannengiesser and W. L. Petersen, eds., *Origen of Alexandria: His World and His Legacy* (Notre Dame, Ind., 1988); R. P. Lawson, trans., *Origen: Commentary on the Song of Songs, and Homilies on the Song of Songs* (ACW 26; Washington, D.C., 1957); J. A. McGuckin, "Caesarea Maritima as Origen Knew It," in R. J. Daly, ed., *Origeniana Quinta* (Louvain, Belgium, 1992), 3–25; idem, "Structural Design and Apologetic Intent in Origen's Commentary on John," in G. Dorival and A. Le Boulluec, eds., *Origeniana Sexta* (Louvain, Belgium, 1995), 441–57; J. A. McGuckin, ed., *The Westminster Handbook to Origen* (Louisville, Ky., 2004); J. W. Trigg, *Origen: The Bible and Philosophy in the Third Century Church* (Atlanta, 1983).

Original Sin   *see* **Fall, Sin, Soteriology**

Orthodoxy

The term "orthodoxy" comes from the Greek term for "correct doctrine" (*orthodoxia*). The word makes its appearance in the fifth-century *patristic* writers to contrast the "tradition of the fathers" with the varieties of "heretical deviance" (false opinion or heterodoxy) that were increasingly being classified as the major historical heresies. Orthodoxy, in patristic theology, is thus the opposite of heresy, and is seen to be the unique possession of the church (an idea that ranges back to the late catholic epistles of the New Testament and was developed intensively by *Irenaeus* and *Origen*), while heresies are the invention of sectarians. In pre-Christian Greek philosophical thought "orthodoxy" referred to a correct conception, whereas heterodoxy simply meant a variant opinion from the norm (not necessarily right or wrong). In the patristic understanding of revealed tradition, heterodoxy, the departure from orthodoxy, is always seen as a culpable lapse into error. Especially evident from the fifth-century conciliar considerations of theology, a sense that the writings of the "Fathers" sustained and represented the tradition of orthodoxy gave an impetus to the careful study and collection of earlier sources and authorities in late antiquity. After the ninth century the word comes to be used as a more common designation of the church (alongside the four "marks" or "notes" of the *church*, as listed in the *creed*, namely: one, holy, *catholic*, and *apostolic*). In a later usage it was a term that was used to connote the Eastern churches (the Orthodox Church) as distinct from the Western Catholic Church (Roman Catholic as it was designated after the Reformation era). When so used, the other marks of the church are also applied. Thus the Eastern churches formally designate themselves as the Holy Catholic Apostolic Orthodox Church of the East.

J. Meyendorff, *The Orthodox Church* (New York, 1962); M. Simon, "From Greek Haeresis to Christian Heresy," in *Early Christian Literature and the Classical Intellectual Tradition* (Paris, 1979), 101–16; T. Ware, *The Orthodox Church* (London, 1963).

Ossius   *see* Hosius of Cordoba

Ousia   *Ousia* is the Greek term for *nature*, a generic word for that which limits the being of a certain type of existent. Following *Aristotle's* teleological views of natures, the early Christians understood human nature as what makes a being essentially "human"; and a dog-nature, for example, that which makes a dog a dog and not any other thing. In Christian debate the term assumed great significance in the *christological* controversies: how could the Christ simultaneously exist in two natures? In reference to created natures (*ousiai*), the nature is the limit set by the creator to the ontological condition of a creature. The *patristic theologians* saw human *ousia* as a dynamic and synthetic combination of many elements (flesh, *soul*, and spirit), which made it unique among all created natures (inanimate

matter, animals, and angels being single realities, not composites). They also saw it as destined for a transcendent union with God (*deification*). Even so, it remained a created nature within limits, as was all other creation. God's *ousia* alone was unlimited, but for that very reason could not be apprehended, since it was devoid of descriptive limitation, the fundamental way all limited being found its definition.

C. Stead, *Divine Substance* (Oxford, 1977); H. A. Wolfson, *The Philosophy of the Church Fathers* (London, 1976), 364–493.

Pachomius (c. 290–346)   Pachomius is traditionally seen as the originator of common life (cenobitic) monasticism: the *ascetic* life lived in a common building (usually a fortified complex) under the rule of a senior figure (higumen or abbot) who directs a common daily rule based around community work and prayer. Pachomius represents the development of cenobitic styles of Christian ascetical life, when previously monasticism had largely been disorganized and more individualist (monachism derives from the Greek world for solitary person). Pachomius was born in Egypt and as a young man was forcibly conscripted into the Roman army. His wretchedness was alleviated one day by the kindness of a Christian community at Chenoboskion in Upper Egypt. When he finished his military service in 313 he returned to the village and was baptized. Some years later he took up the ascetical life under the direction of Apa Palamon the monk. He tells how he was collecting firewood in the deserted village of Tabennisi around 320 when he heard a voice instructing him to build a monastery and be ready to receive many disciples. So, it was built and slowly attracted disciples. Within six years he had to build another house at Pbow, which eventually became the headquarters of a string of eleven Pachomian houses (two for women) along the

Upper Nile. One of these was near the village of Nag Hammadi, source of several gnostic text discoveries, and it is often presumed they represent jettisoned manuscripts from the community's library. The fortunes of the Pachomian houses declined sharply after the fifth century, but his monastic rule and ascetical tradition were very influential on *Basil of Caesarea, John Cassian,* and Caesarius of Arles, and through them was disseminated widely in the church.

A. N. Athanassakis, *The Life of Pachomius* (Missoula, Mont., 1975); D. J. Chitty, *The Desert a City* (Oxford, 1966); P. Rousseau, *Pachomius: The Making of a Community in 4th Century Egypt* (Berkeley, Calif., 1985); A. Veilleux, *Pachomian Koinonia* (vols. 1–3; Kalamazoo, Mich., 1980–1982).

Palladius (c. 365–425)   Palladius was a student of *Evagrius of Pontus.* He first entered the monastic life through the community of the Mount of Olives. He lived in and traveled among the Egyptian desert communities in their golden period, and settled with Evagrius's community. He had to leave Egypt because of his health, and returned to Palestine. He eventually became bishop of Helenopolis in Bithynia, and was exiled in 406 for his support of *John Chrysostom.* His major work, written in 419, was a book written for the Byzantine aristocrat Lausus (*The Lausiac History*), which collected monastic stories, aphorisms, and histories of the major figures of the Egyptian *desert.* It became an immensely popular book in Byzantium, and is a priceless resource for recording desert life, especially giving us most of what is known about Evagrius himself. He also wrote a *Dialogue* to record the life and sufferings of John Chrysostom.

Another Palladius was one of the *deacons* of *Pope Celestine* I who, in 431, was sent to be a bishop "for the Irish believing in Christ" (Prosper of Aquitaine, *Chronicle for the Year 431*). He worked in the south of Ireland, but little is known of his character and work, though later (and unreliable) sources describe him as a martyr (*see Ireland, Patrick*).

E. D. Hunt, "Palladius of Helenopolis: A Party and Its Supporters in the Church of the Late 4th Century," JTS n.s. 24 (1973): 456–80; R. T. Meyer, *Palladius: The Lausiac History* (ACW 34; New York, 1965); idem, *Palladius: Dialogue on the Life of St. John Chrysostom* (ACW 45; New York, 1985).

Papacy   Papacy is a late theological term to refer to the development of Western church theory about the authority and jurisdiction of the *bishop* of *Rome* (deriving from the ancient title of a bishop, "father," *papa*). Most recent theological discussion on the topic takes its departure point from late medieval and early modern perspectives, after the rise of the papal monarchy. In *patristic* times the foundations of a specific theology of the Petrine office, and the authority vested in the bishop of Rome, were evident from an early date, although it is important to read this evidence for what it says in itself, however, not (as has often been the case) primarily for what it adumbrates about the later developments; to read it in the light of antiquity, that is, rather than in the light of anachronistic controversies and post-Reformation apologetics. The Christian movement came to Rome from a very early date indeed. It was already there, probably in Trastevere, the Jewish quarter of the city, even before Peter and Paul's missionary visits in the 40s and 50s of the first century (cf. Acts 2:10). From the second century, however, and largely because of the writings of *Irenaeus,* it became customary to regard Peter and Paul as the twin apostolic founders of the great church. Irenaeus's understanding of *apostolicity* as the foundational pillar of Christian authenticity dealt Rome a double-value significance, and throughout the second and third centuries the prestige of the Roman church continued to rise high. This was not merely because the city was the capital of world empire (though this was an undoubted and positive factor) but because it had already established an international fame as a center of Christian resistance that had already produced large numbers of *martyrs* and *confessors*. The accumulation of a venerable list of *saints,* including several of its early leaders, coincided with the emerging role of the city's Christian community as an authoritative source of appeal for issues of international conflict. Rome by the end of the first century had become a place to look to if one wanted to see how a church should conduct itself. The community had a reputation for sobriety and traditionalism, and it was one that was merited, as the leaders of the various Roman churches (before the mid–second century it is too early to speak of a single Roman church) generally resisted those speculative teachers who later came to be known as the *gnostics.* Irenaeus appealed to Rome on several occasions to represent just this authoritative voice. He is one of the first to articulate that "communion with this church is a guarantee of apostolicity" in the local domain (*Adversus haereses* 3.3.2); it would be a doctrine that would stand at the heart of all later development of papacy, especially when the idea devolved from what Irenaeus actually said (communion with an undoubtedly apostolic church signifies the apostolicity of one's own church) into something he did not actually say: an acknowledgment by the bishop of the Roman church signifies authenticity as a Christian community. When the emphasis is shifted onto the latter aspect it is correct to speak of "papacy" theory. Apart from Irenaeus, the Clementine writings also demonstrated a similar concern of the Roman community to act as a "traditional" grounding and stabilizing force for other communities. Figures such as *Justin* and *Ignatius* also witness to the reverential respect the

Roman church could command. From the outset, therefore, the authority of the Roman bishop was looked for. Just as Rome had long been regarded as the last hope for legal appeal (its law courts were supreme, and all the legal talent of the empire accumulated there), so too the Roman church began to have a reputation as an international court of ecclesiastical appeal. Its traditionalism in Christian affairs underlined this role. From the late second century a series of remarkable popes established and advanced the unprecedented ecclesiastical authority of their city. The first to be known in this regard was Pope *Victor,* who in 190 acted decisively to censure the Asia Minor churches who would not celebrate Pascha on a common date, but preferred their local tradition (the *Quartodecimans controversy*); and he was also credited with decisive action in condemning the appearances of *adoptionist* theology at Rome. In the mid–third century a concept was becoming evident of Peter's special authority as prince of the apostles, and this as having passed to the Petrine successor (in the patristic era the popes invoked the special title "Vicar of Peter"—only much later did this change to "Vicar of Christ"). Pope Stephen invoked the idea to justify the validity of his policy on the admission of heretics' baptisms, against Cyprian's view that heretical *baptism* was invalid. In his controversy with Stephen, *Cyprian* found it necessary to rebut this developing view of the "Petrine Office," a sense of special authority vested in the bishop of Rome as *Petrus Redivivus.* Cyprian argued that while Peter was indeed a special symbol of authority, his preeminence did not pass on to his successors in Rome, but was a general charism that ought to grace every bishop who was "apostolic" as Peter was. Cyprian had to work all the harder on this rebuttal, having only a few years previously published a treatise entitled *On the Unity of the Catholic Church,* which had taken its stand on elevating Peter's confession of faith as the symbol of international Christian unity based around the great church of Rome. Still, powerful leaders at Rome developed the prestige of the papal office as a kind of "superepiscopate." Later in the third century, after the end of the Decian persecution, Pope Dionysius was able to restore order to his devastated community with great efficiency and once again the Roman church emerged as a visible standard for international efforts to stabilize the Christian movement. When the *priests* of *Alexandria* appealed to the pope as a defender of *orthodoxy*, he wrote in the name of a synod of Latin bishops to call his namesake *Dionysius of Alexandria* to give an account of his teaching; and the latter responded to that call. It is in the fourth and fifth centuries, however, that the papacy reached a significantly new level of influence, related to the imperial favor the church now attracted. *Constantine* endowed the Roman church with several buildings, not least the Vatican shrine of St. Peter, which soon became a great place of pilgrimage, adding to the mystique of Peter's abiding presence in Rome (in his tombal relics, and in the spirit of his episcopal successor). Constantine also expected Pope Miltiades (310–314) to resolve the *Donatist* crisis on behalf of the *North African* church, something beyond his ability but showing how the emperor now looked to the pope as the "senior" executive of a worldwide church. Throughout the fourth century the Roman popes consistently exerted their authority in the cause of the Nicene faith, often defending Eastern Nicene theologians such as *Athanasius* or *Marcellus of Ancyra*, to the general annoyance of many Greek hierarchs. When the Nicene faith was confirmed at the end of that century, Rome's reputation for traditional orthodoxy was greatly enhanced, and so too was its own expectation that its voice ought to be heard internationally as a source of true Christian discipline. The more the papacy developed this juridical sense of its influence (as distinct from the moral sense), the more opposition papal theory

began to meet in the East. Constantine himself seemed to change his mind (often), usually taking the road of least resistance in regard to Christian affairs. When he summoned the *Council of Nicaea,* he paid very little attention to the papacy. The *canons* of Nicaea, as they began to set out the principles of juridical order in the churches, demonstrate a sense that administrative rights of bishops ought simply to reproduce the civic hierarchy of imperial organization. The two ideas, one that Rome should have special apostolic rights and the other that the chief imperial centers should be afforded rights of seniority, at first coalesced in the case of Rome, which was both apostolic (doubly so) as well as being the capital; but after the fourth century problems loomed large as other cities in the East gained power and influence while Rome rapidly faded in political eminence. The issue came to a head several times over the relative importances of Rome for the West, and Alexandria or *Constantinople* for the East. While Rome still expected to exercise an office of governance of some sort over all Christian churches, many Eastern churches increasingly regarded Constantinople as having the same significance as Rome for Eastern sees—and a preeminence based on its status as a capital, not on some special apostolic charism. While the Eastern sees would later develop apostolic claims of their own (Constantinople claiming to be founded by St. Andrew, the "first-called"), they generally adopted the theory that all sees were apostolic by virtue of correct doctrine, not by the special case of a Petrine presence or anything comparable. At Rome it was Pope *Damasus* in the late fourth century who brought that Petrine claim to a new focus, and laid down the architecture that his later successors continued to hone to an ever sharper edge, increasingly gaining imperial privileges for their see and primatial authority over other bishoprics in the West. His immediate successor, Siricius, was the first to define the papacy's essential claim (distinct, that is, from the mystical idea of the "Petrine presence"), which was "an office of oversight over all the churches" (*solicitudo omnium ecclesiarum*). Leo and Gregory the Great were subsequently the chief continuators and developers of the theory of papacy, and the progressive decline of Byzantine influence in the early medieval West also gave an immense boost to papal prestige, for its claim to represent *Roma aeterna* and the pure authenticity of Christian faith was increasingly seen (at least in the West) as self-evidently true, socially and intellectually. Nevertheless, from the seventh century onward, those claims were increasingly regarded as both dubious and irrelevant by the Byzantine churches, who in place of Petrine theory had a vigorous synodal and patriarchal system in place. The Eastern churches came to regard the papal claims as honorific, as a matter of local tradition (a *theologoumenon*), or as simply irrelevant. In later centuries, after long ages of effective separation of the Greek and Latin churches, the papacy, which had energetically developed its sense of particular charism in the meantime, emerged no longer as a symbol of unity for the churches, but as a special point of contention over varying ways to interpret *apostolicity*.

J. N. D. Kelly, *The Oxford Dictionary of the Popes* (Oxford, 1986); J. M. R. Tillard, *The Bishop of Rome* (London, 1983); W. Ullmann, "Leo I and the Theme of Papal Primacy," JTS 11 (1960): 25–51.

Papias of Hierapolis (fl. early second century)

One of the *Apostolic Fathers*, said to be a companion of *Polycarp*, and now known only from fragmentary quotations by later authors, Papias of Hierapolis was an early bishop in Asia Minor and held to a *chiliast eschatology*, which brought him the disapproval of later writers, especially *Eusebius of Caesarea*, who both uses and censures him

in the *Ecclesiastical History* as an ancient authority and a rather dim theologian. Papias was a source for early traditions preserved in Eusebius about the composition of the Gospels, which he recounted in his (now lost) treatise: *Exegeses of the Sayings of the Lord.* This seems to have been composed circa 130, and had significant influence on both *Hippolytus* and *Irenaeus,* who thinks of him as an "ancient" witness of apostolic traditions. Papias's views of the order of composition (Hebrew Matthew, and then Mark as the written record of a direct disciple of Peter) had much subsequent influence on ideas of biblical transmission until the modern era. His views represent a form of the doctrine of apostolic succession among bishops and the significance of the "living tradition of the elders," which can also be seen in *Ignatius* and came to a focused form in Irenaeus, both of whom also had roots in Asia Minor, at a similar time.

R. M. Grant, "Papias in Eusebius' Church History," in *Mélanges H.C. Puech* (Paris, 1974), 209–13; J. B. Lightfoot, *The Apostolic Fathers* (London, 1907), 514–35; J. Munck, "Presbyters and Disciples of the Lord in Papias," HTR 52 (1959): 223–43.

Paradise *see* Heaven

Parousia

The Greek New Testament term means "presence" and refers particularly to the empowered presence of the glorious Christ who returns to judge the world at the last day (Matt. 24:3; 1 Cor. 15:23). Parousial (a modern adjective) thus connotes much of the meaning of *eschatological.* In the *patristic* era several writers were engaged over the issue of recognizing when that *Judgment* would occur (*see millenarianism*), but from as early as the first century, as witnessed in Mark 13, it is clear enough that the idea caused much speculation and no little conflict. In patristic writing generally, Parousia meant primarily the act of judgment (*Epistle to Diognetus* 7.6;

Origen, *Commentary on Matthew* 70; Cyril of Jerusalem, *Catechetical Lectures* 15.1–4; John Chrysostom, *Homily on Matthew* 76.3–4), when the martyrs would be vindicated by being manifested as in "Christ's presence" (*Epistle to Diognetus* 7.9). The third-century writers of the *Logos* school, such as *Hippolytus* and *Origen*, were strongly motivated by a desire to offer a broader and more sophisticated eschatological matrix to theologize about Christ's divine "presence" in the continuing saga of world history than that conceived either by biblical literalism, millenarianism, or Montanism. Their spreading impact meant that christological focus soon highly colored the use of the term Parousia, and it increasingly came to denote God's active salvific presence in the world through the *incarnation* of Christ, itself understood as an eschatological act of judgment on history (Ignatius, *Letter to the Philadelphians* 9.2; Justin, *Dialogue with Trypho* 88.2; *First Apology* 48.2; 54.7; Clement of Alexandria, *Stromata* 1.18; 2.16). The Logos theologians, especially Origen, brought this conception of incarnational theology (itself a deep reflection on the Pauline understanding of the presence of Christ as an aspect of *resurrection* glory) to center stage for all subsequent Christian thought.

D. G. Dunbar, "The Delay of the Parousia in Hippolytus," VC 37 (1983): 313–27; R. M. Grant, "The Coming of the Kingdom," JBL 67 (1948): 297–303; A. L. Moore, *The Parousia in the New Testament* (Supplements to Novum Testamentum 13; Leiden, Netherlands, 1966); R. Tevijano-Etcheverria, "Epidemia y Parousia en Origenes," *Scriptorium victoriense* 16 (1969): 313–37.

Patrick (d. c. 460)   Honored as the apostle of Ireland, Patrick was the son of a *deacon* and was kidnaped from southwest Roman Britain as a boy of fifteen and enslaved for six years in the west of Ireland. His misery as a *slave* led him to a deepened faith in Christ, and when he finally escaped and returned home he entered the ranks of the *ascetic clergy.* Around 432 Patrick was sent as a missionary bishop after Palladius, who already ministered to the small Christian community in southern Ireland. From the outset Patrick aimed his mission at the conversion of the Irish pagans in the northeast and northwest of the country. As his church establishment came to be more widely known he was subject to the censure of the British bishops, who raised against him some canonical charges from his youth. He replied in a moving personal testimony now known as the *Confession of St. Patrick.* He also left behind a stringent canonical censure of a British Christian prince (*Letter to the Soldiers of Coroticus*) who had enslaved some of his new converts. Patrick demands acknowledgment that their *baptism* makes enslavement impossible, a heinous offense between Christians, and he imposes *excommunication* for the prince's soldiers who ridiculed his intercessions. As he was one of the most popular saints of *Ireland,* the narrative of Patrick's life subsequently attracted numerous legendary stories that often reflect the missionary impact Christianity was making on the Druidic and folk religions of the pre-Christian Irish. In the tales Patrick appears as a *magician* mightier than anything seen before, who commands allegiance to his strong God. The hymn "Breastplate of St. Patrick" belongs to the eighth century.

L. Bieler, trans., *The Works of St. Patrick* (ACW 17; Washington, D.C., 1953); R. P. C. Hanson, *Saint Patrick: His Origins and Career* (Oxford, 1968); L. De Paor, *Saint Patrick's World* (London, 1993).

Patripassianism   *see* **Monarchianism**

Patristics   Patristics is a modern term deriving from the Latin *patres,* or "fathers" (*see also* **patrology**). Fathers were the bishops or leading monastic elders of the early church. Patristic theology was thus the study of the doctrinal development of the church of the first eight centuries. The usual "cut-off points" were **John of Damascus** in the eighth-century Eastern church and the (rather later) medieval Western theologian Bernard of Clairvaux (often called "the last of the Fathers"). The massive nineteenth-century collections and editions of J. P. Migne (*Patrologia series graeca* and *Patrologia series latina*), comprising hundreds of volumes of Greek and Latin texts, is a virtual "*canon*" of patristic literature. The word and notion of patristics is incomplete, however, for many reasons—not least because it technically neglects every theologian of the early church (and there were many of them) who was not a bishop. Some of the greatest thinkers fell into this category, such as **Origen of Alexandria** and **Jerome,** and not least all of the important women of the early church, such as **Macrina, Syncletica, Olympias,** and **Melania.** The approach to ancient Christian theology as "patristics" led to a certain blindness to the important relevance of the nonofficial and nontextual sources of church history, a neglect that is only recently being addressed. Even so, patristics (understood in its precise sense as the study of episcopal and synodical theology) is not a hopelessly sexist or anachronistic term, and remains an important and valid branch of the theological disciplines, one that enjoyed a renaissance in the twentieth century as many excellent critical editions of primary texts and sophisticated historical analyses have enlivened the field. Patristics as a term of reference also evokes a loaded sense of church history as a pattern of **orthodoxy** versus heresy. The earliest church histories, from **Eusebius of Caesarea** onward, adopted this ideology (witnessed in the Johannine Letters and late catholic Epistles of the New Testament, for example), that the *church* was born in truth and heretics progressively perverted true doctrine. In this schema, great men (always men, it seemed) were raised up in the various generations like the prophets of old to defend orthodoxy against the machinations of the heretics, and these were (retrospectively) recognized as "fathers" of the people, definitive bearers of the charism of true theology. The concept of "patristic witnesses" in this sense is mainly a product of the anti-**Arian** writers of the fourth century, but it came to be adopted passionately by the Greek and Latin churches of later ages. One of the first and classical examples is the **hagiography** of **Antony the Great** written by **Athanasius of Alexandria** (*Life of Antony*), which depicts him as one of the first "fathers" who personally represents a standard of truth, holiness, and orthodoxy. Another is the hagiography of Athanasius by **Gregory of Nazianzus** (*Oration* 21; see also *Oration* 33.5), which lauds him as a father and pillar of orthodoxy for his defense of Nicaea (see also Basil of Caesarea, *Epistle* 140.2). By the fifth century, the concept of "authoritative fathers" is being appealed to specifically and systematically to establish pedigree lines of doctrine (as for example by **Cyril of Alexandria,** who begins to assemble *florilegia* of the "sayings of the orthodox fathers" in his conflict with **Nestorius**), and it comes into the synodical process of the ecumenical *councils,* who more and more see themselves as the defenders and propagators of the "theology of the fathers" (see Canon 7 of the **Council of Ephesus I** [431]; and **Council of Chalcedon** [451], *Definition of the Faith* 2; 4). Patristics in this latter sense corresponds to a certain vision of theology as the "defense and maintenance of orthodoxy," and is particularly favored by Roman Catholic and Eastern Orthodox theologians, whose church traditions still sustain that macroperspective on church history. Patristics in this sense, for example, is more or less equivalent to the concept of "systematic theology" in the Orthodox world.

O. Bardenhewer, *Patrology* (St. Louis, 1908); G. L. Prestige, *Fathers and Heretics* (London, 1940); J. Quasten, *Patrology* (vols. 1–3; Utrecht, Netherlands, 1975).

Patrology   Patrology is literally "the study of the fathers," fathers being the designation of Christian bishops. Originally Abba was a title for spiritual monastic elders, but by the fourth century it came to be appropriated by the leading hierarchs. The study of episcopal theologians of the classical era used to be synonymous with the analysis of their theological writings. Patrology was a nineteenth-century and early–twentieth-century term, now increasingly falling into disuse. It embraced the meaning of the word *patristics* (the study of the theology of the fathers of the church) and also was extended to include the writings of significant theologians of the early church who were not "fathers" or bishops, such as *Clement, Origen, Jerome,* the *Apologists,* and many of the monastic teachers. Next to no writing from significant female teachers has survived from the early church, although there is evidence that there were female teachers, some of whom had gained the title Amma (female of Abba, meaning "Mother-Teacher"), such as Syncletica or Sarra, who both appear only dimly in the collection of the *Apophthegmata Patrum* (Sayings of the "Fathers") but were evidently famous teachers of female ascetic communities in their own day. Patrology, in the sense of the study of patristic theology, had a great renaissance in the last century, but the term has recently fallen into disfavor for several reasons, not least because the study of history as it is pursued in contemporary curricula has demanded that a deeper methodological starting point be adopted than merely the survey of texts and doctrinal statements (which predominated in the old-style patrology), one that embraces a panoply of sociocultural events and is not narrowly channeled on bishops and

emperors and documents. In traditionalist views of patrology, the case of women in the early church, for example, was all but overlooked. The attitudes of the laity and the nonspecialist writers (what earlier ages dismissed as folk religion in Christianity) were not even considered worthy of study. Patrology and patristics have thus given way to a new (but rather vague) definition of the field as the "study of early Christianity" (or, if theology is preferred to be relegated to silence altogether, the "study of late antiquity"); nevertheless the term still retains a valid technical sense, for the detailed and specific analysis of *episcopal* and synodical doctrine still remains a vital task of church history and historical theology. Patrology also had a secondary sense referring to the creation of handbooks of early Christian thought, recounting the lives, writings, and doctrines of the patristic era. In the latter sense this present volume might have been called, in an earlier age, a patrology. Many older versions of patrology still exist and are eminently useful, such as those by Bardenhewer and Altaner. The most popular patrology in several volumes, issued in 1975 and widely valued for its extensive digests of the ancient writers, with bibliographies and synopses of the material, is the *Patrology* of Johannes Quasten, recently supplemented under the editorship of Angelo Di Berardino and brought up to date by the Patristic Institute of the Augustinianum. Di Berardino (who is also the editor of a highly influential *Encyclopedia of Early Christianity*) leads a team that has extended the range of the original volumes to cover the whole history of Greek and Latin Christianity into the early medieval periods, thus making the "New Quasten" the single most authoritative set of patrological handbooks available today. Not all of the volumes are currently available in English translation.

B. Altaner, *Patrology* (London, 1960); O. Bardenhewer, *Patrology* (St. Louis, 1908); J. Quasten, ed., *Patrology* (vols. 1–3,

Utrecht, 1975; vol. 4, ed. A. Di Berardino, Westminster, Md., 1986).

Paulinus of Nola (c. 353–431)

A Roman aristocrat and rhetorician and pupil of Ausonius, Paulinus of Nola was one of the greatest *littérateurs* of his age. Paulinus was the governor of the province of Campania, and after completing his duties married a Spanish aristocrat, Therasia, and retired to live on his estates near Bordeaux. He met the ascetic St. Martin of Tours and became close friends with one of Martin's disciples, the Christian historian Sulpicius Severus, who influenced his growing interest in *asceticism*. Paulinus and his wife Therasia were baptized in 389, and after the death of their only child, they both dedicated themselves to ascetical celibacy, moving to Spain together and beginning to distribute their considerable fortunes. At this time Paulinus renounced the writing of secular poetry, a decision that alarmed his teacher Ausonius and initiated a celebrated exchange of letters on the relation of religion to culture. Paulinus became a *priest* in 394, and he and Therasia left for Campania, where they settled on private estates at Nola, tending the shrine of the (obscure) martyr, St. Felix. He was elected local bishop some time between 403 and 413, and resumed his poetic writings, this time in the service of the cult of St. Felix, composing martyr hymns and liturgical songs. His "conversion" to ascetical Christianity was a *cause célèbre* among the aristocratic circle in which he was well known. Paulinus initiated an extensive series of epistolary exchanges with some of the leading Christian ascetics of his time, including *Ambrose, Jerome,* and *Augustine.* His poetry is significant for revealing the impact the cult of the martyrs had on the church of his time, as well as being, in its own right, among the best of the Christian poetic corpus.

D. E. Trout, *Paulinus of Nola: Life, Letters, and Poems* (Berkeley, Calif., 1999); J. T. Lienhard, *Paulinus of Nola and Early Western Monasticism* (Theophaneia 28; Cologne and Bonn, Germany, 1977); P. G. Walsh, trans., *Letters of St. Paulinus of Nola* (ACW 35–36; Washington, D.C., 1966–1967); idem, *Poems of St. Paulinus of Nola* (ACW 40; Washington, D.C., 1975).

Paul of Samosata (fl. early third century)

Paul was a native of the *Syrian* town of Samosata. From an impoverished background he rose to wealth and prominence as magistrate (Procurator Ducenarius) in the political administration. He was elected bishop of the church of *Antioch* c. 260, at a time when Christian communities were beginning to seek notables for the office, and he carried over into the church his customary signs of social rank. He is said (by scandalized clerical opponents) to have introduced a high throne for the bishop, a raised platform for his tribunal (the apsidal east end of the basilical church), and a retinue of bodyguards and personal secretaries. His role as a teacher in the church soon brought him into conflict with members of his *clergy* and congregation, as he seems to have advanced his theological duties speculatively, interpreting the Scriptures as if giving philosophical commentaries on Christian literature. *Eusebius of Caesarea* (who had access to the acts of the *council* that condemned him) says that Paul taught Jesus was an ordinary man who was inhabited by the Word, and who thus became the Son of God. The Word was the eternal power of the divine wisdom. It was *homoousios* with the divine Father—by which he meant that it was not a distinct *hypostatic* entity, simply another attribute of the divine being. Paul is the first theologian known to have used the word *homoousios* in Christian discourse (its reappearance in the *Christology* debates of the Nicene era, after this inauspicious start, gave the term bad associations for many traditionalists). His Christology is of the classic *Adoptionist* type, and his doctrine of

God and the Word suggests he was a *Monarchian* (he is classed as a "Dynamic Monarchian" insofar as he sees the Word as one of the powers or *dynameis* of God). His most active opponents in the Antiochene church seem to have been *Logos* theologians who followed Origenian doctrines (not least *Gregory Thaumaturgos*). Synods of bishops were held in Antioch in 264 and 268 to condemn Paul's theology and secure his deposition, but his hold over the church was strong enough for him to dismiss the censure and carry on. It was not until an appeal could be made to the emperor Aurelian that his dismissal from the church buildings could be enforced. His sect endured for some time after his death, and *Canon* 19 of the *Council of Nicaea* requires his *clergy* and followers to be *baptized* de novo if they seek admission to the church. Much later he was used as a heretical symbol, and the opponents of *Nestorius* claimed (wrongly) that the latter had resurrected the teaching of Paul on the radical distinction between Jesus and the Word.

H. J. Lawlor, "The Sayings of Paul of Samosata," JTS n.s. 19 (1917–1918): 20–45, 115–20; F. W. Norris, "Paul of Samosata: Procurator Ducenarius," JTS n.s. 35 (1984): 50–70.

Pelagius—Pelagianism

Pelagius was a British ascetic who lived c. 350–425 and taught at *Rome* as a well-respected moral preacher and biblical commentator. His *Commentary on the Thirteen Pauline Epistles* gives a view of his general thought before he was embroiled in a major controversy with *Augustine of Hippo* late in his life, which has ever afterward characterized him as the founder of the *heresy* attached to his name. Pelagius was a moral reformer. A common aspect of his teaching is that God has given the church moral commandments in the Scriptures and in natural conscience, and it is the duty of the disciple to put these into action by faithful obedience. Moral responsiveness, always difficult, is not impossible. God would never have commanded what was not within the ability of his disciples to perform. Accordingly the difficulties in observing moral laws have to be met and answered by significant ascetical training. This progressive determination to keep the commandments is synonymous with true Christianity. Much of this was regarded as wholly unexceptional in many circles of the church of his day. Indeed, although he got into great trouble with the *North African* synods, dominated by Augustine, his archopponent, when he was examined at Jerusalem, the bishop John exonerated him, finding nothing wrong with his *ascetical* teachings. Nevertheless, the clash of Pelagius and Augustine became definitive for much of later Latin Christian thought, and was the catalyst for Augustine's deepest reflections on the theology of *grace* and *redemption.* Pelagius's circle found Augustine's new biography, *The Confessions*, to be rather scandalous. It appeared to them that this was a bishop who did not have the moral fiber necessary to give a good example in the lax condition they saw the churches to be in. They were especially appalled at the many times Augustine seemed to suggest that his moral will was rendered impotent in the face of so many difficulties, and he could only be saved when God came to his assistance and gave him the saving grace to be converted. The phrase "Command what you will, O God, and give what you command" was felt to be particularly objectionable. For Pelagius, this hopelessly confused the assistance God gave to the disciple with the moral power that God expected the disciple to supply (to reform and accept discipline). Pelagius thought that if a disciple persevered in strong discipline and *prayer* he or she would reach a state of stability where even the desire for sin would fade away, a condition of ascetic passionlessness (*apatheia*). The clash with Augustine first came about through one of his followers (Caelestius) introducing controversial theses in North Africa. The latter's examination and censure by the Synod of Carthage in 411 also cast deep shadows over the status of his teacher Pelagius. Caelestius had been appalled at Augustine's view of the transmission of sin through the human race as if it were some form of infection (cf. Augustine's treatise *Guilt and Remission of Sins*, which was his reply to Caelestius) and had made it known that their school regarded sin and sinfulness as wholly a question of conscious moral choice, individually attributable. Children were born in the same state of innocence as Adam was. Around 412 Pelagius wrote a treatise *On Human Nature* to elaborate these views more extensively, and when Augustine criticized it with his own treatise *Nature and Grace*, it was clear that an international quarrel was brewing. The Pelagian circles thought that the Africans were attempting to impose some of their peculiar and extreme views (about original sin and the pervasive effects of the *fall*) on the universal church. Augustine summoned the assistance of *Jerome* against Pelagius, and Jerome (who had already met and fallen out with Pelagius) wrote his own critique, *Dialogues against the Pelagians*, where he attacked them for being more **Stoic** than Christian (he had in mind their views on *apatheia*, or the ability of humans to have remained sinless if they had proved faithful). After Pelagius acquitted himself of charges of heresy (over his views on potential human sinlessness) at the Palestinian synod of 415, Augustine ensured that he was condemned for the same views by Pope Innocent I in 417. The pope's death in that same year, however, led to the case being reviewed by his successor, Pope Zosimus, who was much more sympathetic to Pelagius, and more alarmed than his predecessor by the ascendancy of the African theology. Zosimus rehabilitated both Caelestius and Pelagius, and censured those who were attacking them without proper cause. In the meantime, however, the

Africans had gained the support of the imperial court, and Emperor Honorius issued a decree condemning both thinkers as agitators. Political pressure made Zosimus endorse the ban later that same year and Pelagius then wandered east (perhaps dying in Egypt, where he was not heard from again). While there has been much scholarly debate on what treatises can actually be ascribed to the historical Pelagius, the heresy "Pelagianism" has generally been drawn up in reference to Augustine's theology of grace. Pelagius believed that God gave grace to human beings, certainly, but his primary grace was the freedom to choose and respond. Those who chose the path of goodness would be given further encouragement by God to progress in the spiritual life. Augustine believed that such a view would render Christianity into a simplistic cult of moral "self-improvement." He believed the human race's capacity for free moral choice was so damaged by the ancient (and continuing) fall from grace and enlightenment that even the desire to return to God has first to be supplied by God's prevenient grace. All desire for, and movement toward, the Good was the gift of God, in Augustine's estimate. *John Cassian,* a theologian emanating from the Eastern church, was bemused by the whole controversy as he observed it, and suggested a compromise between the two positions: that human free will cooperated with divine grace (an ascetical theology predominant in the Eastern monastic theologians, and in *Origen*). For the East this has always been received as a common wisdom, although Augustine's views on the priority of divine grace were also accepted (not in Augustine's every formulation by any means, especially not in relation to his radical pessimism about the damage caused to the *soul* by the fall). In the West, Cassian was ever afterward tarred with the brush of Pelagianism, in a form later called "semi-Pelagianism." The issue of Pelagianism was never a large-scale heretical movement at all; more of a manufactured controversy to advance the grace theology of the circle of Augustine. It has, for that reason, never been extensively received as a fruitful discussion in the Eastern church traditions. In the West, however, the Augustinian pessimistic views on the transmission of the contagion of sin through the race, radically damaging human freedom and spiritual capacity, became the standard wisdom. The Augustinian theology of grace was certainly a rhapsodic celebration of the prodigality of God, but by virtue of Pelagius's severe condemnation it was passed on through Latin Christianity at no small cost to the variform concept of human freedom.

G. Bonner, *Augustine and Modern Research on Pelagianism* (Villanova, 1972); P. Brown, "Pelagius and His Supporters: Aims and Environment," JTS 19 (1968): 83–114; J. P. Burns, "Augustine's Role in the Imperial Action against Pelagius," JTS 30 (1979): 67–83; R. Evans, *Four Letters of Pelagius* (London, 1968); J. Morris, "Pelagian Literature," JTS 16 (1965): 26–60; B. R. Rees, *Pelagius: A Reluctant Heretic* (Woodbridge, U.K. and Wolfeboro, N.H., 1988); idem, *The Letters of Pelagius and His Followers* (Woodbridge, U.K. and Rochester, N.Y., 1991).

Penance   The concept of penance derives from the Latin *paenitentia*, repentance. In *patristic* theology it predominantly refers to the system of postbaptismal forgiveness of sins that was adopted by the church and developed from the first century onward, and especially through the third to eighth centuries, when it reached a specific form with some variations in the Eastern and Western churches. The concept of penance covers the related Greek concepts of *metanoia* and *exomologesis* (repentance and confession). The earliest apprehensions of the gospel message understood that forgiveness was central to the *kerygma,* and that it was fundamentally a *grace* of God invoked by the salvific work of Jesus (especially the passion and *resurrection*) and appropriated through the repentance of the believer. The parable of the tax collector and the Pharisee (Luke 18:9–14) demonstrates the high profile that Jesus gave to repentance in humility. The developing organization of the churches led to problems with the concept of repentance, however, as it conflicted in several instances with the powerful sense of the church as the *eschatological* new community of the elect, who had been bought by the blood of Christ and made into his spotless bride, or into the sacred temple of God whose defilement was a sin calling for divine vengeance (1 Cor. 3:16–17; 6:18–20). Even in the Gospel of Matthew there are developing signs that the "problem" of believers who remain "sinners" needs to be addressed. In a text that is generally believed to represent late–first-century reflections, the church (of *Antioch* perhaps) adopted a position of forgiving repeated offenders, up to a certain point, but then disciplining them by treating them as a tax collector (Matt. 18:15–18), which presumably meant imposing some form of *excommunication* on them. In this text the community for the first time claimed the power of "binding and loosing" to be inherited from Jesus as an active disciplinary measure (see also John 20:22–23). Incipient forms of penitential discipline based around exclusion from the community and its prayers (especially the Eucharist) are already visible in the Pauline churches (cf. 1 Cor. 10:21; 11:26–29; 5:1–5, 11–13; 2 Cor. 6:14–18; 2:5–11; 1 Tim. 1:20), and in the Catholic Epistles the sense is clearly growing that the church, as the community of the last age, has no room within it for habitual offenders (1 Pet. 4:7; 2 Pet. 2:20–22; 1 John 3:4–6). This theology grew strongly as the sacrament of *baptism* was elaborated as the archetypal and supreme mystery of forgiveness and initiation, displacing an earlier sense of the *Eucharist* as the preeminent sacrament of reconciliation. The earliest churches so stressed the unrepeatable nature of baptismal regeneration that they were soon faced with particular problems of how to cope with the reality of postbaptismal *sin* among their members (cf. 1 John 1:8–10). While this remained on the level of "interior attitudes" it was not critical, often being addressed by protoascetical solutions such as in the earliest communities of *Syria*, where baptismal initiation was reserved for those who would adopt a celibate and radically ascetic lifestyle. Those who were not able to promise this, especially the young and the *married*, would generally defer baptism until later in life (sometimes to the end of life), thus preserving the church's self-understanding as the initiated community of the saints. Where the sin became a matter of public knowledge (especially the three "unforgivable sins" of murder, adultery, and apostasy), it was sometimes regarded as a sign that the individual had never "properly" been a Christian at all. Not all the churches adopted the Syrian solution, however, and by the fourth century it was regarded as out of harmony with the majority of other churches' baptismal disciplines and faded away; but even into the late fourth century most Christians deferred baptism until the onset of old age or the imminent threat of death. The *Shepherd of Hermas* is a text much concerned with the issue of preserving purity among the church members, and shows an anxiety about the process of seeking forgiveness for regular sins. Such is also a concern of the Johannine Letters (perhaps written at the same period of the late first century and early second century), which introduced the notion of sin in general, which all Christians had to confess, and "sin that is mortal" (1 John 5:15–17), which seems to be a sin so serious that it demonstrated that the sinner was no longer part of the church. The writer of the Johannine Letters probably had schism in mind when he introduced the idea, but the concept of "ordinary sins" and "mortal sins" soon became a commonly held distinction. Texts such as the *Didache* demon-

strate how the earliest penitential system seemed to work, with the idea of "regular sins" being confessed in prayer with *fasting* and *almsgiving* as methods of purification. The era of third-century *persecutions* would change this primitive penitential scheme dramatically. In the aftermath of short and bitter persecutions, considerable numbers of church members lapsed, largely from the basic motive of self-preservation. Their sin had been one of the three "unforgivables," namely, apostasy, and yet in the periods after the restoration of peace many lapsed Christians were petitioning their church congregations to be restored to fellowship, claiming to have repented deeds such as offering incense to the old gods, which they only committed under duress and without any conviction anyway. The church of Carthage in the time of *Cyprian* was particularly exercised with this problem (Cyprian, *De lapsis*), for several of the triumphant confessors (potential martyrs who had survived) regarded it as their prerogative to indicate the Lord's forgiveness to repentant sinners, in contradiction to the commonly established belief that such sinners ought not to be readmitted to eucharistic communion. In some other churches (cf. *Novatianism*), even including Cyprian's own, rigorists held with equal conviction to the position that for postbaptismal serious sin there could be no forgiveness at all. As a result of the chaos of discipline emerging from the third-century persecutions, a system of "graded" penance was established in most churches that allowed those who had fallen during times of duress to return to the Christian assembly in the role of a penitent. *Tertullian* is one of the first to agonize over whether the grave sinner could ever be reestablished. In his treatise *De paenitentia* (7, 9–10, which he would renounce after he became a *Montanist*), he reluctantly acknowledged that one "second" repentance is possible if demonstrated by the adoption of a life of severe penance involving long prayers, fasting, prostration in the churches and before the presbyters, and a special prayer of intercession before God from the church community. After *Constantine* established an international peace for the churches in the fourth century, the system of *canons* governing this process began to be generally agreed through a series of conciliar assemblies. The Western churches had the system more openly arranged, and here it amounted to the stages of (a) petitioning the bishop to be received as a penitent, (b) belonging to the order of penitents for a longer or shorter time (sometimes for the whole of one's life), and (c) final readmission (*reconciliatio*) to eucharistic communion through a ceremony of the laying on of hands (at Maundy Thursday). The entrance into the order of penitents disbarred a person from marital relations or any form of public office and was, accordingly, usually postponed until late in life. *Clergy* could not participate in this process in any sense, the two states being regarded as incompatible, and public wrongdoing among clerics being dealt with by deposition from orders. The system had so many defects within it that a more popular practice arose after the seventh century, first witnessed among the ascetic communities, of confessing one's inner life to a spiritual father or confessor. The confessor (the Irish called him Anam Cara, or Soul Friend) took on a role of high authority over the disciple and imposed "penances" for different offenses, such as periods of fasting, or numerous prostrations, or other acts of self-abnegation. Soon a "tariff" system (certain penances fitted to various sins) became common in the Western churches, where the Irish monks introduced the process more generally. Carolingian clergy tried to resist this Celtic system in favor of retaining the ancient canons, and so the two penitential approaches marked the Western church throughout the patristic era. In the Byzantine world the system of monastic counseling also spread to become the common ecclesiastical process of *confession.* In

both the Greek and Latin churches sometime after the ninth century, the private confession to the soul-guide was absorbed into the formal sacramental process and became established as "sacramental confession," finally administered solely by the *priest* or bishop. The Western church adopted a more ready approach to "penitential commutations," allowing the confessor considerable discretion in imposing retributive penances on the individual. In the Byzantine world the penitential canons (as established in several ascetical writings, notably the canonical letters of *Basil the Great*) were regarded as fixed penalties for various sins and so (because of the severity of these ancient rules) the system of private penance was never as popular there as it would become in the West.

E. Langstadt, "Tertullian's doctrine of sin and the power of absolution in the *De Pudicitia*," SP 2 (1957): 251–57; H. E. W. Turner, *The Patristic Doctrine of Redemption* (London, 1952); C. Vogel, *Le pécheur et la pénitence dans l'Église ancienne* (Paris, 1966); B. Ward, *Harlots of the Desert: A Study of Repentance in Early Monastic Sources* (Kalamazoo, Mich., 1987); L. M. White, "Transactionalism in the Penitential Thought of Gregory the Great," *RQ* 21 (1978): 33–51.

Perichoresis The term literally means "a dancing around something" (the *chora* was the ancient Greek dance in a ring). In *Neoplatonist* technical writing (*see* **Plotinus, Proclus**) it was used to describe the manner in which the soul related to the body and lived within it without being subsumed by it. In Christian theological texts it is most usually translated as "coinherence" or "interpenetration." It is mainly used in the contexts of *Trinitarian* or *christological* language to connote, for example, the dynamic and intimate manner in which the two natures of Christ relate to one another (in the *hypostatic* union), so that one sphere of action (say of the humanity) is distinct from but not disparate from the other (the divinity), rather interactive and correlated in an intensely close relation (*see communion of properties*). *Gregory of Nazianzus* is one of the first to use this type of language (*Epistle* 101; *Orat.* 38.13). In the Trinitarian context the word is referred to the manner in which the three persons (hypostases) dynamically share the self-same nature of Godhead and enjoy dynamic intercommunion in the most intense unity imaginable through the distinct relations, within common being, of Father, Son, and *Holy Spirit. John Chrysostom* is one of the first to employ the image in this domain, and after *John of Damascus* it was standardized as a common term for Byzantine theology.

G. L. Prestige, *God in Patristic Thought* (London, 1952), 297–305; H. A. Wolfson, *The Philosophy of the Church Fathers* (Cambridge, Mass., 1964).

Perpetua and Felicity (d. 203)

Perpetua and Felicity were two women *martyrs* of the *North African* church. Their story is preserved in a remarkable account (*The Passion of Saints Perpetua and Felicity*) that bases itself on the prison diaries (recounting the *dream-visions*) of Perpetua (chaps. 3–10) and the priest Saturus (chaps. 11–13). The two baptismal candidates were arrested in Carthage along with their priest and other *catechumens* (Saturninus, Secundulus, and Revocatus) during the *persecution* of Christians in the reign of Septimius Severus. Felicity and Revocatus were slaves who confessed the faith alongside their Christian owners. Perpetua's story presents the dramatic narrative of a young mother who refuses the authority of her (pagan) father and the attachment she feels to her baby in order to remain faithful to the vow she made to Christ. The incomprehension between the family and the new Christians (they are baptized in prison) is starkly drawn and sets the *confession* of the new religion in an *eschatological* light. Felicity

gives birth in prison and still refuses to recant her confession. Perpetua's visions turn on her dream that she was able to deliver her younger and deceased pagan brother Dinocrates from his pains in *hell* because of her martyr's mediation, and also that her own sufferings (where she will symbolically be transformed into a man for the struggle in the arena) are in reality a battle with demonic forces in which she will be vindicated. The priest has a vision (perhaps equally self-referential) of the heavenly martyr Perpetua settling a conflict that has grown up between a bishop and a priest. The *Passion* is an important martyr-narrative that sought both to make a detailed record of the confession and to demonstrate certain theological points derived from the fearlessness of the martyrs. The themes of constancy and encouragement are prevalent, but the editor also seems particularly interested in advancing the idea that the martyrs demonstrate the enduring work of the *Holy Spirit*, who raises up prophetic visions in the saints whom he tests and refines, and also assures the church of forgiveness through the martyr's mediations. The *Passion* became a standard model of much martyr *hagiography* that followed. Modern interpreters have often wondered if the text derives from *Montanist* circles (female prophets, stress on dreams, and elements where martyrs assume priority over local bishops), but all of these elements could be found in most martyr narratives from Africa (Montanist, *Donatist*, or Catholic), where the cult quickly assumed a great significance. The concept that charismatically graced martyrs and confessors had intercessory power with God that transcended that commanded by a local bishop was exactly the same issue that divided *Cyprian's* church at Carthage fifty years later. Both *Tertullian* (*De anima*) and *Augustine* (*Sermons* 280–283) refer to the tradition of this martyrdom account. The basilical Church of Perpetua and Felicity was one of the largest in Christian Carthage.

M. R. Lefkowitz, "The Motivations for St. Perpetua's Martyrdom," *JAAR* 44 (1976): 417–21; J. A. McGuckin, "Martyr Devotion in the Alexandrian School (Origen to Athanasius)," in *Martyrs and Martyrologies* (Studies in Church History 30; Oxford, 1993), 35–45; repr. in E. Ferguson, ed., *Recent Studies in Church History* (vol. 5; Hamden, Conn., 1999); W. Shewring, trans., *The Passion of Saints Perpetua and Felicity* (London, 1931).

Persecutions   The term derives from the early Roman legal concept (*persequi*) of "prosecuting" dissidents who were regarded as dangerous to the stability of the state. From the viewpoint of the official authorities the Christians were first and foremost a local problem to be dealt with by the normal methods of suppression invoked throughout the empire's large extent (in varying degrees of enforcement depending on the hostility of the local community and the character of the provincial governor and local magistrates). In most sources up to the fourth century (when imperial authorities really did become conscious that the Christian movement represented an international force that had to be contended with), the Roman authorities seem to have been simultaneously bewildered by the tenacity shown by Christians in their refusal to offer conformist sacrifices and angered by their antisocial "misanthropy." This perceived misanthropy led to the earliest Christian communities across a wide range of territories suffering a large degree of local mob resentment, which often spilled out in periods of officially endorsed persecutions. From the viewpoint of the Christians, however, these state persecutions were not primarily a local or merely a legal matter, but a manifestation of the rage of the prince of the world against the elect bride, the church, which was the community of salvation in the last age. Persecutions sponsored by the state, the agent of the "beast," were taken as an *apocalyptic* sign of the

end times, foretold as such by Jesus (Mark 10:17, 39; John 15:17–21), who thus, in the passion narrative, became the archetype of all Christian resistance. As a result the church carefully recorded the *"acts" of the martyrs,* the instances of each community contending with apocalyptic evil, and was very conscious of the importance of having martyrs in each community to validate its powers as a community of the new age. Martyrs were believed to pass immediately from this world into the proximity of the supreme martyr, Christ, and to be able to exercise a powerful ministry of intercession on behalf of their local churches. This is why the recording of the persecutions was precise and (generally) accurate from the outset of Christianity (beginning with the account of the protomartyr Stephen in Acts 7:60, and the execution of James and arrest of Peter in Acts 12:2–3), although the theological attention given to the *eschatological* nature of the persecutions gives them a priority and a significance in ecclesiastical sources that they did not necessarily have in, for example, a secular view of the history of the period. Paul is described by the writer of Acts as being persecuted from city to city (Acts 17:10–13), which really represents the hostility he caused among the local Jewish congregations by his preaching visits there. Several of the early state persecutions were intent on forcing the rising Christian middle class to conform by threatening loss of property and civic rights; others focused only on leading Christian teachers or recent converts, but for the church they were all the same, and in its perspective were always addressed against "the church of Christ" indiscriminately, thus giving the notion of "Roman persecutions" a historical continuity and coherence that they often did not have, being in many cases merely ad hoc responses and tentative policies.

The first of the imperial persecutions was that of Nero, the executioner of Peter and Paul, and always regarded ever after as the archetypal evil genius of a long series of "wicked emperors" to follow. The idea of that series of the wicked kings is brought out brilliantly by *Lactantius* in his treatise *The Deaths of the Persecutors*, where he demonstrates (in parallel to the books of Maccabees) how the evil emperors (as defined entirely by their persecution policies) were cast down by God in violent deaths, whereas the good emperors flourished, most notably *Constantine*, who abolished persecution and so was rewarded by God with supreme power. Nero's persecution in 64 was stimulated by a desire to be seen to be doing something in response to the disastrous fire of *Rome*. As a highly unpopular, foreign, and nonworshiping group, the Christians were an easy target, and were treated with spectacular cruelty designed to placate the anger of the gods while cathartically purging the anger of the city populace. This violent pogrom was restricted to the city itself.

Christian sources (Eusebius, *Ecclesiastical History* 4.26.8; Tertullian, *Apologeticus* 5.4) list Domitian as the second persecutor, in 95. His repressive measures now seem to have been largely aimed at the Roman nobility who were showing a degree of attraction to "Jewish ideas" in morality and worship, a movement Domitian despised as eroding Roman values and traditions. Domitilla, the emperor's niece, was probably a Christian, and was exiled to the island of Ponza, where her "cell" became a cult center in the fourth century (Eusebius, *Ecclesiastical History* 3.18.4; Jerome, *Epistulae* 108.7). Her husband Flavius Clemens was executed for, among other things, "Jewish sympathies." He has been, for a long time, presumed to be *Clement of Rome,* one of the greatest early leaders of the Roman Christians. It is now generally thought that Pope Clement was more likely related to his clan, perhaps as a freedman client. Domitian's desire to deify himself confirmed the worst suspicions of Christians that this was no mere political

accident. The persecution is reflected in several sources (1 Clement 7.1; 59.4; Shepherd of Hermas; Tertullian, *Apologeticus* 5.4; Melito of Sardis in Eusebius, *Ecclesiastical History*. 3:17–18, 4.26.9) and not least in the book of Revelation (Rev. 2:13; 20:4). It was the cause of John's exile to Patmos, and the summoning of the last relatives of Jesus for examination at Rome (cf. Hegesippus, in Eusebius, *Ecclesiastical History* 3.19–20). Christianity was lumped in with "Jewish practices" at this period, though by the end of the first century Roman law would make a distinction between them, one greatly to the detriment of Christianity since it lost any claim it previously had for special consideration.

The next persecution was that recorded under Trajan, whose legate in Bithynia, Pliny the Younger, asked for special instructions in 112–113 (*Epistle* 10.96.2), as he was unhappy at the way locals were vindictively taking the occasion of state censure of Christianity to denounce their enemies out of mere pettiness; especially since his own enquiries, extracted by torturing a deaconess, had revealed they were a fairly harmless movement. Pliny wanted to know if Christians should be executed simply for "profession of the name," or only on account of demonstrable crimes. The imperial reply was to the effect that capital punishment was merited if the accused person refused at a tribunal to retract and "worship our gods," but that Christians ought not to be sought out (*conquirendi non sunt*) like common criminals. Trajan's successor, Hadrian, similarly instructed the proconsul of Asia in 124–125 not to pander to local outcries against the Christians, and to prosecute them only if they committed crimes proven under trial. Hadrian gave to the Christians the right to prosecute their detractors under the laws of calumny.

This rescript calmed the local tendency to denounce Christian groups under vague charges of misanthropy or *magic,* but local outbreaks of hostility still accounted for several other persecutions, some of them vivid in the Christian memory, such as the execution of *Justin* at Rome in 165 or *Polycarp* at Smyrna at the same time (Eusebius, *Church History* 4.15.26, 29; *Martyrdom of Polycarp*), and the martyrs of Lyon in 177 (Eusebius, *Ecclesiastical History* 5.1; 5.2.1–8). Marcus Aurelius, in whose reign these things happened (161–180), is thus credited as the next "persecuting" emperor. During this time (c. 178) the pagan apologist Celsus wrote a treatise called *The True Word*, in which he explained the common hostility against Christians as based on their mutual association, taking secret oaths to support one another, and on their undermining Roman values by negating the gods and refusing public service. For Celsus, they were a society that ought to be sought out and eradicated (cf. Origen, *Contra Celsum* 8.69) for the common good.

In 193 when the Severan dynasty occupied the imperial throne, the pressure against Christians was again eased in a more relaxed policy toward Oriental religions in *Rome*. At this time Christianity resumed its missionary efforts (cf. Tertullian, *Ad nationes* 1.14; *Apologeticus* 18.4) with some success, for a new wave of popular hatred against the church was soon in evidence between 197 and 212, and a series of violent local outbreaks against Christian communities at this period can be seen in Rome, *Alexandria*, and *North Africa*. At Carthage, *Perpetua and Felicity* were among the casualties. They demonstrate a common element in the violence of this time, in that it seems especially to have been directed against recent converts to the movement (see also Eusebius, *Ecclesiastical History* 6.3). Christian writers retrospectively attached much of the symbolic guilt for this to the emperor Septimius Severus, who in 202 had issued a rescript forbidding conversions to either *Judaism* or Christianity. Between 212 and 235 there was another period of peace, culminating in the reign of Alexander Severus (222–235), who tolerated the church. It is from this period

that the first recognizable Christian buildings (such as the Roman *catacombs* and the church at Dura-Europos) are witnessed.

The Severan dynasty was violently overthrown in March 235 by Maximinus Thrax (235–238) with a purge of Alexander's Christian supporters at court (Eusebius, *Ecclesiastical History* 6.28). This also spilled over into a purge of leading Christians at Rome (*Hippolytus* and Pope Pontianus were sentenced to a fatal exile to the salt mines in Sardinia) and perhaps also in Palestine (cf. Origen, *Exhortation to Martyrdom*). Maximinus was himself overthrown by the Gordian dynasty in 238, and although in that year *Origen* (*ComMt.* 24.9; *Hom Mt.* 39) prophesied a future worldwide pogrom against the church, the period proved to be another brief interlude of peace. Philip the Arab, emperor from 244 to 249, has been thought by some to have been a Christian himself.

The assassination of Philip in 249, which brought Decius to the throne (249–251), also brought with it a strong reaction to the growing power of Christians and a determined attempt to kill off the church. Decius wished to lay the blame for Rome's military and political decline at the door of the blatant Christian rejection of Roman values, and in January 250 he ordered that the annual sacrifice on the Capitoline Hill to the gods of Rome should be solemnly observed in all the provincial capitals too. To mark the occasion he arrested many prominent Christian leaders. Fabian of Rome and Babylas of Antioch were martyred, and *Dionysius of Alexandria* and *Cyprian of Carthage* had close escapes. After the first wave, Decius established religious commissions to oversee the observance of regular sacrificial rites and the requirement of citizens to take part in them. This was designed partially to root out Christian objectors, and certificates (*libelli*) became a necessary proof that sacrifice had indeed been offered. Christians who conformed, either by offering incense or

sacrifice (*sacrificati*) or by bribing officials to sell them a certificate (*libellatici*),
were equally regarded by the church as
apostates. Even so, Decius's policy
clearly had a considerable impact and
was the best organized of the persecutions so far. Cyprian gives much information about the period and the
disruption it caused to the life of the
church. Decius was killed in battle with
the Goths in 251 and his successors Gallus and Volusianus at first tried to continue the religious policy (cf. Cyprian,
Ep. 59.8), but it soon ran out of steam and
the church quickly reestablished itself as
can be seen from notable advances in
theological literature and organizational
matters in this period.

The emperor Valerian (253–260),
fighting a losing battle with Persia, tried
once more to insist on religious devotion
to the Roman gods, and in 257 issued an
edict that demanded Christian conformity, and in the following year published an even stronger policy of
suppression. According to its terms
(Cyprian, *Ep.* 80) Christian clergy would
be arrested and summarily executed;
senators and knights who professed
Christianity would lose rank and property; matrons would suffer confiscation
and be exiled; civil servants would be
reduced to slavery and sent to labor
camps. In 258 Cyprian of Carthage was
brought out of house arrest and condemned to die for sacrilege and for pos-
ing as an enemy of the gods of Rome.
The Valerian persecution was not
regarded by the Christians as anything
like as terrible as those of Decius or later
Diocletian, but it probably was one of the
most severe the church ever suffered,
though not of long duration. Valerian
was captured by the Persians at Edessa
in 260. He would be kept as a fattened
hostage for the rest of his life, but after
death his body was flayed and the skin
stuffed and dyed imperial purple to
hang in the temple of the gods as an
offering—a particularly merited punishment as far as the Christians were concerned. His son Gallienus (253–268)

issued a rescript for toleration of the
church in 262, more or less as soon as he
had stabilized the throne. For the next
forty years the church enjoyed political
stability and made great advances.

The next time of crisis, therefore,
struck it with particular force, and so
earned the name of the Great Persecution. This lasted in the Western half of
the empire from 303 to 305, and in the
Eastern empire from 303 to 312. Diocletian introduced a policy of conservative
religious reform as part of a larger pack-
age of measures to stabilize the empire.
It has been argued that members of his
own family were Christian sympathizers, and that may be why his own attitude was ambivalent in regard to a
violent persecution; but his immediate
junior, Caesar Galerius, was more
overtly hostile to the Christian cause,
and persuaded Diocletian to demand
religious conformity by an empirewide
edict in February 303. This still avoided
the death penalty, but ordered the
destruction of Christian churches, the
burning of the Scriptures, the social
degradation of upper-class believers, the
reduction to slavery of civil servants,
and the general loss of legal rights by
professing Christians. An additional
edict soon demanded the arrest of the
clergy, but the prison system was then so
overloaded that this was amended to
require them all to offer sacrifice and
then be set free. Many were tortured to
ensure their conformity. Some became
heroic martyrs at this time (Eusebius,
The Martyrs of Palestine) though some
lapsed, and the destruction of the clerical infrastructure, along with the burning of the churches, proved devastating.
Early in 304, following Diocletian's sickness and temporary retirement, Galerius
stepped up the measures more strictly
and issued an edict demanding that all
citizens should offer a sacrifice and a
libation to the gods under pain of death.
This caused havoc among the Christians
in North Africa (Eusebius, *Ecclesiastical
History* 8.6.10) and resulted in a large
number of executions, burning the

episode into the larger Christian consciousness as the "Great Persecution." In 305 Diocletian and his senior colleague Maximian resigned in the West, and the new leaders were soon distracted by the civil war, during which *Constantine* rose to preeminence, not accidentally as a protector of Christians. In the East, where Galerius was now the senior emperor, the persecution continued. In spring 306 his new junior, Maximin Daia, issued an edict requiring all provincial governors to ensure their people sacrificed. In Palestine this was heavily enforced, and elsewhere it was sporadically observed through 309, after which it became increasingly obvious to all that it was an ineffective policy. In 311 Galerius fell mortally ill and, convinced that he had unwisely angered the Christian God, decided to rescind the policy. He now demanded that Christians should pray for the welfare of the state and for the healing of himself, allowing them to rebuild their churches (Eusebius, *Ecclesiastical History* 8.17.3–10). Six days later he died. His successor, Maximin Daia, took over the command of his territories and, without voiding Galerius's edict, encouraged local authorities to assault Christian communities and any significant leaders. This "half-official" violence accounted for more outbreaks of persecution in Nicomedia, Tyre, and Antioch (Eusebius, *Ecclesiastical History* 9.7.10–11). There was an even more violent episode of oppression in Egypt (Eusebius, *Church History* 9.9.4–5), during which Peter of Alexandria was martyred. The last victim was the famous theologian *Lucian*, bishop of Antioch, who died in January 312. Maximin Daia himself died in 313, just as Constantine had conquered his last Western rival, Maxentius, at Rome. In that same year a formal reconciliation of Constantine and Licinius, now Augustus of the whole East, the Edict of Milan, brought a formal end to the Great Persecution. In the Western empire Constantine now clearly encouraged the Christians. As the latter's aspirations to

supreme power became more and more obvious, Licinius, the Augustus of the Eastern provinces, decided to rely on the alternative power basis of the old religion and its traditional supporters. There were some incipient signs of renewed hostility to the Christians of the East, which Constantine seized on as justification to topple Licinius from power in 324, leaving his way clear to supreme monarchy over the empire. He and his dynasty were, from that point onward, closely associated with the Christian movement, and in the later fourth century the church enjoyed unparalleled peace and growth. There was a brief but halfhearted effort (castigated in *Gregory of Nazianzus's Orations* 4–5) to hinder the church's cause by the emperor Julian (361–363), but the latter's death (probably at the hands of Christian assassins) spelled the end of pagan emperors ordering persecutions against the church, at least in the *patristic* era. In the West there would be a considerable number of further persecutions in the fifth and sixth centuries, as invading Gothic Arian kings made their power felt over native Nicene Catholics; and in Byzantium, zealous Christian emperors imposing their varieties of orthodoxy in later centuries would equally be designated by many sources as "wicked persecutors"; but all of this was strictly "by analogy."

The church had been born into persecution and emerged as a powerful force of resistance through four centuries of difficult circumstances. Ever afterward that memory became for it an archetypal encouragement for its (many) later troubles, and it celebrated its victory in the later fourth century not merely by establishing itself deep in the very fabric of Roman civilization, but particularly by enshrining the memories of its early martyrs in the firmament of an expansive liturgical calendar that canonized the old eschatological view of the "Age of Persecutions."

L. W. Barnard, "Clement of Rome and the Persecution of Domitian," *NTS* 10 (1963):

251–60; T. D. Barnes, "Legislation Against the Christians," JRS 58 (1968): 32–50; W. H. C. Frend, *Martyrdom and Persecution in the Early Church* (Oxford, 1965); P. Keresztes, "The Jews, the Christians, and the Emperor Domitian," VC 27 (1973): 1–28; H. Musurillo, *The Acts of the Christian Martyrs* (Oxford, 1972); A. N. Sherwin-White, "The Early Persecutions and Roman Law—Again," JTS 3 (1952): 199–213; G. E. M. de St. Croix, "Why were the Early Christians persecuted?" *Past and Present* 26 (1963): 6–38; B. W. Workman, *Persecution in the Early Church* (Oxford, 1980).

Person Contemporary thought (particularly after the advances in psychological analysis of the twentieth century) is so fundamentally oriented around ideas of person, personhood, and personality that it is something of a revelation to discover that ancient Greek thought regarded the idea of person as peripheral. *Aristotle* had so centralized the category of the collective nature that the idea of an individual representative of a genus hardly offered anything objectively interesting to the philosopher's consideration. All that could be deduced about humanity was available to collective scrutiny. The investigation of the individual human man or woman, the person, was "accidental" to the classification of the *nature.* It was Christianity of the Byzantine era that radically changed that perspective, and did so largely because of the intense focus on personhood that occurred as a result of the *christological* crisis. The early stages of the christological debate passed by without too much anxiety among Christians that a technical word for "person" was more or less missing from the church's vocabulary. Subjectival unity was simply presumed. In the *creed*, for example, statements about the eternal Son of God (God of God, Light of Light) were simply merged with historical statements about Jesus the Son of God (suffered under Pontius Pilate, died and was buried) without too much consider-

ation. In the early fifth century the sophisticated theology of the Syrian church (*Diodore of Tarsus, Theodore of Mopsuestia*) was brought by *Nestorius of Constantinople* into a serious conflict with the more traditional Alexandrian christological devotion represented by *Cyril of Alexandria.* The result of the debate that followed was a desire to clarify the idea of personal subjectivity as represented in the life of Christ. The *Syrian* church offered the idea of *prosopon* to stand for the individual subject. *Prosopon* was originally the "actor's mask." It connoted a "face." In technical christological use it was that face of personality which a reality presented to the observing outside world. It was thus a very close synonym of the old Latin term *persona*, which had been in use for generations, though never fully defined (Tertullian, *Adversus Praxean*). Nestorius somewhat complicated matters by having a complex theory of how Christ presented various "personality-fronts" to the world depending on whether he acted as the eternal Son of God (*Logos*), the Son of Man (the human Jesus) or the Christ (a complex mixed role, which could be compared to the sacrality of the high priest). All of that is another story (*see* **Council of Ephesus**), but his views were robustly attacked by Cyril of Alexandria, who argued for a single *physis* (concrete reality) of the divine Christ, the result of a synergy of the Word of God with a human life, such that the divine person of the *Trinity* took up a human modality of existence while remaining who he always was, the divine Son ("*mia physis tou theou logou sesarkomene*"). This terminology of single *physis* was quickly rejected by more or less everybody else in the Eastern church, and soon abandoned by Cyril too (though not by his followers in Egypt: *see* **Monophysitism**), who recognized that a word that was a synonym for collective nature (*physis*—as physical attributes) could hardly be expected to stand in as a new definition of personal subjectivity (*physis*—as concrete existent).

Cyril was unwilling to adopt Nestorius's preferred term of *prosopon* because it seemed to him inherently superficial (accidental in the antique philosophical sense), whereas the notion of the personhood of God the Word had to be conveyed by something profoundly concrete and solid (hence his original choice of *physis*). He settled instead for the term *hypostasis*. This communicated the idea of solidity (deep substrate of reality) and was also flexible (and new) enough to connote the idea of personal subject. So it was that *hypostasis* was quickly adopted as the chief Christian term for individual personhood. In the West after 400, *Augustine* turned his attention to the issue of personhood in Christology, and prepared the way for *Boethius* to give a classic definition to the West, that person was "an individual substance of a rational nature." At the *Council of Chalcedon* (451) *prosopon* and *persona* were redefined to have the same meaning of *hypostasis*, and soon only the two latter terms were in active use in the Latin and Greek churches. The Latin tendency to substantize it was combined with the Greek tendency to regard it as a transformative energy of presence. In this way a technical vocabulary of "personhood" entered Western civilization. The function of the hypostasis in Christology was to *deify* the assumed human nature. And so it was that "person," a concept of the divine presence and power that transfigured and transcended, entered philosophy no longer as an "accidental" but as a substantive. From being a philosophically peripheral and accidental term it was destined to assume center stage of religious philosophy.

J. A. McGuckin, *St. Cyril of Alexandria and the Christological Controversy* (Leiden, Netherlands, 1994); M. Nedoncelle, "Prosopon et persona dans l'antiquité classique," RSR 22 (1948): 277–99; M. Richards, "L'introduction du mot hypostase dans la théologie de l'incarnation," MSR 2 (1945): 5–32, 243–70.

Peter the Fuller (d. 488)   A *Monophysite* theologian and bishop of *Antioch*, Peter had been a fuller (clotheswasher) in his early years as a monk in the Monastery of the Acoimetae (Sleepless Ones) at *Constantinople.* He was exiled from the capital because of his strong anti-Chalcedonian views. During the reign of Zeno he returned and was part of the process petitioning for a new *christological* settlement that reduced the significance of the *Council of Chalcedon* (451). During a visit to Antioch Zeno encouraged his attempt to secure the episcopal throne in 470, although the patriarch of Constantinople discovered the plot and had Peter imprisoned in his former monastery, until he escaped in 475 and secured the episcopacy. He was again deposed in 477. In 482 he became a signatory and propagator of Zeno's *Henoticon*, the edict that attempted to broker a christological settlement that did reduce the significance of Chalcedon. Peter was subsequently confirmed in his occupation of Antioch until his death in 488. He caused controversy in his church by making Monophysite amendments to the liturgy. One of the most famous was his addition of the phrase "was crucified for us" to the Trisagion Hymn ("holy God, holy, mighty, holy Immortal, have mercy on us"). His opponents protested that he had thus illegitimately changed a *Trinitarian* hymn into a monochristological referent. His intention was to amplify the significance of the Theopaschite theology of *Cyril of Alexandria* (the theology found in Cyril's *anathemata* attached to the end of his third letter to *Nestorius,* where he stated that "One of the Trinity was crucified in the flesh"), and also to advocate the restoration of Cyril's terminology in place of the Chalcedonian Two Nature language. He is also said to have been the bishop who introduced the custom of reciting the Nicene-Constantinopolitan *Creed* at Sunday services.

W. H. C. Frend, *The Rise of the Monophysite Movement* (Cambridge, 1972), 167–70, 188–90.

Philo of Alexandria (c. 20 B.C.–A.D. 50) A Jewish philosopher and biblical commentator from *Alexandria,* Philo was a slightly older contemporary of Jesus. He belonged to a prominent family at Alexandria and was leader of a delegation to the emperor Caligula (described in his treatise *Legatio ad Gaium*), on behalf of the Jewish community of the city to protest at violence that had been offered to them. He had received the finest Hellenistic education of his time, and his writings show a deep concern to relate the biblical theology of his Jewish heritage to the concerns and insights of Hellenistic metaphysic. His was a highly *Platonized* Alexandrian *Judaism* that had a deep effect on a formative period of Christian thought largely through the Alexandrian Platonists of the Christian period (although a common heritage for some of the Christian writers in the philosophical works of the Middle Platonists can also be presumed). His allegorical approach to the Torah retold the ancient narratives from the viewpoint of a vastly cosmic *Logos theology.* God's supremacy was mediated through his divine Wisdom, which contained in itself all the divine "ideas" and was the source of the entire cosmos. The knowledge of the Logos in the *soul* was seen as the primordial principle of all human understanding, and the root of the soul's desire to return to God. The scriptural revelation (the Mosaic Law) was the pattern of all ethical behavior that rightly orientated a being for the divine ascent. Obeying these prescripts, the soul attained to a "likeness" with God. This massive system (especially the basic prescripts of a Logos theology, which was the motivating force for an allegorical approach to the Bible), and a view of the programmatic of salvation as ascent to spiritual communion with God (*see deification*) had a determinative effect on *Origen of Alexandria,* who followed the main schemata and thoroughly Christianized the ideas, with an inestimable effect on the subsequent history of Christianity. Philo also much influenced *Clement of Alexandria, Eusebius of Caesarea, Jerome,* and especially the ascetical writing of *Gregory of Nyssa,* whose *Life of Moses* is deeply indebted to him.

R. M. Berchman, *From Philo to Origen: Middle Platonism in Transition* (Chico, Calif., 1984); E. R. Goodenough, *An Introduction to Philo Judaeus* (New Haven, Conn., 1940); D. Winston, *Logos and Mystical Theology in Philo of Alexandria* (Cincinnati, 1985); H. A. Wolfson, *Philo* (2 vols.; Cambridge, Mass., 1947).

Philocalia The *Philocalia* was a collection of select passages from *Origen of Alexandria,* mainly focused on his exegetical theory and designed as a manual of instruction for preachers. It was collated and published by *Gregory of Nazianzus* (mentioned in his *Letter* 115) and *Basil of Caesarea* when the two of them were considering how their careers could combine monastic seclusion with service of the *church,* shortly after Gregory's *ordination* in 361, when he visited Basil's monastic settlement in Pontus. The choice of the passages was designed to reduce the more explicitly speculative parts of Origen's thought and show how his brilliant *exegesis* could be allied to the Nicene cause (many *Arians* were also claiming the authority of Origen). The title means "Lover of Beautiful Things." Today it is often called the *Philocalia of Origen* so as not to confuse it with the more popularly known *Philocalia,* which was collated by Nicodemus the Athonite (who was a monk in the eighteenth century). This later *Philocalia* is a major collection of Greek monastic writers from the fourth century to the Byzantine period, and serves as a compendium of *patristic ascetical* and mystical writers.

G. Lewis, *The Philocalia of Origen* (Edinburgh, 1911); J. A. McGuckin, *St. Gregory of Nazianzus: An Intellectual Biography* (New York, 2001), 102–4;

G. Palmer, P Sherrard, and K. Ware, trans., *The Philokalia: The Complete Text of St. Nikodimos of the Holy Mountain, and St. Makarios of Corinth* (5 vols., London, 1979–1997).

Philosophy, the Church and (*See also Aristotelianism, Platonism, Pythagoreanism, Stoicism.*)   From the time of the apostle Paul, who made a critical apologia for faith in the crucified Lord as something that stood in sharp contrast with the "wisdom of the world" (1 Cor. 1:17–25; citing Isa. 29:14), a common *topos*, or often-repeated motif, arose in several early Christian writers that philosophy was incompatible with the faith. The latter conclusion was not what Paul either said or intended, since he himself made use of large amounts of syllogisms and argument-forms taken from the ancient philosophical schools; but it was an idea that was reprised many times in the later *ascetical* writers and has endured throughout much of Christianity's history in some form or another, where philosophy and culture are often paired together and set in opposition to the *kerygma* conceived as a world-denying or cultural-transcending force, rather than as a redemptive leaven within a human cultural matrix. From the beginning of the church, the use of philosophical categories to understand the gospel message was an important and central part of Christian missionary strategy, but there was also considerable friction, especially in the communities of the first two centuries, between those who wished to have a predominantly biblical and imagistic understanding of Christianity and those who wished to apply Hellenistic methods of reasoning in a substantive (or at least systematic) manner, so as to illuminate theological questions in more complex ways than did the biblical poetics. The first of those who brought about the crisis of the church's formal relation to philosophy would later be known as the gnostics. They were the Hellenistically educated private teachers of such large churches as **Rome, Alexandria,** and **Antioch,** and many of their concerns seemed to simpler members of the churches to "fly off" the biblical data like gymnasts from a trampoline. This was partly because many of the philosophical schools of the period of the New Testament were highly eclectic in style and used mythologically based cosmologies (such as the *fall* of spiritual aeons from the heavenly realms) and heavily *allegorical* interpretative methods to explore aspects of theodicy that were common to the church and the ancient schools of wisdom. The alarm of many of the earliest Christian community leaders with this style of "philosophy" and *exegesis* is abundantly evident in some of the late Catholic Epistles (cf. 2 Pet. 1:16) and in writers such as **Clement of Rome** and *Ignatius*; and it reached a critical level in the second-century antignostic fathers such as **Irenaeus,** who applied Paul's warning against "worldly wisdom" precisely to the **gnostic** Christian philosophers as "betrayers" of the simplicity of the faith. The *topos* that philosophy was seen as characteristically complex and humanly clever while the true faith was simple, chaste, and self-authenticating was itself borrowed from the rhetorico-philosophical schools of the period, and thus cannot really be accepted at face value. But up to the end of the second century it did not much matter, since most Christians were of lowly status and poorly educated, and would not have known where the *topoi* of their teachers were taken from. This began to change significantly in the third century, and it is this period that sees several elevated Christian thinkers trying to work out a more complex appreciation of Hellenistic philosophy in the light of biblical revelation. Chief among them was **Clement of Alexandria,** who, in a trilogy of works that were designed to offer Christians a program of higher education (*Protrepticus, Paedagogus,* and *Stromata*), explicitly bemoaned how many Christians regarded teachers of philosophy as "the bogeyman." He had in mind the "simple believers," in whom he wanted to develop a more sophisticated understanding of the faith, but his words could equally have applied to some significant *patristic* thinkers both before and after him, such as *Tatian, Hippolytus,* or *Epiphanius,* who were consistently hostile to the whole idea of "philosophy." Clement set himself the task of showing how the real Christian "gnostic," or illuminated believer, could discern exactly how much of the ancient wisdom was compatible with the faith. He set out a program of describing Christianity as an eclectic school itself that was guided in its discerning choices of philosophical and moral wisdom by the gift of revelation it had received. In his *Protrepticus* Clement clearly intended to catch the attention of the "intelligent seeker after truth" and offer Christian faith as the highest fulfillment of the inner drive and finest aspirations of philosophy. Origen, in the first half of the third century, put this effort on a more systematic basis with his book of *First Principles* designed to show how Christianity addressed the major problems that were treated by the ancient schools of philosophy. Some significant Greek philosophers became converts at the end of the first century and continued to write, now on behalf of the church; *Justin Martyr* and *Aristides* are among the most famous of them. Latin philosopher-converts, such as *Tertullian* or *Lactantius,* were even more robust in their claim that Christianity was not so much the rejection of philosophy, but its fulfillment. Tertullian (despite his often hostile descriptions of philosophy) argued, on the basis of common *Stoic* wisdom, that God had put "divine seeds" in the world in the form of human spiritual consciousness, and he made much of the claim that this general potential for truth had finally come to fruition in Christianity. The incarnation of the supreme World-Reason (the *Logos*) was the reconciliation of the philosophical and religious quests in the form of Christianity.

Lactantius in his *Divine Institutes,* written in the early fourth century, attempted to show how in Christianity alone were found the religious and philosophical "paths" of Hellenism finally reconciled in a religion that was itself a true philosophy: "wisdom perfectly conjoined to religion," as he described it. The early Christian thinkers used Stoicism significantly in elaborating a refined moral theory, Aristotelianism in its logical processes, and Platonism in its cosmology and anthropology. They confidently charted their way through the various waters, affirming and decrying various aspects of the schools. Even at times when the schools are heavily used, it is rarely the case that the Christians took over ancient philosophy wholesale, since always the insights were subjected to the resolving lens of biblical consciousness. Lactantius expressed his simultaneous reliance on and suspicion of Plato by the dictum "He did not so much know God, as dream of him" (*The Divine Institutes* 5.14.13) and his attitude was a common one, demonstrating the great confidence Christian theologians possessed in this period. After the fourth century in Greek and Latin writers it became common to describe Christianity as "our philosophy" (*nostra philosophia*). The general context of the church's attitude to philosophy in the patristic period, therefore, might often appear to be a forced contrast on the one hand between *revelation* considered as a divine gift to the church, which thus possesses the fountain of truth, and on the other hand schools of human philosophy that use physical speculations to vaguely deduce partially true things. In reality this is more an issue of rhetorical apologetics between Christianity and the continuing schools of ancient wisdom than it is an exact description of the true relation of the early church and ancient philosophy. It was not until the early Middle Ages, perhaps, that the church really began to extend its own philosophical systems (until that point it had been profoundly eclectic), but in the classical patristic era the debate between faith and philosophy had already set down clear lines, and was most deeply concerned with the issue of communicating the gospel message to a Hellenistic world using its own cultural media in the process. In the later patristic era, already discernible in *Gregory of Nazianzus* in the fourth century, as well as in Marius Victorinus and *Augustine,* a path was opened up to define philosophy as "faith seeking understanding"; and this conception of philosophy as a "helper" of theological insight was to have a formative effect on the relation of the church to philosophy throughout the Middle Ages.

A. H. Armstrong and R. A. Markus, *Christian Faith and Greek Philosophy* (London, 1964); H. A. Wolfson, *The Philosophy of the Church Fathers* (Cambridge, Mass., 1964).

Philostorgius (c. 368–439)

A disciple of *Eunomius* the neo-Arian and a church historian, Philostorgius was a Cappadocian by birth, but spent most of his life in *Constantinople* and produced a chief work, the *Ecclesiastical History,* which covers the period of the *Arian* controversy (300–430) from the Arian perspective. His work has been fragmented, and survives in an epitome produced in the ninth century by *Photius* (who did not much care for him either as a writer or as a theologian), and in the *Passion of Artemius,* an Arian *martyr.* Philostorgius is a writer with heavy biases, but his pictures of the leading Arians of his day are uniquely valuable.

E. Walford, *The Ecclesiastical History of Sozomen, and also the Ecclesiastical History of Philostorgius as Epitomised by Photius* (London, 1855).

Philoxenus of Mabbug (c. 440–523)

Philoxenus was one of the leaders of the *Monophysite Syrian* church and, with *Peter the Fuller* (who appointed him bishop of Mabbug-Hierapolis in 485) and *Severus of Antioch,* a leading advocate for the advancement of *Cyril of Alexandria's Christology* as a standard for the church, in the face of the Chalcedonian stress on two distinct natures. His works survived in Syriac but still await a comprehensive English edition, which would widely demonstrate his importance as a theologian. His wrote extensively on ascetical spirituality (*Thirteen Discourses on the Christian Life*), on Christology, and on exegesis.

R. C. Chesnut, *Three Monophysite Christologies: Severus of Antioch, Philoxenus of Mabbug, and Jacob of Serug* (Oxford Theological Monographs; Oxford, 1976), 57–112; D. J. Fox, *The Matthew-Luke Commentary of Philoxenus: Text, Translation, and Critical Analysis* (Missoula, Mont., 1979); A. de Halleux, *Philoxène de Mabbog: sa vie, ses écrits, sa théologie* (Louvain, Belgium, 1963); G. Lardreau, *Discours philosophique et discours spirituel: autour de la philosophie spirituelle de Philoxène de Mabboug* (Paris, 1985); E. A. Wallis Budge, *The discourses of Philoxenus, Bishop of Mabbôgh,* A.D. *485–519 (edited from Syriac manuscripts of the sixth and seventh centuries in the British Museum, with an English translation)* (London, 1894).

Photinianism

Photinianism is a theological position, named after Photinus, bishop of Sirmium (d. c. 376), who was deposed for his views on the *person* of Christ at the Council of Sirmium in 351 (Socrates, *Church History* 2.18, 29–30; Sozomen, *Church History* 4.6; Epiphanius, *Refutation of All Heresies* 71). Photinus, a learned rhetorician, had been a pupil of *Marcellus of Ancyra.* Although accepting the virginal birth of Jesus and the accounts of the miracles, he rejected the tenets of preexistent *Logos theology* (for him, the Logos was simply another term for the Father), and he advocated for the view that Jesus was a man who was inspired by God and who represented, in his human life, an extraordinarily luminous revelation of the presence of God. His works were ordered to be destroyed after his deposition and exile, and so it is difficult to know precisely what he taught. Later *patristic* writers used his name to designate as "Photinianism" any view that suggested Jesus was not God, simply a human being, blessed or favored by God. Photinianism might thus correspond to the modern concept of a "prophetic" Christology. Patristic writers retrospectively link him with the earlier *Monarchian* theologian Sabellius, and often make Photinianism synonymous with "Psilanthropism" (from the Greek: *psilos anthropos*), or "Merely a Man" *Christology*. His person was again expressly condemned at the *Council of Constantinople I* (381), and yet again by the imperial decree of Theodosius II in 428.

G. Bardy, "Photine," (DTC 12, pt. 2; Paris, 1935), cols. 1532–36; R. P. C. Hanson, *The Search for the Christian Doctrine of God* (Edinburgh, 1988), 235–38; D. Petavius, *De Photino Haeretico eiusque Damnatione* (Paris, 1636); M. Simonetti, "Studi sull'Arianesimo," *Verba Seniorum* n.s. 5 (1965): 135–59.

Photinus   *see* **Photinianism**

Photius (c. 810–895)   A Constantinopolitan aristocrat and bibliophile, Photius became one of the most important patriarchs of the capital city in the ninth century. Emperor Michael III deposed the patriarch Ignatius in 858 and asked for the diplomat Photius to succeed him, even though he was still a layman. Pope Nicholas I, however, supported Ignatius's legitimacy as patriarch and used the opportunity to assert a strong claim for papal supremacy. The schism that resulted was exacerbated by the dispute that also arose over the newly established Bulgarian church—whether it should look to Roman or Constantinopolitan ecclesiastical jurisdiction. Photius strongly opposed Roman missionaries in Bulgaria, and began to assemble reasons that the Orthodox East had the right claim, an argument which historically resulted in the wider culture of the Orthodox Slav world. In the course of a council at *Constantinople* in 867, Photius's arguments against papal supremacy and the untraditional nature of the Latin *Filioque* theology of the *Trinity* resulted in the Byzantine condemnation of the pope. The ultimate alienation of the Byzantine and Roman churches has often been posited in 1054, but the work of Photius marked the first significant occasion (there had been many prior divisions and would be several others after) that the Eastern and Western churches officially and instinctively drew apart on significant theological issues, particularly related to the manner in which papal authority was felt by the Easterners to have changed the ancient pattern of the Christian Ecumene (*see* **papacy**). Later, in 867, Emperor Basil seized the throne (murdering Michael) and Ignatius was restored to the patriarchate. Ignatius took the opportunity, at a council in Constantinople in 869–870, of anathematizing Photius. Relations with Rome, however, were not improved when Ignatius appointed senior bishops to administer the Bulgarian church. In 877, after Ignatius's death, Photius was reappointed as patriarch, and in 879 a reconciliation with Rome was brought about. In 886, on the accession of Emperor Leo VI, Photius resigned his see and lived in monastic retirement. Throughout his life Photius had been a lover of reading, and in Constantinople he presided over a circle of intellectual friends who read and reviewed literature from antiquity to their own day. His access to the great libraries of the capital was unequaled. The results of his reading circle were published by Photius in his most famous work, *A Thousand Books* (*Myrobiblion*—also known as *The Library*, or *Bibliotheca*). It is a digest and annotated review (often with extracts) of several hundred works, many of which are now known to history only through Photius's comments. The work, therefore, is of inestimable historical importance. His treatise *On the Holy Spirit* became a foundational study for later Eastern Orthodox theology, and one that for centuries to come focused the mind of the Byzantine world on why it held Latin Catholicism in suspicion, both in terms of ecclesiastical organization and in relation to its doctrine of God.

F. Dvornik, *The Photian Schism: History and Legend* (Cambridge, 1948); J. H. Freese, trans., *The Library of Photius (1–165)* (vol. 1; London, 1920); W. T. Treadgold, *The Nature of the Bibliotheca of Photius* (Dumbarton Oaks Studies 18; Washington, D.C., 1980); D. S. White, *Patriarch Photius of Constantinople* (Brookline, Mass., 1981).

Pilgrimage   The word "pilgrimage" derives from the Latin term *peregrinatio*, the undertaking of a foreign journey, and was used by the Christians in the sense of voyaging to see and pray at a specific holy place. The notion is closely related to the practice of praying at the tombs of the greatest **saints** and **martyrs**, an aspect of ancient funeral ritual that the Christians specifically developed in new liturgical ways (*see* **burial**). The shrine of Peter was an early attraction of the Roman church, so too its catacombs, which held the remains of several important martyrs. But many churches, certainly after the spate of **persecutions** in the third and fourth centuries, had local shrines to their own martyrs, and it was generally thought that it was best to pray to one's own saints, who had an interest in the region and in their neighborhood "clients." Pilgrimage to saints' shrines, therefore, was probably in its earliest phases so regionally localized that it had a very low profile. *Origen,* in the third century, showed a lively interest in identifying and visiting some of the notable places of biblical history, but

his was a rare voice (although he had been anticipated by **Hegesippus**), and his example was cited later by **Eusebius of Caesarea,** in the fourth century, as an instance of Origen's exceptional biblical culture. It is really only after the fourth century, when peace was established for the church and it was safe to advertise one's Christian allegiance to the inhabitants of a foreign city, that pilgrimage as such was openly manifested. Then it related primarily to the martyrs' tombs, and increasingly was extended to include a voyage to the monastic sites of Egypt, which **Athanasius** had made popular through his *Life of Antony.* After **Constantine's** building works in Palestine, especially his construction of the Church of the Anastasis-Resurrection (later to be called the Holy Sepulchre), the "Holy Land" started to become a significant concept for Christians, and the idea of a sacred journey to the site of the Lord's passion, **resurrection,** and miracles was encouraged by many writers of the Palestinian church, not least Eusebius. The **Jerusalem** church elaborated a splendid liturgical ritual from this period, and with Latin and **Syrian** monasteries permanently established within the city environs, the church became a genuinely international pilgrimage site, often with trilingual services. One visible result of this was the manner in which liturgical practices from Jerusalem were soon being copied across the Christian world. Some voices, such as **Gregory of Nyssa,** who had himself traveled to see the Holy Land, were skeptical, and Gregory advised his female readers not even to think about traveling (*Epistle* 2.18). The first journal recording a journey to Christian Palestine was that of the "Pilgrim of Bordeaux," composed in 333. One of the most popular, which had a wide readership for centuries afterwards, was the late–fourth century account of the nun **Egeria.** She traveled to most of the biblical sites, many of which were being touted, with dubious historicity, by local monks who already witnessed to the "tourist trade" element of pilgrimage. By the fifth century special pilgrims' guides were being composed to describe the holy places in Palestine; a chief example is that of Eucherius of Lyons. He added to place descriptions suitable biblical passages to read or recite. The pilgrimage centers of *Rome* and Jerusalem were the most famous of all, but the shrines of the martyrs Babylas at *Antioch*, Thekla at Seleukia, Sergius and Bacchus in Syria, Euphemia at Chalcedon, and Menas near *Alexandria* were also well known, and soon the monasteries of famous *ascetics* also began to attract visitors. The community around *Simeon Stylites* in Syria was extensively visited during his lifetime, and other ascetics gained a popular following after their deaths. By the end of the fifth century many churches wanted to expand their local shrines into more internationally significant centers of pilgrimage. A unique example of this was *Constantinople* itself, which progressively began to serve as a magnet for *relics* of the saints, beginning with the relics of the Lord's passion brought there by *Constantine* and Helena. Soon Constantinople had everything in its walls that a Christian pilgrim could wish for (its fame in this regard causing it untold damage at the Fourth Crusade in 1204). It was also soon to be the central Christian locus for monastic life, especially after the barbarian invasions of *Scete* made travel to Egypt unwise. The resistance of the Eastern capital to entertaining transitory visitors, however, made the Holy Land always the more popular venue with foreigners. In Western Christianity after the fifth century, pilgrimage came to be associated with expiation of sins, a concept particularly fostered by the Celtic church, which took the older monastic concept of penitential "exile" (*xeniteia*) to heart. To the ancient aspects of pilgrimage as seeking for intercession at a holy shrine, therefore, came to be added elements of penitential practice, which would be specially developed in the later Middle Ages.

E. D. Hunt, *Holy Land Pilgrimages in the Later Roman Empire, A.D. 312–460* (Oxford, 1982); P. W. L. Walker, *Holy City: Holy Places? Christian Attitudes to Jerusalem and the Holy Land in the 4th Century* (Oxford, 1990); R. L. Wilken, *The Land Called Holy* (New Haven, Conn., and London, 1992).

Platonism   Plato (428–346 B.C.) was a Greek aristocrat and student of Socrates, whose execution as a "subverter of youth" stimulated him to abandon a career in politics and dedicate himself to the life of philosophy, especially as that was concerned with the creation of an ideal society, a new order of state. Between 389 and 367 B.C. he organized his own school in the Grove of Academus near Athens, which gave Platonism its alternative name of the "Academy." In the early dialogues of Plato, Socrates appears as a major actor, setting questions to the reader (in the dramatic form of a dialogue between various characters) that are meant to probe the individual's understanding of basic concepts such as piety, friendship, or love until all the offered definitions have been shown to be defective and bafflement (*aporia*) sets in among the respondents. This state of unknowing then invites the reader to advance into true conceptions by deeper study, having demonstrated the profound need to question received but superficial wisdoms. This educational method Socrates, or rather Plato, called the *maieutic* (midwifery), since it was fundamental to the philosophic task to allow the individual agent "to emerge," not to be dominated in an unreflective assimilation of commonly accepted "truths." The early dialogues (such as *Euthyphro, Lysis*) are particularly concerned with establishing a moral basis of reflection. The good is seen to be that which is truly beneficial; evil is defined as ignorance; virtue is knowledge. The quest for the ideal must direct an ethical life. In the middle period dialogues (*Phaedo, Symposium, Republic*), Plato set out the character of the ideal society and speculated on the nature of true reality as such. Here he posited that ideals such as beauty, truth, or justice exist as real entities outside all material or relative conditions, and are not themselves susceptible to variations imposed either by context or culture. They are absolute standards, always the same. These ideals can be called the Ideas, or Ideal Forms, and are the prototypes that cause their individual manifestations in the world of materiality. Absolute Beauty (Ideal Beauty) is thus the exemplar and root, or common factor, of whatever is beautiful here in our varied experience of "beautiful things." Human beings apprehend the Ideals through intellectual perception (*nous*). Understanding comes from the fact that in a prematerial existence (before the soul was imprisoned in a bodily form), the intellect recognized them directly; and even now the human mind has some "recollection" of them through reminiscences and evocations (anamnesis) provided by material copies (mimesis) of the various absolutes. The theory of the Ideas was not so much emphasized in the later writings of Plato, leading some historians to speculate that he moved away from the notion as it attracted more and more criticism from **Aristotle**. Plato's later successors as heads of the Academy, especially Albinus in the mid–second century A.D., developed the notion in new ways, however, and partly synthesized it with aspects of later Aristotelian thought. Albinus, for example, argued that the Ideas were thoughts in the mind of a supreme Good, or God. It was this form of late Platonic theory that impacted and influenced the Christians. Plato himself developed his theory of Ideas with an increasing emphasis on the manner in which material reality misled the mind from true perception, offering only a frequently illusory reflection of reality. In the *Republic*, he used the image of a fire

that inmates of a cave could see insofar as it cast shadows of their forms on the wall before them as they sat facing the back of the cave. They were so distanced from the "true world," the world of reality outside the cave, that they finally came to think that the shadows were real things and made their deductions about reality from these insubstantial illusions. Plato thus made a strong contrast between material instability and the permanence of the true world. Several of his dialogues (*Phaedo, Phaedrus, Republic, Timaeus*) spoke about the soul in its relation to the body. The soul was envisaged as partly separable from the body in its rational dimension (*to logistikon, nous*) and intrinsically immortal, whereas the body was rooted in the material cosmos, part of flux and illusion. In the *Republic* he described a tripartite soul consisting of a higher part of reason, a "spirited" aspect that is motivated to the good and creative, and then the "desirous" part, which is motivated by acquisition. The last requires the guidance of reason and the discipline of the "spirited" soul, otherwise it falls into dissipation. Philosophy, according to Plato, can give right order to the soul, orientating it away from earthly illusions toward intellectual (noetic) truth. Such an orientation is no less than an ascent to the Good (*to kalon*), or the spiritual world of the Ideas. In the *Gorgias* he spoke of a salvific (***soteriological***) and quasi-religious (or certainly metaphysical) scheme wherein the righteous soul ascends through a cycle of ***reincarnations*** by virtuous living to an escape from material subjugation in a blessed existence. Not all of this amounted to a system, properly so called, but it certainly made for a coherent view of reality that later generations of Platonists developed extensively. Aristotle, one of Plato's own school for a time, made extensive revisions to the Platonic schema, but did not ultimately divert the Academy from its goals. Platonism was perhaps the most dominant form of ancient philosophy, while Aristotelianism was the most extensively "absorbed." Both forms were to make a major impact on Christianity in the *patristic* era. Aristotelian methodology was to be of great importance in Christian logic and *anthropology*, but Plato's ideas on the moral ascent to the Good captured the imagination of some of the earliest and most important Christian intellectuals, who thought they could find here a friend of their religion. Throughout all the periods when Christianity was actively in dialogue with Platonism, notably the second century through the sixth (after that point Platonism became merely a textual reality), none of the Platonists themselves were happy about the manner in which their school had been absorbed and re-presented by Christians. *Plotinus* fought with *gnostics*, Porphyry attacked *Origen,* and *Proclus* (the last leader of the Academy) lamented the manner in which Christianity had so overshadowed the school that Greek culture had been overthrown (he witnessed the final closing of the Academy by order of a Christian emperor). Christians, however, were more than ready to take building materials from anywhere they thought would be useful, and much of the Platonic thought world was adapted for use in theology. Hardly anything of it was left untouched, so thoroughly did Christian thinkers subordinate it to the overall prescripts of their biblically inspired religion, but it is certainly possible to see the major impact Christian Platonism made on the history of theology. Early *Apologists* often claimed Plato as a Christian before his time. That approach was brought to a climactic head in Eusebius's *Preparation for the Gospel*, where he argued that ancient philosophy (especially Platonism) had served as an evangelical catechesis for the world of the pagans (in a manner comparable to the Old Testament for the Jews), and now the intellectual and spiritual aspirations of the Greek world could be fulfilled in the advent of Christianity. Plato's understanding of the transcendent nature of divinity, resolv-

ing into a unicity beyond material forms, was influential to Christians as they too began to describe God's existence in terms that were not merely dependent on the anthropomorphisms of the biblical account. Origen was a careful student of ancient philosophy. He has been often described as the most blatant Platonizer of the patristic era, but a close study of his works shows that he was a careful and critical synthesist. Some aspects of Plato's work were important to him (he particularly emphasizes the metaphysical map of the soul ascending to the Supreme Good as a moral *katharsis*), but in other instances he radically departs from Plato when he considers that the teacher is not compatible with the Scriptures. So, for example, Origen insists on a worldview involving a creation from nothing (*ex nihilo*) to reinforce the biblical understanding of the supremacy of God, over and against the Platonic view of divinity as an agency within a more determinist and eternally preexisting cosmos. The Platonic idea of *philosophy* as a training of the soul to ascend to the Good was also heavily used by other Christians, through the medium of the theory of the Ideas. Plato's sense of the immortality of the soul was also much referred to, although Christians generally did not advocate the natural immortality of the soul as much as its conditional immortality. In the Latin world Marius Victorinus and *Augustine* were enthusiastic advocates of the beneficial effect Neoplatonism could have on Christian self-expression. For the East, Origen, *Gregory of Nyssa, Pseudo-Dionysius,* and *Maximus the Confessor* represent the new Christian Platonism of Byzantium. Plato's view of philosophy as a moral discipline, whereby the soul could rise to true perception, was highly influential on the early Christian *ascetical* movement, who regarded themselves as "true philosophers" using ascetical techniques to distance themselves from material illusions in the cause of advancing noetic insight. In the fourth to sixth centuries Platonism itself took on a deepened religious character of its own in the form of Neoplatonism, but in many senses the Christian monastic movement as represented by its Origenian advocates (such as *Evagrius* and Maximus) was an authentic heir to the earlier Platonic movement. Platonism as a whole, in its profound and indigenous suspicion of material reality, was never quite able to be digested in the generic Christian schemata, which through the foundational medium of the Scriptures, and through the primacy given to the *incarnation* of the *Logos,* actually elevated materiality to a *sacramental* status in a way wholly alien to Platonic values.

R. Arnou, "Platonisme des Pères," (DTC 12; Paris, 1921), 2294–392; S. Lilla, "Platonism and the Fathers," in A. Di Berardino, ed., *Encyclopedia of the Early Church* (vol. 2; Cambridge, 1992), 689–98; J. M. Rist, *Platonism and Its Christian Heritage* (London, 1986); W. D. Ross, *Plato's Theory of Ideas* (Oxford, 1951).

Plotinus   Plotinus, a non-Christian Greek philosopher born in 204, was the founder of the Neoplatonic school of thought. His chief work is the *Enneads.* He studied with Ammonius Saccas in *Alexandria* for eleven years, who earlier had been the teacher of *Origen.* In 244 Plotinus settled in *Rome* as a teacher of philosophy, issuing a series of written works after 253. He attracted, as a disciple, Porphyry, who besides being his editor and apologist was also a strong critic of the manner in which Christians of the time (especially Origen) were making use of *Platonic* ideas. Plotinus was deeply interested in the concept of philosophy as the guide of the soul's ascent to communion with the divine, and although he and his followers were very critical of Christian and *gnostic* teachings, he had a marked influence on several later Christian writers, notably *Ambrose,* Marius Victorinus, and *Augustine.* He died in 270. Porphyry composed his *Life* as a philosophical

hagiography describing him as a true mystic who had achieved moments of divine communion even in this world. Porphyry's text had a motive of discrediting alternative claims to spiritual insight such as those being presented by the Christians, whom he generally disdained. Plotinus differed from earlier receptions of Platonism, notably those presided over by Christians such as Origen, by replacing the view that *nous* (spiritual intellect) was the highest reality, the supreme Good, to which all other consciousness aspired, and substituting for that ideas taken from Plato's *Parmenides,* where the supreme "One" is presented as absolute reality. He identified the supreme Good as beyond being, calling it the "First Hypostasis," which could only be apprehended by negations. The Second Hypostasis was Nous, source of the intelligible world, a principle of reason generated from the One, which is the root of all beauty. The Third Hypostasis was the World-Soul, born from the Nous and serving to inspire rationality within the sensible world, which it constructs and which it infuses with spiritual perception. Plotinus believed that mankind's destiny was a potential for transcendence of this world by reaching a state of passionlessness (*apatheia*) in which a human being found release from the sensory domain and was able to turn the mind purely toward the intelligible world and find communion with the Second Hypostasis. His ideas were taken up by *Gregory of Nyssa* in the latter's concept of *apophatic* theology and the progressive purification of the mind, and they had a continuing influence on other ascetical writers such as *Maximus the Confessor* and *Pseudo-Dionysius,* making an impact on later Byzantine mystical theory. His influence was also particularly marked on late–fourth- and fifth-century *patristic* writers on the *Trinity* (especially *Augustine*), who can be seen to be partly influenced by his notions of the triad of the ascending hierarchy in their conceptions of Trinitarian relations.

A. H. Armstrong, ed., *The Cambridge History of Later Greek and Early Medieval Philosophy* (Cambridge, U.K., 1967), 196–268; S. Lilla, "Platonism and the Fathers," in A. Di Berardino, ed., *Encyclopedia of the Early Church* (vol. 2; Cambridge, 1992), 689–98.

Pneumatology   *see* Holy Spirit

Pneumatomachianism   The term derives from the Greek for "fighters against the Spirit." It was a pejorative designation invented by the *Cappadocian Fathers* to describe a significantly large party of episcopal theologians (there were more than thirty of them present at the *Council of Constantinople I* [381]) who resisted the profession of the *hypostatic* deity of the *Holy Spirit*. Retrospectively they were called the Macedonians, connoting the leadership of one of their most eminent earlier representatives, Macedonius, the bishop of *Constantinople*, who was deposed by an *Arian* synod in that city in 360 (cf. Sozomen, *Church History* 5.14; 4.27; Gregory of Nazianzus, *Oration* 31). Macedonius was one of the *Homoiousian* theologians, who were less than convinced that the concept of consubstantiality ought to be applied to the Son, let alone to the Spirit of God. It was to convince the wavering Homoiousians that Basil of Caesarea wrote his treatise *On the Holy Spirit*. *Gregory of Nazianzus* antagonized the Homoiousian anti-Trinitarian bishops at the Council of Constantinople, calling them "Moabites" illegitimately allowed to enter the councils of the church; but even so he could not persuade the conciliar fathers to adopt his theology explicitly admitting the consubstantiality of the Holy Spirit (the *creed* professed the much vaguer "conglorification"). It seems that it had been the intention of the emperor *Theodosius* to reconcile them if at all possible. If the *homoousion* of the Son had been a bridge too far for this group, the progression toward a *Trinitarian* theology of equal hypostases (such as represented by Gregory of Nazianzus) was altogether too much to take, and the so-called Macedonian party abandoned the council of 381 in its early stages. How close the connection of this party was with the historical Macedonius is very obscure, though the historians *Socrates* and *Sozomen* made that connection. The real leader of the group was *Eustathius of Sebaste,* but he was severely and consistently ignored by the Cappadocians. The title Gregory made up however, "those who fought against the Spirit," was a vivid one that stuck. They have often been associated, as a group, with those whom *Athanasius of Alexandria* had earlier designated as the *Tropici* (the Spirit is only a modality of God, not a separate hypostasis) in his *Letters to Serapion.* They dwindled away as a significant force in Christian politics after the Theodosian Code in 383 deprived them of their churches, although they survived in a small area around the Eastern capital until the fifth century (Sozomen, *Church History* 8.1).

R. P. C. Hanson, *The Search for the Christian Doctrine of God* (Edinburgh, 1988), 760–72; W. D. Hauschild, *Die Pneumatomachen* (diss., University of Hamburg, 1967); M. A. G. Haykin, *The Spirit of God: The Exegesis of 1st and 2nd Corinthians in the Pneumatomachian Controversy of the Fourth Century* (Leiden, Netherlands, 1994).

Polycarp (c. 69–156)   Polycarp is one of the *Apostolic Fathers,* and was the bishop of Smyrna who assisted *Ignatius of Antioch* when he was traveling as a prisoner through Asia Minor. He was an inspiration to *Irenaeus of Lyons,* as a child, and became for him a living example of an apostle of the second generation, thus influencing his theory of the *apostolic succession* (the transmission of authority from the apostles of Christ through to the bishops of the early catholic communities). It was Polycarp who collated and published the writings

of Ignatius. His own letters to Ignatius and to the church at Philippi survive, an example of how the structure of episcopal government of the church was evolving in that period. His writing shows many concerns similar to those evidenced in the Pastoral Epistles of the New Testament. The dramatic account of his arrest, trial, and martyrdom (*Martyrdom of Polycarp*) is one of the first Christian narratives of a **martyr**'s death, and gives witness to the rise of the cult of the martyrs in the early church.

W. R. Schoedel, *Polycarp, Martyrdom of Polycarp, Fragments of Papias* (Camden, 1967).

Praxeas *see* Callistus of Rome, Monarchianism, Tertullian

Prayer The common terms for prayer in Hellenistic religion were preserved in the Christian Latin (*Oratio*, or petition) and only slightly adapted in the Greek (*euche* being replaced by the Pauline term *proseuche*). Many of the same presuppositions were shared between *Judaism*, Christianity, and Hellenism in the period of the early church, not least a belief in the fundamental human need to intercede with the divinity as benefactor (*euergetes*) that demonstrated the essential reverence (*pietas, eusebeia*) that distinguished humanity. The Christians, following Jewish biblical tradition, were much less inclined, however, to develop those common aspects of Hellenistic religion and prayer that could be designated as "aversion rituals," involved with keeping the anger of the gods away from a house or concerned with calling down curses on an enemy. The Christians were also passionately concerned to mark a clear distinction between their calling upon God and that of their Hellenistic neighbors, in terms of the fundamental purity of monotheism that they insisted characterized their prayers (those of the pagans being generally envisaged as addressed to demons). The *church*'s developing concept of prayer was heavily influenced by biblical forms, and not least by the developing *eucharistic* ritual, which gave the early character of its prayers a profoundly "doxological" form: the offering of praise and thanksgiving to God as part of the church's covenant responsibility. In many senses the church subsumed into its understanding of prayer that aspect of covenant theology where Israel understood itself as having, above all else, to preserve the temple sacrificial cult. As in LXX Psalm 21:4, the church sensed that "God is holy, and enthroned on the praises of Israel." Christian prayer, therefore, like much of that of ancient Israel, was first seen as a collective phenomenon more than a private concern: that spiritual consciousness of election and salvation that expressed the church's confession of identity in doxology. The great liturgical prayers of the assembly grew out of this deep sense of identity as the people who were called to sing God's praises and mercies, and the Christians found a ready pattern of such prayer in the biblical texts, especially the psalms and canticles, which were soon quarried for Christian use. The earliest *patristic* references to prayer in the Apostolic writings demonstrate that the **Lord's Prayer** was regularly repeated (and expected to be learned by heart). The **Didache** (chap. 8) requires it to be recited three times a day by every Christian. *Barnabas* also has much in it that refers to the practice of prayer, advising that it ought to be confident, persistent, and above all humble and joyful. The letter, along with the *Didache* and the **Shepherd of Hermas**, witness to the deeply *eschatological* character of prayer in the early church: praying as in the Lukan parable, that they might be awake when the master returns (Luke 12:35–36; cf. *Didache* 16; *Barnabas* 21.3; Shepherd of Hermas, *Similitude* 2.9; see also Tertullian, *De oratione* 5; 29). With **Irenaeus** in the second century, prayers began to be specifically abstracted from the New Testament, and he has many examples, probably of his own making, where he begins to rewrite New Testament texts so that they can serve as formal church prayers, a practice that would henceforth mark most forms of Christian prayer (cf. Irenaeus, *Adversus haereses* 3.6.4; 25.2). In the third century the first explicit theological treatises on the subject of prayer began to appear. Those by **Tertullian** (*De oratione*) and **Origen** (*Peri Euches*) were both the most extensive and the most profound; but **Clement of Alexandria** can perhaps claim to have been the first, composing several fine **christological** prayers within the structure of a **Trinitarian** confession (*Paedagogus* 1.6.42.1–2; 3.12.101) as well as devoting book 7 of his *Stromata* to a consideration of interior prayer as a mystical ascent to communion with God, a concept that had profound impact on Origen and on the later Christian mystical tradition. The treatises of Tertullian and Origen are structurally shaped by a close concern with expounding the meaning of the Lord's Prayer, as too is that of **Cyprian of Carthage** (*The Lord's Prayer*), and probably they grew out of the early practice of instructing **catechumens** in the basics of prayer during the Lenten fast preceding their **baptism.** By the third century certain aspects of Christian prayer were already established. Believers prayed standing up, facing the East as the place of the resurrection, and with arms stretched out and up with the palms facing outwards as a sign of intercession. If confession of sins was being made they prayed kneeling, but after the **Council of Nicaea** kneeling on Sundays was positively discouraged as inappropriate to the glory of the invocation of God. Origen advised that Christians should have a special place set aside for their prayers, and in the apocryphal *Acts of Hipparchas* the text describes how the protagonist painted a **cross** on the inside of the eastern wall of his house where he made his prayer "seven times a day" (a practice advocated in the Psalms). Other treatises on prayer make special mention of solemn prayers in the morning and at evening time. Christians also habitually prayed over meals, continuing the tradition of Jewish food blessings, but now with a profoundly christocentric focus. By the early fourth century the evening prayer is especially associated with the ritual of lighting the household lamps, and a third-century Christian hymn, the *Phos Hilaron*, is still sung to mark the occasion in the Greek vespers service. Morning and evening prayers grew, by the end of the fourth century, into formal rituals of assembly in the churches, and together with the eucharistic service, they became the regular basic structures of Christian prayer, fusing together the elements of communal and personal intercession. After the fourth century forms of prayer and church rituals were greatly extended by the **ascetics,** whose monastic vigils and extensive use of the Psalter took formal Christian prayer into its final, liturgical shape. The ascetical writers of the fourth and fifth centuries also produced an abundance of guidance manuals on interior prayer for the consumption of monastics. Some of the composers of these works, such as **Evagrius** in Egypt, **Pseudo-Macarius** in Syria, **Diadochus** in Greece, **John Cassian** in Marseilles, and Dorotheus in Gaza, left behind masterpieces of mystical literature, generally laying great stress on the need to purify the heart before prayer and to make prayer an earnest and "fiery offering," and on developing the awareness or consciousness of the operation of the **Holy Spirit** within the soul. Origen, Evagrius, and Macarius held a dominant position within this mystical tradition of prayer, and Christian theory generally conceived the ascent of the *soul* to refined spiritual awareness as the progress of the beloved to the "bridal chamber of Christ," in terms redolent of the Song of Songs.

P. Bradshaw, *Daily Prayer in the Early Church* (London, 1981); A. Hamann, *Le Pater expliqué par les pères* (Paris, 1952); idem, *La prière*: tom. 1, *Les origines chrétiennes* (Paris, 1959); R. L. Simpson, *The*

Interpretation of Prayer in the Early Church (Philadelphia, 1965).

Premundane Fall   *see* Fall

Presbyter   *see* Priesthood

Priesthood The word priest derives from the Old English *prester*, which was a version of the New Testament word presbyter, or elder. It is one of the primary triad of words (although there are numerous others such as exorcist, prophet, and so on) that describe the earliest Christian ministerial offices, namely: bishop (*episkopos*), *priest* (*presbyteros*), and *deacon* (*diakonos*). The New Testament Pastoral Letters are the first sources of the descriptions of the Christian presbyterate. The office is not heavily distinguished in the texts from that of the "overseer" or bishop (cf. Acts 20:17, 28; 1 Pet. 5:1–4; Titus 1:5–7), and in many places in the early church the two ministerial roles seem to have been overlapped or even synonymous, although obviously the office of overseer tended always to the singular, while presbyter could often be plural in any given community. The writers of the late first and early second centuries, such as **Clement of Rome** and **Ignatius,** sketch out a picture where churches were governed by a council of elders (probably, originally, simply the old and wise of the communities), from whose number one served as president of the liturgical assembly and had special organizational responsibilities. By the late second century (already witnessed in Ignatius of Antioch's high sense of the special dignity of the bishop as a single representative of the local church), the distinction of the offices of the presbyter and the *episkopos* was becoming more marked. At this time, some of the terms of common Hellenistic usage that had hitherto been avoided by the Christians made their appearance in Christian writing. **Cyprian of Carthage,** for example, who himself was undergoing considerable criticism from his local presbyters, brought into play the notion of *sacerdos*, or high priest, which had formerly been a designation of the priesthood of the pagan cults. Cyprian connected it quite explicitly with the biblical accounts of the high priests of Israel, and gave a strong impetus in the Latin church to the developing theology of the episcopate as a distinct and elevated ministry, and by derivation, also to the theology of priesthood (presbyterate) as a matter of "permanent character," which imaged in a special way in itself the unique priesthood of Christ. The connection of Christian ministers with the **typology** of the priests of the Old Testament was first made by Clement of Rome (*1 Clement* 43–44), but Cyprian developed it apace (cf. *Ep.* 63.14; 3; *The Unity of the Catholic Church* 17). Cyprian also underlined the notion of the priest as the "other Christ" (*alter Christus*), which became important for the West and also contributed to the growing sense of priesthood as something that was primarily claimed by the ordained ministers, who sacramentally iconized Christ in the liturgical ritual of the churches. In the Greek Christian world the word corresponding to the Latin *sacerdos*, that is, *hiereus* (sacrificing priest), never became quite so favored, although in both churches the developing theory of the **Eucharist** as sacrifice contributed greatly to the evolution of the priesthood (both that of the presbyter and that of the *episkopos*) as a matter fundamentally different from the priesthood of believers spoken of in 1 Peter 2:5. The general **patristic** reflection on priesthood before the fourth century had been mainly concerned with the Christians as a whole, manifesting a profoundly different sense of divine worship to God from either Jews or pagans, insofar as they were priests of the "interior offering," that is, a community that exercised priestly reverence to God through moral and rational means. This old idea already appeared archaic when it was resumed on the eve of the **Council of Nicaea** by **Lactantius** in *The Divine Institutes*. **Origen,** in the third century, devoted extensive writing to the idea of true Christian priesthood, and he made a special point (even though an ordained presbyter himself) of maintaining the old idea that the real Christian "priest" was the believer who had drawn close to the supreme Priest, Jesus, and shared in his consecration as illumined and pure worshiper. But in general, the rapid expansion of the fourth-century churches and deepening conceptions of liturgical theology signaled a permanent change in conceptions of priesthood that underlay ordained ministries; and the chief ministers of the church, notably the bishops, presbyters, and deacons, completely subsumed the claim for priesthood (in three degrees) after that century, leaving reflections on the "royal priesthood of believers" in something of a hinterland, often reduced to a brief mention in reference to the theology of *baptism.* The relentless rise and strengthening of the monarchical episcopal office after the third century could not dislodge the ancient character of the council of elder-presbyters, or disrupt the earlier position that had afforded them much the same rights and responsibilities as the *episkopoi.* By the late fourth century when the expansion of the church often demanded that a large city should have more than one worshiping community, or that a suburban hinterland required the building of extra churches (though **Rome** and **Alexandria** had known that context for many years beforehand), it was individual priests who moved out from the *cathedra*-church and became the local eucharistic presidents, basically functioning as rural bishops under the authority of the city bishop. The position afterward became standardized in pastoral practice, as the attempt to secure the unique position of the bishop by ordaining village-bishops (*chorepiskopoi*) to keep the lines clear between presbyters and *episkopoi* simply floundered and was formally abandoned by the end of the fourth century. The consecration of the Eucharist, from the third century onward, became the chief *proprium* of the presbyter and bishop. It was strictly reserved from the deacon or any other Christian minister (even though in the first century it also seems to have been a characteristic of the office of the traveling prophet, and is so mentioned in the *Didache*). After the fourth century the office of presbyter began to accumulate into itself all other manner of blessings (with the exception of ordinations and special consecration ceremonies), and its rights and functions accordingly expanded as the range of other ministries contracted. After the seventh century the primary focus of priestly ministry, both for the Latins and Byzantines, came to be on the eucharistic "sacrificial offering." In recent years much interest has been expressed in the question of whether women ever functioned as presbyters in the early communities. Some **gnostic** Christian churches (Hippolytus, *Refutation of All Heresies* 6.35; Irenaeus, *Adversus haereses* 1.13.1–2; Epiphanius, *Refutation of All Heresies* 42.4; Tertullian, *Prescription against Heretics* 41) and several **Montanist** communities (cf. Cyprian 75.10; Epiphanius, *Refutation of All Heresies* 49.2) seem to have had female presbyters who both baptized and celebrated the **Eucharist.** It may have been this which led the mainstream Catholic communities to react against such a socially innovative advancement of women's public leadership. The sources, however, are very few and vague. It is clear that the very earliest role of female apostolic witnesses gave way in the expansion of Christianity in the Hellenistic city (and thus by the end of the first century) to a system where women's ministries were strictly limited under the aegis of the developing episcopate. With the inclusion of women in the ordained office of deacon (see **Canon** 15 of the **Council of Chalcedon** [451]; *Apostolic Constitutions* 8.20), women clearly exercised priesthood in the Eastern church, in the diaconal degree, at least until until the high medieval period (when political insecurity and antagonistic monastic pressures led to the disappearance of the order as an active cathedral ministry). The Latin theology of priesthood tended to exclude diaconate from its purview of the "three degrees," and the female diaconate was also more quickly suppressed in the West. The question whether women ever exercised priesthood (in the degree of presbyterate) in early Catholic communities remains much discussed.

G. Dix, "Ministry in the Early Church," in K. E. Kirk, ed., *The Apostolic Ministry* (London, 1946), 185–303; E. Ferguson, "Church Order in the Sub-Apostolic Period: A Survey of Interpretations," RQ 11 (1968): 225–48; R. Gryson, *The Ministry of Women in the Early Church* (Collegeville, Minn., 1980); E. G. Jay, "From Presbyter-Bishops to Bishops and Presbyters," TSS 1 (1981): 125–62.

Prisca   *see* **Montanism**

Priscillian of Avila (fl. 370–386)

Priscillian of Avila was a Spanish senator who, c. 370, began a moral renewal movement, encouraging members of his local church to adopt a more *ascetical* and serious life. His movement attracted a lively following, including *clergy*, but seems to have been censured at the Synod of Saragossa in 380 (citing "bad customs" of *fasting* on Sunday, not attending church during Lent, and gathering in mixed groups for biblical reading and study outside of common liturgical meetings). Priscillian was elected, regardless, as bishop of Avila later in that same year. In 381 his enemies secured a sentence of exile against him as a *Manichean* (a common charge of undetermined heresy for that period), and Priscillian and his inner circle traveled to seek a fair hearing at the churches of *Rome* (Pope *Damasus*) and Milan (*Ambrose*). They were not received in either place, but managed to secure from the imperial administration an annulment of their sentence of exile, and so returned to Spain. A synod at Bordeaux again censured him, and Priscil-

lian appealed against its judgment to the imperial court of Maximus at Trier. There, in the secular court in 386, his enemies changed the charge to sorcery, and when he was again found guilty, he was subjected to the legal penalty for that crime, which was execution. The fall of the emperor Maximus in 388 led to the flourishing of the Priscillian movement and Priscillian's spreading reputation as a martyr. His followers were still mentioned as late as the sixth century. Priscillian probably did have a pronounced interest in esoteric spirituality (he is known to have had a lively interest in apocryphal gospels and acts), and this, allied with his vigorous encouragement of a dualistically tinged asceticism and a corresponding disregard for the spiritual worth of *marriage* or ordinary Christian *prayer* practices, was probably what raised the (exaggerated) charges of Manicheism and sorcery against him. His story, however, is chiefly a darkly symbolic moment when the Christians secured the first execution of a religious dissident among themselves.

V. Burrus, *The Making of a Heretic: Gender, Authority, and the Priscillianist Controversy* (Berkeley, Calif., 1995); H. Chadwick, *Priscillian of Avila: The Occult and the Charismatic in the Early Church* (Oxford, 1976).

Proclus   Proclus was a non-Christian *philosopher* born at Byzantium sometime between 409 and 412 (not to be confused with Proclus of Constantinople, who was bishop there 434–446). He became one of the most noted pagan philosophers of his age and was involved, unsuccessfully, in a "classicizing" attempt to restore the worship of the old gods at Athens. This caused his forced retirement from that city for a short period. He was the last great leader of the Neoplatonic school, the Academy. His ideas on the divine Nous, on transcendence, and on spiritual communion had an influence on *Boethius*

and *Pseudo-Dionysius the Areopagite,* who both had studied him closely. He died in 484.

S. Lilla, "Platonism and the Fathers," in A. Di Berardino, ed., *Encyclopedia of the Early Church* (vol. 2; Cambridge, 1992), 689–98; J. M. Rist, *Platonism and Its Christian Heritage* (London, 1985).

Prophet, Christian   *see* **Didache, Hermas, Montanism**

Prosper of Aquitaine (c. 390–455) A Gallic Christian poet, historian, and theologian, Prosper of Aquitaine was one of the first powerful disseminators of the Augustinian theology in the West. Prosper was living near Marseilles when, in 426, the monastic communities associated with **John Cassian** raised objections to the ideas of **grace** and predestination represented in **Augustine's** theology. Prosper undertook Augustine's defense, characterizing his opponents (misleadingly) as "semi-Pelagians." After Augustine's death in 430, he journeyed to Rome to ask Pope Celestine to decide in favor of Augustine's views. Celestine did so generically in a letter to the bishops of Gaul, though falling short of affirming the totality of the Augustinian system (Celestine, *Epistle* 21). Prosper continued the apologia with numerous works between 431 and 435, the year of John Cassian's death. He made several collections of Augustine excerpts, perhaps the first theologian to start the process of making this vast body of work into school-room standard texts and authorities. It was his abridgements that were used in the canons of the Council of Orange (529), an authoritative affirmation that was highly influential in standardizing Augustinianism for the medieval Western church (*see also* **Gregory the Great**). Prosper's *Chronicle of Church History* is based on the works of **Eusebius, Jerome,** and others, but for the years between 425 and 455 it is original and authoritative. It is thought that the

Poem on Divine Providence (discussing the reasons that God allows invasions such as those of the Vandals and Goths) might be his. He also wrote another large theological poem related to the grace controversy (*Carmen de Ingratis*).

P. de Letter, *St. Prosper of Aquitaine: The Call of All Nations* (ACW 14; New York, 1952); J. R. O'Donnell, *Prosper of Aquitaine: Grace and Free Will* (FOTC 7; Washington, D.C., 1949); J. and P. G. Walsh, *Divine Providence and Human Suffering* (trans. of the *Poem on Divine Providence*; Wilmington, Del., 1985), 64–91.

Prudentius (348–c. 410)   Aurelius Prudentius Clemens is one of the most capable of the Latin Christian poets. He was a Spaniard from the region of Tarragona, and probably from a Christian family. Well educated in grammar and rhetoric, he subsequently embarked on the legal profession, but says that "bitter experiences" led him into a career in public administration. Toward the end of his career he served as urban prefect governing two cities. Here he achieved such a reputation that he was entrusted with an unspecified mission (probably as diplomatic attaché, or *proximus*) at the imperial court. He does not specify the details and so it could be either at the Milan court with **Theodosius** (388–391) or possibly at **Rome.** Here he occupied the high status of "Count of the First Order." But at court he also experienced some personal crisis, which he hints at in his writings and which immediately preceded his retirement from public life. We might surmise this was the death of Theodosius, in 395, which ushered in a period of great instability in the imperial administration. He tells of his journey to Rome, which greatly impressed him because of its ancient Christian holy places alongside the noble monuments of Roman civilization. He determined to set in writing how the two things were consonant, and this idea is a key element of his poetry. Prudentius celebrates the *baptism* of *Constantine* as the spiritual coming of age of Rome, and sees Christianity as God's adoption of Roman civilization as a medium for the evangelization of the world. Deeply versed in all the Latin authors and all the pre-Christian poets, Prudentius see his task as being to demonstrate that Christians can take up and purify this tradition, renewing it for a future in Christ. After his visit to Rome, between 401 and 403, he energetically turned to the writing of poetry (although his command of meter suggests he was already a skilled writer). He published his main work, the long poem *Cathemerinon* (*Book of Daily Affairs*), in 405 at the age of fifty-seven. It stands as a classic Christian example of "conversion" narrative in which he describes his turning to a life of retirement, and the cleansing of his soul in simplicity. His other main work is the *Peristephanon* (*Crown of Martyrs*), in which he particularly celebrates the martyrs of three Spanish cities: Tarraconensis (Calahorra), Saragossa, and Tarragona, suggesting the probability that he retired to estates he owned at one of these places. His *Apotheosis* is a hexameter poem on the **incarnation.** He also composed apologetic poetry (against pagans and heretics) and a *Psychomachia* (an extended allegory of the soul's battle against vices).

M. M. van Assendelft, *Sol ecce surgit igneus: A Commentary on the Morning and Evening Hymns of Prudentius (Cathemerinon I.2, 5, 6)* (Groningen, Netherlands, 1976); E. Castelli, "Epic in Prudentius' Poem for the Martyr Eulalia," in E. Castelli, ed., *Re-imagining Christian Origins* (Valley Forge, Pa., 1996), 173–84; M. C. Eagan, *Prudentius* (FOTC 43, 52; Washington, D.C., 1962, 1965); V. Edden, "Prudentius," in J. W. Binns, ed., *Latin Literature of the Fourth Century* (London, 1974), 160–82; B. M. Peebles, *The Poet Prudentius* (New York, 1951); R. M. Pope, *The Hymns of Prudentius Translated* (London, 1905); J. J. Thompson, *Poems of Prudentius* (Loeb Classical Library; 2 vols.; London, 1949, 1963).

Psilanthropism The doctrine that the Christ was purely and "merely" a man (that is, not divine). (*See* **Photinianism.**)

Pulcheria *see* **Council of Ephesus I, Council of Ephesus II, Council of Chalcedon**

Purgatory The word is a Latin Christian term for place of cleansing (*purgatorium*) and refers to the concept of a place of "middle state" between *heaven* and *hell*, reserved for those *souls* who at the time of *death* do not deserve final damnation into the pains of hell, but whose sins are such that they are not considered fit to enter immediately into the joys of paradise. Purgatory was thus envisaged as a place of penitential postdeath purification. The inhabitants of purgatory would one day, when their sins had been sufficiently purified (often it was envisaged that purgatory was comprised of cleansing flames analogous to hell's punitive flames), be liberated and admitted to paradisiacal joy. The doctrine as sketched out above did not assume clear form in the Western church until the eleventh century (in the works of Hildebert. PL.171. 741), although it makes an embryonic appearance much earlier in **Tertullian,** who deduces that the soul which needs cleansing must be made to stay for a short time in Sheol (*De anima* 58). For him this would apply to all souls, except those who were able to go straight to God on account of their martyrdoms. Several other *patristic* writers also speculated that the soul after death would be cleansed by some form of purgative fire (cf. Origen, *Homilies on Numbers* 15; Cyprian, *Ep.* 55.22; Ambrose, *On Psalm* 36.26). This theory of psychic postdeath purification probably developed on the basis of the words of St. Paul (1 Cor. 3:11–15): "fire will test what sort of work each has done"; he goes on to the effect that those who have built upon shoddy foundations "will be saved, but only as through fire." This doctrine of postdeath purification was shared with early rabbinic thought (cf. 2. Macc. 12.38–45). From the beginning of their organized existence, therefore, both the synagogue and the early Christian church prayed extensively for their dead, and many of the most ancient prayers to this effect are still found in the liturgies of the Greek and Latin churches. Purgatory was an idea that received a massive boost by the endorsement given to it by **Augustine.** It was Pope **Gregory the Great,** in the seventh century, however, who elevated what he called the "opinion" of earlier thinkers into a more or less formulated doctrine (*Dialogue* 4.41[39]) that "purgatorial fire will cleanse every elect soul before it comes into the Last *Judgment.*" After that moment the Latin church took the idea more and more into its official preaching, while the Eastern churches continued to regard it as a speculation, a *theologoumenon* that was not part of the central doctrinal *tradition.* The Eastern Christian world generally retained a simpler doctrine of the afterlife where the souls of the elect, even those who were not particularly holy, would be retained in "A place of light, a place of refreshment, a place from which all sorrow and sighing have been banished." This view reflected the statement in Revelation 14:13 that "those who die in the Lord. . . rest from their labors." In short, the state of afterlife as it was envisaged in the early Eastern church was generally a happy and restful condition in which the departed souls of the faithful were not divorced from God, but waited on the Last Judgment with hopeful anticipation, as the time when they would be admitted to a transfigured and paradisiacal condition in proximity to God. After **Origen** (who argued that Christ's descent into hell was a definitive liberation of the souls of the just), the idea (based on Paul's authority) of the saints being "with the Lord" began to account for the prevailing Eastern view changing into a belief that the souls of the just entered after death into the presence of Christ (*see* **heaven, hell**), while

the wicked were cast away from his presence. From the seventh century onward, therefore, the doctrine of purgatory has largely been a distinct *proprium* of the Latin Catholic world.

R. R. Attwell, "From Augustine to Gregory the Great: An Evaluation of the Emergence of the Doctrine of Purgatory," JEH 38 (1987): 173–86; J. Le Goff, *La naissance de purgatoire* (Paris, 1981).

Pythagoreanism Pythagoras was born on the Greek island of Samos in the first half of the sixth century B.C. In the middle of that century he moved to Croton in southern Italy, where he founded a philosophical society, bound to Pythagoras by vows of loyalty, that was closely involved in the political life of the Greek cities of the region. A violent reaction to his movement resulted in the massacre of most of his early followers and his own death (though some say this took place shortly afterward in exile). His early legend established him as a sage and prophet. The lives and accounts of his teaching only came much later, by which time he had become a convenient hook on which to hang many later doctrines and beliefs (some of which accorded to him magical and mystical powers). His followers were described by **Aristotle** in a (now lost) work. The Pythagoreans were collectively known for their dedication to religious *asceticism,* mathematics, music, and cosmology, all of which were closely integrated in their system. They saw in the ordered progression of numbers, for example, the root of all musical harmony (even the harmony of the spheres, which only the initiated could hear) and a pattern for the order of cosmic existence. In the religious domain Pythagoras was believed to have founded a society based around the belief in the transmigration of souls across various earthly forms (human and animal), and that through the observance of particular rules a better *reincarnation* could be achieved.

Some of the rules were explicitly mentioned in ancient sources: namely, the observance of a vegetarian diet, the avoidance of beans (a spiritually auspicious food), the avoidance of picking up things that fell from a table, never to touch a white cock, never to break a loaf of bread. Many attempts existed even in antiquity to explain the reasons for the rules, most of them relying on *allegory* to make sense out of them. In the first century B.C. his school was refounded and is known to modern scholarship as neo-Pythagoreanism. It was this synthesized form of the school that eventually came into contact with Christianity. In the fourth century A.D. there was particular friction between neo-Pythagoreans and Christians, both claiming that their respective founders were divinely gifted healers and sages who were sent to bring the world to a religious-philosophical truth and elevate the common level of humanity. The neo-Pythagorean apologist Iamblichus (fourth century A.D.) wrote a treatise called *On the Pythagorean Life*, which recounts the numerous miracles of Pythagoras and is generally thought to have been inspired by a desire to challenge the ascendancy of Christianity. The concept of the closely bonded society of ascetic religious philosophers was of some interest to the early Christian monks, who also were aware of the benefit of philosophical questions and answers (*chreia*) in the formation of new recruits to the communities. It is an aspect that can be partially seen in the *desert* literature such as the *Apophthegmata Patrum*.

G. Clark, ed., *Iamblichus: On the Pythagorean Life* (Liverpool, U.K., 1989); W. K. C. Guthrie, *A History of Greek Philosophy* (vol. 1; Cambridge, 1962).

Quartodecimans Controversy
The word derives from the Latin for "fourteenth" and refers to the custom in some early churches of following the Jewish liturgical calendar and observing the Christian Passover (that is, Easter) on the 14th day of the month of Nisan, regardless of what day of the week that fell on. Most other churches from earliest times had reserved the festal celebration of Pascha to the nearest Sunday after the date of the Jewish Passover. By the second century the disparity of liturgical practices was becoming a matter of common knowledge internationally, and the Asia Minor churches were specially concerned with defending their own practice of keeping the 14th day, against pressure from other communities to fall in line with Sunday Paschal observance. When he visited *Rome* in 155, *Polycarp* the bishop of Smyrna tried to make the Romans conform to Asian custom, though Pope Anicetus declined, commending Polycarp for the antiquity of his own observance. In the next generation Rome decided that it ought to take the lead in arguing for a greater uniformity in the observance of Pascha, and Pope Victor (189–198) summoned a synod of bishops to discuss the issue and then threatened Polycrates, the bishop of Ephesus, that if his church did not change its practice they would cease to be in communion with them. *Irenaeus of Lyons* protested the harshness of this measure (Eusebius, *Ecclesiastical History* 5.23–25) and the Asian church retained the custom for some time longer. In the fifth century there was still a Quartodecimans sect in Asia Minor, though by this stage it was organized as a separate, schismatical community. The issue is taken to be of interest not only for what it reveals about the growing pattern of episcopal synodical guidance of the churches and the history of liturgical observance, but also for the light it throws on the emergence of a sense, at Rome, that the *papacy* had a special responsibility for international church order.

F. E. Brightman, "The Quartodecimans Question," JTS 25 (1923–1924): 250–70; C. W. Dugmore, "A Note on the Quartodecimans," SP 4; TU 79 (1961):

411–21; T. J. Talley, *The Origins of the Liturgical Year* (New York, 1986), 5–33.

Quicunque Vult   *see* Creeds

Quinisext Council   The Quinisext Council was literally the "Fifth-Sixth" Ecumenical Council, so named because it was a synod that was called retrospectively to add disciplinary canons to the decrees of the Fifth and Sixth Ecumenical Councils (*see* **Councils of Constantinople II and III**); and it did not wish to claim a separate existence within the preexisting scheme of the "Ecumenical Councils," but rather to attach itself to the two previous ones and claim their authority for its own moral reforms. The synod met in the domed hall (Troullos) of the imperial palace at **Constantinople** in 692, and from this location is sometimes known as the Synod in Troullo (a confusing designation since that title also describes the Third Council of Constantinople of 681).

L. D. Davis, *The First Seven Ecumenical Councils: Their History and Theology* (Wilmington, Del., 1987).

Recapitulation   The term derives from the Latin (*recapitulatio*); bringing things round to their starting point, summing up, or bringing full circle. The equivalent Greek term (*anakephalaiosis*) is found in the New Testament literature (Eph. 1:10), where in a pregnant passage God is said to have "gathered up" all things in Christ. *Patristic* interest in the idea derived from a *christological* starting point that envisaged the *incarnational soteriology* as a cosmic mystery of the summation of time and created destiny (cf. 2 Cor. 5:17–18). *Irenaeus* was one of the first who developed the idea (*Adversus haereses* 3.18.1; 3.22.3; *Demonstration of the Apostolic Preaching* 87), using it in his *Adversus haereses* to describe how the incarnation summed up human history insofar as the obedi-ence of Christ repaired the damage caused by the disobedience of Adam, and brought it to a new apex of meaning by the establishment of Christ as cosmic Lord and Head. The restoration of the race to communion with God thus "summed up" the original point of the creation, which God had designed as a path to union but which had fallen, and which was now recapitulated in Christ. By these great cyclical images Irenaeus expanded the Pauline scheme of cosmic soteriology and brought it into a new dimension that would deeply influence later patristic thought, especially after the third century, and particularly in the *Alexandrian* school as seen in *Clement* and *Origen*, whose cosmological vision of theology is indeed spacious. Irenaeus also used the word to describe the way in which the revelation of the New Testament summed up (brought to a head) all the previous *revelations* contained "in shadows" in the Old Testament. This sense of "summary" is based upon its appearance in Romans 13:10, where Christ's commandment of love is said to be the "fulfilling" of the whole law. These two meanings, the soteriological and the hermeneutical, predominate in later patristic thought about recapitulation.

J. Behr, *The Way to Nicaea* (New York, 2001), 122–33; J. T. Nielsen, *Adam and Christ in the Theology of Irenaeus of Lyons* (Assen, Netherlands, 1986).

Redemption   *see* Soteriology

Reincarnation   The doctrine that *souls* migrate to new life forms, once the bodily medium of earthly life is dissolved, was one that dated to prehistoric times in Indian civilizations and also impacted ancient Greek philosophical and religious thought. In the *patristic* era the concept (generally known as *metempsychosis*) was encountered by the *church* in its dialogue with *Platonism* and *Pythagoreanism*. The former had suggested that souls had preexisted in a purely intellectual condition, where they could see the pure state of the Ideal forms, but had then been "imprisoned" in a corporeal form and had fallen to an earthly suffering existence. Knowledge of the truth was, for Plato, a partial remembrance (anamnesis) of pre-earthly existence. By virtuous living (a philosophical life devoted to the quest for the Good) a soul could rise once more to the higher realms. This was not reincarnation as classically conceived, but it had an impact on Christianity, notably in the Alexandrian school, which speculated about the preexistence of souls before their earthly appearance. Among the Origenist monks of the fifth and sixth centuries, especially *Evagrius*, it became a key idea that the soul which had fallen from its spiritual purity (in a preexistent state) would one day rise again to a divinized transcendence. The prosecution of the Origenist monks by a series of episcopal opponents, such as *Epiphanius* and *Theophilus*, and eventually their condemnation by synodical decree in the time of *Justinian* brought an end to speculation along such themes in the later history of patristic thought. Latin theologians, beginning with *Tertullian* (*De anima*) and culminating in *Augustine*, who was specially concerned to refute *Manichean* and Pythagorean forms of reincarnation thought (cf. *On Genesis Literally Interpreted* 7.9.13; 7.11.17; *De civitate Dei* 10.30), discussed whether the soul had been created beforehand by God and then sent specifically into the body after the latter's conception by its earthly parents (Creationism) or whether God had put the souls of all generations in a germinal form in the loins of the ancestors, and so each conception of a new life transmitted bodily existence and also simultaneously "passed on" a soul (Traducianism). Either alternative (the Latins were explicitly concerned to offer only these two opinions as being in harmony with Christian tradition) effectively ruled out reincarnation as an acceptable Christian theory. The Pythagorean school was

more overtly interested in reincarnation, in the sense of the possible transmigration of souls. By an *ascetic* and intellectually disciplined life the Pythagorean sages tried to ensure a better reincarnation in the next life. *Origen* considered the doctrine in his *Peri archon* 1.8.4 and on several other occasions (*Commentary on Romans* 6.6.8; *Commentary on Matthew* 11.17; *Against Celsus* 3.75; 4.83; 5.49; 8.30; cf. 1.20) and always rejected it as a foolish notion, since for him the purpose of the soul's existence was to ascend to God, and the common theme of reincarnation, he argued, was that each life was more or less a forgetting of the past one, which meant that spiritual identity could not be sustained. Origen was particularly acerbic about the possibility of a human soul lapsing, because of sins, into an irrational animal body. Here Origen was engaging in a direct philosophical attack on the Pythagoreans. In later years his intellectually duller enemies *Epiphanius* and *Jerome* (with blatant disregard of his explicit text) tried to make him responsible for holding such a theory (Augustine also believed he had done so), and they were effective in the sense that this became a common belief about "Origen the heretic." No significant Christian thinker ever adopted a theory remotely like reincarnation, not least because of the great stress the theologians of the early church placed upon the concept of the Final *Judgment* (cf. Augustine *De civitate Dei* 21.17), and also because the idea of a constant progression through various corporeal shells is at variance with the centrality of the concept of the *resurrection* of the body.

M. C. Albrecht, "Reincarnation and the Early Church," *Update: New Religious Movements* 7, 2 (1983): 34–39; L. Lies, "Origenes und Reinkarnation," *Zeitschrift für katholische Theologie* 121 (1999): 139–58, 249–68; R. Roukema, "Transmigration of Souls," in J. A. McGuckin, ed., *The Westminster Handbook to Origen* (Louisville, Ky., 2004).

Relics   The term relic (Latin: *reliquiae;* Greek: *leipsanta*) is usually applied to the material remains of *saints* after their deaths; or it refers to materials that belonged to the holy person and had been in regular contact, such as clothes. Things that had touched the relics of a saint were also valued (Latin: *brandea*) and the latter were often worn in crosses around the neck (also a favored place for carrying dust from the Holy Land). These came, in the Latin *church,* to be called "second-class relics." The most important of all Christian relics was the *cross* of the Lord, which later tradition associated with St. Helen, mother of *Constantine* who visited the Holy Land in 326. It was the era of Constantine, which saw the rapid spread of the cult of relics in the church, although the practice of venerating the bodies of the *martyrs* (which was the probable origin of the Christian practice of relic devotion) was established well before the fourth century. After the Peace of the Church, in the aftermath of the persecutions, the building of shrines for the martyrs, and the desire of churches to have such local shrines, led to a veritable explosion in the significance of relics. Soon it was a common thing (compulsory after the eighth century and still so for the Greek and Latin churches) that every altar in every church had to have relics of the saints placed within it. The early Christians saw biblical precedents for the cult of relics in the Elijah story. His cloak was passed on to Elisha and transferred the power of miracle and prophecy (2 Kgs. 2:14), and his bones also had the power to raise the dead (2 Kgs. 13:21). A cult of relics of St. Paul (his handkerchief) is also observable even in Acts 19:12. Hellenistic religion knew something similar in reference to the cult of the great heroes, whose tombs (such as that of Theseus at Athens) were believed to have healing powers. *Eusebius of Caesarea* (*Ecclesiastical History* 1.8.6.7) says he has to frequently disabuse pagans that Christian *martyria* were not simply versions of hero-worship, where the devotees offered divine honors to the dead. But the danger of this mistake among the pagans of his day did not deter him from the liturgical practice of honoring the martyrs. Generally, however, Hellenistic civilization (it was certainly true of Roman culture) looked with horror on the notion of kissing the bones of the dead, regarding it as something defiling. Julian the Apostate made fun of the Christian concern for relics of the saints, calling their churches "charnel houses" (cf. Cyril of Alexandria, *Contra Julianum* 1.6). For such reasons the dismemberment of relics (donating parts to different churches) was practiced for generations in the Eastern church before it was ever felt to be appropriate in the more conservative West. One of the first evidences of the concern for gathering the relics of martyrs comes in the second-century *Martyrdom of Polycarp* (c. 156–157), which speaks of his relics as "more valuable than precious stones and finer than gold that has been refined" (chap. 18). Martyrs were felt to have such great power of heavenly intercession that many Christians wanted to be buried next to them, ready for the last day. It is a practice that can be discerned in the orientation of graves in ancient Christian cemeteries wherever there are martyrgraves present. There were voices of opposition to this. *Origen,* for example, though firmly advocating the heavenly power of the martyrs, was not eager to encourage a liturgical cult of their relics. His remarks discountenancing that cult already show that it was prevalent in his own church in third-century Caesarea, but that he at least regarded it as something appropriate only for the ignorant (cf. Origen, *Exhortation to Martyrdom* 30). The fourth-century Council of Gangra anathematized those who "despised relic veneration," which again is not only a testimony to the rise of the cult, but also shows there was some degree of resistance at that time. One of the several complaints about church abuses by Vigilantius of Toulouse in the early fifth century referred to the veneration of relics, which (if *Jerome* is to be trusted) he saw as a revival of idolatry. Jerome gave him such a castigation in his *Adversus Vigilantium* (406) that few protesting voices were ever raised again on the matter in the patristic era. Many writers at this time begin to mention how relics were common and highly prized in both the Eastern and Western churches (cf. Theodoret, *Epistles* 131, 145; Paulinus of Nola, *Epistle* 32.17). In the Latin church before the pillaging of Constantinople in 1204, when thousands of portable relics were distributed in the West, relic veneration had generally been a "tombal" matter; that is, they were either lodged in the altar or in the tomb of the saint. After the Fourth Crusade, the practice of venerating portable reliquaries became more common. The latter practice had always been common for the Byzantine world. Here, after the *iconoclastic* crisis of the eighth and ninth centuries, relic veneration gave way considerably before the rise of the popularity of icon veneration, although both liturgical practices are still much in evidence in Orthodoxy today. *Patristic* reflection on the significance of relics generally concluded that they ought to be venerated since the saints, when alive, were the special friends of Christ; and now that they had been transfigured in heavenly glory, their earthly bodies were sacramental anticipations of the glorified body that Christ would give them at the end. In the meantime, as his martyrs and friends, they were expected to work benefits (like heavenly patrons) for their local churches here on earth. Some patristic theologians (such as the ninth-century Theodore the Studite) also used the theory of deification to argue that even the bones of the saints were charged with the power of sanctity that the *Holy Spirit* had worked in them while alive, and which would now be released to those who prayed before them with faith. Most later theologians

were careful to draw the distinction in relic veneration between *latreia* and *douleia* (*see* **Council of Nicaea II**). The first (worship) is reserved only for God. The second (veneration) can legitimately be given to God's saints through their holy relics. In the seventh century Isidore of Seville synopsized the whole of this patristic teaching on relics in his *De Ecclesiae Officiis* (1.25.1–6).

P. Brown, "Relics and Social Status in the Age of Gregory of Tours," in *Society and the Holy in Late Antiquity* (Berkeley, Calif., 1982), 222–50; idem, *The Cult of the Saints: Its Rise and Function in Latin Christianity* (Chicago, 1987); H. Leclercq, "Reliques et reliquaires," in F. Cabrol and H. Leclercq, eds., *Dictionnaire d'Archéologie Chrétienne et de Liturgie* vol. 14, pt. 2; Paris, 1948), cols. 2294–359.

Resurrection   The Latin term means to rise or get up once more. The New Testament and **patristic** Greek word is *anastasis*, again from the root "to stand up once more." In the Scriptures it is often used as a symbol of God lifting up a person into glory after disaster (or restoring them to health), and in the Gospels it is predominantly a reference to the glory (*doxa*) of Jesus after his passion and death. It is significant to note that the word's primary meaning ought to be rendered as "glorification," or lifting up again (that is, before specifically associating it with "lifting up from death"), because within the Gospel texts the meaning of *anastasis* as the returning to life of Jesus' crucified body becomes so dominant that within later Christian usage the word almost exclusively means "resurrection from the dead." Even so, the idea that *anastasis*-glory can be expressed through, not necessarily exclusively by, the resurrection to life of the dead body is a powerful and rich theology within the New Testament, and care should be taken that the perspective is not lost. Other ways of the "glorification" of Jesus after the passion are described in the Scriptures through the narratives of ascension (*analepsis,* another word for "lifting up"), or the narratives of angelic transformation (resurrection appearances), or the powerful descent of the **Holy Spirit** (Pentecost), all of which accumulate in earliest Christian theology to form a nexus of "stories of glorification" whereby Jesus' *anastasis*-exaltation is described in a variety of dimensions. To restrict our understanding of *anastasis*-glory solely to the resurrection of the body to life thus diminishes the complexity and richness of the foundational New Testament evidence. In the patristic era, while this tendency to focus on the bodily return to life is a predominant aspect (the miracle of Jesus' resurrection from the dead becomes the ultimate miracle in the series of miracles that mark his earthly ministry), there is, nevertheless, a profound sense that the resurrection is not just another in a foregoing series of astounding "signs" Jesus gave; rather, that it is the "ultimate sign" of the ministry of Jesus. The narrative of the resurrection of Lazarus in John 12 attempts to describe this theology in relation to its own account of the resurrection-glory, which it offers at the end of the Gospel, positing the resurrection of the Lord as the power that saves the world and gives birth to the church as the end-time community of salvation. In the Johannine resurrection accounts it can be noted that the resurrectional appearances, the gift of the Spirit, and the return of the body to transfigured life are all described as "exaltation events" of the single Pascha Sunday. Resurrection in late Jewish thought was accepted by several schools, particularly the Pharisees (cf. Josephus, *Jewish War* 18.11–22), as it had been theologized by the **apocalyptic** movement from the time of the book of Daniel. Jesus was a robust defender of the idea (Mark 12:18–27). The notion of the calling back to life of the just (Dan. 12:1–2; 2 Macc. 7) so that their fidelity could be rewarded by God (and often even of the wicked too so that their infidelity could be punished; cf. Rev. 20:11–

15) was thus something that marked *eschatological* Judaism in the time of Jesus. The resurrection of the just, however, was understood to be something that would mark the end time, that is, the eschaton, when world history would be rolled up by God, and the kingdom of God would be definitively manifested. No one could "live again" in late Judaic thought before the general resurrection. Only the greatest of the great prophets (it was attributed in the time of Josephus to Moses, Elijah, and Enoch—hence the purpose of the transfiguration story in Mark 9) might be summoned by God to live in the first heaven as quasi-angelic beings. The early Christian announcement of the bodily resurrection of Jesus was thus something more than a simple statement that Jesus had been raised back to life by God after his brutal execution; it was a specific claim that in restoring Jesus to bodily life (though the texts are very careful to claim that this bodily life is no mere continuation of his former biological and chronological life), God had definitively inaugurated the last age in and through his exaltation of Jesus. For the early Christians, therefore, in Jesus' resurrection the end time has arrived, and the risen Jesus is thus constituted the Lord of the eschaton who uses the resurrection appearance to commission the **church.** It is this precise and potent mix of theological claims that underlies the New Testament **kerygma** of the resurrection, whether that is expressed in some of the New Testament accounts in the style of "God raised Jesus from the dead" (Acts 2:24) or in the Johannine style of "I lay down my own life, I have power to take it up again" (John 10:17–18). Patristic thought on the resurrection of Jesus increasingly focuses on the Johannine and Pauline (cf. Phil. 2:6–11) aspects, namely, that the resurrection was a definitive conquering of **death** and **sin.** One of the earliest apologetic contexts was the struggle to insist, over and against many currents in second-century **Gnosticism,** that resurrection involved the true body: both that

of Jesus (that is, he physically rose from the dead) and that of the disciple (who would also be raised in the flesh on the last day by virtue of the *grace* of the resurrection). The purely "spiritualized" view of *anastasis* (the risen Jesus is typically described in gnostic texts as a luminous and shape-shifting figure who has left corporeality behind: *Acts of Thomas* 27; *Apocryphon of John* 2.1.32–2.9) can be seen most clearly in the *Treatise on the Resurrection* in the Nag Hammadi gnostic literature. Here the symbol of resurrection was wholly a psychic matter, only symbolically referred to the body, since true resurrection was the ultimate liberation from all materiality. This idea was already troublesome to Luke, who seems to have explicitly wished to rebut the notion that Jesus' resurrection was simply a "visionary experience" for some disciples (Luke 24:36–45). The patristic writers of the earliest centuries were also very concerned to refute this kind of teaching, and as a result of their apologetic anxieties they greatly stressed the rising to life of Jesus' body as a central aspect of the resurrection story (*Epistle to the Apostles* 11; 24–26). One of the main accounts in this vein was *Tertullian's* treatise on *The Resurrection of the Flesh*, and the same idea can be seen throughout *Irenaeus* (cf. *Adversus haereses* 5.7.1–2; 5.13.1). The tendency was given a second boost later in the classical patristic age in the course of the anti-Origenist controversy, when theologians such as *Methodius of Olympus* and *Epiphanius* wrote to attack what they felt to be *Origen's* underestimation of the "physicality" of the resurrection. This predominantly apologetic approach from the earliest level of patristic writers, nevertheless, did not lose sight of the wider implication of the eschatological kerygma, because, following on Paul's message, most of the patristic writers emphasized the way in which death had been corporately broken in the rising to life of the body of the Lord of life. Through the breaking of death's stranglehold over humanity, in the particular instance of Jesus' resurrection, the grace of immortality was understood to be given back to the world in the locus of the church. The idea was prevalent in Origen (*De principiis* 2.10–11), but *Athanasius of Alexandria* was one of the first who expressed the idea of redemptive exchange graphically with full insistence on the physical resurrection as the locus of humanity's redemption. Athanasius, in his treatise *On the Incarnation*, described the resurrection as the method whereby life was infused back again into the human race, which had hitherto been chained to corruption and death. The idea became prominent in all later writers, notably the great Alexandrian theologian *Cyril,* who connected the resurrection experience to the ongoing *eucharistic* life of the Christians, seeing in the eucharistic mysteries the medicine of immortality (*pharmakia tes athanasias*), which communicated the power of resurrection to the bodies of the faithful in anticipation of their final redemption through the gateway of the grave. By insisting on the physical transfiguration of the body alongside the *soul's* hope for immortal life in the resurrection grace of Jesus, the church forged its own clear path in the face of much of the received wisdom of the Hellenism of the time. The idea of a transfigured body seemed ridiculous to many sophisticated thinkers who believed in the philosophical axiom of the immortality of the soul. In developing its theology of the risen body (of the faithful), the church insisted that the human soul was only conditionally immortal (Tatian, *Oration* 5.3–6.1; 13–16; Irenaeus, *Adversus haereses* 5.3.2–13; Justin, *First Apology* 18–19; Theophilus, *To Autolycus* 1.7–8). Just as the body was transfigured by the grace of resurrection, so too would the soul be immortalized by the same power. The concept became the classical substructure of all later patristic *soteriology.* It is, perhaps, most graphically demonstrated in the ancient liturgies, which thereby became extended celebrations of the resurrection of Jesus as the commencement of the Lord's dominion in the manifested kingdom of God, and the deliverance of the first-fruits of the *grace* of life, in and through the eschatological, *sacramental* appropriation of that *mystery.*

A. H. C. Van Eijk, "Resurrection-Language: Its Various Meanings in Early Christian Literature," SP 12 (1975): 271–76; E. Gebremedhin, *Life-Giving Blessing: An Enquiry into the Eucharistic Doctrine of Cyril of Alexandria* (Uppsala, Sweden, 1977); J. A. McGuckin, *The Transfiguration of Christ in Scripture and Tradition* (New York, 1986); idem, *St. Cyril of Alexandria and the Christological Controversy: Its History, Theology, and Texts* (Leiden, Netherlands, 1994); J. E. McWilliam Dewart, *Death and Resurrection: Message of the Fathers of the Church* (Wilmington, Del., 1986).

Revelation The term derives from the Latin (*revelatio*), literally the lifting away of a veil from a thing to expose it to view. It is thus the direct translation of the Greek New Testament and *patristic* term apocalypse (*apokalypsis*), but it grew in patristic theology to have a much wider range of associations than the term apocalypse (which remained fixed in the context of its eschatological origins, suggesting an ecstatic and dramatic prophetic initiation; cf. Dan. 10:1–12; Rev. 4f.). Revelation became the generic word for the entire *economy* of God's salvation, including the "preparatory teachings" of the whole nexus of the Old Testament, but especially the complex of New Testament writings, which collectively became the scriptural corpus of "revelation." Revelation in this wider sense was connoted by the Greek terms epiphany, manifestation, or illumination (*epiphaneia, phanerosis, photismos*). Revelation considered objectively, therefore, was more or less the *canon of Scripture,* but was also transmitted by prophetic charism in the church. There thus arose a tension in the patristic treatment of this theme (still apparent in Orthodox and Catholic theology) between, on the one hand, revelation considered as definitively ended with the closing of the canon of Scripture (or the close of the *Apostolic* age, as the patristic writers would have expressed it) and, on the other hand, the dynamic power of revelation still being vitally experienced in the ongoing life of the *church* (not as a mere reception of a body of truths, but as an ever-new and lived experience of God's revealed presence in various generations of the church). In Eastern Christian theology the idea of revelation both as closed deposit of truth and as continuing experience of the mysterious God who reveals himself in a mystery of presence to the church is expressed by the notion of *tradition* (*paradosis*). It has a deeply dynamic sense that is absent from most contemporary appreciations of the idea and the word. Old Testament conceptions of revelation were expressed in a large variety of images. Appearances of angelic messengers (Gen. 16:7, 9–11; Judg. 6:20) or didactic *dreams* (Exod. 33:22; Num. 24:4; Isa. 6:1f; Gen. 28:1f; 1 Sam. 28:6) all served as some of the media of the interrelation between God and Israel in Judaic thought. The sense that God would "speak a word" to Israel was, however, one of the most pervasive of all biblical ideas, and was brought to a pitch in the prophetic claim to "speak for" God (cf. Gen. 1:28; Exod. 7:13; 2 Kgs. 1:3; Dan. 9:2; Amos 3:1). So, for example, Jeremiah is told by God to write down all the things God has spoken to him (Jer. 30:2). Already in the Old Testament the concept of Scripture as the paradigmatic medium of revelation was well established, though never (as would be the case in the New Testament too) was it the sole or exclusive medium of revelation. Both the Testaments consider revelation not so much as a communication of a body of true facts about God, rather as a series of encounters with the living God, who reaches out to his own people and gives them life and salvation in that very reaching out. The New Testament took that fundamental structure of biblical revelation theology to a new pitch by insisting that the ultimate salvific outreach of God to the world was in the person of Jesus, whose death inaugurated a new covenant, a new access (*prosagoge*) to the divine presence. The Gospels thus present Jesus as the supreme gateway of revealed truth, the authentic path to the experience of God (Matt. 11:27; Luke 10:21–22; John 16:12–15). His own teachings, life, death, and *resurrection* thereby became supremely revelatory for the Christian movement after him (Heb. 1:1–4), and the fullness of revelation was anticipated only to be finally delivered when the Parousia of the Son of Man occurred at the end time (Luke 17:30). The writings of the *Apostolic Fathers* generally demonstrate a diffused sense of revelation, largely continuing the New Testament sense that in Christ a new age of salvation has dawned. As yet there was little focused interest in determining a closed canon of Christian Scriptures, or any desire to elevate a specific theology of revelation, since it was not, as such, a controverted matter. *Ignatius of Antioch* repeated the Pauline sense that God has finally revealed himself in his own Son: "There is one God who has manifested himself through his Son, Jesus Christ, who is his very Word, proceeding from silence, who in all respects was well pleasing to the one who sent him" (*To the Magnesians* 8.2). Ignatius and especially Irenaeus were concerned with the preservation of the integrity of this *kerygma* in a dangerously hostile and intellectually relativized world, and thus several of the earliest patristic writings insist on the need for the church's obedience to the word once heard. Obedience and faithfulness preserve intact the message so definitively delivered. This becomes a central theme of the second-century fathers who speak about the "chain of apostolic tradition," which preserves the spiritual vitality of God's revelation (*Didache* 4.1; *Barnabas* 9.9; *1 Clement* 2.1; Ignatius, *To the Ephesians* 15.2; Irenaeus, *Haer*. 1.8.1; 1.10.2; 2.9.1). In the next gen-

eration, when the church's relationship to the Hellenistic world was becoming more of a pressing intellectual issue, several of the *Apologists* reflected on the nature of revelation as the source of the "authority" of the church's teachings about God, the universe, and salvation. The idea of revelation in this period thus became predominantly concerned with an apologetic defense of legitimacy of teaching. Several of the Apologists, such as *Justin Martyr* and *Tertullian* (it would be brought to a resolution in the work of *Origen*), elevated the scheme of the immanent *Logos* that permeated all human life to be the ground and basis of all truth and wisdom. By demonstrating Jesus as the creative Logos personified (Justin, *Second Apology* 6.3) and the source of all sacred revelation (Justin, *Dialogue with Trypho* 62.4), they were able to make the claim that although they were a very recent religious group, and apparently possessed of few educated leaders, nevertheless their teaching was at once, ancient, true, and powerful; indeed, that it was the sole source of religious wisdom since their Lord was Wisdom itself (Justin, *First Apology* 13.3; 63.13; *Dialogue with Trypho* 121.4). The older idea (perhaps now addressed more to Christian readers than Hellenes) that the *incarnation* was the apex of the way God spoke to his people was not forgotten, however (Justin, *Dialogue with Trypho* 127.4; *First Apology* 63; Irenaeus, *Adversus haereses* 4.20.5), and would soon come to a pitch in the incarnational *Christology* of the fourth century. In this era the Fathers were able to stand back a little from the apologetic contexts of the previous centuries, and so elaborated a more systematic view of revelation, one that was active on several fronts. They began to articulate a specific view of canonicity of the Bible, for example, with the scriptural teachings as the supreme manifestations of apostolic truth, being the key (in Christ) to the whole revelation of the corpus of Scripture. They also reflected on the act of incarnation as supreme revelatory locus. In this respect,

Athanasius and *Cyril,* in the fourth and fifth centuries, elaborated strong defenses of the "once-for-all-ness" of the incarnation as supreme revelation of the person and presence of God in Christ. Athanasius in his *Contra gentes* and the *Cappadocian Fathers* (especially Basil's *Hexaemeron*) were also interested in showing how the creation could be taken as a book of God's revelations addressed to all and sundry, a preparation for the deeper revelations that were hidden within the church. These exercises in singing of the beauty of God manifested by the beautiful cosmos were rooted in the Old Testament but grew out of it to be the beginnings of a long Christian tradition of apologetics; namely, that all humanity, not just a section, receives divine revelation, and the resistance of the sense of divine presence in a human life is thus a choice that cannot be ascribed to ignorance or lack of opportunity. After Athanasius, the idea of the true *image of God* as rooted in the deepest recesses of the human heart became a common theme in patristic writing and was taken to refined heights by *Gregory of Nazianzus* and *Augustine.* Revelation was thus in the most transcendent media (apostolic illuminations reserved from the general run of humanity) and in the most immanent media (open to anyone who could scrutinize the purified soul). Most of Greek patristic writing continued this rich vein of transcendent-immanentism. Several of the Latin theologians after the fourth century developed the theme in their reflections on the nature of revelation that there was an inherent tension between faith and speculative knowledge. It became a much-repeated idea in Latin thought thereafter, and this aspect of revelation as the authoritative underpinning of faith in the face of the limits of human reason marked the later Latin theology of revelation decisively (*see philosophy*).

J. Barr, *Revelation in History* (Nashville, 1976); A. Dulles, *Revelation Theology: A History* (New York, 1969); M. Harl, *Origène et la fonction révélatrice du Verbe incarné* (Paris, 1958); P. Stockmeier, *Offenbarung in der fruhchristlichen Kirche* (HDG 1, 1a; Freiburg, Germany, 1971), 27–87.

Romanos the Melodist (fl. c. 540.; d. after 555)

One of the major Byzantine Christian liturgical poets, Romanos the Melodist was a *Syrian* by birth, possibly a Jewish convert to Christianity. He was ordained *deacon* at Beirut and came to *Constantinople* at the end of Anastasius's reign c. 515. He was the most famous Christian musician in the age of *Justinian.* His speciality was the *kontakion* (the name means "a sermon on a roll"), basically a long biblical hymn that became a standard element of liturgical style in his day but was later reduced in significance, although it still has a place in the liturgical offices of the Eastern church. Romanos represents Syrian midrashic style in his poetic renderings of the biblical narratives, playing on the drama of the events he poetically and paraphrastically retells, and using heightened contrasts and paradoxes to convey the sense of wonder and mystery of the story of salvation. His "Christmas Hymn" and his "Hymn of the Virgin's Lament" are used today in the great feasts of the Orthodox Church at Christmas and Great Friday of Holy Week.

S. Brock, "From Ephrem to Romanos," in E. A. Livingstone, ed. (SP 20; Louvain, Belgium, 1989), 139–51; M. Carpenter, trans., *Romanos the Melodist* (2 vols.; Columbus, Ohio, 1970–1973); E. Lash, trans., *St. Romanos the Melodist: Kontakia on the Life of Christ* (New York, 1996); J. A. McGuckin, *At the Lighting of the Lamps* (Harrisburg, Pa., 1997); C. Trypanis, *The Penguin Book of Greek Verse* (London, 1971), 392–414.

Rome

At the time of the appearance of Christianity Rome was the single greatest city of the empire and proved the accuracy of the dictum that "All roads lead to Rome." In the affairs of the Christian church in the first two centuries only *Alexandria* and *Antioch* could rival its importance, but it is about Roman Christianity that we have the first and best records. Jews and interested "righteous Gentiles" from Rome were present in *Jerusalem* for the first Pentecost (Acts 2:10), and doubtless the earliest adherents of the Roman Christian movement, from the middle of the first century, were located in the extremely large Jewish quarter in Trastevere. Tradition has it that Peter visited and preached there circa A.D. 42 (perhaps the transfiguration narrative was the actual burden of his preaching ministry and caused sufficient controversy to initiate a reaction that stimulated the issuing of Mark's Gospel: cf. McGuckin 1987). The historian Suetonius also mentions a riot among Christian believers during the imperium of Claudius (*Divus Claudius* 25.4) that issued in a large expulsion of Jews from the capital. By the time Paul wrote his Epistle to the Romans (ca. A.D. 58) the Christian community was well established, and judging from the contents of the letter, it was here that centrally important issues for the future of the Christian movement were being decided, notably the issue of Jewish-Gentile relations in the early church. If the Syrian Christians were conservative on the matter (namely, the tradition of James at Jerusalem, and of Peter at Antioch), the Roman church (soon to be heavily influenced by Pauline trends in theology, as evidenced in the Gospels of Mark and Luke–Acts) pushed the policy of extensive "gentilization" most energetically. The city's earliest Christian communities seem to have been varied and based in a number of house churches. It would not be until late in the second century that one could begin to speak about a more unified church of Rome, although the *patristic* historians (especially *Eusebius of Caesarea*) retrospectively imposed such an order on Roman affairs in drawing up a

list of episcopal succession that derived from Peter. The lists of bishops at Rome is certainly one of the most ancient of all the surviving churches, but the impression it gives of a single *church* with a coherent policy from the beginning is misleading. Punitive persecution first fell on the Christian communities in the time of Nero, who was sufficiently aware of them as a new sect, generally disliked, to be able to use them as a scapegoat. Burning his hostages alive was meant as a dreadful placation of the anger of the gods; and who better than a poor, oriental, and perceivedly "misanthropic" group of foreigners who had denied worship to the gods of Rome (Tacitus, *Annales* 15.44; *First Clement* 6; see *persecutions*)? Tradition has it that Peter and Paul both perished at this time: Peter in the Circus of Nero on Vatican Hill, and Paul outside the city walls. Once again, in the reign of Domitian in A.D. 95, the Roman church was targeted for punishment (Eusebius, *Ecclesiastical History* 4.26.8; Tertullian, *Apologeticus* 5.4), showing that it had endured and grown. It was still largely Jewish and poor, but already was drawing considerable interest from the higher ranks, and Domitian's measures were designed to offset the attraction of "Jewish ideas" among the nobility. It is thought that the emperor's niece, Domitilla, may have been a Christian; and that if the aristocrat Flavius Clemens, who lost his life at this time, was not a Christian himself, then one of his freedmen certainly was, the Flavius Clemens (*Clement of Rome*) who is known to history as one of the early popes, and who wrote an important letter to the church of Corinth in the name of the Roman Christians. The Clementine letter reflects an urban church that is well organized and is already attempting to serve as a forum for international organization among Christians. These two characteristics would long remain typical of this community. After the fall of Jerusalem in A.D. 70, several of the surviving Jewish priests were brought as captives to

Rome. It is possible that another important Roman theologian and writer, Hermas, was one of these. He too rose to become a freedman and had some kind of charge of the Roman church, possibly as one of the early prophets. The Muratorian Canon says that he was the brother of Pope Pius (141–154). His book (*The Shepherd of Hermas*) was for a long time regarded as an equivalent of Scripture. Pope *Victor* in 189 was the first leader of the Roman Church who was Latin-speaking. He received delegations from Lyons, led by St. *Irenaeus*, and issued general instructions concerning the *Quartodecimans controversy*. This latter attempt to impose a uniform date for the liturgical observance of Pascha shows that the tradition of an international oversight of the churches had lasted at Rome. This was entirely a natural thing, given that all legal cases tended to end up at Rome for their final adjudication. Rome was the court of last appeal in the mentality of the whole empire, and it is no surprise that Christians began to look to the church of the world's greatest city as both a trendsetter and a force of conservatism and "good order," the virtues that, civically speaking, Rome was famed for. At the beginning of the second century (c. 110–117) *Ignatius of Antioch* was martyred there, as was *Justin Martyr* in c. 165. The list of Roman martyrs would grow ever longer, and in its earliest phases the Roman church was renowned more for its famed martyrs than for being the locus of the two great apostles, Peter and Paul; but from the third century onward it was this latter claim (that Rome was the see of Peter, and the spiritual home of Paul), that the city church used more and more in its projected self-image. During the course of the second century the church of Rome was forced to respond to a complex series of teachers of *gnostic* tradition (*Marcion* and *Valentinus*) and radical Syrian *ascetical* views (*Tatian* and *Hegesippus; see also* *Encratite*). As a center of *paideia*, the city attracted all manner of philosophers,

and the richness and diversity of the theologians who gathered there reflected the global religious views that were represented in the city. The Roman church leaders at this period responded to gnostic trends quite forcibly and sternly, advocating a conservative view of tradition. Soon the church would be famed for its conservatism; and this became another reason underlying its increasing popularity as an international court of appeal for all matters ecclesiastical. The rise of *Logos theology* at Rome in the early third century caused a crisis with the conservative leadership, who overreacted to it in such a way that they set out views that were quickly sidelined and dismissed as archaic *Monarchianism*. *Hippolytus* the theologian clashed with Pope *Callistus* (217–222) over the question whether Monarchianism or Logos theology should have the precedence. Another problem of the same period was how a disciplinary process should be organized to deal with the number of Christians who had lapsed under *persecution*. Rome set the tone for the whole penitential process of early Christianity, generally taking a moderate and balanced view, and persevering for its defense in the face of all manner of zealotry and exclusivism. *Novatian* was another leading Logos theologian who brought the community to a serious schism on account of disciplinary procedures. The pope at this time, Cornelius (251–253), and his successor Stephen (253–257) did much to advance thinking on the nature of the church as the ark of salvation, which thus required a system of *penance* to deal with the realities of sinfulness among its members. Controversies with Novatian and *Cyprian of Carthage* did much to sharpen the awareness of the higher Roman *clergy* of the need for an inclusivist ecclesiology over and against the demands of rigorists that sinners must be excluded from the elect community. At the end of the third century the Valerian persecution once more devastated the leadership of the Roman church. It had no long-term effect on its policy or vitality, however, a sign of its considerable extension by that period; and indeed under Cornelius there were a recorded forty-six *presbyters* and seven **deacons** constituting the official leadership (Eusebius, *Ecclesiastical History* 6.43.11). Pope Xystus II and all his deacons were tortured and put to death in 258 (including the celebrated deacon Laurence, who is said to have joked with his torturers as they roasted him against a flame so that he would reveal the church's treasury: "Turn me over. I am done on this side"). By the late third century the property owned by the Roman church and its poor relief were both considerable. After Xystus, **Pope Dionysius** (259–268) intervened in the affairs of the great church of Alexandria, requiring its bishop, **Dionysius**, to explain himself on matters of **Trinitarian** theology, which he did in a series of letters. The Great Persecution of Diocletian fell upon the Roman church leadership with great severity and caused immense turmoil among clergy and faithful. Much property was confiscated and many lapses happened, along with a cluster of more martyrs (whose numbers tended to be amplified retrospectively). With the seizure of power by Maxentius in 306, and the extension of the civil war waged by **Constantine**, the persecution of Christians abated at Rome, and a large number of lapsed once more clamored to be admitted to communion. The disturbances in the church at this time caused the exile of the successive popes Marcellus (308–309) and Eusebius (310). But the fourth century soon ushered in a period of great peace and prosperity for the church. Much property that had been confiscated was returned to Pope Miltiades (311–314) and Constantine's victory at the Milvian bridge, when he seized Rome, and subsequently the publication of the Edict of Milan (313) established the Christians as a corporation permitted to receive legacies and own title. From that moment on, the Roman church grew rapidly in wealth and political weight, so that it was a force to be reckoned with by Christian and pagan alike. In 382 the emperor Gratian made a dramatic symbolic move by removing (in accordance with Christian demands) the pagan altar to divine Victory from the Roman senate house. This marked the rapid decline of the fortunes of classical paganism at Rome, although the old religion was culturally embedded and thus lingered on for a considerable time. Its symbolic fate is illustrated, nevertheless, by the fact that the great bronze doors of the Roman senate house are now the main entrance portals to the Basilica of St. John Lateran. The leadership of the Roman church throughout the fourth century became increasingly conscious of its "rights" in the face of the equally strong development of the Eastern churches under Constantine's patronage. Perhaps the removal of the capital of the empire from Rome to **Constantinople** also gave the city a frisson of presentiment at its future fate as a declining giant. Although no one in the early fourth century probably saw it, or believed it possible, that great epoch that promised peace and prosperity would really set in motion the beginning of a great political decline for Rome, which in some senses would culminate in the fall of the Western capital to the forces of Attila the Hun in the fifth century. But for years earlier the grass had been growing in the gutters of imperial buildings at Rome as Constantinople was being paved with new marble, and the city bishops of "Old Rome" repeatedly protested their sidelining as international arbiters of the faith. The real dynamic movement in Christianity, however, had passed to synodical meetings largely held in the East and conducted under imperial patronage in the Greek language. Through the fourth to the sixth century the popes generally adopted the role of loud and important but nonetheless extraneous commentators to the development of ecumenical **Christology** and Trinitarianism that took place in the

East. The old reputation of the city as a bastion of conservative *orthodoxy* proved to be of inestimable benefit to the fourth century Eastern Nicene party led by *Athanasius* and later by the *Cappadocian Fathers.* If it had not been for the support of the West, orchestrated by Rome, the Greek Nicenes could never have overcome the weight of the *Arian* opposition listed against them. In the same period Rome was extending its program of building churches and beginning to contemplate the takeover of redundant pagan temples, although it was always more cautious in this regard than other places in the Christian world. As the budding fortunes of Milan and Ravenna placed Rome further in the political shadows, the theory of *papacy* developed more overtly. At first the popes were seen to be the Vicars of St. Peter, and a quasi-mystical view of the abiding presence of the apostle martyr within the church, in the form of his episcopal successors, started to develop. Much later this would be stepped up to them becoming known as the Vicars of Christ (*see Gelasius*). The authority and wisdom of many great popes in the dark period when the city was sacked by invading barbarians and, in 476, subjected to barbarian rule set the precedent for what would happen generally after the age of *Justinian.* Starting in the sixth-century wars between the Gothic masters of Italy and the Byzantine armies, which wanted to reclaim Rome, the inhabitants of the city were progressively reduced to extreme poverty. In the early seventh century the papacy took up the power vacuum left in Italy by the twin forces of the collapse of effective Byzantine rule and the rise of the Lombard warlords. In the person and work of Pope *Gregory the Great,* the long history of the papal monarchy would symbolically begin, setting the terms of most of the subsequent character of Latin Christianity in the patristic era, and its constant orbit around the ever-centralizing force of the Roman church.

R. Beny and P. Gunn, *The Churches of Rome* (New York, 1981); R. Brown and J. P. Meier, *Antioch and Rome: New Testament Cradles of Catholic Christianity* (New York, 1983); R. Krautheimer, *Rome: Portrait of a City, 312–1308* (Princeton, N.J., 1980); J. A. McGuckin, *The Transfiguration of Christ in Scripture and Tradition* (New York, 1987); T. F. X. Noble, *The Republic of St. Peter: The Birth of the Papal State, 680–825* (Philadelphia, 1984); C. Pietri, *Roma Christiana: Recherches sur l'Église de Rome, son organisation, sa politique, son idéologie de Miltiade à Sixte III (311–440)* (Rome, 1976).

Rufinus of Aquileia   *see* **Jerome**

Rule of Faith   *see* **Apostolicity, Irenaeus of Lyons, Tradition**

Sabellianism   *see* **Monarchianism**

Sabellius   *see* **Monarchianism**

Sacrament   The Latin term *sacramentum* originally meant a "sacred thing" (*sacer*) or an initiation confirmed by a sacred oath. In secular use it denoted the entrance of a candidate into the military life, a ritual that was observed with both oaths and religious sacrifices. It was introduced into theological language in the Latin church only. It never had a corresponding synonym in Greek, but was increasingly used by the Latins to convey the meaning of the Greek term "mystery" (*mysterion*). It first appeared in discussions of the ritual of *baptism* to describe the sacred character of the obligations the candidate had now accepted and the profession of faith by which they had bound themselves to the service of Christ. Soon it was developed as a distinctly Christian technical term, covering much of the range of the Greek Bible's use of *mysterion*, the "mystery of salvation." By the time of *Augustine* the word had come to designate most of the Christian rites: baptism, *Eucharist, marriage, ordination,* anointing, and *penance.*

O. Casel, "Zum wort sacramentum," JLW 8 (1928): 225–32; T. M. Finn, *Early Christian Baptism and the Catechumenate* (Wilmington, Del., 1989); J. De Ghellinck, *Pour l'histoire du mot "Sacramentum"* (Louvain, Belgium, and Paris, 1924); D. J. Sheerin, *The Eucharist* (Wilmington, Del., 1986).

Saints   The New Testament, following biblical precedents (Pss. 16:3; 34:9; 89:5), calls the members of the *church* Christ's "saints" (Greek: *hagioi;* Latin: *sancti*), or more precisely Christ's sanctified, to denote the effects of salvation diffused in the church. The congregation of the saints was especially seen (again in terms derived from the Old Testament) as a "kingdom of priests and a holy nation" (Exod. 19:6; 1 Pet. 2:9; Rev. 20:6). Christ's great work of redemption, in his passion and *resurrection,* was seen to have consecrated the Christian faithful. It was a sanctification that was shared in by the church from its fundamental source, which was Christ's own holiness: a holiness he had invoked over the church as his commissioned community (as for example in John 17:17). All holiness within that community was the gift of the same *Holy Spirit* whom Jesus had sent to make the church the firstfruits of cosmic salvation. Concepts of holiness as something individuals could aspire to in an individual way, as a personal merit or suchlike, were alien to the deep sense of holiness as consecration and as a free *grace* from God in Christ. For the first three centuries of Christian life this idea of the sanctity of Christ's Church, collectively understood, predominated in Christian thinking. It was known also that the faithful martyrs had been elevated to a special place in *heaven,* from which they would intercede for the community of faithful still struggling on earth (cf. Rev. 2:26–27; 6:9f). From this basis, the age of *persecutions* that would mark the church from the second to the fourth century also made an impact on the understanding of sanctity among Christians. The persecu-

tions demonstrated quite dramatically that many in the congregations were only nominally attached to the movement, while others were heroically dedicated, even to the point of torture and death. These martyrs soon attracted great veneration. Some of the first noncanonical writings of the Christians were the Acts (the *Martyrdom of Polycarp,* from c. 156, is one of the first) recording their trials and executions, and in the time of peace their tombs were specially venerated, in the lively hope that they would look down on their former communities and help them. The martyr thus emerges as the first "saint" in the sense of specially holy and powerful patron. The idea of active patronage would soon extend, from the fourth century onward, to include (besides public martyrs) the growing ranks of *ascetics* and bishops. In both cases the expectation was that the holy man or woman demonstrated heroic levels of commitment, was validated by God by distinct signs of favor (the *hagiographies* of this era list the saint's signs and wonders, often modeled on the New Testament narratives), and could serve as a patron to the Christians who took his or her life as a model for reflection. One of the first texts elevating monastic ascetics into the category of the special "saint" was *Athanasius's Life of Antony.* Later in the fourth century *Gregory of Nazianzus* would effect something similar by transforming the Hellenistic funeral encomium into a form of hagiography. His sermons on his deceased brother Caesarius and sister Gorgonia are early examples of the putative canonization of ordinary Christians (neither was in any sense a martyr or really an ascetic). In most cases in this transitional period the traditional Roman language of patronage and benefit is clearly marked: the saint is addressed as a new form of local hero who will care for his people. After the fifth century hagiography became immensely popular in Christian literature, and numerous examples survive. The veneration of the saints was described as *douleia* (reverence) to distinguish it explicitly from the worship (*latreia*) that was due to God alone. The sense that veneration of the saint as the "friend of God" was an act of reverence for God too, since the saint manifested the single holiness of the Christ, retained the old idea of the church's collective sanctification. By the late fourth century specific reference to the saints had entered the liturgies of the Latin and Greek churches, and the calendar of liturgical feasts celebrating them began to spread out so as to cover the whole year. Sulpicius Severus records how he had a vision of St. Martin of Tours standing among the apostles and prophets and giving his own heavenly blessing to the faithful as they gathered for prayer (Suplicius, *Epistles* 2; 4; 16). In both the Latin and Greek liturgies this intercessory role of the saints and martyrs became increasingly central after the fifth century.

P. Brown, *The Cult of the Saints: Its Rise and Function in Latin Christianity* (Chicago, 1981); idem, "The Rise and Function of the Holy Man in Late Antiquity," JRS 61 (1971): 80–101; J. H. Corbett, "The Saint as Patron in the Work of Gregory of Tours," JMH 7 (1981): 1–13; A. G. Elliott, *Roads to Paradise: Reading the Lives of the Early Saints* (Hanover, 1987).

Salvation *see* Soteriology

Scete

A desert area with several salt lakes to the southeast of *Alexandria* and equidistant from Alexandria and Cairo. It is today known as Wadi al Natroun, which has led to several confusions of ancient Scete with *Nitria*, another monastic settlement further to the east (the modern El Barnugi). It was a place where *Macarius of Alexandria* settled in 330, and there attracted numerous monastic followers. From that time onward it was one of the three most important spiritual and theological centers of Egyptian monasticism (along with Nitria and Kellia) until the barbarian devastations of the fifth century. Four ancient monasteries still survive in the area.

D. J. Chitty, *The Desert a City* (London, 1977); H. G. Evelyn-White, *History of the Monasteries of Nitria and Scetis* (3 vols.; New York, 1932).

Schism

The term derives from the Greek word (*schisma*) for a rent or a tear in fabric: a division. It began life as a word for dissent within the community, but soon became almost exclusively used as a precise term for a division in the *church* that is caused by reasons other than theological. The latter would result in a division over basic matters of the interpretation of the faith, and would usually be called a heresy (Greek: *hairesis*). Schism was a rupture of church communion (most usually seen in an actual breaking of sacramental communion between various communities or individuals) based on a matter of church discipline or moral integrity or suchlike. *Jerome* was the first to put forward this definition (Jerome, *On the Letter to Titus* 3.1–11), and for the East Basil's dictum that schism was a nonheretical matter that had brought about a separation from the local church that was repairable passed into Eastern canon law (Basil, *Epistle* 188, Canon 1). However, some, such as *Cyprian*, do not reflect such a clean distinction, seeing schismatics and heretics as two sides of the same coin (Cyprian, *Epistles* 33; 66.5). *Augustine* came to the conclusion after years of fruitless overtures to the *Donatists* that schism would always result in heresy in the end (Augustine, *Against Cresconius* 2.4). The *Arians* were always seen to be a heresy from the perspective of the Nicene theologians, whereas the Novatians (who held that the main body of churches had compromised their purity and their sacramental forms) were always regarded as a schismatic group by the Nicenes. For their part the

Novatian communities regarded the mainstream as heretical. The *catholic* communities in *North Africa* in the time of Augustine regarded the Donatists as schismatics, whereas the Donatists themselves regarded the catholics, more severely, as having lapsed from the church, and from *sacramental* efficacy. In the *patristic* era, however, the concept of a merely juridical lapse was not always clearly distinguishable from theological reasons for divisions, and throughout the patristic period the reconciliation of heretics and schismatics was dealt with by church authorities predominantly in an "economical" manner: proceeding as would best fit the situation. Often it was required that returning heretics should be (re)baptized, while schismatics could be received by *chrismation* and a statement of faith. Most writers of the patristic period regarded schism as a serious matter, a sin against the **Holy Spirit** who demanded union in the church, but nevertheless a matter that could be solved by internal reconciliations; but many (on the basis of the Johannine Letters, where the schismatics are said never to have belonged to the church in the first place) called into question the validity of the claim of the schismatic group to retain even vestiges of the identity of church. Cyprian's treatise *The Unity of the Catholic Church* is one of the earliest and most substantial patristic treatments on the issue of schism and ecclesial identity. Augustine was also much exercised by the problem in his own relations with the Donatists. He gave to the Western church a more eirenical view of schism as a lapse of charity not involving serious theological causes, which could be reconciled juridically. That optimistic view was never so universally sustained in the Eastern church, whose *canons* often presume that the lapse into schism is itself a serious theological disruption of the *mystery* of the church, which endangers the continuing ecclesial identity of those who broke away. Several patristic writers say that schism always is the result of pride and desire to rule (*philarchia*) (cf. Basil, *Contra Eunomium* 1.13; Chrysostom, *In Ephes* 4, *Hom.* 11.4–5; Theodoret, *On First Corinthians* 11.18).

E. Ferguson, "Attitudes to Schism at the Council of Nicaea 325," in D. Baker, ed., *Schism, Heresy, and Religious Protest* (Cambridge, 172), 57–63; S. L. Greenslade, *Schism in the Early Church* (London, 1964).

Severus of Antioch (c. 465–538)

Leader of the *Syrian* so-called "*Monophysite*" party, as a young man Severus studied rhetoric at **Alexandria** and Beirut, received **baptism** in 488, and entered monastic life at Gaza. He came to **Constantinople** as a monk around 508 and, in the period when the imperial *Henoticon* was being advanced, interceded successfully with Emperor Anastasius for tolerance of the strongly Cyrilline, anti-Chalcedonian monastic party. In 512 he became patriarch of **Antioch** and was looked to as a powerful theologian who might mediate reconciliation for the post-Chalcedonian *christological* crisis then prevalent in the Eastern church. On the accession of Emperor Justin I in 518 he was deposed and lived in Alexandria. *Justinian's* attempts to reconcile him to his own christological settlement in the capital in 535 proved fruitless, and he was condemned at the Synod of Constantinople in 536. His writings were ordered to be burned. Retiring again to Egypt, he died soon afterwards. Severus's thought shows him to be a careful disciple of *Cyril of Alexandria*, especially insisting on the mystical unity of the Christ (Cyril's *mia physis* theology) as a paradigm of human deification. He took it as axiomatic that if one confessed the existence of two **natures** in Christ after the *incarnate* union, one could not believe that a union had taken place. His theology is much closer to that of the Council of Constantinople II (553) than he would ever have admitted, but the apparently divisive language of *Leo's Tome* made the **Council of Chalcedon** synonymous with **Nestorianism** as far as he was concerned. Because of his anti-Chalcedonian stance, his works (mainly christological and apologetic) remained extant only in Syriac, and thus largely unknown to the classical tradition. Like *Philoxenus of Mabbug* he was one of the most interesting thinkers of the Justinianic period.

W. H. C. Frend, *The Rise of the Monophysite Movement* (Cambridge, 1972); A. Grillmeier, *Christ in Christian Tradition* (vol. 2; Atlanta, 1987), 269–84; I. R. Torrance, *Christology after Chalcedon: Severus of Antioch and Sergius the Monophysite* (Norwich, U.K., 1988).

Sexual Ethics The earliest ages of the church were powerfully influenced by the teachings on sexual ethics set out in the Old Testament. These were a varied and complex set of instructions, ritual prohibitions, and law codes, gathered together across centuries, and not always coherent or systematic in any philosophical manner. Thus, while homosexuality was an "abomination to the LORD" (Lev. 18:22) in the ancient code, so too was the eating of ostrich and shellfish (Lev. 11:10, 13–16), and the commission of adultery was punishable by death (Lev. 20:10). The first prescript the church retained in its ethical code without adaptation (other than sporadically agonizing over the rightness of attaching severe civic penalties to it after the fifth-century Justinianic revision of the law code), but the others were passed over and radically re-contextualized. And yet, all the prescripts expressed in the code of Leviticus 18, in the context of ancient Israel, had the same standing ethically speaking. If they were not necessarily coherent in their totality as an ethical philosophy, they were coherent as subordinate aspects of the keeping of covenant ritual. Sin was what was forbidden by the

sacred law. Something was thus a matter of sin because it was the expressly revealed will of God that had been countermanded by human choice. Virtue was obedience: sin was prideful rebellion. All sin was one thing, and so too all virtue. This dominant theme of ethical thinking, what we might call Israel's concern for ritual purity and fidelity to the law, was also the basic substructure of all Christian thinking for the first three centuries until it came into the age of the **Apologists,** who first started to make a conscious dialogue with Hellenistic philosophy on matters of theology, cosmology, and ethics. The transition from covenant ethic to situation (or deed-centered) ethics was not always a happy one for the church, and indeed the two levels of thinking are still abundantly present in most areas, sometimes complementing one another, sometimes hindering each other's logical development. The adaptation of sexual ethics within the church was highly problematized because, on the one hand, Christianity adopted the authoritative voice of the Old Testament as revealed literature, while on the other hand, it simultaneously unraveled the "totalist" authority of the law in the light of the gospel, which it was progressively reflecting on. Several times Jesus commented on sexuality. The pericope of the woman caught in adultery (John 8:2–11) was an example of his radical and highly enigmatic doctrine of compassion that, without explicitly saying as much, countermanded the Levitical decree that adultery be punishable by death (a move of revisionism that had already occurred in the Judaism of his day). But the strict following of Jesus' words did not always help the early church to a clear position on sexual ethics, for he also has numerous anti-familial and antimarriage statements (Matt. 8:21–22; 10:21; 35–37; 19:10–12; Luke 8:10–21; 11:27–28) attributed to him in the Gospels (*see* **marriage**). These the church did not follow (despite always having a constant tendency to the *ascetical*), for it rendered most of his straight commendations (such as to leave wife and children) into "ideal recommendations," and although the church enshrined celibacy as the highest state for a Christian, it is undeniable that marriage, sexual love, and *family* life have been just as central and celebrated in Christianity as in *Judaism* before it (though admittedly not in its rhetorical or canonical tradition). First Timothy 4:3, written perhaps in the early second century, was already concerned to offset the growing tendency, visible in the apocryphal gospels, for example, to present celibacy as a fundamental and universal Christian obligation, and the letter actually offers marriage as the norm for the *church*, as a critical response. It is an important matter of interpretation, of course, to decide what was the original context of the obviously grouped cluster of Jesus-sayings recommending ascetic celibacy and social detachment. By the time the Gospels were composed in the middle of the first century, they were clearly being recommended to the church in general as dominical sayings of universal application; if not as commandments, at least as ideals that ought to be aspired to by all disciples. If, however, the sayings originated from Jesus as addressed primarily to his inner circle of immediate disciples, then he was probably calling followers to his side as missionaries and informing them that the requirements of attendance on his preaching ministry would foreclose normal family life. Such is the context we glimpse with Peter and the others who dramatically leave their families and their livelihoods (Mark 1:16–20), although after the *resurrection* they return to Galilee and seem quite able to use their boats once more (John 21:1–3). We thus might be led to think in terms of temporary celibacy for the sake of the itinerant preaching ministry. That no women are mentioned as wives of the disciples, except almost accidentally as in the case of Peter's mother-in-law (Mark 1:30), is not unusual in ancient sources, where women were all too frequently wholly transparent. The overall climate of Jesus' teachings on marriage, celibacy, and family seem clearly enough to relate to the overwhelming demands of the kingdom of God. Paul continued this *exegesis* dramatically in 1 Corinthians 7, where he was asked for advice from members of the church on whether fathers should be concerned to arrange marriages for their daughters, and he replied that it would be a better state to remain single, considering the nearness of the end time. The *eschatological* imperative thus informed and sharpened the earliest Christian thinking on sexual ethics, while never completely dismantling the earlier and more pervasive cultic concern for ritual purity that is found within the law. Jesus' statement that the thought of adultery was tantamount to adultery of the heart (Matt. 5:27–28) was generally received by *patristic* ethicists as making the inner motive synonymous with the deed, a factor that was underlined by such recommendations as given in Mark 7:1–23, where Jesus commends the inner attitude as more significant than the outer observance in a passage of sharp criticism on Pharisaic observance of the law. Often what originated as wry observations from Jesus on matters of the heart's motivations were elevated, in early Christian ethical thinking, to become "dominical laws." The difficulty in this latter process, an attempt at a straightforward reception of Old Testament cultic ethics, now glossed by authoritative dominical revisions ("You have heard it said ... but now I say to you," Matt. 5:21), was that even when the church gathered together all the dominical sayings about ethical matters they were not a comprehensive commentary on the whole range of the Old Testament law, nor were they ever intended to be such. Even so, the reflections of Jesus that the kingdom's nearness demands a standard higher than the old informed much Christian thinking on sexual-ethical matters, such as marital fidelity, chastity, contraception, and abortion. Many of the Fathers recommended "passionlessness" as the best state to aim for (Ignatius, *To Polycarp* 5.2; Tertullian, *De anima* 27; *Against Marcion* 1.29; Clement of Alexandria, *Paedagogus* 2.10.91; *Stromata* 3.5.42–44; 3.7.57; 3.11.71; 3.12.87; Augustine, *De civitate Dei* 14; and passim in *Marriage and Concupiscence*); that is, an avoidance of sexual passion even in a marriage, and while they rarely went further than this "rhetorical" intrusion into familial love (it would be different after the eighth century, when confessional laws progressively invaded family life more forensically and much more punitively), it nevertheless set a long-lasting and lugubrious tone in early Christianity that sex and spirituality did not mix well. The Fathers were generally repeating a long-standing Hellenistic rhetorical presupposition that the life of the sophist, the wise adviser on ethical and philosophical matters, ought to be marked by radical detachment from the affairs of this world, especially marriage and the bringing up of children. The ideal is dominant in **Stoic** ethical reflection, and from this channel it had a considerable impact on the rhetorical tradition of Christian ethics in the patristic age. Most of the writers were, of course, single ascetics, either philosopher-monks or celibate bishops. Their texts on the same theme of dispassion mount up to a large and dominant voice. The even greater *vox populi*, that is, the day-to-day practice of the married Christians who made up the vast majority of the churches of the time, is simply not heard. They were neither rhetoricians or theologians in the main, and the fact is we have no textual evidence representing what must have been the normal and normative reality of innumerable Christian couples who loved one another, found their love spiritually illuminating, and regarded the rhetoric of celibacy as merely a partial view. An argument from silence is always dubious, of course, but here one feels it can and needs to be made. The imbalance on this front has left its mark on Christian-

ity even to the present day. Most patristic statements about the ethics of lovemaking in marriage are concerned with the concept (again Stoic-inspired) of "natural law." The value of an act is determined by its compatibility with the natural purpose. Eating is ethically good when concerned with sustenance of the body, ethically wrong when concerned with gourmet self-pleasuring. Thus, sexual intercourse is right and proper only when it is aimed at physical procreation of children (Justin, *First Apology* 29; Athenagoras, *Legatio pro Christianis* 33; Clement of Alexandria, *Paedagogus* 2.10.83, 92–93; 2.10.91, 95–96; *Stromata* 3.7.58; 3.12.79; Augustine, *De civitate Dei* 14.23; *Marriage and Concupiscence* 1.5.4; 1.16.14; 1.17.15). While this nature-technological language was being developed in patristics during the strong ascent of the ascetical movement, thus from the second through the fifth century, the older biblical sense of two becoming one flesh as a joyful sign of the vitality of creation, or of the covenant of God with Israel, was being forgotten. It is still discernible in the elevation of marriage in parts of the pastoral literature as a sign of Christ's own love for the church (Eph. 5:25) and is presented in such ways in the Eastern marriage liturgy; and through such scriptural and liturgical texts it was never wholly overrun by the juggernaut of the ascetical movement; but it was undoubtedly overshadowed. The loud surrounding context of Hellenistic sexuality, inspired either by pagan cult or existentialist relativism, that faced the church of the early centuries perhaps explained the need for stern rhetoric on such matters from the early Christian teachers. Abortion, contraception, and child exposure were classed together by many Christian theologians as the wicked results of a surrender to sexual license and were regularly condemned. The severe and unremitting condemnation of abortion and infanticide was a visible mark of the early church that made it stand out among contemporary Hellenistic society, where abortion was practiced widely and without second thought (*Didache* 2.2; *Barnabas* 19; Athenagoras, *Legation* 29; 35; Justin, *First Apology* 27; 29; Tertullian, *Apologeticus* 9; Clement of Alexandria, *Paedagogus* 2.10.96; Jerome, *Epistle* 22.13; Augustine, *On Marriage and Concupiscence* 1.17.15; Basil the Great, *Epistle* 188.2; *Apostolic Constitutions* 7.3; John Chrysostom, *Homily 24 on Romans*). Throughout this period the ascetical movement managed to increase pressure against second marriages where the previous spouse had died. Only with reluctance did the fourth-century bishops finally license it as a concession to those who lacked sufficient self-control (Justin, *First Apology* 15; Athenagoras, *Legation* 33; Tertullian, *To His Wife* 1.7; *On Chastity* 5–6; 9; 12; *On Monogamy*; Jerome, *Epistle* 54.4.2; 79.10.4; Chrysostom, *On Not Marrying Twice* 1). A few writers, such as *Jovinian*, thought that this elevation of the ascetic ideal denigrated marriage in an unhealthy manner. But the former's public castigation by Jerome was a damper ever afterwards on all who dared to think the same. *Julian of Eclanum*, himself a married bishop (and thus one of the last of this class of bishops before the wholesale absorption of the office into the ranks of the ascetics in the late fourth and early fifth century), wrote a poem proclaiming the joys of marriage shortly after his own nuptials. He was sharply criticized for it by *Augustine*, and in his monumental fall in the *Pelagian* controversy, he took with him one of the last ecclesiastical voices, for centuries to come, that would celebrate marital love. Augustine, one of those who took an extremely severe view of the need to control concupiscence, even in the marital state, was the single writer of the Latin tradition who was most popularized, and thus brought this puritanical view into general reception. His view was that passionlessness was an ideal reflected in Adam and Eve, who, although they possessed sexual organs, had these entirely at the control of their will, and used them only for the

service of producing children when necessary (that is, after their *fall* from *grace*). Sex, for Augustine, was a lamentable admission of sinfulness and alienation from the divine; and while marital intercourse was within the range of forgivable sins, it was inevitably and always smeared over by guilt and lustful disobedience (Augustine, *De civitate Dei* 14; *Against Faustus* 15.7; 22.84; *On Marriage and Concupiscence* 1.16.14; 1.17.15; *Against Julian of Eclanum* 2.15.7; 2.16.7; 2.30.26; 4.12.2; 6.59.19). Marriage was clearly the friction point between church leaders, the large Christian masses, and contemporary ethical attitudes. This is why marriage legislation is the dominant locus of ethical reflection on sexuality in the early church, beginning with the Council of Elvira in 306. The prescripts on marriage that Jesus gave had an impact on Christians from the outset, as can be seen from the way the various Gospels already show textual variations in the reception of the "hard saying" of the Lord about the impossibility of divorce (Mark 10:1–12). This *logion* was received in the Latin church as a basic element of canon law without much further reflection. In the Eastern church it was received differently and by the fourth century was absorbed into Roman Christian law, which allowed marriages up to three times. *Gregory of Nazianzus* in his *Oration* 37 to Theodosius, where he argued forcibly for the retention of current Eastern canon law, not the imposition of the stricter Latin canon law, gave an exegesis of the divorce sayings where he eloquently demanded that Jesus' intentionality must be contextualized. For Gregory, that context, determining what the Lord would require of his church in the present day, was governed and shaped by Jesus' overall character as a lawgiver of deep compassion, constantly motivated by loving concern for the welfare of his people. On these grounds, Gregory argued, the more compassionate "economy" of the Eastern canonical position on marriage law ought to be preferred to the more rigid

Western interpretation, because the merciful economy more faithfully represents the deepest intent of the compassionate lawgiver than does the strict observance of the word as law. Gregory was a rare, empathetic, and subtle voice in the annals of patristic ethics, however. Most of explicit sexual reflection in the classical patristic age, from the third century to the fifth, is contextualized under the umbrella of the burgeoning ascetical movement and shows little other than a machismo-ethics of celibates fighting against sexual desire as if it were the greatest evil imaginable. That highly charged sexual ethic informs most of the *desert* literature, such as the *Apophthegmata Patrum*, and it needs to be appreciated for what it represented, namely, a uniquely Christian adaptation of the original eschatological message of Jesus; an awareness of the proximity of the kingdom, which demands all and was now expressed for the monks in the radical surrender of familial love and sexual fulfilment. Even so, it cannot be taken as a satisfactory answer, let alone a balanced response, to Christian sexual ethics globally considered. After the late fourth century little further attention was formally given to the issue, as it was felt that it could be addressed through the extension of canon laws; and dogmatic concerns then generally overshadowed most patristic writing. In this way a profoundly significant area of human experience, and also a matter of what we might call Jesus' insights into creation theology (cf. Mark 10:6–8), covenant fidelity, and human spirituality became subordinated to a burgeoning juridical mentality.

D. S. Bailey, *Sexual Relation in Christian Thought* (New York, 1959); P. Brown, *The Body and Society: Men, Women, and Sexual Renunciation in Early Christianity* (New York, 1988); E. Levin, *Sex and Society in the World of the Orthodox Slavs* (Ithaca, N.Y., 1995); V. J. Popishil, *Divorce and Remarriage* (London, 1967); A. Rouselle, *Porneia: On Desire and the Body in Antiquity* (London, 1988).

Shenoudi of Atripe (also Sinouthi, Shenoute, Shenuti, Sinouti; c. 350–466) One of the leading monks of Upper Egypt, and a powerful force in the monastic evangelization of the country, Shenoudi of Atripe was an active supporter of *Cyril of Alexandria* and accompanied him to the *Council of Ephesus*, subsequently moving on to agitate (successfully) for Cyril's vindication at *Constantinople* in the aftermath of the council. In 377 Shenoudi was inducted into monastic life by his uncle Pgol who had founded the White Monastery on the Nile. He became superior of the community in 388, and massively expanded it to over 2,000 monks and almost the same number of nuns. He headed a severe regime, where floggings were common for infringements. He is thought to be the first to require of monastics a written profession, a practice that later became very common in monastic life. Shenoudi is the founder of Coptic *Christology* and Coptic theological literature. Before the discovery in the twentieth century of new documents, he was uniformly dismissed as a sideline figure dabbling in *magic.* The texts show a popular theologian encouraging a deep Jesus devotion, someone who was also a powerful local leader who protected his people from raiding tribes and negotiated for them with imperial authorities, using his network of relations with Cyril and *Dioscorus of Alexandria.* He attacked *Nestorius* and was an opponent of the (intellectual) Origenist monks of Egypt. The violence and the thaumaturgical legends associated inescapably with his name have prejudiced many European scholars against him, but they open an important window on the process of the rapid evangelization of Egypt in this period. His writings that have survived (all in Coptic, which ensured his neglect by international Christianity) all come from the scriptorium of the White Monastery, but are now scattered among twenty modern libraries, and still await a complete edition. Shenoudi's *Life* was composed by his immediate successor Besa.

D. N. Bell, trans., *Besa: The Life of Shenoute* (CS vol. 73; Kalamazoo, Mich. 1983); A. Grillmeier and T. Hainthaler, *Christ in Christian Tradition* (vol. 2, pt. 4; Louisville, Ky., 1996), 167–228; J. Limbi, "The State of Research on the Career of Shenoute of Atripe," in B. A. Pearson and J. E. Goehring, eds., *The Roots of Egyptian Christianity* (Philadelphia, 1986), 258–70.

Shepherd of Hermas   *see* Hermas

Sin   Sin is the normal translation of the Greek New Testament term *hamartia*, which etymologically means a missing of the mark, an error; and also of the Latin *peccatum*, which means a fault. Early Christianity did not focus on the nature of sin very much, although it was always conscious (a tendency that continued to mark *patristic* theology) that sin was first and foremost a matter of disobedience of God's commands, and thus a rebellion against the covenant of mercy. In this respect it took to heart the strong moral line developed by the prophets of the Old Testament to interiorize the theology of covenant obedience, a theme that can be discerned in all the later Scriptures. The earliest writings of the *Apostolic Fathers* were heavily influenced by the quasi-*apocalyptic* idea of the "two ways" (of good and evil, life and death) that were set before individuals. The *church* offered itself as the community of those who were following the way of life (*Didache* 1.1–6; 2; *Barnabas* 18–21; Shepherd of Hermas *Mandates*). For the first three centuries the concept of the church as the end-time elect who had been given space for repentance was very strong and seen above all in the earliest theologies of baptism as a dynamic rescue of the believers from the spiritual and physical *death* caused by the prevalence of sin in the cosmos. *Baptism* was associated most strongly with the concept of Christ's *resurrectional* power as Lord of the church, refashioning a community of *saints* who would be liberated from the corruption caused by sin. The

strong link in patristic thought between sin and death is exemplified clearly in *Origen's* theology and **Athanasius of Alexandria's** *On the Incarnation*, where the latter describes how the Christian life is meant to be an ever-deepening assimilation into the immortal power of the risen Lord, while sin is an endemic force that drags humanity down into corruption (*ptharsia*) and death. Monastic *asceticism* after the late fourth century turned its attention to the problem of sin as it marked a new level of psychological awareness in the *desert* communities of zealous celibates. Theologians such as *Evagrius* highly amplified the practice of moral scrutiny, and the concept of the mystery of sin (the manner in which it would never simply "go away," and how it had attractive powers over human beings) became a focus of interest. Evagrius and others began to theorize that as holy behavior was due to Christ's work and the assistance of angels, so the pervasiveness of sin was partly the fault of demonic attacks on the faithful. In the fourth century, Syrian ascetics such as Pseudo-Macarius (*see* **Macarius the Great** 2) developed the idea of sin as a dragon lurking in the human heart, sometimes sleeping because of grace, but never to be taken lightly. Several Eastern theologians after that time were at pains to resist this "Messalian" tendency and lay a great stress on the free character of human sinfulness. In the West things were different. In the fifth century *Augustine* also turned his attention to the problem of sin, once more from the vantage point of an introspective ascetic. His theology of *grace* and redemption, sharpened by his conflict with the optimistic moralist *Pelagius,* set the tone for most of Latin Christianity after him, which saw sin as a debilitating pandemic among the human race that caused radical losses of spiritual capacity in human beings that could only be healed by the equally radical intervention of God's grace. Augustine's strong influence over later thinkers ensured that the **North African** *theologoumenon* of original sin entered the mainstream Latin tradition. This was the idea that sin spread like a disease from the first parents through the race by means of sexual concupiscence, so that all newborn babies were guilty and needed baptismal forgiveness. After Augustine, many Latin church leaders tended to presume that sin was almost a natural proclivity of human beings and that the works of grace were *miraculous* in contrast. Eastern Christianity never adopted such a widespread pessimism about the extent and spread of sin. Origen and Athanasius, in the Alexandrian tradition, both argued strongly that even though humanity had fallen, the potentiality for divine vision remained intact within the innermost soul, and the power of the resurrection of Christ would shine through in abundance if the disciple gave obedience with generosity of heart. Origen never failed to insist that sin was always a matter of free choice, and that on the basis of choice humans would be judged (*Peri archon* 3.1). Most patristic reflection on sin remained at the individual level. The social justice sermons of many of the great Fathers (notably *John Chrysostom,* who castigated the venality of the rich and their neglect of the poor) work from a presuppositional basis of rights of possession, and the needful advocacy of individual philanthropy. Modern ethical concerns with "institutional sin" were largely unknown, although there was always a lively sense in the early Christian writers that sin was not something entirely interior and individual, but rather something of cosmic dimensionality, in which the church was caught up in no less than an *apocalyptic* battle with evil and the forces of evil that hated the extension of the kingdom of God. Many of the Eastern Christian prayers also regularly spoke of the confession of sins "voluntary and involuntary, committed in knowledge or in ignorance," which served to demonstrate a sophisticated awareness of the complexities of the human heart and soul in the perennial matter of following, or avoiding, the demands of the gospel.

W. Babcock, "Augustine on Sin and Moral Agency," JRE 16 (1988): 28–55; J. P. Burns, ed., *Theological Anthropology* (Philadelphia, 1981); S. Lyonnet and L. Sabourin, *Sin, Redemption, and Sacrifice: A Biblical and Patristic Study* (Analecta Biblica 48; Rome, 1970).

Sinai   The Mountain of Sinai (where the law was given to Moses) was identified by the Christians at the site of "Mount Moses" (modern Jebel Musa) in the south of the desert region between Egypt and Palestine. Monastics were already there when *Egeria* made her pilgrimage in the late fourth century. Christian ascetics set up a number of desert communities in the Sinai region (the whole of the peninsula), which were related in a close nexus; with hermits being supported by the larger cenobitic establishments. The two most significant communal centers were the Monastery of Raithu on the Red Sea coast and the Monastery of the Burning Bush at the foot of Mount Sinai. Both foundations served as focal points for a lively ascetic culture that became textually witnessed in the *Ladder of Divine Ascent* by *John Climacus,* one of the most significant abbots of Sinai. Against a background of growing political instability in the Egyptian desert and the decline of once-flourishing monasticism there, the emperor *Justinian* authorized the massive fortification of the Sinai monastery, and the buildings now remain as a remarkable testimony to sixth-century Byzantine Christianity. The monastery was later renamed St. Catherine's, and was associated with the legend that the saint's body was flown by angels to the top of an adjacent peak, where it was found by one of the monks, who brought it back to the church below. The original dedication of the burning bush especially celebrated Mary's role as the *Theotokos* (in Christian symbolism she was the antitype of the bush that was never consumed although it contained the divine presence within). Justinian's work ensured that the Sinai monastery remained a strong Chalcedonian presence even after Egypt was lost to the Byzantine Empire. The clergy at Sinai maintained connections with *Jerusalem* rather than with *Alexandria.* Eventually, although always tiny, Sinai was given the status of an autocephalous church, headed by the abbot, who has always since then been an archbishop. The Sinai monastery today is the receptacle for masterworks of early Christian iconography, and its collection of manuscripts is of inestimable importance. The apsidal mosaic from the sixth-century monastery church shows Jesus transfigured, thus associating the other mountain of glory (Tabor) with the peak of Sinai (since Moses appeared on both). The famed Codex Sinaiticus was purloined from here by Tischendorf to become an important basis for modern critical editions of the New Testament. Both it and the Codex Vaticanus probably represent the surviving remains of the biblical pandects ordered by *Constantine* for the new churches he was building, and which were copied at Caesarea under the supervision of *Eusebius of Caesarea.*

O. Baddeley and E. Brunner, *The Monastery of St. Catherine* (London, 1996); V. N. Beneshevich, *Monumenta Sinaitica, archaeologica et paleographica* (Russian text; vol. 1; Leningrad, Russia, 1925); G. H. Forsyth, K. Weitzmann, et al., *The Monastery of St. Catherine at Mount Sinai: The Church and Fortress of Justinian* (Ann Arbor, Mich., 1974); J. Galey, *Sinai and the Monastery of St. Catherine* (Cairo, 1985); K. A. Manafis, ed., *Sinai: Treasures of the Monastery of St. Catherine* (Athens, 1990); J. A. McGuckin, *The Enigma of the Christ Icon Panel at St. Catherine's at Sinai: A Call for Re-Appraisal* (*Union Seminary Quarterly Review* 52, 3–4; 1999): 29–47; K. Weitzmann, *Studies in the Arts at Sinai* (Princeton, N.J., 1982).

Slavery   The practice of enslaving others, especially the conquered peoples of war, was basic to the ancient Roman-Hellenistic economy, and was widely practiced. Laws that punished slave revolts with brutal cruelty reflect the political realization of ancient society that slaves probably outnumbered the free citizens in the imperial urban centers, and did so by a very large margin in the rural regions. The harsh penalties for revolt and escape (the same as that inflicted on Jesus) reflect the perennial anxiety of the system. *Aristotle* had laid down a basis for philosophical and moral reflection on the issues of freedom and slavery, which had long been absorbed into the consciousness of Hellenistic society. It drew a picture that the pursuit of virtue (*arete*) was fundamentally necessary for the acquisition of true humanity. Only those who had achieved virtue by the practice of learned reflection in *philosophy* could be human, properly speaking, and those only should vote to determine the affairs of the city-state. By this he intended to restrict political rights to the landowning classes, who were the only ones in ancient Greek society who could afford the leisure for study, largely because they used slave labor on their farms and in their work houses. This definition implicitly categorizes the truly human as the rich, the free poor as less than human, and the slaves (who did the laborious tasks) as subhuman. Aristotle further reflected that this division of humanity was undoubtedly a "natural" phenomenon, and society thus reflected inherent natural divisions of humanity into those who were either fully or defectively human; that is, the masters and the subordinate. The concern for treatment of slaves under such an ethico-philosophical system, therefore, was comparable to the sensible treatment of domestic animals. The welfare of the slave (let alone any concept of human rights) was not predominant; what really mattered was the wise balance of the owner, who could treat each element of his estate (or city) in the moderation that produced the golden mean of peaceful prosperity. Later Greek thought, especially *Stoicism* around the Christian era, had added nuances to this generic position, mainly in the way that humane treatment of slaves was advocated as a common decency. Stoicism was more aware of the idea of common humanity between slave and slave owner, but while this new theme of compassion for the suffering (cf. Seneca, *Moral Epistles* 47) found a resonance within Christianity, it was not sufficient in itself to dislodge the older, Aristotelian views. This fundamentally economic context of reflection on slavery was the dominant ethos in which the early church appeared. The Christians, of course, inherited much Old Testament legislation about slaves (Exod. 21:2–11; Deut. 15:12–18; Lev. 25:44–46; Num. 31:25–47; Josh. 9:22–27; Ezra 8:20), which was also concerned with their humane treatment, and in some cases with sabbatical manumissions of Israelite slaves (foreign slaves were permitted to be enslaved permanently in Israel). But the generic impact of the Old Testament on this matter was never as instructive as contemporary Hellenistic practice, except that the very example of biblical legislation in the Old Testament for the condition of slavery seemed to some thinkers in the church a partial legitimization of the affair (although slavery in Israel was never as extensive as in Hellenism). This may partly account for the general inability of patristic theologians (and Christian thinkers for centuries afterwards) to come to the apparently logical end of their generic antislavery sentiment, that is, an outright condemnation of the whole business. *Gregory of Nyssa* is the only one of the major fathers who regarded slavery as offensive in the eyes of God and openly contested the rights of a master over a slave (*Homily 4 on Ecclesiastes*), although *Gregory of Nazianzus* regarded it as a lamentable institution that reflected the moral chaos of the world at odds with God's law (*Carmina* [*Theologica*] 1.2.36). By this he implied that slavery was not part of the ethic of the Kingdom. In this he is followed by several leading *patristic* theologians (cf. John Chrysostom, *Homilies 1–3 on Philemon*). The *Donatists* were a Christian secession movement in *North Africa* that expressed great hostility to slave owners (the colonial Roman oppressors) and sometimes invaded the country estates to liberate the slaves and punish harsh slave masters. Eustathius of Sebaste also tried to introduce monastic reforms that abolished social distinctions within his communities, refusing to admit that the status of slavery had relevance within the Christian community. But Eustathius attracted the hostility of local *bishops* for his itinerant habits, and the Donatists drew down on themselves even harsher penalties for political insurrection from the Roman imperial authorities. *Augustine* regarded the existence of slavery as a direct result of original sin (*De civitate Dei* 19.15–16), part of the pervasive suffering the human race had brought upon itself. This pessimism may account for why Augustine, who was personally greatly concerned with the plight of slaves and expended much effort and church money to ransom young children captured by African slave traders (*Epistle* 10, Divjak collection), still never censured the institution outright. Numerous wealthy Christian bishops, including Gregory of Nazianzus, owned slaves. Gregory's will records the manumission of his family slaves and their endowment with gold as a pension, but this was a posthumous graciousness. *Patrick,* who had once been enslaved himself, regarded the act of enslavement (even in war) as an excommunicable offense. The condition of a slave varied greatly in the Roman Empire, from the position of an indentured servant (often such city slaves could become wealthy and important social figures) to something little better than animal labor in the imperial mines or on large country estates. Families were never so cruelly dissipated as was the case in early modern slavery, and there were several routes out of ancient slavery (usually available only to those who could accumulate money through business transactions), but it was generally a condition that reflected the poorest of the poor in ancient society. The servile class was meant to work for all others, not for themselves. The church made some impact on this condition, even if it did not see the necessity to call for its abolition. It legitimated slave marriages by canon law, in the face of Roman attitudes, which gave them the secondary legal status of concubinage. Doubtless because so many slaves formed the ranks of the early urban communities, the church was also one of the most flexible organizations in ancient society in its readiness to accept slaves or former slaves as community leaders. Pope *Callistus* was himself a manumitted slave, as was the author of the *Shepherd of Hermas,* who also rose to a prominent position in the Roman church through the patronage of his slave owner. Callistus was much censured by other Christian writers for allowing, in the church, marriages of slaves to Roman freedwomen (prohibited under secular law). His attitude here was clearly one of spiritual (if not temporal) equality, a theme he had learned from his reading of Paul, who simultaneously instructs Onesimus to return to his master from whom he had escaped (Letter to Philemon) and also writes that in Christ there is no longer free or slave (1 Cor. 12:13; Gal. 3:28; Col. 3:11). Paul at least encouraged Philemon to think of manumitting Onesimus rather than punishing him. The later Pauline tradition, in the early second century, seemed to have become afraid that its spiritual attitude of equality in Christ might attract the unwelcome attention of the secular powers, for there is a renewed concern in the deutero-Pauline literature and Catholic Epistles to calm down any potential unrest by requiring good Christian

slaves to be obedient to their masters (Eph. 6:5–8; Col. 3:22–25; 1 Tim. 6:1–2; Titus 2:9–10; 1 Pet. 2:18–25). In 316 and 323, *Constantine* authorized the church as a legal body that could manumit slaves. There is not extensive evidence that it arranged the liberation of massive numbers of them (it had to be done with the owner's consent), but the theme of most fourth-century patristic writings, especially *John Chrysostom,* is to urge a liberal attitude among the rich toward the idea of freeing slaves (John Chrysostom, *Homily on First Corinthians* 40.5; Augustine, *Homily* 31.6). A slave was not permitted to receive *ordination* in the post-Constantinian canons, but the emperor *Justinian* in the sixth century allowed monasteries to protect slaves who had fled, and if they had stayed in the monastery as a monk for three years, they were legally freed of all former obligations. By the time of the late sixth century and onward the fabric of the empire had declined so drastically in economic terms that the whole system of slavery under the Christian empire had begun to fall apart, and was progressively replaced by early feudal systems of indentured labor, the institution of serfdom that would last throughout the Middle Ages in both East and West.

W. Buckland, *The Roman Law of Slavery* (Cambridge, 1908); G. Corcoran, *St. Augustine on Slavery* (Rome, 1985); G. de Ste. Croix, "Early Christian Attitudes to Property and Slavery," in D. Baker, ed., *Church, Society, and Politics* (Oxford, 1975), 1–38; S. Talamo, *La schiavitù secondo I Padri della Chiesa* (Rome, 1927); W. L. Westermann, *The Slave Systems of Greek and Roman Antiquity* (Philadelphia, 1955).

Socrates Scholasticus (c. 380–450) An important church historian of the fifth century, Socrates was a resident of *Constantinople* all of his life and had a centralist view of church affairs. He was a layman and a lawyer of wide political and religious sympathies (he saw oracles, pagan and Christian, as a common religious experience). He wished to continue the historical writing of *Eusebius of Caesarea* into his own age, and accordingly composed his own *Ecclesiastical History* in seven books (each covering the reign of an emperor) between 438 and 443. It is for this he is famous. It made him the chief historian of his age. His work covers the period of church affairs from 306 to 439. Socrates is a careful historian with good judgment and has a lively sense of the need to cite his sources accurately. He uses the works of *Athanasius* as well as a collection of church councils (*Synagoge*) assembled in 375 by Sabinus of Heraclea, whom he criticizes for his tendency to suppress evidence he does not ideologically like. Socrates was a Christian *Platonist* by inclination, and in all his writing he favors the ecclesiastical intelligentsia, especially *Origen* and his later disciples. He has the prejudice of the Constantinopolitan looking down on the provincial, and it comes out especially in his views of *Syrian* and Egyptian Christian affairs. He seems to have some association with the rigorist *Novatian* church in the city, and always portrays their affairs (otherwise negligible) with sympathy. He has a classical Byzantine view that history is the record of disturbances to the God-given plan of peace for the church (some see his plain style as a deliberate preference for a nondistracting medium of historical narrative), and he ends his work hoping that the future may have "nothing worthy of record" for historians.

G. F. Chesnut, *The First Christian Histories: Eusebius, Socrates, Sozomen, Theodoret, and Evagrius* (2d ed., Macon, Ga., 1986); A. C. Zenos, *The Ecclesiastical History of Socrates* (NPNF, 2d ser., vol. 2; New York, 1890).

Soteriology

A modern term derived from the Greek word for salvation (*soteria*), soteriology refers to the doctrine or theology of salvation. It is much used in contemporary *patristic* analysis, since most of the ancients held dynamic and active views of the Christian *mystery* as an ongoing process of God's salvation of the cosmos. In older books the term "redemption" (redemptive theology) predominated, but the concept of redemption, or the buying back of a slave, is merely one image (albeit a New Testament one) alongside many others in patristic writing that is used to convey the vast scheme and many methods of how God called the world back to *grace*. Many of the ancients begin their theological deductions from the soteriological effects. Taking *Christology*, for example, they do not argue in the abstract about the *person* and *nature* of Christ, but consider what the *incarnation* concretely effected for the human race (*see* *deification*). As a macrotheoretical structure that underlies the Christian *kerygma*, soteriology was never something that became a specific focus of attention in early Christian history. As such it was never specifically defined in the dogmatic or conciliar traditions, although there are recognizable and recurring themes by which it was approached, notably illumination, purification, redemption, divinization, victory, and reconciliation. There are also an abundance of iconic and textual images by which the idea is sketched out, such as the good shepherd, the man of sorrows, the bread of life, and so on. The whole range of Scriptures, with their rich association of suggestive typologies, encouraged an expansive and poetic approach. The earliest patristic soteriologies of the second century focused on the glorious descent of the heavenly Lord to save his people from demonic oppression. The christological hymns in Ephesians and Colossians represent the shape of this schema, and it is still clearly present in the terms of *Athanasius's De incarnatione* of the fourth century (for since they were never the center of controversy most of the soteriological images were progressively overlapped rather than ejected). Athanasius describes the divine choice of the cross as necessary to entrap the "aerial demons." But his overall schema in the *De incarnatione* shows other influences for, as a result of the **gnostic** crisis, theologians such as **Irenaeus, Tertullian** and **Ignatius of Antioch** had already turned their focus on the incarnation of God in the flesh as the quintessential act of God's salvation; and the incarnation, understood soteriologically and dynamically, never lost its central position in Christian thought thereafter. Athanasius again put it succinctly when he described the assumption of human nature by the divine Word as first and foremost an act of "re-creation" of corrupted humanity. The enfleshment of God was the deification of mankind, a saving and stabilization of a formerly corrupted nature doomed to death. For Athanasius the incarnation was the root cause of the immortalization of the race (often called the "physical theory" of atonement). Many of the Greek philosophical teachers, such as **Clement** and **Origen of Alexandria,** invested heavily in a pedagogical soteriology. Christ, as true Word, was the reason and principle of all existence. His incarnation served to give mankind the teaching and example necessary to turn back to the true life. The same idea in more sober form is found in many of the Latin writers, such as Tertullian, **Cyprian,** and **Lactantius.** The pedagogical strain of much patristic writing is easily noted, and often combined with other soteriological themes and ideas. It came to a flowering in the Byzantine ascetical writers of the fifth century and afterward. In the hands of such as **Dionysius the (Pseudo) Areopagite** and **Maximus the Confessor,** the ascetical pedagogical theme was combined with a deeply liturgical (*sacramental*) and mystical approach (union with Christ the Paschal Victor), which dominated most Greek thought of the late Middle Ages onward. In the Latin West many of the earlier wide range of soteriological images came increasingly to be restricted until the ideas of redemptive sacrificial substitution predominated.

J. Rivière, *The Doctrine of Atonement* (2 vols.; St. Louis, 1909); B. Studer, "Soteriologie in der Schrift und Patristik," vol. 3, sec. 2a in *Handbuch der Dogmengeschichte* (Freiburg, Germany, 1978); H. E. W. Turner, *The Patristic Doctrine of Redemption* (London, 1952).

Soul   The soul (Latin: *anima*; Greek: *psyche*) was a fundamental concept for **patristic** thought, foundational, in a sense, for its **mystical, anthropological,** and **soteriological** schemas, but one where a number of unresolved issues can be witnessed in most of the writers. This is partly because in this aspect the Christian intellectual tradition involved a very mixed prior heritage. The biblical data on soul, and that of the various Greek philosophical schools, accumulated to a very disparate body of teaching. The earliest centuries of the patristic era were spent trying to synthesize much of this body of evidences. In the Old Testament the concept of soul is broached in a variety of ways. The texts often use the word *nephesh* to describe the breath of life in a human being, as that distinctive life force which God inspirated into clay to make a living creature (Gen. 2:7). But most commonly, Christian writers wished to use the term spirit (Greek: *pneuma*) to connote this aspect of the divinely graced life force within, that element which distinguished a living human being from, say, animals. This aspect is not apparent in much of early Hebraic theology, necessarily, or in the majority of New Testament references to "soul," which simply use it in biblical fashion to refer to the creature, but it became a notable aspect of later Christian reflections that were being articulated in a context of Greek thought, which had long speculated on the inner makeup of human consciousness. The distinction of soul and spirit remained always a tenuous one in Christian reflection. In regard to the influence of Hellenism, three great schools had, long before Christianity's appearance, elevated a distinct rivalry in regard to the question of the human soul. Plato taught that the *psyche* tragically fell into a material embodied existence from a previous spiritual life, where it was able, with unwavering clarity, to behold the Ideal Forms. Trapped in a body ("the body a prison" was the *Platonic* motto), the soul suffered all manner of ills, not least the inability to perceive truth with any surety. Its basic task was to transcend material illusion and return to its former dignity by asserting control through its rational power (soul as *to logistikon*) over the "lower soul," which was the aesthetic center of life. The soul, for Plato, was eternal and self-moving (at least in its superior aspects as *to logistikon*). *Aristotelianism* had, in distinction, argued strongly that the soul was a fundamental part of the inner entelechy of the human nature, not a separate alien spark trapped within a material form. It was born along with the body and was the life force that made the whole organism grow to its determined end. As an acorn has an inner force to drive it to its natural *telos* (the oak tree), so did the human soul serve to guide the development of a human through the stages of embryo to that of thinking, rational being. *Stoicism,* in turn, argued that the soul was the life principle (comparable to the "directive" aspect of Platonism: *to hegemonikon*), which originated from the reconstitution of cosmic elements after great cyclical conflagrations. The soul was the locus of the divine spark of *Logos,* which permeated each living being endowed with reason. It was thus the principle of reason within a human and the seat of divinity within the mortal form. It was material in nature, as Aristotle had said, but not material in the sense that base matter was, insofar as the soul had a special "fiery nature," which was refined and subtle. Each approach

to soul from the various schools held attractions for different patristic theologians. Plato gave a strong focus on the inherent immortality of the soul. At first this was resisted by many Christians as incompatible with the gospel message, and the concept of the "conditional immortality" of the soul was preferred: namely, that God would elevate the human being into immortal life (and not merely the soul but the body too), if (and only if) the creature was obedient to the covenant. Only after the third century did the presupposition of the soul's immortality became more commonly accepted in the Christian world. The dominant figures of *Augustine* and *Origen* were very influential for this development. In its turn, Stoicism gave to the church an attractive basis for reflecting on the manner in which the soul was the inner locus of the divinity: the place where the spark of Logos resided. It was not a far step to connect this with the vibrant New Testament image of the soul as the temple of the *Holy Spirit,* the place within where God indwelt the creature. Paul himself had seen the connection, and many of his own reflections on the psyche and the soul were influenced by that same mix of philosophical ideas current at the time, which would be available to the patristic theologians after him. For their part, they were the additional heirs of that Pauline synthetic language of soul-spirit-body (cf. 1 Cor. 6:20; 7:34; 1 Thess. 5:23), and even though it may have been a somewhat naïve attempt by Paul to reconcile some of the fluid ideas of his time on spiritual anthropology, nevertheless, because it was from an apostle it immediately became authoritative to the patristic tradition and shaped it to a degree. For its part, Aristotelianism gave to the church a strong sense of the soul as dynamic life force, directing the development of a whole organism, that is, its physical and emotional as well as its intellective and moral progress. The soul as an integrative center of moral awareness and choice was thus taken in from Aristotelianism and heavily used in Christian ethics, as well as in the later monastic writings on *ascetical* purification of the heart, as a primary preparation for mystical apprehension of God. All of this Christian articulation of a doctrine of soul was a vast philosophical and religious synthesis. It did not happen consciously, or with refined systematical coherence, perhaps, but nevertheless evolved over several centuries as significant Christian intellectuals tried to make interventions in the great disputes about the origin and nature of the soul as they were playing out in the ancient world. *Justin Martyr* was one of the first of the Fathers to take up specific interest in question. He criticized Platonic immortality theory by arguing that God created souls, they did not eternally preexist, and that the soul would be immortal only by God's gift, not because of its own life force (*Dialogue with Trypho* 4–5). Irenaeus, noting this, underlined the theology as a sharp characteristic dividing the biblical sense of creaturehood from the Platonic sense of the soul's self-subsistence (*Haer.* 2.19, 29, 33–34). *Irenaeus* also made moves to synthesize aspects of Stoicism, by arguing that the soul is the directive force (*hegemonikon*) in a human life, but not as Plato thought, for it is an integral function of the entire soul to be directed to God, not a separate aspect of a mere part of the soul (Plato's *to logistikon*). The Irenaean *exegesis* of the Pauline tripartite psychology of soul, body, and spirit interpreted it emphatically that spirit in this instance (1 Thess. 5:23) means the indwelling divine Spirit, not a separate humano-divine spirit as the Stoics (and perhaps some of his contemporary Christian gnostics) had suggested (*Haer.* 5.6.9). *Tertullian* was soon to put most of this Christian theology together in a compact treatise entitled *On the Soul*. He thought, from biblical premises, that the soul did not preexist at all but was transmitted to the child through the semen of the father in the act of conception, a view (Traducianism) that thereafter fought

with the alternative Christian belief that it was directly created by God at conception (Creationism) and put into the conceived embryo as God's direct consecration of each life. It was this Creationist presupposition that made abortion so evil an act in the mind of the early church. Tertullian also thought that the Stoics were probably right that this human soul was a very refined and ethereal substance, but not wholly "spirit" (that is, immaterial). It was the work of Origen that dramatically challenged *Tertullian*'s view. He was vividly aware that the soul was one of the great philosophical problems of the age, and outlined the varieties of belief on the subject in his *Commentary on the Canticle of Canticles* 1.8, and also in the preface to his *De principiis*. Origen taught that the soul was wholly incorporeal in its nature, had preexisted the material world, and was sent to earth, embodied, to fulfill its punishment for earlier sins in the heavenly domain. As such, it had the task of disciplining the body and thereby fixing its own reorientation to the divine. The soul was the seat and center of the creature as a spiritual entity, and was itself the locus of the *image of God* within mankind. After Origen the idea that the soul was a refined material substance more or less evaporated from Christian theology (cf. Origen, *Dialogue with Heracleides*). His ideas on the soul's preexistence were rejected soon after his time, but his thesis that the soul was the inner icon of God, immortal and ascentive, became the substrate for all later reflections, as it was perceived to be a brilliant synthesis, not only of the best of the various Greek schools themselves, but also a reconciliation of the philosophical problem of the soul with the overall thrust of the biblical account of the creature under God. In the West, Tertullian's thesis remained the most developed treatment on the idea until the time of Augustine, who revisited it in the light of later developments (*The Immortality of the Soul; The Soul and Its Origin; The Magnitude of the Soul*). Augustine was always beset by doubts as to the soul's origin. He was attracted to the idea of its preexistence but felt he could not subscribe to such a view as a bishop. Equally he was repelled by Tertullian's view of the soul's refined materiality, but still he relied on the theory of Traducianism to account for the transmission of original sin, something he felt was not incompatible with a Creationist view (as *Gregory of Nyssa* had already argued in *On the Soul and Resurrection*). He regularly entertained the idea that the soul was created by God directly, but was always unsure when this happened: whether at the act of creation or individual conception he was never sure. Augustine's own hesitations led to the idea being received in the West as something of a perennial "problem," an unresolved issue. It attracted some other thinkers, most notably a fine treatise *On the State of the Soul* by Claudius Mamertus, and one *On the Soul* by Cassiodorus; but generally speaking, the tendency before and after Augustine was that the church moved to a common consensus on creationism: that God directly created each soul, and that this direct touch of the "finger of God" accounted for the divine destiny of humankind, as distinct from all other life-forms on the earth. In the East after the fourth century the idea of soul was taken up energetically in the monastic writings. *Pseudo-Macarius* and *Evagrius* particularly influenced the reception of the widespread belief that the soul was the fundamental locus of the vision of God. The Pauline trichotomy of body-soul-spirit led the ascetical writers to regard the soul as a "midway station" between the bodily and spiritual motivations of an individual. The later ascetic writers, such as *Dionysius the Areopagite* and *Maximus the Confessor,* particularly illuminated the issue of the relation between soul and spirit by the concept of progressive *deification,* and hierarchical ascents to the deity.

E. L. Fortin, *Christianisme et culture philosophique au V-ième siècle: La querelle de l'âme humaine en Occident* (Paris, 1959); R. Markus, *Christian Faith and Greek Philosophy* (New York, 1964), 43–58; R. J. O'Connell, *The Origin of the Soul in Augustine's Later Works* (New York, 1987); R. Roukema, "Souls," in J. A. McGuckin, ed., *The Westminster Handbook to Origen* (Louisville, Ky., 2004).

Sozomen (fl. early fifth century) Salamon Hermias Sozomen was an important historian of the fourth-century church and the *Arian* crisis that troubled it. Sozomen was a native of Gaza who was educated by monks and, although he always preserved a deep affection for *ascetics* and a lively interest in monastic affairs in his writings, he remained a layman and was not particularly interested in the intellectual issues involved in the major theological controversies he records (although he writes from the viewpoint of the triumph of the Nicenes). He came to *Constantinople* c. 425, where he practiced law and was personally present during the crisis instigated by *Nestorius.* He shows in his writings a constant theme of criticism of bishops who abuse their powers. In 443 he composed his *Ecclesiastical History* and dedicated it to Emperor Theodosius II. His work covers the years from 325 to 425. It lacks an ending, which some have seen as evidence of the censorship of the imperial court for materials relating to the Theodosian dynasty's contemporary church policy. Sozomen depended on *Socrates'* *Ecclesiastical History,* which had just been published in the capital, and often uses it without acknowledgment. He is not as good as Socrates for isolating, acknowledging, or citing his other sources either, although his interest in church affairs among the *Armenians,* Goths, and Saracens is unique, and his clearer focus on significant affairs in the capital city (and in the Western *church*) is more acute than his rival. When he differs from Socrates he clearly has access to other materials, but it is now difficult to know what these were. His literary style is much more lively than that of Socrates (which is probably why he decided to write an alternative history in the first place), but he is the inferior scholar of the two. He sees the Byzantine church as God's establishment, with the emperors as sacred defenders of *orthodoxy.* He is very interested in recounting *hagiographical* stories as evidence of God's continuing involvement in the minutiae of history.

G. F. Chesnut, *The First Christian Histories: Eusebius, Socrates, Sozomen, Theodoret, and Evagrius* (2d ed., Macon, Ga., 1986); G. Downey, "The Perspective of the Early Church Historians," GRBS 6 (1965): 63–66; C. D. Hartranft, trans., *Sozomen: The Ecclesiastical History* (NPNF 2d ser.; New York, 1890).

Stoicism   A school of ancient Greek philosophy that derived from Zeno (c. 333–262 B.C.). It took its name from the Painted Colonnade (Stoa Poikile) at Athens, where Zeno first taught. Its major figures apart from its founder were Chrysippus, Panaetius, Posidonius, and Seneca (the Roman tutor of Nero). Stoicism evolved considerably over its long existence but was one of the dynamic influences on early Christian thinkers, for it was one of the most highly respected *philosophical* systems at the time of the appearance of the *church.* The Stoic view that the world was infused with divine sparks from the ultimate *Logos,* the immanent principle of divine order and reason which indwelt the souls of rational human beings, was an idea that the Christian Logos theologians adapted enthusiastically to their own ends. So too was the extensive system of Stoic ethics. The Stoics taught that order and synonymity with *nature* were primary ethical imperatives. The theory of Natural Law, also adapted to biblical prescripts, became of immense value to *patristic* thinkers. The pervasiveness of Logos as a common bond (a divine principle) marking our common humanity was a distinctive

mark of the Stoic school, which was thus one of the few philosophical movements in antiquity to speak openly about the equality of all rational human beings, and the inconsistency of social distinctions (not least *slavery*). Friendship was highly emphasized as the bond of charity that underpinned society. Such ideas also found a strong resonance among Christians. The school was deeply interested in logic and syllogistic argument. In the fourth century many of the Greek Fathers, not least *Gregory of Nazianzus* in his *Five Theological Orations* (*Orations* 27–31), used Stoic and Aristotelian logical rules to develop a systematic approach to major doctrines such as *Trinity* and *Christology. Tertullian* and *Lactantius* are among the Latin Fathers who show most influence of Stoicism in their works. The comparisons between Christian values and Stoic ethical ideals were so marked that later Christians forged a set of letters purporting to be a correspondence between St. Paul and his contemporary the Stoic philosopher Seneca. The Stoic cosmology, which envisaged the world as proceeding from one great fiery conflagration to another, with divine sparks of Logos scattering after each conflagration into *souls* and finally being drawn back together, is really like some vast Panentheist system. In its totality it was wholly opposed to Christianity, and not one of the Fathers adopted Stoic elements without substantively revising them. Nevertheless, in this philosophical system, as with much of *Platonism,* several of the patristic thinkers (especially *Justin Martyr, Clement of Alexandria, Origen,* and *Eusebius of Caesarea*) found here a form of propaideusis of the gospel message: if not an anticipation, at least a friendly element in Hellenistic society that could be positively adapted for the purposes of the Christian evangelistic mission.

J. M. Rist, *The Stoics* (Berkeley, Calif., 1978); M. Spanneut, *Le Stoicisme des pères de l'église: de Clément de Rome à Clément d'Alexandrie* (Paris, 1957); R. M. Wenley,

Stoicism and Its Influence (New York, 1963).

Stylites   *see* **Symeon Stylites**

Subordinationism

The term is a common retrospective concept used to denote theologians of the early *church* who affirmed the divinity of the Son or Spirit of God, but conceived it somehow as a lesser form of divinity than that of the Father. It is a modern concept that is so vague that it does not illuminate much of the theology of the pre-Nicene teachers, where a subordinationist presupposition was widely and unreflectively shared. The notion of "subordinationism" as wholly incompatible with the ascription of deity (in other words, the attribution of Godhead absolutely precludes limitations) was an insight that really rose to the fore in the *Arian* crisis of the fourth century. *Athanasius of Alexandria* and the *Cappadocian Fathers* were chiefly responsible for arguing how its implications could be expressed in terms of *Homoousian Christology* and the *Trinitarian* theology of three coequal divine *hypostases* sharing the same *nature*. After the fourth century Niceno-Constantinopolitan settlements, subordinationism was officially excluded from *patristic* conciliar orthodoxy.

A. Grillmeier, *Christ in Christian Tradition* (vol. 1; London, 1975); W. Marcus, *Der Subordinatianismus* (Munich, Germany, 1963); J. N. Rowe, *Origen's Doctrine of Subordination: A Study in Origen's Christology* (New York, 1987).

Symeon Stylites

(c. 390–459) The first, and most famous, of the Stylite *ascetics* who lived exposed to the elements in a life of ascetical penance on top of columns (*styloi*). They were attended by disciples who sent up food for the recluse and controlled the people who came to seek his advice and prayers.

Symeon began as a *Syrian* monk in monasteries near *Antioch* and eventually took to a form of eremitical life in the open air. He occupied a column drum but soon progressively raised it to avoid the press of crowds who came to him for intercession. His great fame, even in his own lifetime, classically exemplifies the rise of the cult of the holy man in the Near East. Western authors and monastics (especially *Benedict*) disapproved of the sensationalism of the Syrian forms of ascesis. Symeon had a notable impact on the church and imperial authorities of his time. His objections prevented Theodosius II from restoring synagogues to the Jews of Antioch, and he influenced Emperor Leo I to support the Chalcedonian cause in *Christology*. Extensive ruins still survive (including the base of his pillar) from the monastic complex that grew up around him (Qal'at Sim'an). Symeon's pupil, Daniel the Stylite (d. c. 493), set up his own column in *Constantinople* and exercised a similarly influential ministry there. There was later another Symeon the Stylite (the "Younger"; d. c. 596), who set up his column to the west of Antioch and became a cult figure for Byzantine *hagiography*.

R. Doran, trans., *Symeon Stylites: The Biographies* (Kalamazoo, Mich., 1988); S. Ashbrook Harvey, "The Sense of a Stylite: Perspectives on Simeon the Elder," VC 42 (1988): 376–94.

Synaxarion

The liturgical book of saints' lives, used by the Eastern Orthodox churches, arranged in short episodes for the appointed feasts of the year. The life of the saint of the day is read at the service of Orthros (Matins).

Synaxis

The Greek word is more or less a Christian invention signifying the assembly of believers, especially as gathered together for the *Eucharist*. By the fourth century, as can be seen in the writings of *Basil of Caesarea* (*Hom 1. on Ps.*

28) or *John Chrysostom* (*Hom. Act.* 29), it came to be a technical term for the Eucharist, especially the rite of communion within the divine *liturgy.* In Greek and Latin monastic usage of the fifth century it also acquired a secondary meaning of the assembly of monastics for prayer, particularly vigil services or services based on the Psalter (*Apophthegmata Patrum PG.65.*220), though the primary meaning of the term in the East and West remained that of the eucharistic assembly or the eucharistic rite itself.

E. Peretto, "Synaxis," in A. Di Berardino, ed., *Encyclopedia of the Early Church* (Cambridge, 1992).

Syncletica   One of the few "Desert Mothers" (*see* **asceticism, desert**), who have left behind an imprint (albeit small) on the textual tradition of Sayings of the Desert Fathers (*Apophthegmata Patrum*). This in itself suggests the large level of her original historical importance, given the more or less wholesale invisibility of early Christian women in the textually transmitted record of Christian origins. If Antony is called the "father of monks," Syncletica can rightly be called the "mother of female ascetics," and indeed Mother was one of the earliest titles ascribed to her by her disciples (*Amma*). She had a *Life* written about her, which was formerly attributed to **Athanasius the Great,** and while it is no longer commonly seen as by him, it is nevertheless of similar antiquity, and probably predates *Gregory of Nyssa's Life of Macrina,* thus making it the first recorded Christian woman's biography. Syncletica was a wealthy heiress who from an early age had lived at home as a consecrated *virgin.* On her inheritance of her merchant family's wealth, she devoted the money to establishing a common-life (cenobitic) house at **Alexandria** for female ascetics, which she headed, and where she gave spiritual teachings. She is therefore the first known female cenobitic founder for women's monasticism (*see* **Pachomius**).

Her few sayings that have survived illustrate a lively and independent spirit, who was revered in her time as an enlightened spiritual guide.

E. Bryson Bongie, trans., *The Life and Regimen of the Blessed and Holy Teacher Syncletica* (Toronto, 1997); K. Corrigan, "Syncletica and Macrina: Two Early Lives of Women Saints," *Vox Benedictina* 6, 3 (1989): 241–56.

Syria (*See also* **Antioch, Aphrahat, Asceticism, Bardesanes, Diodore, Encratism, Ibas, Jacob of Serug, Nestorius, Philoxenus, Severus, Tatian, Theodore, Theodoret, Virgins.**)   The ancient church of Syria was the cradle of Gentile Christianity. It was at the great city of **Antioch,** the capital of the Roman province, that Paul's ministry of preaching was first commissioned and financed, there that Peter took up residence, and there too that the Jesus movement was first called "Christian." It is most likely that the Gospel of Matthew was the liturgical book commissioned and produced by the Antiochene church. Syrian theology in the late first and early second centuries continued the highly charged **apocalyptic** character of the earliest Christian **kerygma.** Some of its early theologians such as Tatian, and his Encratite tendencies, demonstrate the way in which the first pattern of baptismal initiations in the Syrian church tended to be highly ascetic, only admitting to full church membership those who would enter the community of the *Ihidaya* and elect to be the celibate sons and daughters of the covenant. It was also in Syria that the monastic movement began to develop in the third century, beginning with virgin ascetics living secluded lives in the cities and spreading to clusters of nomadic monks living on the outskirts of villages and small towns. The countryside of the Syrian church (mountainous and difficult to traverse) extended from Antioch eastward to Persia, south to the Holy

Land, and northwest to Cappadocia and Armenia. It was in these directions that the Syrian church looked and found its natural alliances. Rome and Egypt were always "far away" both intellectually and politically, and throughout the patristic era a rivalry existed between the Syrians and the Alexandrians that had far-reaching consequences when, after the *Council of Ephesus I* (431), Alexandrian theologians managed to have the Syrian *christological* tradition censured and sidelined. During the *Arian* crisis, leaders of the Syrian church such as *Eustathius, Meletius of Antioch,* and *Eusebius of Samosata* nurtured a young body of intellectual clergy, including *Basil of Caesarea, Gregory of Nazianzus,* and *Diodore of Tarsus,* and formed them as bishops to take on the fight after them and bring the Nicene movement to a successful resolution at the *Council of Constantinople I* (381). The great city of Antioch was always Greek-speaking and fully hellenized in its *philosophy* and culture, but the local people also spoke Syriac. The writings of Syriac-speaking theologians such as Bardesanes, Ephrem, and Jacob of Serug show a vividly poetic and imagistic character that other parts of the Greco-Roman world of early Christianity could not equal. That influence came into Byzantine liturgical poetry through the medium of the Syrian *Romanos the Melodist.* Some of the greatest rhetoricians of the Syrian church in the late fourth and fifth centuries, not least *John Chrysostom,* wrote in pure Greek, though John is also known to have preached bilingually when he was a priest at Antioch. After the *christological* crises of the fourth and fifth centuries, allied with an increasing loss of political control from the Byzantine capital, the affairs of the Syrian Christians became more and more detached from the ambit of Constantinople and the Latin-Byzantine churches. The rising tide of Islam further isolated Syrian Christianity, and after the seventh century its history became one of relentless shrinkage under Islamic domination. In its powerful years, from the third to the sixth centuries, Syrian Christianity was a strongly evangelistic church, and sent missionaries to China, Persia, *Ethiopia,* and *India.*

W. S. McCullough, *A Short History of Syriac Christianity to the Rise of Islam* (Chico, Calif., 1982); R. Murray, *Symbols of Church and Kingdom: A Study in Early Syriac Tradition* (London, 1975); W. Wright, *A Short History of Syriac Literature* (London, 1894).

Tall Brothers (fl. 400)   The Egyptian monks Dioscorus (bishop of Hermopolis), Ammonius, Eusebius, and Euthymius were collectively known as the Tall Brothers both because of their height and because of their leading stature as intellectual theologians of the Origenian tradition (most heavily influenced by *Evagrius of Pontus,* whose recent death possibly encouraged the city authorities to move against his school). They came into conflict with *Theophilus,* the dominant archbishop of *Alexandria,* who censured them in 401, sparking off a long-running conflict among the Eastern monastic communities (over theological issues as well as attitudes to the episcopal control of monks) known as Origenism. They took their complaint to the canonical court of *John Chrysostom* at *Constantinople,* which Theophilus resented greatly, as his church had never fully consented to the canons of the *Council of Constantinople I* (381) that technically gave Constantinople legal precedence over Alexandria. Theophilus made the appeal of the Tall Brothers the occasion for a large delegation to the capital including himself, his nephew *Cyril of Alexandria,* and numerous suffragan bishops, where he orchestrated the deposition of John himself at the infamous Synod of the Oak (Chalcedon) in 403.

C. D. Hartranft, trans., *Sozomen: The Ecclesiastical History* (NPNF 2d ser.; New York, 1890).

Tatian One of the second-century *Apologists,* Tatian was a rhetorician from east *Syria* who converted to the Christian faith, and devoted the rest of his career to making a strong defense of it as a supreme philosophy that showed up all other paths to the truth. His *Oration to the Greeks* presents a strong castigation of contemporary morality and the inability of the Greek philosophical culture to come to the focus of a serious life. He was particularly critical of the manner in which *Rome* presumed it had a monopoly on culture, defining all external forces (including the Christians) as mere barbarians. As a result of his strong rhetoric on this theme he is often elevated as one of the early theological voices opposing any theological value in human culture (though it is an exaggerated view of his work). He is also an example of the strongly *ascetical* form of early *Syrian* Christianity. He advocated views that discouraged marriage for believers and demanded vegetarianism. In the *Encratite* views he espoused he was probably not too "out of the ordinary" in an early Syrian Christian context, though later Church Fathers looked at him askance, suggesting he had been influenced by *gnostic* ideas (Eusebius, *Ecclesiastical History* 4.29; Epiphanius, *Refutation of All Heresies* 1.3). He produced a synopsis harmonization of the four Gospels called the *Diatessaron,* which had great vogue in the Syrian churches for the next two centuries. Having traveled extensively, meeting with *Justin Martyr* at Rome, he spent his last years in Mesopotamia, where he headed a theological school.

G. F. Hawthorne, "Tatian and His Discourse to the Greeks," HTR 57 (1964): 161–88.

Tertullian (c. 160–225) Quintus Septimius Florens Tertullianus was a major Latin *apologist* from *North Africa,* who made a formative impact on the estab-

lishment of a technical Latin Christian vocabulary. His was a brilliant and pugnacious legal mind set to the service of the church in the era of *persecutions,* and despite his later (apparent) move to *Montanism,* his reputation as one of the founding minds of orthodox Latin theology was maintained by his successors, including *Cyprian, Lactantius,* and *Augustine.* He was the son of a centurion serving in Roman Africa and as a young man pursued a legal career at Rome. In middle age he was converted to Christianity, probably in Carthage (*Jerome* says he became a priest), and his knowledge of both Latin and Greek enabled him to make a study of the international Christian tradition. His style in apologetic is terse, and relies on caricature and ridicule (a standard element of lawroom argument in his day). It is not usually safe to deduce his opponents' real positions from Tertullian's way of dragging them round the room, but when he was not engaging in an explicit denunciation of foes outside or inside the church, he showed himself to be a reflective theologian. He had a gift for the telling phrase, and many of them still echo in the minds of Christians. Warning the authorities that their persecution policy was futile, he said, "The blood of martyrs is seed [for the church]." Speaking of the mystery of why God would reveal himself in the crucified and resurrected Christ, he argued: "I believe it precisely because it is absurd." Scornfully dismissing the ridicule of contemporary philosophers for the Christian movement, he replied: "What has Athens to do with Jerusalem?" And in his treatise *The Soul's Testimony,* where he argued that natural life is an instinctual witness to the divine presence, he made the bold apologetic statement: "The *soul* is naturally Christian." Modern readers find the dramatic style, his cultural rigorism (again not untypical of the general attitude in the African church), and his frequent misogyny to be barriers when reading him today. He enriched the

Latin theological literature by his knowledge of ecclesiastical customs and controversies from the East, not least by raising **Logos theology** to prominence in his theological schema. From around 205 his writings show an increasing respect for Montanist ideas, but the style of Montanism as it was then influential in North Africa was a much-moderated form of the original Asia Minor movement, and there is no clear indication that he ever broke from the catholic community. His major works include the *Apology* (written c. 197), where he makes a passionate appeal for legal toleration of Christianity. In a series of moral works addressed to Christians (*The Shows, The Crown, Idolatry, Repentance*), he severely warns them of the dangers of assimilation to the corrupt standards of contemporary society, and warns against adopting a military profession (largely because of the requirement to worship the imperial genius, though also with a conviction that such a life is contrary to the eirenic gospel). He wrote a work arguing (from the legal principle of prescription as "preliminary ruling out of order") that heresies could not be considered part of the Christian world at all (*Prescription against Heretics*). He followed **Irenaeus** in setting the principle of the **apostolic succession** as the proof of where **catholic** Christianity resided de facto. It was to have the effect of massively reinforcing the importance of catholic orthodoxy in the definition of the church. He composed a series of works attacking the ideas of the **gnostics** and **Marcion** (*Against Marcion, Against Hermogenes, The Resurrection of the Flesh, The Flesh of Christ*), taking up the central theme that Christ's incarnation was a true material reality that vindicated the material world and gave the promise of true resurrection to believers. He wrote a major attack (*Against Praxeas*) on the **Monarchians** addressed to one Praxeas (a "Busybody"), which was probably not a real name (it might be an ironic way of ridiculing Pope **Callistus** of Rome, his

contemporary, whom **Hippolytus** (a Logos theologian he respected) had also accused of Monarchianism. In this work Tertullian set out the foundations for what would become the Latin doctrine of the Trinity. He shows how Modalism is unscriptural, and sets out to explain how the Word and Spirit emanate as distinct **persons** from the Father, all possessing the same **nature**. His approach to **Christology** understood natures in the sense of legal possessions, which set Latin thought on a long path: Christ possesses two natures, but is only one person. His treatise *Baptism* gives interesting illumination about early–third-century liturgical practice (he dislikes infant **baptism**, which was becoming more common). His work *The Soul* introduces the idea of Traducianism, the concept that the soul was handed down along with all other aspects of life, from parent to child. It was a door that led to the concept of the transmission of "original sin" like a stain of guilt. It would be developed significantly by **Augustine** in his argument with **Pelagius**, and would come to cast a certain pessimistic shadow over all subsequent Latin thought. In his final years the renewed interest in eschatology and an increasing strain of rigorism marked what have been called his "Montanist period" works (*Monogamy, Exhortation to Chastity, On Fasting, Modesty*). This latter treatise was written c. 200 in anger at the bishop of Carthage's intention (like that of Pope Callistus) to allow the forgiveness of serious sexual sins to lapsed Christians (*see penance*).

T. D. Barnes, *Tertullian: A Historical and Literary Study* (Oxford, 1971); P. Holmes and S. Thelwell, trans., *Works of Tertullian* (ANF 3–4; Edinburgh, 1885); J. Morgan, *The Importance of Tertullian in the Development of Christian Dogma* (London, 1928); E. Osborn, *Tertullian: First Theologian of the West* (Cambridge, 1977); R. Roberts, *The Theology of Tertullian* (London, 1924).

Thaumaturgos   *see* **Gregory Thaumaturgos**

Theodore of Mopsuestia (350–428)

Theodore was the chief student of **Diodore of Tarsus** and was, along with him, one of the chief Syrian biblical interpreters in the "Antiochene School." Diodore and Theodore were to be posthumously caught up in the crisis over **Christology** after the **Council of Ephesus I** (431), when Theodore's younger students **Nestorius** and **Theodoret** opposed **Cyril of Alexandria.** The condemnation of Theodore at the **Council of Constantinople II** in 553 caused the loss of the majority of his biblical writings. Theodore's surviving exegesis shows a style that stresses the literal-moral reading of the biblical narratives through a careful historico-grammatical hermeneutic. His writing has a dynamic force comparable to that of **John Chrysostom.** Theodore was (perhaps) a friend of Chrysostom's (if he is the recipient of the *Exhortation to Theodore after His Fall*) and had resolved to follow a retired ascetical life after they completed rhetorical studies with the teacher Libanius. His decision to try for a political career instead stimulated Chrysostom to write to call him back to church service. In 383 Theodore was ordained priest, and in 392 was consecrated bishop of Mopsuestia in (Syrian) Cilicia. Throughout his life (and afterward in the Syrian church) he was regarded with high respect as "the Interpreter," and his theological authority was unchallenged in the annals of the Syrian writers. After Ephesus 431 Cyril of Alexandria consistently attacked his reputation as a precursor of "Nestorianism," and this caused his overshadowing in the Greek-speaking world. Even today there is no complete edition of his writings in English. Most of the nondoctrinal and nonexegetical works have been lost apart from three ascetical treatises: *On Priesthood*, *To the Monks*, and *Perfect Direction.* His theological work was in the pro-Nicene tradition, and his chief anti-Arian treatise was a *Defense of*

Basil against Eunomius (in which he followed the lead of **Gregory of Nyssa**). His *Dispute with the Macedonians* also survives in large part in a Syriac version. It derived from a public debate held in 392 at Anazarbus. An important anti-Apollinarist work entitled *The Assumer and the Assumed* is completely lost. Its title suggests the strong application of the New Testament titular Christology, which caused him to be censured later (since it was taken as synonymous with Diodore's "two subject" Christology, even though it was meant as a more careful restatement of his teacher's formulations). Theodore became aware of the Pelagian crisis and composed the treatise *Against Those Who Defend Original Sin.* He concluded that the Augustinian doctrine on this point is hostile to Christian tradition and accordingly gave a welcome to Bishop **Julian of Eclanum,** whom he thought had been unjustly condemned by the **papacy.** His chief work on theology was the fifteen books of *On the Incarnation.* It was a systematic exposition of Christology with attacks on the **neo-Arians** and **Apollinarists.** It was rediscovered in Syriac in 1905 and lost again in the course of the 1914–1918 war. It is now presumed destroyed and, being unpublished, is one of the great literary tragedies of the twentieth century. There are only fragments of the work that survive in other ancient treatises which refer to it. Another christological work (which comes at the same issue from liturgical and catechetical angles) was his *Catechetical Homilies.* This was rediscovered in Syriac version in 1932 and was published soon after. Theodore was noted for his robust attack on the "excesses" of Alexandrian allegorism. He preferred what he regarded as a "straightforward" reading of the text's historical-moral meaning. Most of his exegetical work has been lost. The catalogue originally included commentaries on Genesis and the remaining books of the Pentateuch, Psalms, major and minor prophets, Job, Ecclesiastes, and a letter on the Song of Songs, as well as

Matthew, Luke, John, Acts, and the major and minor Pauline Epistles. All that survives from this body of biblical work is Greek fragments from the *Genesis Commentary,* chaps. 1–3; the *Commentary on the Minor Prophets* (in the original Greek text); *Commentary on John* (in a Syriac version); *Commentary on Paul's Minor Epistles* (in a Latin version); fragments from the *Commentary on Paul's Major Epistles*; and a modern reconstruction by Devreesse (relating to the first eighty psalms only), gathered from various sources, of the *Commentary on the Psalms.* Theodore's custom was to preface his detailed comments on a biblical text with a generic preface where he outlined the book's overall character (its ethos), and discussed its author and the context in which it was composed. This is very similar to the standard (*Aristotelian*) *canons* for literary comment, which had been established in the Great Library at Alexandria. His comments on the Psalms show that he had already noted that many of the episodes narrated in the Psalms (such as the invasion of Jerusalem) were later than David's time, but were still composed by David, he argues, since he is traditionally known as the author of the Psalms, and so was acting proleptically in visionary terms as a prophet when he spoke of these things. There is rarely any explicit doctrinal application in Theodore's exegeses. Most of his writings become, as a result, an extended paraphrase of the biblical story. He especially wishes to root out the (Origenian) habit of cross-relating texts from different scriptural books, and regularly fights against number-symbolism, denying it has any mystical associations whatsoever. Theodore retains the Alexandrian sense of typology (*see allegory*) as underlying some passages of the Bible, but massively reduces the scope and extent of the types as compared to the Alexandrians. His chief legitimate types are Jonah as a symbolic foretelling of the death and resurrection of Jesus; the exodus as a type of the Passover of Christ; and the bronze serpent as a symbol of the passion. In short, he either follows a New Testament precedent or a liturgically established tradition. Whereas Athanasius had taken the whole book of Psalms to have christological reference, Theodore says there are only four psalms that can be so interpreted (Pss. 2; 8; 44 = 45; and 109 = 110). Numerous Old Testament texts that had, until his time, commonly been taken christocentrically or ecclesiologically (such as Malachi 4:2. (= 3:20 in the LXX—the Sun of Righteousness), he says can be entirely explicated as having reference to events that were accomplished in the time of the prophets themselves. He is the only patristic commentator who denies that the bride and groom of the Song of Songs is a reference to Christ and the church. He tries to give a systematic rule to explain when *typology* should be followed and when avoided. To be useful as a type, he argues, the Old Testament episode must (a) have obvious correlations with its New Testament anti-type, (b) be inferior in its import and contextual weight to the New Testament episode it adumbrates, and (c) have a good moral impact that can be applied sensibly in preaching. Theodore's very heavy restriction on the use of the Old Testament for typological interconnections demonstrates his generic preference for reading the Hebrew Bible as a closed system that maintained a pre-Christian religious dispensation, which was superior to Hellenism but was destined to give way before the coming of the new covenant. The latter was ushered in by the newly revealed doctrine of the *Trinity.* Christ's *incarnation* reveals the new *economy* between God and humanity (synopsized in the doctrine and belief of the Trinity, into which a new race would be baptized) and is a new holy text that brings its own meaning, illuminating the old, not being illuminated by it. He lays over all his *exegeses* a macrocontext of his doctrine of the Two Ages. Christ's incarnation ushers in the future age. The New Testament is, therefore, the initiation of the next age and looks to the future, never to the past. Typology, for Theodore, is a theological trend that seems to want to make the New Testament tied to the Old. But he sees the latter as a series of books that cannot do other than look to the past. As they are rooted in history, they have to be historically unraveled. But since the New Testament is focused in another direction, looking to an *apocalyptic* future, proleptically charged, then it cannot be explicated by history since it explicates history itself, and can only be interpreted in the light of *eschatology*. His established custom of reading the text literally and sequentially makes his *Commentary on John* one of the least inspiring versions of that Gospel in patristic literature. Some see his polarized sense of the strong difference between the two Testaments as helping his understanding of Pauline thought. Previous Pauline exegesis had tried to harmonize all aspects of Paul with the Old Testament because of widespread anti-Marcionite anxiety. John Chrysostom and Theodore are probably the best of the ancient commentators on Paul. Modern commentators, not always seeing the point of his distinction between historical and transhistorical hermeneutics, have often (quite wrongly) hailed him as a precursor of modern historical-critical biblical interpretation.

R. Devreesse, ed., *Le Commentaire de Theodore de Mopsueste sur les Psaumes* (Rome, 1933); A. Mingana, ed., *The Commentary of Theodore of Mopsuestia on the Nicene Creed* (vol. 2; Cambridge, 1932); R. A. Norris, *Manhood and Christ* (Oxford, 1963); H. B. Swete, ed., *Theodori episcopi Mopsuesteni in epistulas B. Pauli commentarii* (vols. 1–2; Cambridge, 1880–1882); H. N. Von Sprenger, ed., *Theodori episcopi Mopsuesteni Commentarius in XII Prophetas* (Gottingen, Germany, 1977); D. Z. Zaharopoulos, *Theodore Mopsuestia on the Bible* (New York, 1989).

Theodoret of Cyrrhus (c. 393–460)

Theodoret was a Syrian bishop and the-

ologian who was deeply involved in the *christological* controversy between *Cyril of Alexandria* and *Nestorius* (*Council of Ephesus I* [431]). He represented (much more than Nestorius) a balanced form of the Syrian theological tradition and was engaged by patriarch John of Antioch to make a reasoned statement of why the Syrians found Cyril's "One Nature" Christology offensive. Theodoret attacked Cyril for his preference for the use of the word *hypostasis* to designate the principle of single subjectivity in Christ, thinking that it led the mind toward an overly materialist, or essentialist, view of what was fundamentally a spiritual mystery of union. In his late christological writings such as *The Beggarman* (*Eranistes*), he quietly changed his opinion and acceded to the hypostasis language that Cyril had established as an international standard. He always believed Cyril's position was defective, and the *Eranistes*, written in 447, three years after Cyril's death, was meant as an attack on his reputation. It brought him into conflict with *Dioscorus of Alexandria*, who orchestrated his legal confinement to his Syrian diocese (as a trouble-maker), and then secured his deposition at the *Council of Ephesus II* (449). He was reinstated (though with much controversy, and only after he was reluctantly compelled to anathematize his friend Nestorius) at the *Council of Chalcedon* (451); but his name was symbolic of all focused "Two Nature" resistance to the Cyrilline christological doctrine, and his enemies ensured that he would be posthumously anathematized as a "Nestorian" at the *Council of Constantinople II* (553) (*see Three Chapters controversy*). He was born at Antioch and educated by monks, becoming an ascetic bishop at the small Syrian town of Cyrrhus in 423. At Cyrrhus (sometimes wrongly written as Cyrus in recent books), a small town in the Syrian hinterland, he undertook many public building works (bridges he constructed are still standing in the area) and was active as a writer. His *History of the Monks of Syria* is an important source for the lives of leading Syrian ascetics of his day. He also composed a *Church History* that covers the years 323–428, with special reference to the Syrian patriarchate.

B. Jackson, trans., *The Ecclesiastical History, Dialogues, and Letters of Theodoret* (NPNF 2d ser.; New York, 1892); J. A. McGuckin, *St. Cyril of Alexandria and the Christological Controversy* (Leiden, Netherlands, 1994); R. M. Price, trans., *Theodoret of Cyrrhus: A History of the Monks of Syria* (Kalamazoo, Mich., 1986); R. V. Sellers, *Two Ancient Christologies* (London, 1954).

Theodosius the Great (346–395)

Theodosius I was a Spanish general whom Gratian appointed to supreme power (379) in the Eastern provinces after the disastrous death of the emperor Valens (378), who was trying to prevent massive influxes of Gothic tribes into the Roman Empire. By virtue of his military campaigns and by political treaty he pacified the Visigoths and admitted them into the Roman army (a policy that would later have severe disintegrative effects in the West). On Gratian's death in 383 Theodosius became the last Augustus of the undivided empire. He acknowledged the rebellion of Maximus in 384, but eventually came westward to defeat him and assist the junior emperor Valentinian II. In 390 he sent a punitive expedition against Thessalonica, whose citizens had murdered the military governor, and many citizens were slaughtered. It was the occasion of the insistence of *Ambrose of Milan* that he should do penance before he could be admitted to communion—a canonical action that was later amplified as a symbol of the moral superiority of the bishops over emperors. Having returned to the capital at *Constantinople* in 391, Theodosius undertook a second campaign in the West in 394 to suppress the pagan revolt under the imperial pretender Eugenius. He died at Milan early in the next year. He was remembered by Christians mainly as the first of a series of powerful "orthodox" emperors (his Western roots made Nicenism the ancestral faith of his family) who came into the Eastern world and imposed a sharp change of policy after a long series of pro-Arian rulers. His policy reversal was seen markedly in the career of *Gregory of Nazianzus,* whose occupancy of the see of Constantinople Theodosius confirmed after ejecting the Arian incumbent Demophilus. Theodosius called the *Council of Constantinople* (381) to settle *christological* and *Trinitarian* controversies, and afterward progressively penalized the profession of *Arianism.* He was the first of the Christian emperors so openly to penalize "paganism," a pugnacity that resulted from the fact that he was unusually baptized early in his reign, having given up hope of life after an illness contracted during his campaign in Thessalonica on his way to take his Eastern capital. He instructed, in the *canons* of the Council of Constantinople, that the Eastern capital should be given equal precedence with Rome in church affairs, something that reflected political realities, but which long remained a source of friction between the Eastern and Western churches. With the encouragement of several hierarchs (such as Ambrose of Milan), Theodosius legally prohibited animal sacrifice and legalized the church's sequestration of many pagan temples. He was succeeded by his son Arcadius (395–408). Theodosius II (408–450), his grandson, continued the dynasty's policy for a strong support of orthodoxy.

N. Q. King, *The Emperor Theodosius and the Establishment of Christianity* (London, 1961); C. E. V. Nixon, *Pacatus: Panegyric to the Emperor Theodosius* (Liverpool, U.K., 1987); S. Williams and G. Friell, *Theodosius: The Empire at Bay* (New Haven, Conn., 1995).

Theodotus the Banker   *see* Monarchianism

Theodotus the Cobbler (or Tanner) *see* Monarchianism

Theodotus the Gnostic *see* Gnosticism, Valentinus

Theophilus of Antioch Theophilus was bishop of *Antioch* in the late second century, and was one of the *Apologists*. Of his writings there survives a work of apology entitled *To Autolycus* (see Eusebius, *Ecclesiastical History* 4.24; Jerome, *On Illustrious Men* 25; *Epistle* 121.6.15). In it Theophilus tried to demonstrate the superiority of the religion of Christ and its views on morality and the origins of the world, in contrast with the Olympian myths, which, he argued, taught only examples of immorality and idolatry. His is the first Christian exposition of the book of Genesis as a creation theology. He developed *Logos theology* more than any Christian thinker had before him, and was thus a precursor of the predominance of the Logos school in the next century (*see* **Clement of Alexandria, Hippolytus, Origen**). In reference to the doctrine of creation Theophilus speaks of a time when God's Logos was immanent within him in an undifferentiated way (*Logos endiathetos*), but then sees the Logos as extrapolated, for the purposes of the creation of the cosmos, through the medium of holy wisdom (*Logos prophorikos*). He thus is an early exponent of *Trinitarian* theology as a manner of conceiving the *economy* of God's *salvation* of the world. In his works the term Triad (*trias*) makes it theological debut.

R. M. Grant, *Theophilus of Antioch: Ad Autolycum* (Oxford, 1970); R. Rogers, *Theophilus of Antioch: The Life and Thought of a Second-Century Bishop* (Lanham, Md., 2000).

Theotokos The Greek term means "God-birther." It is usually translated as Mother of God (Latin: *Mater Dei*; Greek:

Mēter Theou), though in fact this older title was displaced (at least in Greek-speaking Christianity) by the immense popularity of the Theotokos title after the fifth century. It began as an Egyptian Christian title for the *Virgin Mary* that was probably designed to offset common pagan use of the same term to designate Isis (the "mother of the god" Horus). It moved internationally, through the works of *Origen* and others, to enter common Christian usage in the early fifth century. When *Nestorius* came to his new see at *Constantinople* in 428, he discovered that it was a popular term of piety there, and he took it in hand to suppress it, arguing that it was a paganism that did not do justice to the complexities of the Christian doctrine of the incarnation. Mary was not the "Mother of God," he argued, since God has no origin; rather she was the mother of Jesus, or even the Mother of Christ (*Christotokos*). When the news of this came to the ears of *Cyril of Alexandria*, he recognized an attack on his own ecclesial tradition of piety: not merely Marian devotion, but the whole Egyptian-Alexandrian tradition of high *Christology*, which was accustomed to using strong juxtaposed paradoxes (such as "God in swaddling bands," or the "sufferings of God") to express the dynamic of the salvation effected in the divine *incarnation.* Cyril rose to the occasion and defended the title Theotokos as the supreme safeguard of a belief in the deity of Jesus. To Nestorius's claim that Theotokos was not "strictly accurate" theology, he replied that "If Mary is not, strictly speaking (*akribos*) the Mother of God (Theotokos), then the one who was born from her is not, strictly speaking, God." So the battle was joined, and the result was the *Council of Ephesus I* (431), where the title Theotokos was endorsed as an ecumenical expression of faith in the divinity of Jesus and the special reverence that ought to be afforded to the Virgin Mother of God. It was reaffirmed as an "ecumenical" theology at the *Council of Chalcedon* (451).

G. A. Maloney, "Mary and the Church as Seen by the Early Fathers," *Diakonia* 9 (1974): 6–19; J. A. McGuckin, "The Paradox of the Virgin-Theotokos: Evangelism and Imperial Politics in the 5th Century Byzantine World," *Maria: A Journal of Marian Theology* 3 (autumn 2001): 5–23; idem, *St. Cyril of Alexandria and the Christological Controversy* (Leiden, Netherlands, 1994).

Three Chapters Controversy (sixth century)   The Three Chapters were texts from the leading Syrian "Two Nature" theologians: *Theodore of Mopsuestia, Theodoret of Cyrrhus,* and *Ibas of Edessa.* All, in their own way, were vehement opponents of the "One Nature" *Christology* propagated by Cyril of Alexandria, which was in the ascendancy at the *Councils of Ephesus* (431, 449) and in a moderated form at the *Council of Constantinople II* (553). More or less as soon as the *Council of Ephesus I* (431) was concluded, Cyril realized that his deposition of *Nestorius* was hardly an achievement when the entire Syrian patriarchate seemed to share his theological sentiments about the duality of natures in Christ (something he took, wrongly, to be tantamount to a confession of double subjectivity in Christ— the heresy of Nestorius). The Syrians, by contrast, regarded his own insistence on the single personality of Christ to be a claim that Christ only had one single *nature* (presumably a hybrid of divine and human). In this they too were mistaken, as neither position was what the other school was advocating; but the confusions of an imprecise and unestablished terminology severely hindered open communication, apart from the fact that many political scores were in the process of being settled. Cyril, after 431, turned his attentions to denigrating the wider Syrian tradition in the persons of their deceased "great teachers" Theodore and *Diodore.* Theodoret and Ibas took to themselves the task of denigrating Cyril. After years of christologi-

cal confusion, and division of the churches in the Eastern church, the emperor *Justinian* believed that a reconciliation between the moderate Monophysites (strongly Cyrilline) and the Eastern Chalcedonians (also strongly Cyrilline) could be effected by symbolically denouncing the (now dead) Syrian opponents of Cyril. He issued a christological edict to this effect in 543–544 (confirmed at the council of 553). The policy alienated *Rome,* which saw in it a disguised attempt to reduce the significance of the divisive *Council of Chalcedon* (451), and ultimately it did not achieve the reconciliation it sought after. Even so the writings (chapters) of the three were used as evidence to anathematize their persons, thus deeply alienating many parts of the *Syrian* church, which was thus accelerated in its progressive departure from the imperial Christian world.

W. H. C. Frend, *The Rise of the Monophysite Movement* (Cambridge, 1972), 274–82.

Timothy Aelurus (d. 477)   Timothy Aelurus was *Monophysite* patriarch of *Alexandria* from 457 to 460, when he was replaced on the throne by the Chalcedonian Timothy Salofaciolus (the "Wobble-Hat" or the "White-Hat"), and again assuming the throne between 475 and 477. He himself was known as Timothy the "Cat" or the "Weasel" (Aelurus), either from his small stature (according to his friends) or from his creeping political tendencies (according to his enemies). He had been part of the entourage of *Dioscorus* at the *Council of Ephesus II* (449), and was himself an important leader of the resistance to the *Council of Chalcedon* (451) in Egypt, and prefigured the tradition of *Severus of Antioch,* preferring a reversion to the theology of *Cyril of Alexandria* as the *christological* standard for the church. Timothy Wobble-Hat assumed the patriarchal throne again on the death of Aelurus, demonstrating how severely the

Council of Chalcedon had divided and destabilized the Egyptian church in this period.

R. Y. Ebied and L. R. Wickham, "A Collection of Unpublished Letters of Timothy Aelurus," JTS (n.s.) 21 (1970): 321–69; idem, "Timothy Aelurus: Against the Definition of the Council of Chalcedon," in C. Laga, ed., *After Chalcedon* (Louvain, Belgium, 1985), 115–66.

Tome of Leo   *see* **Christology, Council of Chalcedon [451], Leo the Great**

Trade Routes   Christianity spread through the ancient world with considerable rapidity. At the end of the first century (an impression gained from viewing the recorded sites of known church communities—conveniently listed in the end maps of Van der Meer and Mohrmann), it was a religion that had moved through the range of Diaspora synagogues and was like a loosely connected string of pearls within the empire. By the mid–third century it had evolved into a socially rooted macrocommunity that had already laid down international channels of interchurch communication, and was a force that had to be reckoned with by wider society (the era of the *persecutions* attests this most clearly). Within a century after this, it would subvert the very governmental system itself, founding a new Christian imperium in the process. The wonderment of the spread of the new religion was not lost on the Christians themselves. Thinkers such as *Melito of Sardis, Hippolytus,* and *Origen* thought that it was a great *mystery* of the *economy* of God that *Rome* had provided so many roads and interconnected cities for the easy spread of the gospel to mankind (*Eusebius of Caesarea* would express this classically in his fourth-century work, *Preparation for the Gospel*). Here they all reflected the common conception of Mediterranean thinkers that the empire of Rome was the *oikoumene*—the limits of the world. The Roman mind-set, in one sense, saw nothing beyond that boundary (all those not of the empire were "bearded ones," that is, barbarians). Our modern conception of "the world" might lead us to wonder what it would have been like if the major *patristic* writers were less centered on the Mediterranean as a "Roman lake" and more interested in the vast domains that lay outside: the Celtic territories to the north (Germany, Gaul, Britain, and Ireland); the immense land of China and India to the southeast; the whole vastness of sub-Saharan Africa; the mountainous passes to Persia; or the caravan routes through Arabia. The map of world Christianity will show, of course, that those territories outlying the Roman Empire were not only peripheral mentally and geographically to the ancient conception of the *oikoumene*, but proved, historically, to be less durable in terms of missionary outreach, or church endurance. Christianity could survive bitter persecutions, if brief enough, but centuries of sustained hostility and systemic oppression could evidently wipe out the vestiges of once vibrant churches, as can be proven all too readily today in terms of Asia Minor Christianity, Syrian Christianity, the ruined cities in the sand that were once the world of *Augustine,* or the church of the Middle East, which once had the eye of the world upon it, waiting for news of the latest *liturgical* styles (*see Jerusalem*). The central locus of the Christian church (once firmly rooted in Asia Minor around the hub of *Constantinople*) has progressively been eroded and pushed westward so that its epicenter is now, probably, somewhere in the southern states of the United States. Innumerable factors can account for this, not least the progressive erosion of Eastern Christianity before the advance of Islam. That was a powerful factor from the seventh century onward, and although it reached critical proportions for Byzantine Christianity after the eleventh century, its impact had been more devastating much earlier for the Christians of the world east of Syria. The armies of Islam had not materialized out of nowhere, of course; Turkic traders had already settled Asia Minor generations before, and the final advance of the Ottoman armies was merely the last act in a long drama of the erosion of Byzantium as the supremely great trade power (and therefore sea and military power) of the Eastern world. As its ships declined so did its hold on the religious loyalties of its once-great domains. The spread or decline of Christian communities was closely related to the ancient trade routes. Down the trade routes, both those of sea and land, followed the armies or ships of the great powers who protected the routes. War in antiquity, as today, was not about honor or territory, but security and the tribute of cash or taxes. If we followed the routes we would have a far better picture of the spread of the church in the patristic era than any we can construct retrospectively from contemporary, Euro-American–dominated visions that lead us to the anachronistic position that Christians today are often surprised to hear that the church existed in Africa probably from the first century, in a most sophisticated indigenous culture, or that it was a powerful religion in Iraq in the third, one that could even send out missionaries to mainland China before the seventh century. The western migration of Christianity (or maybe we should call it a "forced march") has been so marked in the early modern centuries that it is all too easy to forget that Christianity was originally a religion *ex oriente*. The trade routes are thus relevant for our purposes of reimagining Christian origins. First of all, they can be considered as a sea revolution around the Mediterranean. Christianity soon populated the shores in a complete circle. Palestine was insignificant in most regards (except for its religious symbolism) and the churches there did not really flourish powerfully until the building of pilgrimage centers in the fourth century. This was because

Palestine had little to trade. It would register on the map of the church mainly for its *deserts* and its shrines. The real centers of the church were the trading posts: the great Mediterranean cities of *Rome, Alexandria,* Carthage, each with outlying territories that brought to the local urban centers their own lively trade with the farthest-flung posts of empire. *North Africa,* Latin-speaking and conservative in nature, was closely bonded with its natural trade center of Rome, and so the whole character of earliest Latin Christianity was formed. Rome also traded extensively with the East, through the sea routes to Asia Minor and the Greek mainland. All of the major seaports of the Asian coast—Pergamum, Smyrna, Ephesus, Miletus, and then on the southern coast through to Antioch and Beirut—were significant from the earliest ages of Christianity (many of them appearing in the book of Revelation). They were cities in constant contact with Rome and Alexandria as the great magnets of Mediterranean trade. So it is, for example, that we find *Irenaeus,* an Asia Minor Christian, as bishop of Lyons in Gaul, advocating for Christians of his Asian homeland with the pope in Rome as early as the second century. The great thinkers, such as *Justin* the Samaritan philosopher, *Ignatius* the captive bishop, *Hippolytus* the first international theologian (*Origen* too), *Marcion* the millionaire ship-owner, or the many *gnostic* Didaskaloi, all were attracted to Rome to try to make their name, and in the process changed and deepened the discourse of Christianity. The great imperial roads stretched out from city to city in stations crossing the land mass of Asia Minor, always ready to send massed armies in forced marches to the eastern borders in Mesopotamia. In peaceful times the same roads carried the produce of the East westward, also connecting up with the Silk Road in the northeast into China. In the south, the journey through Arabia to India was supplemented by the sea routes from the Red Sea (always poised for connection with Alexandria and **Ethiopia** and the great Christian culture of **Nubia** [Sudan], which lay interposed between them and served as a filter of Christianity into the heart of Africa). The first settled Christian communities of Persia clustered around the mouth of the Persian Gulf and then spread out in a crescent, reaching northwest along the camel caravan routes to the interior, and on to Samarkand. The same sea routes from Ethiopia along the Arabian coast connected with **India** and account for the first settlement of Christians there along the eastern coastal regions: a connection between India and Syria dating back to at least the third century that still marks the history and culture of the ancient church of Ethiopia. More adventurously, perhaps, because it was a voyage into the fearful unknown, ships left the Gibraltar straits and headed out into the wild Atlantic to travel north for tin and silver from the British Isles. So connections were made that were once vibrant between the pre-Roman churches of southern Britain and **Ireland** and the Coptic communities of the Mediterranean southern littoral. The church in the Celtic Irish and British islands clung like moss in the wild weather to the rocks and endured through three foundational periods (Roman colonial, Celtic, papal Saxon) from the first century to the seventh (still evident in its mix of Celtic and Roman traditions), eventually stabilizing in its last refoundation in Britain and Ireland, again after economic invasion by the "Men of the North," the Normans of the eleventh century. The Byzantines, by strategic political alliances, extended the Christian culture progressively to the north, even as they were losing ground to the southeast to Islam. The tenth-century fur traders of Rus, and even Scandinavia, were progressively drawn into their orbit, and finally stabilized as a great Christian culture that could not be burned out by the successive raids of the peoples of the ever-farther north, the Mongols, who could never escape their

nomadic mentalities and thus were ill fitted to found an enduring system such as the church had learned from Roman urban examples. China was always a high wall. It could be approached only by the Silk Road, and was never colonized along its coastal towns as it was simply too far to reach. Christianity loved to move through the poor and immigrant communities of the large port cities to which it sailed and traveled with the goods of the world. Our vision of the spread of Christianity is often romantically linked to missionaries and monks: apostles sailing out with one or two companions to plant a *cross* and build a church. This is so largely because the understanding of Christian missionary outreach is still so partial and unknown that one often relies on biblical paradigms and legendary stories to account for the great deal that we simply do not know. The reality is that the greatest of all Christian missionaries have been the ancient Christian merchants, travelers, sailors, soldiers and their accompanying families, and then the monks who stayed there to serve them and their needs, and the clergy who finally built the churches to mark their arrival as a wealth-owning minority. One of the aspects of the genius of Christianity has always been its readiness to move and begin again, always interested to be where the stir of life, commerce, and culture can be felt.

R. Foltz, *Religions of the Silk Road: Overland Trade and Cultural Exchange from Antiquity to the 15th Century* (New York, 1999); A. H. M. Jones, *The Roman Economy: Studies in Ancient Economic and Administrative History* (Totowa, N.J., 1974); E. Van der Meer and C. Mohrmann, *Atlas of the Early Christian World* (London, 1958).

Tradition   The Latin term (*traditio*) and the Greek counterpart (*paradosis*) both acquired technical meanings from the New Testament onward (cf. the significant use of the word *paradosis* in

1 Cor. 11:23) signifying tradition as the central core of evangelical experience that was communicated from Jesus to the apostles and through them to the Christian world. Tradition was elevated by *Irenaeus* in the second century as the ultimate safeguard against *gnostic* "innovations," in an age when Christian self-identity was being publicly challenged by numerous streams of redefinition. It was he who, in the *Adversus haereses*, popularized the model of tradition as a conservatory force (not necessarily a conservative one) that guarded the transmission of the message of salvation through a regularly constituted order (*taxis*) from Jesus, to the apostles, to the early episcopal teachers such as himself, who maintained the apostolic succession of the *kerygma*. Tradition in the Irenaean sense was the vital force of authentic evangelism, much more than it was the conservative mechanism whereby the church from generation to generation was able to filter out what it felt was harmful, or inauthentic, to its central self-identity (what could be called its integral "tradition"). Jesus himself was noticeably less than patient with those who could not differentiate between the "customs of men" and the perennial demands of the Word of God alive in his generation. His anger was directed at those who resisted the dynamic process of the saving Spirit, by opposing to it deliberately "deadening" appeals to past "traditions" (Mark 7:13). In his argument with the Pharisees over the significance of traditions, Jesus was not opposing a developmental sense of theology to a "static" or "traditionalist" one; rather, he was opposing a concept of living tradition to a traditionalist attitude that opportunistically served to screen the elect community from the ever-present demands of God over his people. In the apostolic age, St. Paul operated with a double sense of tradition. At some times he is conscious of how carefully he must deliver to others "what I myself received" (1 Cor. 11:2, 23; 15:1–4), especially when it concerns tra-

ditions about the Lord, or *liturgical* process. At other times, in advancing the cause of the church's effective preaching of the message of salvation he is more than conscious of how the risen Lord has empowered him to "seize the moment" (*kairos*), and how he himself authoritatively transmits his own contribution to the tradition, with the authority of no less than Christ, whom he serves apostolically. The first concept of tradition Paul sees as an unchanging verity. The second he sees as economically related to the saving kerygma, and changing across the times as the servant of the efficient proclamation of the gospel in various conditions (1 Cor. 7:10–12, 25, 40). In his times of conflict with other apostolic missionaries of the Jerusalem church, who resisted his boldly "innovative" apostolate to the Gentiles, Paul is ready to use this missionary sense of tradition not merely as a flexible kerygmatic tool ("I have become all things to all people," 1 Cor. 9:22), but even in a fixed and canonical sense. He warns his disciples in several places to keep fast to the traditions he gave them, and to keep away from those who did not live accordingly (1 Thess. 2:15; 3:6). The generation after Paul, less confident than their teacher, represents a correspondingly more cautious attitude and speaks of that "deposit" of tradition that has to be preserved by the church with nothing added or taken away (1 Tim. 6:20). The sense of kerygmatic adaptability was being conditioned at this period, on the cusp of the first and second centuries, by an imminent sense of the end times approaching. In the writings of *Clement of Rome*, later in that same generation, one witnesses the first attempt to make the tradition synonymous with that which the presbyters and bishops of the church both represent and protect. This first attempt to make the tradition aligned very closely with "authoritative preaching" on the part of church leaders was really the first formally elaborated *patristic* concept of tradition (more exactly a doctrine of the episcopal inheritance of the charism of authority). It proved insufficiently flexible to meet the large range of challenges to church unity that the second century threw out. In the following generation, witnessed both in **Tertullian** and **Irenaeus,** who were much exercised with the problem of how to distinguish authentic tradition from heretical imposture, the broader principle of an appeal to the community's sense of basic truths was more noticeably elevated. For Irenaeus the question of what was true tradition could be proven by appeal to the record of the main apostolic centers, the ancient and leading churches. He further developed his thought by suggesting that the apostolic churches possessed the "charism of truth" in a special way (*Adversus haereses* 4.26.2). This was manifested above all in the manner in which they interpreted the Scriptures: soberly, and with *catholic* consensus. In this context he developed his famous image of the interpretative "key" (*hypothesis*), which the church owned but which others do not possess. It was to grow into the fuller patristic concept of the *mens ecclesiae*, the "mind of the church," what **Athanasius** was later to call the church's *dianoia* and its instinctive sense of the true intentionality (*skopos*) of both Scripture and tradition, that is, the comprehensive overview given to the Spirit-illumined faithful, which was radically partialized and distorted by **heretical** dissidents. For Irenaeus, the heretics were those who did not possess the "key" to the Scriptures. They reassembled the pieces of a mosaic (he uses the idea of a mosaic of a king) and made it up again from the original parts but now representing a dog's head, foolishly claiming that they were authentic because their mosaic bits were original (*Adversus haereses* 1.8.1). Irenaeus added further to the fundamental vocabulary of the theology of tradition when he developed the argument that the key to biblical interpretation was the "canon of truth" (*Adversus haereses* 3.2.1), which in the Latin version of his works gave to the West (decisively so in the hands of Ter-

tullian) the principle of the Rule of Faith: *Regula Fidei,* or *Regula Veritatis.* This *Regula,* Irenaeus says, is the strongest refutation of gnostic variability, for it is maintained in all the churches and goes back to the apostles. Apostolic succession, then, is not primarily a matter of succession of individual bishops one after another, but the succession of apostolic teaching from the time of apostles to the present. In the third century Origen adopted most of Irenaeus's sense of living tradition, but further developed the Irenaean emphasis on the necessity of Spirit-filled guardians of the tradition. For **Origen,** however, this was not necessarily the bishops; rather, those Christians who had been purified and illuminated by God, so as to serve publicly and visibly as authoritative teachers. Nevertheless, by the middle of the fourth century the episcopal principle and that of the inspired theologian were both wearing rather thin as reliable ways to interpret the scriptural intent in a time of crisis. When the **Arian** controversy hit the church it reacted instinctively by appealing to an older process of solving problems from the end of the second century: that is, by holding regional synods where the church leaders would decisively address problems and offer solutions in a synodal consensus. At first the "international" (ecumenical) synodical principle had a hopeful beginning, but soon **Constantine's** restless policy changes and the strife of bishops left the aspirations for public harmony in tatters. The fourth century saw the hope of an ecumenically led principle of synodical government hopelessly compromised as one synod countermanded and anathematized another. Throughout this period, whether for the perceived good or ill, Christian emperors had increasingly taken charge of the "policing" of Christian orthodoxy. Often they used leading bishops to show the way, or they themselves endorsed synods, called them into being, or enforced them; but all in all their own role as the "God-graced emperor" and "defender of the faith" emerged as a distinctive new force in the preservation and definition of "tradition." Many theologians have not sufficiently recognized, perhaps being unwilling to do so, that the Byzantine emperors were very serious in regard to their role as guardians and protectors of the faith, using predominantly a legal approach to the issue of the charism of authenticity. Nonetheless, they played a radical role in the church from the fourth to the fifteenth centuries, and in Romania and Russia, even beyond. To this extent the Christian emperors were in a large measure the historical heirs, or at least co-heirs, of the synodical principle of defining Christian tradition. The question over the identifying marks of tradition rose again acutely at the end of the Arian period over the issue of the deity of the Holy Spirit. Here significant theologians such as *Athanasius, Basil,* and *Gregory of Nazianzus* all consciously theologized about the way in which tradition could make new statements about fundamental matters of faith that had not been explicitly witnessed hitherto. Gregory's *Oration* 31 describes his own role in proclaiming the *homoousion* of the *Holy Spirit* (despite any lack of precedent) as a herald of God speaking in the time of a new "seismic shaking" of the world order. Similarly Basil (typically more cautiously) appeals to the range of "unwritten traditions" in the church's liturgical life (*On the Holy Spirit* 27) to justify the principle that the real inner life of the church (its core tradition) is something more extensive than its *canonical* or written traditions. This more or less stabilized the ancient church's overall doctrine of tradition apart from two last movements, one Eastern and the other Western. The christological crisis of the fifth century was so fast and furious, and subtle, that many of the same problems over discerning "true tradition" that had occupied Irenaeus rose again in this period. The fifth century answer (as manifested in the Acts of the *Councils* from *Ephesus*

[431] to *Nicaea II* in 787) was to assemble dossiers of patristic evidences. The very notion of patristic theology was born in this era. Fathers of the church were regarded as possessing significantly elevated authority, and when accumulated in a *florilegium*, collectively they made a powerful testimony for authentic tradition. After this period, most Latin and Greek theology was constructed on the basis of assembling *florilegia*. In the West, *Augustine's* long fight with the *Donatists* had led him to elevate the principle of catholicity (a universal solidarity as opposed to a provincial regionalism) as a handy guide to authentic tradition. Catholicity was thus a necessary factor alongside antiquity (apostolic or scriptural status). This view of truth manifested by its geographical extension was always closely allied with the principle of communion with the Roman See in the Western churches. It led inexorably to the famous formula of *Vincent of Lerins,* commenting on Augustine, who argued that "oral tradition" must always be subordinated to scripture (Vincent of Lerins, *Commonitorium* 2.1–2) as being purely its *exegesis.* It was he who also defined the authentic Christian tradition as that which is held to be such "by everyone, always, and in all places." It gave rise in later Latin thought to the doctrine of the clear distinction of Scripture and tradition (as two sources of Christian kerygma). The Eastern churches never followed the latter path, seeing always Scripture itself as one of the first (but not exclusive) manifestations of the core tradition of the gospel kerygma, of which the inner life of the church was certainly another, as were also the other principles of tradition-discernment it had elevated across the centuries: namely, the scriptural, the apostolic, the episcopal, the synodical, the conciliar, the pneumatic, the imperial, and the legal. The Christian doctrine of tradition is thus an ancient and richly complex idea, which is no less than an investigation of the inner roots of Christian consciousness in history.

L. Bouyer, "The Fathers of the Church on Tradition and Scripture," *Eastern Churches Quarterly* (entire volume dedicated to Scripture and tradition) 7 (1947); D. van den Eynde, *Les normes de l'enseignement chrétien dans la littérature patristique des trois premiers siècles* (Gembloux, Belgium, and Paris, 1933); G. Florovsky, *Bible, Church, and Tradition: An Eastern Orthodox View* (vol. 1 of *Collected Works*; Belmont, Mass., 1971); R. P. C. Hanson, *Origen's Doctrine of Tradition* (London, 1954); idem, *Tradition in the Early Church* (London, 1962); E. F. van Leer, *Tradition and Scripture in the Early Church* (Assen, Netherlands, 1954); J. A. McGuckin, "Eschaton and Kerygma: The Future of the Past in the Present Kairos: The Concept of Living Tradition in Orthodox Theology," SVTQ 42, 3–4 (winter 1998): 225–71; B. Reynders, "Paradosis: Le progrès de l'idée de tradition jusqu'à S. Irenée," Recherches de théologie ancienne et mediévale. 5. 1933. 155–91.

Trinity   The word "Trinity" derives from the Latin term (*trinitas*), which is a neologism combining the notions of threeness and oneness, a "tri-unity." The normal Greek term for the Trinity (*trias:* the threeness or triad) does not hold the same semantic tension in itself, though for the *patristic* era both the Latin and Greek theologies of the Trinity are essentially the same with minor variations of stress. The concept of God as Trinity, a threefold unity, is a distinctive mark of the church's patristic theological culture. It is the quintessential refinement of the specifically Christian doctrine of God. Although it was rooted in biblical foundations, the classical Christian doctrine of Trinity did not begin to emerge until the second century, and after that point it moved forward with gathering momentum. Even so, it was not fully and formally articulated, doctrinally, until the *Arian* controversy of the fourth century had forced theologians to make a definitive statement of belief in the manner of Trinitarian relations and the character (particularly the status) of the *persons* of the Trinity. These two position-statements make up the substance of the formal definition of Trinity as it emerged in the writings of *Gregory of Nazianzus,* the president of the first *Council of Constantinople.* Gregory was the theologian who brought the important work of *Hippolytus, Origen,* and *Athanasius of Alexandria* to a resolution, with a Nicene *christological* basis underpinning his theology of three perfectly coequal divine persons (*hypostases*), all sharing the selfsame divine nature (*ousia*). Put more succinctly: he advocated a vision of God where the Son and *Holy Spirit* were *homoousion* with the Father, though hypostatically distinct. The roots of Christian Trinitarianism lay in the many scriptural references to the Son and Spirit of God. The latter are diverse and often enigmatic, but it was clear in the main that they referred to a supremely holy power of the divine presence at work in the world, especially when it was a question of creation or sanctification. The Spirit of God infused life and raised up prophets and heroes of the Old Covenant. For the Christian writers these two attributes remained fixed in their minds. The "Spirit of God" became especially the power of divine sanctification and inspiration. Most of the New Testament references to the Spirit of God fall within this ambit. But it was the centrality of Jesus' teachings on the nature of God as Father, and his own implicit status as Son, that really provided the first focus point for Christian reflection on the concept of God as revealed in Christ. The relation of the Son to the Father thus provided a basic structure of Binitarian thought in relation to God, and it was undoubtedly this christological question that demanded all the attention of the first two centuries of the church's intellectual life: How could God be one if faith acclaimed the Son as divine also? Two equally firm statements the church adhered to, that God was One (1 Cor. 8:4–6; Acts 17:24–29; Gal. 3:20), and also that Jesus his Son was ineluctably and agentively involved in the divine presence and work (that is, God considered both as Creator and Savior: Col. 2:15–20; Phil. 2:6–11), set the terms for a substantively new doctrine of God. This tended to keep explicit reflection about the several biblical references to the Spirit of God, or Paraclete, in a liminal condition at this period. The earliest levels of *"subordinationist"* Christology, which regarded the Son as a created agent of God (a supreme angel, comparable to the Philonic sense of *Logos*), had some extension in Christian circles, but the clash of the Monarchians and the Logos theologians in the third century brought that older, poetic way of speaking about Jesus as God's servant to a fatal impasse. Second-century *Monarchianism* was very strong in its insistence that the divine power was unique; but the general Christian consensus that this unique monarchy had been shared (a not inconsistent position) in the person of the Savior led to general dissatisfaction with the view that Jesus was merely another prophet or angelic mediator. The church's sense that in the salvation effected by Christ a new revelation for a new age had dawned had in a real sense broken a mold. The *Apologists* were among the first to rethink the issue of the problem of God, and used the concept of Trinity as a way of articulating God's outreach to the world. Their vision of the supreme Father using his own Word as demiurgic power of order and rationality in the cosmos, and then the Spirit also assisting in that refinement of the revelation of God through his creative work, provided a basis for Trinitarian thought that actually explained something (rather than simply being a *mystery* in and of itself). Trinity theology in the Apologists, therefore, was a vibrant theology of the creation process understood as a progressive *revelation* and an ongoing work of salvation. The scheme only worked by implicitly presenting God, in some sense, as "scaling down" as the extrapolations progressed. Thus the

Son was less than the Father, and the Spirit less than the Son in much of pre-Nicene presupposition. By that "scaling down" the incomprehensible God actually became partly comprehensible. The pre-Nicene subordinationism, therefore, was not so much seen as a scandal of impiety, but as a powerfully *"economic"* theology to explain how God bridged a chasm between the uncreated and the created. The work of *Theophilus of Antioch* is very important in this respect. His distinction of the Logos as being immanent within God (*Logos endiathetos*), and then "expressed" for the purposes of creation (*Logos prophorikos*) employed *Stoic* cosmology to illuminate the gospel (*To Autolycus* 2.10, 22). Similar ideas can be found in *Athenagoras* (*Legation* 10) and *Justin Martyr,* who is aware of the issue of the single God, "and another who is called God, his Logos, alongside him" (*Dialogue with Trypho* 56.4), but does not advance much further to resolve the obvious problem. Theophilus is the first to use the word Triad (*trias*) in reference to God. His Trinity is God, his Word, and his Wisdom. In most of the Apologists this presupposition that the Trinity is the extrapolation of the divine Wisdom in the act of creation leads to regular and frequent confusions of the Word and the Spirit (cf. Justin, *First Apology* 33.6). The increasing readiness of theologians to speak of the Father, Word, and Spirit-Wisdom as three divine entities was not matched, however, by a corresponding clarity on how this could be reconciled with monotheism. *Irenaeus,* a subtle and biblical thinker in many respects, demonstrates this particularly in regard to his Trinitarian language. In the *Adversus haereses* he describes the Son and Spirit as the "two hands of God," which he used as powers in the work of creation, and regularly alludes to the Son and the Spirit-Wisdom, even speculating that the Son was generated from God before (not in the act of) the creation. But nowhere does he step outside biblical categories or phraseology. His apparently hypostatic language about the Spirit as a distinct entity is heavily based on the Old Testament Sophia texts (not least Sirach 24). The rise of this hypostatic language in relation to the three divine "persons" was resisted heavily by conservative Christian thinkers at Rome, such as Noetus, Praxeas, and the Theodoti. These, now collectively known as the Monarchians, feared the developing Logos-Wisdom theology as introducing a plurality of Godheads into the faith. One of their solutions, presented by the school that came to be known as Modalist Monarchians, was to deny any distinctions (except terminological) between the three persons whom Christian piety regularly referred to. All were the same God under different titles, reflecting appreciation of different parts of God's work. Another group (the so-called Dynamic Monarchians, such as *Paul of Samosata*) resolved the issue of Jesus being called "God" by speaking of his adoption into deity by the indwelling Spirit, which accounted for his inspiration and his godly status as God-bearer (*theophoros*). The Monarchian school thus raised a challenge to the whole legacy of the Apologists, without offering any equally powerful clarity or theological utility of their own. The strength of the Monarchians was merely that they "tidied up" loose ends of discourse. But they were not felt to have matched the sense of radical newness in the God whom Jesus had revealed, which the Apologists had alluded to in their broadly cosmic theologies. As such the Monarchians in their turn soon became the object of severe attack by a powerful new school of Christian thinkers, whom history has since designated the Logos theologians. The first were *Hippolytus* of Rome, who issued his treatise *Contra haeresin Noeti* to clarify problems in Trinitarian theology, and *Tertullian,* who wrote *Adversus Praxean* for similar reasons. Both theologians explicitly defended the distinct hypostatic existence of the Son, and argued that he was with God before the creation, not merely issued from the

Father for the sake of creation. Both of these early works on the Trinity are essentially extended christological investigations. In each of them the level of reflection on the person and status of the Spirit is much less developed. Tertullian introduced a set of rules and formulae that would ever after be retained by Latin Christianity and would be the first manifestation of a tendency to approach difficult matters of Christian theology (and the Trinity is certainly that) by the medium of formulaic utterances (later dogmatic *creeds*). Tertullian is the first to use the word *trinitas* (*Adversus Praxean* 3). For him the root of unity and monarchy in the Godhead is provided by the commonality of substance (*substantia*). The Son and Spirit share that single divine substance of the Father. They have his being, and for this reason they are both God in their own turn, but not a numbering of Gods apart from the One God. The Father, Son, and Spirit are each separate persons (*personae*), a word that did not mean the modern sense of psychic subject, rather the notion of the "presentation of a face." He also used numerous images to describe the personal relations as a progressive outreach, such as the singleness yet distinctness of the root, stem, and fruit. The organic life of the plant thus gave an image of unity (single substance), which was expressed in varieties of economic sequence (*gradus*) in accordance with the role and function of each part of a whole. In this way the divine persons could be one in essence and glory, and three in *economic* effect and character. Tertullian described the principle of the salvific economy as that which "distributed the unity into a trinity" (*Adversus Praxean* 2). His work provided a brilliant set of new terms and linguistic structures that permanently marked Latin thought; but for the century following him his choice of technical language caused a rift with the Greeks, who had adopted the same general process but regarded the word *hypostasis* as the key term that described the separate persons. For a Greek, *sub-*

stantia was the direct etymological equivalent of *hypostasis*; and because of this many in the East misheard the Latins to be teaching a perverse doctrine of "three substances and one person." The issue would only be clarified laboriously by the controversial exchange of letters between Bishops **Dionysius of Rome** and **Dionysius of Alexandria** in the mid–third century. Earlier in that same century **Novatian** of Rome (*On the Trinity*) and Origen of Alexandria (*De principiis*) had taken already Trinitarian theology a stage further. Novatian argued that as fatherhood is integral and essential to his being, then if God was always God, then he was always a father, and so the Son preexisted eternally. The same idea was taken to a new pitch by Origen who made the timeless (and thus eternal) generation of the Son a key point of his system. If the Son was produced from God before the creation, he cannot be part of the creation that he then initiates, and is thus uncreated and divine, though certainly "begotten" by the Father and economically agentive, along with the divine Spirit, in the work of creation and redemption. Origen generally had little to say on the Spirit, but he did insist on two chief points: first, that the ancient tradition of the church regarded the Spirit also as clearly divine and hypostatically distinct, and second, that the Spirit of God was that power of sanctification and prophetic charism in the church which was given through Christ to the world (as in John 16:7–15). Origen believed that the Logos–Son of God was begotten precisely to be a lesser image of the unapproachable God's radiance. So, even in his work (much more profound in its range than that of the Apologists before him), there still remains a deep subordinationism at the core of the system. The Logos is a version of God that can be comprehended by the world (like a smaller version of a colossal statue). This subordinationism (for example, he calls the Logos a "second god" in *Against Celsus* 5.39) is not, for him, a defect but the whole purpose of

how the Trinity functions as God's power of salvation and revelation. Origen's work had a wide reception in the East. The Latin world was content to rest with the formularies of Tertullian and besides, other matters occupied it as *persecuting* emperors turned their attentions on the church in both East and West. In the early fourth century one of the close readers of Origen, the Alexandrian priest **Arius,** clashed with another Origenian theologian, his bishop Alexander, and so sparked off a vital period of theological exchange and clarifications. Alexander's interpretation of Origenian Christology had been to emphasize the latter's position on the eternal generation of the Son of God, as uncreated yet begotten. The approach of Arius was, in contrast, to stress the subordinationism that Origen felt was integral to the effectiveness of the economy of revelation. Arius also added other theological strands, not least a pressing of statements to their logical ends (logical method would always be a characteristic of the later Arians too). For Arius, if Christ was an inferior divine being to the Father, he could not be God in the same sense at all. He took his stand with a biblical proof text (soon the controversy would result in a war of scriptural proof texts), namely, John 17:3: "The Father is greater than I." He also adduced Colossians 1:15 and Proverbs 8:22 to argue that the Son of God was a creature. The starkness of his claims produced a crisis, tantamount to panic, among Christian theologians across the world. The argument caused immense divisions, and was finally resolved only in partial stages. Significant among them was the victory of Alexander's party at the **Council of Nicaea I** in 325, when the word *homoousios* was adopted and given creedal authority as a concise statement of the "full deity" of the Son. Immediately after Nicaea, many of those who signed the creed "wandered off," both intellectually and politically, as the imperial family changed its policies in relation to christological orthodoxy. The

Nicene party of the East held firm, however, and was given a flamboyant figurehead in the person of *Athanasius of Alexandria,* who gained the much-needed support of the Western churches for his theology of the *homoousion.* In 362 Athanasius tried to bring some coherence to the scattered parties of anti-Arians, and in an important synod at Alexandria that year substantive matters were addressed and terms were agreed on. It was then commonly accepted that the *homoousion* of the Son was critical (the coessentiality of the Father and the Logos), but the role and person of the Spirit also came into question. At the same time Athanasius began to sketch out (most tentatively to be sure, since he was terrified of losing the fragile unity he had secured on the christological front) a doctrinal summation of belief on the Holy Spirit. His *Letters to Serapion concerning the Holy Spirit* censured Egyptians in his archdiocese who accepted the *homoousion* of the Son but believed the Spirit was a creature. These letters drew attention to the "functions" of the Spirit of God (creation, inspiration of prophets, creation of the Scripture, power of the *incarnation,* and sanctification of the world) and concluded that since central Christian belief accepted the Spirit as the sanctifying power that "*deified*" the believer in baptism, then the Spirit had to be God, since no creature could sanctify and divinize another (*Orations against the Arians* 3.24: "Only by participating in the Spirit are we caught up into the Godhead"). His death in 373 took him away from the arena, but the prestige of his name after the final victory of the Nicene cause at the council in 381 ensured that this theology of the fully divine Holy Spirit could be facilitated in the work of Gregory of Nazianzus. During the time Athanasius was negotiating with the wider band of Eastern theologians (the Homoiousians led by Basil of Ancyra), a Western bishop was present in the East, *Hilary of Poitiers,* who was able to take a close interest in the intellectual developments

and enthusiastically endorsed the coming together of the *Homoiousians* and the *Homoousians.* In his treatise *On the Trinity,* Hilary explained these refined movements for a wider Latin audience, and suggested that the two schools were actually complementary and mutually necessary. His book served to cement together the fortunes of Latin and Greek Trinitarian theology thereafter, with both churches presuming they had the self-same doctrine, although significant thematic differences can be discerned between the later Greek and Latin forms of Trinitarian thought. The *Cappadocian Fathers (Basil of Caesarea, Gregory of Nazianzus,* and *Gregory of Nyssa)* represent the classical resolution of all this long development. Each of them was heavily involved in the intellectual battle with the final stages of Arianism, and had especially taken in hand the school of *Eunomius* and *Aetius,* which argued that Christ and the Spirit were creatures, however exalted they might be. Basil repeated much of Athanasius's argument that the evidence of the wider Christian tradition of liturgy and prayer argued strongly, even if implicitly, that the Spirit of God was divine, just as the Son of God was divine and consubstantial with the Father. Basil did not attribute the *homoousion* to the Spirit, but it was clear from his highly influential book *On the Holy Spirit* that there was no longer any ambivalence possible. His colleague Gregory of Nazianzus spelled it out even more clearly: "How long will we hold the light under a bushel measure?" he protested, demanding that the church should recognize the full divinity of the Son and Spirit as well as their coequality and consubstantiality. Gregory's explication of his position in his *Five Theological Orations (Orations* 27–31) became ever afterward the classical locus of Greek patristic doctrine on the Trinity (it would later be synopsized and simplified by *John of Damascus* in his summa *On the Orthodox Faith).* For Gregory, the issue of coequality was critically important. His thought marks the end of three centuries of implicit subordinationism. In Gregory's Trinitarianism the Father is the primary cause of the Trinity. He is the *arche*, or principle of the Godhead, in and for himself, and in the Son and the Spirit alike. Because of this the Son and Spirit possess the Father's own being. They are that which God the Father is, and they are that because God the Father is that. But Father, Son, and Spirit are distinct divine hypostases. This is because they are what the Father is but not who the Father is. The Father relates to the Son and vice versa, in the manner of the mysterious, loving, but very specific Father-Son dynamic. The Son originates from the Father "by being begotten of the Father." This mode of eternal filial origination is his distinct hypostatic character (the meaning of his Sonship). The Spirit equally issues from the Father, who is thus supreme *arche* of both in direct and unmediated form (which is why the East was always so worried about the *filioque* clause), and from this issuing he too takes his distinct hypostatic identity (through the manner of the originating) as well as his divine being (which is the divine being of the Father). The Spirit's mode of origin is not the same as that of the Son (which is why he is distinct from the Son). While the Son is begotten, Gregory says, the Spirit is "processed" (taking his cue from John 15:26). This direct procession from the Father confers on him the fullness of deity, and thus the Spirit and Son are fully and coequally God, but each in a distinctly different hypostatic realization of the selfsame deity: none other than the deity of the Father. Thus the divine nature is not a common property for three distinct beings (a thing we might designate as a set of properties attributable to "a god"), but rather a personal being (that of the Father) that is hypostatically realized by the Son and Spirit as they each derive from him and relate back to him. The Father's causality in the divine Trinity (in a sense, his dynamic function as "source of the Godhead") is synony-

mous with his own essential energy as "God who is Father," that is, begetter and processor (of the divine hypostases). The creation, in this sophisticated theology of triple monism, proceeds as a work of the whole Trinity. Gregory's work was a brilliant and complex theory that itself frequently warns that to engage too much in theological reflection leads one into the danger of dazzling the mind by speaking about mysteries that even angels cannot comprehend. After him the idea of Trinitarianism would be fixed by two factors. The first would be the wide adoption of his own theology (much more so than the *creed* of the *Council of Constantinople* 381, which skirts the real questions of Trinitarian relations, and which had greatly disappointed Gregory's expectations of it); the second was the binding power of the Eastern liturgies, which were replete with Trinitarian doxologies. In the West, a final act was waiting to unroll, which in a sense brought Western theology of the Trinity to a similar resolution to that achieved by the Cappadocians. *Augustine*, at the end of his life, took his long-standing belief in the soul as the inner manifestation of the works of God (the *soul* as the *image of God*) to a new pitch in explaining the Trinity to his readers in terms derived from spiritual psychology. The spiritual life of humans, Augustine argued in his treatise *The Trinity*, retains traces of the Trinity's presence (*vestigia trinitatis*) within it, almost as if they were small icons manifesting the Godhead. There are several of these, such as the inner unity that existed between human memory, intellect, and will. Three distinct things, one single power and reality. Augustine's depiction of the Trinity as the deepest substrate of the human spiritual life caught the imagination of the West. His work was really an extended commentary on the structures of Trinitarian thought as they had reached him, but he brought the whole to a magnificent resolution. Like the Cappadocians he emphasized the issues of Trinitarian coequality and identity of essence, giving them a high relief. He also laid great stress on the manner in which the three persons co-inhere in mutuality of love, thereby setting a tendency in Latin thought after him to consider the Trinity as the supreme example of the ontology of communion. It was important for Augustine, in defending this mutual *perichoresis* of persons, that the Spirit should be seen to relate identically to God the Father and Son, and for this reason Augustine argued that the East had got it wrong: the Spirit "proceeded from the Father *and* from the Son" (*filioque*) as an expression of the mutuality of their love. At the time he wrote, the Greeks no longer read Latin, and Augustine, as we know, had great problems in reading Greek. The issue would thus simmer in the dark for centuries to come and only develop as a problem in later centuries (*see* **Photius**). At the dawn of the sixth century a Gallic Augustinian disciple decided to summarise the trinitarian teaching of his master in a condensed credal form (really a schoolroom device more than a creed). The result was the dense confession later known as the Athanasian Creed, or the *Quicunque Vult*. It became a popular synopsis of one of the most difficult and brilliant books of Augustine, but had the unfortunate tendency to resolve the great mystery of the Trinity to a set of riddle-like syllogisms that were somewhat distanced from their original powerfully soteriological and spiritual context. This would have a detrimental long-term effect on Western Trinitarian thought, even though, as in the East, much Trinitarian devotion was preserved along earlier and simpler lines, in the liturgical prayers and great offices of Latin Christianity. After the Cappadocians and Augustine, there was a definite sense among Christians of both East and West that perhaps they had gone as far as they dare to go in Trinitarian speculations, and the tendency was, after that point, to more or less repeat the formularies, without necessarily understanding the dynamics of the economy. It led to a certain ossification in the

church's Trinitarian confessions in later ages, which was certainly not present in the original arguments.

B. Bobrinskoy, *The Mystery of the Trinity* (New York, 2001); R. P. C. Hanson, *The Search for the Christian Doctrine of God* (Edinburgh, 1988); B. Lonergan, *The Way to Nicaea* (London, 1976); G. L. Prestige, *God in Patristic Thought* (London, 1952); T. F. Torrance, *The Trinitarian Faith: The Evangelical Theology of the Ancient Catholic Church* (Edinburgh, 1988); H. A. Wolfson, *The Philosophy of the Church Fathers* (vol. 1; Cambridge, Mass., 1964).

Tropology (Tropological Reading)　*see* Allegory

Two Swords Theory　*see* Gelasius

Tyconius

Tyconius (fl. 370–400)　A North African layman and theological apologist of the *Donatist* community, Tyconius was a moderate thinker who began to question the Donatist movement's fundamental belief that the church was quintessentially the community of the pure, and concretely manifested only by believers who were in good standing in the Donatist communities. He composed a book, now lost (*On the Inner Warfare*), that argued the church was a mixed community of sinners and saints destined to spread over the whole world. This earned him the censure of his bishop (Parmenian) and condemnation at the Donatist Synod of Carthage in 380. It simultaneously brought him to the attention of the more eirenically minded members of the *catholic* community in **North Africa**, particularly **Augustine**, who encountered his work soon after he himself returned to Africa in 388. Tyconius made a lasting mark on church history through his influence on Augustine, which was mediated through his ecclesiology and his exegetical work. Tyconius was the first Latin writer to elaborate a systematic *Book of Rules* to guide biblical interpreters. Augustine incorporated his seven rules into his own *De doctrina chris-tiana* (3.30–42; *see also Ep.* 41), and thereby ensured Tyconius's transmission as an important authority for the West. His rules see the purpose of *exegesis* as the discovery of the key "mystery of Scripture," which is the revelation of the church, the mystical culmination of all history and historical *revelation*, which will be consummated, after history, in the purification of all sinners in the eschaton. The rules revolve around the pole idea of ecclesial interpretation of the Scriptures. All that refers to Christ's body, for example, can be taken to refer to the *church* (Rule 1). Christ's body is twofold (two natures), which symbolizes the division of the church in present history into saints and sinners (Rule 2). References in the Scripture to issues of grace and law are to be interpreted in the light of the distinction of letter and spirit (Rule 3). Commentators must carefully distinguish references to genus and species, and not mistake or confound them. An example is the promise of the "new heart" in Ezekiel 36:23, which refers not to Israel's renewal but to God's gift of the church to the world, made potent through the *sacrament* of *baptism* (Rule 4). Tyconius also speaks of how to treat number symbolism (Rule 5); why biblical writers often recapitulate their stories (Rule 6); and how to distinguish references to the body of Christ, as distinct from the body of Satan (Rule 7). This ecclesiocentric approach to Scripture dominated the Western medieval imagination. Tyconius also wrote a *Commentary on Revelation* (now lost), which took a highly spiritualist approach and influenced Bede.

P. M. Bright, *The Book of Rules of Tyconius: Its Purpose and Inner Logic* (Notre Dame, Ind., 1988); F. C. Burkitt, *The Book of Rules of Tyconius* (Cambridge, 1894; repr. 1967); A. B. Sharpe, "Tyconius and St. Augustine," *Dublin Review* 132 (1903): 64–72.

Typology (typological reading)   *see* **Allegory**

Valentinus (fl. 120–160)   Perhaps the leading Christian *gnostic* teacher, Valentinus was famed for his brilliant intellectual and rhetorical skills. His rejection by the church at *Rome* and other major Christian communities was the spark that clarified the difference between *orthodox* and gnostic theologies (even though there was, of course, a wide variety at that time in both the ideas of *catholicity* and gnosticism). Valentinus is thus the catalyst of the whole concept of the *tradition* of orthodoxy, regardless of the interest his ideas have in their own right. He was a native of *Alexandria* who took up a teaching position at Rome sometime between 136 and 140. He seems to have left for Cyprus in 160, according to *Eusebius* and *Tertullian,* largely because of the hostility toward him from the Roman church. He became identified as the archheretic in the Christian apologetic literature and almost nothing of his original work remains, although his system was described (and ridiculed) by several hostile witnesses, especially *Irenaeus.* The discoveries of gnostic literature at Nag Hammadi in the twentieth century were a major event, as many scholars now believe that the *Gospel of Truth* is a work by him, or at least reflecting his teaching in a substantial way. His theology teaches that the divine world, or *pleroma*, is a summation of thirty powers or aeons. From the primordial pair (a male-female syzygy called Ineffable and Silence) a second syzygy emanates, and from this four comes a second set of four, making the eight of the First Ogdoad. Eleven pairs of male-female aeons emanate in turn, which produces the completion of the thirty. The youngest and last of them all is Sophia (Wisdom). As the lowest emanation she is defective, or lacking, and is restless. Her wandering error produces the (disaster of the) material cosmos and the god of the material world, the demiurge, who is named as "God" in the Old Testament. This is a daimonic lower power who lords it over the world, keeping souls imprisoned in ignorance by seeking adoration as the true and supreme divinity. In the process of Sophia's disastrous production of the material cosmos some spirit-existence became entrapped in matter. One of the higher aeons, the compassionate heavenly Christ, sent down the Savior Jesus to liberate *souls* from their material imprisonment. Those who comprehend the message are enlightened and saved. Those who cling to material forms continue their enslavement to the demiurge in a sorrowful and broken world that is robbed of spiritual significance and devoid of the potential for psychic progress. The believers are classed, according to their level of enlightenment (or gnosis), as Materials, Psychics, or Spirituals. The Spirituals are those who have the secret for the final ascent to reunion with the higher aeons after death. Valentinus's system is a typically *Platonized* expression of the problem of the one and the many, envisaging a descending hierarchy of emanations to mediate between the high God and the daimonic powers of the material world. Valentinus, however, combines a Platonic metaphysic with major elements of the Christian *salvation* story, and gives his understanding of the life of Jesus a profoundly cosmic significance. The orthodox opponents of his scheme resisted him chiefly on the grounds that he had disconnected the Jesus story from history and wrenched it away from the seamless context of the Hebrew Scriptures, but they were also deeply influenced by the majestic way Valentinus had explained the metaphysical and universal implications of the Christian message of salvation. Important thinkers, such as *Clement of Alexandria* and *Origen*, set out to rehabilitate that cosmic scale in their own work and reclaim some of the insights for orthodox tradition. The gnostics were, for example, an important early stimulus for Christians to think seriously about how they could appropriate the message of the Hebrew Scriptures to the gospel story and the preaching of the divine *incarnation*.

Valentinus left behind him two schools of disciples. The so-called Western school, including Ptolemy and **Heracleon** (the first known Christian to leave a biblical commentary as preserved in Origen's *Commentary on John*), and the Eastern school presided over by Marcus and Theodotus (whose writings are discussed by Clement of Alexandria in his *Excerpts from Theodotus*).

H. Jonas, *The Gnostic Religion: The Message of the Alien God and the Beginnings of Christianity* (2d ed.; Boston, 1963); B. Layton, ed., *The Rediscovery of Gnosis* (Proceedings of the International Conference on Gnosticism at Yale University, March 28–31, 1978; Leiden, 1980); K. Rudolph, *Gnosis: The Nature and History of Gnosticism* (San Francisco, 1983).

Venantius Fortunatus (c. 530–610) A bishop of Poitiers and Christian poet, Venantius Fortunatus wrote works including the *Pange Lingua*, perhaps the most famous of Western **eucharistic** hymns, and the *Vexilla Regis*, which he wrote to celebrate the occasion, in 596, when a **relic** of the true **cross** was presented to the convent at Poitiers founded by Radegunde, the Frankish Queen, where Venantius first served as a **priest**. He also wrote several works of **hagiography**, especially developing the cult of St. Martin of Tours. His mystical writings are among the first Latin Catholic works to introduce the idea of the erotic quest of God, which would become a keynote of later medieval thought.

P. J. Godman, *Poets and Emperors: Frankish Politics and Carolingian Poetry* (Oxford, 1987), 1–37; F. J. E. Raby, *A History of Christian Latin Poetry* (2d ed.; Oxford, 1953), 86–95.

Vestments   Vestments distinguishing the Christian *clergy*, either in terms of special clothing worn in normal life or special clothes worn for the *liturgical* celebrations, do not seem to have been much in evidence before the third century. In the pre-Nicene church, and up to the third century, white clothes were preferred for church meetings (the *toga virilis* of the Roman middle class), and thus the officiants seemed to have used their best clothes for the occasion (cf. Clement of Alexandria, *Stromata* 4.22.141, 4; *Hippolytan Canons* 37; Jerome, *Against the Pelagians* 1.29). On special occasions in the Byzantine era, a toga or tunic would be worn with special embroidery on the borders; a pattern that can still be observed in almost all forms of ecclesiastical dress. *Origen* is one of the first to speak of special vestments worn during the raising up of prayer (Origen, *Homilies on Leviticus* 4.6), but the import of his text is disputed, whether he is conscious of the practice of the Church of his day in using special liturgical vestments, or whether he is primarily referring, in a symbolist manner, to the way in which the Christian at prayer is "clothed" in newness in the Pauline manner. *Jerome* says something similar in the fourth century (*Commentary on Ezekiel* 13.44.17f.: "Divine religion is clothed in one fashion for service, and in another fashion for day-to-day life"). The general import of most references to clerical dress from the late third to the fourth century, however, accumulates to a constant rhetorical refrain to stop clergy increasing the splendor of their garments as the time of the church's peace gave a greater sense of security and a more ready willingness to be recognized (cf. Theodoret of Cyrrhus, *Ecclesiastical History* 2.23). After *Cyprian* and Origen in the third century, a great wave of Old Testament symbolism came into the church, specifically connected with the liturgical cult, and doubtless the rise in favor for special liturgical garments (those, that is, that would be worn only in the church itself) emanates from this time. In the ancient temple rituals the distinctive dress of the priests and Levites was prescribed. One chief reason for this was to keep a strict ritual purity, so that day-to-day defilements would not be brought into the holy place. Christian *bishops, priests,* and *deacons* widely adopted distinctive garments after the later fourth and fifth centuries, but in each case the minor distinctions of office were worn over the traditional Roman dress of high officials. In regard to matters of dress in general and church robes in particular, Christian clergy seem to have been very conservative and to have retained elements of clothing style that secular society had long before discarded. As long tunics went out of fashion in early Byzantium, they were retained among the clergy and so became a distinctive form of ecclesiastical vestment almost by default. So, for example, the most visible garments such as the alb (Greek: *sticharion*) or the chasuble (Greek: *phelonion*) were simply normal outdoor wear for late antique Roman gentlemen. Bishops were distinguished by the omophorion (pallium in the West, though this was reserved for the pope and archbishops there), a broad stole worn over the neck and over the outer garment. In place of the *phelonion* the bishops of the East adopted the *sakkos*, a shorter tunic of gold cloth sewn along the seams with bells in a manner reminiscent of the description of the garments of the high priest of Israel. The priests wore a distinctive stole (Greek: *epitrachelion*) around the neck and hanging down in front, underneath the *phelonion*. In the ninth century it also began to be joined as a single piece with pomegranate-shaped buttons (reminiscent of Levitical descriptions). The deacons (to mark their status as symbolic "Levites") wore a long stole-like garment (*orarion*), but only over the right shoulder, and at certain times during the liturgy it was crossed over in front and behind to symbolize the wings of angels. *Gregory of Nazianzus* in 380 is one of the first to note the appearance of these changes of specifics (*Carmen De Vita Sua* 862), which he attributes with some wryness to the hybris of the archbishop of Alexandria, who had adopted, it seemed, a white linen vestment, a distinctive turbanlike headwear (again reminiscent of the high priest of Israel), and even the jewelled ephod on the breast. But Gregory also notes that he himself was criticized for wearing shabby clothes (as he felt befitted an *ascetic*) during his time as bishop at *Constantinople* (*Oration* 33). *Augustine* expressed a similar view, informing his correspondents and congregation that any precious cloth given to him for use in church he would sell in order to spend on the poor (the argument ought not to be pressed too heavily as he wrote in a time of refugee crisis; *Epistle* 263.1; *Homily* 356.13). Pope Celestine in the fifth century wrote against the custom, then creeping in to the church, of distinguishing the different grades of clergy by varieties of splendid garments. Again this ought not to be absolutized, for the bishops of Gaul had taken over what he regarded as the papal prerogative of wearing the pallium, and it was this that caused his irritation. Clergy, Celestine wrote, "must be distinguished from the people, by their teaching, not their clothing, by the purity of their minds, rather than their dress" (Celestine, *Ep.* 4.1.2). But by the end of the fifth century it was common everywhere to reserve special garments for church use, and from the sixth century synodical *canons* began to appear to regulate the clerical vestments that ought to be worn (Canon 12, Council of Narbonne, A.D. 589; Canon 27, Second Troullan Council of Constantinople, A.D. 691). After the sixth century what had been fought against as a clerical hubris had become a canonical necessity. The old warnings against "pride" were replaced with admonitions for clergy to make the service of the liturgy splendid in every respect. The adoption of vestments certainly influenced the increasing sense of sacrality around the priesthood and the connection of Christian liturgy with Old Testament "types." The old sense that simplicity and sobriety ought to prevail in the vestments for use at the altar was preserved, however, and recurs in the sixteenth canon of the *Council of Nicaea II* (787), which once again prohibits the use of "showy colors." After

the ninth century the varieties of colors that should be worn to manifest different church "seasons," and the high symbolism attached to different aspects of clerical vestment (usually variously rendered into symbols of the passion of Jesus) were developed extensively.

J. Mayo, *A History of Ecclesiastical Dress* (New York, 1984); V. Pavan, "Liturgical Vestments," in A. Di Berardino, ed., *Encyclopedia of the Early Church* (vol. 2; Cambridge, 1992), 864–66; C. E. Pocknee, *Liturgical Vesture: Its Origins and Development* (London, 1960).

Victor of Rome   *see* Irenaeus, Papacy, Quartodecimans Controversy

Vincent of Lerins (d. before 450)

A monk of the island community of Lerins, Vincent was author of the influential work *Commonitorium*. He was one of the objectors to the ascendancy of the Augustinian theology of *grace* whom *Prosper of Aquitaine* attacked. In his apologetic writing (*Commonitorium* 2.3) he devised a rule for which he is most famous: the so-called Vincentian Canon, which tries to define what is meant by authentic *catholic tradition* (as distinct from *heresy*, or a mere *theologoumenon*—an opinion which even though legitimate is not binding on catholic Christians). The canon states that catholicity in faith is determined by three criteria that have to be equally witnessed in any constitutive proposition. It has to be a thing that the church has held as "an object of belief everywhere, always, and by everybody." If a given belief is not attested by a universal, an antique, and a consensual character it cannot be imposed as a central article of faith. The Vincentian Canon enjoyed an immense significance in later Western thought, and became heavily applied by Catholic theologians arguing against Reformation divines. As a practical principle it is almost impossible to adjudicate historically, and has been progressively neglected in modern discourse.

J. A. McGuckin, "Eschaton and Kerygma: The Future of the Past in the Present Kairos: The Concept of Living Tradition in Orthodox Theology," SVTQ 42, 3–4 (winter 1998): 225–71; B. S. Moxon, *The Commonitorium of Vincent of Lerins* (Cambridge, 1915); J. Pelikan, *The Christian Tradition: A History of the Development of Doctrine* (vol. 1; Chicago, 1971), 333–39.

Virgin Mary

Mary was an object of intense fascination and devotion for the Christian movement, from its earliest origins. The cult of the Blessed Virgin reached very high proportions, encouraged greatly by the great *ascetical* rhetoricians of the classic *patristic* era of the fourth and fifth centuries, but there was hardly a generation of the early church where a focused interest in Mary of Nazareth can not be observed, especially if one takes into account the graffiti at the earliest pilgrimage centers, as well as the high theological texts of the patristic theologians. Given the general truth that the gospel texts record only one figure in any dimensionality (that is, Jesus), whenever a disciple appears in some kind of higher textual relief besides Jesus (usually Peter or Paul, thus reflecting great tensions in the transmission of authority in the earliest communities), then close attention ought to be given. Texts such as Mark 10:35–40, where James and John are given center stage for a little while (albeit Mark proceeds to criticize them in his own editorial redaction), are generally taken to reflect the posthumous encomia of martyred disciples, which the church assembled in the early to mid–first century and which were already "traditional" by the time the Gospel accounts were set into writing in the latter part of that century. In this light, the appearances in the New Testament text of Mary the mother of Jesus stand out as exceptionally crafted and deeply text-modeled. Far more than any other original disciple (including Peter, but with the exception of the "second-generation" disciple Paul, to whom the author of Acts devoted an extraordinarily large *hagiography*), Mary appears as the preeminent New Testament character who is used to advance the narrative of the saving deeds of Jesus. On the basis of the argument that any "modeled" disciple in the earliest level of texts demonstrates a prior significant impact on the shaping of the proto-Christian movement, it is entirely logical to deduce that the historical Mary had an important and pivotal role to play, not only on the formation of Jesus himself but also in the development of the Jesus movement after him. Such a conclusion is given symbolical articulation in texts such as Luke 2:51; Acts 1:14; and John 19:26, but can also be discerned in the manner in which Josephus (not generally an advocate of the "Jesus movement"), in his *Jewish Antiquities*, regarded Jesus and James his brother, as two eventful personalities of *Judaism* of his era. The first he records as a "lamentable thing" (at least in the original version of his text insofar as this can be deduced) (*Antiquities* 18.3), the second as one of the outstanding Torah interpreters of the age. The standing of Mary within this familial "school of Torah" can not be attributed to accident; thus her first historical appearance ought to be instanced as "Torah matriarch" in the earliest circles around Jesus. In the perspectives of the evangelists, Mary first appears as the "mother of the chosen one." Her figure is set out in the birth narratives of Matthew and Luke in forms drawn from a mixture of the biblical archetypes of the barren woman who prays and is given the blessing of a great prophetic leader (as with Hannah and her child Samuel), and the women of Israel's history who formed the chain of generations leading to the Messiah (as in the accounts of the genealogy of Jesus). In the infancy narratives she appears as the reflective disciple "who treasures these things in her heart" (Luke 2:19; 2:33; 2:52), and fulfills the role of one who is destined, as is her child, to bear a vocation of suffering (Luke 2:35). Thus even in the synoptic tradition (and so a generation before the Fourth Gospel underlines it), Mary exemplifies the role of faithful witness (*martys*) in the **kerygma** of the passion of Christ. Parts of the Markan tradition reflect a certain degree of veiled hostility to Mary and the family of Jesus (one first notes the absence of a birth narrative, but see also Mark 3:19–35), which may well be attributable to the manner in which the Markan accounts reflect a generically "Pauline" gospel in an era when Paul's conflicts with James and the family of Jesus, over issues of the right reception of Gentiles into Christianity, had been well publicized. Mark takes the side of the Pauline tradition, that faith made for a deeper bond of "family" with Jesus than did blood; but the power of a blood-relation with Jesus cannot be underestimated in the earliest history of the Jesus movement, especially in Palestine before the destruction of the temple in A.D. 70. In this era Mary's significance must already have been highly elevated. Without it, it cannot be doubted but that Christian preachers would have circumvented the traditional stories of Jesus' virginal birth. Doubtless this aspect of the tradition enhances the glory of Jesus, and reflects the prestige attached to Mary as Virgin Bride of God (as Israel had always aspired to be), but even so, the attachment of a narrative of Jesus not being fathered "normally" was an apologetic burden Christians must often have wished away (as can be seen in the controversies attending it in Jewish Christian apologetics for the centuries following). The Johannine accounts of Mary depict her as the facilitator of the public manifestation of Jesus' glory at Cana in Galilee (John 2:1–12) and again at the cross (John 19:25–27), where she appears as archetypal "woman" (the new Eve) who becomes the legal cipher of the validation of the kerygmatic message of the beloved disciple (that is, John's inheritance of Jesus' mother instances his legitimacy in the succession of Jesus' Torah teaching). This embryonic theology was extensively developed in the second century by *Irenaeus* (*Adversus haereses* 3.22.4; 3.18.1; 5.19.1) and *Justin Martyr* (*Dialogue with Trypho* 100.4–6), who both draw out the explicit parallel of Mary as the new Eve who reverses the fall of the first, just as her son, the Second Adam, repairs the fall of Adam's race. In neither theologian is there any suggestion of elevating Mary as an independent salvific principle. Her role as "antitype" in the process of salvation (*see allegory*) is always presented as one of the firstfruits of the redemptive work of her Son. In *Ignatius of Antioch* also (*To the Ephesians* 18.2; 7.2; 19.1; *To the Trallians* 9.1; *To the Smyrnaeans* 1.1), the same stress is found on the notion of Mary's faithful work as primary disciple. Ignatius, much preoccupied with the problem of *Docetism* in the churches, uses Mary to emphasize Jesus' true humanity. Thus, for all the earliest patristic witnesses, Mary appears theologically as a *christological* witness; an aspect that is enshrined in her Byzantine title as *Hodegitria:* the one who "shows the way" to her son. A similar nexus of ideas is developed in Tertullian, who begins to lay stress on the *virginity* of Mary as a principle of pristine newness that was appropriate to the coming of the *incarnate Logos,* who was set on "making all things new" in the process of incarnation (Tertullian, *The Flesh of Christ* 17). It was *Origen* who heavily popularized the church's use of the title Mother of God (*Theotokos*), but it would be *Cyril of Alexandria* in the fifth century who transformed this title into a major oecumenical *confession* of faith at the *Council of Ephesus I* (431). After that point both the Latin and Eastern churches always used this title as the primary reference to the Virgin Mary. Other titles that were also commonly in use were "Immaculate One" (*Achrantos, Panagia*) and "Ever-Virgin" (*Aeiparthenos*); both titles were also given ecumenical synodical weight at *Constantinople II* in 553, and at *Nicaea II* in 787. The fourth-century ascetical writers saw in Mary's virginity a model for the withdrawal of the ascetic from the affairs of the world. This was allied, as they noted, with Mary's tendency, as described in Luke, to "treasure things in her heart." She thus became for the ascetics of the West (especially *Ambrose* and *Jerome*) as well as the East (especially Proclus of Constantinople and *John of Damascus*) the archetypal hesychast (reflective mystic), and mother of all virgin ascetics. After the fifth century her position in the devotional and liturgical life of the church, and finally in its iconography (*see art*), reflected her powerful hold over the imagination of both clergy and laity in ancient Christianity. After her son (and it is interesting to note that all her iconography depicts her as Empress Mother—*Basilissa*) she was approached as the most potent of all intercessors; the supreme *saint* who could command the ear of Christ, and thus intercede for the suffering on earth, just as she had once interceded successfully for a poor couple in Cana, and gained for them (and for the world) an abundance of new wine. The Second Council of Nicaea (787) defined the veneration that ought to be afforded to Mary as exceeding that which should be given to the saints. While worship (*latreia*) could be given to God alone; and veneration (*douleia*) should be offered to the saints; the special glory of the Virgin (whom the Byzantine liturgical prayers described as "our tainted nature's solitary boast") called for an appropriate *hyperdoulia* or "most elevated reverence."

R. E. Brown, et al., eds., *Mary in the New Testament* (New York, 1978); S. A. Campos, ed., *Corpus Marianum Patristicum* (6 vols. in 7; Burgos, Spain, 1970–1981); H. Graef, *Mary: A History of Doctrine and Devotion* (2 vols.; New York, 1963–1965); J. McHugh, *The Mother of Jesus in the New Testament* (New York, 1975); P. F. Palmer, *Mary in the Documents of the Church* (Philadelphia, 1952).

Virgins Christianity in its earliest forms, in the *Syrian apocalypticism* that underlies the New Testament texts for example, strongly advocated a hesitant attitude to world culture. In the Johannine Gospel tradition the very term "world" (*kosmos*) is used as a cipher for all the forces that are apathetic, or even hostile, to the message of salvation (John 1:10; 14:17; 15:18–19; 17:25). Jesus' strong message of prioritizing the kingdom and its demands before all other concerns, even the sacred duties and ties of familial responsibilities (Matt. 19:29), found a ready audience in the earliest structures of the church, and the existence of consecrated virgins (male and female) who lived zealous ascetic lives in the heart of the various local communities seems to have been an aspect of organized Christian life from at least the early second century in Syria, long before the fourth-century monastic movement popularized this lifestyle and made it institutionally central to the Christian church of the ancient era. Jesus' sayings about subordinating sexual desire to the demands of the kingdom (Matt. 19:12) and Paul's recommendations of virginity as a suitable response to the proximity of the end times (1 Cor. 7:25–31) can be seen to be reflected in parts of the early Christian tradition, such as witnessed in the book of Revelation (Rev. 14:4), where virgins are presented as the pure of heart, the core elect of the church who closely attend the heavenly Christ, and who are the firstfruits of all the redeemed. A passing mention in Acts 21:9 also tells us that the evangelist Philip had four daughters who were virgin prophets (two of them remained active as such all their lives according to Eusebius in his *Ecclesiastical History* 5.24.2). This aspect of Christian virgins using their ascetical lifestyle to advance a highly apocalyptic office as "witnesses" of the gospel marks a very early and very strong tie in Christian thought between the idea of evangelical detachment from the cares of the passing world and the renunciatory sign of sexual abstinence. In other words earliest Christianity elevates sexual abstinence not as a social factor (Paul used that idea in his general recommendation of the single life as a "useful state" in 1 Cor. 7:28) but as a distinct *eschatological* "sign of contradiction" (the lifestyle is described as such by **Athanasius** at the end of his *De incarnatione*). The virgins seemed to have lived in the heart of the urban communities of the first four centuries, if they were female, sheltered within the house of parents or other family. In Syria, there is some evidence to suggest that full initiation in the church, through baptismal consecration for example, was reserved precisely for those who had renounced marital love. This practice was abandoned in the late third century and would soon be denounced as *Encratism,* but it may have been the case that only celibate *ascetics* ("spiritual virgins" if not actual virgins) were admitted to full communion as the Ihidaya, the solitary "Sons and Daughters of the Covenant." The two *Pseudo-Clementines* show that virginal communities were fairly common in Syria in the third century. Such a tradition where only the ascetics could be baptized would actually result in the leadership of the earliest Syrian communities being increasingly dominated by ascetic virgins. Although the female virgins were sequestered at home, they appeared in the churches for regular prayers, which they often organized, and so their impact on the public life and rituals of the church must have been considerable. Once male Christians adopted the celibate lifestyle and symbolically took over the office of "spiritual virgins," they dramatically brought this office out from the domestic zone into the public domain and set the stage for what would be more common after the fourth century, that is, the increasingly wholesale co-option of ecclesiastical offices by male celibate ascetics. The Syrian text *Letter to the Virgins*, in protesting against the practice of male and female celibates sharing the same household (see also Canon 3 of the **Council of Nicaea**), is an interesting sidelight on the origins of organized ascetical communities; where it seems that female ascetics gathered in communities and availed themselves of the social protection of their male brethren. Ignatius was one of the first writers to caution against the "pride of virgins" (*To Polycarp* 5.2), which suggests that he had occasion to rue their social influence at Antioch and was penning words of wisdom to his younger episcopal colleague **Polycarp.** The *Apostolic Tradition* of **Hippolytus** also speaks of an order of Virgins who live at home, under the spiritual guidance of the bishop. After the explosion of the ascetical life in the fourth century, many Christian women increasingly looked to an organized monastic community as an attractive and powerful Christian vocation. *Patristic* rhetoricians, themselves increasingly representing the ascetic class, drew up extensive treatises recommending the virginal life as something even superior to *marriage. Cyprian* was the first to write in these terms (*The Dress of Virgins*), and Tertullian gives much information in his treatise *The Veiling of Virgins*. After his and Cyprian's writings on virginity, it seems that the custom of "taking the veil" and the wearing of simple clothes became the distinguishing outward habit of the Christian virgins. *Methodius of Olympus* at the end of the third century also composed a Christian version of Plato's *Symposium*, entitled *The Banquet of the Ten Virgins*, where he gives an extended encomium of the virginal life. One of the classic accounts of the "superiority" of the ascetical virginal life is given in Gregory of Nazianzen's poem "In Praise of Virginity" (*Carmen* 1.2.1). After **Gregory the Great** reiterated this view in his *Dialogues* it became an established attitude in Latin Christianity up to the high Middle Ages. *Gregory of Nyssa, Ambrose, Basil of Ancyra, John Chrysostom,* and *Augustine* all wrote extensive treatises on virginity. Gregory of Nyssa's *Life of Macrina*, his sister, also attests to a remarkable phenomenon in the fourth-century church, where several prominent and powerfully wealthy women (*Syncletica*, for example, *Macrina, Melania the Elder, Olympias of Constantinople*, or the fifth-century empress Pulcheria) used the virginal life as a means of retaining personal control of familial properties and extending the limited range of self-determination available for women in ancient society. It is paradoxical but nevertheless true that the adoption of an ascetical virginal lifestyle by Christian women in all-female communities was a liberating social move for most of them. The power of the virgin *saint* as intercessor became a notable factor in early Christian *hagiography* and *iconography* (the north wall of San Apollinare Nuovo at Ravenna illustrates it). This was even more true when that virgin saint was also a martyr, as several of the earliest female ascetics were, doubtless because they attracted the attentions of the persecutors precisely because of their local notoriety as Christians. The extent of female virgins in the lists of the early martyrs is remarkable. Most of the patristic writings, all of them by men, laud virginity as a "spiritual betrothal" to Christ. Thus even in celebrating the ascetic renunciation of marriage, the male theologians conceive of it in marital terms. There is little to suggest otherwise from the rare female voices that managed to be textualized.

P. Brown, *The Body and Society: Men, Women, and Sexual Renunciation in Early Christianity* (New York, 1988); H. von Campenhausen, *Tradition and Life in the Church* (Philadelphia, 1968), 90–122; S. Elm, *Virgins of God: The Making of Asceticism in Late Antiquity* (New York, 1994); J. A. McNamara, *A New Song: Celibate Women in the First Three Christian Centuries* (New York, 1983); J. E. Salisbury, *Church Fathers: Independent Virgins* (New York, 1991); C. H. Turner, "Ministries of Women in the Primitive Church: Widow, Deaconess, and Virgin, in the First Four Christian Centuries," in H. N. Bate, ed., *Catholic and Apostolic* (London, 1931), 316–51.

Virtue The Latin *virtus* signifies strength, integrity, or "manliness." It is the equivalent of the Greek term *arete*, which had a much larger and longer preexistence in the pre-Christian philosophical tradition. *Aristotle*, in particular with his *Nicomachean Ethics*, set the tone for most of Hellenism's moral reflection. It was this mingled with massive elements of *Stoic* moral teaching that the Christians adopted as the basic structure of most of their ethical thinking. The particular Christian elements of the moral scheme (often ad hoc and organically developmental rather than systematically extrapolated) were constituted by biblical structures such as the law as a divine commandment (renewed and internalized in the New Testament), the *apocalyptic judgment* of God, and the specific dictates of Christ's teachings and those of the apostles. The Hellenistic background of thought on virtue suggested that the life of a human being was poised between two tendencies: to virtue or vice. The way of vice was easy and debilitating. The path to virtue was a struggle that required constant vigilance and effort, hence it was described as a warrior's path and advocated for the Greek youth as equally important, in terms of civic and human development, as military training in the Palaestra.

The idea of the twofold path (the polar tracks of good and evil) was already well known from ancient Christian writings, not least Paul the apostle and the *Didache.* This fit well with the Greco-Roman conception of the life of virtue as civic and human refinement. The *Clementine Letters* are an early example of the Roman household code (obedience to authority and a regular commitment to moral improvement) given a new Christian makeover. *Philo* was an important bridge in reconciling the terms of Stoic moral theory with the biblical accounts, and his influence was determinative for later Christian exegetes, especially *Origen of Alexandria.* In the *On Life of Moses*, for example, Philo describes the eponymous biblical figure in terms of a moral hero whose example is to be emulated and whose life marks the progressive stages of *arete*, advancing through all the virtues as his intelligence becomes more acute, until in the end his refinement is so great that the capacity for the encounter with God is given to him. *Gregory of Nyssa* would reproduce much of this scheme in his own *Life of Moses*, underscoring the Christian identification of the heights of virtue with *mystical* union with God, and thus making it a profoundly theological concept at root. Origen made a deeper synthesis of the Hellenistic moral philosophies and the biblical revelation by decisively identifying Christ as the supreme virtue: not just the highest example of a virtuous life, but rather the embodiment of virtue in his capacity as *Logos* enfleshed within history. The life of virtue was thus synonymous with the life in Christ, mystical appropriation to Christ being the goal and fulfillment of the moral life. The disciples of Origen spread this scheme as a fundamental substructure of *patristic* theology after him. *Gregory of Nazianzus,* for example, spends much time in his *Five Theological Orations* (*Orations* 27–31) describing how the gospel calls the disciple to a progressive moral and intellectual refinement. The two are always seen as inseparable, and are explained on the basis that morality is an embodied expression of the spirit: the regular image used to justify the synergy being the manner in which the soul is inseparable from the body. *Augustine* and *Ambrose* took over the Hellenistic conception of the chief virtues, and in Latin moral writing particularly the idea of the "cardinal virtues" became popular: prudence, temperance, fortitude, and justice. In later writers these were often compared and contrasted (the former being regarded as common to nonbelievers) with the "theological virtues": faith, hope, and charity (seen to be specifically reserved in their fullness to the initiated and illuminated). Christian writers after the fourth century especially adopted

Stoic moral encomia in ascetical terms. The life of *ascesis* now emerged as a supreme example of the true "philosophical" life (that is, the life of virtue). So great was the ascetical impetus that nonascetical Christian lifestyles had a hard time gaining a hearing, although loud protests in *Rome* from influential *married* aristocrats had the effect of toning down some of *Jerome's* most exaggerated attacks on sexuality. Even so, after many treatises lauding monasticism and virginity as the "highest" of lifestyles, the concept of asceticism as inherently superior form of Christian virtue found an official sanction in the seventh century under *Gregory the Great,* and was structured into Greek and Latin Christianity for centuries thereafter. One of the distinctive Christian strands of ascetical moral writing was the listing of vices (a taxonomy of the moral life), which is first seen in *Evagrius of Pontus,* and was brought to the West by his disciple *John Cassian.* The Evagrian stress on identification of vices and virtues in the inner life of the ascetic had a profound effect in developing psychological introspection and inner consciousness in western civilization: what would later be called the "formation of conscience." The monastic writers also had the insight that progress in the moral life needed a community context, and a wise guide to assist, scrutinize, and correct the person who wished to live a life of moral advancement. The early Christian writers called this guide the higumen (director), or (as in ancient Christian Ireland) the Anam Cara or soul friend.

T. Spidlik, *The Spirituality of the Christian East* (Kalamazoo, Mich., 1986).

Visions　The concept of visions (*optasia, orama*) as a significant part of theological apprehension has always had a checkered history within Christianity, certainly so within *patristic* literature. While most of the Fathers regard the visions and epiphanies of the Old Testament (such as the burning bush, or the Sinai revelations) as straightforwardly historical events, they were less than ready to continue that epiphanic tradition on into the New Testament, even though there were numerous occasions when the disciples "saw" phenomenal visions, notably the transfiguration event (Mark 9) or the **resurrection** appearances. In most cases, even when commenting on the visionary experiences of the Old Testament prophets (cf. Hippolytus, *Commentarium in Danielem* 4.36.1), wherein the various prophets saw things with their bodily eyes, and thereby learned deeper spiritual messages, which they then communicated by their preaching, the patristic commentators regularly employ the phrase "they were accounted worthy of such visions," implying both that the present generation may not be accounted so worthy (since epiphanic vision had clearly declined as a vehicle of theological articulation in later Christian centuries), and also that the preaching of the word was a vastly superior form of discourse, of which the vision was merely a particular prelude. Thus, if the vision was removed, the task of preaching could still continue; and in some cases (it was argued) it could even be purer as a result. Even so, some of the earliest theologians, particularly those of **Syrian** origin such as the writer of the **Shepherd of Hermas,** clearly regarded visions as a fundamental mechanism of prophetic insight and discourse. But the contrast between Hermas and his near-contemporary **Clement of Rome** could not be more marked. Here in the latter is the theme of sobriety and rational argument taken to a pitch. Vision is set aside, and this partly accounts for the rapid fall into disfavor of the once-famous Shepherd. The vision is more lively in the apocryphal literature, but largely because this is heavily based upon earlier Syrian models of **apocalyptic** narratives (cf. the *Apocalypse of* Paul); but the trend runs out quickly as the apoc-

rypha are themselves marginalized. The seventh-century revival of the genre of "vision of the afterlife" can similarly be explained in Christian literature as sub-apocalyptic retrospective with many elements borrowed from Virgil's *Aeneid,* book 6 (cf. Gregory the Great, *Dialogue* 4.37–38; *Visio Baronti;* Gregory of Tours, *History of the Franks* 4.33; 7.1). For **Clement of Alexandria, Hippolytus,** and **Origen,** leaders of the **Logos** school, the transition is becoming more or less fixed: the "word" (a play on the synonymity of Logos and rational discourse) is to predominate absolutely over the lower apprehensive categories such as sensation (*aesthesis*) or vision (*optasia*), and this as part of the vocation of the Church to ascend beyond bodily things to a "conception" of the truth in spirit. After them the use of the word "vision" in Christian theology normally means "intellectual conception." Origen's interpretation of the Transfiguration of Christ spends much time discussing how the chosen Apostles were enabled to "see the glory of Christ" but not with bodily eyes, rather with eyes of the spirit given to them for the occasion; in other words their visions were not *optasia* at all, but were rather acute intellectual-spiritual penetrations of the veil of the flesh (which veiled the eyes of the other apostles so that they could not behold the glory of Jesus at all) (cf. *Contra Celsum* 4.16; 6.68; *Homilies on Genesis* 1.7; *Commentary on Matthew* 12.36–43). In the ascetical movement of the fourth century Origenian disciples such as **Evagrius** underlined this theological approach and warned against reliance on visionary phenomena in the life of the monk. Visions were given low currency, and frequently appear as one of the temptations for a monk to guard against: the rising of delusions, which were often inspired by demonic activity. Evagrius fixed this anxiety about visions in the Christian ascetical literature after him. One suspects that visions, so much a part of ordinary Hellenistic paganism, had a wider currency in popular Christian life in the first five centuries, but the rhetorical transmission of all accounts of Christian visions tends to mute and transmute them into a distinction between "waking *dreams*" and "dreams of the night." Visions still occurred in *hagiographical* literature but, along with prophetic dreams, they were generally rendered theologically peripheral by the fourth century; and this despite the manner in which *Antony* is portrayed as a clairvoyant visionary in Athanasius's *Life of Antony*. In the *Alphabetical Collection* of the Sayings of the Fathers (the spiritual literature of the fourth-century Egyptian *desert*), a story attributed to Abba Olympius demonstrates the passing over the cusp in regard to visions among the Christians. The tale concerns the dialogue between a priest of Isis and two young monks. The pagan priest is puzzled to hear that such ascetics have no regular "vision of their god," since he regards this phenomenon as a suitable thing for zealous devotees. The monks are so disturbed by the conversation that they return to their elders for advice, and receive the admonition that visions are only for the righteous who have worked hard to be purified. The moral of the tale is a generic call for monks to double their efforts at purifying asceticism, not to worry about receiving visions; and as such it is entirely in line with the Evagrian tradition. Even so, this attitude to the primacy of the word must have made Christians stand out distinctively from much of the pagan religiosity around them. The *Montanists* of the second century showed a brief revival of the category of prophetic vision, but even by the second generation of Latin Montanism (as demonstrated in the African *Passion of Perpetua and Felicity*), vision has been definitively transmuted into dream, and after that point, each successive attempt in the history of Christianity to revive the concept of vision as a major vehicle of revelation becomes merely a temporary response to a critical situation.

M. Aubrun, "Caractères et portée religieuse et sociale des 'Visiones' en Occident du VI-ième au XI-ième siecle," Cahiers de Civilisation Mediévale 22, 2 (1980): 109–30; R. Lane-Fox, *Pagans and Christians* (New York, 1987), esp. chaps. 4–5, 8; J. A. MacCulloch, *Early Christian Visions of the Other World* (Edinburgh, 1912).

War It is doubtless because of its inheritance of the Old Testament as its scriptural book of prayer that so many warlike images passed on into early Christianity. They were regularly used to describe the "battle" for gospel fidelity (though mainly transmuted into personal symbols of inner struggle). The constant presuppositions of the Old Testament that the land mattered, and was an actual physical land that had to be fought over, or that God would rout the forces of evil violently and with justice to establish the *apocalyptic* kingdom (casting down the "empires" as in the book of Daniel), or that God ought to be entrusted to extend his strong right hand and crush his foes permeated into the church's consciousness. Jesus himself has many sayings that seem to suggest he had a nonviolent attitude. He describes wars and revolts as parts of the inescapable order of the world, but as matters that cannot frustrate the divine plan for the cosmos (Mark 13:7–8). Earthly unrest and violence are not an expression of the irrefragable might of the powerful, rather an incitement to the intervention of God in justice, within history. In this Jesus follows the classical doctrine of the prophets, albeit with a definite *eschatological* sharpening. He is very skeptical as to the utility of political military might, and among his recorded sayings is one that appears to be a mockery of the supreme "hero" of the Hellenistic world, Alexander the Great (Mark 8:36) as well as a cold view of the profession of soldiering, with his dictum that "whoever lives by the sword shall die by the sword." And yet many of the parables use the image of a king who expresses his will by force of arms; and this as a symbol of how God will vindicate himself over Israel. The political program of God's overthrowing earthly power (understood of course as *Rome*) to vindicate the righteous was, however, a vision that was best kept quiet in the context of the Roman Empire. Apart from the book of Revelation, which produces its call for violent vengeance from God in the light of a recent and savage *persecution*, most Christian writings of the earliest period are remarkably pacific, and advocate communities to conform to the political authorities peaceably. Such is the message of Paul, who encourages his Christians to be good citizens, and taxpayers, and to pray for the welfare of the rulers. Similarly in the Pastoral Epistles, and 1 and 2 *Clement*, the churches ought to be models of good citizenship. Military images, which abound in Paul more than most New Testament writers (1 Thess. 5:8; Rom. 13:12; Eph. 6:10–17; 2 Tim. 2:3), are generally rendered into allegories of spiritual readiness. *Clement of Rome*, in his *Letter to the Corinthians*, composed just after Domitian's persecution c. 96–98, still expresses admiration for the military profession (Clement, *To the Corinthians* 37). The Roman military, a profession that was known for particular brutality and oppression in a world generally inured to it, retained something of an aura about it, partly because the stories of Jesus' admiration for the centurion's faith (Luke 7:1–10), Peter's baptism of the centurion Cornelius (Acts 10), and the testimony of the captain of guards at the crucifixion (Mark 15:39) all showed how the message of faith could transform the military. Of course, if the gospel message ever became popular with the middle ranks of Roman soldiery, it could only be a matter of time before Christianity permeated into the very substructure of the empire. This it did, of course; and in regard to early

church attitudes to war it is instructive to see the earliest levels of cautious noninvolvement give way in the third century to a first position that is generally hostile to war, and then in turn give way to an attitude that is much more ready to accept a role in the shaping of the destiny of Rome. The final stage is nothing less than the final subversion of the empire by Christianity in the age of *Constantine*. After that point *patristic* writers generally speak only about moderating the moral evils of war. Although *Tatian* was always deeply hostile to the military profession (*Oration to the Greeks* 11.1; 19.2; 23.12), it is really *Tertullian* who was the first patristic writer to engage the problem of war as an ethical notion. At first he was open-minded about the profession of arms (*Apologeticus* 30.4), but in his later work his view changed to the position that soldiering was inherently incompatible with belief in Christ. Part of this can be explained from the constant requirements of a soldier to engage in pagan cultic acts (*Idolatry* 19; *The Crown*, passim); but the fundamental aspect of a life dedicated to sustaining power, whether morally so or not, can not be excised from his thinking. *Clement of Alexandria* was equally forthright: soldiering was nothing other than a machination of the devil (*Stromata* 5.126.5), and he is echoed by *Cyprian of Carthage* (*To Donatus* 6). Both writers had the benefit of seeing how easily the machinery of the state could be turned against the church. The Latin apologist *Lactantius* is a rare voice, however, because his objections to the military are not concerned, as are the others, with individual matters of right and wrong, but with a more global view. He denounces war as evil because it is the machinery of murder (*The Divine Institutes* 6.20.15–17) attempting to masquerade as patriotism or a special category of "invasion." He wryly notes that if an individual pillaged and killed a neighbor, he would be denounced as heartless, but if a nation (he is criticizing the great

Roman heroes) wades in blood as it subdues other lands and peoples, it is generally praised as a great "peacemaker." Yet Lactantius in his *Deaths of the Persecutors* advocates and supports Constantine as God's chosen ruler. For him God has elevated this emperor above all others because he alone protected and nurtured the church. Even so, **Constantine** rose to power by a bloody ascent through civil war and familial murders. **Eusebius of Caesarea,** another of Constantine's panegyricists, cannot deny that war is an unmitigated calamity (*Ecclesiastical History* 1.2), but he seamlessly slides over issues as he depicts Constantine as Roman Imperator, now receiving blessing from a new god of war, no longer Mars but Christ, as he instructs his soldiers to write the new divine cipher of the *cross* on their shields (Eusebius, *Life of Constantine* 2.4; 4.56). The Constantinian age changed attitudes. Christians were now a dominant force within the army and the imperial court, a fact that alarmed Diocletian and Galerius considerably, and led to the outbreak of the Great **Persecution.** They were such a force that even years of purges could not shift them, and after Constantine they would not be ready to relinquish power again. After the fourth century, however, they had to face a new context of ethical reflection. It was easy enough for theorists to argue a radical pacifist position before the church had responsibility for being the moral guidance of the state, but how could Christianity now claim to guide a new political order without a readiness to bless war? Would it not be the case, as Celsus had once mockingly claimed in the second century (cf. Origen, *Contra Celsum* 8.68–71), that if there ever was Christian emperor, he would have to be hopelessly pacifist and thus leave Rome to be ravaged by its enemies? The patristic writers of the fourth century show their awareness of the new problem only gradually and partially. Several, such as Eusebius of Caesarea, were perhaps content to allow the God of the armies to

change from pagan to Christian, and then continue with military politics much as before. But the change was nevertheless marked. A much more pacific philosophy had entered into the heart of Roman moral thinking in the Christian empire. It is instructive to see how later Byzantine ages always preferred negotiated settlement to force of arms; and it is one of the fundamental reasons historians beginning with Ammianus Marcellinus in the fifth century, and continued by Gibbon in the eighteenth, have denounced Christianity as the force that destabilized the empire, because of its condemnation of the idea of aggressive war and its advancement of the justification for military action being lodged solely in the concept of self-defense. The latter idea is epitomized by **Basil of Caesarea,** who agonized over the whole idea of war, as something that is inherently incompatible with the gospel of love. It was a concept that he already found in the earliest collection of **canons** (*Apostolic Tradition* 16; *Canons of Hippolytus* 14.74). Basil, however, was bishop of a military town at an important crossroads on the road to the unstable eastern frontier, and in his time his people were suffering from raids of local warlords. His solution to the problem was to urge his local Christian soldiers to form war parties and punish the perpetrators of the attacks. If they spilled blood, however, they would be debarred from communion for several years. Yet, if they refused to fight, they would be equally guilty in the eyes of God, for they would be responsible for not protecting the innocent. **Clergy,** who represented the church as a "pure type" of Christian, were under no circumstances ever allowed to take up arms or engage in violence or killing. If they spilled blood, they could not function any longer as ministers of the altar. Basil's canonical letters set the tone for this approach to war in most of late Eastern Christianity, avoiding any suggestion of a "just war" theory, in favor of a view that regarded it as the least of evils that needed to be adopted to safeguard the good of protecting the innocent. Some of the later Latin writers were more overtly "patriotic." *Ambrose of Milan* praised the very idea of military faithfulness, and set it as an example to his congregation. He also lists the strength of a warrior among the chief virtues he can think of (*De officiis ministrorum* 1.129). Gregory of Tours was even more explicitly warlike. He is, indeed, one of the first examples of a bellicose bishop, a type that would make its appearance more extensively in the early Middle Ages. Gregory urges Christian princes not to hesitate to make war when necessary for the defense or extension of the faith. Aware that the Latin tradition, now poised in his day between Tertullian's bristly pacifism and the new accusation that Christianity had led to Rome's fall (*De civitate Dei*), simply had to be given some systematic coherence, *Augustine* set himself the task of thinking out a position more coherent than situation ethics. He was the first to attempt a moral justification of the profession of arms. He took the basic ideas of "just war" from Cicero (Augustine, *Epistle* 138.15; *Against Faustus the Manichaean* 22.69–76) and set out what would be the terms and conditions of a Christian "just war." Most writers of the Latin church followed him after that point. The East continued its canonical approach, more individually focused, but always resisting the idea that war, as such, could ever be legitimated in the abstract.

R. H. Bainton, "The Early Church and War," HTR 39 (1946): 189–212; C. J. Cadoux, *The Early Christian Attitude to War* (London, 1919; repr. New York, 1982); W. L. Elster, "The New Law of Christ and Early Pacifism," in W. M. Swartley, ed., *Essays on War and Peace: The Bible and Early Church* (Elkhart, Ind., 1986), 108–29; J. Fontaine, "Christians and Military Service in the Early Church," Concilium 7 (1965): 107–19; J. Friesen, "War and Peace in the Patristic Age," in W. M. Swartley, ed., *Essays on War and Peace: The Bible and Early Church* (Elkhart, Ind., 1986), 130–54; A. von Harnack, *Militia Christi: The Christian Religion and the Military in the First Three Centuries* (orig. German ed., 1905; ET Philadelphia, 1985); H. T. McElwain, *Augustine's Doctrine of War in Relation to Earlier Ecclesiastical Writers* (Rome, 1972); L. J. Swift, *The Early Fathers on War and Military Service* (Message of the Fathers of the Church; Wilmington, Del., 1983).

Wealth   *Aristotle,* in a widely received aphorism, had defined the true human being as the one who had sufficient leisure to attend to *philosophy* and practice virtue by reflective meditation. This meant a radical reaffirmation of the traditional Greek view that "real humanity" began at the level of landowner. Slaves and indentured laborers were frequently criticized in Hellenic letters, the first as being subhuman, the second as being "feminized" because of their drudgery (and thus equally subhuman in Greek consciousness by lacking virility, *andreia*). Poverty was generally seen by the ancient Greeks as a curse from the gods, or at best a sign of the indifference of the gods to the common people. The idea that the poor, by virtue of their plight, were a worthy object of attention, solace, or compassion was a thoroughly "un-Hellenistic" notion. The gift of real humanity through the possession of sufficient patrimony was a sacred gift of the gods, which had to be defended at all costs (hence the severe oppression of ancient slaves) and celebrated without shame. Excessive spending was not virtuous, not because of hubris, but because the correct use of the patrimony (usufruct) was a critical ethical matter. The basic corpus of wealth had to be passed on intact, if not amplified, so that successive generations of one's family could enjoy the same liberty. These ethical parameters about the morals of wealth, the distinctions surrounding patrimony and usufruct, determined almost all the later moral discussion on wealth through the Christian centuries up to the late Middle Ages. Christianity had a hard time introducing the idea that the very concept of the human **person** was not (philosophically and morally) a subset of the notion of societal standing and wealth. It is debatable, of course, whether it ever got that philosophical and religious message across to society at large, and whether it was ever really moved by its own vision of simple equality in its own internal affairs (the problem is witnessed as early as James 2:1–26; and 1 Cor. 11:19–22). The biblical philosophy of wealth was very different from this brittle pagan Greek view. The Scriptures of Israel recurrently demonstrate a God who has a marked concern for justice to the poor (at least the poor of Israel). This does not necessarily accumulate to a generic reflection on human worth as such, but is more of a set of reflections on fidelity to the covenant: watching out for the poor in the body of the elect. There is some movement that can be witnessed in the Bible in terms of the abstract concept of protecting the "stranger in your midst," but even this does not accumulate to a systematic philosophy of philanthropy. Even so, the biblical tradition that God was the defender of the poor, the orphan, and the widow (Lev. 19:10; 1 Sam. 2:8; Ps. 72:12; 82:3; 113:7; Prov. 14:31; Isa. 3:15) made from the very start a great fissure in the Hellenistic tradition when Christianity brought biblical ethics to play in the Greek world. The biblico-apocalyptic strand of God's *judgment* on the rich oppressor (Luke 12:16–21) and the theme of God's deliverance of the downtrodden are both clearly and frequently witnessed in Jesus' teachings. What is more, many of Jesus' sayings appear to advocate a disregard for the claims of wealth and possessions (Mark 10:25; Luke 12:22–35). Disciples are invited to follow at the cost of possessions and sedentary lifestyle. Some of the statements that at first sight appear to make Jesus argue for a radical abandonment of wealth (Mark 10:21–31) are better interpreted as instructions to the first generation of missionary travelers, whose lifestyle moving from area to area necessarily involved them with hardship and poverty (*see also* **sexual ethics**). Parts of the gospel witness a concern to transmute several of these "poverty statements" into the form of generic spiritual advice. A classic example is how the injunction "Blessed are you who are poor" (Luke 6:20) seems eventually to have become rendered as "Blessed are the poor in spirit" (Matt. 5:3). Along with many other examples of Jesus' sayings, the Hellenistic trend to interpret literature *allegorically* made for a progressively "spiritualizing" approach to Jesus' difficult commandments, especially when they refer to wealth and possession. One of the first examples of such an allegorizing approach appears in the evangelist's symbolical retelling of Jesus' parable of the Sower and the Seed in Mark 4. The allegorical retelling of the editor (Mark 4:13–20, as distinct from the original parable of Jesus, Mark 4:2–9) adds in the detail that the thorns that choke faith are the "cares of the world, and the lure of wealth." Here, we see the Gospel story being reapplied for an increasingly affluent city church in the late first century. Roman persecutors in the third century knew that they ought to target their first opposition to the Jesus movement by refined financial penalties (it was less dramatic than throwing Christians to the lions but more effective from the imperial standpoint), and it is clear from the accounts of these early *persecutions* that the financial penalties involved caused many Christians to lapse, an indication of how affluent the church was becoming. Banking systems thus soon came to be a source of friction for the Christians, as they had to face up to the wider ethical implications of wealth. The only time Jesus ever encountered an organized banking system led to most unhappy results, as the account of his casting out the money changers from the underground arcades of the temple clearly shows. For the early church the idea of

charging interest on a loan was a fundamental evil, a further oppression of a
person who had fallen into wretched-
ness. This earliest moral outrage against
usury was progressively abandoned by
both Christianity and *Judaism,* but both
systems initially saw this opportunistic
oppression as a fundamental apostasy
from the covenant. In early Christianity
it was regarded almost as an unforgivable sin. In contradistinction, the free
distribution of wealth to the needy (first
those of the Christian community but
then often to those outside the community, beginning with the widows, the
sick, and the orphans) was seen as a
renewal of *baptismal* commitment, and
as such a source of the forgiveness of
sins. Until the institution of a system of
penance in the late third century, "*almsgiving*" was the only source of institutionalized "forgiveness of sin ritual"
among the Christians. The first *patristic*
writer to reflect systematically on the
question of wealth was *Clement of
Alexandria* in the mid–second century.
Clement was addressing his wealthy
patrons, and for affluent Christian circles in *Alexandria* he wrote a "table
manners guide" (*Paedagogus*). His other
treatise, *Quis dives salvetur (Salvation
of the Rich*), is the first attempt (based
on Mark 10) to develop a theology of
wealth that is not founded on principles
of *apocalyptic* renunciation. Clement
argues in this treatise that Jesus was an
intelligent philosopher, and so when he
advocated the avoidance of wealth for
his disciples he knew that this would be
socially ruining if it was meant as a universal commandment. Therefore, what
the Teacher "really meant" was to issue
a challenge to his hearers to interpret him less hyperbolically: that a righteous disciple should be "relatively
detached" from possessions. Clement
argues (honestly and well in his context)
that total impoverishment is an unremit-
ted human evil. Moderate wealth (an
honest income, honestly earned) is, by
contrast, a salutary blessing for society.
Christians, according to Clement, ought
to work hard, earn honest wages, and
bring up their own households in moderation, while providing philanthropic
support to outside society from their
labors. This attitude calls down God's
blessing, and makes the disciple that rich
man who finds salvation, as adumbrated
in Jesus' enigmatic teaching in Mark 10.
In many senses Clement is right that the
words of Jesus on wealth renunciation
must be regarded as a "parable" to be
exegeted, but his legitimation of wealth
as a spiritual symbol lost some of the
light of passion that infused Jesus' apocalyptic clarities. In the fourth century,
Gregory of Nazianzus's Oration 14: *On
Love for the Poor* was a major landmark in
Christian reflection on the social duty of
Christians to provide philanthropy in a
society lacking even basic social welfare.
Gregory here argues the case that the
poor person is de facto the *image of God,*
intrinsically equal to all other human
beings and worthy of care. Even if all the
rest of human society cannot see the connection between poverty and merit (the
poor man was deservedly so for most
Greek society as one who had evidently
been cursed by the gods), nevertheless
the Christians must begin to see and
make that connection. The Christian
philanthropist who supports the help-
less poor, Gregory argues, at that instant
acts like God (mercifully and phi-
lanthropically) and demonstrates the
perfect example of true discipleship.
Gregory himself was a very wealthy
man. This *Oration* was part of his collaboration with *Basil of Caesarea,* another
immensely wealthy *bishop* of the fourth
century, to build a new hospital complex
at Caesarea. It was a task they accomplished with the aid of massive interventions from the imperial treasury, thus
setting a pattern for ages to come in
terms of the church's direct engagement
with social welfare. Despite his radical
social message, Gregory himself was
deeply rooted in the Hellenistic ideas of
patrimony. He goes on to argue that patrimony is given to individuals by God. It
is the mark of a perfect man to despise

wealth (an old sophistical theme), but God also commands love as the primary virtue, and both the rich and moderately wealthy have a duty to share their beneficence with those who suffer from not having money: especially lepers, widows, and orphans. The expenditure of wealth for the poor is a mark of greatest eminence and earns a Christian (that is, the wealthy Christian, whom Gregory is addressing here) a tabernacle in heaven. The orations of the Cappadocians mark a new awareness in the patristic world that bishops must be the "friends of the poor" (*philoptochoi*), that is, founders and funders of the church and its charitable enterprises. This, of course, meant that they had to be rich and powerful, and such was a pattern that developed apace after the fourth century. The sermons of **John Chrysostom** are among the best of numerous patristic writings that castigate the superfluous excesses of the rich in the face of the sufferings of the poor. This predominantly ad hominem rhetoric brought in its train a generic view that the correct approach to the ethics of wealth was to consider its application, rather than the processes of its systemic accumulation. In general, the conflict between the many disparate elements in Christian practice and theory in regard to the possession and use of wealth has never really been resolved, from antiquity to the present. Even so, that tension has also served as a motivating factor of some considerable force in the varieties of Christian society. One thing at least is certain: wealth (its use, its renunciation, its acquisition and protection) is a fundamental force in defining the character and setting the goals not only for an individual human life, but even for entire societal systems. In analyzing how wealth and the rich are esteemed within society and within the church, one sees revealed the essential "treasure" of a person and a whole social fabric ("Where your treasure is, there your heart will be also," Matt. 6:21). This arena of human life and passion is, accordingly, one of the clearest manifes-

tations of how seriously church or individuals appropriate the values established by the charter of the gospel. Although the problem of wealth was addressed in the patristic corpus, most of those attempted answers (to renounce it completely, to employ it so as to act charitably, or to allow the church to serve as a source of philanthropy, or even to learn detachment and moderation) do not begin to do justice to the centrality of a perennial question. The image of the rich young man who met Jesus but went away downcast (Mark 10:21–22) has remained to haunt Christian consciousness to the present.

D. Batson, *The Treasure Chest of the Early Christians* (Grand Rapids, 2001); I. Giordani, *The Social Message of the Early Church Fathers* (Peterson, N.J., 1944); S. R. Holman, *The Hungry Are Dying: Beggars and Bishops in Roman Cappadocia* (Oxford, 2001); J. A. McGuckin, "The Vine and the Elm Tree: The Patristic Interpretation of Jesus' Teaching on Wealth," in W. J. Sheils and D. Wood, eds., *The Church and Wealth* (Studies in Church History 24; Oxford, 1987), 1–14; P. Phan, *Social Thought* (Message of the Fathers of the Church 20; Wilmington, Del., 1984); J. de Santa Ana, *Good News to the Poor: The Challenge of the Poor in the History of the Church* (New York, 1979); M. Sheather, "Pronouncements of the Cappadocians on Issues of Poverty and Wealth," in P. Allen, et al., eds., *Prayer and Spirituality in the Early Church* (Everton Park, Australia, 1998); W. Shewring, *Rich and Poor in Christian Tradition* (London, 1966); G. Uhlhorn, *Christian Charity in the Ancient Church* (New York, 1883).

Widows   The prevalence of widows in the Christian communities of late antiquity was a natural result of the custom of Roman marriage where older men often espoused very young girls. On the death of the husband, the legal wealth-holder, the familial property (when it existed in the first place) sidestepped the widow and was recirculated along the line of the nearest male inheritors. It thus followed that both widows who had no patrimony and those who had formerly been wealthy were often rendered destitute by the deaths of their husbands. With little prospect of earning anything themselves, they were a particularly vulnerable class (and had been regarded as such from Old Testament times, as can be seen in Exod. 22:22; Deut. 10:18). Early Christian writers urged the need for a careful effort on the part of local church communities to protect widows financially (James 1:27; Shepherd of Hermas, *Mandate* 8.10; *Similitudes* 1.8; 5.3; Ignatius, *To Polycarp* 4; *First Clement* 8; *Apostolic Constitutions* 4.2). Even by the second century, as evidenced in the earliest form of instructions for recognition as a "Christian widow" (1 Tim. 5:9–10), the plight of being a widow had transmuted into something else within the communities: namely, the concept of the widow as the elder woman who had special time and availability for *prayer* and charitable action on behalf of the local church. It was a development that is first witnessed in the *Pseudo-Clementine Recognitions* (6.15), where it is attributed to the apostle Peter, and may thus have originated in the church of *Antioch*. *Patristic* texts suggest that the offices of nursing the sick, evangelizing and catechizing pagan women who were interested in the church, and administering *alms* among the women of the town were frequently exercised by the widows (Clement of Alexandria, *Stromata* 3; *Apostolic Constitutions* 3.5), who thus emerge as a distinctive class of early Christian ministers. *Origen,* in the third century, explicitly acknowledges them as a class of official ministers in the church of Caesarea in his day (*Commentary on John* 32.7). Widowhood as a ministerial office thus grew out of an early attempt to institute a welfare dole. By the fourth century it began to be the subject of patristic reflection, especially in *John Chrysostom's* homily *The Widow Is Chosen* (*Vidua eligatur*), where he notes how

the state of a despised and impoverished social class had been reversed and elevated by the honor the church gave to it. In *Syrian* literature widows are called the "altars of God," which suggests that they were probably the first core of that class of "praying women" who seem to have extended the times the church officially gathered for worship (the beginnings of the *liturgical* offices of prayer alongside the eucharistic congregations), which was later taken over by the increase of female ascetics (*see virgins*). The office of widow seems to have quietly fallen into abeyance by the middle of the fourth century, when its duties were more or less taken over by the office of female *deacons.*

C. Methuen, "Widows, Bishops, and the Struggle for Authority in the Didascalia Apostolorum," JEH 46, 2 (1995): 197–213; C. Osiek, "The Widow as Altar: The Rise and Fall of a Symbol," TSC (1983): 159–69; B. B. Thurston, *The Widows: A Women's Ministry in the Early Church* (Minneapolis, 1989); C. H. Turner, "Ministries of Women in the Primitive Church: Widow, Deaconess, and Virgin, in the First Four Christian Centuries," in H. N. Bate, ed., *Catholic and Apostolic* (London, 1931), 316–51.

Will   The idea of the human will (Latin: *voluntas*; Greek: *thelema*), or ability to choose freely that which is good or evil (and implicitly the ability to shape by assent or dissent one's place within the order God has established for the world) is a central idea in the Christian conception of *anthropology* and *soteriology.* Many biblical sources, governed as they were by the overpowering sense of God's mastering dominion of the created cosmos, had a tendency to Predestinarianism. In the early Christian era this was allied with a deep-seated fatalism prevalent in many aspects of Hellenistic religion. The will of the gods was seen to be implacable. *Philosophers* increasingly regarded the notion of individual *prayer*, or freedom of personal choice, as simplistic metaphysics. The *gnostic* Christians amplified this fatalism in such a way that a reaction was caused among the early *patristic* theologians, such as *Irenaeus* and *Justin Martyr,* who were alarmed that the tendency to regard individuals as ciphers in a cosmic battle already predetermined would impoverish the concept of conversion and moral commitment required of believers. They thus set out to explain how the idea of radical "salvation" (that which God gave to an incapacitated humanity, which was beyond its own helping) could be reconciled with the notion of God's invitation to humans to respond to his *grace* in a freely chosen path of moral and intellectual obedience (the concept of "covenant" as obedience to the law). *Origen* was one of the first antignostic theoreticians to insist that the principle of the freedom of the human will lay at the root of the whole metaphysical order. It was, he said, because God had allowed all cosmic destiny to depend on the free assent of angels and humans that the *fall* was allowed to damage the beauty of the creation's order. God had foreseen and permitted this to accommodate creaturely freedom. For Origen, all of angelic life after the fall, and all of human life on the terrestrial plane, was thereafter a therapeutic training of the will to obey God, no longer in innocence but in penitent fidelity. Allowing for numerous lapses of individuals through their lifetime, Origen envisaged the return of fallen *souls* to God as an inevitable ascent and progress back to the source of life. Thus, ultimately (his doctrine of *apokatastasis*), all intelligent creation would be harmoniously united with the deity once more, in perfect communion of their wills with God's: and the cosmos, which once fell into disunity because of creaturely freedom, would nevertheless find harmony again through God's assistance and vindication of that freedom. For Origen all the different degrees of intelligence, giftedness, and social condition that existed on earth were a direct result of free will (not accidental fate), since God assigned a human destiny and condition to individuals in accordance with the degree of the lapse of their preexistent will that had taken place before the soul's embodiment. Ingenious though this scheme was, it ran into great controversy from the early third century onward. After Origen it was more or less abandoned in all Christian writers, who therefore had to think out again the implications of reconciling the problem of God's invincible providence with the vagaries of human freedom. Origen again supplied the key here, for his treatise *On Prayer*, without recourse to the theory of preexistence, had demanded a clear distinction be drawn between God's foreknowledge and God's providence. Thus it was possible for patristic theologians to argue that God shaped his providential plan for the cosmos around and within the vagaries of the human choices, which he foresaw his creaturely friends and enemies making in their lifetimes. *Augustine* wrestled with the problem of free will, most famously in his *Confessions*, where he describes the strangely mysterious path of a human freedom developing under the shaping providence of God. His solution, that the only real human freedom was that which God permitted the soul, became constitutive of later Christian thought. In Greek patristic writing the same idea was approached more in terms of its mirror reflection: namely that human freedom was not a given reality, and that the human being started off from a basis of profound "enslavements" to habits and prejudices. The ability to become intellectually and morally free was a mysterious work of grace in which the believer had to collaborate intimately and with great faithfulness (the Greek East was never so wary as Augustine about the issue of "collaboration" with the divine). Only when the soul had achieved union with God could there be any hope for freedom, for only then could individuals claim to have transcended all the determinative habits and obsessions that previously ruled them. In the seventh century the conciliar *christological* crisis (over the unity of Christ) ran over some of this same ground. The Third *Council of Constantinople* (680–681) and much of the writing of *Maximus the Confessor* were concerned with the nature of Christ's will. How many wills did Christ possess? If he had a divine will only, it seemed that his unity of personal action was assured. But then without a human will how could he be said authentically to have experienced human life? Maximus the Confessor made an important distinction between natural will and gnomic will. Natural will was comparable to that which Adam had in the paradisiacal garden, when he walked hand in hand with God and innocently chose the good as an immortal being. Gnomic will occurred after the fall. Gnomic will was a deduced choice. One could no longer, as a fallen creature, instinctively choose the divine, the right. One had to deduce it, and often even then had to force oneself to follow such a choice. Gnomic will was that principle of volition now rooted in every human being. In Christ, Maximus argued, there was no gnomic will, only natural will. But it was truly a human will: one that made all of Christ's human choices instinctively orientated to the divine will. Thus, although Christ had two wills, one divine (as the *Logos* of God ruling the cosmos) and another human (manifested, for example, in the fearful decision of Jesus in the garden to accept the cup of suffering), there was nevertheless in Christ a permanent and absolute unity of will: Christ never for a moment deviated from the choice for good, because his human life was so radically in communion with the life of God. In this pattern he gave to humanity the potential for the redemption of will: the redefinition of human freedom as perfect communion with God. The council of 681 endorsed this theology of the will of Christ, and incidentally thus gave a further impetus to the notion of human freedom as a divine quality. It has not been much elaborated in modern theological thought, but it is surely one of the most important implications of late patristic theology and philosophy.

T. D. J. Chappell, *Aristotle and Augustine on Freedom: Two Theories of Freedom, Voluntary Action, and Akrasia* (New York, 1995); W. L. Craig, *Divine Fore-Knowledge and Human Freedom* (Leiden, Netherlands, and New York, 1990); V. L. Harrison, *Grace and Human Freedom According to St. Gregory of Nyssa* (Lewiston, N.Y., 1992).

Women, Early Christian

(*See anthropology, asceticism, Cassia, deacons, Egeria, family, Macrina, marriage, Melania, Montanism, Olympias, Perpetua and Felicity, Pulcheria, sexual ethics, Syncletica, Virgin Mary, virgins, widows.*) *Patristic* writing followed many of the social customs and intellectual presuppositions of the ancient Greek world. In that intellectual universe women were of the "private" domain, while men were of the "public" domain. The home, and domestic interiority, were seen as "female" by the Greek mind, and the open space of the *agora*, together with association in public and (most important for our present purposes) "discourse" (*logos*), was seen as a male phenomenon. Textuality (the Greeks always understood the "word" as a proclaimed discourse) was thus part of the male domain. And textuality became the primary historical record. It is clear enough that wealthy women in antiquity were educated, and textual; but it was never a common thing for women to be educated, at least not in the higher levels of a rhetorical school in one of the great cities. This leads inevitably to the great problem of the "textual invisibility" of women (or comparatively speaking anyway) in the records of Greco-Roman society, and especially in the annals of Christianity in the early period. Women are spoken of, extensively so, but always from the male perspective. The stage dramas of ancient

Greek literature summarize the problem exactly: the characters who present the views of women are using words entirely supplied to them by male authors, for the exclusive benefit of male viewers, and are themselves (as the law required) male actors impersonating females. In the early church, women were disadvantaged by this ubiquitous Greek invisibility. Women were married young, in their midteens, to considerably older men who enjoyed extensive authority over them, socially as well as financially (*see widows*). Their families made the decision of marriage for them, and with a life ahead of childbirth and domestic labor, without sophisticated medicines, the death rate was high. It would not be unusual for a woman to be regarded as being in advanced old age by her late forties. As women played no great part in the formation of the great patristic textual tradition (being closed out of the major leadership offices of bishop and priest in antiquity), they have largely been passed over in history, up to the twentieth century, and the story of the church in the patristic era has been a one-sided and heavily patriarchal one. The mid– to late twentieth century, however, has witnessed a remarkable flowering of women's studies, not least in the domain of early church life. The significant presence of women apostles in the earliest Jesus movement has been reclaimed for the record by many notable feminist biblical scholars, and decades of scholarship by skilled women patristic theologians and historians of late antiquity have only recently begun to make a mark, excavating the dust of the "Greek silence" to reveal a fuller picture of the impact women had on early Christianity from the postbiblical age to the early Middle Ages. As a result of that pioneering work, it has become clear that asceticism was taken and used by many early Christian women as a channel for self-development that allowed them new vistas of opportunity. Today the path of virginity might look to us as a narrowing of prospects, but the liberation from

marriage and the capacity to determine one's own financial and social identity (*see wealth*) were nurtured imaginatively by important female ascetics (several of whom were respected teachers; *see Macrina, Melania, Olympias, Syncletica*). The *church*'s acclamation of virginal life thus offered new options above and beyond domestic drudgery. The autonomy and partial independence offered in the ascetical circles made the fourth century an important era for the development of Christian women, though successive centuries saw the gradual erosion of those rights as episcopal authorities brought all forms of ascetical communities under their *canonical* control. The scholarly attempt to break the silence about early Christian women meets increasing difficulties, however, as it begins to move away from the fruitful ground of the place of Christian women in asceticism, or the occupancy of ministerial offices such as *deacon*, prophet, or widow, and now begins to move out into the issues of women in general social standing, familial life, and Christian social networks. The problems are the perennial ones: not enough archaeological data and not enough textual record. But what is being produced is enlivening the whole field of patristics, dragging it into the wider world of late antique social, religious, and philosophical research. The present enthusiasm of a new generation of women scholars of Christian antiquity promises to bear a fruitful harvest in decades to come.

V. Burrus, *Chastity as Autonomy* (Studies in Women and Religion 23; Lewiston, N.Y., 1987); A. Cameron and A. Kuhrt, eds., *Images of Women in Antiquity* (Detroit, 1983), esp. chaps. 11, 17, and 18; E. Castelli, "Virginity and Its Meaning for Women's Sexuality in Early Christianity," *Journal of Feminist Studies in Religion* 2 (1986): 61–88; E. A. Clark, *Women in the Early Church* (Wilmington, Del., 1983); idem, *Ascetic Piety and Women's Faith* (Lewiston, N.Y., 1986); G. Clark, *Women in*

Late Antiquity: Pagan and Christian Lifestyles (Oxford, 1993); G. Cloke, *This Female Man of God: Women and Spiritual Power in the Patristic Age 350–450* (London, 1995); S. Elm, *Virgins of God: The Making of Asceticism in Late Antiquity* (Oxford, 1994); V. Harrison, "The Feminine Man in Late Antique Ascetic Piety," *Union Seminary Quarterly Review* 48, 3–4 (1994): 49–71; A. Kadel, *Matrology: A Bibliography of Writings by Christian Women from the 1st to 15th Centuries* (New York, 1982); R. S. Kramer, *Maenads, Martyrs, Matrons, Monastics: A Source-Book on Women's Religions in the Greco-Roman World* (Philadelphia, 1988); J. Lang, *Ministers of Grace: Women in the Early Church* (London, 1989); J. Laporte, *The Role of Women in Early Christianity* (Lewiston, N.Y., 1982); V. Limberis, *Divine Heiress: The Virgin Mary and the Creation of Christian Constantinople* (New York, 1994); J. A. McNamara, "Muffled Voices: The Lives of Consecrated Women in the Fourth Century," in J. A. Nichols and L. T. Shank, eds., *Medieval Religious Women: Distant Echoes* (Kalamazoo, Mich., 1984); P. S. Pantel, *From Ancient Goddesses to Christian Saints* (trans. A. Goldhammer; vol. 1. of G. Duby and M. Perrot, eds., *A History of Women* [Cambridge, Mass., 1992]); J. Rowlandson, *Women and Society in Greek and Roman Egypt: A Sourcebook* (Cambridge, 1998); R. R. Ruether, "Misogynism and Virginal Feminism in the Fathers of the Church," in R. Ruether, eds., *Religion and Sexism: Images of Woman in the Jewish and Christian Traditions* (New York, 1974); D. Sawyer, *Women and Religion in the First Christian Centuries* (New York, 1996); D. M. Scholer, *Women in Early Christianity* (New York, 1993); L. Schottroff, *Lydia's Impatient Sisters: A Feminist Social History of Early Christianity* (trans. B. and M. Rumscheidt; Louisville, Ky., 1995); G. N. Stanton, *Women in the Earliest Churches* (Cambridge, 1988).